# THE RISE OF THE
# LATINO VOTE

# The Rise of the Latino Vote

## A History

Benjamin Francis-Fallon

*Published in Cooperation with the*
*William P. Clements Center for Southwest Studies,*
*Southern Methodist University*

Harvard University Press

Cambridge, Massachusetts
London, England
2019

*Library of Congress Cataloging-in-Publication Data*

Names: Francis-Fallon, Benjamin, 1979– author.
Title: The rise of the Latino vote : a history / Benjamin Francis-Fallon.
Description: Cambridge, Massachusetts : Harvard University Press, 2019. |
    Includes bibliographical references and index.
Identifiers: LCCN 2019014635 | ISBN 9780674737440
Subjects: LCSH: Hispanic Americans—Political activity. | Hispanic
    Americans—Ethnic identity. | Hispanic Americans—Suffrage. | Hispanic
    Americans—Politics and government—20th century.
Classification: LCC E184.S75 F717 2019 | DDC 305.868/073—dc23
LC record available at https://lccn.loc.gov/2019014635

*For Liz*

# Contents

# THE RISE OF THE
# LATINO VOTE

# Introduction

> As I peer into the future and I see this crass materialism that is beginning to infect and poison American life, and in fact imperil and endanger its very essence of liberty and freedom, I see this great Hispanic people of the Southwest then rendering their great contribution, because of the nature of their being, spiritual, idealistic, they will contribute to offsetting the destructive and noxious effects of this crass materialism. They, like a giant stream that for generations and years and centuries flows underground unseen by human eye, will through some event, fortuitous event, suddenly arise to the full surface, in full flood and majestic grandeur.
>
> —Walt Whitman to the Citizens of Santa Fe, New Mexico, ca. 1865

Latinos entered the national political consciousness burdened by extraordinary expectations. For decades, scores of influential journalists, civil rights advocates, and political professionals have, in echoes of Whitman, imagined a people poised to transform the country. One can look back to the *Time* magazine cover in October 1978, which imposed upon a collage of faces, most of them brown, the words "Hispanic Americans" and a prediction: "soon the biggest minority." The cover story examined Miami, Los Angeles, and New York, profiling the nation's Cuban Americans, Mexican Americans, and Puerto Ricans, respectively (the story judged a fourth group, "the 'Illegals,'" a separate population altogether). Their shared Spanish language, Catholic faith, and strong, patriarchal families, the magazine asserted, were altering American life. But more than cultural change was on the horizon. According to *Time,* the "Hispanics'" influence on US democracy would be striking. Their "very numbers guarantee that they will play an increasingly important role in shaping the nation's politics and policies," proclaimed the magazine. "Just as black power was a reality of the 1960s, so the quest for latino [*sic*] power may well become a political watchword" in the 1980s. It was this group's "Turn in the Sun."[1]

The expectations have not diminished. Consider the hundreds if not thousands of times in the ensuing decades that newspapers and magazines, blogs, or television commentators have referred to the "Latino vote" or "Hispanic vote" as the "sleeping giant" of American politics. Or look, for instance, to another *Time* magazine cover, this one from March 2012, which promised to explain "Why Latinos Will Pick the Next President." Whether high Latino turnout has tipped the balance in favor of a presidential candidate, as many observers claimed after Barack Obama's 2012 reelection, or whether a predicted "Hispanic Voter Surge" mysteriously failed to appear, as has been said in the 2016 election of Donald J. Trump, it has become impossible to analyze the contest for power in the United States without accounting for the Latino vote. The Latino population's expected growth and the widespread belief that "demography is political destiny" ensure that this electorate will remain central to the conversation for the foreseeable future.[2]

Embedded in discussions of the now-ubiquitous Latino vote are certain assumptions. Foremost among these notions is that New Mexicans who trace their ancestry to sixteenth-century Spanish explorers, Puerto Ricans who migrated to the Bronx in the 1950s, Cuban exiles in Miami, and Salvadoran refugees in Washington, DC, share fundamental political interests and a distinct position with respect to other societal groups. But there is more. As political scientist Cristina Beltrán has noted, countless analysts and politically active Latinos have ascribed to these diverse populations a sort of "common collective consciousness," and held that these communities' natural and fullest empowerment can thus only be achieved through formation (or recognition) of a shared ethnoracial bond and a commitment to achieving political "unity" from coast to coast.[3] Within the confines of the US political system, the thinking goes, a group destiny awaits fulfillment.

Despite the widespread incorporation of the Latino vote in the political lexicon, and a "Latino politics" with unity as its lodestar, both are relatively recent creations. As late as 1960, the people said to comprise the Latino vote rarely claimed to be a single community, political or otherwise. In the Southwest alone, ethnic Mexicans embraced a variety of identities in politics and daily life. They referred to themselves as "Spanish Americans,"

"Latin Americans," or "Mexican Americans," depending in large part upon the state in which they resided. Most mainland Puerto Ricans were far removed from these conversations. Concentrated in East Coast cities, they constructed Puerto Rican political identities amid a nominal US citizenship and deep connections to a beloved homeland, one whose government actively promoted and channeled their patriotic identification with the island in service of its own objectives. Cuban exiles in Florida and elsewhere arrived en masse in later years. In flight from a revolution and expecting only temporary residence in the United States, they were far more concerned with recovering their homeland than with the other two groups' affairs.

Nor did the federal government recognize these various peoples as a collective entity. This was partly because the United States conquered or otherwise absorbed the core Latino populations in different eras (i.e., Mexicans from the mid-1800s, Puerto Ricans after 1898, and Cubans after 1959) and mostly in different regions of its mainland (i.e., the Southwest, the Northeast, and the Southeast, respectively). Set upon particular political trajectories, leaders of these distant communities developed few relationships. There was also the fact that a nontrivial portion of these populations thought ethnic politics distasteful or counterproductive. Many self-identified as "Americans" and some as "whites." And regardless of their *personal* identification, like other ethnic spokespeople of their time, many influential Hispanic Americans at midcentury were wary of any *official* efforts to separate them from the American mainstream. Mexican-American leaders had vehemently opposed the creation of a "Mexican" category on birth certificates and censuses, for example, fearing the distinction would license additional prejudice against their people. Federal officials heeded these protests, and classified most Mexican Americans (and later mainland Puerto Ricans) as regionally defined subsets of the country's "white" population. This meant that even as late as 1969, no nationwide census category distinguished them. Those wishing to make the case that this was a people central to national affairs, or to mobilize them to pursue a common agenda, were hamstrung by a lack of hard data as to their numbers, their location, and their condition.

In short, the "Latino vote" did not exist before 1960 because—at least, as a subject of national political analysis and policy conversation—the "Latino" did not meaningfully exist. And the "Latino" did not yet exist because the "Latino vote" did not yet exist.

This book explores how the two were created together, transforming American democracy and the image of a nation. Many people assume that the emergence of the Latino vote was the inevitable consequence of immigration-fueled demographic growth. Yet it was never preordained that Hispanics or Latinos would come to be seen as a prominent national political constituency. Rather, the Latino vote was painstakingly created over more than two decades. Beginning roughly in 1960, a collection of political actors—from grassroots activists to US presidents—labored to mold all "Spanish-speaking Americans" (as they often denoted themselves)—irrespective of national origin, immigration status, skin color, or even language—into a single US minority group and political constituency. These architects of Latino politics defined this pan-ethnic group's public identity on the middle ground between traditional assimilation and the race- and class-conscious nationalisms of Chicano, Puerto Rican, and Cuban movements. They productively mined the ambiguity in whether they were building a *coalition* of existing peoples or instead articulating the values and desires of a new of US-based *community* that transcended national origins. As Latino leaders gained familiarity with one another and sponsorship from party elites in the 1970s, their collaboration produced policy agendas that simultaneously reflected and constituted their people's collective will. Activists and elected officials cemented their alliances by fashioning a host of new organizations that distributed power among their respective communities so unequal in size. The relationships built and differences negotiated, identities defined and harmonized, platforms and institutions created and promoted, drew liberal Democrats and conservative Republicans alike into a self-reinforcing consensus that "Spanish-speaking Americans" (later "Hispanics" or "Latinos") constituted a unique civil rights constituency, electoral bloc, and statistical population. I argue that these political endeavors were decisive in the construction of Latino peoplehood in the United States.

Relentlessly repudiating color blindness, self-described "Latino" and "Hispanic" officials and activists played a central role in pushing the United States into the age of multicultural politics. Again, the obstacles were formidable. In the 1960s, the Democratic Party was home to most Latino voters. However, Democrats were facing immense pressure to satisfy the black freedom movement's urgent demands without losing the support of white working people in the North or their party's traditional base in the white South. Many resisted the claims of another "national minority" group. Even influential liberals at first counseled that Mexican Americans and Puerto

Ricans would achieve civil equality and economic progress by underscoring their commonality with other Americans, not by seeking official recognition of their cultural difference or policies targeting their unique disadvantages. These liberals espoused a "civic nationalism" that offered inclusion in the American nation to all who embraced the egalitarian ideals expressed in the Declaration of Independence and the Constitution. They believed that their creed, when combined with the economic security policies enacted in Franklin D. Roosevelt's New Deal, gave outsiders the means to join the American mainstream.[4] But by the late 1960s, the party's prolonged marginalization of Mexican Americans and Puerto Ricans underscored how different the two peoples remained from other Americans, and revealed how similar they were to each other. They responded by forming a pan-ethnic alliance that rejected racial assimilation and transcended the country's black-white binary, winning for their nationwide "Latino" constituency recognition as a pillar of a reconstructed Democratic Party. Yet even as Latinos helped fashion a multicultural party from the ashes of the Roosevelt coalition, they sought less to discard the New Deal than to renovate it. They creatively wove their demands for group recognition and cultural autonomy into broader arguments to preserve and extend the federal commitment to economic fairness that had been the material foundation of civic nationalism since the Great Depression. Their vision of democracy spoke to class *and* cultural concerns.

The forging of Latino politics transformed the Republican Party as well. In the late 1960s, a self-described "Hispanic Republican Movement" began to emerge, primarily through the sponsorship of GOP moderates from the Southwest. Embracing a middle-class conception of pan-ethnic community and likewise resisting color-blind politics, its equation of individual success with group progress and inclusion proved an influential formula. Yet this movement's leaders were forced to wage their own struggle to maintain their recognized place in an increasingly conservative party, one whose commitment to expanding civil rights and minority representation were certainly not a given. Hispanic Republicans ultimately promoted a multicultural conservatism that buttressed the rollback of liberal economic policy while attenuating but also masking—at least in part—the degree to which racialized conceptions of nationalism were finding a comfortable home in the GOP. By replacing a dwindling African American constituency in northern industrial states with a Sunbelt minority expected to be a more congenial coalition partner to the party's growing base of white conservatives, the

Republican "Hispanic strategy" facilitated the post–World War II era's monumental political realignment.

Thus the emergence of Latino politics both contributed to the collapse of the New Deal order *and* embedded parts of that very order's economic vision in the era that ensued. The multicultural democracy emerging from the 1960s was at once more traditionally liberal *and* more conservative than many analysts have recognized.

Even as the making of the Latino vote helped to summon into official existence a national Latino or Hispanic political community and identity, it also worked to undermine the coherence and stability of that identity. Forging *Latinidad* (roughly, Latino-ness) in the political system made its content subject to ideological redefinition and its representative institutions vulnerable to manipulation by powerful interests—US presidents especially—eager to control rather than to empower the constituency. Party leaders dutifully spoke of Hispanic political unification. But presidents and aspirants to the office were as willing to divide Latino constituencies from one another, through ranking or exclusion, as they were to promote their solidarity. The shifting priorities of party elites—whether due to the strategic needs of an election or to the rise of new party leaders possessed of different geographic or ideological backgrounds—often exposed or exacerbated internal hierarchies latent in the embryonic Latino political community. Presidential influence aligned what was an insurgent force at the dawn of the 1960s with establishment objectives by the 1980s. The burgeoning Latino *vote* was accepted fact; independent Latino *power* was far more elusive.

A deep archival investigation of Latino or Hispanic pan-ethnicity's construction and deployment in national politics, this book embraces Cristina Beltrán's view of *Latinidad* as, in her words, "something we *do* rather than something we *are*."[5] In so doing, it advances our understanding of the character, inner workings, and significance of what is now commonly known as "Latino politics" in a number of interrelated and important ways.

First, it shows that the creation of Latino politics—and with it the nationalization of Hispanic or Latino pan-ethnicity—began much earlier than scholars have acknowledged. Studies of the emergence and institutionalization of a Hispanic category have located it in the late 1960s or primarily in the late 1970s, with a corresponding debut of the "Latino vote" in the 1980s or later.[6] Yet Mexican-American and Puerto Rican political activists and elected officials had begun forging a national voting bloc as early as 1960. They had thoroughly institutionalized bipartisan courtship of the "Spanish-speaking Vote" in more or less its current form by 1972. Moreover, though far less uniform and omnipresent than they would become, pan-ethnic identifiers appeared in federal statistical practices by the early 1960s and were in some awkward use by Democratic presidents throughout that decade.

This alternative chronology points to a different set of historical agents, intentions, and chains of causation in the making of the nation's Hispanic minority constituency. In the debate over its meaning in the US context, some scholars have attributed to Hispanic identity a largely negative or defensive quality. A tendency within this school of thought, often emerging from local or regional studies, regards its assertion as an act of racial positioning. According to one scholar, ethnic Mexicans in the age of Jim Crow used it "to arrogate to themselves the privileges of whiteness," and a place on the safe side of the color line. Another argues that Puerto Ricans in New York City adopted it in the 1970s to declare their communities, once staunch allies of African Americans, now "mutually incompatible with 'blackness.'"[7] Scholars who look to the national picture, in contrast, tend to ascribe to Chicano and Puerto Rican nationalists an outsized role in propelling pan-ethnicity to national prominence. According to these interpretations, radical activism beginning in the latter half of the 1960s drove the state to impose upon a mostly unwilling society an inauthentic, "stigmatizing," and conservative "Hispanic" identity as a means of "undercutting" or casting "back into invisibility" these dynamic social movements.[8]

This book, however, calls for seeing the national "Spanish-speaking" political project more for what it was than what it was not. The creators of Latino politics and prime advocates for the recognition of Hispanic pan-ethnicity on which their project rested were liberal congressmen from the Southwest and New York. Shaped by the New Deal and its legacies, they were skilled builders of interracial coalitions. Constructing and institutionalizing Latino unity on a national scale—principally between Mexican Americans and Puerto Ricans—was a practical and logical extension of their earlier political work in New York and Los Angeles. Their "Spanish-speaking" political project scrupulously avoided claims to "whiteness," regularly asserted (over the opposition of many Democrats) the permanency of their minority status, and in crucial moments forged key partnerships with black legislators. Their adoption of pan-ethnicity accelerated *simultaneously* with the challenges of radical social movements of Chicanos and

Puerto Ricans, and for a time they used radicalism as a foil. But liberals' advocacy for, as examples, a "Cabinet Committee on Opportunities for Spanish-Speaking People" or a national "Spanish-speaking Coalition" owed primarily to more mundane causes, respectively, the structure of Congress and the election of the first Puerto Rican to serve as a voting member in the House of Representatives. Certainly those Republicans who played a vital role in institutionalizing Hispanic pan-ethnicity found that, in their world, the need to consolidate the support of conservative Cuban nationalists—not to fend off Chicano leftists—was paramount. By and large, the architects of the Hispanic constituency were far more intent on establishing new pan-ethnic alliances that could enable them to renegotiate their weak standing within the parties than they were with suppressing radical formulations of ethnicity emerging in their districts and regions.

Identifying the makers of the Latino electorate and clarifying their intentions, this book shows that the constituency emerged as the result of forces more eclectic, creative, and on occasion democratic than has previously been recognized. Scholars have rightly identified the "strategic use of ambiguity" and the "disregard for specificity" that have characterized efforts to promote a unified Latino or Hispanic collective. Undoubtedly, a focus on the public image of *Latinidad* that lobbyists, media officials, and many politicians projected indicates a powerful urge to "homogenize" distinct communities, foreclose deliberations, and minimize dissenting opinion.[9] But this book shows that the internal workings of Latino politics were—at least at times—much more varied, open, and contested than the face that Latinos showed, either to their powerful allies or enemies. Far from effectively silencing internal disagreements, the Latino political project fostered vigorous debate on the nature and needs of a people, and was highly diverse as to its purposes, structures, and meanings. That is, Mexican Americans, Puerto Ricans, and eventually Cubans deliberated and organized their way toward a common place in US democracy. This was the making of "Latino politics."

The book proceeds in eleven mostly chronological chapters. Chapters 1–3 explore the debut of Mexican-American, Puerto Rican, and Cuban political communities on the national stage in the 1960s. Taken together, they examine the ways in which these communities' various quests for recognition from local and national elites at once sharpened their senses of singularity *and* encouraged their occasional embrace of pan-ethnic orientations and imagery, all while fostering their collective inclusion in official organizations and categories that masked highly unequal distributions of status within the larger group. Chapter 1 introduces the places that came to form the core of the imagined national electoral constituency and the leaders they elevated to national prominence by the early 1960s. Portraits of northern New Mexico, South Texas, Los Angeles, New York City, and Miami illuminate the sheer variety of distinct Latino political projects ongoing in these places during the post–World War II years, and the intensification of many of these distinctions heading into the 1960s. They also reveal certain parallel political experiences, however, and how similar obstacles faced by ethnic Mexicans and Puerto Ricans drew them ever more into wider political conversations and networks. Chapter 2 marks the full investment of these communities, as well as the Cuban refugee population, in the national political arena. Liberal multiracial coalitions in urban Mexican America and Puerto Rican New York produced leaders who could, for a brief time and mostly in appearance, represent a united "Latin American" electorate. The "Viva Kennedy" effort of 1960 enshrined the presidential campaign as the central ritual in the fashioning of Latino political unity and identity. Yet John F. Kennedy's Cold War preoccupations combined with the basic separateness of Mexican-American, Puerto Rican, and Cuban political projects to further assign various "Latin American" constituencies to different spheres of political activity. Chapter 3 examines how Mexican Americans, Puerto Ricans, and Lyndon Johnson negotiated the place of "Spanish Americans" amid the civil rights progress and rising racial backlash of the mid-1960s. As black activism surged, Mexican Americans laid claim to being a comparable "national minority." Puerto Ricans used their concentrated population and alliances with African Americans to win protection for their people in the 1965 Voting Rights Act. Disappointed that traditional Democrats seemed bent on containing rather than empowering them, these constituencies' distinct options for political defection— conservative Republicans courted Mexican Americans with an anti-black appeal, while liberal Republicans courted Puerto Ricans as another liberal, urban, and progovernment civil rights constituency, like African Americans—worked against a pan-Hispanic consolidation in the Republican Party. But Johnson himself had only limited interest in uniting these groups, seeing in them more of a hierarchy than a harmony. The president regarded Mexican Americans as America's "second largest minority," first among, or even spokespersons for, the nation's "Spanish-surnamed" population.

Though gulfs separated traditional Mexican-American and Puerto Rican leaders, and a tradition of executive manipulation of Hispanic pan-ethnicity had been established, mainstream politicians pushed to enshrine their common interests and supposedly shared identity in the workings of government, and then to activate the latter for political gain. Chapters 4–7 analyze the rapid consolidation of a "Spanish-speaking" political identity in the wake of the Democratic coalition's collapse in 1968. They focus on Latino elected officials' construction of a "Spanish-speaking" advocacy body and subsequent attempts to forge a national "Spanish-speaking Coalition," as well as Republicans' first comprehensive efforts to "capture" what they called "the Spanish Speaking Vote." Chapter 4 investigates the rapid institutionalization of pan-ethnicity in 1969. As radical Chicanos and Puerto Ricans explored their own visions of "Latino" unity, and typically assigned it a low priority, liberal ethnic Mexicans forged bipartisan consensus to create a Cabinet Committee on Opportunities for Spanish-Speaking People, with proportional representation from the nation's three main Latino communities. Meanwhile, Richard Nixon inadvertently abetted the pan-ethnic project by pressuring the Bureau of the Census to redraw the nation's statistical portrait to reflect the importance of "Spanish Origin" people. Chapter 5 shows the Nixon White House finding difficulty reconciling its primary aim of converting Mexican-American voters with the ideals of fair treatment for all "Spanish-speaking Americans" to which Congress—and his own statements—had committed the president. Mastery of the "Spanish-speaking concept," as Republicans called it, lay in devising a broad middle-class appeal, one that identified the "Spanish-speaking" ethnic orientation as consistent with Republican individualism, while distributing material benefits to those national origin groups most essential to the president's "New Majority." In Chapter 6, Mexican-American and Puerto Rican congressmen convened activists from around the country in an effort to mold them into a "Spanish-speaking Coalition" that could counter Nixon's appeal and hold the balance of power in national elections. The "Unidos" conference energized many of its participants, and its democratic deliberations yielded a basic left-liberal "Spanish-speaking" policy agenda. The conference also established a temporary system of national "Spanish-speaking" representation, egalitarian with respect to Mexican Americans and Puerto

Ricans but exclusionary toward Cubans. Chicano and Puerto Rican nationalists' demands led liberals to withdraw their support for independent
"Spanish-speaking" politics. However, the liberals ensured the "Unidos"
platform and the coalition's representational logic would live on in the
Democratic Party and in the 1972 campaign of George McGovern. As
Chapter 7 shows, however, it was the Nixon administration that initially
made the most of the "Spanish-speaking concept." A campaign team nicknamed the "Brown Mafia" tendered federal patronage and racially charged
appeals in nearly equal measure, and by and large avoided nationalist
dustups. Nixon's team wooed Mexican Americans with an ethnic *and*
class—middle-class—appeal, winning a record percentage of the "Spanish-
speaking Vote" in 1972. This was a targeted conversion, however. The campaign's contempt for Puerto Rican voters exposed and exacerbated the fis-
sures within the emerging electorate. Meanwhile, the Watergate
investigation intensified the legacy of 1972 in Cuban America by further
alienating that political community from liberal Democrats and encouraging its leaders to seek a place of influence in the nation's "Spanish-
speaking" politics.

Chapters 8–11 examine how self-described Latinos and Hispanics in both
parties secured their people's place in a multicultural democracy. These
chapters evaluate their battles to enable their visions of *Latinidad* to prosper
and achieve victories against, or as part of, a rising tide of political conservatism that challenged so many of the assumptions, strategies, and intragroup relationships established in the years before Watergate. Chapter 8
focuses on Republicans in the middle years of the 1970s. It shows how even
as the Nixon administration crumbled, moderate party activists led by Mexican Americans carried forward a vision of political participation in which
individual economic uplift, Hispanic unity, and the GOP were mutually
reinforcing. The leaders of this "Hispanic Republican Movement" cemented
their presence in a new Republican National Hispanic Assembly. Nonetheless, they found GOP Hispanic politics complicated by two factors then
coming onto the political scene: undocumented immigration and a Cuban-
American constituency increasingly committed to influencing domestic politics and often in alliance with the party's right-wing insurgents. Chapter 9
examines how Latino elected officials spent those same years of the Ford
administration fighting to prevent Democrats from retreating from their
commitment to a multicultural party. In a series of mutually reinforcing

steps, they ensured permanence of the new participatory channel they had cut in the political system. By allying with black congressmen, they passed a renewed Voting Rights Act that protected their "language minority." They also legislated national statistical recognition of their people that could not be withdrawn by a capricious president, pushing the bureaucracy ever closer to adopting a national "Hispanic" category. And they redoubled the pressure on their party by uniting its Latino officeholders in a new National Association of Latino Democratic Officials. Chapter 10 examines the collision of their Latino political project with a Democratic Party not only in retreat from the policies and commitments that had guided it since the New Deal, but also, even at this late point, reluctant to assume identification with another national minority constituency. In response to Jimmy Carter's color-blind "new" liberalism, Latino Democrats creatively interwove demands for ethnic recognition with calls for universal economic uplift. Their synthesis of economic and cultural security, coupled with their elaboration of a "Hispanic" opposition to Carter's immigration policies, dislodged the administration from its selective color-blindness, and encouraged it to enlist its allies in a "Hispanic" defense of his administration. These new "Hispanic American Democrats" protected the president from a left-wing challenge, that of another Kennedy, and surrounded traditionally and economically liberal "Latino" positions with a socially liberal Hispanic blueprint fit for the 1980s and beyond. Chapter 11 analyzes another leadership transition. Hispanic Republicans engaged in their own battles over who would lead their collective endeavor and define the character of their political community. In a pathbreaking presidential run by GOP fundraiser Benjamin Fernandez, moderate Mexican-American Republicans redefined themselves and the Hispanic political character to keep pace with the party's rightward march. Yet these "New Hispanic Conservatives" could not abide the Reaganites' attacks on the policies that had promoted Hispanic inclusion in government and society. Nor could they defend their institutions from a coordinated attempt by loyal Reaganite Cubans to supplant them as the leading voice of Hispanic Republicanism. The result was a turn away from many of Hispanic Republicanism's previous strategies and techniques of appeal, and a political party's thorough recasting of a people's image and values along highly conservative lines.

The Epilogue brings the story of the "Latino vote" to the present day. It suggests that the long history of supposed electoral underachievement by

America's largest minority, articulated in national news stories, community debates, and by political organizers, has served in and of itself as a catalyst for Hispanic solidarity, one that could eventually help Latinos live up to their perceived electoral potential.

For now, however, we turn to investigate the years before "Latino Politics," to introduce the political communities that would come to play the greatest role in forming the "Latino vote."

## A Note on Terminology

To understand the political development of Latino pan-ethnicity requires close attention to names. Those subjects of this book who identified with pan-ethnic terms described themselves and their people variously as "Spanish-speaking," "Spanish-surnamed," "Hispanic," or "Latino." Some had clear preferences. For them, one or another of these terms was a more authentic reflection of themselves and their political values. Others used these terms interchangeably. Whenever possible, I refer to individuals and the peoples for whom they spoke by the terms they embraced at that time. This means I describe the Democrats who founded their party's "Latino Caucus" as "Latinos"; leaders of the Republican National Hispanic Assembly I generally refer to as "Hispanics." When it would not have offended the subjects in question to add a little variety, I use these two terms (and "Spanish-speaking") interchangeably. Still, an author must make choices. As the title suggests, my preference for discussing the emerging sense of common purpose and, for some, collective identity among Mexican Americans, Puerto Ricans, and Cubans is to use "Latino." Like the term "Hispanic," "Latino" was in widespread circulation by the later years explored in this study. Yet it seemed to reflect better the preferences of both the institutional actors *and* the grassroots populations who were then and after coming to grips with a societal expectation that their various communities together constituted a US minority group. While "Latinx" is gaining important recognition as a term of gender inclusion, I feel uncomfortable applying it to individuals in the past who had no exposure to the designation.

National origin terms also merit brief discussion. While a variety of local identities were present in Mexican communities of the United States, to limit confusion I generally refer to the broad group of individuals of Mexican origin who were born in the United States or who became naturalized

US citizens as "Mexican Americans." The term "ethnic Mexicans" refers to Mexican immigrants and Mexican Americans alike. I apply "Chicano" to the ethnic Mexican activists who adopted that designation in the movement of that name that reached its height in the late 1960s and early 1970s. Shifting to Caribbean origins, because so few Cuban exiles imagined they would remain permanently in the United States upon their arrival, I write mostly of "Cubans" and not "Cuban Americans." Many Cubans did take up US citizenship throughout the 1970s, however, and so it is at that point in the book that I begin to employ "Cuban American" as well. Finally, there is almost no tradition of Puerto Ricans as hyphenates. Possessing US citizenship and roots in a homeland politically designated as a "free associated state," they will appear in these pages as "Puerto Ricans" or, occasionally, "Boricuas," regardless of their birthplace or residence.

1

# The Many Political Communities of Latino America

A look back on the United States of America over most of the twentieth century reveals much more "politics by Latinos" than it does "Latino politics." Even in the heartland and demographic core of what became the nation's "Hispanic" or "Latino" population, the US Southwest, there was more debate than consensus as to what held together the region's political communities of ethnic Mexicans. The demands of pursuing power in places as varied as Los Angeles, the mountains of northern New Mexico, or the border counties of South Texas combined with residents' diverse historical experiences, especially with Mexican migration, to nurture distinct ethnic orientations and political outlooks. Well into the decades after World War II, these traditional factors joined new ones in challenging any notion of a singular and unified "Mexican-American" agenda.

A national politics rooted in a broader *Latinidad* was another prospect altogether. By the early 1960s, a Puerto Rican "Great Migration" to the mainland and waves of exiles fleeing revolutionary Cuba had raised for some analysts the possibility of understanding and, perhaps, mobilizing these peoples as a collective. The country's leading Mexican-American intellectual, George I. Sánchez, offered his doubts:

> They are just too many different peoples to be adequately covered under one umbrella. While they could be called, loosely, "Americans who speak Spanish" they would have to be treated in separate categories . . . though a Cuban in Florida and a Mexican in Laredo both speak Spanish, they really have little else in common (even though both may be aliens or citizens, or a combination).[1]

As he had earlier written, for these groups to "appear to be culturally homogeneous," required "a veritable shotgun wedding."[2]

Yet for all of Sánchez's skepticism about their *peoplehood*, at least some of the foundations of a Hispanic *constituency* can be seen emerging in the post–World War II years, a potential collectivity rooted in common experiences as much as in perceived cultural similarity. In the middle third of the twentieth century, the most important contributors to making the Latino vote, ethnic Mexicans and Puerto Ricans, underwent a number of similar processes and transformations, and encountered many comparable political obstacles, almost always at the hands of Democrats. They weighed and tested the value of an assertive ethnicity in a society still fully invested in white supremacy and Anglo conformity. Some developed radical critiques of American capitalism and racism. They probed a variety of alliances with other "Latins," but also with labor, African Americans, and white liberals. They conceived and reconceived of unity and what it demanded, and located themselves and their distinctiveness within the parameters of citizenship in the Cold War United States. And they arrived at the dawn of the 1960s far from powerful and often very poor.

For all their common experiences, however, their traditional practices of political self-fashioning and the largely local contexts in which they defined and articulated their communities' will led them not to coalescence, not at first. Instead, the middle third of the twentieth century witnessed ethnic Mexicans and Puerto Ricans asserting themselves as distinct and dominant Hispanic minorities in their core regions of residence. Despite the multinational Spanish-speaking populations still observable in places such as New York or San Francisco, demographic dominance of the core national origin groups fueled senses of local and state-level supremacy that fixed political peoples with places. New York was Puerto Rican. California and Texas were *Mexicano*. The "fact" of regional turf and a related need to bring these ostensibly undifferentiated national origin communities into a national network would become mostly unquestioned assumptions of Latino politics in coming years.

Cuban exile politics emerged on a completely different timeline and out of vastly different conditions. Its practitioners' relationship to the US color line was unique. It posed distinct questions to, and opportunities for, not only municipal or state officials (as was most often the case for ethnic Mexicans and Puerto Ricans) but also the national government. Yet for the notion of a unified national "Latin" constituency, as it might have been called, the end result was similar. As of 1960, the enormity of the exile migration and its concentration in Miami advanced the spatial distinction of Latino political communities that reinforced their diverse ethnopolitical orientations and self-images. Moreover, the incorporation of Cubans as exiles, as well as clients or Cold War proxies of the federal government, imparted a trajectory to their political development in the United States that ensured they would long operate apart from, yet still exert influence on, the currents of what became "Latino politics."

☆ ☆

The Mexican-American contribution to Latino politics would derive in crucial measure from a desire to be seen as truly "national." In 1960, more than 110 years after annexation and war turned Mexico's northern hinterland into the US Southwest, this people held just a limited claim on the nation's consciousness. A sizable number of ethnic Mexicans had established communities in the industrial Midwest, but the majority lived in the Southwest, a region still gaining prominence in the nation's political economy. They existed beyond the sight of many academics, advertisers, and policymakers, enigmatic and easily misunderstood, if mentioned at all. George I. Sánchez, in his 1940 study of New Mexicans, called this group a "Forgotten People."[3] More than a quarter of a century later, the *Atlantic Monthly* would run an oft-cited piece identifying them as "A Minority Nobody Knows."[4]

Mexican Americans were in this respect quite unlike the African Americans to whom they would often be compared in the years ahead. The history of black enslavement, and the overwhelming nativity of black Americans, had long compelled black and white to reckon with their status and identity in the United States. The "Great Migration" of African Americans to northern cities had established this group's incontrovertibly national character and transformed the Democratic Party. Moreover, dramatic mobilizations for black freedom and fair treatment in the postwar years challenged the American order, including the country's claim to lead the free world during the Cold War.[5]

It was not that Mexican Americans at the dawn of the 1960s did not wish to transform their people's place in society. At a time of great national prosperity, ethnic Mexicans suffered the effects of widespread and generational economic discrimination. For decades, bigotry had restricted Mexican-American and Mexican immigrant alike to the lowest-paid and dirtiest jobs. Prejudice had usually excluded them from American trade unions or consigned them to segregated locals. Even if they were allowed to perform the same labor as "Americans" (many of whom were, in fact, European immigrants), dual-wage systems had ensured that, no matter their citizenship, "Mexicans" would be paid less.[6] In Texas, where the inequalities were the most extreme, Mexican-American workers in 1960 averaged as little as 61 cents for every dollar an Anglo counterpart made. The median annual income for a Mexican-American family in the Lone Star state hovered around the national poverty line. Even in comparatively liberal California, significant disparities still existed between the earnings of these "Spanish surname" Americans, as they were known in official statistics, and "whites."[7]

Workplace discrimination wove itself into a larger web of injustice. Poverty and Anglo bias confined ethnic Mexicans to the rundown homes, unpaved roads, and open sewers of "Mexican" districts in many towns and cities. In 1960, almost 30 percent of the dwellings where Mexican Americans made their rest were "dilapidated or deteriorating," four times the rate for Anglo domiciles in the Southwest. Notwithstanding some victories in litigation, segregated and inferior schools were common. Anglos saw little reason to invest in children they marked for a future of low-wage work. The future US president Lyndon Baines Johnson became the principal of a "Mexican" school in Cotulla, Texas, while still a college student. His enthusiasm was unquestionable; his lack of credentials went largely unquestioned. In the US Southwest of 1960, a full 28 percent of Mexican Americans above the age of fourteen were "functional illiterates," possessing, at most, four years of formal education. An education, moreover, was little protection against daily reminders to stay in one's humble place. Movie theaters often relegated Mexican people to balconies or seats with obstructed views. The public swimming pool might tolerate their presence, on the day before the water was to be changed. Restaurants that were mannerly enough to have taken down their signs warning "No Dogs or Mexicans Allowed" could still make plain—and with no legal repercussion—those who would and would not be enjoying service. Policemen and immigration agents could abuse ethnic Mexicans with basic impunity.[8]

Mexican Americans struggled to obtain the power sufficient to overturn these conditions in the local and state elections. Their communities usually contained large numbers of noncitizens, ineligible to vote and thus unable to use the political system to advance their interests. Language, literacy, and residency requirements further constrained their exercise of the franchise. Poll taxes and intimidation discouraged many more potential voters. Where political bosses prevailed, they had little interest in bankrolling Mexican-American mobilizations. And since most Mexican communities were working-class in character, they tended to lack the financial resources to pursue an independent agenda. When Mexican Americans did successfully cast a ballot, gerrymandering or at-large election strategies divided or diluted their votes, denying them the chance to elect candidates who would represent their interests.[9]

Yet if Mexican America in the aggregate suffered socioeconomic and political exclusion, it was hardly foreordained that Mexican Americans would see themselves as one and unite across the Southwest (and indeed the country) to address their collective woes. As one scholar has noted, a "variety of historically constituted social boundaries" had arisen in the Southwest over centuries, with numerous local terms employed to describe and divide people of Mexican and Spanish ancestry. These identities were a testament to the multiple group loyalties brought by Spanish colonists and the uneven incorporation of New Spain's (and later Mexico's) northern provinces in their respective political communities. They also resulted from distinct experiences with and responses to the in-migration of both "Anglos" and Mexican nationals. Not only correlated to location, the names ethnic Mexicans used to describe themselves served as comments on status, skin color, linguistic style, citizenship, or wealth, among other characteristics.[10] These separate trajectories militated against the establishment of an ethnic consensus in favor of Mexican-American political empowerment on a regional scale. Political power would have to come, first, from below.

Nowhere did independent Mexican-American power threaten the status quo more than in Texas. There, ruling Democrats had a long history of methodically controlling Mexican-American votes to ensure no challenges to the dominant system of racial subordination. With the state's embrace of Jim Crow and its anti-Mexican cousin in discrimination, Juan Crow, officials in 1902 instituted a poll tax that was roughly equivalent to a Mexican worker's daily wage. In 1923 Democrats closed their primary elections to anyone who was not "white."[11] Given these constraints, Mexican-American political participation, when it existed at all, tended to be mediated by political machines. In South Texas, where most Tejanos lived, Anglo political *patrones* derived power and fortunes by delivering the Mexican vote, en masse, to the statewide candidates who paid the highest price. These *patrones'* Mexican-American "sub-bosses" procured those votes by doling out loans and favors, paying poll taxes, and handing out cash on Election Day. Most anything went. The machines voted dead men, and they brought Mexican nationals across the border by the truckload to cast ballots. Many times, citizens did not need to bother heading to the polls at all; the machine voted *for* them. To challenge the South Texas machines, especially before World War II, was to court violent reprisal. Meanwhile, Anglos in other counties made machine corruption a pretext to disfranchise *all* Mexican Americans on the grounds that a "tainted Mexican vote" undermined the political system. Nevertheless, the system had its benefits. Playing their humble role allowed Mexican Americans to become "city councilmen, constables, tax collectors, hide inspectors, justices of the peace, county commissioners, treasurers, and public attorneys," in addition to affording them the less prestigious but still remunerative work of building roads and sweeping streets. And in counties where Mexican people were incorporated in the machine, they experienced less physical segregation and social isolation. The price was the surrender of independent political influence, the hope of statewide power, and the chance of reforming the society that held Mexican people in second-class status.[12]

Machines ruled New Mexico as well, but in a somewhat more benevolent fashion. A land unattractive to Anglo fortune hunters in the nineteenth century, its Spanish-speaking elite, concentrated in mountainous northern counties, had managed to retain much of its land after the US conquest. Marshaling the allegiance of their "peon" laborers, these "Hispano" or "Spanish-American" landowners (preferred self-identifications in the state) kept a certain amount of power. They played a key role at New Mexico's 1910 statehood convention. The thirty-two Hispanos (all Republicans) on hand helped draft a constitution that outlawed school segregation, and guaranteed the right to vote, hold office, and serve on juries, regardless of "religion, race, language or color, or inability to speak, read, or write the English or Spanish languages." These safeguards forced both major parties to promote Hispano candidates for office, thereby ensuring their visible representation.[13] More than symbolism was at work, though. In rituals that any Bronx ward heeler could have grasped, Hispano *patrones* secured voter loyalty by dispensing favors, loans, and cash payments to individuals, and subsidies to community celebrations and religious festivals. Amid wide-spread poverty, public sector employment was an especially valuable political currency, and one that kept average Hispanos connected to the political system. When the Depression struck and the impoverished masses flocked to the comfort of New Deal patronage and programs (almost a third of the state was on relief in 1935) the long-ruling Republicans were routed.[14]

In 1930, a longtime Democratic Party worker, state legislator (and seventh-grade dropout-turned lawyer) named Dionisio "Dennis" Chavez rode the wave of popular frustration with Republicans to the US House of Representatives. Chavez joined the US Senate in 1935 and managed re-election five times. He defended the New Deal and Hispano civil rights with equal vigor.[15] This was a matter of increasing importance. Anglo migration from the South and Midwest accelerated in the years after World War II, eroding the Hispanos' demographic advantage. While most of the newcomers were Democrats, their willingness to respect the state's traditional power-sharing arrangements and Hispano civil rights was hardly assured.[16] Thus while New Mexico's Hispanos may have been the most politically integrated of all Spanish-speaking Americans, even they had reason to regard their modest sociopolitical status as fragile.[17]

Alternatives to political machines were themselves quite varied. In South Texas after World War I, a budding cadre of Mexican-American shop-keepers, craftsmen, and professionals began to experiment with new forms of independent quasi-political organization.[18] The combined migration into South Texas of southern and midwestern Anglos unwilling to accommodate even the faintest hint of Mexican-American political participation and social equality, and of the vast numbers of poor Mexicans fleeing the upheaval of a revolution in that country, concerned them greatly. Viewing themselves "as a small nucleus of enlightenment,"[19] the Texans formed the League of United Latin American Citizens (LULAC) in 1929. They yearned to win a measure of equality from Anglo society by dressing well, becoming educated, speaking English, and living clean and upright lives. LULAC aimed to cultivate "the best, purest and most perfect type of a true and loyal citizen of the United States of America."[20]

In the face of a body politic obsessed with purging its inferior "races," the label "Latin American" itself suggested an ethnic status that differed little from that of, say, Irish American. Indeed, many LULAC members insisted that they were white, a matter of no small consequence in Jim Crow

Texas.[21] LULAC was officially nonpartisan and did not endorse candidates. But it did register voters and organize poll tax drives, exhorting its members to support "men who show by their deeds, respect and consideration for our people."[22] LULAC filed lawsuits opposing segregation and jury exclusion.[23] Offering social interaction, cultural recognition, and a route to a civic voice, the group grew rapidly in the 1930s. By World War II, it had more than eighty councils (chapters) across the Southwest and was active in Kansas as well.[24]

Whereas LULAC's "acquiescent" character reflected its origins in the restrictive atmosphere of South Texas, a bolder attempt to mobilize "Spanish-speaking" solidarity came out of Depression-era Los Angeles.[25] The city's ethnic Mexican population had a high proportion of immigrants but lacked traditional working-class routes to political incorporation; nonpartisan municipal elections and the city's sprawling geography worked against the formation of party machines.[26] This lack of integration left the political field somewhat open for experimentation. During the 1930s, the city's culture industry radiated radicalism, and its industrializing economy became more heavily unionized. Indeed, across the region, left-wing trade unions were fanning out to the Southwest's fields, packinghouses and canneries, its mines and smelters, and its garment sweatshops. These unions, often affiliated with an upstart labor federation called the Congress of Industrial Organizations (CIO), broke with US labor tradition and welcomed Mexicans and Mexican Americans—crucially including women—into their ranks. They were the working-class foundation for El Congreso de Pueblos de Habla Española (the Congress of Spanish-Speaking Peoples).[27] Established in 1939 and modeled after other left-wing "Popular Front" groups, this broad coalition of liberals, trade unionists, and Communists empowered its supporters to challenge the twin structures of economic exploitation and racial subordination. Fusing class and culture consciousness, El Congreso advocated for striking workers as it demanded an educational system that nurtured its members' language and heritage. Opening its ranks to Mexican citizens, a practice shunned by LULAC, it did urge them to naturalize and vote in US elections.

Displacing American citizenship as a precondition for membership and the essence of self-identification, El Congreso crossed other boundaries as well. By invoking a community of "Spanish-speaking people," it sought to transcend the longstanding divisions among Mexican-descended people in the Southwest, while reaching out to Puerto Ricans and other Latinos who resided mainly in the East.[28] These groups' various problems were, according to El Congreso, "differences of degree rather than kind." This choice reflected the strong imprint of the labor organizer Luisa Moreno. Her own national origin (Guatemala) and experiences organizing Mexican-American farmworkers in Texas, Puerto Ricans in the garment shops of New York, and the Cuban and Spanish cigar factory workers in Tampa convinced her of the need for pan-Hispanic organization.[29] Such inclusiveness could be seen here and there during the pre–World War II period, as certain cities, such as New York, possessed a rough balance of migrants from the Spanish-speaking world.[30]

Its ethnic ecumenism notwithstanding, El Congreso struggled for survival. Lack of money and organizers, rivalries with more conservative Mexican-American organizations, and the Southwest's vast geography were key obstacles to its expansion beyond Los Angeles. Furthermore, while Communist ties inspired its radical critique, the leadership's adherence to the Moscow party line alienated liberals and gave conservative opponents ammunition with which to attack it.[31] World War II and the Cold War were deeply inhospitable to El Congreso. Anticommunist labor organizations raided its union base. Redbaiting government crusaders hounded its leaders, who sought exile or were deported for reasons ranging from minor immigration violations to their past or present Communist sympathies.[32] As other labor-centric movements for racial justice would find, the small space that had been opened for their critique during the tumult of the Depression was narrowing rapidly.[33]

☆ ☆

Though World War II and the Cold War foreclosed more sweeping solutions to the plight of Mexican Americans—and in the case of El Congreso, all Spanish-speaking peoples—they also presented new opportunities to mobilize them around common understandings. During those years, Mexican Americans and the region most of them called home were integrated into national life in new ways. After the Japanese attack on Pearl Harbor, the federal government's war purchases lifted the economy out of the Depression and spread industrialization across the Southwest. Seeking steady jobs on military bases, in bomber factories or shipyards, in the oilfields or countless other war-related industries, Mexican Americans escaped the repressive countryside and became an urban people. They still did the dirty work and had little chance for promotion. But the tight wartime labor market (unemployment was 1.2 percent in 1944) and government contracting rules brought them improved wages and new benefits such as health coverage and vacations. Moreover, those who served abroad were forever changed. Returning more worldly and confident, Mexican-American soldiers used the GI Bill to attend college and Veterans Administration loans to secure property. Many found stable jobs in the Southwest's burgeoning military-industrial complex and became pillars of a growing Mexican-American middle class. Like black veterans, they argued that it was unacceptable to risk their lives for the country in a war against Nazi racism only to return to a world of second-class citizenship. Their country's Cold War pretentions to leading a free and democratic world against the Soviets upped the ante; the "American" way was not supposed to tolerate bigotry.[34]

In 1948, Mexican-American veterans in South Texas established the American G.I. Forum. Under the leadership of a Corpus Christi physician and World War II veteran named Hector P. García, the group soon formed dozens of chapters. The Forum achieved a national reputation for protesting a South Texas funeral home's refusal to hold a wake for a Mexican American killed in action, on the proprietor's grounds that "the whites would not like it."[35] Though the Forum was, on balance, a more forceful voice than LULAC, it was political in ways that reflected its place and time. Early on its chapters encouraged Mexican Americans to pay their poll tax and cast a ballot, but stayed out of machine-controlled counties. It was officially nonpartisan and, like LULAC, cautiously favored litigation to attack Mexican Americans' social exclusion. Reflecting both the prevailing hostility to independent political action and its own yearning for inclusion in the nation, the Forum cast electoral participation as a civic duty rather than a quest for ethnic power. Its patriotic name was a needed shield against reprisals from those concerned it was organizing "Meskins" as a bloc. All the Forumeers aspired to, it suggested, was their rights as loyal Americans.[36]

As Forumeers well knew, embracing the American nation was often a necessary protection against bigoted forces who labeled any and all civil rights organizing as a sinister Communist conspiracy, and who fought back with, among other tools, their own version of Cold War authority.

As it was, holding the nation to its democratic ideals did not preclude ethnic politics as much as it did channel it. Indeed, subsuming

Mexican-American political ambitions in larger questions of what the country owed *all* its people—a "civic nationalist" strategy—coupled with the basic demands of local politics in Texas and California to foster Mexican Americans' participation in transformational coalitions. By aligning with other outsiders seeking both group power and the fulfillment of their American rights, Mexican Americans achieved watershed victories for political independence.

San Antonio was scene of one such breakthrough. A landscape fundamentally reordered by the wartime defense boom, its overall population grew by more than 50 percent during the 1940s.[37] By the time of Viva Kennedy, it held the second largest Mexican population in the country, after that of Los Angeles. Ethnic Mexicans seeking opportunity there found little equality, however. Restrictive covenants and homeowner prejudice confined most to the city's West Side barrio. Poor conditions there meant shorter, sicker lives, and unspeakable needless suffering. The city's Democratic political machine had proven itself loath to address such inequities and was losing its grip in the rapidly growing city.[38] Businessmen organized an ostensibly nonpartisan "Good Government League" to seize the reins of power, but their aims were promoting growth and investment, not social justice. Vying with both the machine and the business class was a coalition of Mexican Americans, blacks, and white liberals, intent upon making civil rights, a higher minimum wage, and a fair share of public spending in their neighborhoods the new mission of local government.[39]

"Local" issues had greater significance, however. The fight for a voice in San Antonio was inextricably tied to a larger effort among liberal Texas Democrats to align their state's party with the national Democratic Party's liberal wing, and to extend the New Deal fully to the South. In a one-party state, failure to do so would mean they would remain captive to the state's conservative "Establishment," which one historian has described as "a loosely knit plutocracy comprised mainly of Anglo businessmen, oilmen, bankers and lawyers . . . dedicated to a regressive tax structure, low corporate taxes, antilabor laws," and to "oppression" of the state's black and Mexican populations.[40]

It was in this context that a liberal and interracial coalition helped launch the career of Henry Barbosa González. Born in 1916 to parents who had fled the Mexican Revolution, Henry B., as he was known, grew up in a political household. His father, once mayor of a small Durango city, served as managing editor of *La Prensa,* the city's only Spanish-language daily. Intellectuals frequented the González house, exposing young Henry to political, historical, and philosophical discussion.[41] He trained in law,[42] and after serving a stint as a radio and cable censor in World War II, ran a liberal gamut of housing, education, religious, and labor work. These positions allowed González to develop a vast network of contacts and a reputation for advocacy.[43]

Through it all, this son of immigrants developed a political style that blended universal and ethnic appeals, civic nationalism with a subtext. In his first race, for the state assembly in 1950, he pledged to be a genuine voice for the "common citizen—the wage earner" and not the "country club set." At the same time, he cultivated Mexican Americans' loyalty with Spanish-language advertisements stressing that "a vote for Henry B. González is one more step to the unification and defense of *nuestra Raza* [our people]."[44] Though González lost that race, he would parlay his charismatic and bilingual campaign style, effective on radio and on television, to a city council seat in 1953. Recognizable in his white shoes and a white suit, councilman González was a steadfast liberal, fighting the burning of library books deemed "communist-tinged,"[45] working to desegregate public facilities, and opposing utility rate increases.[46]

In 1956, González and Bexar County liberals set their sights on a seat in the Texas Senate, a body in which no ethnic Mexican had sat in more than a century. Henry B. counted on the liberal political organization then being established by attorney and activist Albert Peña. Having turned San Antonio's sclerotic LULAC Council #2 into an activist political organization, Peña launched an all-out poll tax drive. In coalition with black leaders on the city's east side, they expanded the electorate just enough for González to scrape out a Democratic primary win over a candidate backed by one of the state's biggest power brokers, US senator Lyndon B. Johnson.[47] Battling accusations that he was a "left-winger" and "creeping socialist," González defeated his Republican general election opponent as well, drawing upon Mexican-American, black, and Anglo support.[48]

From his first days in Austin, González continued to inspire and be inspired by the liberal insurgency against Texas's conservative Democrats. In 1957, state legislators were playing their part in the campaign of "massive resistance" to the *Brown v. Board of Education* decision.[49] They introduced a noxious series of bills that denied funds to integrated schools, set aside public money to send students to segregated private schools, barred NAACP members from public employment, and required advocates of integration to register with the state. González and Senator Abraham Kazen fought the measures with filibusters lasting as long as 36 hours. Henry B. upbraided his colleagues for trying to deny an equal education to the children of patriotic minorities, who had sacrificed so much during wartime. He called one of the bills "odious to any free society."[50] Despite being unable to foil the bulk of the segregationist agenda, the filibusters captured national attention.[51] González won an NAACP "Man of the Year" award for his defense of racial equality and constitutional freedoms.[52] For civic nationalists such as González, Mexican-American progress in postwar Texas was intimately tied to the fate of other marginal groups.

González's civic nationalist defense of labor, integration, and civil rights for all Americans made him a hero to liberal Texans, regardless of ethnoracial background. The Democrats of Texas, the party's organized liberal wing, redoubled its efforts to oust segregationist incumbent governor, Price Daniel, in 1958. González launched his own campaign, pledging to "make every citizen a first class citizen."[53] The liberal *Texas Observer* made clear the enormity of his burden. "By the customary standards of Texas politics," it noted, "González has three handicaps: he is a Mexican, he is Catholic, and he is for integration."[54] Barnstorming the massive state in his old station wagon, González tried to reassure voters that he was no special interest candidate. "I have not and will not ever use a public office to promote any group," he promised one crowd. Of a Rio Grande Valley man who had hugged him and pledged his vote, all "because my name is González," he said, "I don't see how I could do that man much good." Like many liberals of his day— even more so given his need to impress the state's Anglo electorate—he stressed that it was "the issues" alone that mattered.[55] His broad and egalitarian platform called for aid to education, improved health care, higher taxes on gas pipelines, and federal support for school lunches.[56]

Yet as in his city council run, Henry B. found ways to benefit from his ethnic appeal. One Spanish-language flier touted his Catholicism and seven children, encouraging voters to take pride in making him the state's first "Latin American" governor.[57] And with political campaigns being a form of entertainment—especially in midcentury Texas—González was known to employ mariachi musicians to enliven his rallies.[58] Then there were the González *corridos*, ballads adapted to serve as musical endorsements. One such ditty, patriotically dated July 4, 1958, extolled the virtues of this "estadounidense de ascendencia mexicana" (US American of Mexican descent):

| | |
|---|---|
| Recordemos nuestra Historia, | Let us remember our history, |
| sin olvidar el pasado, | without forgetting the past, |
| refresquemos la memoria | Let us refresh the memory, |
| en el momento presentado. | in the present moment. |
| . . . | . . . |
| En todita una centuria, | In all of a century, |
| nunca habia habido otro igual | there had never been another equal, |
| ni su nombre se repudia, | nor his name repudiated |
| porque ha de ser inmortal. | because he is to be immortal. |
| . . . | . . . |
| Si tenemos patriotismo, | If we have patriotism, |
| a GONZÁLEZ no olvidemos, | we won't forget González, |
| ataviados de CIVISMO | adorned in public spirit, |
| ahora lo demostraremos. | We will show it now. |

There was no contradiction between Mexican-American pride and the duties of national citizenship, asserted the *corrido*. In fact, a vote for this honorable and worthy man seamlessly expressed both ethnic and national loyalty.[59]

Henry B. González lost the Democratic primary to Price Daniel by more than half a million votes.[60] Yet in garnering more than 200,000 votes statewide, he proved himself a force in Democratic politics, and a key link between Mexican Americans and the liberal movement in Texas and beyond.[61]

In Los Angeles, Mexican Americans felt a similar sense of urgency for an equal place in their city and nation, and for a more liberal and inclusive Democratic Party. As in San Antonio, World War II and the Cold War defense buildup rapidly reshaped life, fueling industrialization and regional growth. Citrus groves became subdivisions, and L.A. became the nation's fourth largest city and home to the greatest urban concentration of Mexican-origin people in the United States.[62] Yet as late as 1950, the city was still 81 percent white and only about 8 percent Mexican and 9 percent African American.[63] Most politicians felt little need to court Mexican votes, let alone

Henry B. González campaign flyer, ca. 1961. González's pledge to serve *"all* Texas" deflected Anglo conservatives' charges that he was only an "ethnic" candidate while at the same time speaking to his multiracial coalition of labor, liberal, and minority constituents. Courtesy of Henry B. González Papers, e_hbg_0033, Dolph Briscoe Center for American History, University of Texas, Austin.

support their candidacies. The metropolis was becoming famous for its motion pictures, endless freeways, and futuristic aerospace industry. Yet Thomas Edison was hard at work on the lightbulb the last time a Mexican American had sat on its city council.[64]

In 1947, a thirty-year-old social worker named Edward Ross Roybal set about restoring Mexican-American representation in Los Angeles. "Eddie" Roybal, as most knew him then, was a wiry man with a warm smile and a thinning head of dark, wavy, swept-back hair. He had been born into an old New Mexico Hispano family, the son of a cabinet maker, in 1916, the same year as Henry B. González. In the early 1920s, his parents moved with their eight children to Los Angeles, settling in the polyglot east side neighborhood of Boyle Heights. Roybal graduated high school, joined the Civilian Conservation Corps during the Depression, and then studied at UCLA and Southwestern University Law School. He spent the last year and a half of World War II in the army, and afterward found work running a mobile X-ray unit for the California Tuberculosis Association. He won a position on the Los Angeles Democratic Central Committee, and another social service job, closer to home, directing the health education unit of the Los Angeles County Tuberculosis and Health Association. His performance in this respectable public position convinced several politically involved doctors and Mexican-American businessmen that Roybal was suited for office.[65]

The ninth council district was the place. Even in the postwar boom years, the ninth was a jumble of blue-collar ethnic American insecurity. High levels of unemployment plagued its residents. Its private home stock was poor, much of it rentals and without running water. What the district lacked in material amenities it made up for in human diversity, however. In 1947, the population of Roybal's Boyle Heights was 40 percent ethnic Mexican. The neighborhood was also nicknamed the city's "Lower East Side" because of its large Jewish population. What's more, the ninth encompassed Chinatown, Little Tokyo, as well as predominantly African American and Anglo neighborhoods.[66]

As in San Antonio, for a Mexican American to win required a multiracial coalition. Roybal's 1947 campaign set the diverse constituency's shared issues within a framework of civic nationalism. He pledged bread-and-butter constituent service, and a voice against police brutality. Campaign cards pressed into the palms of voters listed three things: his name, "veteran," and "progressive." With his campaign button a patriotic red, white, and blue, Roybal made clear he was not a Communist, and he was not a foreigner.[67]

He was also not a winner. But defeat in 1947 was educational, and his third-place showing convinced Roybal and his disappointed supporters to reconstitute their campaign committee as a group they called the Community Political Organization. Around this time, Saul Alinsky, the patron saint of American community organizing and leader of the Industrial Areas Foundation, was taking an interest in east side Los Angeles. With financial support from west side Jewish donors, he hired the gifted organizer Fred Ross (later instrumental in building the United Farm Workers) to work with the city's budding Mexican-American leadership. Thus was born the main vehicle for Mexican-American civic participation in Los Angeles during the 1950s, the newly renamed Community Service Organization (CSO).[68] Under Roybal's chairmanship, the CSO drew liberal anti-Communist trade unions, the Catholic clergy, professionals, and business-people into its broad coalition. Nearly every night, it seemed, the CSO held a house meeting, soliciting community concerns and convincing average people to take part in its program of "mass-based civic action."[69]

These efforts soon bore fruit. In his 1949 campaign, Roybal again promised to fight for an equitable distribution of city services and a life free from discrimination and police brutality.[70] Japanese community leaders backed him, and one of the city's two black newspapers gave its endorsement.[71] Donations and volunteers came from needle trade and steelworker unions.[72] Most important of all, between the 1947 and 1949 elections, the CSO convinced more than 15,000 district voters—most of them Mexican Americans—to register.[73] His opponent race-baited the New Mexico–born Roybal, maligning him as a "Mexican" unworthy of a seat in government. And no matter how patriotic Roybal proclaimed himself to be, his campaign to include the outsider in the city's mainstream merely made him, in his opponent's eyes, a "Communist in disguise."[74] Yet more than 82 percent of the district's eligible voters turned out (compared with 39 percent in 1945), making Roybal, by an almost two-to-one margin, the city's first councilman of Mexican heritage since 1881.[75] Befitting a victor whose coalition included Jews, labor, and other minority support, he said he intended to "represent all the people in my district—one of the most cosmopolitan in our city."[76]

Like other civic nationalists of his day, Councilman Roybal tried to make Cold War patriotism a basis for reform, and not simply reaction. He was

Edward Roybal and his family celebrating victory in his 1949 campaign for Los Angeles City Council. The first ethnic Mexican to serve on the council since the nineteenth century, Roybal was a staunch defender of his multiracial constituency's civil rights and liberties, labor rights, and access to municipal services. © Roybal Family Trust. From the Edward R. Roybal Papers, Collection 107. Courtesy of the UCLA Chicano Studies Research Center.

the only councilman to vote against requiring Communists to register with the authorities, which he denounced as a "thought-control" measure.[77] He bravely condemned the commonplace brutality of Los Angeles policemen, and helped establish the American Civil Liberties Union chapter in East Los Angeles during the height of the Cold War.[78] He fought workplace discrimination on patriotic grounds, arguing that a citywide Fair Employment Practices Commission was needed to prevent "communist influences" from finding "a fertile breeding ground" in the City of Angels. Continuing to permit employers the "freedom" to deny someone a job on the basis of ethnic or racial background would only "give further credence to the belief that racial and religious discrimination is too thoroughly established in our economy to be outlawed," declared Roybal.[79]

Even as Roybal mined the civic nationalist tradition to affirm his entire coalition and advance their rights as Americans, he was hardly colorblind. Indeed, his election to a council consisting of thirteen white Protestants and one Irish Catholic (all were men) was uniquely important for *his* group.[80] He had acknowledged as much at his swearing-in ceremony when he announced that it was "the first time in 70 years that a Mexican American has taken office in this city hall." Roybal's self-identification as "Mexican American"—the term of choice among his California constituents— illustrated that inclusion need not depend on asserting a "Spanish" or "Latin American" cultural identity at the expense of one's "Mexican" roots. Indeed, it subtly endorsed the claims of all Mexican people, regardless of their origins, to a decent life in the United States. Perhaps the closest parallel might be African Americans' later embrace of "black" instead of "Negro." To Mexican Americans in California, it was a declaration of ethnic pride and independence.[81]

Like Henry B. González, Edward Roybal became a well-known liberal, a fighter for a multiracial, blue-collar constituency, and a thorn in the side of interests (including many Democrats) who would rather that issues such as discrimination not enter the political system. And just as in San Antonio, Roybal's rise called attention to the barriers that Mexican Americans (and liberals more generally) still faced in the state Democratic Party. The California Democratic Council, a liberal party organization similar to the Democrats of Texas, helped Roybal receive the Democratic nomination for lieutenant governor in 1954. He outperformed the party's gubernatorial candidate, but felt that Democratic regulars withheld their full support, resulting in his loss.[82] Party power brokers seemed unwilling to support a "Mexican" for statewide office.

As frustration mounted, the CSO organized. It added chapters across the state and even expanded to Arizona. Holding citizenship classes and registering voters, the group was raising Mexican Americans' political profile. As Roybal told its 1957 convention, "The sleeping giant is beginning to awaken, and it will not be long before his strength begins to be felt in the state and local elections."[83] The 1958 elections challenged this optimism. Democrats rode rampant, but a Mexican-American candidate for secretary of state suffered the party's lone statewide defeat. Roybal, too, lost a narrow battle for a Los Angeles County Supervisor seat that year, stoking his sense of grievance against party insiders. Completing the insult, the state's new governor, the liberal Edmund G. "Pat" Brown, offered Mexican Americans little in the way of patronage appointments. California created a Fair Employment Practices Commission to combat workplace discrimination, but Brown, suggesting the extent to which politicians still considered civil rights the province of African Americans, failed to name a single Mexican American to its five-member board. The legislature proved similarly unresponsive. The CSO's main priority, securing old-age pensions for noncitizens, was going nowhere.[84]

Greater autonomy was necessary. "We felt that the time had come to organize an independent electoral organization," recalled the CSO's Bert Corona, "based on the needs of the community and not on the electoral needs of the Democratic Party."[85] In 1959, Roybal began lining up Hispanic supporters within the California Democratic Council. And in April 1960, 150 mostly middle-class professionals and trade unionists descended upon Fresno to found the Mexican American Political Association (MAPA). This nonpartisan group dedicated itself to achieving "the social, economic, cultural and civic betterment of Mexican-Americans and all other Spanish-speaking Americans through political action."[86] Electing Edward Roybal their first president, MAPA activists believed they were taking a bold step toward political independence in their state.

Yet, to expand the scale of organization revealed persistent disparities in the ways that ethnic Mexicans understood their relationships to Mexico, other "Spanish-speaking Americans," and to the wider society. For instance, at MAPA's founding convention it was the new organization's name that produced the "most heated discussion." A minority of California delegates had roots in Puerto Rico or elsewhere in Latin America. They wished those to be acknowledged in the organization's name. But as MAPA activist Henry López recalled, "there had been . . . too many people evading the use of the word Mexican, as though there was something shameful about it." He recalls explaining the stakes to the others: "'Listen, we love you, we want you, but for our special psychological reason we have got to confirm this as Mexican American.'"[87]

The trouble in building a statewide organization was only magnified at the regional level. Ethnic Mexicans who gathered in 1958 to build a south-western political coalition failed, the MAPA activist Bert Corona recalled, "largely—and foolishly—because we couldn't agree on a name for the group." According to Corona, "the Texans wanted 'Latin American,' the New Mexicans wanted 'Spanish-speaking,' the Arizonans wanted 'Hispanic' or 'Latin American,' the Coloradoans wanted 'Hispanic,' and we in California wanted 'Mexican.'"[88]

While Corona chalked their collective failure up to "provincialism," it was, as we have seen, a provincialism with deep and tangled roots. The various political identities that Mexican Americans embraced not only tied them to places but also served as proxies for political orientation and faction. With the Southwest's ethnic Mexican communities vying to determine their collective destiny, disagreements over goals or strategy could easily appear "ethnic" in nature. That is, the Texans' adoption of "Latin American" or "Spanish-speaking" was, for Corona and many others, evidence not of their political socialization in a conservative state but of their lack of ethnic honesty. The implication was that if *Latin Americans* stopped being ashamed about who they *were*, they would advocate the political approach that *Mexican Americans* in California demanded.[89]

☆ ☆

As Mexican Americans struggled for political voice in the postwar years, events were unfolding in the East that would alter their prospects for empowerment. The foundation of the change was laid decades earlier in the Caribbean. After the United States' 1898 war with Spain had made Puerto Rico a US colony, the island's inhabitants came north to fill the openings in the low-wage workforce created by immigration restriction laws passed in the 1920s. Much like their Mexican contemporaries, they were the migrants admitted in an era of otherwise largely closed borders. Those who settled the New York *colonias* in those early decades became janitors and maids, as well as porters and seamstresses and factory operatives. They built lives for themselves in the tenements of uptown Manhattan's East Harlem, downtown near the cigar factories of Chelsea, and across the East River in Brooklyn, where they took jobs on the waterfront and in the borough's Navy Yard.[90]

Like other newcomers before them, these early migrants sought protection from abuses by employers, landlords, and other petty tyrants whose indiscretions have many an urban Democrat made. And like their predecessors, they organized clubs that traded their votes for social services, job referrals, housing help, legal and medical assistance, and entertainment. Since at that time they composed but a modest portion of the city's multinational Spanish-speaking population, some of these associations were pan-Hispanic in nature, including the city's populations of Cubans, Spaniards, and other Latin Americans. Many had a more specific identity, however. The "Puerto Rican Democratic Club," for instance, announced its ethnic composition by name. Still others were christened after Puerto Rican political heroes.[91] Mainland Puerto Ricans before World War II were thus both practical in seeking alliances and much like other migrants in drawing political inspiration from their homeland.

Unique was that their homeland belonged to the United States. Since 1917, Puerto Rican birth had conferred US citizenship, and thus the right to participate in local, state, and federal elections. For Puerto Ricans, US citizenship and a shared island background could therefore promote political solidarity and effectiveness. On the other hand, unresolved questions about Puerto Rico's political status—whether its people should seek independence, statehood, or some other form of political autonomy—could just as easily divide the migrant community. Most Puerto Rican migrants and their children were practically idealistic. They built political relationships that addressed their immediate needs while promoting justice—however they defined it—for their homeland. Certainly, a number of New York politicos encouraged Puerto Rican migrants to believe that backing the local party organizations would not only better their day-to-day lives but also give them a say in shaping the island's destiny. In the early 1970s, Brooklyn political boss Carlos Tapia recalled the diasporic political connection of earlier decades in this way:

So that when some unfortunate Puerto Rican is arrested by the police I can ask some politicians to talk to the judge on his behalf. So that I can ask the same politician to help some poor Puerto Rican who needs medical attention in some municipal hospital. . . . I am looking ahead for my people in Puerto Rico also and that is what every one of us should have in mind. The only way for our island to get political recognition is through the Puerto Ricans here in New York and in other states of the Union. Someday the Puerto Ricans in New York and in many other states of the United States, will by their political power get what our brothers on the island will never get, congressmen who in exchange for our help to elect them will have to help our beloved Puerto Rico.[92]

"Political recognition," however, was not simply yielded. Many officials perceived Puerto Ricans as a transient population and thus made few efforts to incorporate them. Others actively discouraged their influence. Those who wished to suppress the Puerto Rican vote had an important tool at their disposal. Enacted in 1921, a time of fevered antiimmigrant passion, New York State's literacy test limited voter registration to those who could demonstrate an eighth-grade education, or pass a "stringent" test of their English-language reading and writing ability given by the state Board of Regents.[93] One result: it would not be until 1954 that Tammany Hall, New York's Democratic machine, named a Puerto Rican to a party leadership position.[94] And it would take until the 1960s for Democrats to nominate a Puerto Rican for a seat on the city council, in which they held twenty-four of twenty-five places.[95]

A dearth of representatives in positions of authority inspired calls to summon Puerto Rican unity to challenge the machine.[96] One writer considered the state of affairs during the Depression and concluded that there was a stark choice: "Who are we going to serve? The Jews? American Negroes?" His answer: "NO. Puerto Ricans."[97] In 1934, a lawyer and onetime postal worker named Oscar García Rivera declared that "the time has come to vote for a Puerto Rican," someone "who represents the collective sentiments of the 50,000 or more Spanish-speakers" residing in the upper Manhattan *barrio*. To "fixate" on party labels, he said, was folly. Answering his plea, East Harlem sent García Rivera to the New York State Assembly in 1937 on the Republican line (with strong labor and left backing).[98] He became the first Puerto Rican to hold elected office in the country.

Puerto Ricans' pursuit of an independent agenda during the 1930s was about more than simply putting one of their own in office, however.

Rather, the trauma of the Depression underscored Puerto Ricans' efforts to connect their mainland situation and that of the island, and strengthened their access to the political and intellectual resources needed to pursue ethnic goals within a broader analysis of economic injustice and colonial exploitation. A radical Italian-American politician named Vito Marcantonio championed this critique. Marcantonio had been Mayor Fiorello LaGuardia's campaign manager, and had ties to the Communist Party.[99] He represented East Harlem in the US House of Representatives every year but two from 1934 to 1950 because of his strong support for New Deal labor and social legislation, and because of his fervent constituent service, which often extended beyond his district to Puerto Rico itself. Marcantonio was "de facto Congressman for Puerto Rico" on serious policy questions as well. He demanded that the US government restore Spanish-language instruction in Puerto Rico's schools as fervently as he defended progressive taxation, rent control, and old-age pensions in New York. He introduced legislation calling for Puerto Rican independence and later won the extension of New Deal benefits to the island's population. Paralleling his leftist contemporaries in El Congreso, his class *and* culture-conscious politics rested on an ability to connect his constituents' everyday experiences of economic exploitation and racism to Puerto Rico's status as, in his words, a "slave colony" that bore the "scars of imperialist control."[100] Marcantonio's ability to reflect Puerto Ricans' antiracist and anticolonial linkage of mainland and homeland furthered New York Puerto Ricans' socialization as a left-leaning and politically insurgent constituency.

Yet as it had for El Congreso in the Southwest (and many other leftists across America), this strategy ran headlong into dramatic changes underway during World War II and the early postwar era. At the tail end of the Depression, the political dynast Luis Muñoz Marín helped found a new island political party. The Partido Popular Democrático (PPD) was a populist coalition of urban workers, farmers, and the middle class. Its leaders shared many values and interests with the New Dealers in Washington. When Muñoz Marín became the island's first elected governor in 1948, the one-time independence advocate set about establishing the island as a "free associated state." Under the "commonwealth" arrangement, talk of US imperialism was officially a dead letter. For Muñoz Marín's staunch anti-Communist regime, foreign investment, not the extirpation of colonial rule, were the keys to alleviating Puerto Ricans' enduring poverty.[101] The PPD soon inaugurated a development plan, known in English as "Operation Bootstrap," which made Puerto Rico into "an almost tax-free environment." US capital flowed in to reap returns; a vast restructuring of island life ensued. Light manufacturing expanded, wages increased, and literacy spread its blessings. Health improved and average life expectancy skyrocketed (from forty-six to sixty-nine years between 1940 and 1960). But with modernization came an actual decline in the number of jobs on the island. For elites, the unemployed now constituted evidence that the island was "overpopulated."[102] Puerto Rican officials induced air carriers to lower their fares in order to facilitate an exodus. Mainland wages, however unremarkable, more than paid for the trip aboard the *vuelos quiquiruiquí*, or "cockadoodle-doo" flights, that left the island late at night and landed in New York at the break of dawn.[103]

Almost a quarter of the island's workforce left during the 1950s. New York in turn claimed 612,574 Puerto Rican residents by the start of the next decade, almost ten times the number it had just twenty years before.[104] The astonishing undertaking became known in community lore as the "Great Migration."

The newcomers occupied a precarious economic and social position. Like other migrants to the urban North at the time, Puerto Ricans labored in industries mechanizing or in decline. Male and female migrants alike were very poorly paid, and in the 1950s, Puerto Rican men were out of work at roughly twice the rate of white men. Puerto Ricans with darker skin had an even more difficult time finding jobs, particularly skilled positions.[105] Immigration restriction had created the openings in the low-wage labor force that Puerto Ricans came to fill. It also meant that many New Yorkers, now a generation or more removed from their own immigrant past, had little sympathy for Puerto Ricans' struggles. Poor and often of African descent, the migrants were cursed by society. Politicians and journalists disparaged the Puerto Ricans as unfit to reside in their metropolis, railing against their use of city welfare funds, and their alleged tendencies toward poor health, stupidity, and criminality.[106] Hysterical accounts of Harlem "reeking" of the newcomers graced the pages of *Life*. Fear-mongering exaggerations of their numbers—human beings appearing as "swarms"—did too.[107] In a city short on housing, they were blamed and called an "overcrowded" and "overdiseased" people.[108]

Easily manipulated at the polls, it was said, they seemed to lack any political maturity or capacity. In attacking the radical congressman Vito Marcantonio, the Hearst *Daily Mirror* described his base as the "hordes of Puerto Ricans enticed here from their home island for the value of their votes, and subjected to pitiful poverty," swelling the city welfare rolls.[109] Their greatest champion was a crook, and they were little more than welfare chiselers. The city had a "Puerto Rican problem."[110] The space for radicalism, already small, was narrowed further when Puerto Rican independence activists attempted to assassinate US president Harry Truman in November 1950. A week later, a coalition candidate selected by the Democratic, Republican, and Liberal parties, and with support of the PPD, defeated their nemesis Marcantonio handily.[111]

If left-wing denunciations of the relationship between US colonialism and the mainland Puerto Rican condition proved too much for political elites and not a few voters, the challenge nonetheless forced the Democratic machine and its island allies to collaborate on an alternative.[112] Just a few weeks before the 1949 mayoral elections, incumbent William O'Dwyer, a Tammany Democrat running against Marcantonio, established a Mayor's Advisory Committee on Puerto Rican Affairs (MACPRA). It offered nearly three-dozen community figures from the respectable press, professions, labor, and the Puerto Rican government entrée to city officials. The committee would supposedly foster Puerto Ricans' "mutual self-help and advancement."[113] In practical terms, MACPRA members served as extensions of the regular Democratic organization. Their groups brought in votes and in turn channeled municipal services to the community.[114] The MACPRA alliance also paid off with a sizable number of positions in the city's Welfare Department,[115] from which Puerto Ricans were expected to minister to community needs without unduly upsetting local power arrangements.[116]

The island government supplemented these efforts in 1951, when it reconstituted a three-year-old government body as the new Migration Division of the Puerto Rican Department of Labor. The Division placed Puerto Rican migrants in agricultural, domestic, and industrial employment, and made efforts to defend Puerto Ricans from prejudice and mistreatment.[117] It was also a voter turnout operation. Come election time, the Division would "blanket Puerto Rican neighborhoods with leaflets," advertise on Spanish-language radio, and arrange for "a squad of soapbox orators to encourage voting and explain voting procedures."[118] The right kinds of Democrats were, of course, appreciative.

The PPD's efforts to weave Puerto Ricans into the fabric of New York life and politics constituted a multifaceted experiment in adapting US civic nationalism to the migrants' unique situation. The Puerto Rican government sought to mold its people in the image of prior generations of immigrants without letting them lose sight of their Puerto Rican identity. Hence, the Migration Division held that Puerto Rican migrants were no separate "race" but rather possessors of a distinct culture. They were following the same arduous path of adjustment to urban life that previous newcomers had traveled and would, the Division reassured, only seem out of place for a little while. To spur them along, the Division promoted annual "Learn English" campaigns for children and adults. Uncertain if Puerto Ricans' condition, as one historian puts it, "justified an assertive ethnic posture," the Division did not demand bilingual education programs.[119] It was essential to realize, said its director Joseph Monserrat, that "very often our concentration on differences ignores what to me is a basic fact: that people . . . are more alike than they are different."[120]

The Division's efforts to speed Puerto Ricans' incorporation into American society went hand in hand with the PPD's larger project of reconfiguring Puerto Rican nationalism in the context of the commonwealth arrangement. In service of this aim, the island government adopted a national flag and anthem, and commenced Puerto Rican participation in international sports competitions in the late 1940s. It established an Institute of Puerto Rican Culture in 1955, with a publishing arm to revive out-of-print titles by Puerto Ricans, a national archive, and a mission to spotlight traditional Puerto Rican crafts and music. This official repository and herald celebrated the Puerto Rican "personality," and recast the island's racial divisions as "the mixing, in harmonious synthesis," of its Taíno, Spanish, and African cultural inheritances.[121] The Puerto Rican government had thus developed multiple mechanisms for influencing the lives of its diaspora, instilling pride in being Puerto Rican while harmonizing that identity—including its complex racial configuration—with midcentury Americanism.

However, as Marcantonio's following indicated, mainland Puerto Ricans did not blindly accept the intellectual and political leadership of island elites or their US backers. Over the course of the 1950s, they began to seize control of their community's agenda and institutions, blending the Puerto Rican solidarity being nurtured by the island government with their own New York reality. New leaders and organizations were coming to the fore. Some of these were in tune with LULAC or the National Urban League, a contemporary black organization, in that they preached the virtues of education and self-help, and improving the public's image of Puerto Ricans. While less radical than earlier leaders such as Marcantonio, they were also less wedded to the Migration Division's mandate of making the PPD and local Democrats look good. At least some among them were restless to shine a more critical light on the injustice and poverty in which so many Puerto Rican migrants lived.[122]

Another faction that sometimes overlapped looked to beat the machines at their own game. It was led by the fiery labor organizer Gilberto Gerena Valentín, a former Marcantonio assistant. In the early 1950s, Gerena organized a network of hometown clubs. These met weary migrants at Idlewild airport, and connected them with funds, food, apartments, furniture, and much-needed winter clothing. The Congress of Puerto Rican Hometowns held concerts and dances, card-playing nights, and other social activities. Social worker allies in the city's Welfare Department helped it in aiding its constituencies. The hope, according to Gerena, was that the Congress would be a "vehicle for empowerment" for Puerto Ricans and for reform causes more generally. Within a few years, its clubs represented seventy-eight Puerto Rican hometowns, a promising base from which to challenge the group's marginalization.[123]

Just as numerically dominant Mexican Americans in California believed it vital to assert their ethnic identity in MAPA, so did Puerto Ricans, growing rapidly in number, lay claim to supremacy in New York's Spanish-speaking institutions throughout the 1950s. New York City's annual Hispanic Parade was inaugurated in the mid-1950s and patterned after similar Irish and Italian community spectacles. But it lasted just two years before the Congress and others demanded its name be changed to the "Puerto Rican Parade." Its sponsors believed that doing so better acknowledged the Puerto Ricans' central position in the city's Hispanic life.[124] Although the parade was advertised as honoring Puerto Ricans' contributions to the city, the name change and their participation was a declaration of political intent—they were not going away, they were going to be aggressive in defending *their* interests, and they would matter going forward, just as the

Italians and Irish mattered.[125] Even the less politically assertive organizations began to declare "Puerto Rican" to be their essential identity. A split in the Hispanic Young Adult Association, a youth uplift organization, led to the establishment of a new group, the Puerto Rican Association for Community Affairs in 1956.[126] And in another change that reflected the new ethnic balance, the Puerto Rican–Hispanic Leadership Forum, established in 1957, had by 1964 become simply the Puerto Rican Forum.[127]

Reinforcing the detachment of Puerto Ricans from a larger "Hispanic" New York was an evolving approach to the color line. Puerto Ricans, especially those with lighter skin, had long expressed an ambivalence or trepidation about being associated with African Americans. The attitude endured into the postwar era, as denunciations of the migrant community led many who could do so to espouse a cultural identity of Spanish, Hispanic, or Latino.[128] Yet as time passed, many Puerto Ricans had begun to realize that American society would not acknowledge them as a "white" people, no matter how much they acculturated. And by the 1950s black political and social gains had begun to remove some of the stigma of association. Leftists tried their hardest to promote coalitions among the two populations. In the 1950s, the Communist Party's Harlem office issued pamphlets on "the Struggle for Puerto Rican Representation, and for Negro-Puerto Rican unity" in New York. Even the moderates of the Migration Division joined with the NAACP to promote a "Conference on Problems of Negroes and Puerto Ricans in New York State."[129] Blacks became key allies of Puerto Ricans in a fight to end discrimination in the largely female garment industry and its male-dominated unions. Their common neighborhoods and poverty also led Puerto Rican and black women to settlement houses, where they organized to fight to save their neighborhoods from disinvestment and decay.[130] In short, even as the island government cultivated a distinct Puerto Rican identity, Negro and Puerto Rican were becoming, for many activists, twinned concepts, if not one and the same at least possessing common interests.

Even as their portion of the New York electorate was expanding greatly, and their activists becoming increasingly dynamic, Puerto Ricans entered the 1960s facing a number of challenges. The Puerto Rican left was alive but diminished. The group's middle and upper classes were small. Racial antagonisms, including some within the Puerto Rican population itself, remained salient and potentially divisive. A literacy test hampered Puerto

Ricans' attempts to vote, and competition with other organized Democratic constituencies was intense. The government of their homeland intervened in Puerto Rican political life, sometimes for their benefit but more often with its own priorities in mind. In sum, Puerto Ricans may have been more important to the city than ever, yet they still faced abundant obstacles to exercising effective control over their own lives and communities.

☆ ☆

The counterpoint and eventual complication to the political projects of Mexican Americans and Puerto Ricans came due to revolutionary transformations unfolding on the island of Cuba. On January 1, 1959, Fidel Castro's forces triumphed in ending the brutal reign of the once-US-backed dictator Fulgencio Batista. Over the ensuing two years, Cuba's new rulers eliminated their conservative predecessors and moderate rivals, either by firing squad, imprisonment, or coerced exodus. They set about restructuring the economy to address rampant inequality and the country's dependence upon the United States. Rents were dropped and wages raised for many workers. Landowners absorbed new limits on the size of their holdings, and, in a cycle of action and retaliation, US firms found many of their assets subject to compensated nationalization. Cuban leaders placed Communists in key positions in their government and, clearly aware of the repercussions of their unabashedly leftist program, sought Soviet help in consolidating their revolution before Cold Warriors in Washington could reverse it. As one historian puts it, Castro's revolution "had introduced the Cold War to the Western Hemisphere."[131]

While the implications for Latino politics would take some time to reveal themselves, the revolution's impact on the US Spanish-speaking population was swift. There were perhaps 125,000 Cuban émigrés about the country as 1958 turned to 1959, with anywhere from 30,000 to 50,000 present in Miami. Between the revolution's triumph and the Cuban Missile Crisis of late 1962, roughly 250,000 of their countrymen joined them in the United States.[132] The first Cubans to depart were high officials and prominent backers of the deposed Batista regime. Some learned the game was up while ringing in 1959 with the departing dictator himself; wasting no time, a cohort was even observed arriving in the United States still dressed in their New Year's Eve finery.[133] In the coming weeks and months, a cadre of wealthy commercial elites and plantation owners would take their leave of a revolution intent on rearranging the social pyramid to their detriment. It was not only the elite who fled, however. Within the first two years of Castro's victory, many in the middle classes grew disillusioned with the island's transformation. Even those who had initially supported the overthrow of Batista recoiled at the new government's use of violence against a range of dissenters, its eager incorporation of Communists, and its increasing anticlericalism. When experienced alongside the expropriation of businesses and urban housing reforms, these factors resulted in white-collar workers and merchants of the Cuban middle class boarding aircraft bound for destinations abroad. As the revolution extended itself into nearly every aspect of society over the next two years, a large number of skilled and semi-skilled working-class Cubans chose to follow the middle classes.[134] By late 1961, strict curtailment of their religious mission or imprisonment and expulsion resulted in the additional departure of a few thousand priests and nuns who had maintained the island's Catholic churches, seminaries, and schools, many of these emigres destined for the United States.[135]

The refugees' movement occurred in a larger Cold War framework with Washington and Havana, exiles fled to Spain and Puerto Rico, and Cuban communities arose in the New York metropolitan area and a few other scattered locales. But Cuban America's symbolic and demographic core would coalesce in South Florida. Indeed, no US location absorbed the number of Cubans tossed by political storms like Florida, and Miami specifically. By 1980, Miami housed the second largest concentration of Cubans in the world, after Havana.[136]

Miami became the capital of exilic Cuba for several reasons. The city's proximity to the island was an obvious selling point for emigres expecting only a temporary stay in the United States. Indeed, for decades, Cuban exiles of various stripes had recognized South Florida's value as a political staging ground, a place of refuge from which they planned to return to transform power relations on the island.[137] But Miami was deeply familiar in other respects. It was a principal hub of US–Cuba trade, and as such well known to the island's businessmen.[138] Moreover, 50,000 Cubans were among the more than 100,000 Latin American tourists who each year flocked to enjoy the shopping, beaches, and nightlife of the city, the self-styled "Gateway to the Americas."[139] By the time of the mass Cuban influx, Miami was already a "burgeoning Pan-American metropolis."[140]

Miami had been undergoing a working-class Latinization as well in the decade before the Cuban Revolution. During the 1950s, the city's growing garment industry attracted Cuban and Puerto Rican factory workers, and agricultural laborers established a growing presence near the fields and groves on the city's periphery.[141] By 1960, Dade County hosted dozens of grocery stores catering to a Latin American clientele.[142] To accommodate these newcomers' spiritual needs, the Catholic Diocese of Miami had assembled a modest cadre of priests who could hear parishioners' confessions in Spanish, as well as a smaller number of clergy who could conduct Mass in the tongue.[143]

The refugees thus arrived in a city containing two Caribbean Latino populations—Cubans and Puerto Ricans—in rough demographic balance, and several much smaller pockets of Central and South Americans. In 1958, the *Miami Herald* held that Dade County's "Latin Americans" numbered 85,000, with roughly 30,000 of these Puerto Rican and 46,000 identified as Cuban, the next largest constituency being Colombians.[144] But in shades of the Puerto Rican "Great Migration" to New York City, as more than a thousand Cubans landed in the United States each week in the three years after 1959, they helped ensure that Miami was not to be defined by its Puerto Rican population any more than New York was to be defined by its pre–World War II Spanish community.

As they became Miami's most visible "Latin" population, the Cuban exiles' encounter with race was complex and distinct from that experienced by most Mexican or Puerto Rican migrants. The majority of the first wave of exiles to come to the United States saw themselves as white. Afro-Cubans constituted more than a quarter of the island's population, but tended to remain there in expectation of better lives under Castro's professed racial egalitarianism, and those who did leave the island often did not choose to settle in the southern city of Miami.[145] It was a Jim Crow town where African Americans couldn't ride courthouse elevators, try on clothes in downtown department stores, or attend school with white children. It was also a place in which Spanish-speakers had for some time enjoyed certain privileges unavailable to US blacks. The "Gateway to the Americas" could not afford thorough discrimination against a prime tourist and investor constituency. And so it furnished Latin Americans, even some of dark skin it seems, relatively unfettered access to an otherwise segregated hospitality industry, public beaches, as well as to exclusive institutions of learning such as the University of Miami.[146]

But if the tourist industry conferred favorable status on Spanish-speaking visitors, and if this suggested that Cubans might easily claim the privileges of "whiteness," the status of Miami's resident Puerto Rican population pointed to a potentially less rosy social position for Cubans. By 1954, the *Miami Herald* identified a brewing "Puerto Rican problem," evidenced in the migrants' poverty, educational challenges, poor housing, high unemployment rates, and in their potential to contribute a spike in juvenile delinquency.[147] The subject remained in the news in the ensuing years. On the eve of the Cuban exodus, concerned local officials of the Dade County Council of Community Relations would speak not only of the need to address Puerto Ricans' problems with sanitation, overcrowded housing, and crime but of the urgency of addressing "the problems of all Latin American residents in Greater Miami."[148] And after the Cubans began arriving en masse, many destitute, responding to a lack of housing by doubling or tripling up, worried observers looked to New York. A local television documentary on the refugees, "Crisis, Amigo," aired in late 1961, gave voice to concerned residents, such as the one who declared that "the Cubans are going to take over Miami . . . just like the Puerto Ricans took over New York City." The documentary explained that the conditions "Miamians fear will create slums not unlike New York's Puerto Rican district" and "a health hazard and a breeding ground for juvenile delinquency which we are told will grow to alarming proportions."[149]

In contrast, journalists who worked to enhance the early exiles' image often compared them favorably to Puerto Ricans. One *Newsweek* article, entitled "They're OK," reassured readers that Cuban schoolchildren came "mainly from middle-class homes (as contrasted with most of the Puerto Ricans in the New York schools)."[150] While comparisons to Puerto Ricans could be positive or negative, and while some news outlets did observe individuals of African descent among the exiles,[151] it was undoubtedly to the early exiles' advantage that most were white. As one historian has observed, the "peculiarities of the Cuban refugee flow defused objections . . . about the race" of the newcomers to Miami.[152]

☆ ☆

Emigration to the United States was crucial to the Cold War dynamic, as both Cuba and the United States encouraged opponents of the new regime to leave the island. Castro taunted the *gusanos* (worms), the Cubans who by packing their wormlike duffel bags and crossing the Florida Straits had put narrow personal interests ahead of the good of the *patria*.[153] But he knew that exporting the majority of the regime's most ardent opponents was good for the revolution. Likewise viewing Cuban émigrés as Cold War assets, US policymakers celebrated and facilitated the exodus. "Every refugee who comes out [of Cuba] is a vote for our society and a vote against their society," declared one Republican congressman in 1959.[154] Virtually all Cubans who sought entry to the United States in the next few years were admitted, whether via tourist or student visas, or by having "visa waivers" signed by supportive Immigration and Nationalization Service officials.[155] At the same time, their stay was always understood as temporary. As a powerful congressman with an immigration bailiwick put it in August 1960, to grant permanent resident status to the exiles "would imply that we consider the present situation in Cuba as a permanent one" a view that was at odds with American "national interest and foreign policy."[156] Few US officials imagined or desired that Cubans would become a permanent element of the American family.

Still, the Cubans who fled for American shores were more than simply pawns in the Cold War game. As one historian has argued, Cubans saw themselves as "actors in a complex world struggle between authoritarianism and democracy, between communism and free enterprise."[157] Their experiences nurtured in them profound and mutually reinforcing senses of patriotic identity and personal victimhood. For many Cubans, feelings that Castro had betrayed the revolutionary goals they once supported only heightened these emotions.[158] The notion that their stay in the United States was only temporary was more than consistent with US foreign policy. It was fundamental to Cuban patriotism, serving as a powerful psychological balm as they awaited the day of their return to their homeland.

These were not immigrants, then, but rather exiles. However, while exile identity shared a common anti-Castro theme, the exiles themselves were far from a unified political community. Representing dozens of factions, an extraordinary number of political organizations flourished among them. These ran the spectrum from authoritarian to moderate to liberal reformists. While some had backed the Batista dictatorship, a number sought the restoration of democracy that had preceded it, while still others agreed with the early ambitions of the Castro-led insurgency, including its calls for land reform and other economically egalitarian measures.[159] Each of these factions vied to assert its vision and leadership upon the exile community so as to hasten its return to the island so close to them.

Violence was critical to exile politics. Envisioning themselves as heirs to nineteenth-century independence heroes and the true revolutionary patriots of the day, a sector of Cuban leaders set themselves to liberate their nation from what they viewed as the powerful Communist forces directing Castro from beyond the hemisphere. From bases in Florida and other parts of the Caribbean, they conducted sabotage on the Cuban economy—aerial bombings of sugar mills were a passion—and armed attacks on island political and military targets.[160]

Fearful of the repercussions of Castro's revolution *and* unauthorized armed excursions emanating from American territory, Washington aimed to channel the Cubans' patriotism and paramilitary zeal. In March 1960, President Dwight Eisenhower approved a CIA proposal to assemble an exile military force and train it for an invasion of Cuba in the following year. The goal was to foment a larger uprising that would, according to its exponents in the Agency and their optimistic Cuban sources, topple Castro's government. The CIA paired this attempt at martial unification with the political unification of various exile factions under something resembling a government in exile. The result was the Frente Revolucionario Democrático, the Democratic Revolutionary Front, a collection of most of the moderate to liberal exile leadership. It was they who were to assume administration of Cuban life upon the assumed success of the US-backed military assault on the island.[161]

☆ ☆

Thus while Mexican Americans and Puerto Ricans dedicated themselves to persuading party leaders and elected officials to devote them a space for *participation* within US governing structures, American state power was elsewhere attempting to mold Cuban exiles into a unified leadership that would return *to govern a nation*. These were quite different projects.

Yet even as Cuban exile fighters trained in camps across the Caribbean basin, and as Cuban exile political elites prepared themselves to implement their visions of reform on a post-Castro Cuba, their countrymen were struggling to rebuild, if only for a short while, their Cuban lives in South Florida. Whatever racial privileges they may have enjoyed, most Cubans' day-to-day lives in Miami were hardly simple. Perhaps only a third of the first wave possessed resources to buy homes in cash or hire representation to protect their assets or secure long-term legal status in the United States.[162] And some less-affluent Cubans could rely upon family and friends to house, clothe, and advocate for them as they sought to establish lives in Florida. The far more common experience—especially as Cuba's government increased restrictions on departures during 1961—was for exiles to arrive in Miami with practically no financial resources and little sense of where to lay their heads. Locating a means of self-support was another question altogether.[163] Tourist visas, upon which many exiles relied at first, did not allow their holders to seek legal employment. The exiles arrived during an economic recession, too, which further limited their job prospects. Indeed, some 40 percent of Cubans surveyed by the federal government in late 1960 reported themselves in need of some combination of housing, clothing, and food.[164]

A comprehensive response was sorely needed. The Eisenhower administration, however, made few plans for integrating the refugees in domestic life (military resolutions to their presence in South Florida were, as we have seen, another matter).[165] Florida maintained a decidedly ungenerous public welfare system,[166] too, and by virtue of their status the Cubans had no early recourse to city or state services beyond emergency medical attention.[167] It was left to local actors, religious sectors in the main, to provide for the Cubans. The Catholic Church spent roughly $200,000 on their cause in the first two years of the exile influx. A church breadline fed 300 exiles daily. The Church delivered English classes, operated a health clinic, a dental clinic, provided child care services, and worked overtime to provide emergency housing and food baskets. Such a burden was unsustainable, however. Before two years of the migration had passed, it was clear that local systems were being overwhelmed.[168]

The search for solutions to an international crisis with deeply localized consequences caused the Cuban exile population and Miami's leadership to look ever more to Washington. By the fall of 1960, the community leaders who had been spearheading the relief efforts had assembled themselves into a "Cuban Refugee Committee." The committee attempted to forge a collaboration between themselves and national leaders within the framework of Cold War policies and thinking. Its chairman wrote to the president, imploring Eisenhower to recognize the "unique and critical situation" the city now faced. Dade County had "become a 'front-line' in the cold war tactics of the Communist world," he explained, and as such a response to the Cuban refugee situation could not fall on local actors alone. Miami mayor and Cuban Refugee Committee member Robert King High too made clear the federal government's responsibility to aid his community—now a "bastion against communism"—in addressing the refugees' needs.[169]

This characterization of the refugees and their hosts aligned with Washington's conceptualization of the exile population. In late 1960, the outgoing Eisenhower administration initiated an investigation into the Cuban refugee situation. Laying the foundation for a federal understanding of US-resident Cubans as a Cold War constituency—and not as members of a domestic "minority"—the president designated Tracy Voorhees, who had a few years earlier coordinated resettlement of Hungarians fleeing the Soviet Union's crackdown on their 1956 revolution, to head up the inquiry.[170] Voorhees' initial skepticism about a large federal role in distributing local aid and his ambition to resettle the Cubans across the country did in no way preclude a sense that the situation in Miami was "most critical."[171] When Voorhees delivered his report to the outgoing President Eisenhower in early 1961, he declared that the "ever-mounting Cuban population obviously has overrun the community's capacity to cope with it." Indeed, as the expert determined, "the problem is now a national one."[172]

☆ ☆

At the start of the 1960s, there were many political projects underway in Latino America. The Southwest's ethnic Mexicans faced the daunting task of developing political alliances amid divergent experiences with Mexican immigration, a profusion of ethnic orientations, and a variety of local political incorporations, most of which strongly resisted their assertions of independence. Divisions between these ethnic Mexicans and the Puerto Ricans of the East Coast were greater still. The latter's geographic concentration in New York City meant less the need to unite a political community across vast space and experience, as was a frequent objective in Mexican America. Rather, it required mainland Puerto Ricans—overwhelmingly a community of recent migrants—to determine the extent of their independence from two powerful forces: their homeland's government and the local bosses of the Democratic Party with which it was aligned. While highly politicized, the Cuban exiles of Florida focused little on local political integration, and instead devoted their energies to securing their return to a Cuba free of Fidel Castro and his version of revolution.

Soon enough, however, the distinct and localized political projects of ethnic Mexicans and Puerto Ricans at least would make an important and seemingly collaborative debut on the national stage.

# 2

# Viva Kennedy and the Nationalization of "Latin American" Politics

In October 1960, a group of Mexican-American and Puerto Rican leaders gathered around presidential candidate John F. Kennedy in a ballroom at New York's elegant Waldorf Astoria hotel. Dressed in their finest suits, the men smiled upon the presidential hopeful with a mixture of adoration and expectation. These were leaders of the "Viva Kennedy" campaign, a national effort to register and turn out Mexican-American and Puerto Rican voters for the Democratic ticket in that year's presidential election. It was a month before the voting, with hardly any space between Kennedy and his Republican opponent, Vice President Richard Nixon. That a nationwide "Latin American" political community seemed to be united behind a single candidate was a powerful prospect. Hands of many hues converged, binding them to the Irish American in pursuit of the common goal of victory. With a broad grin gracing his tanned face, Kennedy joined them in awaiting a nearby camera's flash.

What remains is an image of unity and a pretension to sameness, a political collaboration that simultaneously conveys the impression of peoplehood. Yet the picture obscured much about Latino politics up to that point. As we have seen, the men who huddled around Kennedy that night at the Waldorf represented quite distinct constituencies. Ethnic Mexican leaders had long struggled to harmonize and unify their distinct ethnopolitical projects. They would have had even fewer established relationships with the Puerto Ricans whose hands they held in unity that night. The absence of representatives of the Cuban exile community, largely concentrated in Florida yet with many members of its diaspora in the New York area, indicates their distance from this conversation.

Yet, as the image attests, Mexican Americans' and Puerto Ricans' diligent organizing and electioneering throughout the middle third of the

Just weeks away from Election Day 1960, presidential candidate John F. Kennedy joined Mexican-American and Puerto Rican supporters in New York for his campaign's National Conference on Constitutional Rights. *Left to right:* Ralph Estrada (Alianza Hispano-Americana), Felipe N. Torres (New York State assemblyman), Henry B. González (Texas state senator), Kennedy, Dr. Hector P. García (American G.I. Forum), Henry López (MAPA), José Ramos (New York State assemblyman), and an unidentified supporter. Forum News Bulletin, Courtesy of Dr. Hector P. García Papers, Special Collections and Archives, Bell Library, Texas A&M University–Corpus Christi.

twentieth century, so shaped by national political processes and trends, was finally opening the possibility that they themselves could influence national politics. Most influential were the pathbreaking electoral victories of the 1940s and 1950s, in which Mexican Americans framed their demands within a larger language of patriotic Americanism, forged local and statewide coalitions with blacks and white liberals, and secured new political footholds in Texas and California that complemented the "Hispano" base that endured in New Mexico. Ironically enough, these victories won in the name of all Americans underscored their group's very distinctiveness. When coupled with persistent local opposition to their empowerment, the postwar electoral breakthroughs tempted rising ethnic politicos, presidential candidates, and their advisors to assemble these separate communities of ethnic Mexicans and Puerto Ricans into a pan-ethnic voting bloc ostensibly national in scope. The "Viva Kennedy" campaign encouraged them to collaborate in what was, as yet, largely a fiction, the nationwide "Latin American" constituency.

Their debut on the national political stage was equal part exhilarating experiment and painful chastening. This assertion of centrality to the nation and to the man who became its principal leader came tied to an aspiration to use that proximity to power to enhance individual careers and status, and to gain a lever with local forces who for so long impeded their progress and who cared so little about their people's concerns. Betrayal marked the experience. A victorious Democratic presidential candidate had little use for a mobilized "Latin American" constituency once the votes had been counted. Made to realize their weakness in the Democratic Party was national as well as local, Mexican-American activists debated anew what transformations—ideological, organizational, personal—could make them an independent force to be reckoned with across the Southwest, a people whose power would gain the respect of officeholders from the American president on down.

Cubans were another matter. Indeed, Kennedy's relations with Cuban exiles revealed that the White House was not wholly disinvested in promoting *a* "Latin American" constituency's leadership, prosperity, and unity, provided that its political energies directed themselves entirely in service of US foreign policy objectives. In time, however, Cubans' sense of having been victims of Kennedy's betrayal would dwarf the ill will the administration's neglect generated in Mexican America. In both the Southwest and South Florida, however, the distance between a president's promises and what he delivered served to underscore feelings of ethnic distinctiveness and reinforce the separate political projects then underway.

Beyond ensconcing the presidential campaign (and the campaigners' subsequent disillusionment) as the central ritual of political Hispanicity, Viva Kennedy set the stage for a repositioning of Mexican-American and Puerto Rican political representation. By facilitating the election of a small cohort of Mexican-American congressmen, supporters of Kennedy, it linked the separate political projects of the Southwest to the national in more than temporary ways. Moreover, abetting the rise of one highly influential Puerto Rican politician, it furthered the process of incorporation in New York. All told, participation in Viva Kennedy advanced the nationalization of Mexican-American politics while deepening the localization of Puerto Rican politics, encouraging few meaningful ties and often enough an ambivalent, if not competitive, relationship in the years ahead.

☆ ☆

To conceive of a nationwide "Latin" or "Latin American" vote in 1960 was to reckon with a multistate blend of constituencies self-identified as Mexican American, Latin American, Hispano, and Puerto Rican, among other identities. It was to encompass both liberal reformers and machine insiders. It was to imply that local communities that were then forging coalitions with African Americans or Jews or labor unionists or Japanese Americans should instead see their natural political alliances—at least for a time—as national, with other "Latins," some living thousands of miles away. Given the difficulty even ethnic Mexicans had in forming southwestern coalitions, it was not an obvious choice.

Such was the state of affairs in Mexican America and Puerto Rican New York when Massachusetts senator John F. Kennedy selected Lyndon B. Johnson of Texas, then the US Senate Majority Leader, to be his running mate in the 1960 presidential election. The national Democratic Party's support for civil rights had caused southern Democrats to back Republicans or "Dixiecrats" in previous presidential elections, and Johnson was there to allay his fellow southerners' suspicions. The uncertain loyalty of conservative whites nevertheless meant that the Southwest's Mexican-American voters were increasingly important to a Democratic victory. This was especially so in Texas, but also in California, home state of the Republican candidate, Vice President Richard Nixon. New York's Puerto Ricans could hardly be overlooked either. They were concentrated in the "grand prize of the electoral college." Its 45 electoral votes could decide the race, expected to be very close in November.[1] In sum, any loss of traditional Democratic support could prove fatal to the Kennedy/Johnson campaign.

As the 1960 campaign entered its final phase, it was Mexican-American elected officials who brought forward the notion of a separate undertaking to mobilize their people. The party itself had planned no meaningful assembly of Latino delegates for the 1960 Democratic National Convention in Los Angeles, where John F. Kennedy secured the nomination. Instead, Henry B. González and Edward Roybal discussed the matter with New Mexico senator Dennis Chavez. The three then sought out campaign manager Robert Kennedy. Little record of their conversation exists, but as the leading historian of the "Viva Kennedy" campaign has put it, their proposal was a sort of parallel voter turnout effort that would "shed light on the needs of the Mexican American," particularly in the areas of jobs and schools. Robert Kennedy quickly endorsed the plan, dangling high-level presidential appointments as a reward for Mexican Americans who brought the campaign to victory.[2]

Thus was born "Viva Kennedy." Official leadership of the auxiliary campaign was soon placed in the hands of James Carlos McCormick. The son-in-law of a prominent Arizona Mexican-American leader, McCormick had come to the campaign's attention after volunteering for Senator Kennedy and organizing a local chapter of the American G.I. Forum (AGIF) in Washington, DC. After returning from the convention, he opened an office on K Street,[3] from which he oversaw the campaign's enlistment of sixteen "national cochairmen," three quarters of whom represented states west of the Mississippi.[4] Their message was to highlight the candidate's party affiliation, his interest in Latin America, and his liberalism, especially his concern for the poor. It would imply that his Irish heritage gave him insight into the experience of being an outsider in America. And while it would not play up his religion, it would "not discourage" voters from embracing Kennedy as the "Catholic" candidate. An AGIF member drew a campaign emblem featuring the Massachusetts senator, grinning and mounted atop a burro, having donned a great sombrero emblazoned with the words "Viva Kennedy."[5]

Viva Kennedy was eclectic, bolstering insurgents where it had to, but calling upon establishment politicians where it could. The campaign tapped the Southwest's most prominent Hispano leaders, New Mexico Senator Dennis Chavez and Representative Joseph Montoya, as "National Honorary Chairmen." Though he was by then in his seventies and the fifth-ranking US senator, Chavez stumped for the ticket in countless locations across the Southwest and Midwest. He delivered two speeches at every stop: one in English that skewered Republicans for lacking concern with rising inequality, and one in Spanish praising Kennedy's humanity and the duties of the Mexican-American citizen.[6] He urged Mexican Americans to see electoral politics as the key to changing their conditions, often reminding them that though they "may complain about police brutality and discrimination," without voting they would "deserve what [they] get."[7]

In California, Viva Kennedy strengthened the campaign for Mexican-American political independence by naming its Mexican American Political Association's (MAPA) Edward Roybal and Henry López as state chairmen. Using money from the state's labor federation, Roybal's Community Service Organization hired twenty organizers and registered 140,000 Mexican-American voters, almost 50 percent more than had previously been on state voting rolls. Roybal too delivered speeches across the Southwest and as far as Illinois, praising Kennedy as a true friend of the Mexican American. It was "this public image of friendship and honor" between Kennedy and Mexican-American leaders—largely the latter's creation—that was central in reaching a sizable segment of Mexican Americans otherwise unconnected to the campaign's issues.[8]

The candidate could hardly turn down any endorsement of his authentic connection with Mexican people. Jacqueline Kennedy may have swayed some voters by endorsing her husband in Spanish-language campaign advertisements. But as Viva Kennedy campaigner Sal Castro recalled, the sum of John Kennedy's response to a pulsating crowd of Los Angeles admirers, delivered in an accent well at home across the country in Boston, was just this: "'Viver!' That's all he said: 'Viver!'"[9]

In Texas, "Viva Kennedy" balanced the Democrats' moderate and liberal factions, employing promising politicians and prominent civil rights activists as chairmen and coordinators. It recruited the AGIF's leader, Hector P. García, bolstering forces loyal primarily to Lyndon Johnson. The involvement of Henry B. González and Albert Peña Jr. of San Antonio nurtured the Texas party's liberal wing. From the League of United Latin American Citizens (LULAC) and AGIF chapters sprang forth many "Viva Kennedy" clubs. Recruited to the campaign's "Latin American division" by McCormick, Peña went far and wide in South Texas, urging labor and civil rights colleagues to establish the voter groups and ensure a strong *liberal* Mexican-American showing in November. Johnson's presence on the ticket no doubt eased tensions with local county bosses, but for Peña the real significance of Viva Kennedy was its boost to Mexican-American political autonomy. "We decided that we were not going to accept any money from anybody. We were going to do it on our own. We sold one dollar memberships. . . . If you didn't have a dollar, you became a member anyway."[10]

☆ ☆

While "Viva Kennedy" emerged from and was concentrated in Mexican America, the national nature of both the presidential campaign and the Democratic Party still linked it to the New York Puerto Rican community, albeit in highly qualified ways. Two of Viva Kennedy's sixteen "national cochairmen" were New York Puerto Ricans; they were a local district leader and a state assemblyman aligned with Tammany Hall and the Bronx Democratic machine, respectively.[11] Yet this linkage belied the extent to which local considerations constrained the reach of Viva Kennedy. The Democratic National Committee's "Nationalities Division" employed an organizer, Pedro A. Sanjuan, to drive Puerto Rican turnout. Havana born of elite pedigree and almost fifteen years a citizen of the United States, in possession of a master's degree from Harvard and married to the daughter of a powerful US diplomat for Latin America,[12] Sanjuan later recalled the specificity of his efforts. Materials the campaign disseminated among Mexican Americans were unusable with Puerto Ricans, who possessed "a completely different mentality," he remembered. Although Sanjuan occasionally invoked the slogan, and while a Puerto Rican Viva Kennedy cochairman might clasp hands with a Tejano and John F. Kennedy for a photo opportunity, "there was no Viva Kennedy organization in New York, really."[13]

There were similarities. As among Mexican Americans in parts of the Southwest, Kennedy outreach to Puerto Ricans had to negotiate intense political rivalries between liberal insurgents and Democratic regulars.[14] Herman Badillo was aligned with the former. Born in 1929 in Caguas, Puerto Rico, he was orphaned by the age of five after both his parents succumbed to tuberculosis. He later came to New York, where he studied business and law. He was handsome, tall, thin, and a fine speaker of English. His appearance was such that he was on at least one occasion mistaken for being an Italian by East Harlem's political insiders.[15] Like others, he saw in the Kennedy campaign a golden opportunity to break out of old patron-client relationships, to build community power, and to advance his own career.[16] He aspired to unseat the Italian Americans who ran East Harlem, believing they did so with little regard for the area's large black and Puerto Rican populations. The Kennedys knew that the machine politicians feared adding voters who might challenge their control. But the presidential campaign's interest was in high minority turnout. Sensing his opportunity, Badillo loosely connected himself not with Viva Kennedy but to another campaign auxiliary—Citizens for Kennedy—the vehicle for party reformers. As Sanjuan recalled, Badillo "seemed to be a difficult, tough, intelligent Puerto Rican, exactly what the Puerto Ricans needed."[17] And so the campaign disbursed the funds that allowed Badillo to establish "East Harlem Citizens for Kennedy" in a storefront headquarters. As Badillo remembered, "I proceeded to get a sound truck to go around the district, telling people in Spanish and in English that they could register to vote. . . . It was a very bitter campaign, because . . . they [local Democratic leaders] didn't want to have any Puerto Ricans or blacks registered. So it was a question of them trying to push them out and me trying to push them in."[18]

But the campaign's insurgent quality was muted by the party's reliance upon established leaders. It was the state's two official Viva Kennedy co-chairmen, Democratic regulars, who in August welcomed Robert Kennedy to Spanish Harlem and the Tammany-affiliated Caribe Democratic Club. The candidate's brother proclaimed himself *simpático* by a friendly butchering of his limited Spanish repertoire, and by stressing his origins in—and production of—a large family. "I was one of nine children myself; so I think we can keep up with the Puerto Ricans," he joked to the Democratic activists. He strolled Lexington Avenue surrounded by hundreds of young Puerto Ricans, followers who would become constituents when he was elected to the US Senate in 1964.[19]

On Columbus Day, John F. Kennedy made his own stop in El Barrio. A day scheduled for breakfast with Eleanor Roosevelt and a lunchtime march in the Columbus Day Parade included an afternoon visit to Spanish Harlem's 116th Street and Lexington Avenue. This was the "Lucky Corner" that leftist congressman Vito Marcantonio had made hallowed political ground for the city's Puerto Ricans.[20] There was deep concern to ensure that Kennedy understood the ethnopolitical situation in this part of Harlem, separate in population and orientation from the better-known African American neighborhood to its west. Italian-American party regulars still clung to the offices of city councilman, state assemblyman, and congressman in East Harlem, largely by sidelining politically the Puerto Ricans whose votes Kennedy might need to carry the state. Pedro Sanjuan recalled telling the advance men:

put them all [the party regulars] on the stand, but don't you make any mistake about it: the people that are going to be there are *not* going to be Italians; they're going to be Puerto Ricans. And they're not going to be Negroes; they're going to be Puerto Ricans; black Puerto Ricans but not American Negroes, you see. And we better . . . gear the speech to that.

Bribing the police for permission to drive their sound trucks around the densely populated neighborhood, the campaign magnetized an estimated twenty thousand people to the rally.[21]

After a nod to the machine politicians on the dais, Kennedy's short address combined bread-and-butter appeals on the minimum wage, housing, and social security with jabs at Nixon's supposed neglect of Latin America. The crowd applauded when Kennedy identified himself and his family's journey from Ireland with that of the Puerto Rican migrants: "My forefathers came here 100 years ago, you came maybe this year or last year or 10 years ago," he said. But all sought the promise of equality, "the same chance, the same opportunity to educate your children, the same chance to work at decent wages, the same chance to live in decent housing, the same chance to live in a strong America, the same chance to stand and identify yourselves with freedom. . . . That is why we are all here, me, you and all of us, all of us."[22] While John Kennedy was a hit, Herman Badillo recalled that the biggest cheers again went for Jackie, who addressed the throngs in what was remembered as excellent Spanish.[23]

Republicans were unwilling to cede Harlem, however. Two years before Kennedy's visit, the liberal Republican Nelson Rockefeller had walked those same streets in search of votes. He had addressed three thousand Puerto Ricans, in Spanish, scoring Democratic bosses, praising the island's governor, Luis Muñoz Marín, and promising better and more affordable housing, a freeze in subway fares, and access to welfare with no waiting period. At the conclusion of his remarks, he leapt into the crowd and was swept up on Puerto Rican shoulders, on his way to victory and control of the Empire State.[24] Republicans hoped to transfer some of the governor's popularity to Nixon. Rodman Rockefeller, Nelson's bilingual son, opened an office in Harlem to reach out to Puerto Rican and African American voters on behalf of the GOP ticket.[25] And on Columbus Day, Republican vice presidential candidate Henry Cabot Lodge Jr. stepped to the stage on the

"Lucky Corner" just a couple of hours after Kennedy had passed through. Lodge, aware he was in "Harlem" and beholding an audience containing at least a number of dark-skinned faces, offered a discourse heavy on pledges to the "Negro," including that Nixon would name the first black cabinet member if elected. The two-thousand or so spectators offered what was described, most charitably, as "little response" to Lodge, poorly briefed on his audience.[26]

In Democratic minds, the challenge was always registration. As Pedro Sanjuan put it, "these are people who—it isn't a question of their voting for Republicans. It's either that they vote for us or they don't vote at all."[27] In addition to the grassroots work done by reformers like Herman Badillo, Puerto Rico's government conducted its own registration drive through its Migration Division office. Though ostensibly nonpartisan, the Partido Popular Democrático's (PPD) allegiance to the US Democratic Party and a basic understanding of Puerto Ricans' political tendencies suggests clear intention to benefit Kennedy and Johnson.[28] The city's two major Spanish-language newspapers, *El Diario* and *La Prensa,* also abetted the registration effort. "The most important thing" the Kennedy campaign did, according to Sanjuan, was convince newspapers to pay for buses that would "just literally take people off the street and bus them to the registration locations," where campaign monitors were stationed to ensure that Puerto Ricans were not shown the door before they could register.[29] There was reason to be concerned. News reports came in that citizens of East Harlem attempting to register or take the literacy test waited on "discouragingly long lines" that snaked around and outside of the elementary schools that served as polling places. Registration cards ran out. There were not enough literacy tests to go around.[30]

Despite local obstructionism, the drive produced impressive results. On the eve of the 1960 election, the *New York Times* reported that over 230,000 Puerto Ricans had registered in the city's five boroughs alone. It was a remarkable number. Just eight years earlier, only 35,000 of 250,000 eligible Puerto Ricans had taken this step for the contest between Dwight Eisenhower and Adlai Stevenson.[31]

☆ ☆

Kennedy's victory in the historically close 1960 presidential election was in no small part due to Puerto Rican and Mexican-American votes. The

Democrat took New York and its forty-five electoral votes by less than 400,000 votes out of more than seven million cast.[32] Puerto Ricans gave him 77 percent of their votes. And the 85 percent that Mexican Americans gave Kennedy nationally was higher than that given by practically every other ethnoracial segment of the electorate. It was even higher than Kennedy's tally among the Irish.[33] Most importantly, Mexican Americans gave the Democratic ticket 91 percent of their votes in Texas, a 200,000-vote cushion in a state Kennedy carried by only 50,000.[34]

While an election postmortem declared that the country's "Spanish-American vote"[35] proved crucial to the outcome, more specific interpretations existed. In New York, Puerto Rican leaders spoke with pride and possibility, now that the migration was fulfilling the responsibilities of citizenship. "We are a young community," said Joseph Monserrat, head of the Puerto Rican government's Migration Division. "We will solidify and accelerate the relatively rapid progress we have made."[36] Mexican Americans, too, felt they had arrived. Kennedy himself had wired his congratulations to a Texas Viva Kennedy leader, saying that "the margin of victory" the clubs gave him in South Texas was of "prominent significance" in winning the state. As the AGIF's newspaper put it, "Mr. Kennedy rode the Mexican burro into the presidency."[37]

If Mexican-American and Puerto Rican leaders largely interpreted Kennedy's victory as one for their own specific national origin communities (and if Mexican Americans perceived themselves as the biggest contributors), it should hardly be surprising. Viva Kennedy began after the Democratic convention and thus lasted only a few months. And while Dennis Chavez, Henry B. González, Ed Roybal, and other spokespeople campaigned *across* some of these communities, including in a handful of places in the industrial Midwest where relatively modestly sized mixed communities of Mexican Americans and Puerto Ricans existed, it appears exceedingly rare that Mexican-American activists came together with leaders of New York's Puerto Rican community, let alone coordinated their efforts in any sustained fashion. As Pedro Sanjuan recalled, "I don't know how much the Viva Kennedy thing in New Mexico and California amounted to, but in New York City it did not amount to anything."[38] Viva Kennedy was intended to elect John Kennedy, first and foremost. If it stimulated a broader Latino unity or a pan-Hispanic consciousness going forward, this was largely incidental. The political communities of Mexican Americans and Puerto Ricans remained at once essential to the Democratic future, but meaningfully distinct.

☆ ☆

Though those communities were pivotal to the Kennedy victory, it was still another "Latin American" community that came to exert the greatest influence on the Kennedy presidency. With its leaders' avowed intention to return to Cuba by force, not to seek integration in the US political system, the Cuban exile population in the United States, growing by more than a thousand per week, challenged most clearly the notion of a collective "Latin American" domestic constituency. As President Kennedy took a central role in the Cuban exile drama, and as Cuba furnished the defining foreign policy moments of a presidency oriented toward external affairs, it further ensured that Cuban America would develop on a separate path from Mexican America and Puerto Rican America.

Obliquely addressed in Viva Kennedy, Cuba occupied a prominent role in the wider 1960 campaign. As the scale of the revolutionary government's radicalism and outreach to Moscow became known, Kennedy relentlessly battered his opponent, Vice President Richard Nixon, for his complicity in "a disaster that threatens the security of the whole Western Hemisphere." Castro's regime of "Communist menace," he lectured, was "permitted to arise under our very noses, only 90 miles from our shores."[39] Whether in South Florida or the industrial heartland, Kennedy seldom passed up the chance to burnish his reputation as a fighter who would restore American superiority in the Cold War and regain the respect supposedly squandered by the sitting administration. In October 1960, for example, he pledged to a Johnstown, Pennsylvania, crowd that he would get tough with Castro and his Soviet patron Nikita Khrushchev, that he would not allow the United States "to be pushed around any longer."[40] Fodder in three of four presidential debates, Cuba's geopolitical alignment was an issue of unequivocal national political significance.

The victorious Kennedy inherited a US-based Cuban population expecting to return and a government geared up to facilitate that objective through armed force. Indeed, while Viva Kennedy campaigners exhorted audiences to vote in the hope of becoming full American citizens, Cuban exiles were set to receive CIA training in weaponry, explosives, and radio communications, and to be spirited across the straits of Florida to sabotage the Cuban economy and pave the way for the eventual toppling of Castro.[41] During the transition period, CIA briefers told the president-elect of the Eisenhower administration's efforts to raise and train an exile brigade to invade Cuba.[42] And on the day before Kennedy's inauguration, Eisenhower delivered his successor something very close to an order. "We cannot let the present government there go on," declared the five-star general, probably the nation's greatest living war hero.[43] Candidate Kennedy vowed to unleash exile saboteurs and other clandestine military operatives, calling them "fighters for freedom" who were unjustly inhibited by the Eisenhower administration's timidity.[44] In April 1961 came the chance for the new president to leave his mark on the hemisphere.

But it was also a chance for the Cuban exiles. Indeed, when an amphibious invasion force of some 1,400 US-trained Cuban exiles landed at the Bay of Pigs in April 1961, it was an enactment of Cuban exile patriotism on a dramatic, if doomed, scale. The members of Brigade 2506 imagined themselves as true national heroes, soldiers who continued the revolution against authoritarianism and the police state, who endeavored to secure educational and religious freedom, the hopeful saviors of a nation being sold out to the Russians.[45] They wore Catholic nationalism literally on their sleeves: their uniforms were emblazoned with a shoulder patch—a shield on which was inscribed a billowing Cuban flag set in front of a white Latin cross.[46] Accompanying the forces were three priests. One held in his possession a proclamation that read that the brigade was returning to Cuba "in the name of God" and declared that its "struggle is that of those who believe in God against the atheists, the struggle of democracy against communism."[47] For those who led it, that is, the invasion was more than simply an act of US Cold War aggression.

What followed was, from a US and Cuban exile perspective, an unmitigated disaster. From the hubris of the planners who naively predicted the invasion would spark a popular uprising against Castro to the utter lack of secrecy that made the invaders' training activities front page news from New York to Havana *months* in advance of the actual landing of troops, various aspects of the folly have been amply recounted elsewhere.[48] Suffice it to say, the Cuban government was as prepared as it was informed. Militias and neighborhood watch committees participated in a roundup of individuals feared likely to collaborate with the invaders. Perhaps one hundred thousand "suspected dissidents" were detained.[49]

Whether a different US invasion strategy for Brigade 2506 would have toppled Castro is not knowable. What is known is that Kennedy prioritized the ability to deny that the invaders were his proxies. It was this overarching ambition that led Kennedy to endorse a landing site of dubious strategic value. Most consequential, it was Kennedy's withdrawal of US air support that could have disabled the small and antiquated Cuban air force, and denial of air cover during the attempted beach landing, that exposed the *brigadistas* and their plodding vessels to withering machine gun fire from above.[50] With their ammunition supply exhausted, scores of brigade soldiers took to the nearby woods and swamps, where they were bombarded by Cuban artillery shells and pursued by machine-gunning militiamen and helicopters. There, subsistence over several days rested upon a remarkable survival diet of raw lizard meat, snake flesh, and the occasional chicken, washed down with the blood of reptiles and the soldiers' own urinary excretion.[51] When all was said and done, some 140 brigade soldiers were dead and almost 1,200 had been captured.[52] Prison sentences of thirty years awaited the survivors.[53]

Kennedy took public blame for the debacle, while privately raging at the intelligence and military figures—"those sons-of-bitches with all the fruit salad [military decorations]"—who had advised him that the invasion would succeed.[54] Within the White House, the sense of shame and culpability was palpable. Of the soldiers whose invasion he had authorized, Kennedy told one aid, "They trusted me. And they're in prison now because I fucked up. . . . I have to get them out."[55] Though Kennedy did not pay an initial cost in wider public support for the Bay of Pigs, it was clear to his advisor Arthur Schlesinger that both the president and his brother Robert were motivated by "concern for the domestic political implications of Castro and Cuba."[56] Republicans were soon enough hammering away at the administration's "disastrous" coup attempt.[57]

An experience of shame and embarrassment for Kennedy was one that Cubans experienced as a profound betrayal. The Miami community had long imagined, according to Schlesinger, that "the logic of the situation" would always mandate "the US to send in Marines to make sure that the invasion is a success."[58] That nothing of the sort occurred—that it would become clear that the United States had actively withheld support out of a fear of appearing to directly engage in a conflict it was orchestrating—was devastating.[59] In the eyes of the brigade commander, José "Pepe" San Román,

Kennedy's choice to foreswear air support set the outcome: "we were sure of going to our death." In the absence of air support, recalled another leader, it was "just like sending a bunch of human beings to get killed."[60] Brigadistas sensed that they had been lied to, but allowed to go in nonetheless. Imprisonment in Cuba did little to improve the soldiers' assessment of their experience. According to the soldiers' family members, who visited them during their months of confinement, "the majority of the Brigade has a marked anti-U.S. feeling."[61]

Adding to the indignity, the invasion served primarily to further Castro's consolidation of power. Enemies of the regime were exposed and imprisoned, if not executed. And the foreign-sponsored invasion "tapped into the deepest well of Cuban nationalism," one historian writes, providing the Cuban government a clear enemy against which to identify its revolution and to mobilize its populace in order to transform the island.[62] The Cuban Revolution was on firmer ground than ever.

For this foreign policy president, containing the public relations fallout from the debacle was essential. It meant securing the continued loyalty and cooperation of the Cuban Revolutionary Council (CRC), the successor to the Frente Revolucionario Democrático as the CIA's not-quite-government in exile. This political arm of the US-backed counterrevolutionary army had endured a harsh lesson in its powerlessness during the invasion, with exile leaders held under virtual house arrest and the CIA "issuing battle communiqués to the press in their name."[63] Hoping to prevent them from going to the press with full details on the Americans' folly and their own mistreatment, Kennedy met with the Cubans in the Oval Office. The president shared the rosy intelligence he had received that indicated the brigade's ability to function with minimal American support. He faced the grieving father who already knew his son's life had been lost during the invasion, whose words summed up the situation: "You have been taken for a ride, Mr. President and this Council has been taken for a ride." Kennedy was soon to confide to Richard Nixon that having to face the Cuban exiles was "the worst experience of my life."[64]

In the longer term, the administration sought ways to strengthen the Cubans' organizational and military capacity to serve as assets in covert efforts to discredit and bring down the Cuban government. A few days after the invasion, Kennedy declared that "the Cuban people have not yet spoken their final piece," and that the Cuban Revolutionary Council would "continue to speak up for a free and independent Cuba."[65] In private, Kennedy met with CRC leaders and, as one recalled the encounter, "planned the immediate future of Cuba." The president committed to, among other things, recruiting Cuban volunteer soldiers to train with diverse US military units for the purposes of eventually uniting them under "their natural leaders" when the time came to invade Cuba once more.[66] The CRC also became the US government's representative for refugee affairs. And in October 1961, the White House took the additional step of making it the official conduit through which financial assistance would flow to the hundreds of exile organizations that had sprung up in Miami and elsewhere in the United States in the previous years.[67] The CRC was to serve as the "superstructure which sits atop" the multitude of exile organizations.[68]

For an administration whose pride was deeply wounded by its failure to eliminate Castro, it was essential that the exile population's posture remain oriented toward return. The CRC collaborated in articulating this homeland orientation to official Washington. The administration's designated spokesperson for the exile community was CRC chairman Dr. José Miró Cardona, an attorney who had served briefly as prime minister of Cuba in the early days after the revolution's triumph. The first witness to testify in the Senate Judiciary Committee's hearings on the Cuban refugee situation in December 1961, Cardona committed the Cubans of Florida to a mindset and agenda premised upon return above all other objectives. The exile, he said, had "but one wish, one idea, one obsession—to go back to his country as soon as possible." And the exile preferred "to fight and die" in service of return, rather than to attempt to reconstitute life "in a friendly but foreign country."[69] There was a basic harmony of interests here. Cuban exiles wanted to return home, and Kennedy wanted them to want to return home.

Cuban exile leaders expected to see action, and the White House continued to prepare them for it. In November 1961, Kennedy approved a new program intended to unseat Castro. Overseen by his brother Robert, by then the US attorney general, "Operation Mongoose" was "a multifaceted campaign of overt diplomatic and economic pressure to isolate and impoverish the island, and covert paramilitary operations to overthrow the Communist regime."[70] Little expense was spared. At a cost upwards of $50 million per year, the CIA implanted a station on the South Campus of the University of Miami, an operation so large that it was second in size only to the Agency's Langley, Virginia, headquarters. Operating under the front name of Zenith Technical Enterprises, Inc. and known among operators as JM/WAVE, the Miami facility boasted some four hundred US employees, who in turn supported and tried to manage thousands of exile operatives. In addition to operating dozens of front businesses, the CIA's Miami station counted airplanes and, in one estimation, a fleet of boats that constituted the Caribbean's "third largest navy."[71] As the planners of Operation Mongoose made clear, "the development of Cuban resources" existed "for the purpose of facilitating and supporting" a necessary US "intervention and to provide a preparation and justification for it."[72]

As Washington intensified efforts to overthrow Castro, it took ever-more interest in the matter of promoting Cuban exile "unity." As far as the CIA was concerned, the "mercurial character" of the refugee political community made this very difficult.[73] The Agency reported in May 1962 that the number of organizations into which Cubans grouped themselves, in the United States and abroad, numbered more than two hundred. The exiles themselves were "divided and quarrelsome." Their organizations presented a "confused picture" of breakups and reformations that agents described as "kaleidoscopic."[74] In a subsequent analysis, the agency concluded that while the number of organizations had grown, their overall "effectiveness" had diminished. As US observers saw it, political life for many exile organizations consisted mostly of lashing out at Washington's "do nothing policy" toward Cuba.[75] In late 1962, Kennedy and the Joint Chiefs of Staff discussed the Cuban situation, and determined that, "these various groups sit down there [in Florida], stew in their own juice, elect committees, become emotionally upset, and then finally call upon somebody in Washington to let off their steam."[76] The planners of Operation Mongoose had hoped that CIA aid to the Cuban Revolutionary Council would "provide a degree of cohesion within the exile community."[77] But with the CRC's leadership increasingly scorned and its utility in question, the administration talked about finding a new "focal point" for exile organization.[78]

Continuing to structure Cuban exile politics along martial lines, Kennedy and his top military brass looked to the fighters to be that "focal point." For a year and a half, almost 1,200 soldiers of Brigade 2506 languished in Cuban prisons. However, in late 1962, thanks to the actions of Cuban exile activists, administration hands, and corporate leaders, the Cuban government accepted a ransom of $53 million worth of goods, mostly a mixture of food and medical supplies.[79] As Kennedy relaxed in Palm Beach in late December, he received a delegation of recently released brigade leaders. Following the meeting, their commander, Pepe San Román, announced that Kennedy would be heading to Miami to inspect the returned invasion force. Another *brigadista*, Erneido Oliva, stated that Kennedy would be receiving "the greatest treasure" in the brigade's possession, the flag the soldiers flew for three days over their command post on Playa Girón.[80]

On December 29, 1962, John F. Kennedy celebrated the brigade's release, serving in his own right as "focal point" of Cuban exile politics. Once again enacting their own version of Cuban patriotism for an international audience, the soldiers stood at attention in khaki dress uniforms at the fifty-yard line of Miami's Orange Bowl stadium. Some 35,000 family members and other supporters cheered them on. A white convertible ferried Kennedy and his wife Jackie onto the field. A reporter noted the contrast between Jackie's "young and radiant visage" and that of the soldiers, just weeks removed from incarceration, who were "old before their time, and white with prison's pallor." Binding the wound, the first couple shook hands with the brigade's leaders. The national anthems of Cuba and the United States opened the ceremonies. Delivering the invocation, San Román set the terms of the soldiers' sacrifice, past and future. The brigade, white crosses on their left shoulders, were "offer[ing] ourselves to God and to the free world as warriors in the battle against communism." It was then that Oliva presented Kennedy with the flag, "temporarily deposit[ed]" with the president for his "safekeeping." The half-filled stadium erupted. "Guerra! Guerra!" [War! War!] "Libertad! Libertad! Libertad!" [Liberty! Liberty! Liberty!][81]

As Kennedy inspected a battle flag that depicted a soldier hurtling forward into battle, rifle and fixed bayonet thrust ahead, he saw reflected back his own vision of a Cuban exile unity achieved through military leadership and an unstinting focus on return. Kennedy's prepared text made few promises, but his seemingly ad-libbed response was another matter. "I can assure you," he vowed to his audience, "that this flag will be returned to this Brigade in a free Havana."[82] Cries of joy erupted. Kennedy praised the brigade's military heroism, and the broader community's sacrifice to live in exile. That they were Americans in the hemispheric sense, but quite apart from the US Americans, the president made clear. He called upon the Cubans to "submerge [momentary] differences in a common united front" and work "to the united end that Cuba is free." That the brigade and its

The recently released prisoners of the Brigade 2506 invasion force present their battle flag to President John F. Kennedy in Miami's Orange Bowl stadium, December 1962.
ST-C75-8-62, White House Photographs, JFK Library.

"spirit" should remain vibrant was essential. In preparing the Cuban people for their eventual return, the brigade was "the point of the spear."[83]

Though in the Cuban Missile Crisis resolution of just two months prior Kennedy had seemingly pledged not to invade the island again, the Orange Bowl ceremony conveyed a different message. The *Miami Herald* reported that Kennedy's remarks "brought a vast new wave of hope" to the exiles. "What more could he have said?" the paper quoted one Cuban exile leader. "We are reborn right now."[84] An editorial excitedly argued that Kennedy's "strong words—words of commitment" had "bound the United States in honor to help wrest Cuba from the foul tyranny which infests it." On the field of the Orange Bowl, the president's "policy on Cuba (as they say in football) has turned the corner and is outside, with clear running room ahead."[85] For CRC leader Cardona, Kennedy's remarks "were vibrant, strong, decisive, and binding," a clear "commitment to Cuba [made] before the world." The CRC expected to be part of a war of liberation, Kennedy's noninvasion pledge be damned.[86]

But it was not to be. A significant portion of the Cuban invasion brigade ended up incorporated in the US armed services. And in the months after the Orange Bowl celebration, exiles returned to raiding Cuban targets, especially focusing on infrastructure. CIA-sponsored exiles had a relatively free hand in these activities. But some exiles sought their targets without CIA approval, often with disastrous consequences. The Kennedy administration was forced to declare that the raids were "neither supported nor condoned by this Government," and to commit itself in March 1963 "to insure that such raids are not launched, manned, or equipped from U.S. territory." Efforts to constrain them in turn strained relations between Cuban Americans and the administration, which was turning its attention to Southeast Asia.[87]

Maintaining the Cuban exile as a Cold War asset poised to return always required more than weapons and explosives training. From the start of his administration, it was clear that Kennedy accepted the premise of Eisenhower's administrator Tracy Voorhees that the Cuban refugees' material needs constituted a "national" concern.[88] Within a week of being sworn in as president, he instructed his secretary of Health, Education, and Welfare, Abraham Ribicoff, to assume management of federal refugee aid. Ribicoff was to personally inspect the situation to ensure that the proper services were being delivered and opportunities fostered, all with the understanding that the federal government intended "to expedite their voluntary return [to Cuba] as soon as conditions there facilitate that."[89] Delivered just a week later, Ribicoff's report concluded that local authorities and charities were no longer able to cope with the massive refugee influx. Matters justified a stronger federal role in managing the Cuban migration. Washington's ensuing commitment encompassed a vast array of provision: direct aid to individuals, job training and placement, health services, school aid, food distribution, and funds to relocate some refugees to areas where their incorporation could be more easily managed.[90] By the end of

February 1961, refugees were receiving the first of their biweekly assistance checks.[91] Eisenhower had appropriated $1 million for refugee aid. Kennedy added almost $18 million for 1961. Spending tens of millions of dollars in each of the next few years, the program would ultimately provide roughly $2 billion in assistance to over 700,000 Cuban emigres.[92]

Just as continued US aid to clandestine paramilitary actors nurtured Cuban exile identity and patriotism, so did the activities of the Cuban Refugee Program (CRP). In a strictly legal sense, federal benefits were conditioned upon Cubanness. Whether one was a traditional Cuban immigrant or an exile in "parole" status, that person was eligible for CRP aid.[93] Only when a Cuban became a naturalized citizen of the United States did the CRP's responsibility to that person end. That is, Cuban exiles actually *lost* benefits by becoming American citizens.[94] Further, Cubans in Miami received benefits at a special Cuban Emergency Refugee Center, the old headquarters of the *Miami News,* a building that would in time become known as the "Freedom Tower."[95]

If Brigade 2506 projected the image of Cuban exile valor, the soldier poised to fight his way back to freedom in his homeland, the CRP cultivated the image of the average Cuban refugee residing in the United States. Sensitivity to charges that Cubans were leeching off of US taxpayers was significant. The line repeated by administration officials was that Cubans were a "proud and resourceful people," who would not otherwise be seeking assistance were it not for the unusual circumstances of their arrival in America.[96] Indeed, lest the public associate Cubans with dependency, federal officials took pains to release data on the amount of federal dollars the Cubans *refused* to accept, as well as those Cubans who repaid the earlier assistance they had received.[97] Cuban Refugee Program publications could—and did, at least in effect and possibly in intent—make use of the Cubans' phenotypic whiteness in constructing the image of benefits recipient as bootstrapper.

US officials buttressed their aid to Cubans with an expectation of breaking up the largest concentration of them. Ribicoff's mandate had from the start included funding refugee resettlement to areas beyond Miami. The perceived urgency of this situation rose with each passing day. As of late 1961, "xenophobia" directed at the refugees was "growing," according to one astute local observer, *Miami Herald* reporter Juanita Greene. Unemployment in South Florida was high—7 percent in 1962—and job competition intense. African American leaders spoke for populations being wedged out of certain economic sectors in favor of exile workers. What was worse, the exiles were reaping the benefits of special federal programs unavailable to the city's black population, US citizens of long standing. The expectation of return that had made federal support politically saleable to the Kennedy administration made it odd and unfair to many black Miamians. According to a local Urban League leader, African Americans "question[ed] why they [Cubans] receive special treatment as a group when they plan only to remain until the situation in Cuba changes to their satisfaction."[98] Also, despite significant federal disbursements to local authorities, the fiscal costs of refugee services were noticeable, and perhaps more so to a native population chafing at having to live side by side with a people quite content to carry on their Caribbean cultural traditions on American soil.[99] Though many would eventually return, by the summer of 1963, perhaps more than a third of the Cuban Refugee Center's 165,000 registered clients had left Miami. Added urgency emerged the following year when the White House announced that Miami's unemployed Cubans would cease to receive federal aid if they did not migrate to cities where work could be more easily found.[100] By the middle of 1964, the program had supposedly relocated more than 80,000 refugees, transforming them into "self-supporting members" of some 1,800 communities across the country.[101]

While resettlement appealed to the desires of many local voters and their representatives, some exile leaders saw the matter quite differently. Already doubting the Kennedy administration's commitment to Cuban liberation, resettlement appeared to be a strategy to shatter the exile community's solidarity, cover for another betrayal. Resigning from chairmanship of the CRC in April 1963, José Miró Cardona listed "the speedy relocation, outright dispersal of Cubans" along with Washington's new constraints on "the establishment . . . of revolutionary Cuban bases of operation" and the "persecution of revolutionaries" as important shifts in US policy toward the exiles. Such actions were among those that conveyed a clear indication that "the Cuban struggle is in the process of being liquidated by the government [of the United States]."[102]

The sense of betrayal stayed with Cardona. A few years before his death, he was to write of US presidential involvement in his homeland, a sentiment that had become something of a common sense among the exiles:

"one American, Teddy Roosevelt, helped Cuba's Independence; another, John F. Kennedy handed her to Russia."[103]

☆ ☆

While Cuban leaders in the United States nurtured an exile politics that pointed toward the day when they could restore themselves to their island homeland, Mexican Americans and Puerto Ricans redoubled their efforts to secure places within the halls of American power. If the Viva Kennedy campaign was at best a temporary linkage of these mostly distinct political communities, it did bolster the hopes that at least ethnic Mexicans had laid the foundation for a new level of political unity. And having made common cause as never before, they expected to see their demonstration of electoral influence honored by Democrats in Washington.

Campaign pledges and the Kennedy administration's focus on Cuba and Latin America more generally raised expectations that the new president would recognize that Mexican Americans could represent the United States in a variety of important capacities. Viva Kennedy volunteers had been promised that their campaign labors entitled them to judgeships, ambassadorships, as well as other less prestigious but still well paid federal posts. Acting on Carlos McCormick's advice, a number of Kennedy campaigners sought positions in the State Department.[104]

While in past years many of these same leaders might have emphasized their bona fides as "Americans" first, and possibly their "whiteness," they now demonstrated an increasing comfort in linking their qualifications for public office to their ethnic backgrounds. Avoiding the unseemly appearance of asking for patronage as an explicit quid pro quo for campaign efforts, they asserted that their unique "Latin American" cultural attributes and sensibilities merited special consideration.[105] Many spoke about how "Americans of Latin American origin"[106] could prove vital to the fight against Communism in Latin America. LULAC national president Frank Valdez, for example, reminded Kennedy that they could be of great service in South America, "where the ethnic background and the language are one and the same." A San Antonio LULAC leader suggested that Mexican Americans' knowledge of Latin Americans' "habits, traits, characteristics and most of all their emotionalism" would make them ideal ambassadors to the region. The US-born Latin Americans, resolved LULAC as an organization, "have an insight to their problems and generally know how they think."[107]

The Kennedy administration's decisions tested the strength of this argument for "Latin American" cultural homology. The Cuban revolution had elevated Puerto Rico's strategic importance to US Cold War policymakers. Kennedy intended the island to be a "meeting place and workshop" for the United States and Latin America, a showcase for US-led anti-Communist development in the hemisphere.[108] Two men from the island's Democratic-aligned PPD leadership therefore gained high-profile diplomatic posts in his administration. Arturo Morales Carrión, Puerto Rico's (Cuban-born) secretary of state, was named Assistant Secretary of State for Latin America. Teodoro Moscoso (born in Spain but living most of his life in Puerto Rico), who had spent the previous decade in charge of Operation Bootstrap, was picked to be ambassador to Venezuela and to head up Kennedy's Latin American development program, the Alliance for Progress.[109] Believing Kennedy in debt to the numerically dominant element of Viva Kennedy, Mexican-American leaders were indignant. During the campaign, Hector P. García told Democratic National Committee members that the United States had done a poor job selling democracy in the hemisphere "because we are not making use of our greatest salesman of Democracy" the "Americans of Latin American origin."[110] But when Moscoso's visit to Venezuela in the summer of 1961 touched off riots, Dr. García's remarks—"I think that by now Kennedy would be realizing . . . that the only people that they respect in Latin America are the Mexicans"—suggested the boundaries of his political community.[111]

As of June 1961, Spanish-surnamed Americans filled only four key administration diplomatic posts, and only one of these belonged to a Mexican American from Viva Kennedy, El Paso mayor Raymond Telles.[112] A group of Viva Kennedy leaders publicly accused the administration of going back on its word, even claiming that their exclusion from decision-making positions had indirectly led the administration to blunder into the Bay of Pigs fiasco.[113] Kennedy acknowledged that Mexican Americans represented a "great reservoir of talent," especially for the Foreign Service, but did little to change the situation.[114]

In truth, the 1960 election was so close that any number of constituencies might have seen their votes as decisive in the Democratic victory. Bert Corona remembered Kennedy as a "Boston political animal" whose administration "didn't understand Mexicans."[115] It seems reasonable to believe that the Kennedy brothers then viewed Mexican Americans much like they did

African Americans, as akin to "classic machine politics urban ethnic voters, rather than an oppressed group with a moral claim to justice."[116] Moreover, realpolitik may explain the administration's patronage decisions as much as cultural ignorance does. The Democrats were still largely the party of northern cities and the South. In 1960, Pennsylvania provided Kennedy the same number of electoral votes as California had given Nixon, and each offered eight more than Texas's twenty-four votes. New York, with its forty-five electoral votes, added more to a candidate's tally than Texas, New Mexico, Nevada, Colorado, and Arizona combined. Massachusetts gave a candidate almost the same amount of electoral votes as the last four of these southwestern states. Since fifteen of eighteen Viva Kennedy coordinators came from the Southwest, their campaign efforts, however important, may have done little to dispel the notion that Mexican Americans were basically a distant and regional concern, one that could wait for more central Democratic constituencies to be rewarded.

Fueled by a sense of betrayal at the highest levels of government, Mexican-American activists and leaders redoubled their efforts to form organizations that could capitalize on their demographic strength and location. In the spring of 1961, Viva Kennedy leaders in Texas established a statewide organization called Mexican Americans for Political Action. Dr. Hector P. García, a Lyndon Johnson ally, became its "national" organizer and Bexar County Commissioner Albert Peña Jr., again representing liberals, its state chairman. In March 1961, the Texas activists met in Phoenix with California's MAPA, hoping to join forces and transform the Viva Kennedy network into a permanent southwestern political powerhouse. Chaired by James Carlos Mc-Cormick, the Phoenix conference balanced the Texas and California factions by naming García its president and Edward Roybal its vice president.[117]

The struggle to create political institutions advancing an independent ethnic Mexican agenda initiated wide-ranging deliberations over the nature of their peoplehood. In Phoenix, Dr. García surmised that having leapt into the national political arena in 1960, the Viva Kennedy backers now found themselves "locked in a battle with the men of great power in our country." Only through "united strength" could "*la raza*" prevail. Power required forming an organization "national" in scope, "political" in nature, and "NONPARTISAN" in orientation. If García's nationwide ambition and his invocation of *la raza* suggested his openness to pan-Hispanic alliances, he closed his remarks with an even more explicit call: "We need to be united. There is no difference between Spanish-speaking Texans, Californians, and New Yorkers because we all suffer and travel the same road. They used us."[118]

Despite García's occasional connection of Mexican-American and Puerto Rican interests, a consensus on a collective self-definition proved elusive. Lingering questions of ethnic terminology, so laced with political meaning but submerged in Viva Kennedy, resurfaced with a vengeance. The activists spent the bulk of the Phoenix conference debating what to call their new political group. Roybal's Californians believed in "empowering the term" they had chosen for themselves—Mexican American—thereby "eliminating its stigma." But for others this was too much. The Phoenix contingent, in the end, called themselves the "Political Association of Spanish-speaking Organizations" (PASO) as a sort of placeholder. Yet at the group's next meeting in Las Vegas, the former Viva Kennedy campaigners once again quickly fell into dispute over how to understand and represent their collective endeavor. Carlos McCormick counseled them that presidential recognition rested on their ability to adopt a collective posture with respect to other societal groups. In their internal debate, all PASO leaders noted that African Americans had achieved comparatively great gains by declaring themselves a "colored people." As one activist noted, liberals who claimed not to "see any color" found that the NAACP effectively "pointed out . . . the color" they needed to see.[119] However, a vocal contingent wanted ethnicity out of the naming altogether, preferring to emphasize the group's "Americanism." Was "Spanish-speaking a correct name to adopt by a group of Americans that seek to place themselves before the nation as fellow Americans on an equal basis with any other group of Americans?" asked a delegate from Arizona. In contrast, a Nevadan said it would be "very foolish to not in some way identify ourselves by name because we are going to be identified anyway." There was no escaping certain facts, he claimed: "When I am running for office people immediately recognize that I am Mexican." McCormick, however, argued that a national organization could not have "Mexican" in the title without alienating Puerto Ricans, and that "Spanish-speaking" was a descriptor that all in the group "can be proud of." It was preferable to the condescending "Latin American," for instance, "a tag that they put on our people in Texas and feel they are doing us a favor." At the end of the day, he said, groups such as the NAACP had chosen to identify themselves and were "doing better than us." While few in the room would disagree, an accord proved elusive. In the end, Texans called their group PASO and Californians retained the MAPA name. Lacking funds and the active participation of elected officials—Roybal, nominally the PASO vice president, did not attend the Nevada meeting—Mexican-American political organizations remained without a formula to constitute themselves as a national force, absent a Democratic presidential candidate's blessing.[120]

☆ ☆

Elected officials fared better in translating their support for Kennedy into an ascent to the national political arena. Though the unification of Mexican-American political forces faltered, and a pan-Hispanic coalition was even farther off, these politicians capitalized upon their Kennedy campaign activism to expand the Mexican-American presence in Congress. The process cemented their status as assets to national Democrats, players in state and local politics, and emblems of a multicultural democracy.

Mindful of the Democrats' needs in Texas, President Kennedy cleared a path for Henry B. González to ascend to the ranks of the national government. In the fall of 1961, the president appointed San Antonio's sitting congressman to a federal judgeship, and endorsed the state senator González in his successful primary campaign, raising the possibility that González could become the first Mexican American to represent the state in the US House of Representatives. The stakes for the party were high. The state Democrats' conservative-liberal split was becoming irreconcilable, and Mexican Americans were absolutely essential to liberal hopes. Conservative Democrats had twice handed the state to Dwight Eisenhower (1952, 1956) rather than vote for the liberal Adlai Stevenson. And in the special election for Lyndon Johnson's senate seat held in early 1961, many liberals refused to vote for the conservatives' choice, oil man William "Dollar Bill" Blakley. As a result, a conservative Houston political scientist named John Tower became the first Republican to represent the state in the upper chamber since Reconstruction. Sensing an opportunity to build off of Tower's historic victory, the GOP sent former president Dwight Eisenhower to Texas in support of González's general election opponent, John Goode. Eager to defend Democratic territory and maintain his own influence in Texas, Vice President Johnson stumped for Henry B. Newspapers portrayed the race as a referendum on the new administration and on the future of Republicanism in Texas.

The image of American democracy, especially in Latin America, informed the White House's intervention. Though the civic nationalist González portrayed himself as the choice for all Texans, Lyndon Johnson sold him as an ethnic asset to Cold War America. Sending González to Washington would give proof, the vice president told crowds, that Americans "can elect a man to the United States congress regardless of his race." Johnson promised that if González won, Kennedy would send him "throughout the hemisphere to show people what can happen in the land of the free and the home of the brave." For those inclined to discriminate, Johnson called on voters to join their countrymen in looking beyond the prejudices of the past.[121] Leaving nothing to chance, Johnson called upon Mexican president Adolfo López Mateos to ensure that Cantínflas, Mexico's favorite film star, would excite the masses at González's election-eve rally.[122] John Goode held his own fiesta, but it failed to captivate the city's West Side barrio. The ten kegs of beer and 200 dozen tamales in which he invested returned only 16 votes in one precinct. The results became the grist for a memorable Democratic riposte: "They drink Goode's beer, they eat Goode's tamales, then go to the polls and vote for González."[123] In the end, Henry B. took nearly 53,000 of 95,000 votes, roughly 56 percent, recreating his winning coalition of Mexican-American, African American, liberal Anglo, and labor support.[124] While Texas Republicans later claimed they never had a chance against "a Mexican in a Mexican town," they had clearly hoped for a much better result.[125]

If Texas was political property national Democrats hoped that Mexican Americans would help them maintain, the fast-growing state of California appeared the party's future, an inheritance to manage wisely. Out of power for most of the twentieth century, state Democrats had steamrolled their opponents in the 1958 elections. When California gained eight House seats thanks to congressional reapportionment (pushing the state's total to thirty-eight) after the 1960 census, the Democratic-controlled state legislature redrew the state's thirtieth district to include Edward Roybal's city council territory.[126] The new district was roughly 60 percent Democratic, though only 9 percent Mexican American.[127] Setting his sights on Washington, Roybal battled William Fitzgerald, a Loyola University professor, in the 1962 primary. Although Fitzgerald was supported by state assembly kingpin Jesse Unruh, Roybal won the primary as he had won his previous campaigns, with support from African American and Jewish voters and the district's Mexican Americans, and with aid from the Los Angeles County Federation of Labor and other liberals in the state Democratic Party. It was a New Deal coalition similar to González's.[128] In the general election, Roybal highlighted his connection to Kennedy and touted the president's endorsement. He received at least three supportive campaign visits from members of the president's Cabinet, another important sign of the administration's eagerness to see him elected.[129] In the end, he defeated the nine-term Republican incumbent, Gordon McDonough, with 56.7 percent of the vote.[130] As he had been the first Mexican American to serve on the Los Angeles City Council in the twentieth century, so did he become the first Mexican American sent to the House of Representatives from California since the 1870s.[131]

While González and Roybal clearly benefited from Kennedy's backing, such support was about more than simply paying off campaign debts. To Democratic elites intent upon portraying their party in its traditional role as champion of the underdog, the Catholic, the immigrant, and, increasingly, the "minority," González and Roybal were valuable allies and resources going forward. They served as important symbols of the party's inclusiveness, and as magnets to maintain and attract ethnic votes to Democrats in statewide and national races at a time when the party's traditional strongholds in the Northeast were beginning to lose power and as the formerly "Solid South" could no longer be counted on to support liberal Democrats for the White House. The administration, criticized for failing to recognize its Mexican-American supporters with positions of influence, instead summoned the image of an alliance with ethnic Mexican legislators as proof of their shared commitment to the group's "progress."

Mainland Puerto Ricans did not elect one of their own to the US Congress during this period.[132] However, Herman Badillo experienced an ascent in New York politics comparable to the triumphs of Mexican-American legislators in the Southwest. After the 1960 election, the thirty-one-year-old Badillo converted his East Harlem Citizens for Kennedy storefront into the East Harlem John F. Kennedy Club. He vowed to "draw people from all racial groups to work for the betterment of the community, not for any particular racial group." His immediate target was the incumbent of the 16th state assembly district, Alfred E. Santangelo, a long-time Tammany Democrat, whom he charged with running the district purely in the interests of its Italian-American residents.[133] Although Badillo lost to

**OUR GOAL IS PROGRESS**

President Kennedy at the White House with Congressmen Joseph M. Montoya of New Mexico (left), Edward R. Roybal of California and Henry B. Gonzalez of Texas.

The Kennedy administration promotes itself and the former Viva Kennedy campaigners who by 1963 would comprise the ethnic Mexican contingent in the US House of Representatives. *Left to right:* Joseph Montoya, John F. Kennedy, Edward Roybal, Henry B. González. Courtesy of Henry B. González Papers, e_hbg_0035, Dolph Briscoe Center for American History, University of Texas, Austin.

Santangelo in a bitterly contested election to represent the district in the Democratic state committee—by 75 votes out of more than 2,800 cast—he was on the rise.[134] Badillo was only thirty-two years of age when Mayor Robert F. Wagner Jr. made him the first Puerto Rican to serve as a city commissioner. The job of Deputy Commissioner of Real Estate paid a tidy $15,000 salary, and Badillo later became the city's first Commissioner of Relocation, in charge of managing the human displacement that attended urban renewal and infrastructure projects.[135]

Badillo's growing political network and recognition portended even bigger things. In 1965, at age thirty-six, he won a close race for Bronx borough president against a candidate backed by the Bronx Democratic machine. To put matters in perspective, the Bronx had almost 1.5 million residents in 1960, making it twice as large as San Francisco and one-and-a-half times as populous as Houston. It had almost three times as many residents as San Antonio, and six times the population of El Paso. Were the Bronx its own city, it would have been the sixth largest in the country in 1960.[136] It was like many northern cities, in that it was a place of minority political advancement only after it had suffered serious neglect and begun to manifest signs of urban crisis. Nevertheless, that its leader was now a Puerto Rican was, to many, an important sign of inclusion. For the city's leading

Spanish-language daily, *El Diario-La Prensa,* the election marked the moment that the Puerto Rican people had "finally become first class citizens." The victory reverberated as far as Badillo's island hometown of Caguas. In one island power broker's words, it was "a starting point towards a new horizon of progress and happiness for Puerto Ricans in New York."[137]

☆ ☆

The nationalization of the Mexican-American and, to a far lesser extent, Puerto Rican political communities that the Kennedy campaign fostered was as close to the birth moment for "Latino politics" as one can identify. But Viva Kennedy was more a reflection of the possible than any confirmed alliance or developed articulation of a "Latin American" or "Spanish American" political community. Furthermore, the nonparticipation of Cubans in this project reflected and portended their distinct trajectory, reinforced during the Kennedy administration (and beyond) by political violence and extraordinary federal aid premised upon and conditioning their sense of national origin distinctiveness and impermanence in the United States.

The demobilization of the nascent electorate and the neglect of many of those who presumed themselves its leaders did not reverse the nationalization of Mexican-American politics, or dampen the urge among some to utilize the focusing energy of the presidential campaign to construct a powerful constituency, whether Mexican-American or more broadly pan-ethnic. And while they lagged behind other Democratic constituencies in patronage and party visibility, their association with the national Democrats John F. Kennedy and Lyndon B. Johnson served to elevate politicians from Mexican America to the national stage. These elected officials, sometimes in spite of their own stated desires, served as symbols of their peoples' incorporation in the Democratic Party and progress in American life.

Though it ultimately revealed how many obstacles remained to the realization of an enduring and independent nationwide "Latino vote," and its outcomes may have only encouraged divergent political projects in the Southwest and New York, the national political opening of 1960 forever entwined the political destinies of Mexican Americans and Puerto Ricans. While they would continue to operate in distinct spheres throughout the 1960s, their separate political conversations, conducted in local vernaculars, did begin to converge on common subjects. One of these was civil rights, the focus of the next chapter.

# 3

# Civil Rights and the Recognition of a "National Minority"

Rising to address the 1963 state convention of the Political Association of Spanish-speaking Organizations (PASO), successor to the Viva Kennedy clubs in Texas, Albert Peña made a point that few in the room could deny. With the black freedom movement at full tilt, its marchers facing beatings and water cannons and police dogs, their sacrifice etched in gripping images shown on televisions across the world, Peña declared that the "number one issue" facing Texas and the country in June 1963 was ensuring what he called "Civil Rights for everyone." Peña's definition of "civil rights" transcended formal legal equality. It meant "the right to vote, the right to a job, decent wages and hours, the right to an education, adequate housing and the best of medical care; and what is more important, equal opportunities to obtain all these things."[1]

As Peña saw it, to achieve this broad package of civil rights required ethnic Mexicans to clarify the relationship between their community and the country at large. "We are Americans. We are proud to be called Americans. And we insist on being treated like Americans," he said. But to achieve the better America of which he spoke, ethnic Mexicans had first to accept that they were a minority group. It was a venerable American tradition, he explained. If "the Irish in Boston, the Italians in New York, the Negroes everywhere" could do it, so could the Mexican people of the United States. By organizing themselves as a distinct minority bloc, they would deliver a message to the Anglos whose control of government had for so long prevented Mexican Americans from advancing. Times had changed. In the new civil rights era, said Peña, "the price of our vote is recognition and representation."[2]

The national impetus of Viva Kennedy had raised hopes in Mexican America, but delivered far less than had been promised. As the failed efforts to organize a southwestern Mexican-American political organization after the 1960 campaign revealed, and as Peña's remarks confirmed, even in 1963 many Mexican-American leaders remained unconvinced that an assertive ethnic sensibility was necessary to their political empowerment.

Nevertheless, Peña's plea for Mexican Americans to adopt a "minority" mindset to complement their insistent Americanism shows how, by the early 1960s, civil rights progress had become fundamentally entwined with political recognition and representation. As the federal government expanded its civil rights efforts, largely in response to African American protests, it created new venues for ethnic Mexicans to assert claims on the White House. Between elections, they used these to confront the administration that had so baldly slighted them following Kennedy's victory. Appealing to a simple liberal logic that "national origin" discrimination was no less pernicious than "race" discrimination, that no "group" must be helped less than another, their leaders hoped to transcend their historic organizational and ethnic disunity, and end their status as an afterthought, regional minority.

As the Kennedy administration strained to balance its dependence on white support with its growing commitment to black freedom, it proved unwilling to assume identification with another vocal minority constituency. The ticket that carried the closest presidential election in history by mobilizing Hispanic pan-ethnicity now confronted assertive Mexican Americans with a wall of colorblindness. But a fundamental change was underway. The civil rights revolution was integrating southwestern political communities and organizations ever more under the demand to be recognized as a national minority—the Mexican American.

The revolution in civil rights had more uncertain consequences for the group that officials for a time called "Spanish Americans." In the face of assertions of "Mexican-American" identity, Washington often reflected back a pan-ethnic image. For instance, federal civil rights enforcers by 1962 established a "Spanish American" category, amalgamating Mexican Americans and Puerto Ricans (among others) into a singular type of discrimination victim. And even as Lyndon Johnson appointed a Mexican-American civil rights leader to the federal government's leading anti-discrimination board in 1967, and tapped him to lead a federal "Inter-Agency Committee on Mexican American Affairs" that recognized them by name as the country's "second largest minority group," the president still expected the committee to serve the interests of all "Spanish-surnamed Americans" as well.[3]

Yet this long-sought recognition from Washington did little to reflect or foster "Spanish American" coalescence at the elite or grassroots levels. While Mexican Americans asserted a collective identity on the national civil rights stage to achieve justice from white society and a certain sense of equality with African Americans, Puerto Ricans continued to draw upon the local and interracial strategies of the pre–Viva Kennedy era. They translated their concentrated strength in New York into recognition as a protected minority in the Voting Rights Act of 1965, and into achieving breakthroughs in local political representation. The potential partners each encountered in the quest for political independence pushed Mexican Americans and Puerto Ricans who sought to punish traditional Democrats into very different orbits. Mexican Americans who entertained crossing party lines in the Southwest faced the option of supporting conservative Republicans who promised the "recognition and representation" that Democrats had long withheld. Puerto Ricans, in contrast, could and did defect to liberal "reform" Democrats or liberal Republicans. Because the latter were ever more the archenemies of the same southwestern conservatives then wooing Mexican Americans, a "Spanish American" unification under Republican auspices was not in the offing.

But little integration of the two populations would come from Democrats either. At times respecting Mexican Americans' and Puerto Ricans' senses of difference from each other, and always wary of a pan-Hispanic mobilization after an election was complete, Presidents Kennedy and Johnson more often divided or even ranked the two populations than they did encourage them to form an enduring pan-ethnic bloc. Johnson's creation of a committee named for Mexican Americans but ostensibly charged with advocating for all "Spanish-surnamed Americans" was more than ambiguous. It reflected the president's sense that recognizing the named people's demographic strength and location in key states was an essential task of the nation's leader. Even if "Spanish-surnamed Americans" were more similar than they were different, certain members of this group were clearly more important than others in the president's eyes.[4]

☆ ☆

Albert Peña approached the Kennedy presidency eager for a period of great civil rights progress. The liberal San Antonio activist was one of the few Mexican Americans to attend the Democratic Party's 1960 convention, at which he and fellow Democrats committed their party to undertaking landmark civil rights reform. The Democratic Platform of 1960 pledged to hasten the desegregation of southern schools, provide fair access to voting booths and the housing market, and "break down artificial and arbitrary barriers to employment based on age, race, sex, religion, or national origin."[5] When Peña and many others organized "Viva Kennedy" clubs, to bring about this future was an essential element of their motivation.

The party's conservative southern barons held different ideas, however. Reluctant to challenge this untiring bulwark of racial hierarchy in the Congress with a meaningful civil rights bill, President Kennedy at first confined himself to issuing an executive order that barred workplace discrimination only in federal worksites and those of the government's contractors.[6] To bring what it called "affirmative action" to bear on the problem, Kennedy's executive order created something called the President's Committee on Equal Employment Opportunity (PCEEO). Vice President Johnson was placed in charge. What "affirmative action" meant in practice was yet to be fleshed out.[7]

While ethnopolitical heterogeneity continued to constrain Mexican Americans' attempts at organizational unification, the PCEEO operated in a manner similar to Viva Kennedy, collapsing distinctions among a broad swath of Spanish-speaking populations. For instance, though the body's initial employment censuses listed separate categories for "Spanish-Americans" and for Puerto Ricans,[8] by 1962 it amalgamated the groups into a single civil rights category: "Spanish-Americans."[9] Techniques used to collect employment data consolidated these communities even further. Because state laws barred employers from asking workers to declare their race, PCEEO surveys relied upon employers to make visual observations of their workforce's ethnoracial composition. Bureaucratic practices such as these in effect nullified national origin, skin color, or class differences within the larger "Spanish-American" category. As sociologist John Skrentny has observed, this practice made "a white Cuban" and a "dark brown Mexican *indio*" a part of the same official minority.[10]

This instance of the bureaucracy constructing "Spanish-Americans" as a national minority did not mean that the constructed group rated as a civil rights priority. Of all those selected to sit on the PCEEO, including a dozen individuals chosen to reflect a variety of economic, gender, racial, and religious constituencies, none were Mexican American or Puerto Rican.[11] And though the PCEEO would garner early praise for negotiating voluntary anti-discrimination agreements with several major employers, its main focus was the plight of African Americans, especially those in the Southeast.[12] According to the PCEEO's own records, only 2.1 percent of the more than 4,000 complaints it received during its first two-plus years came from Spanish-speaking Americans.[13]

The PCEEO's racial and regional emphases, and its corresponding lack of attention to Mexican-American concerns, pricked the Viva Kennedy leaders who still smarted from the president's patronage snubs and yearned for any acknowledgment from Washington that their people mattered. In an early internal evaluation of the committee, the American G.I. Forum (AGIF) determined that "the emphasis appears to be all on discrimination against Negroes."[14] The group's Washington, DC, director, Rudy Ramos, lambasted the PCEEO for devoting "98% plus direct work for one minority group," for it came "at the expense of others equally as deserving." A former Viva Kennedy coordinator himself, he implied that blacks were essentially abusing the system. "Please notice that we do not publicize every event to which we have legitimate complaints as opposed to the group mentioned in paragraph one," he noted. Mexican Americans, he claimed archly, "do as much as we can to solve our own problems."[15]

As they presented "Spanish American" and "Negro" as mutually exclusive but ostensibly equal national minority populations, federal civil rights policies helped modify the terms of Mexican-American political contestation. For those leaders of the AGIF persuasion, who had long sought to ameliorate discrimination by asserting their personal dignity, sacrifice, patriotism, and at times by claiming "whiteness," civil rights initiatives provided new resources with which to stake a claim on the national consciousness.[16] Discrimination was a universal wrong, but it appeared that the PCEEO was not dedicated to fighting discrimination everywhere it occurred. The PCEEO had inadvertently illuminated a new social reality: government and its contractors discriminating in the workplace, *and* government bias in investigating the wrongdoing.

The sense that black civil rights gains of the early 1960s were coming at Mexican Americans' expense emerged most powerfully in Los Angeles. In previous decades, Southern California's defense-fueled economy had drawn migrants from far and wide. African Americans, whose numbers in California had grown 91 percent during the 1950s, were eagerly demanding a fair share of economic opportunity from the state's many government contractors.[17] In the summer of 1963, reports circulated that these contractors were so intent on avoiding civil rights complaints that they held on to their black employees at all costs and, whether to meet payroll, adjust for production changes, or for any other reason, chose to fire Mexican Americans instead. The same pattern was supposedly at work in hiring. As a member of the California Democratic Central Committee claimed, "When Negroes apply for jobs, employers are afraid not to hire them for fear of retaliation and so, in some cases, fire Mexican-Americans to make space for the Negro." Sixty Mexican-American leaders in Los Angeles held a closed-door meeting to respond to the situation. One contingent wanted to form a united front of Mexican-American and African American civil rights organizations. But according to an account of the meeting, "several of the more conservative Mexican-American leaders strongly oppose[d] any 'mixing' of Mexican-American and Negro grievances."[18]

For a variety of California Mexican-American community interests, inequities in civil rights enforcement inspired a collective call upon Democratic elites to recognize their people's centrality to national life. Fifty Mexican-American leaders in the state formed a diverse coalition representing civil rights and community groups, lawyers' associations, chambers of commerce, and social work agencies. They demanded that Vice President Johnson sit down with them and acknowledge their particular issues. "Who is not aware of the plight of the Negro?" said coalition member George Borrell, whose new "Equal Opportunity Foundation" had formed to advocate for Mexican Americans in discrimination cases. "Conversely, who is aware of the plight of the Mexican-American?"[19] The coalition's activism emerged from California conditions, but the national civil rights initiative helped it shed light on all Mexican Americans' plight. "Today's Mexican-American family" reported the *New York Times* on the occasion of Johnson's subsequent visit, was "trapped in degrees of second-class citizenship and deprivation." Their lowly status assumed a bitter new dimension in light of blacks' civil rights gains. Though they were "almost as underprivileged as Negroes," their leaders felt that "nobody seems to be worrying about them." Even worse, civil rights enforcement was having a perverse effect on them. "Word is circulating that the employers' new refrain is: 'You're fired—and a Negro's hired.'"[20]

Vice President Johnson's staff viewed the Mexican-American coalition as originating from less lofty concerns, however. Johnson aide George

Reedy's sources, among them freshman representative Edward Roybal, convinced him that the number one issue was not equal employment per se. It was "appointments—that means political patronage." In Reedy's estimation, "THIS IS THE THING THEY ARE REALLY INTERESTED IN AND EVERYTHING ELSE IS SECONDARY."[21] The Californians had worked hard for Kennedy in 1960, and felt "double-crossed" by his administration. They were purportedly irate that the White House published a pamphlet touting the president's record of appointments to commissions, postmasters, embassies, and the like, under the title "Spanish-speaking Americans: A People Progressing."[22] They were not progressing. They believed that all of the jobs— or at least those they prized—had gone to Puerto Ricans or to Mexican Americans from other states.[23] As one coalition member told a reporter, they had demanded the meeting in order to remind Johnson in person that they had been "literally forgotten once we helped the administration get into office."[24] According to Roybal, at least some within the California coalition were ready to "start plugging for the Republican party."[25]

Yet, if "patronage" was in fact the coalition's main goal, it had to be thought of expansively, and in relation to the new vocabulary that Mexican Americans were embracing in discussing their difference with powerful officials. AGIF representatives on the coalition did describe a shared "ethnic background" that poised their people "to make a great contribution" to the civil service, and called for the country to "profit from [the] bi-lingual and bi-cultural traits of our ethnic group" in hemispheric relations. The coalition expressed its distinct interests on other fronts, however. The bracero program constituted an "attack on family life," which made it "a threat to the civilization in which our culture has its roots." The coalition also argued for programs to combat Mexican Americans' high youth dropout rate, itself in part a function of "adjusting to a different culture." These culturally based claims appeared alongside requests that Johnson pressure California's Democratic leaders to include Mexican Americans in the party hierarchy and to support their candidacies for elective office. They wanted positions of influence in the Democratic National Committee as well. They were a political minority, too.[26]

The Kennedy administration was busy fighting off charges that its anti-discrimination policies, including a recently submitted civil rights bill, constituted a racial quota system for blacks. It mostly rejected Mexican Americans' pleas. Addressing the coalition in August 1963, Vice President

Johnson, who claimed an intimate understanding of the Mexican-American condition thanks to his Texas roots, who campaigned for the group's votes on the basis of their ethnic particularity, now envisioned them as only temporarily different.[27] Language barriers existed, of course. But that did not confer any special "minority" status on Mexican Americans. In fact, he told the audience, "all of us have been a minority at one point," minority being a synonym for "underprivileged." What was needed was, he said, "to merge with other social sectors, to work, and to rise to a higher station in life." Color-conscious policy—treating "each minority as something distinct and apart from the rest of the community"—would never solve the problem, he claimed. Johnson also issued a warning about the conflict brewing between blacks and Mexican Americans: "the surest way to keep minorities in a minority status—to freeze an unyielding pattern of discrimination— is for minorities to pit themselves against other minorities." He challenged the Mexican Americans to file more discrimination complaints if the circumstances merited it. But fighting African Americans, or anyone else, was bound to be counterproductive. According to Johnson, the society's progress depended "precisely on the harmony of all elements of which it is composed."[28]

The administration's defensive liberalism was again on display when over two thousand people gathered in Los Angeles on November 15, 1963, for the PCEEO conference on equal employment in the Southwest. Again, Johnson lamented the endurance of "artificial barriers" to opportunity, but decried the strategy of "promoting minorities" as dangerous, and "merely another way of freezing the minority group status system in perpetuity." Anthony J. Celebrezze, Kennedy's secretary of Health, Education, and Welfare, echoed these remarks, with a special addendum for Mexican Americans. If they simply adopted the European immigrants' resolve to integrate themselves into the larger society, he said, they would have similar success. "You are making a mistake when you say others should feel sorry for you," he scolded the community leaders in attendance.[29]

Roughly half the Los Angeles audience was Mexican American, and in no mood for a color-blind vision of equal opportunity that implied that they could—or should—cease belonging to a minority. Displaying the "highly political temperament" that Johnson's assistant Reedy feared, Mexican-American spokesmen angrily rejoined that their people had been in the

Southwest for generations.[30] They had attempted assimilation. Despite their efforts to prove they were just like other Americans, however, they still suffered discrimination. One man defended his people's right to "retain their cultural background because they are indiginous [sic] to the country."[31] According to one California political insider, the assimilation gaffe, "coupled with the general dominence [sic] of the conference by the Negro at least in terms of numbers," had left Mexican Americans with "a sour taste in their mouths."[32]

. While a color-blind civic nationalism and assimilationist vision undoubtedly appealed to a segment of the room—as we have seen, the idea of being considered a "minority" did not come easily to some—Democrats' campaigns, patronage decisions, and civil rights priorities had been sending a different message. What the government rewarded, it seemed harder to deny, was not mere individual merit, or even group dignity and patriotism. It was group power.

Civil rights organizing across the Southwest was proving in some respects easier than the electoral organizing Mexican Americans were attempting at the same time. Compared to the complicated mechanics of mobilizing for a series of elections, in which usually Anglo candidates might be expected to deliver *on behalf of* Mexican-American constituents, the simplicity of marshaling the data that emerged from the authoritative national state stood out. And the process of convincing the White House to take them as seriously as it did African Americans diminished the salience of local and state rivalries that had frustrated so many previous efforts to unite Mexican Americans. Following the conference, sixty community leaders organized a follow-up meeting of their own to plan "a permanent Southwestern Mexican-American organization."[33] The Kennedy administration, hoping to contain Mexican Americans' surge toward political independence, had instead spurred it on.

☆ ☆

The Republican Party was hoping to hasten the split. Just two months before, on September 16, 1963—Mexican Independence Day—Barry Goldwater was perched atop an open white convertible, a political star on the emerald field of Dodger Stadium. The Arizona senator had not formally announced a presidential run, but he was acting the part of candidate. The conservative hotbed of Southern California was vital to his hopes of securing the Republican nomination. As he and wife Peggy slowly circled the field, they waved to the "wildly cheering Dodger stadium throng" that had paid a dollar a piece to see their hero in person. Forty thousand screams went up. Were they shouting for Goldwater or for the out-of-town result (Dodgers over Cardinals) just posted on the stadium's giant scoreboard? Regardless, the mood in Los Angeles was bright.[34]

Though Goldwater was an outspoken opponent of federal civil rights enforcement, the Los Angeles gathering was no bonfire of racial backlash. In point of fact, organizers billed the engagement as a "Republican Fiesta," with "mariachi bands and Mexican dancers" supplying the warm-up entertainment.[35] The rector of an East Los Angeles mission delivered the invocation, and did so in Spanish. Goldwater then followed with his own tribute to Mexican independence, in Spanish as well, before proceeding with English-language attacks on Kennedy and moderate Republicans.[36] The Democratic Party, he charged, used a "gingerbread monstrosity of programs and promises" to placate its "warring factions." But its coalition was a "house of trick cards." It was Democrats, Goldwater implied, who had "bred racial discontent in this land." Republicans, in contrast, welcomed voters of all backgrounds. But theirs was to be a party "controlled by principle."[37]

It was the glorious culmination of a busy day. For breakfast, Goldwater had enjoyed eggs and grits with Billy Graham. Then he attended a "coffee klatsch" with members of the NAACP and Urban League. In a press conference afterward he conceded that most black votes would go to the Democrats, but felt confident he could erode Kennedy's support among Spanish-speaking Americans. That view had come to him from John Flores, the man in charge of his "Latinos con Goldwater" operation. Flores was no conservative ideologue; he was a consultant. He had worked for Dwight Eisenhower's campaigns, and later to drum up Latino votes for Lyndon Johnson in the 1960 primaries. Now advertising himself as a disillusioned former Viva Kennedy leader, Flores played to Latinos' resentment, sounding the theme that their longtime support for Democrats had been taken for granted, that their people had been used. Rolling out the new organization just days after the Dodger Stadium rally, Flores proclaimed the Arizonan's chances of prying the "Spanish-speaking vote" away from Kennedy to be "very good," because "our people . . . have not received proper representation or any recognition for their efforts."[38]

For only some of Goldwater's Latino supporters was patronage a decisive issue, however. Goldwater's staunchest Latino backer in the crucial Golden State was probably Tirso del Junco, a thirty-nine-year-old Cuban émigré. Born into the island's political elite (his uncle was an ambassador and former mayor of Havana) he trained in medicine in Cuba and the United States. Settling in southern California a decade before the Cuban Revolution, he found himself in the epicenter of a burgeoning grassroots conservative movement whose motive force was anti-Communism.[39] Fidel Castro's rise to power in 1959 reinforced the affinity between the young physician, his place, and this movement. When not attending to surgery at Queen of Angels hospital, del Junco made himself a mainstay of the region's right-wing lecture circuit. His time as a University of Havana classmate of Castro, and his later experience as medical support for the Bay of Pigs invasion, conferred upon him a special credibility to address the dangers of laxity in the face of Communism. He spread the word at women's club meetings, Newman guild gatherings, and CYO luncheons, most in the reactionary hotbed of Orange County. In 1961, del Junco featured in a weeklong red-hunting revival, the Southern California School of Anti-Communism. He headlined along with far-right intellectual Cleon Skousen, singer Pat Boone, and the actor Ronald Reagan, who would later become his friend and political benefactor. For del Junco, staving off the Communist advance had clear domestic implications. As the Goldwater insurgency gained strength into 1964, del Junco joined party leaders in fostering the growth of "Republicans of Latin Extraction," a new group whose intention was to align the constituency with a "limited government" philosophy.[40]

While "Latinos con Goldwater" was ostensibly national in scope, the candidate himself was an unlikely focal point for Latino unity. Tirso del Junco, as a Cuban, came from a minority background within the nascent Latino electorate, an even smaller slice of the constituency, given Cubans' extremely low rates of naturalization at the time. And though outspoken, he was significantly more conservative than the vast majority of the Mexican-American voters in the state of California. Suggesting the variety of factions at work within the Republican Party, several committees arose to support the candidate, with each reflecting a distinct ethnic orientation or constituency. There was the statewide "Latin Americans for Goldwater-Miller" with which del Junco was affiliated. But there was also a "Mexican-American Committee for Goldwater-Miller," as well as a "Hispanic Citizens for Goldwater," not to mention "Latino Youth for Goldwater."[41]

A truly national "Latinos con Goldwater" was even more difficult to imagine because the Arizonan's principal rival for the GOP presidential nomination, New York governor Nelson Rockefeller, had for several years been building a Puerto Rican following through his liberal stewardship of the Empire State. His previous campaigns had shown Rockefeller that the New York City Puerto Rican electorate had a strong appetite for energetic government, one that could deliver improved housing, fight job discrimination, support higher wages, and offer better schools and medical care.[42] This was not the province of Goldwater or the Republicans of Latin Extraction. Indeed, if Goldwater saw the New Deal coalition as a "house of trick cards," Rockefeller identified himself with Franklin Roosevelt. Among other things, this meant pursuing urban votes, drawing upon "minority" support, and connecting both to him through patronage networks. "Let's face it," he told a roomful of Puerto Rican leaders in 1961, "patronage is the lifeblood of politics." By working with him and his organization, Rockefeller pledged, Puerto Ricans could gain access to the jobs and positions of prestige that would secure their leadership and advance their people's position, just as had the countless other "minority groups" of the old Roosevelt coalition.[43]

And Rockefeller was not interested in Puerto Rican votes alone. Having nearly run against Nixon in 1960, and with 1964 on his mind, Rockefeller "made several exploratory campaign trips to California in the early 1960s to test the political waters by meeting with some Mexican-American Republican leaders." With a fortune at his disposal, the governor established a "Latin American" outreach program more comprehensive than that of his Republican opponent. His "Latin Americans for Rockefeller" campaign arm would in time open up a headquarters in Los Angeles, and claim chapters across the Southwest, as well as in Illinois, Pennsylvania, and of course New York.[44]

While liberal and conservative Republican challengers vied to mobilize and define the "Latin-American" electorate in their respective images, the incumbent John F. Kennedy attempted to secure its loyalty in a Democratic Party roiled by the question of civil rights. Although Kennedy's rights agenda was criticized from the left—including by the Republican Rockefeller—for being narrow in ambition and dawdling in execution, it hardly received a pass from the right, including conservatives in the president's own party. Kennedy figured his support for integration and, since early 1963, a federal civil rights bill, would cost him much of the South. But he was determined to hold onto Texas, where liberal and conservative Democrats remained locked in combat over who would rule the party and thus the state. Vice President Johnson had long tried to hold the factions together, but his grip on Lone Star politics had been slipping ever since he became vice president.[45] Kennedy, needing the state's warring parties to reconcile, and seeking to raise money for the 1964 campaign, traveled with Johnson there a week after the PCEEO hearings in Los Angeles.[46]

Acknowledging Mexican Americans' importance to victory in Texas, on November 21, 1963, after a full day spent in tarmac greetings, building dedications, and ceremonial dinners, the presidential retinue entered the Grand Ballroom at the Rice Hotel in Houston, honored guests of the League of United Latin American Citizens (LULAC). The president fidgeted as he shook hands with the LULACers. He made brief remarks to the assembled, praise for the group's self-help traditions and its value in "remind[ing] Americans of the very important links that we have with our sister Republics in this hemisphere."[47] The first lady addressed the audience in Spanish and without notes. Lyndon Johnson smiled in the background. A band serenaded the dignitaries with a *corrido* in honor of the president:

| | |
|---|---|
| Dios le ha dado gran dominio | God has given him a great dominion |
| Para poder gobernar, | To be able to govern, |
| El ha guiado los destinos | He has guided the destinies |
| De esta América sin paz. | Of this restless America. |
| Kennedy, Kennedy, Kennedy, | Kennedy, Kennedy, Kennedy |
| Hombre de fuerza y valor, | man of strength and valor. |
| Todo tu pueblo te aclama | All of your people acclaim you |
| Porque eres su salvador. | Because you are their savior.[48] |

The president left amid a crush of photographers and well-wishers. Most of the audience filed out, but some men lingered to discuss what had transpired. Presidents did not bother to visit a Mexican-American organization, but this one did.[49] For a night in Texas, it might have seemed possible that the administration's problems, the Republican advance on Mexican-American voters one of many, might be forgotten.

John F. Kennedy's life was extinguished the next day in Dallas. In the wake of the assassination, a wave of Kennedy-themed *corridos* could be heard in Texas and elsewhere. Many were performed live, while others poured forth lamentations through southwestern radios and jukeboxes. The ballads made the slain Irish Catholic president into a brother outsider, a representative of the Mexican Americans and their struggle for full recognition in US society. His achievement of the presidency had been a victory for them. His vision for a cooperative hemisphere validated them by making their ancestral homeland a national priority. Performers railed against the "cowardly assassin" who had left humanity aghast and the world "weeping."[50]

As John F. Kennedy passed from disappointment to martyr, it fell to Lyndon Johnson to satisfy the Mexican-American yearning for recognition. A Texan who spoke often of his lifelong association with Mexican-American people, he would be under particular scrutiny to better Kennedy's record. Within nine months the national government under Johnson's leadership had taken dramatic steps forward in the fight for a more equal society. The Civil Rights Act of 1964 outlawed several forms of discrimination with deep roots in national life. Moreover, the Economic Opportunity Act of 1964 promised considerable infusions of federal dollars to empower communities to battle poverty, a condition that many recognized was the legacy of decades, if not centuries, of unfair treatment of minority peoples. Deeply insecure in his position and in the possibility of reelection, the vice president who had publicly pretended that Mexican Americans were not a unique civil rights constituency had become a presidential candidate fully aware of his obligation to acknowledge them as an electoral one. "We've been miserable to the Mexicans," he remarked to his assistant secretary of state in the spring of 1964. They were "all raising hell that you've got Negros [*sic*] all over government but you haven't got any Mexicans," he told Secretary of Defense Robert McNamara. The president's realization that "we got 'em dying all over the world as privates but we never do put any of them in these top jobs" helped persuade McNamara to name a Mexican American, Daniel Luevano, as assistant secretary of the Army. Johnson also broached the idea of a Mexican American serving as his ambassador to Mexico, as prominent a diplomatic post as could be imagined for the status-conscious Mexican-American leadership.

Nevertheless, his state department's argument that "the Mexicans don't like what they call '*pochan*,'" that is, a Mexican American, appears to have carried the day.[51] An overall increase in the number of Mexican Americans employed in the federal government—perhaps some 2,000 from the summer of 1964 to that of 1965—was less controversial.[52] Such use of the incumbency was intimately connected to Democrats' efforts to encourage Mexican-American electoral mobilization.

☆ ☆

Lyndon Johnson and Mexican Americans would each use 1964 to advance their own objectives. Not waiting for a top-down campaign, Mexican Americans began organizing their own "Viva Johnson" clubs in the spring of 1964, the better to muster their forces for state and local elections.[53] The president authorized a national "Viva Johnson" campaign to commence in mid-September of 1964, choosing World War II veteran and AGIF leader Vicente Ximenes to head up the effort. Raised in the South Texas town of Floresville, Ximenes attended high school with the family of the state's future governor, John Connally. He learned the rules of politics from his own father, a local political figure. In his youth, he had tacked Lyndon B. Johnson campaign posters to mesquite trees during the big man's congressional races. "Ethnic politics was the name of the game" where he came from, he was to recall.[54] Now, Johnson asked him to play the game writ large.

As the "Viva Johnson" campaign began, it remained unclear that it would take on even the limited veneer of a national pan-Hispanic initiative that "Viva Kennedy" had been. The campaign Ximenes directed was overwhelmingly southwestern in its orientation. Its national cochairmen were Joseph Montoya, Henry B. González, and Edward Roybal, Democratic congressmen from the region. And though perhaps 300 "Viva Johnson" clubs formed, the leading historian of Johnson's relationship with Mexican Americans suggests few—and possibly none—were based in the Northeast.[55] A Democratic National Committee Spanish-language brochure spoke ecumenically of Johnson's commitment to "expanding opportunities for North Americans of Mexican descent and Spanish-speaking people," but its list of more than eighty Johnson administration appointees contained just a handful of names from beyond the great Southwest.[56] At least one "Viva Johnson" recruitment flyer simplified both constituency and intention to a remarkable extent:

A. We have three objectives:
1. Elect Johnson-Humphrey ticket
2. Elect Johnson-Humphrey ticket
3. Elect Johnson-Humphrey ticket

B. *Because* Johnson-Humphrey believe in:
1. Peace and prosperity
2. Peace and prosperity
3. Peace and prosperity

C. *And* Johnson-Humphrey favor
1. Progress for Mexican-American
2. Progress for Mexican-American
3. Progress for Mexican-American

Join the Great Society
Join the VIVA JOHNSON CLUB[57]

A detailed accounting of the unique circumstances of the "Latin American" voter it was not. But against Republican nominee Barry Goldwater, it was more than enough. In his forty-four-state victory, Johnson took roughly 90 percent of the Mexican-American vote and 86 percent of Puerto Rican ballots. While Mexican-American turnout dipped from its 1960 level, New York's Puerto Ricans maintained their turnout, even in the lopsided election, thanks both to the US Senate candidacy of Robert F. Kennedy and an intensive voter-registration effort that helped support it.[58]

☆ ☆

Despite their collective contribution to Johnson's landslide, Mexican Americans found few institutional supporters for maintaining their mobilization, or even rewards for their efforts. Vicente Ximenes lobbied the Democratic National Committee to maintain at least a monthly newsletter that could link local activists after the election. Yet from the vantage point of the party's leader in the White House, the task of governing could go on just fine without a bloc of organized Mexican Americans, let alone one that united all the nation's Latino Democrats.[59] Having withdrawn his support for their collective endeavor, the reelected president delivered little high-status patronage their way. Ximenes described himself as "embarrassed" at how little pull he could exert on behalf of Mexican Americans seeking positions with the administration.[60] And at the grassroots level, Johnson's War on Poverty continued to be fought without them in leadership positions. There were more than 1,100 employees of the Office of Economic Opportunity as of the summer of 1965, but the number of Mexican Americans was in single digits.[61]

Eager for any sign from Washington that their group and its needs registered as of national significance, Mexican-American leaders looked to the implementation of the Civil Rights Act of 1964. Title VII of the Act banned employment discrimination on the basis of race, color, religion, sex, or national origin, and created an Equal Employment Opportunity Commission (EEOC) to enforce the law. The EEOC promised to be better funded and better staffed than the PCEEO that Johnson had led as vice president. And because it covered private sector employers, it would be farther reaching. In President Johnson's telling, the new law was a measure national in scope and purpose, "a challenge to all of us to go to work in our communities and our States, in our homes and in our hearts, to eliminate the last vestiges of injustice in our beloved country."[62] Such rhetoric no doubt stirred many Mexican Americans' hopes for a broad attack on the discrimination they had long endured.

Yet Mexican Americans were again to observe a federal anti-discrimination force built without representation from their communities. The five-member EEOC, which Johnson claimed represented "a broad cross-section of America," included three Euro Americans and two African Americans. Its lone "Spanish-surnamed" commissioner, Aileen C. Hernandez, was a black New Yorker, the daughter of Jamaican immigrants, whose surname came courtesy of a four-year marriage to a Los Angeles garment cutter. Lower-level staffing at the EEOC was little more inclusive. Managers overseeing an applicant pool of thousands had great discretion in choosing the first waves of federal discrimination fighters. They selected only a few Latinos for an EEOC staff that grew to 227 employees by the middle of 1967. The Commission's actions followed a familiar pattern. In its first year, the EEOC recommended investigations into 3,773 alleged cases of discrimination, but only 50 of these involved "national origin" discrimination claims (25 of these were filed under the category of Mexican American, one under Cuban, and eight under "Latin American"). In contrast, more than 2,000 complaints were for racial discrimination against African Americans. And 1,600 were for sex discrimination. It was not until 1970 that the EEOC provided general guidelines about what, in fact, constituted national origin discrimination.[63]

Federal efforts to contain Mexican-American displeasure at these conditions only drove leaders to further coordination. In response to a deluge of complaints, EEOC chairman Franklin D. Roosevelt Jr. invited Mexican Americans to an EEOC conference in Albuquerque in April 1966. Leaders of groups from across the Southwest, including PASO, MAPA, LULAC, the AGIF, and the Los Angeles–based Community Service Organization (CSO), all gathered ahead of the conference to sketch out an oppositional strategy. They soon discovered that only one EEOC commissioner would be present, a Republican named Richard Graham. It was hardly the level of recognition a national civil rights constituency would seem to merit. Graham apparently suggested that only "direct and drastic action" would compel the Johnson administration to acknowledge their grievances. Channeling their feelings of disrespect into action, the leaders had by 5:00 in the morning outlined a coalition structure, planned a rump conference, devised a media plan with press releases, and worked up a list of resolutions to present to the Johnson administration.[64]

Less than an hour into the next day's program, they leveled their charges. "Our employment problems are severe and complex," charged LULAC's assertive new national president, Alfred Hernández, "yet we have no one on the commission with any insight into them." "I find it difficult to see how the commission can go out and enforce laws on fair employment when it practices discrimination itself against the Mexican-American," said Dr. Miguel Montes of San Fernando's Latin-American Civic Association. Augustine Flores, the AGIF's national president and another Californian, demanded the appointment of an EEOC commissioner who had "special insight into the unique employment problems of our bilingual, bicultural group." They called for the EEOC to hire more Mexican Americans, to open offices where large numbers of their people lived, and to investigate "800 major national companies in the Pacific Southwest" that allegedly refused to hire Mexican Americans. No longer should the commission simply wait for the complaints of individuals. In a sign of their determination to force their way onto the national stage, the protesting leaders demanded inclusion at the White House Conference on Civil Rights, an event planned for black leaders in June. Then they walked out, calling themselves the "Mexican American Ad Hoc Committee on Equal Employment Opportunity."[65]

New ground had been broken. Mexican-American civil rights leaders had chosen confrontation with the government, many for the first time. In addition, given the number of southwestern coalitions that had fallen apart because the members disagreed over their ethnic identity, that leaders from around the Southwest could join together as a "Mexican American" committee was significant.[66] According to one proud walkout organizer, "It has always been said that Mexican-Americans can't get together—that if you put three of us in a room to form an organization, we end up with three organizations." But, he proclaimed, their actions had put an end to that "myth."[67] Augustine Flores agreed that failures to organize a broad Mexican-American political movement were a thing of the past, "because we have one common goal now—dissatisfaction with the power structure all over the Southwest."[68] They celebrated the walkout as "El Grito de Albuquerque" ("The Cry of Albuquerque"), suggesting it was a modern version of "El Grito de Dolores," the 1810 uprising often credited with sparking Mexican independence from Spain. Grandiose perhaps, but it was clear the time for parochialism had passed.[69]

The emboldened civil rights leaders pressed to maintain their credibility in the eyes of an increasingly restless ethnic Mexican population. Following the protest, they requested a meeting with President Johnson, and repeated their demand for an invitation to the upcoming White House Conference on Civil Rights, warning that the "Mexican-American Community emotion is such" that their exclusion could be dangerous.[70] Besides linking their cause with that of Mexican independence, they likened their efforts to an ongoing social justice struggle that was then captivating Mexican Americans with its willingness to confront entrenched economic power, the farmworker movement led by former CSO organizer Cesar Chavez. Said one walkout leader: "The first and hardest steps toward unity have been taken, in Albuquerque and in Delano [home of the 1965 Grape Strike and Boycott], where Mexican-Americans have taken a leadership role" in establishing organizations dedicated to their community's interests.[71] Honoring their walkout with a banquet at a Los Angeles hotel, the speakers showed solidarity with the poor farmworker's plight by wearing huaraches, the sandal of the Mexican rural classes.[72]

Although they placed their protest within a larger narrative of ethnic Mexican activism, their aims were anything but separatist. As the national government expanded its efforts on behalf of minorities, including in its War on Poverty, the activists moved beyond earlier complaints about a lack of ambassadorships and other high-level appointments to scrutinize their lack of incorporation in the broader federal workforce. They were convinced its ethnoracial composition and its programmatic responsiveness were deeply related. On April 22, 1966, the Ad Hoc Committee filed a complaint with the Civil Service Commission charging the EEOC with bias. The great symbol of the federal effort to end discrimination against American workers had only two Mexican Americans on a staff of over 150, evidence of "shameful discrimination against Mexican-Americans because of our national origin." No mere oversight, it was "premeditated exclusion of Mexican-Americans" and it had been "carried out meticulously." Though EEOC Commissioners had obviously been chosen to represent certain important segments of society, none was a Mexican American. This, despite the fact that "the Mexican-American ethnic group" was "the nation's second largest minority group in size."[73]

For leaders of a group calling itself America's "second largest minority," the quest for representation in the Great Society required continuing to confront what appeared to be African Americans' entrenched position as Democratic policymakers' number one concern. "Your commission seems to be concerned only with the Negro," complained George I. Sánchez to EEOC chairman Roosevelt. Although he conceded that "we still are not doing enough to do justice" for African Americans, Sánchez protested that, "we have done *nothing* for some six million Americans of Mexican descent." Their present conditions were galling because they were longstanding Americans. "We were here, as Indians, from time immemorial. As Europeans, we were here long before Jamestown and Plymouth Rock," the professor explained to FDR's namesake. In leaving the Mexican immigrant experience unaddressed, and comparing his people to African Americans, Sánchez—who in the past had seen the diversity in the country's ethnic Mexican populations as defining—now asserted that ethnic Mexicans in the United States were a single people, whose claim on the nation was second to none.[74]

The reconceptualization of Mexican Americans as a homogeneous minority, national in importance and comparable to African Americans, was gaining currency for a variety of reasons. For some observers who were eager to see conflict, an emerging Mexican-American consciousness would undermine the Democratic coalition. In the *Washington Post,* the influential columnists Rowland Evans and Robert Novak called the Albuquerque walkout "the Mexican Revolt," one "in the nature of warning" to Democrats. Mexican Americans, they wrote, "feel they have been ignored" by the federal government, particularly so as a result of "the Great Society's preoccupation with the Negro question." "Unless the Johnson Administration starts taking the Mexican-Americans seriously the revolt will grow."[75] Others viewed the political consequences as less important than the policy implications, but still emphasized the national dimension of Mexican-American unrest and its relationship to African American progress. Leo Grebler of UCLA's Mexican-American Study Project argued that policymakers had been so "preoccupied by their concern over Negroes" that they had overlooked an important shift. They had failed "to recognize that this group, despite its concentration in the Southwest, is emerging as a national minority" with unique needs that "cannot be equated with those of Negroes." Discrimination, poverty, and poor educational outcomes, he claimed, "can no longer be brushed off as matters of only regional significance. They are problems of the nation-at-large."[76]

Just how much policymakers' supposed "preoccupation" with black concerns perpetuated Mexican Americans' social marginality was open to debate. What soon became apparent, however, was that Mexican Americans would not receive equal billing with African Americans. Johnson reneged on his earlier pledge to invite their leaders to the scheduled June 1966 White House Conference on Civil Rights. He pledged to hold another conference "of the same type for their [Mexican Americans'] problems" instead.[77]

Being told there was no place for them at the government's major civil rights summit was a major blow to Mexican-American leaders. Blaming their exclusion on "THE BIG SIX" (the nation's black civil rights leadership), the AGIF's Rudy Ramos urged a militant response. He formed a group named "Civil Rights for All Americans—Now," and sought an injunction that would prevent the conference from opening on the grounds that it constituted "government activity that discriminates against Mexican-Americans." If that were to fail, he called upon Mexican-American organizations to picket the event. The Forum's board of directors approved and "numerous Negro grass root [*sic*] organizations" promised to join the picketing, he claimed.[78] But others were far less sanguine about the enterprise. Fearing reasonably enough that the picketing "could be misconstrued by those forces that want to see the minority groups fighting amongst themselves," the Ad Hoc Committee refrained from endorsing Ramos's plan.[79]

The coalition saved face in late May, when President Johnson invited its leaders to the White House. He plied the activists with drink, regaled them with stories, showed them movies (of himself on official trips), and gave them a grand tour of the premises in which he encouraged them to test the firmness of Lincoln's bed. When they finally got down to business, MAPA's Bert Corona recalled, Johnson's advisors seemed receptive to establishing a federal committee to focus specifically on Mexican-American concerns. The president also pledged to make his secretary, a Mexican American, a direct conduit for their communications.[80] After the White House meeting, Johnson received their recommendations for a Mexican American to serve on the EEOC. He also assigned staff to plan a White House Conference that would put them and their issues in the national spotlight. "None of us had gone to the White House with any illusions," remembered Corona. Still, "we were pleased with the concrete results concerning the agency." He, for one, believed that "it signaled a new and national position for Mexican-Americans."[81]

The administration made other gestures of concern for Mexican Americans as the 1966 elections approached. It held a few conference-planning sessions with community leaders. And Civil Service Commissioner John Macy had his "talent scouts" on hand to offer patronage positions to the best of them.[82] The planning itself appears to have been mostly for show, however, as Johnson repeatedly made it known to his top domestic assistant, Joseph Califano, that there would be no White House conference per se.[83] The president thought that the White House could encourage Mexican Americans to coordinate their efforts, but did not want to be accountable to their demands. "The more [meetings] you have the more trouble you have," he told Califano. Better for the White House not to "get in it."[84] In addition to planning for a conference that might never occur, the White House announced in September that it was on the verge of establishing a federal panel that would improve the War on Poverty's performance among Mexican Americans. Cesar Chavez, too, was rumored to be in line for an "extremely high federal appointment." The FBI was even sent to Delano, supposedly to perform a background check as part of the hiring procedure.[85]

However, no Mexican-American EEOC commissioner was forthcoming, and no schedule was set for a White House Conference. After months of protesting, the Mexican-American activists were nowhere.[86]

☆ ☆

Puerto Ricans, too, grew ever more willing to embrace a "minority" status during the 1960s, though their route to recognition and power was different from that of Mexican Americans. Because around two-thirds of all mainland Puerto Ricans lived in New York City,[87] their task was to mobilize their concentrated strength, rather than to establish ethnic alliances across a sizable number of cultural and political jurisdictions. The geography of the political parties also shaped Puerto Ricans' options in distinct ways. Though obtaining independence from Democrats was an objective they shared with Mexican Americans, two-party politics did not require Puerto Ricans to experiment with an ideological conversion to something like Goldwater conservatism. Moderate Republicans such as Nelson Rockefeller wanted their votes and were willing to extend civil rights, patronage, and an array of social programs to this needy constituency in order to get them. The existence of the labor-supported Liberal Party in New York City further allowed some Puerto Ricans to oppose Democratic regulars while still supporting progressive candidates.

These differences in the political landscape interacted with the distinct circumstances of Puerto Rican communities to frame how the group's leaders related to the black civil rights struggle. First, large numbers of Puerto Ricans were of African descent, and thus encountered the American color line in consequential ways. For example, the New York social worker and antipoverty activist Manuel Diaz's skin was sufficiently dark for him to be refused restaurant service in the US South, the type of experience that heightened many Puerto Ricans' sense of "kinship" with American blacks.[88] Close physical proximity in neighborhoods and a common sense of victimization by urban renewal policies further linked US blacks and Puerto Ricans. Limited access to much of the trade union movement (and certainly from its leadership), also worked to break down some barriers between the two groups. A persistent weakness vis-à-vis a Euro-American-dominated municipal government also favored "black-brown" reformist electoral coalitions of the sort that backed liberals such as Herman Badillo. A persistent Puerto Rican radical tradition should not be overlooked either in framing Puerto Ricans' struggles as connected to those of African Americans. The leftist Gilberto Gerena Valentín, veteran of the Vito Marcantonio organization, was a bridge between Puerto Rican organizations and progressive labor sectors, and he helped steer part of the community toward building ties with African Americans.

Thus while many of their Mexican-American counterparts pursued Washington's acknowledgment that they were a "national" minority on par with African Americans, the most influential mainland Puerto Rican activists and politicians typically dwelled less on such comparisons. Instead, through the conscious labors of Gerena, Manny Diaz, and others, prominent acts of solidarity linked Puerto Ricans and African Americans in the early 1960s. One example was the famed March on Washington for Jobs and Freedom. Organizing in concert with hometown associations, labor activists, and social workers, Gerena and Diaz brought busloads of their people from across the Northeast to Washington, DC, for the August 1963 event. There the Puerto Ricans marched along Constitution Avenue, waving the flag of their homeland. Some men paired their suits and ties with the *pava*, a straw hat deeply symbolic of the island's rural classes. As they neared the Lincoln Memorial, they began to sing their national anthem, "La Borinqueña."[89] Mounting the stage that Martin Luther King Jr. used to deliver his famous "I Have a Dream" speech, Gerena addressed the multitudes in Spanish.[90] For many Puerto Ricans, the trip constituted an affirmation of their place as an American minority, one whose destiny was inextricably linked with that of African Americans.[91]

The March on Washington was not the only moment of convergence. The following year, the same leaders who propelled Puerto Rican participation in the civil rights march led their people alongside African Americans in protesting inferior educations being delivered by New York City schools.[92] Though they differed in their objectives—black leaders were promoting integration and Puerto Ricans considered language accommodations more essential—hundreds of thousands of black and Puerto Rican children dramatized their collective need for a better education by staying home, or attending Freedom Schools, on February 3, 1964.[93] Collaboration then deepened in the early stages of the War on Poverty. Sharing resources and knowledge with black groups in their joint pursuit of city and federal resources to combat privation helped sharpen Puerto Ricans' sense of themselves as both "a working-class community and a racialized ethnic group," one for whom assimilation into the white American mainstream was becoming less and less a goal.[94]

New York Puerto Ricans' civil rights activism resonated at the national legislative level as well, reinforcing the group's association with African Americans while simultaneously underscoring Puerto Ricans' uniqueness. This time, the civil rights issue was voting. On March 15, 1965, just days after black marchers absorbed the brutal blows of state troopers and county men in Selma, Alabama, Lyndon Johnson urged Congress to pass a Voting Rights Act without delay. In his address, the president praised the black protestors for having "awakened the conscience of this Nation." He invoked his days teaching in that "small Mexican-American school" in Cotulla, Texas to explain his personal inspiration to build a more just nation, equal access to the ballot being a central ingredient.[95]

Yet it was not Mexican Americans in Cotulla, but rather Puerto Ricans in New York, who established a clear legislative link between their cause and that of southern blacks in 1965. For years, Puerto Ricans had been lobbying to end New York State's literacy test. The congressional debate over national voting legislation afforded them the chance to capitalize upon their geographic concentration and importance to liberals in both parties. Within a couple of weeks of Johnson's March 1965 address to Congress, Herman Badillo, Gerena, and voting rights attorney and organizer Irma Vidal Santaella led a delegation to Washington. In late March they testified before the House of Representatives in the hope of unlocking their group's electoral power. Badillo spoke for Puerto Ricans, denouncing the legacy of "bigotry and race superiority" that had inspired the state's literacy qualification in the earlier part of the century. He challenged the "myth . . . that a citizen can be an intelligent, well-informed voter only if he is literate in English," and defended the Puerto Rican's integration in American life, irrespective of his or her physical location.

> When any New Yorker opens a newspaper in the subway to read about Dr. Martin Luther King in Selma or President Johnson in Johnson City you can be certain that his neighbor, reading a Spanish language newspaper is reading the same news—not only that, but his cousin riding a bus to work in San Juan is also doing precisely the same.

Badillo attested to Puerto Ricans' solid citizenship, their record of military service, and patriotism. If anyone doubted Puerto Ricans' fitness to exercise self-government, and many did, Badillo drew upon the island as a resource, calling it "a society that has blended a rich Hispanic heritage with a system of government," under the commonwealth, that was patterned after the United States' own. While emphasizing the perniciousness of the literacy test for Puerto Ricans, Badillo nonetheless claimed his testimony "applie[d] with equal force" to New York's "Negro citizens," themselves disfranchised by the schemes and "devices" of local politicians.[96]

Given Puerto Ricans' density in the second largest electoral college state, their mass enfranchisement appeared to the administration a tantalizing get. Conferring with the president in early April, Attorney General Nicolas Katzenbach thrilled at the partisan prospects of including them in any forthcoming voting law: "I'd love to do it, Mr. President, to get those Puerto Ricans in New York voting. . . . You know it could be the difference in New York in any close year. They're all Democrats." Johnson wanted bipartisan support for the bill, however, and Katzenbach doubted that GOP liberals would ever sponsor the creation of at least a half a million voters whose first order of business would be to bury them at the ballot box.[97] Force Republicans to take a stand on the issue, one way or another, argued Johnson. "I'd give them hell on that Puerto Rican thing. I'd make them back up and run. . . . I'd let Bobby [Kennedy] give it to them in the Senate and I'd let the ablest man I had in the House just shove it, and shove it, shove it."[98]

Some Republicans proved willing to be shoved. Since the Goldwater debacle, the party's Rockefeller wing had been arguing that the GOP's return to national influence lay not among conservatives in the South and West, the Goldwater stalwarts, but in a much more liberal "Northern strategy."[99] Supporting Puerto Rican enfranchisement was of a piece with these Republicans' attempt to prove they could compete for the northeastern urban vote, and thus command their party's center of gravity.

In a major test of the "Northern strategy," US representative John Lindsay, a tall and elegant liberal Republican backed by Rockefeller, was running for mayor of New York City that fall. He would need Puerto Rican votes. New York's senior senator, Jacob Javits, was Lindsay's campaign cochairman, and a fellow civil rights supporter. In May, Javits joined with his junior colleague, the Democrat Robert Kennedy, to sponsor an amendment that would free the Puerto Rican vote from the literacy test. The supporters of what became Section 4(e) of the Voting Rights Act acknowledged the unfairness of educating the children of Puerto Rico in Spanish, and then judging this education insufficient for Puerto Ricans to exercise their US citizenship when they migrated to the mainland. "That his [the Puerto Rican's] schooling takes place in Spanish is not up to him, but is due to the fact that the U.S. Government has chosen to encourage the cultural autonomy of Puerto Rico, to make Puerto Rico a showcase for all of Latin America," Kennedy explained to his senate colleagues.[100] For his part, Javits denied any fear of the partisan consequences of 4(e). He expressed his pride in proposing a change that would "make a great difference in the feeling of acceptance, in the feeling of belonging, in the feeling of participation of 300,000 potential voters."[101] Kennedy aide Peter Edelman recalled that Javits's support gave the amendment the sought-after bipartisan appeal. Puerto Ricans' concentration further implied the change's impact would be limited. "And what it turned out was that it was essentially a New York amendment that the two senators from New York wanted; those kinds of things tend to provoke less opposition," Edelman later said.[102] In fact, the measure prevailed 48 to 19 in the Senate.[103]

With the new law in place, the New York City municipal elections of 1965 marked an important turning point in Puerto Rican politics, and ultimately in national Hispanic politics. Fewer than 10,000 Puerto Ricans may have used section 4(e) to become New York State voters that year.[104] Yet they may have been the difference in helping Herman Badillo, at age thirty-six, win a close primary contest (one report had the margin as less than 200 votes) for Bronx borough president against an African American candidate backed by the Democratic machine.[105] His background and alignment with "reform" Democrats won Badillo significant Puerto Rican support, but also that of black and Jewish voters fed up with boss politics. After triumphing over an Italian-American Republican in the general election by a mere 2,086 votes, Badillo promised to work for a liberal agenda: "schools, housing, hospitals, minimum wage, transportation, [and] low-income students" upon taking office.[106]

While Badillo's coalition was multiethnic and his ambition ecumenical, there was no denying his victory's import for the Puerto Rican community. The cover of El Diario–La Prensa, the city's largest Spanish-language daily, depicted the triumphant Badillo embracing his family beneath an oversized headline that read, "Gracias Boricuas Dice Badillo" ("Thank you, Boricuas, says Badillo").[107] The newspaper lauded Puerto Ricans for rising to the moment, "the very first time that the language barrier was lowered,"

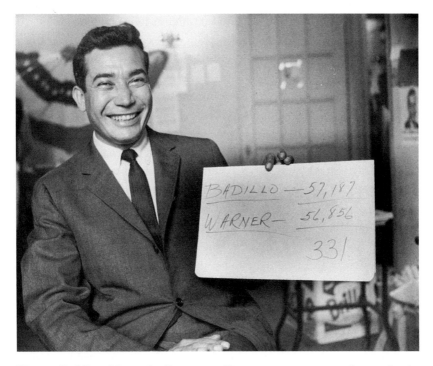

Herman Badillo celebrates his Democratic Party primary victory in the race for the Bronx borough presidency, 1965. Another liberal candidacy backed by a multiracial coalition, Badillo's win was also a watershed moment in mainland Puerto Ricans' municipal representation. Photo by Ossie Leviness/NY Daily News Archive via Getty Images.

and celebrating their long-delayed arrival as "first-class citizens," no longer "discriminated upon for reasons of language or place of birth."[108]

In that same election, Puerto Ricans joined with African Americans and liberal Jewish voters to elect John Lindsay, running as a "fusion" candidate (he had the nomination of the Republican and labor-backed Liberal parties), their mayor. Contrary to expectations that Puerto Ricans were entirely a Democratic constituency, newspapers reported that around 25 percent of their voters cast a ballot for Lindsay rather than the machine candidate, Democrat Abraham Beame, or the conservative writer William F. Buckley.[109] Stanley Ross, editor of *El Tiempo*, the city's Republican-leaning Spanish-language daily, claimed Lindsay's Puerto Rican tally was closer to 40 percent.[110] Demonstrating the ideological flexibility of the political consultant, John Flores coordinated Lindsay's Spanish-speaking outreach program. Reprising his "Latinos con Goldwater" formula this time as "Latinos con Lindsay," he even kept the earlier committee's red, white, and green campaign letterhead. Though this color scheme would have more appeal to Mexican Americans than Puerto Ricans, it was the promise on the page bottom that mattered most: "Representation—Justice—Opportunity."[111]

These words indicated that the line of attack in the city election would be similar to that which Flores used against national Democrats. Lindsay campaign flyers called Puerto Ricans a group "taken for granted at election time and ignored the rest of the time." Spanish-language radio spots took aim at "the cynical political machine" that "uses your votes like a stepping-stone and then ignores you."[112] Playing with an intentional mispronunciation of Beame's name—flyers referred to him as "el frijol" (the bean)—Lindsay's campaign blamed the Democrat and his allies for "20 years of bad housing, bad schools, bad hospitals, bad welfare services, a water crisis, little protection from crime, and a lack of job opportunities."[113] They promised instead a "5-Point Program for Action on Puerto Rican Affairs," the first article of which was for important government jobs to go to Puerto Ricans. The second was more positions of influence in the city's antipoverty efforts. The remaining pledges spoke to increasing Spanish-speaking voter registration using the new voting rights provisions Lindsay had backed, a boost to low-income housing, and job training centers to be placed in poor neighborhoods.[114] Addressing Puerto Rican organizations on the campaign trail, Lindsay spoke proudly of his role in championing civil rights legislation while in Congress, specifically including the Voting Rights Act provisions for Puerto Ricans. His proposed board to investigate allegations of police brutality was yet another "burning issue" he believed would win him Puerto Rican support.[115]

After winning an election in which he promised to end the era in which Puerto Ricans were "taken for granted politically by the entrenched machinery of a one-party political monopoly," the new mayor had work to do. In January 1966, Lindsay promised to triple the number of Puerto Ricans working in city government.[116] Yet when seventy-five community leaders and activists met with him the following month to ensure that Puerto Ricans would maintain and expand their footholds in municipal government,

Lindsay instead told them that "no particular ethnic group owns any job" in his city hall. He encouraged the Puerto Ricans to see themselves as Americans first.[117] Gilberto Gerena Valentín's National Association for Puerto Rican Civil Rights claimed to be "shocked at the seeming inability of" Lindsay's administration "to find qualified Puerto Ricans" to serve in city government.[118]

At issue was who would lead Puerto Ricans. Lindsay recognized the Puerto Rican government as a resource for policy improvements for the city's Puerto Ricans, and named Teodoro Moscoso (of Operation Bootstrap and the Alliance for Progress) as a consultant on Puerto Rican affairs, further alienating mainland leaders. Badillo accused the mayor of an outworn strategy of "by-passing the Puerto Ricans in New York" and employing unaccountable island leaders to represent the New York community.[119] A mayoral aide replied that Lindsay had no intention "to dictate leaders or rules to the Puerto Rican community." But city hall had been planning precisely that. Campaign strategist John Flores had been working since at least February 1966 to form a body reflective of the diversity within "the city's Spanish speaking community." He was devising an executive committee, he told the mayor, "which will take matters direct [*sic*] to your attention." At Lindsay's request, Flores convened "about 70 Puerto Ricans, Cubans, Dominicans, Colombians and other Latin Americans," many of them the mayor's campaign supporters, the following month. They formed a "Hispano-American Committee" they hoped would, according to newspaper accounts "speak for the entire Hispanic community of New York" in its dealings with Lindsay's government.[120]

Though hoping to foster a community faction that could rival the liberals and leftists aligned with Badillo and Gerena, Lindsay had to nod to the fact that his campaign backers were not the best-known Puerto Rican leaders. By that summer he had named Manny Diaz to the city's Police Review Board and Gerena to its Commission on Human Rights, the latter responsible for enforcing the city's anti-discrimination laws.[121] Moreover, after vociferous objections from New York leaders, he agreed to cancel the proposed conference with the government of Puerto Rico and instead hold a policy summit on New York Puerto Ricans, one planned and executed in concert with the migrant community's leadership.[122] These were hard-won acknowledgements that the New York–based leadership could indeed represent their own community.

Challenges to the Puerto Rican–African American alliance were to emerge, in part due to competition for antipoverty funds. The issue of defining a mainland Puerto Rican leadership and agenda persisted. Yet the view from 1966 suggested that Puerto Ricans were conscious of their own place as a minority group, liberal in their agenda, and an increasingly sought-after constituency by state politicians and those with presidential ambitions.

Thus it was hardly surprising to see Governor Nelson Rockefeller, running for reelection, marching up Fifth Avenue in late June 1966, a prominent guest in the city's Puerto Rican parade. As the incumbent traversed the forty-block route, he held both arms high in the air and greeted the estimated 200,000 parade watchers in Spanish. This same crowd that would erupt at seeing the liberal senator Robert Kennedy marching alongside fellow Democrat Herman Badillo had no trouble praising their Republican governor. "El Rocky," they chanted back. Somewhere along the route, Rockefeller spotted his likely fall opponent, the machine-backed president of the New York City Council, Frank O'Connor. Encircled by cheering Puerto Ricans, O'Connor was "standing stock still," with "the bemused air of an Irish Catholic priest trapped in a New Orleans Mardi Gras parade." The buoyant Rockefeller plunged into the throng, playfully teasing the Puerto Ricans in Spanish about their habitual Democratic loyalties, and shouting "Viva O'Connor" before then rejoining the procession. Upon completing the march, he returned to the reviewing stand on the parade queen's float, receiving a well-photographed kiss on the cheek.[123]

Rockefeller wooed reform-minded Democrats, the kind who supported Badillo and who cast a vote for Lindsay. Indeed, Rockefeller hoped to build upon Lindsay's success. His 1966 campaign employed the same consultant, John Flores, who established a Comité Accion Hispano Americana (Hispanic American Action Committee), led by a Lindsay supporter. The committee touted Rockefeller's expansive implementation of the Medicaid program, his signing of a state minimum wage law (the first in the nation), and his support for college financial aid, low-income housing, and rent control, coupling these with praise for Rockefeller's willingness to fight a "war without quarter" against narcotics use. "PROTECT THESE BENEFITS!" Puerto Ricans were warned. The well-financed Rockefeller campaign also set up a "Democratas Hispanos Para Rockefeller" wing, with headquarters on the fringe of the Rockefeller Center complex in Manhattan. Its endorsements came from men such as Bronx assemblyman Salvatore Almeida, a reform Democrat. Almeida excoriated "the Machine Bosses" for neglecting Puerto

Ricans, and praised the "progressive governor" for advancing those same policies mentioned above. Campaign publicity meant for El Barrio voters cast doubt on O'Connor's commitment to the poor. The Democrat had earlier in his career supported a one-year waiting period before city residents became eligible for welfare, a deeply punitive position in the migrant community. East Harlem campaign literature made an especially candid appeal to "Stick with Rocky." "Since most of us are poor," it read, "Don't trust O'Connor."[124]

When all was said and done, Rockefeller supporters in New York reported that the campaign performed "beautifully in the Spanish-speaking community." They claimed a "total vote in the Spanish-speaking areas" of "about 50%." Even "in the blindly Democratic sections in East Harlem," they boasted of taking a third of the vote, a result they considered "fantastic for a Republican."[125] A liberal message, it seemed clear to Rockefeller's Puerto Rican supporters, could indeed convince a Latino constituency to cross party lines.

☆ ☆

While Nelson Rockefeller marched with New York's Puerto Ricans as the standard bearer of a liberal Republicanism, Ronald Reagan carried a different message through the streets of East Los Angeles. On a warm October day in 1966, the former actor was seeking Mexican-American support in his campaign to become governor of California. Guiding him along the barrio's crowded sidewalks were two Mexican-American supporters from his "Viva Reagan" committee, one a prominent doctor and the other a local television personality. A hired mariachi band struggled gamely to keep up as Reagan made his way in and out of stores, signing autographs and pumping hands. The candidate addressed the students and instructors of a beauty college via loudspeaker. He hugged strangers. Along the way, his campaign workers met a show of force from supporters of California's liberal Democratic governor, Edmund "Pat" Brown. Jostling with their rivals for space, the Reaganites held aloft placards tendering East Los Angeles a simple message: "Ya Basta!"[126]

"Enough already!" The slogan's combination of stridency and generality accommodated a variety of contemporary resentments. Some would have heard it as a rebuke to the state's open housing law, then a controversial concern in California politics.[127] Or was it the new civil rights laws the liberal Congress had passed? Had enough of street crime, welfare dependency, riots, campus protests, drug use, or sexual liberation? The challenger's argument was simple. Liberal government was failing to respond to social change and instability, and even encouraging and rewarding the disruptions. Voters could pull the lever for Ronald Reagan—inexperienced, perhaps, but with the fortitude to fight back.

Ronald Reagan was not the first politician that year to serve East Los Angeles a helping of backlash politics, however. Los Angeles mayor Sam Yorty had run to Pat Brown's right during the Democratic gubernatorial primary. He criticized the sitting governor for being "soft" on an array of societal menaces, including Communists, criminals, rioters, and Vietnam War protestors. And though Yorty had failed to win the nomination, he had done well in East Los Angeles. His success there led Reagan's strategists to believe that many Mexican Americans would support a Republican candidate who talked tough against Brown's supposedly "irresponsible" liberalism.[128] The leader of Yorty's Mexican-American campaign, Dr. Francisco Bravo, was soon invited to head up "Mexican-American Democrats for Reagan." "Ya Basta!" was his idea.[129] He stood with Reagan that day in East Los Angeles as the candidate contrasted Yorty's record of support for Mexican Americans with Governor Brown's sorry history of neglect.[130] The state's Democratic rulers, the argument went, practiced favoritism and tolerated chaos—even rewarded mayhem—but Mexican Americans could expect consideration, fairness, and order from a Governor Reagan. This message was not expected to resonate with the state's large African American population, whom the challenger implicitly impugned as illegitimate beneficiaries of the Democrats' perfidy. As one of Reagan's campaign managers was to recall many years later, "We did a lot of work in the Mexican-American community. Almost none in the black." The reason: they believed "there were no votes there to speak of."[131]

Yet Reagan based his appeal to Mexican Americans on more than what they opposed. As he campaigned before Mexican-American audiences, the Republican offered a pluralistic conservatism. His conception of the group blended ideas of immigrant incorporation with Western individualism. While acknowledging the Mexican presence in California before US statehood, he nonetheless placed Mexican people within a lineage of immigrants, just like himself. Since he was an "American of Irish-English descent," he found no quarrel with "Americans of Mexican descent," having a "double loyalty," which he defined as "a love for the land of our beginning, and a love for this, our present country." He praised them for having "kept alive with great pride the customs, the language, and the traditions of your mother country." He pledged a "special effort" to assist Spanish-speaking students acclimating themselves to the classroom, a plan that sounded much like bilingual education, though he did not call it by that name. He celebrated their patriotism, their willingness "as free Americans" and "responsible citizens" to fight for their land. Their sacrifice of lives, including those in Vietnam ("this present brutal war") stood out, and recognizing this earned Reagan applause. His Mexican-American audiences clapped wildly when Reagan attacked high property taxes. They cheered when he promised a state welfare system "that helps . . . [welfare recipients] to help themselves so they can get back to being self-supporting with dignity and self-respect." He bashed Governor Brown for encouraging Mexican Americans to see themselves "as a group apart . . . as a kind of voting bloc" that the Democrat could "use to perpetuate himself in power," and then vowed to better the governor's record of bringing Mexican Americans into state government and to set up a state agency focused on their bilingual community's needs. His audience roared with his denunciations of the Democrats' failures, their "unkept promises." As he closed, all that needed be said was, "Ya Basta! . . . we've had it.'"[132]

As Ronald Reagan made incursions into Democratic strongholds in California, fellow conservative Republican John Tower employed a curious mix of color-blind politics and support for affirmative action to secure Mexican-American votes in Texas. In 1966, Tower was locked in a tight battle to hold the Senate seat he had won after Lyndon Johnson became vice president. He wanted Tejano votes. Though he had voted against the Civil Rights Act just two years before, he believed he could get them by requiring the EEOC to have at least one commissioner of "Latin American heritage." EEOC commissioners, he argued, "should be qualified to understand and assess the nature" of discrimination in all parts of the country. Echoing the arguments of Mexican-American civil rights advocates, Tower claimed that "Latin Americans" brought unique and necessary talents to Title VII enforcement. He therefore urged the president to provide the commission with "maximum feasible representation" of "all the various groups throughout our Nation" and, incongruously, that he manage to do so "without regard to race, color, religion, sex, or national origin."[133] In another obvious jab at Johnson, Tower went on the record supporting Mexican Americans'

California gubernatorial candidate Ronald Reagan campaigns in East Los Angeles in October 1966. Reagan blended hard-line positions against social unrest and welfare dependency with praise for Mexican Americans' dignity and independence, and their contributions to California's development. Photo by Steve Fontinini. Copyright © 1966 Los Angeles Times.

inclusion in the White House Conference on Civil Rights, scheduled to be held in June 1966.[134]

Tower and at least some of the Tejano establishment had found a use for each other. Citing the senator's plan for the EEOC, as well as his support for farmworker legislation and immigration restriction, LULAC president William Bonilla formed a group called "Democrats for Tower."[135] Although he hesitated to criticize Johnson directly, Bonilla claimed it was time for Mexican Americans to stop giving Democrats their votes without "being recognized in Austin or Washington." Mexican Americans needed to "vote intelligently and not be herded to the polls" by *patrones* or "special interest groups," the civil rights leader claimed. A two-party strategy would demonstrate political maturity, wisdom, and independence.[136] "Amigo-Crats for Tower" took out space in LULAC publications.[137] A large Tower campaign ad in the October 1966 issue of *LULAC Extra* featured the Republican with Father Antonio González, "spiritual leader" of the Texas Valley Farmworkers, and reprinted a news article describing his support for "fair treatment of . . . persons of Mexican and Latin American heritage" in matters of equal employment.[138]

When the ballots were tallied in November 1966, Republicans gained eight governorships, forty-seven seats in the House of Representatives and three in the Senate, effectively ending the Great Society. Riots in Watts, the war in Vietnam, rising crime levels, youth rebellion, and a broader backlash against civil rights contributed to the outcome. But Republicans' courtship of Mexican Americans, which incorporated these issues, appeared to have paid off as well. John Tower prevailed over his conservative Democratic opponent, despite the latter having been the choice of both Johnson and Texas's popular governor, John Connally. One estimate has Tower pulling 18 percent of Mexican-American votes. Another, offered by a Tower campaign leader, puts the number closer to a third of their statewide support.[139] Reagan's million-vote margin over Pat Brown (good for a fifteen point victory) in the 1966 election confirmed the political headwinds that liberals faced in the Golden State. Estimates of the conservative's success among Mexican Americans vary widely, from a respectable 22 percent to a remarkable 40 percent.[140] Was this the sign that Mexican Americans had, at last, had enough?

☆ ☆

Mexican-American leaders wanted Democrats to think so. They viewed the party's devastation in the 1966 elections as the logical outcome of its neglect of their people. Dr. Hector P. García, frustrated Johnson loyalist, warned of dire consequences if groups such as his AGIF did not immediately become a clear presidential priority. "Unless you help me and my friends . . . the backbone, the main stay, and grass roots of the Viva Johnson clubs," García warned the White House, "President Johnson will not even carry Texas in 1968."[141] Reagan's sweeping victory in California augured further danger. Vice President Hubert Humphrey reported "important defections in the Mexican-American vote" there. He relayed to Johnson the Mexican American Political Association's contention that the Mexican-American vote for Reagan "may have been a kind of protest against Negro advances."[142] If so, this was ominous news for the Democratic coalition.

Lyndon Johnson remained unmoved. "Tell the Vice President that we have heard all this year in and year out," he ordered an assistant.[143] But despite his bluster, how Johnson might recognize Mexican Americans' importance would remain a White House concern. With his own reelection campaign to consider, Johnson's wish, according to top domestic aide Joseph Califano, was to find someone who would "actively take charge of the Mexican American problem and keep it away from the White House."[144] At this time, Dr. García and the Mexican-American establishment insisted upon a "political Mexican-American" to serve on the Equal Employment Opportunity Commission, someone who could redirect the federal anti-discrimination fight their people's way.[145]

Satisfying both Johnson and Mexican-American leaders proved inordinately complex and time-consuming, however. Civil Service Commissioner John Macy, who vetted Johnson's major appointments, described "the magnitude of the problem" that the divisions in Mexican America caused: "On the one hand, a candidate acceptable to a given group of Mexican-Americans tends to be unacceptable to certain other political forces. On the other hand, a candidate with political support in one State may be unknown to Mexican-American groups in other parts of the Southwest." Then there were questions of authenticity. The White House rejected one otherwise highly regarded candidate because he came from "an old New Mexico family." This raised doubts that he could build "genuine rapport with the group most affected by employment discrimination." There were considerations of temperament as well. The candidate had to prove "neither so well assimilated that [he] can be accused of being an Uncle Tom, nor so militant and vitriolic that [he] cannot bring to the Commission a rational attitude." Finally, there was the president's overarching criterion for appointments. As his chief of staff, Bill Moyers, put it, Johnson looked for "someone who's the best but *indisputably* loyal." The administration had received its "first firm candidate" in June 1966. By March 1967, when García wrote his letter threatening to abandon Johnson's reelection effort, Macy's "talent scouts" were on their sixteenth potential Mexican-American EEOC commissioner.[146]

The choice was there all along. As the war in Vietnam eroded his popularity at home, Johnson sought out a man who had been a loyal soldier, both to the president and his country: AGIF leader and "Viva Johnson" coordinator Vicente Ximenes. In April 1967, Johnson named this "proven friend and operator" to be the first Mexican American to serve as an EEOC commissioner, the highest-ranking person of his background in the executive branch.[147]

His was a balancing act. Although he had been appointed because of intense lobbying by Mexican-American leaders, Ximenes described having "no plan to be the Mexican-American guy on the commission." He would enforce the law as vigorously in Atlanta as he would in Albuquerque, he said.[148] Yet while Ximenes pledged scrupulous neutrality in earning his EEOC salary, a second (unpaid) position called upon him to be a determined ethnic advocate. On the day that Ximenes was sworn in to his EEOC post (June 9, 1967), the president announced that he would take charge of a brand new cabinet-level committee called the Inter-Agency Committee on Mexican American Affairs (ICMAA). In this role, he was tasked with coordinating cabinet-level federal departments (e.g., Labor; Health, Education, and Welfare; and Agriculture) and the broader War on Poverty in service of a sweeping mandate: to "assure that Federal programs are reaching the Mexican Americans . . . and to seek out new programs that may be necessary to handle problems that are unique to the Mexican American community."[149]

The White House had made Ximenes the face of a national minority in government, but let no one mistake this for power. Johnson's private description of Ximenes at the time dripped with the Anglo paternalism that had long characterized Texas politics: "he is for me, he's from my place, and we raised him." The president even referred to Ximenes, then in his mid-forties, as a "boy of mine."[150] Ximenes had been a willing party to the exchange, though, rewarded after the 1964 campaign with a position as deputy director of the USAID mission in Panama, the type of foreign service job the Viva Kennedy campaigners had craved. And however unequal the relationship was, he had been playing the game long enough to know the dual nature of Johnson's expectations. The president had given him the task of advancing his people's interests in government while also defending the president from any charges of insufficient devotion to those interests.

Those interests were located, by and large, in the Southwest. Though the ICMAA's purview would in time include all "Spanish-surnamed Americans," its true intention was to elevate Mexican Americans' national profile. The new organization's name showed this clearly. So did a report released by Johnson's cabinet entitled "The Mexican-American, A New Focus on Opportunity." Coinciding with the committee's press rollout, it was a compilation of Johnson's efforts on behalf of Mexican Americans, and included the dozens he had named to high-level appointments. And it was unambiguous as to this population's unique importance. "More than 5 million strong," it announced, Mexican Americans were "the second largest minority group in our country."[151] Johnson, who had in 1963 publicly warned Mexican Americans against portraying themselves as a permanent "minority," now appeared to recognize a different reality.

Showing a more flexible liberalism, the White House hoped that acknowledging Mexican Americans' distinctiveness would keep them devoted to the national project. The administration nestled its recognition of ethnic difference within a larger "search for equal opportunity and first-class American citizenship" that all could recognize as essential to their collective well-being.[152] In fact, part of the report, "The Mexican American, a New Focus on Opportunity," is boilerplate used for War on Poverty speeches that Johnson delivered in Appalachia. Both poor whites and Mexican Americans, the report's composition thus implied, "want education and training . . . want a job and a wage which will let them provide for their family . . . want their children to escape the poverty which has afflicted them. They want, in short, to be a part of a great nation, and that nation will never be great until all the people are a part of it."[153]

This desire to legitimize Mexican Americans' ethnic claims without jeopardizing their allegiance to the nation—and Johnson as its steward—guided Ximenes's efforts. Speaking before southwestern audiences, he described the ICMAA as the institutional embodiment of Mexican Americans' new assertiveness. To self-identify as "Mexican American," and not to "seek cover under some other term," he declared, showed pride and progress. With "Mexican American" in its name, his committee constituted "one measure" of victory over a history of "self-denial."[154] While recognizing that ethnic names reflected political sensibilities, Ximenes articulated a vision of group pride that was validated in a partnership between a people and their government. Mexicans in the Southwest, he argued, must transcend the region's long-standing ethnic divisions and form a single community whose rights would be protected by national officials. He told his fellow AGIF members that though northern New Mexico and South Texas might have problems, "what is important to understand about all these regions is that they all have a common factor, and that is that the majority of their inhabitants are Spanish speaking." They all had shown "strength and virtue" amid a distinct history of injustices in the United States. And they all would see their problems ultimately resolved by the United States government. If only "all Mexican Americans cooperate[d] with the Committee and the Commission," he said, they could at last "discover a new place in this society for the forgotten people of the United States—the Mexican Americans."[155] Working through official channels was not a sellout, but rather how national minorities got things done.

Intended to bolster Johnson's support in the Southwest, the ICMAA nonetheless raised hopes for a wider reconstruction of America's ethnic landscape in which all "Spanish-speaking" people joined together as one. Upon learning of the new committee, the Los Angeles Spanish-language newspaper *La Opinión,* the largest Spanish-language daily in the country, praised the development. It was concrete proof that Mexican Americans (implicitly contrasting the group with African Americans) could make gains without acting "in a sweeping or violent manner." This victory for moderation held great possibility. "At the risk of sounding overly optimistic," the editorial "dare[d] to predict that this will be the basis for the unification of all the Spanish-speaking, without distinction since, (whether we admit it or not), the goals of the Mexican Americans coincide with those of the other Spanish-speaking communities, at least as it relates to the political-social-economic field."[156]

The sentiment had important adherents in government as well. Senator Joseph Montoya of New Mexico believed that the "Mexican Americans" for whom Ximenes spoke belonged to a larger collectivity that included the "already large Spanish-speaking communities" then "growing in Florida, New York, and the Midwest." It was not simply the Mexican-American, but rather the "Spanish-speaking community of our Nation" that constituted the "second-largest minority in our land."[157] As a whole, they suffered from poor schools, language barriers, and inadequate training for work. And a key part of Ximenes's task, as Montoya saw it, was molding these disparate Spanish-speaking communities into one powerful force.

President Lyndon Johnson with longtime backer Vicente Ximenes. To recognize Mexican Americans as a national minority group on par with African Americans, Johnson named Ximenes to serve on the Equal Employment Opportunity Commission and as chairman of a new Inter-Agency Committee on Mexican American Affairs. Courtesy of LBJ Library, Austin, Texas.

The pan-Hispanic perspective Montoya had adopted was also gaining acceptance among liberal political activists. Once devoted to organizing Mexican Americans first ("If we couldn't do that, how could we offer strength and support to other groups"), MAPA's Bert Corona recalled trying to convince the Johnson administration, "that we were no longer a regional minority, but were now a national minority, from coast to coast and border to border." He wanted a committee that would "represent all of the Spanish-speaking." After the ICMAA's unveiling, MAPA announced it would be forming a coalition with likeminded Puerto Ricans in New York, including Manny Diaz and Gilberto Gerena Valentín. Together through independent political action, they meant to force all levels of government to "recognize the problems of our people and begin to develop programs specifically directed and designed by Spanish-speaking Americans."[158]

Reflecting his patron's political needs and his own familiarity, Ximenes was primarily focused on the Mexican American. He devoted time to criticizing advertising executives for their negative portrayals of Mexican people.[159] His ICMAA publicly supported collective bargaining rights and minimum wages for farmworkers, and expressed its desire to eliminate "green card commuters," whom it described as "citizens of nearby countries who compete with U.S. citizens for jobs." Under Ximenes, it claimed to have helped increase Mexican-American hiring at post offices, and to have shaped congressional initiatives such as the bilingual education appropriation. The ICMAA also took credit for advancing the cause of migrant education and manpower programs, to fight "hard-core [un]employment" in thirteen southwestern cities.[160] Under Ximenes's leadership, the ICMAA worked to reduce the percentage of federal jobs requiring a written examination, and pressed for intensified recruitment of Spanish-speaking consultants as well as permanent civil servants. For fairness, it lobbied that those already in the government's employ receive training and accelerated promotions. And it acted as an adjunct to departmental personnel offices, publishing directories of "Spanish-speaking" college graduates, and running its own employment pool so that "talented members of the Mexican American community" could latch on in the civil service.[161] Ever mindful to show progress, the ICMAA centralized federal employment demographics and collected statistics on how federal programs were helping Mexican Americans, and then publicized these as evidence of Johnson's care and concern.[162]

But treating the ICMAA as the instrument of Mexican Americans' collective energies frustrated those people the White House left unrecognized. The administration evidently received enough letters and phone calls charging the ICMAA with neglecting other "Spanish Americans" that a generic letter had to be created to respond to the criticisms. In contrast to Ximenes's speeches to Mexican Americans, which underscored the importance of his being a "Mexican American" committee, the dispatch downplays the name, and declares no "intention to detract from any other Spanish-speaking group." At the same time, his people, the Mexican Americans, were unlike "other ethnic groups" with "similar, but perhaps more avenues for solution of their problems." Whether Ximenes feared devoting scarce resources to Cuban exiles, already covered under the Cuban Refugee Program, or to Puerto Ricans, birthright citizens whose island government often presumed to speak for them, is unclear. Certain, however, was his belief that it had been "extremely important and imperative to focus on the Mexican American and his need."[163]

Ximenes employed the pan-Hispanic orientation selectively. Seeking to assuage Puerto Ricans' misgivings about his office, Ximenes traveled to New York City in early 1968. While in the Southwest he had invoked the region's unique history and the urgency of asserting a Mexican-American identity; in Gotham he remarked that, "our problems can be categorized, not by nationality groupings, but only by rural and urban demands." Invoking Henry B. González's preferred nomenclature, he urged the Puerto Ricans to see themselves as fellow "Americans of Spanish surname," whose "identical sense of personal dignity and the worth of family life" and whose common struggles pointed to a shared sense of peoplehood. "We can travel from Santa Fe, New Mexico to Santa Fe, Puerto Rico, and finally to Santa Fe, Ecuador," he argued. "These links are indisputable," he averred, "regardless of the country from which our parents came or of the section of this country in which they settled to live."[164]

Ximenes found deemphasizing nationality and embracing the idea of a national "Spanish-surnamed" minority group useful in addressing the national bureaucracy as well. As the Albuquerque walkout demonstrated, the federal workforce's composition illuminated Mexican Americans' perception that Johnson's policies were not being neutrally implemented. This sentiment interacted powerfully with their long-standing quests for government recognition of the political and societal importance of the Mexican American. Yet in the demand for civil service representation proportional to their percentage of the general population, a pan-Hispanic orientation meant larger numbers, and possibly more jobs. Accordingly, despite his personal and professional emphasis on Mexican Americans, Ximenes advocated a comprehensive program of affirmative action to combat underrepresentation of "Americans of Spanish surname" in the bureaucracy. Informing the Department of Health, Education, and Welfare about this broader group in 1968, he argued that "the American of Spanish surname" may have had family in the Southwest for centuries, or be a recent immigrant. "His parentage may have its roots in Mexico, South America, Puerto Rico, Spain or a combination of these." But regardless of how "varied . . . his origins are . . . the Spanish surnamed American shares a basic culture and a common language," and a life distinct from "the accepted American middle-class tradition." This national minority group's inclusion was a prerequisite for bureaucratic efficiency, he asserted. "Until our people gain better representation in both policy-making and technical positions, we cannot expect our government to become permanently responsible on a day-to-day basis."[165]

If the fight for federal employment advanced the notion that all "Americans of Spanish surname" (and not simply Mexican Americans) were indeed a national minority, the big prize in presidential recognition, the White House conference, revealed something else entirely. Planning for the event had begun in the fall of 1966, when Johnson was attempting to soothe the anger of Mexican Americans excluded from the major conference he held for black leaders earlier that summer. It was then that New York mayor John Lindsay's courtship of Puerto Ricans caught the White House's attention. Lindsay, who was rumored to have presidential aspirations, had been planning a conference for Puerto Ricans, which inspired some White House aides to consider preempting it.[166] Hoping to address Mexican-American and Puerto Rican policy concerns together, presidential staffers held a series of separate planning sessions with leaders from each of the two populations in the fall of 1966. The administration had little foreknowledge of the people it was to meet, but soon learned how difficult it would be to develop a common approach.

The first and most basic challenge was that they could not convince the two groups to work together. Mexican-American leaders, resentful at being shut out from black civil rights events, "balked rather vehemently" at including Puerto Ricans in their conference.[167] Staff felt that "the Mexicans are very reluctant to accept the Puerto Ricans, and the latter expect (rightfully) some attention of their own."[168] The two constituencies also appeared to want different things from government. For example, reported one planner, "Puerto Ricans are concerned with Urban Renewal, but most Mexican Americans are not; Mexican Americans worry about border problems; Puerto Ricans to [sic] not." Any conference probably ought to be divided into Mexican-American and Puerto Rican segments, went the determination.[169]

In the end, opponents of a joint White House Conference on Mexican Americans and Puerto Ricans prevailed. Dropping the latter from the agenda altogether, the administration renamed the proposed event the "White House Conference on Problems of the Mexican-American."[170] The decision revealed the limits of Hispanic solidarity at the national level in 1966. Mexican Americans' public discourse of themselves as an aggrieved minority—the nation's second largest—had been forged in part by their competition with African Americans. As yet it was too much for them to widen their circle of group loyalty to include a people largely alien to them, even fellow "Spanish Americans."

Though the administration still sought to get "off the hook" for its pledge to hold the conference, Johnson softened his stance as his political situation further deteriorated after 1966.[171] The president authorized Ximenes to grant Mexican Americans an audience with his administration, but the location would be El Paso, not the White House. Johnson intended to be nearby anyway for a ceremony with Mexican president Gustavo Díaz Ordaz.[172] Ximenes invited LULAC, the AGIF, the CSO, and Texas's PASO to plan the event and serve as "monitors" for hearings that would outline Mexican Americans' unique needs in several areas: Agriculture, Labor, Economic Development, Housing, Health, Education, and the War on Poverty.[173]

Most of the agenda had no specific national origin requirement. The educators, social service providers, and other professionals who were invited wanted to focus federal attention on housing, bilingual education, federal employment, and manpower training programs. And the two most important goals they identified were increasing the numbers of "bilingual and bi-cultural policy makers, administrators and community workers in the Federal Government," and expanding bilingualism in "all phases of public activities, especially education," objectives that certainly interested Puerto Ricans and other Latinos.[174]

Yet Ximenes's determination to spotlight Mexican-American interests was clear. As Manny Diaz recalled, "two thousand people attended from the Southwest and six New York Puerto Ricans. We were well received by our Mexican friends but it was not our conference." The closing presentation, cut short so that attendees could be bused to the edge of the Rio Grande to serve as an audience for Johnson and the Mexican president, could only have reinforced this feeling.[175]

If Johnson's goal was to cement the loyalty of the traditional Mexican-American leadership by acknowledging their special history and problems, and convincing them that the solutions lay in faith in government and in incremental social reform managed from above, there was reason for skepticism. Johnson had never given the ICMAA the actual power to compel his cabinet heads to even meet with Ximenes, let alone require

Mexican-American inclusion in federal programs. The group was already largely bypassed by the War on Poverty. It was more difficult still to reconcile a promised federal attack on the injustices the Mexican American endured with the massive funding cuts to the Office of Economic Opportunity and Community Action Programs that Johnson had made in order to sustain the military effort in Vietnam.

The more progressive Mexican-American organizations had grown fed up with the erosion of support for domestic reform. While the AGIF was reportedly still "99.9 percent safely pro-Johnson" in 1967, MAPA's more oppositional leaders saw the El Paso conference as a "window dressing" event. It was for "safe" leaders, those unconditionally devoted to the president and his policies. With many *Mapistas* gravitating toward an impending challenge to Johnson by Minnesota's Democratic senator Eugene McCarthy, the organization boycotted the conference.[176] Cesar Chavez had also declined his invitation, on the grounds that the administration had not fought for farmworkers to have collective bargaining rights and protection for their strikes. A spokesman summed up the union's attitude: "those guys in Washington don't really want to help us."[177] When Vice President Humphrey's opening speech to the conference praised the recent activism in Mexican-American communities as nothing less than "a new awakening of 'la raza,'" set to yield "some of the greatest social reforms this nation has yet known," it was met with pickets outside.[178] Protestors carried signs reading, "Today We Demonstrate—Tomorrow We Revolt" and "'Conferencia de titeres' (Conference of Puppets)." Even many participants on the inside passed around pins whose message declared their first allegiance: *"Primero la Raza, Después Viva LBJ."*[179] The interests of the Mexican American must come before those of the president.

In opposition to a government seeking to manage but not empower their people, some chose to walk out and join a rival assembly in downtown El Paso. Farmworker advocate and scholar Ernesto Galarza chaired the rump conference. Galarza, who had testified at the official hearings, wanted "a strong Inter-agency committee," not one that was "a rubber stamp" for an administration tepid in its commitment to helping them.[180] The rival meeting concluded that the answer would be found in autonomous political action. According to Bert Corona, it was there that politically active Mexican Americans first adopted "Raza Unida" (united people) as a rallying cry.[181] Activists later agreed on a set of principles for

Mexican-American self-organization, "El Plan de la Raza Unida." Pledging "loyalty to the Constitutional Democracy,"[182] it nonetheless stressed the need for full cultural independence. "We affirm our dedication to our heritage, a bilingual culture, and assert our right to be members of La Raza Unida anywhere," it claimed. It was a potent alternative to the old practice of a divided Southwest, in which "Latin Americans" argued with Hispanos and Mexican Americans over their relationship to one another and what label constituted ethnic authenticity.[183]

☆　☆

As they sought recognition from political elites in the months and years after Viva Kennedy, Mexican Americans and Puerto Ricans separately defined their stances toward the movement for civil rights that was then transforming the country. For traditional Mexican-American leaders, black civil rights progress—and their belief in their own comparative neglect—was galvanizing. It encouraged them to set aside long-standing disagreements over the nature of their community, to claim the status of America's "second largest minority," and to vocally challenge a president raised to view them as his political wards. Mexican Americans found conservative Republicans eager to convert their grievances—toward liberals and blacks, as Republicans understood them—into votes for the GOP. Puerto Rican leaders faced a different set of options. Their concentration in New York recommended continued emphasis on local, and to a lesser degree, state politicking. Seen as a linchpin to Democratic presidential victory in New York State, they nonetheless came of political age in the 1960s as a priority constituency for liberal Republicans as well. Thanks to their utility to both parties and their dedicated effort to align their struggle with that of black activists operating locally, they won federal voting rights protection in 1965 just as surely as did the African American marchers in Selma.

Under fire from the right and left, President Johnson attempted to hold his coalition together by offering Mexican Americans official recognition as the country's "second largest minority." He appointed a Mexican American, Vicente Ximenes, to the EEOC, and called upon him to lead a new ICMAA, which the president claimed would enable government to tackle this group's unique policy needs. This was a belated acknowledgment that Mexican Americans were a true minority and would not be assimilated, and that they had a distinct relationship to the state. Yet it still rested on a view of the group as being a fundamentally loyal and patriotic subset of US citizens. Despite its name, the ICMAA purported to serve all "Spanish-surnamed Americans" as well. As such, it drew some Mexican-American and Puerto Rican leaders together, if on unequal terms. And it raised hopes, particularly among Puerto Ricans, that their collaboration under federal auspices could improve life in both communities.

For all the ways that national developments shaped their communities, then, Mexican-American and Puerto Rican political prospects were complex and evolving in unique ways. They would continue to overlap, but also diverge, as the New Deal coalition collapsed, as radical movements sought to redefine "national" politics in each community, and as liberals and conservatives alike became more assertive in molding them into a single constituency.

# 4

# Becoming Spanish-Speaking, Becoming Spanish Origin

It was 1968, and a speaker arose to rail against the assimilationists and the Americanizers. He was disgusted, he said, with their attempts to "eradicate the ancestral minority culture[s]" of so many people. It was an "egregious repercussion" of bigotry for children to reject their ethnic heritage, when such was "an heirloom to prize." The haughty arbiters of Americanism had not expunged all precious diversity from the land, however. "A distinctive Spanish-Indian-Mexican culture" had managed to survive. "The strain of the Spanish Conquistador and the Aztec warrior lives in America today," the speaker avowed defiantly.[1]

These impassioned words belonged to no radical activist. Rather, the speaker was United States senator Joseph Davies Tydings, a Democrat from Maryland. The occasion was the US Congress's approval of a joint resolution calling upon the president to proclaim each week of September 15 and 16—independence days in Central America and Mexico—a "National Hispanic Heritage Week." Tydings praised the initiative, and the new Public Law 90-498 that instructed the country's institutions, "especially the educational community," to honor the week "with appropriate ceremonies and activities."[2]

The logic of national ethnic celebrations necessitated that all be aware that this pan-ethnic group derived its praiseworthiness from its contributions to the national project. The "Hispanic heritage" was evident in great scientists, politicians, artists, athletes, and businessmen, people who left an "indelible Hispanic influence" on the entire country. According to Tydings, even the average group member possessed deeply ingrained values that were aligned with the national interest. The many honors these people won in battle, for instance, proved that "patriotism, courage and bravery," were traits "sacrosanct in the Hispanic culture." The senator's urge to celebrate converted transnational agricultural workers into good ethnic Americans. Those "Mexican-Americans who toil long hours in the hot sun for meager, below minimum standard wages" showed that, as a people, they had fully embraced the "value" of "hard work."[3] Hispanic Americans, so often disparaged in racist tales of the West or in damaging stereotypes of poverty-stricken ghetto dwellers—as obstacles to national progress—now found themselves embraced as part of an alternative history of noble cultural attributes deployed in the national service.

This story of heroic humility was of little use, however, if young people failed to acknowledge it. Tydings wanted the "new generation of Hispano-Americans," rather than taking the road of rebellion, to see themselves as "but the latest in the long line of contributors" to America. "National Hispanic Heritage Week" ceremonies would help them "recognize that the American culture truly is an amalgam of many and variegated cultures," including, of course, their own. With pride in their ancestors' dedication to the country, and recognized as an integral component of the national culture, they could go on "to make their own meaningful contribution" to its future.[4]

In the late 1960s, federal officials more thoroughly and officially integrated the hitherto varied and mostly distinct Latino populations, constructing them as a singular component of a new American pluralism. Joining the newly established National Hispanic Heritage Week were a pan-ethnic Cabinet Committee on Opportunities for Spanish-Speaking People (formerly the Inter-Agency Committee on Mexican American Affairs), as well as a new "Spanish Origin" census category. As we have seen, pan-ethnic categories existed for several years on the menu of options the federal government employed to delineate or appeal to Mexican Americans, Puerto Ricans, and other "Spanish Americans." Moreover, as this chapter shows, even radical nationalists were themselves at times experimenting with organizational endeavors and visions of community that encompassed Chicanos and Puerto Ricans under what they sometimes identified as a "Latino" umbrella. The fact that Chicano and Puerto Rican nationalists did not, for many good reasons, see a left-wing Latino coalescence as a *primary* objective should not obscure that pan-ethnicity at times appeared to be a sensible resource for activists engaging in national coalition politics.

This was even more true for mainstream elected officials by the late 1960s. Indeed, when Hispanic pan-ethnicity gained serious traction in the federal government, it did so not only because it simplified governance (though it did) but because a new political order afforded a number of officials new space and incentive to claim to represent the aspirations of all "Hispanic" or "Spanish-speaking" Americans. Upon the departure of Lyndon Johnson, a southwestern president who had long presumed control over Mexican Americans' politics, liberal Democrats Sen. Joseph Montoya and Rep. Edward Roybal seized the initiative. Beginning in early 1969, they led a bipartisan legislative coalition that included deeply conservative Republicans in creating a representative pan-Hispanic lobbying organization within the federal government, the Cabinet Committee on Opportunities for Spanish-Speaking People. Whereas the Chicano and Puerto Rican radicals who experimented with panethnic organization envisioned "Latino" solidarity as a form of *coalition* (a special one perhaps), but not necessarily more urgent than an alliance with black or American Indians, or poor whites, the congressmen imagined a different project. It was to forge at once a *constituency* and a *community,* solidifying the orientation of Mexican Americans and Puerto Ricans (and to a far lesser extent Cubans) toward each other, and to an extent away from a variety of other allies and identities, by coordinating federal knowledge of, and aid to, their collective population. Radical nationalism influenced this process, it is true. Congressmen invoked the specter of unrest as a justification for achieving state recognition of the more modest and patriotic (for the United States) visions of pan-ethnic community. The congressmen and their allies devised a narrative of pan-ethnic community suggesting transhistorical cultural traits aligning the "Spanish-speaking" with forces of order, and in opposition to the riotous and troubled America of the late 1960s. Inhabiting a new space between a black minority that supposedly threatened violence to achieve government assistance and a stereotypical "model minority" that did not seek state assistance to succeed, the "Spanish-speaking" people achieved full national recognition, for a time, as a sort of *deserving* minority, worthy of government aid that would further its own self-help traditions.

Emerging from the executive branch, the second crucial institutionalization of Hispanic pan-ethnicity was far less deliberative or intentional, yet even more enduring. While the Congress was debating the need for a "Spanish-speaking" lobby in 1969, the new president, Richard Nixon, compelled the Bureau of the Census to enumerate his favored "Spanish-speaking" electoral constituency, Mexican Americans, from coast to coast. While honoring a campaign commitment to recognize Mexican Americans as a truly national minority, Nixon's intervention unintentionally led to their amalgamation into a larger statistical category of "Spanish Origin" Americans. Like the Cabinet Committee on Opportunities for Spanish-Speaking People, the resulting statistical *population* of "Spanish Origin" Americans furnished the image of a pan-ethnic minority national in scope, diverse in characteristics, but bound both together and to reshape the United States of America.

☆ ☆

As Joseph Tydings's invocation for Hispanic Heritage Week suggested, a significant segment of US elites had acknowledged by 1968 that their country's diversity required official recognition. US social movements, including those led by Mexican Americans and Puerto Ricans, had ignited a revolution in civil rights during previous years. Their struggles had ensured that minority peoples would feel a heightened sense of group consciousness, and that they would expect their distinct communities and identities to be explicitly addressed in their dealings with all levels of American government. A purely color-blind vision of American citizenship was a thing of the past. A multicultural America was being born.

There was still a certain imaginative quality to National Hispanic Heritage Week. Prior to 1969, liberal Mexican Americans and Puerto Ricans did not, in the main, describe themselves as belonging to a collective. They tended to operate at different levels of politics and claim different concerns, allies, and rivals. In some presidential campaigns, they had collaborated in manufacturing the image of a national constituency, but had seldom sought to build effective pan-Hispanic coalitions to press for shared gains from the national government. Most of their political conditions and aspirations helped their leaders to see themselves as more different than similar. On the other hand, the basic demographic growth of various communities of Latin American origin throughout the 1960s tempted Washington. In fact, one of the stated justifications for establishing a "National Hispanic Heritage Week" was the census's finding that large numbers of Americans bore "Spanish surnames, especially in our Southwestern States and in New York City."[5]

However, while Hispanic Heritage Week suggested Washington's hopes to contain societal unrest within a reconstructed Americanism that valued the nation's many official cultures, such top-down Hispanic pan-ethnicity competed with emerging grassroots movements that challenged the basic justice and righteousness of the American order. Tactical and ideological differences of the sort that often divided generations of African Americans in the age of Black Power were playing themselves out in Mexican-American and Puerto Rican communities as well. Those elected officials and civil rights leaders who had long endeavored to collapse the distance between Mexican and American, or who asserted a "Spanish American" identity, confronted a new generation of activists who often felt differently.

For many young ethnic Mexicans, and not a few parents in the age of Vietnam, America and its institutions seemed to have been indifferent to their oppression, if not the direct cause of it. Many felt as if they had never known true citizenship and equality, but instead poverty, bad schools, racist cops, and biased draft boards. They rejected the belief that the United States was a fundamentally benevolent nation. They were unwilling to wait for those who kept saying that progress was just around the corner. A number understood themselves as a conquered people, whose lands were colonized by nineteenth-century Anglo invaders. As such they had no obligation to the United States and its institutions. They had a duty to resist. Taking inspiration from a vast array of sources, including Black Power activists, Cesar Chavez, and Mao Zedong among others, they embraced a militant critique of US citizenship and patriotism, affirming a primary bond with fellow ethnic Mexicans. Their symbols of power were Emiliano Zapata and the Mexican tricolor, not Jack Kennedy and Old Glory. In place of the numerous solidarities that characterized the Spanish- and Mexican-descended people of the Southwest, many of these activists embraced the term "Chicano." Although its origins have been disputed, the term had strong association with working-class and poor Mexicans. The younger generation embraced this once-pejorative self-designation in order to show their solidarity with those same souls, to reject assimilation, and to "establish a genealogical tie to a militant, Aztec warrior past."[6]

The Chicano movement made its mark in key nodes of Mexican-American liberalism, such as northern New Mexico. There, the longtime incorporation of "Hispano" Americans in politics existed alongside some of the most extreme poverty in the country. The county of Rio Arriba, for instance, the size of Connecticut and ethnic Mexican in majority, had in 1968 an unemployment rate of 28 percent, more than eight times the national average. Three-quarters of its residents lived without flush toilets.[7] Identifying landlessness as the principal cause of Hispano poverty, an itinerant Pentecostal preacher named Reies López Tijerina dedicated himself to restoring to poor New Mexicans the lands lost as a result of the nineteenth-century US conquest of northern Mexico. In the early 1960s, Tijerina founded an organization called the Alianza Federal de Mercedes (the Federal Land Grant Alliance). It first tried to recover Spanish and Mexican land grants through the courts, claiming that vast parcels had passed into Anglo hands illegally and in violation of treaty obligations.[8]

Recovery of the grants was linked to cultural recovery as well. For Tijerina and many of his followers, the quest affirmed the separate history and cultural distinctiveness of those he called the "Indo-Hispanic" people, a community of "not Spaniards, not Indians," but rather "a new breed" born of their interaction in the Southwest.[9] As the decade wore on and legal strategy bore little fruit, the Alianza took up armed land occupations and confrontations with the state. In one episode, depending upon one's politics famed or notorious, which occurred just days before Vicente Ximenes was sworn in to protect the White House from "Mexican" problems, Tijerina's armed band entered the Rio Arriba County courthouse to make a citizen's arrest of the district attorney. The courthouse raid produced a hostage situation and manhunt. Though it ended in Tijerina's arrest, the raid only increased his celebrity among the generation of militant activists seeking new means of mobilizing ethnic solidarity to redress the social and economic condition of ethnic Mexicans in the Southwest.[10]

Tijerina and his *Aliancistas* looked upon their state's political arrangements and concluded that Senator Joseph Montoya was not qualified to lead the New Mexicans. The senator was, they argued, in the pocket of the timber and land lobbies. Tijerina remarked in 1967 that cozying up to the state's powerful economic interests had rendered Montoya "a stranger . . . to the Spanish Americans." Tijerina pledged to "remove him from office" when he stood for reelection in 1970. "As much as we hate to fight one of our brothers, we must admit every race has a Judas," he said. Montoya was his people's "greatest Judas."[11] The following year, Alianza members could be seen picketing the politician in Albuquerque. Blending international and domestic concerns, the protestors called their senator to account for supporting the country's war in Vietnam and held signs calling him the "Powder Milk Senator," a reference to the numbers of his constituents lacking land and thus unable to subsist without welfare.[12]

The Alianza challenged the established electoral order in 1968, when Tijerina ran for governor of New Mexico with the backing of a newly formed People's Constitutional Party. The candidate transcended his core issue of land rights to embrace a working-class agenda, including urban concerns such as civilian review of the police, welfare rights, discrimination in the draft, and incorporating Mexican history and culture in school curricula. Though Tijerina was ultimately removed from the ballot, his party appears to have drawn enough Hispano votes away from the Democratic candidate, himself a Hispano, that the Republican incumbent, David Cargo, retained his gubernatorial office.[13] Even in defeat, then, the Alianza could make the difference.

As Tijerina's movement gained force and adopted more confrontational tactics, erstwhile Democrats repudiated mainstream politics and embraced cultural nationalism. Rodolfo "Corky" Gonzales was one. A former prize fighter and bail bondsman, he had coordinated the Colorado Viva Kennedy effort in 1960 and Denver's participation in the War on Poverty.[14] He was among the leaders who had walked out of the Albuquerque Equal Employment Opportunity Commission (EEOC) conference in 1966 in protest. Later, he resigned his War on Poverty post and a promising future in Democratic politics. In its place, he chose confrontation with an establishment he claimed had done little to solve his people's problems but much to turn them into "lackeys, political boot-lickers and prostitutes."[15] In addition to founding the "Crusade for Justice," a center of cultural revival and self-help organizing for Denver Chicanos, Gonzales penned one of the movement's most influential anthems, *I Am Joaquín/Yo Soy Joaquín.* The 1967 poem instructs readers to reject assimilation and its attendant "American social neurosis" in favor of fortifying the beloved ethnic community for "cultural survival."[16] Similar to Tijerina's "Indo-Hispano" concept, the poem is a celebration of *mestizaje,* an attempt to make a vision of blood ties uniting ethnic Mexicans as the basis for authentic and powerful group action.

Fired by these ideas and more, new political players mobilized previously overlooked constituencies to challenge local establishments at the ballot box. In San Antonio, the Mexican American Youth Organization (MAYO) began to organize disaffected young people, many of them gang members. MAYO united them with students, neighborhood residents, and politicians around a Chicano "liberation strategy." Embracing principles of *carnalismo* (brotherhood) and their need to be a *"raza unida"* (united people) in the face of external threats, MAYO activists took a dim view of those leaders from LULAC and the American G.I. Forum (AGIF) who humbly and patriotically expected Lyndon Johnson to address their problems. From the rump conference to the administration's 1967 El Paso summit, they addressed the old guard: "We have studied and seen your ways of improving the lot of the Chicano. We are not impressed. If nothing happens from this [conference], you'll have to step aside or we'll walk over you." In the coming months, MAYO commenced political attacks against the city's power structure, especially Rep. Henry B. González. One activist's brother conceded that, "to our parents and their generation, Henry B. was a hero, a pioneer." Yet MAYO saw him as a conservative and obstacle to their goal of Chicano self-determination.[17] By 1969, his refusal to lend public support to the farmworkers on strike in the Rio Grande Valley (he claimed it was because the strike was beyond his district boundary), or to take a stand in favor of Chicano school walkouts led MAYO to ask a pointed question, "Where is Henry B."? González's onetime ally, Bexar County commissioner (and PASO activist) Albert Peña threw his support to MAYO, and endorsed the charge that González had "forgotten the people who elected him." In local races held in early 1969, MAYO ran candidates pledging to defend Chicano interests against the city's Democratic establishment. The largely Mexican-American West Side turned out in surprisingly large numbers for them. Though none of the MAYO candidates won, the group had injected a new unpredictability into the city's political arrangements. Within a year, MAYO activists would complete their rejection of establishment politicians, founding La Raza Unida, a third party dedicated to mobilizing the Chicano people of South Texas and beyond.[18]

☆ ☆

Configurations of opposition similar to those of the Chicano movement were emerging in Puerto Rican communities. Amid a worsening of conditions, mainland Puerto Ricans were seeing a need for new and more assertive means of generating power. In New York, for example, an extraordinarily young community—in 1968, the median age of a New York Puerto Rican was nineteen, less than half the figure for whites—was absorbing new waves of migration from the island as the urban crisis delivered itself full bore. Factory jobs were fleeing the city, public jobs were scarce, and desperation was mounting. Perhaps a third of Puerto Ricans in the city benefited from welfare programs in 1967, and by the decade's end more than half of its Puerto Rican families were officially impoverished. Antipoverty programs initiated during the mid-1960s helped build community leadership, but these initiatives continued to get short shrift from city leaders. Despite their growing incorporation in political life, the city's liberal officials were slow to address what historian Lorrin Thomas calls "Puerto Ricans' intensifying sense of disempowerment." As the situation worsened, the island's nationalist movement began strengthening linkages between the homeland and the mainland. The aim was to engage the latter ever more in the former's liberation. The war in Vietnam played a focusing role. Island-based nationalists sought to knit together the many young Puerto Ricans who opposed being drafted to serve in that conflict. Already disenchanted by the war and their people's status, young Puerto Ricans, many of them students on City University of New York campuses, developed closer ties with black power activists. And concerned with a host of other local community issues such as grassroots antipoverty efforts, higher education access, and "community control" of local schools, they began forming radical organizations in 1966 and 1967. Like their leftist forebears, they would come to understand a connection between US domination of Puerto Rico and their own place in American society, and seek solutions that would liberate Puerto Ricans everywhere from oppression.[19]

And around that time in Chicago, leaders of a mostly Puerto Rican street gang called the Young Lords were reconstituting themselves as a community and political organization. Their minds eclectically drew upon black nationalism, Puerto Rico's historic independence struggle, strands of Marxism, and a whole host of other "fragments of leftist political theory." The Lords had been formed in the late 1950s to defend Puerto Rican migrants from Chicago's many rival youth gangs. But like their minority peers elsewhere, the accumulated pressures of urban renewal and displacement, police brutality, poverty, war in Southeast Asia, and persistent local racism infused them with a political consciousness over the coming years. And in a manner that would have been familiar to those who supported Vito Marcantonio, or to the New Yorkers they would meet in the coming years, they were beginning to draw connections between Puerto Ricans' lives of poverty and inequality on the mainland and their homeland's status as a US colony. So it was that when Lords leader José "Cha Cha" Jiménez left prison in early 1968, having heightened his political awareness and sharpened his critique of injustice, he joined with other likeminded Lords to change the group's name to the Young Lords Organization (YLO). Instead of a "simple street gang" they were to commit themselves to self-determination in their neighborhoods and, for some, a path of revolution.[20]

While drawing inspiration from Puerto Rico's independence movement, Chicago's Young Lords exhibited a flexible ethnic orientation. The Lords' critique of colonial exploitation was broad, supporting "self-determination for all Latinos," not simply Puerto Ricans.[21] The group welcomed into its ranks ethnic Mexicans, who also inhabited the city in large numbers, and even embraced Mexican revolutionary icons such as Emiliano Zapata. The Lords counted a small number of Euro-Americans as members and allies as well. Having identified capitalism as central to the problems they endured encouraged them to downplay the use of racial markers for group membership.

The group's reluctance to make race a resource was for other good reasons. As historian Lilia Fernández observes, Puerto Ricans were themselves so highly diverse in physical appearance (Jiménez, for example, could pass as white) that this "made a rigid understanding of race and racial boundaries absolutely untenable" in the group's conception of itself and its mission. This set them apart from those Chicano activists who defined their group identity by its European-Indian hybridity (and typically made little reference to the African presence in New Spain and Mexico). Indeed, the Lords were emerging as a highly complex amalgam, espousing "a politics that was nationalist, panethnic, anti-imperialist, multiracial, and grounded in the working class."[22]

Bearing distinct ethnopolitical orientations, Chicano and Puerto Rican leftists found themselves occasionally drawn together in the New Left milieu of the late-1960s. One such moment came when civil rights, antiwar, and antipoverty activists convened in Chicago over the 1967 Labor Day weekend for the National Conference on New Politics, intending to forge an interracial coalition that could drain enough votes from the left to end Lyndon Johnson's presidency in 1968. With African Americans and white antiwar activists highly organized, MAYO's José Angel Gutiérrez recalls that "there was an effort to try to start a dialogue [between Chicanos and Puerto Ricans] because this was going to be yet another meeting where it's going to be a black/white agenda going up."[23] Corky Gonzales invited the Puerto Ricans in attendance to operate as a "Latino" caucus, in part as a means of ensuring that Chicano issues received recognition.[24] Although these overtures went largely unrequited, the conference's creation of a

"Spanish-speaking interests" panel implied that Mexican-American and Puerto Rican concerns belonged together (or perhaps simply did not merit separate attention).[25] Reies Tijerina used the session to address the two groups' commonalities with respect to the black struggle, but he also stressed their distinctiveness from one another. A similar struggle for linguistic self-determination joined Chicanos and Puerto Ricans, he said, even as "the demand of the Puerto Rican for independence is different from the Mexican's demands."[26] Delegates approved Tijerina's resolution that the United States "restore" the Treaty of Guadalupe Hidalgo, which had conferred protections upon those Mexicans absorbed into the United States during the war of the 1840s. And they separately resolved that the United States "immediately withdraw its occupation forces from Puerto Rico and grant this suffering nation full political and economic independence." Tijerina's solution to "unite all these [Chicanos and Puerto Ricans] with the Negro, the Indian, and the 'good Anglos,' in order to change our condition" reflected that as of late 1967, those Mexican Americans and Puerto Ricans then openly challenging the beneficence of the United States considered their movements at once comparable in relation to others, potential coalition partners, but also operating largely along separate tracks.[27]

The Poor People's Campaign of 1968 again brought parts of the Chicano and Puerto Rican lefts into contact, again recognized each community's unique stories, and again envisioned these as fundaments of an interracial coalition politics, not necessarily a pan-Latino one. Announced by Martin Luther King Jr. in December 1967, this event would bring an interracial army of the poor to the nation's capital, dramatizing the need for a genuine federal intervention into the persistence of poverty in the midst of American plenty. King made overtures to various marginal groups, calling for "participation by representatives of the millions of non-Negro poor: Indians, Mexican-Americans, Puerto Ricans, Appalachian whites, and others." When King invited their leaders to Atlanta on March 14, 1968, to strategize their precise involvement, the Chicanos and Puerto Ricans shared a skepticism that their people would be truly incorporated in the black-led effort. Chicano leaders such as Tijerina demanded not only an equal voice in campaign decisionmaking, but for issues such as land grant recovery to be officially included as Poor People's Campaign objectives. Speaking for the "particular and rather unique problems" of Puerto Ricans, Gilberto Gerena Valentín labored to convince some black leaders present that bilingual education and an official stance on Puerto Rico's "political status" were not objectives, in his words, "too narrow" for the wider coalition.[28]

However, the shared desire to "negotiate for a space" from the black leadership, as Gutiérrez put it, apparently did little to stimulate a reconsideration of Chicanos' and Puerto Ricans' relationships to each other. Indeed, after King's assassination in April, the Poor People's Campaign largely reflected and reinforced their senses of themselves as distinct communities. An eight-day Western Caravan bringing most of the Chicanos, including Reies Tijerina and Corky Gonzales, arrived in the capital on May 23, 1968. Fresh from days of bonding on the road, the Chicanos joined a large number of American Indians in taking up residence in a school near the main protest encampment, Resurrection City. Arriving three weeks later, ninety buses of Puerto Ricans acted more as reinforcements to the Poor People's Campaign than as core participants. They had been unwilling to put off preparations for New York's annual Puerto Rican Parade, a highly political June event in which the community articulated its needs to powerful city and state politicians.[29] In Washington, thousands of Puerto Ricans held their own march and rally on the national mall, several days before the Poor People's Campaign's culminating "Solidarity Day" activities. Puerto Rican flags and the *pava* were ubiquitous, as were shouts of "Viva Puerto Rico." Although Reies Tijerina did address the rally along with King's successor, Rev. Ralph Abernathy, the Puerto Ricans' separate arrival and action underscored the extent to which that group found it essential to have its particular patriotic identity recognized in the broader movement of the poor.[30] So it was with the Chicanos. Operating distinctly from the black leadership and its followers (as well as from Puerto Ricans), historian Gordon Mantler argues, their "experience became a key building block for the developing Chicano movement, increasing its sophistication and strength by building and deepening relationships among activists."[31]

The coalitional nature of the Poor People's Campaign and the organizing that followed again held out the prospect for coordinating Chicano and Puerto Rican struggles. Aiming to convince student activists that they were no longer an American ethnic group, but a Chicano nation in desperate need of self-determination, Corky Gonzales assembled in excess of a thousand young people in March 1969 at his Chicano Youth Liberation Conference in Denver.[32] Puerto Rican student activists from

New York made the long trip to Denver, as did bus- and carloads of Puerto Ricans and other Latinos from Chicago. Such effort suggested their interest in at least a *collaboration*. The intensification of nationalist theorizing among Chicanos complicated such efforts, however. The conference's seminal product and road map for Chicano nationalism, "El Plan Espiritual de Aztlán," sought to replace virtually every aspect of the US presence in the Chicano's life with a just and authentic alternative. First, it disputed US sovereignty over the Southwest. Activists renamed the region "Aztlán," after the mythical homeland of the Aztec Empire. They called upon Chicanos to begin "reclaiming the land" of their "forefathers," dispossessed by "the brutal 'gringo' invasion of our territories" during the nineteenth century. As a practical matter, reclamation often meant a search for ethnic autonomy rather than an independent state, although the latter had its supporters. Chicanos' adoption of Aztlán as part of their "origin myth," and their commitment to separate political action on behalf of a *"raza nueva"* (new people) were part and parcel of a new perspective on racial identity.[33] El Plan would have none of the previous generation's tendency to identify as Caucasian. It drew sharp racial distinctions between the Chicanos, "a bronze people with a bronze culture," and the "foreign Europeans" who exploited their community. To amplify racial pride and make it politically useful meant mapping certain cultural values onto skin color. As a "mestizo" nation, Chicanos were said to possess "cultural values of life, family, and home" that could defeat the "gringo dollar value system." Part of the search for community control was to reject the two-party system, an "animal with two heads that feed from the same trough." El Plan called instead for a Chicano political party dedicated to representing the "Familia de la Raza."[34]

Though some would contend they belonged to this same ethnoracial family, young Puerto Rican leftists had difficulty seeing their connection to the racial orientation and cultural nationalism then emerging from the Southwest. The conference's overriding concern with defining the nature and boundaries of Chicano life struck some of the Puerto Ricans as misguidedly narrow. One YLO member believed the Chicano activists to be "too nationalistic," and a group that mistakenly "saw everything from a racial or cultural point of view."[35] As the Lords newspaper put it, "culture isn't the whole answer." Their people suffered "usually because we are poor, not because of our race."[36]

As it was, while the conference's Puerto Rican contingents were being introduced to the Southwest's Chicano peoples, Chicano nationalism inadvertently facilitated a contrasting organizational formation and sense of solidarity among Puerto Ricans. According to the recollections of some of the founding members, it was in Denver that the New York activists first met Young Lords leader José "Cha Cha" Jiménez, for momentous example. And having viewed the separateness of the Chicano project first hand, the New York Puerto Rican contingent gravitated to Jiménez and the Young Lords. They next went to Chicago to confer with the group's leader, and not long after began to merge their separate student organizations into a New York chapter of the YLO.[37] With purple berets and a militant raised fist salute, their announced aim was "to serve and protect the best interests of the Puerto Rican community."[38]

In the fall of 1969, the renamed "Young Lords Party" (YLP) released its "13 Point Program and Platform," which underscored the important similarities as well as divergences from the core sensibilities of Chicano activism.[39] Calling for community control of land, institutions, and education, they vowed to resist "cultural, as well as economic genocide by the yanqui."[40] But whereas the Plan de Aztlán made room for the Chicano middle classes, the Lords blended their critique of colonial power relations with a pointed jab at "capitalists and alliances with traitors." In their place, and in place of the "poverty pimps" and "street workers" offering liberal government aid, the Lords proposed a socialist society.[41]

Chicanos figured in the elaboration of the Lords' political program as important coalition partners, with the YLP offering them assistance in the struggle "against gringo domination and its (puppet) generals." But as staunch internationalists, this alliance took place within the framework of a larger solidarity with the oppressed people of the "Third World." The "Latins . . . Black people, Indians, and Asians" who "slaved to build the wealth of this country" and others around the globe formed "one nation under oppression."[42] In the coming year, the Young Lords would conceive of Puerto Ricans as a "divided nation," one-third on the US mainland and two-thirds on the island. Within this understanding, liberation of the mainland community was inextricably linked to the fate of the movement for Puerto Rico's political independence.[43]

As of 1969, then, the radical movements and organizations of Chicanos and Puerto Ricans conceived of their liberation projects as connected but in fundamental ways independent. Both sets of movements inhabited an inchoate world of alliances and sympathies, where blacks, American Indians, and even poor whites provided coalition partners. Such interracial alliances were considered little more or less natural than any geared around a shared "Latino" ethnic orientation. Moreover, their self-images still derived strength from their invocation of shared historical events, of heroes and martyrs, of national flags and quasi-national symbols. Most of these symbols in turn corresponded to places. When Chicano activists imagined a homeland, they dreamed not of the Antilles but of the greater US Southwest, of Aztlán. Likewise, despite their internationalist and pan-Hispanic impulses, the Young Lords wore buttons depicting a raised fist clutching a rifle, against the silhouette of Puerto Rico, and the words "Yo Tengo Puerto Rico En Mi Corazon" ("I have Puerto Rico in my heart").[44] The inability and in some cases unwillingness of Chicanos and Puerto Ricans to collaborate on a pan-Latino project from the left, no doubt for many important reasons, kept open a space for traditional civil rights leaders and elected officials, within and without these communities, to construct a vision of "Spanish-speaking" solidarity along very different lines.

☆ ☆

The creative convulsions of political thinking and organization emerging from the Puerto Rican and Chicano lefts only occasionally merged, but still influenced those liberal elected officials who had become symbols of group progress during the postwar civic nationalist era. These liberals had by the late 1960s become the establishment, and the Chicano movement inspired them to amplify or rearticulate their vision of the proper relationship between ethnic identity and Americanism.

For example, when MAYO activists accused San Antonio's Henry B. González of selling out the West Side barrio, the congressman fought back with a vengeance. As historian David Montejano has shown, González enlisted informants to report on MAYO's activities, and worked with the San Antonio Police Department and the FBI to build a case against the group. He further collaborated with other congressmen and the IRS to challenge the Ford Foundation's tax-exempt status—it had indirectly funded MAYO—and to pass legislation aimed at preventing any future foundation grants being given to groups like the Mexican American Youth Organization.[45]

González waged a public war against MAYO as well. Drawing upon the civic nationalist tradition of the New Deal and Great Society, he tried to delegitimize the group's philosophy and tactics. MAYO posed a threat, he claimed, because it "demand[ed] an allegiance to race above all else." The group's leaders were little more than "brown Bilbos,"[46] who practiced "reverse racism." MAYO leader José Angel Gutiérrez had spoken of a "vicious cultural genocide being inflicted upon La Raza by gringos and their institutions." But for González, talk of "cultural genocide" was distraction. "The real issue," he claimed, was finding a way to "defeat poverty and hopelessness and despair." To González, justice had a national economic dimension, but not a specific cultural dimension. Rather, it was "decent work at decent wages for all who want work; decent support for those who cannot support themselves"; equal opportunity in schools and impartial administration of the law; it was "decent homes, adequate streets and public services." To Chicanos who claimed that the United States was a lost cause for them, González replied with optimism. "I have seen too much proof that there is a residue of good will in this country. . . . I have seen, taken part in, and been the beneficiary of too much progress to deny its existence, or to say that we are incapable of it. I cannot find evidence that there is any country in the world that matches the progress of this one," he said.[47]

While Henry B. González's civic nationalism was capacious, it demanded conformity, both ideological and cultural. He belittled MAYO as a bunch of imitation radicals, phonies who "affect[ed] the Castro manner—berets, beards, fatigues, and so on," and who "play[ed] at revolution." He red-baited the publishers of radical Chicano newspapers, dismissing their ideas as, in essence, the product of outside agitation. Their "hate sheets," he claimed, did little but "reflect the language of Castro," and echoed a politics "that is alien to our area of the country." González went even further, however, to align Americans of Spanish surname with the American nation. Lambasting foundations for subsidizing Mexican-American organizing efforts, he continued to assert that there was no single organization that could speak for "such a disparate" and "pluralistic group" as the Mexican Americans of the Southwest. González even questioned that there was even a separate cause for "what he [Gutiérrez] calls the Mexican-American." The congressman, in contrast, claimed the standard of "classless, raceless politics."[48] All that was needed was to be American.

Senator Joseph Montoya responded to pressures from the left in some similar ways at first. Like other "Spanish American" politicians, the New Mexico Democrat had maintained influence in the state in part by a calculated distancing of himself from "Mexican" people. In his world, the Hispano's loyalty to the United States could never be questioned. As Reies López Tijerina and his land grant movement gained notoriety in 1967, Montoya denounced the leader in the strongest of terms. The nation's ranking "Spanish American" elected official called Tijerina an "exploiter, discredited charlatan, imposter, racist and creature of darkness." The senator labeled the activist an "enemy of the United States" for calling attention to the poverty of New Mexicans when abroad. Montoya declared that "if he doesn't like a nation and what it stands for he can get to [sic] hell out." Montoya took particular offense at Tijerina's efforts to forge alliances with black radicals. This guardian of "Hispano" dignity avowed that his people "make no alliances with Black Nationalists who hate America. We do not lie down in the gutter with Ron Karenges [sic], Stokely Carmichaels, and Rat [sic] Browns who seek to put another wound in America's body." "The Spanish people of New Mexico," he would say, possessed "patriotism and love of country."[49]

Yet thanks to the efforts of activists such as Tijerina and his followers, the lone Hispano in the US Senate found it impossible to escape the notion that he was a representative of a larger group of minority people. Mexican Americans' struggles were gaining greater attention in the nation, and Chicano protest in his state only increased the pressure to highlight the steps he was taking for his people. Criticized by Tijerina for neglecting his own kind, he declared himself to be "the only one publicly taking up the cause of the Spanish-speaking people of the United States." In the same breath, however, he vowed "to act as an American for Americans, whether they be of Mexican descent or Anglo descent or anything else."[50]

How he would reconcile his ethnic advocacy and his Americanism would not only define his political fate as he stood for reelection in 1970 but also shape the future of "Hispano" politics in the United States. Eight years of Democratic control of the White House was ending. With Lyndon Johnson no longer in a position to try to channel "Spanish-surnamed" political energies into support for his liberal nationalist program, a new space to lead was opening.

Montoya's bid for national leadership came in the first days of 1969. It was then that the ninety-first US Congress began debating the fate of Johnson's Inter-Agency Committee on Mexican American Affairs (ICMAA). As the representative of Mexican Americans in the federal bureaucracy, the committee held tremendous symbolic significance. It was substantively meaningful too because Mexican-American leaders had not yet established a significant lobbying presence in Washington. Yet its existence rested on executive whim. While the new president, Richard Nixon, would replace its chairman, Vicente Ximenes, with a supporter of his own, a Los Angeles attorney named Martin Castillo, he was uncommitted to retaining the ICMAA. Seizing the initiative, Montoya introduced legislation to make the ICMAA a statutory committee, one that would continue its work regardless of whether the president gave it his backing.

Support for the idea was substantial. Montoya's S. 740 had seventeen Senate cosponsors, including four Republicans. Some of the cosponsors came from the Southwest, including liberal Democrat Ralph Yarborough of Texas, California's two senators (one Democrat and one Republican), as well as the two Republicans from Arizona, Barry Goldwater and Paul Fannin. Other sponsors were found in less likely locations, including Wyoming, Arkansas, and Iowa. Senate liberals with small Mexican-American constituencies but grand political ambitions joined in as well, with Edward Kennedy, Walter Mondale, and Eugene McCarthy all backing the legislation.[51] Presidential hopefuls Birch Bayh of Indiana and Maine's Edmund Muskie later signed on, though South Dakota's George McGovern did not.[52] By September 1969, Montoya's bill would have thirty-nine cosponsors in the Senate, almost a quarter of them Republicans.

Bipartisan Senate support reflected the strong backing for the committee among mainstream individuals and organizations in Mexican America. Indeed, despite the ICMAA's shortcomings, moderate Mexican Americans defended it vigorously. In lobbying the Senate, Louis P. Tellez, former national chairman of the AGIF, called it a source of "inspiration," and a means of getting long-awaited "recognition and help."[53] José P. Lopez of the Albuquerque AGIF mentioned its "unprecedented accomplishments," particularly in affirmative action. To keep the committee would serve both group and country, "assisting many many more in becoming fully contributing functioning persons."[54] Similarly, a California job training professional argued that making the committee permanent "would bring a new hope to the countless thousands of Mexican Americans who lack communications skills, of [sic] vocationally deprived, and dislike receiving welfare benefits."[55] For others, the ICMAA's existence conveyed a powerful message about Mexican Americans' social worth. As the Los Angeles physician and Ronald Reagan supporter Francisco Bravo judged, prior to the ICMAA "we were like little children adrift with no one paying any attention to us or performing meaningful tasks for us." The ICMAA conferred a degree of maturity, legitimacy, and respect upon Mexican Americans and their causes.[56]

As Montoya's bill moved forward in the summer of 1969, Puerto Ricans showed that the ICMAA was important by protesting for greater inclusion in its activities. The tales of accomplishment the Johnson administration had told only underscored the very limited sense in which the committee appeared to be working for Puerto Ricans. This created feelings ironically similar to those many Mexican Americans had articulated just a few years before, as they perceived government favoritism toward African Americans in civil rights enforcement efforts. New York leader Manny Diaz testified before the Senate that ICMAA chairman Vicente Ximenes's "well-intentioned commitment" to do more for Puerto Ricans had been "largely meaningless," thanks to what he called "political and institutional pressures." He complained that merely extending the committee's lifespan would leave Puerto Ricans, whether on the mainland or the island, with "no platform or advocate in government to address their needs and grievances."[57] Echoing this concern, a coalition of Puerto Ricans from across several states wrote to complain about Montoya's original bill. One member, José Antonio Vasquez, claimed its contents "very clearly express discrimination in the past of the Mexicans toward others."[58] Citing their "little 'representation'" in Washington, it was even more important to make explicit the inclusion of Puerto Ricans.[59] The coalition furnished its own bill, one that clearly defined the committee's mandate as pan-ethnic, to cover "all Spanish Americans and not merely just the Mexicans."[60]

With Puerto Ricans seeking inclusion and Montoya aspiring to the role of national spokesman for "Spanish Americans," the stage was set for consolidation. In contrast to Johnson's southwestern-oriented ICMAA, Montoya declared the need for a "community advocate" whose "constituency will be nationwide—wherever there are Spanish-speaking Americans." The goal was now to "expand upon the functions" of the ICMAA, he said, "by involving all Americans of similar ethnic or cultural background."[61]

As the first witness to testify in Senate hearings on his legislation in June of 1969, he laid out the dilemma and implied his understanding of the people he aimed to protect:

> the Spanish-Speaking American is proud of his heritage. If he is of Mexican extraction he wants to be remembered as such. If he is a descendent from Spain, he is proud of it and wants to be remembered that way. If from Puerto Rico, the same thing. If from another Latin American country, likewise. So that it is important that he have an agency, which is to look out for his welfare, symbolically represent him as well as theoretically and actually represent him.

They required a term that was "all inclusive and should offend no-one." Montoya proposed renaming the organization the "Interagency Committee on Hispanic American Affairs."[62]

Although Montoya presented the choice as natural, to establish a federal institution for several populations whose members, as he acknowledged, saw themselves as distinct, and whose leaders had shown great reluctance to work together, was an act of creation. And like all elite-sponsored ethnic creations, it required highlighting or inventing commonalities, and minimizing, dismissing, and forgetting differences. The highest-ranking elected official belonging to the community being forged, Montoya conceded that the estimated ten million "Spanish-speaking Americans" exhibited "striking" heterogeneity. "As a group," he told his colleagues, they ranged "from native born Mexican Americans and Puerto Ricans to emigrants from Latin America." Nevertheless, he claimed that "their similarities in language and culture" were "also striking."[63] They all shared "the same background, language, and surnames," he testified. Regardless of "his ethnic origin," the senator testified, "the Spanish-speaking American" constituted "the second largest minority in America, representing 5% of our population."[64]

Montoya nonetheless based this amalgamated population's claim for justice and recognition on the historical narrative of the Southwest. The New Mexican offered an extended discourse on Spanish explorers and joked that his people had been on their land so long that "When the Pilgrims landed at Plymouth Rock, the Spanish were there to feed them pinto beans!" Over time, they had "been pushed into menial jobs, into poor education, into barrios" and remained "caught in a vicious circle" of deprivation. But they were more deeply rooted than all but "the Indian." The "Spanish speaking" were "a part of the American dream . . . American citizens, and have been for generations."[65]

Despite Montoya's best efforts, the efficacy of placing all of the "Spanish-speaking Americans" together came under scrutiny during senate hearings. Mooring multiple populations to a southwestern story did little to obscure that the peoples in question remained largely unfamiliar to one another. Montoya himself described Puerto Ricans as "newcomers from a predominantly rural society," a group unused to the "increasingly high level of technological sophistication" they encountered on the mainland. If the New Mexican perceived most Puerto Ricans as having just left the farm, the New Yorker Manny Diaz seemed to think that few Mexicans had ever seen the city. When asked if the two groups could work together to resolve common grievances, Diaz responded that there was "one essential difference" between the two populations. "The Puerto Rican is by and large an urban animal," he claimed, one who "engages the economy in industrial areas in the manufacturing field." By contrast, he believed that Mexican Americans were "largely focused on agricultural endeavors." The image of the poor rural Mexican, however, was a slur to new ICMAA chairman Martin Castillo. He replied angrily that his people had "long ago been converted into an urban population." He rebuked the "Easterners" for "misconceptualiz[ing] about the Mexican-American to the extent that they do." His brief time in Washington had given him the distinct impression that policymakers knew about Puerto Ricans but had no clue about Mexican Americans. "The Eastern mind believes my community is some kind of a cross between an Eskimo and a Patagonian" living in a place "out there somewhere," he fumed.[66]

Such confusion and defensiveness reflected the novelty of the undertaking and the persistent sense of difference among representatives of each community. Montoya argued that Puerto Ricans had a "parallel" experience to "other Spanish-speaking Americans." Castillo, in contrast, stressed that he had been "brought here as a Mexican American," the most important group since, "in terms of number, we have the most people." And Vicente Ximenes may have told the Senate subcommittee that he "could write a speech to be delivered to the Mexican Americans of East Los Angeles and make the same speech to the Puerto Ricans in New York or Spanish Americans in New Mexico" because they all shared "poverty plus language, custom, history, and culture and background." But as he acknowledged, labels reflected something essential about how the groups saw themselves. Their similar needs notwithstanding, Ximenes still recoiled at the attempt to rename the ICMAA to reflect the pan-ethnic identity of "Hispanic-Americans." In his view, having "Mexican-American" in its name "hits at the large numbers of people who have the problem which we talk about." Castillo argued that to change the name of the Mexican American Affairs committee—"the only thing we have ever had"—would be "a step back into anonymity." "The term 'Hispanic-American,'" he declared, "is ridiculous."[67]

Yet the system of pluralist politics taking shape favored synthesis. The "eastern mind" of subcommittee chairman Abraham Ribicoff, a Connecticut liberal, was just the sort of thing a new bureaucrat in Washington was going to have to understand if he wanted to be successful. Ribicoff admonished the assembled Mexican Americans and Puerto Ricans for not working out their differences. "You represent segments of a community, and you are looking for the same objective," he informed them. As part of this lecture, he urged the witnesses to sit down for "a long lunch," during which they could determine a name for the new committee.[68] It was as if they were siblings arguing over what color their room would be painted, and not virtual strangers being asked to determine how millions of other strangers would be jointly represented in their country's federal government. Those differences of region and nationality, those unique histories, the context for millions of lives and the meanings attached to them, so important to the panelists, all began to be melted away in a congressional hearing room.

While Mexican-American and Puerto Rican leaders debated their relationship to one another, the legislators moved ahead, evoking fears of ethnic strife and flattering their responsible minority constituents. Liberal and conservative supporters of fusing these communities in one government agency both justified their intervention as necessary to prevent society from losing the Spanish-speaking people to anger and violence, a contagion supposedly threatening to spread from African Americans. Having recently returned from California, Ribicoff stressed the need for government to take steps to stem "what they call the Chicano problem." He had observed that the "Mexican-American is learning, rightfully so, from the pressures brought by the Negro." Nevertheless, he hoped that "we have the wisdom . . . not to see our history with regard to the blacks repeated" or "compounded now with the Spanish-speaking people."[69] The archconservative Barry Goldwater, too, feared that without government help, "radicals will be able to excite the Mexican-American to the point that he might attempt what we have seen the blacks attempt." Although the chances of this happening were small, since this people "come to this country because they love this country," it was not worth taking the risk when the Congress was in a position to help.[70]

Eager to see his legislation through and to solidify his support at home, Montoya did little to allay these suspicions. Instead, he warned that a "growing discontent and unrest among very responsible individuals and groups . . . is both justified and long overdue and *must* be taken seriously." To ignore this sentiment now, he cautioned his colleagues, would lead to "serious civil disturbances throughout this Nation." Yet even as he predicted riots, Montoya endeavored to define this national minority in ways that would resonate with more conservative audiences. In so doing, he invoked characteristics that would yield the broadest sympathy from his colleagues without straining the plausibility of a common bond existing among these disparate peoples. The "Spanish-speaking American" did not "want special treatment" or "charity" or "handouts." Such things "rob[bed] him of his man-hood, of his initiative, of his strong pride which is his birth right," said Montoya. "But neither does he want to forever be relegated to a third class citizenship behind white America and Black America. All he wants is equality."[71] Support, he argued, would "prove that the free market economy and our whole system of Government can work for everyone, regardless of historical or ethnic origin."[72]

As Montoya delineated the Spanish-speaking American's character for his fellow senators, sympathetic members of the House variously interpreted this group's makeup for their colleagues. Apparently, a number of lawmakers did not understand, or did not believe, that the Spanish-speaking were a native population with longstanding claims, but were instead fixated on the likelihood that a committee working on their behalf would aid undocumented immigrants. Los Angeles's Chet Holifield felt compelled to explain that, rather than "depress[ing] the wage level of other segments of our society," the committee would "build up the vocational skills and the educational levels of . . . American citizens and legal residents" belonging to the "Spanish-speaking group." With this aid, they could "share more abundantly in our normal American standard of living." Edward Roybal enlightened his colleagues that the bill's beneficiaries were "not foreigners to this land" but "Americans who can trace their ancestry here in the United States to a time before the Pilgrims landed on Plymouth Rock." At the same time, Roybal claimed, they were "Americans who have come from every Latin American country to enrich the culture of our Nation." Regardless of their origins, from fighting in wars to contributing to the country's economic development, they had proven they belonged.[73]

While Roybal acknowledged that immigration was part of the story, others seemed to deny it altogether in defining this people as exceptionally worthy of aid. California Republican Charles E. Wiggins argued that immigrant processes did not really apply to this monolingual group. They were "unique," he said, because "Spanish is their only language and as such they do not have the advantages of other hyphenated Americans."[74] To those who blamed this minority group for its relative lack of progress, John Erlenborn, an Illinois Republican, defended cultural pluralism. "The Spanish speaking were the first to come to this country," he said. "They have resisted assimilation into the culture of this country—that is, a complete assimilation—and they maintain their own life style and culture," a condition that he considered "healthy."[75] The politicians seldom dwelt on how the group came to be a part of "this country," but it was clear that members of both parties had for the time being given up on assimilation as a precondition for government assistance.

The structure of Congress ensured that while the southwestern origin story was useful, it was not sufficient. Representatives from the Northeast also defended Puerto Ricans' special need for a federal advocate. New Jersey's Joseph Minish added his praise for "our residents of Puerto Rican descent" who suffered "inattention and neglect" that were shameful given the ways in which their "industry, vitality, and pride, have contributed vastly to the quality of our national life." Representing the Lower East Side of Manhattan, Leonard Farbstein lauded his Puerto Rican constituents' "progressive spirit and hardworking character." They suffered poverty, and he demanded that Congress act to provide them with a "special agency to handle their side of the problem, because their difficulties are different and need to be treated differently."[76]

If Mexican Americans claimed historical precedence and Puerto Ricans had unique problems, the congressional debate knitted the two groups together around a vague set of supposedly common cultural dispositions. Quiescence was one. In the eyes of congressional advocates, this minority represented the antithesis of the disorder and disenchantment of the late 1960s. Roybal, for instance, called them "law-abiding Americans who have not resorted to riot and civil disobedience and need just a little help to enable them to lift themselves from their present status of poverty and neglect."[77] Others set their supposedly timeless patience against the alleged impatience, propensity to violent protest, and cultures of dependency belonging to other groups, presumably African Americans but also antiwar activists. In the juxtaposition, the deserving group came off as docile, spectators in their own lives. Holifield, who claimed to have "lived among these people most of my life," considered them both "gentle and kindly . . . a religious-type people" who "err on the side of gentility and timidness if they err at all." Rather than "burn down buildings and break windows . . . they suffer in silence." Such dignified people deserved "some encouragement" from government. Illinois Republican Thomas Railsback agreed. He repeated the praise for the "gentle, kind, timid, and deeply religious people" who do not "demonstrate in the streets, burn down buildings, and break windows." Though "often frustrated at their lot," they were "always striving toward self-help. . . . They do not ask that others do what they themselves can do." Roman Pucinski of Chicago also marveled at how, even as "they suffer their indignities and they are exploited," they were "the only group that almost never ask for a handout." This favorable discourse even aroused a rare effort to associate Cuban exiles with Mexican Americans and Puerto Ricans. William C. Cramer, the first Republican representative from Florida since Reconstruction, repeated the view that "Americans of Spanish heritage have proved a law-abiding minority" and expressed his pride "to welcome freedom-loving Cubans to my State and Nation." No handout was this. "They have earned all the support we can give them," said Cramer.[78]

It was a remarkable display in many respects. The 1966 Division Street Riots in Pucinski's Chicago saw "Spanish-speaking Americans" engage in days of street battle against city police. The following year, the barrio of Spanish Harlem erupted in riots following a police shooting of a young Puerto Rican man.[79] In 1968, thousands of Chicano students had walked out of Los Angeles schools to protest against racism and a miserable quality of education. The LA students had backing from the Brown Berets, a militant Chicano organization that drew upon the style and philosophy of the Black Panthers.[80] Reies Tijerina's followers were armed and occupying national forests. The farmworker movement was an enormous protest led by a Mexican American. In short, there was ample evidence to contradict the rosy portrayal of Spanish-speaking Americans' docility that the congressmen had put forward.

But they were aiming to please a different segment of the population. It was true that black, Chicano, and Puerto Rican radicalism worried legislators, but electoral activism by mainstream Mexican-American and Puerto Rican groups was probably foremost in their minds. Elected officials could usually do little to convert the radicals. But they could win or maintain the support of the working and middle classes that were drawn to organizations such as LULAC and ASPIRA. Their desire for the votes they could win and their willingness to traffic in stereotypes, even if these were intended to be positive, worked together. It allowed them to ignore the youth challenge almost entirely, while still paying a tribute to their constituents' sense of ethnic distinctiveness.

Conservative voices did rise against the plan. Iowa Republican Harold Royce Gross criticized the bill on cultural and fiscal grounds, wondering aloud if his colleagues would refuse to create a Cabinet committee for Polish speakers, or one for Scandinavians, Germans, or even Swahili speakers. "Are they going to teach languages under this program or is it to promote basket weaving," he sarcastically inquired. Most of his concern, however, stemmed from the program's costs. Given "the billions we are spewing out on social and welfare programs," Gross claimed to be "surprised that there is a rock down in the southwest part of the country that has not been turned over so that they could find another place to plant some money." "When," asked the Iowan, "do we let somebody lift themselves up by their own bootstraps?"[81]

Gross was no match, however, for the bipartisan coalition in support of such decent and honorable Americans. Arizona Republican Sam Steiger reminded him that American pluralism implied a commitment to fairness. The bill, he said, would help rectify inequities in federal attention to minority populations. "In terms of simple equity," said Steiger, "if we are going to attempt to solve the problems of a minority then we must attempt to solve the problems of all minorities, and we must not have a situation where we have a favorite minority."[82] Yet for all the talk that funding a new ICMAA was just about ensuring equal treatment, the debate revealed that many congressmen had indeed a "favorite minority."

The outcome of the congressional deliberation reflected both a will to distinguish the Spanish-speaking Americans from other population groups as well as an awareness of the legislature's accountability to several distinct populations. The "Cabinet Committee on Opportunities for Spanish-Speaking People" (CCOSS), as the ICMAA was to be renamed, adopted a linguistic definition of group solidarity. This compromise concealed important dilemmas. First, neither group membership nor the conditions that led to demands for federal intervention necessarily went away with English language acquisition. Mexican Americans and Puerto Ricans, the bill's principal beneficiaries, were racialized minorities. At the same time, while much of the Chicano movement had proposed to understand their people as a racial group, and rally them together around ideas of shared physical appearance, this was hardly a unanimous view, especially among the Mexican-American political elite who represented their group to the state. Moreover, racial ascription was even more obviously complicated in the US national context because Puerto Ricans and Cubans, from islands whose economies were once built on imported African slave labor, brought even greater phenotypic variation to the "Spanish-speaking" population. Then there was the fact that a significant core of the early Cuban emigres likely slotted into the American racial system as "whites."

As a final compromise, the bill also created an "Advisory Council on Spanish-Speaking Americans." Appointed by the president, it would consist of nine people deemed "representative of the Mexican American, Puerto Rican American, Cuban American, and other elements of the Spanish-speaking and Spanish-surnamed community in the United States."[83] This was the best the Congress could do at the time to respect the important differences among the many peoples it was attempting to amalgamate for the purpose of organizing their relationship to the state.

Henry B. González was not pleased with the development. When the House approved Montoya's S. 740 by an almost four-to-one margin in December 1969, he angrily made his way to the well and denounced the new committee as a "third-rate Bureau of Indian Affairs." The CCOSS would be "a fine agent for political gamesmanship," he predicted, a "press agent for a politically astute administration." But it would do little to resolve the problems of the Southwest, "where most of these people live." The majority had simply created "a token, a false hope, a vague promise." The CCOSS would substitute for action rather than catalyze it, "imprison[ing] hope and freeze[ing] into permanence the injustices that afflict the Spanish surnamed." In the face of those injustices, the CCOSS was akin to "feeding soup with your finger . . . enough to taste but not enough to satisfy hunger."[84]

The Nixon administration, once inclined to let the committee die, now appeared set to make the most of it. From the Western White House in San Clemente, the president signed the Cabinet Committee into law—"con gusto," his signing statement declared—on New Year's Eve, 1969. Lyndon Johnson's brand of nationalism had conceived of Appalachia and the Rio Grande Valley as largely interchangeable in their economic marginality, with each in need of government's helping hand to integrate vast populations into national life. In contrast, Nixon viewed bilingual education, "enlisting [the] support of the private sector," and "assisting Spanish-speaking people to launch their own businesses" as the way forward. Borrowing from the congressional playbook, he lauded as many as ten million of "our people [who] draw upon a Mexican, Puerto Rican, or Cuban heritage," for showing "admirable respect for law, strong family and religious ties, and a proud individualism."[85]

☆ ☆

While Congress was establishing collective representation for the "Spanish-speaking" and defining this "community's" public persona in the process, much about the emerging minority remained unknown. As of 1969, the country's statistical system recognized Mexican Americans and Puerto Ricans as discrete regional subsets of the American population, rather than a nationwide entity. Moreover, due to the techniques used to classify them, in particular a tradition of listing them as part of the "white" population, their place in the nation, and the extent of their social disadvantage, were often difficult to discern. A 1968 article in the social science journal *Trans-Action* noted the problem that census data was often of limited use in analyzing the "characteristics of the large populations in Texas, California, New York, and Illinois—the Mexican-Americans and the Puerto Ricans—who are counted as whites." "How many are there? How poor are they?" it asked. The answer: "We simply do not know." Informed public policy would require a way "to separate Latins from the white population statistically."[86]

Although the authors imagined "Latins" as a collective, the separate histories of ethnic Mexicans and Puerto Ricans made their statistical unity and distinction from "white" America anything but simple. While the Bureau of the Census had since 1880 employed a "country of birth and country of birth of parents" identifier, Mexican Americans had fought against additional statistical practices that they believed might further their social subordination. In the best-known example, they strenuously resisted the Bureau of the Census's creation of a separate Mexican "race" classification in 1930. The Mexican government, eager to be seen as protecting its citizens abroad and also concerned that such a designation could lead to restrictions on Mexican migration, also vehemently opposed the new category.[87] Defiance occurred at the grassroots as well, with northern New Mexico and southern Colorado's self-identified "Spanish-Americans" refusing to assign themselves to the "Mexican" category.[88] In response to these objections, the Bureau dropped Mexican "race" from its 1940 census in favor of a new identifier: "Persons of Spanish Mother Tongue."[89] This classification suggested a more flexible view of Mexican America as rooted in linguistic affinity rather than in inherited racial characteristics. Instructions to census enumerators further embedded Mexican people within the country's statistical majority: "Mexicans are to be returned as white, unless definitely of Indian or other nonwhite race."[90]

For 1950, the Bureau took a different tack. In addition to asking its question on country of birth or parental country of birth, that year's census compared the surnames of respondents in California, Arizona, New Mexico, Colorado, and Texas to a list of those that immigration authorities had compiled while processing the deportation of hundreds of thousands of ethnic Mexicans during Depression-era repatriation campaigns.[91] Those that matched would belong to the new statistical population, "Persons of Spanish Surname."[92] They, too, would be classified as "white" unless they were "definitely Indian or other nonwhite race."[93]

The category appealed to statisticians and Mexican Americans alike. The former approved of its apparent objectivity—either a person's surname matched one on the list or it did not—and in its potential for discerning southwesterners who no longer spoke Spanish, but who may have maintained a distinct Spanish-Mexican culture. Exogamous ethnic Mexican women would likely be erased from the data. Yet the surname technique also obviated the need to aggregate the many subregional identifications (e.g., Latin American, Spanish American, Mexican American, Hispano, etc.) that characterized Mexican America. The term also was broadly consistent with the assimilationist sentiment and legal strategy of the contemporary Mexican-American leadership. LULAC continued to admit only US citizens to membership. Along with the AGIF, they argued that their people were patriotic and upright Americans, and therefore entitled to full social privileges. The statistic did not compromise their citizenship-based claims by official suggestion that they had any allegiance to a foreign state. Nor did it classify them as nonwhites, a distinction of crucial importance as they sought to maintain their access to Jim Crow facilities, to participate in Texas politics, and to litigate against school segregation. The renowned scholar-activist George I. Sánchez, himself a former LULAC president, informed the Bureau that he was "very pleased" with the surname technique,[94] which was "far superior" to the 1930 and 1940 methods.[95] In 1953, he hailed the data it yielded as "extremely valuable."[96]

Reflecting Puerto Ricans' distinct historical experiences, the Bureau employed a different methodology for measuring them on the mainland, one that it developed after the makers of the island's "Great Migration" began heading for work in northern industry and agriculture after World War II. In 1953, the Bureau of the Census published a special report on mainland Puerto Ricans.[97] In 1960, the census asked New York state residents a separate question on their origin, giving them three choices: the United States, Puerto Rico, or elsewhere. That same year, the Bureau began a subtle expansion of the racial spectrum occupied by "persons of Latin descent." Coinciding with this massive surge of population from an island with significant numbers of African-descended individuals, it instructed enumerators that, "Puerto Ricans, Mexicans or other persons of Latin descent would be classified as 'White' unless they were definitely Negro, Indian, or some other race." Thus it was that "Negro," and not just Indian or white, had become something that "persons of Latin descent" could be, according to the census.[98]

The statistical basis for conceiving of "Spanish-speaking Americans" as the nation's second largest minority was not yet laid, however. By the late 1960s, the federal government's image of Mexican Americans and Puerto Ricans consisted of nearly 10-year-old data on White Persons of Spanish Surname in the Southwest, and Persons of Puerto Rican birth or Parentage in New York.[99] A special report that repackaged the 1960 data, *We, the*

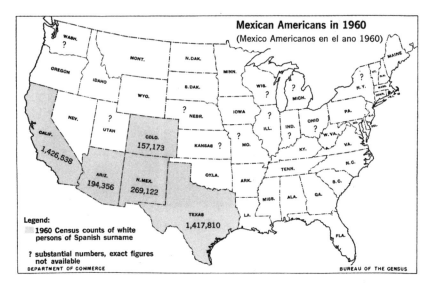

**Mexican Americans in 1960**
(Mexico Americanos en el ano 1960)

CALIF. 1,426,538
ARIZ. 194,356
N. MEX. 269,122
COLO. 157,173
TEXAS 1,417,810

**Legend:**
1960 Census counts of white persons of Spanish surname

? substantial numbers, exact figures not available

DEPARTMENT OF COMMERCE                    BUREAU OF THE CENSUS

Until the late 1960s, federal statistics identified Mexican Americans as a regional population. The dearth of official knowledge reflected in the chart shown above became a rallying cry for activists and elected officials who sought to include this population in federal programs and to harness its political power. U.S. Bureau of the Census. *We, the Mexican Americans/Nosotros, Los México Americanos* (Washington, DC: Government Printing Office, 1970), 2.

*Mexican Americans/Nosotros, Los México Americanos,* revealed the extent to which federal statistical knowledge regarded even Mexican Americans as a regional population. A prominent illustration suggests the group's presence in sixteen states, but provides data for only five of these (Texas, New Mexico, Colorado, Arizona, and California). For several other states across the West, the industrial Midwest, as well as New York, the map showed only question marks. If this was a national minority, statistical confirmation was still forthcoming.

As useful as these procedures may have once seemed, they were wholly out of place in the late 1960s. The Bureau was planning to use these same limited techniques again in 1970, but the profound transformations in Mexican-American ethnic consciousness and civil rights strategy of the 1960s had rendered "White Persons of Spanish Surname" hopelessly outdated. As we have seen, Mexican-American civil rights leaders had begun to consider it essential to present themselves to the government *as Mexican*

*Americans*. They recognized that their people's share of federal resources was contingent upon them appearing to be a national minority group. This in turn required data that demonstrated their difference from the majority. And with the Chicano movement winning supporters by challenging the notion that ethnic Mexicans belonged with "whites," statistically or otherwise, "White persons of Spanish surname" seemed sterile and insensitive. Its geographical limitations added further insult, since large communities of "Spanish surname" in the Midwest went unidentified.

Puerto Rican leaders, too, had reason to complain. If they lived outside of eight states (the southwestern five, New York, and for 1970 Pennsylvania and New Jersey), the third generation stood a decent chance of being made to appear part of white or black America's statistical portrait, much like the majority of "foreign stock" individuals. The federal government was slowly but surely erasing their distinctiveness, and thus their need, from the record. The gaps in governmental knowledge, largely born of separate histories of migration, Mexican-American integrationist sentiment, and budgetary realities, appeared now as an affront maintained only by bureaucratic inertia.

Liberal Mexican Americans and their representatives pressured presidents, congressional leaders, and bureaucrats to change the system. In 1967, members of the Johnson cabinet, having received the message, urged the Bureau to collect more information on "ethnic origin, particularly the identification of Mexican-Americans."[100] In 1969, EEOC commissioner Vicente Ximenes lobbied Census director A. Ross Eckler to expand coverage of Mexican Americans beyond the Southwest.[101] Advancing new arguments to demand greater personal freedom on census forms, Mexican Americans objected that the old system violated their "right" to identify themselves as they saw fit. Ximenes publicly criticized the Bureau for denying the Mexican American "the prerogative to indicate his ethnic group," and for instead choosing "it without his consent or knowledge."[102] The demands intensified as the 1970 census approached. In April 1969, Texas Democratic senator Ralph Yarborough protested that the Bureau appeared more concerned with "determining the number [of] toilets, bathtubs and showers in the United States than they are the number of Puerto Ricans, Latins and Mexican Americans." He demanded "salient questions" to "clearly identify each of the Spanish-speaking groups," and asserted the people's "right of self-identification."[103] The following month, Herman Gallegos, the

MAPA activist and executive director of the Southwest Council of La Raza, a newly created lobbying and research organization, bemoaned "flagrant discrimination" in the census. Forms allowed "several other minority groups," including Filipinos, Hawaiians, and Koreans, to identify their ethnic origin, but did not extend that "right" to "Spanish-surnamed, Spanish-speaking minorities." Without a major change, he argued, the "Hispanic community" would remain "an invisible minority when seeking assistance and recognition." Gallegos's followers demanded that "the question titled Color or Race be changed to read Race, Color, or Ethnic Origin" and to provide "a breakout of the groups of Spanish heritage such as Mexican-Americans, Puerto Ricans, Cubans, Central Americans, South Americans, etc." Including ethnicity as coequal with race in US life elevated, but did not substantially distinguish, it. In some sense, Gallegos sought to make a quasi-racial Hispanic group, which was an act of distinguishing black Hispanics from African Americans, white Hispanics from Anglos, Indo-Hispanics from American Indians, while muting the differences in lived experiences and influences among and within each. National origins did not impede this broader ethnic feeling. Instead, they were its component parts, distinct for the purposes of intragroup analysis, yet aggregable for the more important comparison with dominant groups.[104]

Fearing their omission from the national stage for another decade, Mexican Americans and Puerto Ricans opposed the old system during hearings of the House Subcommittee on Census and Statistics, held in Los Angeles in May 1969. Witnesses included academics, civil rights advocates, nonprofit workers, and elected officials. They derided the current system as, as one of them put it, "the 'guestimate' approach" to the Mexican American's "statistical identity." They rebuked the census for setting arbitrary geographic limits on counting their people. Fueled by a desire to assert their "right" to self-identify, they criticized the Spanish surname category for being inaccurate, devoid of cultural content, and potentially misleading. One witness called the surname technique "an offense to many Mexican-Americans who claim a culture of their own." The implications of the Bureau's decision would be far-reaching. Deeply enmeshed in these questions as a member of the UCLA Mexican American Study Project, political scientist Ralph Guzman claimed that all parties involved confronted a choice "between bureaucratic convenience and social justice . . . between a governmental agency as servant or master."[105]

As the creation of the Cabinet Committee on Opportunities for Spanish-Speaking People showed, the rights and recognition of Mexican Americans existed in tension with the possible power of pan-ethnicity. Upon hearing that a nationwide pan-Hispanic identifier might be forthcoming, witnesses argued that it would be unacceptable unless they could list the specific national origin with which they identified. Guzman called this "the right of freedom of choice." "If we must invade people's privacy," he explained, "why . . . racially categorize people without even giving them a choice of what they would like to be called." It was also a question of fairness. One witness described how "many, much smaller ethnic designations have found their way into the form," such as several Asian nationalities that were already listed. Closely related to fairness was a soft form of nationalism. Most of the witnesses were Mexican American, and wanted that designation to appear clearly in the record. Including them under a broad pan-ethnic term, along with the Cubans already gaining a reputation for prosperity, for example, ran the risk of painting "a false picture" that their people had made it "into the mainstream of American life," said one group.[106]

The argument that respect for individuals' preferences promoted fairness and accuracy did not preclude concerned parties from seeking data tabulations that promoted greater group power. Guzman argued that the "range of identities that Mexicans choose, depending on where they live" justified allowing them to identify as "Latin-American" or "Spanish-American" or "Mexican" or "Mexican-American." But he portrayed some of these identities as forms of false consciousness, lamenting that "not all Mexicans—because of what American society has done to the Mexican people—consider themselves Mexican." Accordingly, he wanted to be able to "compress these categories in a number of ways, and still count the Mexican in Texas who might be forced to cloak himself with a euphemism like Latin American."[107] An individual's right to identify himself was essential, but it was not always the end of the story.

Unsurprisingly, the witnesses exhibited diverse attitudes toward the idea of Hispanic solidarity. Guzman, for instance, claimed that the "Mexican-American community" was "the second largest minority in the Nation." "We do not object to the Puerto Rican people," he said, but they were best understood as "ethnic cousins" whose "model does not fit the Mexican model." Others, however, adopted a pan-ethnic approach. For Rep. Edward Roybal, the "Spanish-speaking community" constituted "the second largest ethnic minority in the United States and an important and significant component of our overall population." Roybal's long-time colleague in California political organizing, Herman Gallegos, too claimed "the Hispanic community" as "the second largest minority in the United States." A Puerto Rican witness, Ricardo Callejo, of the Spanish-Speaking Political Association, opened the community to "anyone who is willing to answer truthfully that they are either Spanish surnamed or Spanish speaking."[108]

The Bureau of the Census opposed the desired modifications for several reasons. First, any change to existing statistical practices would cost a great deal of money. And cost-conscious bureaucrats knew that "at budget time, the Census Bureau must stand in a chow line with other bureaus of the Commerce Department . . . and then travel to Congress, where there is even less interest" in its needs.[109] Moreover, its statisticians believed that their traditional techniques were superior to self-identification. In any case, a new question would have to meet their professional standards, and there was not enough time before the decennial census to perform a satisfactory test.[110] In late March 1969, the Bureau's statisticians remained committed to the existing means of counting the nation's "Spanish-speaking" peoples.[111]

As the public struggle to define America's second-largest minority played out among activists, elected officials, and bureaucrats, the Nixon White House put its weight behind consolidation. By May, word came that the 1970 Census would for the first time likely include a nationwide question to identify the country's population of "Spanish Origin." Conrad Taueber, then associate director of the Bureau, remembered it as a case of interference from above. He recalled years later that the 1970 forms had already been finalized "when the order came down that we were to ask a direct question, have the people identify themselves as Hispanics" [*sic*].[112] Most of the forms had been printed, but "the 5-percent schedule had barely started at the printers when we pulled it back and threw in the question which hadn't been tested in the field—under orders." The statisticians considered the new question deeply problematic, and clearly resented the political interference. But, explained Taueber, they could not "get away from the people in New Mexico, Arizona, and South Texas," referring to those residents who had been in the Southwest so long they were not distinguished by Spanish language or parental nativity. Ironically, it was these Americans' deep roots in the United States that justified a question about their "origin."[113]

While Bureau statisticians lamented the politicization of their craft, many others hailed the forthcoming measure as a major triumph for justice and recognition of their people. Hector P. García, founder of the AGIF, called it "a great success." "We have been working since 1961 to let the people in Washington know of our Spanish-surname minority. This will let them know we exist," he claimed, "for good or for bad, and whether we have problems or not."[114] Vicente Ximenes deemed it "a great victory," one that left him "completely satisfied."[115] Senator Yarborough said that the data "will be of great help" in improving health care, housing, and bilingual education.[116] The enthusiasm was broadly shared. The *Dallas Morning News* editorial page applauded the replacement of "woefully out of date" statistical methods. "Economically, sociologically, and politically," it argued, "it is important to spell out the ethnic situation in this and other states." With scarcely concealed boosterism, the editorial expected the new numbers to be "especially helpful to Texas," which was, after all, a "home for millions of Latin descent."[117]

Notwithstanding this initial praise, the prospect of a more comprehensive statistical picture of "Spanish Origin" Americans was dimmed in practice. Only a five-percent sample of households received the long-form census containing the "Spanish Origin" question. Most encountered an enumeration process intended to designate them as "white." With the help of the Mexican American Political Association and legal aid workers, "three impoverished East Bay Spanish-Americans" sued the Bureau in federal court to stop the census. They cited the absence of a "Mexican-American" or "Hispano-American" entry on the race question as evidence of "invidious discrimination."[118] Texas activists, too, complained of "just getting lumped in with the Anglos, among the whites." They argued this was "an obvious attempt to shut the Chicanos completely out" of federal antipoverty efforts.[119] Back in California, the AGIF convinced several state senators to introduce a resolution chastising the Bureau for not properly distinguishing the Mexican Americans in statistics. They claimed that this group "constitute[d] the largest racial minority in the United States," and called upon Mexican Americans to mark "other" and then write in "Mexican-American" on the race question.[120]

While some activist Mexican Americans embraced a racialized statistical identity and distrustfully awaited the results of the 1970 census, the federal government further subsumed them in a national language-based

**Table 4.1.** Spanish Origin Population for the United States, Five Southwestern States, and Remainder, November 1969 (Numbers in thousands)

| Origin | United States | | Five southwestern states | | Remainder of United States | |
|---|---|---|---|---|---|---|
| | Number | Percent | Number | Percent | Number | Percent |
| **Total** | 9,230 | 100.0 | 5,507 | 100.0 | 3,723 | 100.0 |
| Mexican | 5,073 | 55.0 | 4,360 | 79.2 | 713 | 19.1 |
| Puerto Rican | 1,454 | 15.8 | 61 | 1.1 | 1,393 | 37.4 |
| Cuban | 565 | 6.1 | 82 | 1.5 | 483 | 13.0 |
| Central or South American | 556 | 6.0 | 170 | 3.1 | 386 | 10.4 |
| Other Spanish | 1,582 | 17.1 | 835 | 15.2 | 748 | 20.1 |

*Source:* US Bureau of the Census, *Persons of Spanish Origin in the United States: November 1969* (Washington, DC: US Government Printing Office, 1971), table 1.

minority. In the spring of 1971, the Bureau of the Census released the results of its first use of the "Spanish Origin" identifier. The report, *Persons of Spanish Origin in the United States: November 1969,* looked quite different from *We, the Mexican Americans.* Gone was the singular focus on Mexican Americans. But gone, too, were the many question marks. The sample survey found that there were 9.2 million persons in the country (excluding such "outlying areas" as Puerto Rico) who spoke Spanish at home, reported Spanish as their mother tongue, or who identified as being of "Spanish Origin." They were approximately 5 percent of the country's population.[121] More than five million of these were judged to be of Mexican origin, while approximately 1.5 million were Puerto Rican. About 565,000 were Cuban, roughly the same amount as in the "Central and South American" category. There were actually more "Other Spanish" tallied than Puerto Ricans. Roughly 80 percent of Mexican origin people resided in the five southwestern states. Further delineating the population, the report noted that rarely did a member of one national origin subgroup choose to marry a member from another. Only 5 percent of marriages of "Spanish Origin" Americans occurred across two of the five categories.[122]

In presenting the data, the Bureau negotiated a complex relationship between language and identity. For a group coming to be rendered as "Spanish-speaking Americans," the report's title page contained a jarring illustration—more than half of respondents did not speak Spanish, even in their own homes. Almost a third reported English as their mother tongue. Fewer than half of those citing an "origin" in Mexico spoke Spanish at home. More than 80 percent of "Other Spanish" Americans spoke a language other than Spanish at home. Cuban American and mainland Puerto Rican communities, however, contained high percentages of Spanish speakers due to their relatively recent migrations. They thus made the "Spanish Origin" population appear more "Spanish-speaking." The Bureau presented the national language data as evidence of an entire pan-ethnic group's historical propensity toward ethnic differentiation. "The continued use of Spanish is an indicator of the strength of those bonds which tie Spanish persons to each other and to their past," it argued.[123]

The new statistic exerted its own power in other ways, recasting the components of a multicultural American nation. Though the report showed that about 80 percent of the population was born in the United States, "or in outlying areas of the United States,"[124] the *New York Times* informed readers that 5 percent of the country's people had now "identif[ied] themselves as having an origin in a Spanish-speaking country." This group constituted "America's second largest minority," though "probably its least visible" one. The article made no mention of discrepancies in income or unemployment or language within the group. It did not mention any differences in racial identification. Instead, it portrayed the "Spanish Origin" population as a "nation within a nation, the size of Belgium or Chile." Previous methods of measuring these populations, once lauded for their objectivity, now came in for criticism. "Most experts agreed that the [old] methods were imprecise," the *Times* noted, before mentioning that even these new statistics had come under fire from "Spanish leaders." Antonio Rodríguez, executive director of the Cabinet Committee on Opportunities for Spanish-Speaking People, was the first "Spanish leader" whose expert opinion it cited. Rodríguez suggested that the Bureau may have failed to count almost three million of his people, which if true meant a staggering undercount of almost a third.[125] With new statistics showing a national population of "Spanish Origin" Americans, and advocates from the Cabinet Committee serving to interpret them, America's ethnic boundaries were being redrawn.

☆ ☆

In the late 1960s, dynamic movements of Chicanos and Puerto Ricans raised hopes for self-determination for each group. To posit that the essential orientation of Chicanos and Boricuas ought to be toward each other held out the prospect of a united "Latino" front against US militarism, Anglo capitalism, and the supposed deceit of assimilation. But the challenges of coordinating the movements' distinct tendencies—such as the rural reclamation of Reies Tijerina, the urban-rooted cultural nationalism of Corky Gonzales, the third-party electoral activism of MAYO, and the largely self-taught revolutionary Marxism of the Young Lords and their "divided nation" theory—meant that a left-wing Latino synthesis would appear elusive if not counterproductive. This asked these activists to forget too much about what they valued in politics, the other peoples they knew as vital allies, as well as what made them unique. It was also to subordinate their ties to the places that gave them their clearest sense of who they were, and the sharpest focus on their pathways to liberation.

Along a spectrum of officials and interested parties ranging from New Deal liberals to Barry Goldwater, the public debates over whether and, if so, how the United States government should represent Mexican Americans, Puerto Ricans, Cubans, and others of Latin American descent illustrated the discomfort that many still felt toward regarding them as a single community. Yet led by southwestern legislators and their allies, there was underway a process of institutionalizing these groups' ostensible ethnic bond. Filtered through the Congress's own structural realities, politicians elaborated a broad definition of "Spanish-speaking" solidarity for the state to safeguard and promote. While Congress established a pan-Hispanic advocate in the CCOSS, a powerful nudge from a Republican president ensconced a "Spanish Origin" identity in the nation's statistical system. The White House put its imprimatur on a new knowledge that would redefine Mexican Americans, Puerto Ricans, Cubans, and by extension the American people.

In constructing this pan-ethnic constituency, the congressmen not only seemed to suggest that all "Spanish-speaking Americans" should envision themselves as one and act accordingly in their dealings with the federal government. At least in theory, their action also obligated the new Republican president, Richard Nixon, to treat the diverse components of Spanish-speaking America equitably. As these changes took hold, elected officials and political activists would try to convert the seemingly vast potential of this newly recognized minority group into votes that would allow them to control the institutions of government.

# 5

# Mastering the "Spanish-Speaking Concept"

Two weeks before he was sworn in as president of the United States, Richard Nixon received a warning from Barry Goldwater. "These people are watching us," wrote the Arizona conservative, "to see if we will treat them the way the Democrats have." Goldwater urged Nixon to honor, and without delay, his campaign pledge to convene a White House conference on Mexican Americans. In a nod to changing ethnic sensibilities, the senator also advised the president-elect "that Mexican-Americans be referred to with that title." "Latin-American," on the other hand, should be used in reference to South America. For Goldwater, Mexican Americans nonetheless gained greater prominence as part of a "Spanish speaking" population national in dimensions. "Did you know New York is the biggest Spanish speaking city," Goldwater queried, "and did you realize that we have over six million Americans with Mexican or Spanish names?" "You will hear a lot on this subject from me, so the faster you move, the less bother I will be."[1]

Nixon would not have needed Goldwater's advice. He took only about 10 percent of the national "Spanish-speaking" vote in 1968. His campaign-trail recollections of a youth spent among Mexican Americans had delivered even less in Texas. Thanks in part to the end of the poll tax, 20 percent more Mexican Americans voted there in 1968 than had cast a ballot in 1960. They rose up in force to thwart Nixon. In a state he lost by fewer than 40,000 votes to Vice President Hubert Humphrey, Nixon lost Tejanos by a 300,000-vote margin.[2] A modest improvement from this 7 percent showing would go a long way toward switching Texas's twenty-five (and counting) electoral votes to the Republican column. Several other states in the Southwest and Midwest appeared close enough that they, too, could be tipped or secured with a decent showing among Mexican Americans. And there was reason for the optimistic to believe this was possible. Nixon tallied 40 percent of Spanish-American votes in New Mexico.[3]

Richard Nixon had not been elected president of the Southwest, however. Over its first two years, his administration would struggle to reconcile its intentions to convert that region's Mexican Americans from their Democratic loyalties with the newly minted expectation of governing in the interests of all the nation's "Spanish-speaking Americans." On one hand, partisan allies and the administration's own doubts about the likelihood of wooing Puerto Ricans to his brand of Republicanism led the White House to focus on dislodging Mexican Americans from the Democratic Party, usually by pitting them against African Americans. However, advocates for Puerto Ricans and Cubans complicated what might be called the administration's "Mexican-American strategy." Drawing inspiration from the pan-Hispanic promise of the Cabinet Committee on Opportunities for Spanish-Speaking People (CCOSS), they demanded parity, not with African Americans, but with Mexican Americans. The White House showed its acceptance of pan-Hispanic politics by developing special programs geared toward the upwardly mobile of all Spanish-speaking communities. While Mexican-American, Puerto Rican, and Cuban leaders were often (and with good reason) skeptical that assistance to one was assistance to all, the White House moved ahead in governing these groups. Through the CCOSS and other federal offices, it was learning where the various populations resided and in what numbers, what concerns they had; and it was learning how to manage their relationships with each other. It was developing a "Spanish-speaking strategy."

☆ ☆

By the time of Richard Nixon's inauguration in January 1969, official recognition of the country's diversity was becoming an ever-more influential factor in American life and politics. As Nixon's "Southern Strategy" amassed white votes at the cost of black ones, the Mexican-American vote appeared to be an important asset to Republicanism in an increasingly multicultural democracy. Indeed, it was not by accident that Nixon mentioned a "Mexican" child in the same breath as Polish and Italian children in his acceptance speech to the 1968 Republican National Convention. These ethnics were all just as American as Richard Nixon, and they all had an important role to play in his party's future.[4]

Yet the remark also suggested that, while southwestern Republicans at times talked of a national Spanish-speaking population, certain constituencies within that population appeared to them far worthier than others. Richard Nixon had resided for various lengths of time in the key nodes of Spanish-speaking America, and had ample time to conclude as much. Following his 1962 loss in California's gubernatorial race, Nixon had moved to New York. There he began the long resurrection of his political career while working for a major Wall Street law firm. In the core of mainland Puerto Rican settlement, he no doubt observed that the most prominent Republicans to have made inroads with this constituency were his rival, the progressive New York governor Nelson Rockefeller, and Rockefeller's liberal protégé, New York City mayor John Lindsay. Neither Nixon nor the party's southwestern conservatives to his right had any desire to strengthen their nemeses' Spanish-speaking constituency, thought to be liberal in its fiber. Nixon spent a good deal of time in South Florida as well, often accompanied by his Cuban-American confidante, Charles "Bebe" Rebozo. Days spent fishing, and chatting with Rebozo over martinis and grilled steaks in Key Biscayne, not to mention Nixon's long-standing reputation as one of the nation's most ardent anti-Communists, might have recommended a more central role for Cubans in his "Spanish-speaking" appeal.[5] But while Miami's Cubans did support Nixon's 1968 campaign, and were making initial forays into municipal politics around that time, so many still awaited a return to their homeland that they had comparatively low naturalization rates, and thus formed a very small portion of the electorate. It was not certain that they desired to be recognized in league with Puerto Ricans or Mexicans either.[6]

Mexican Americans were a different, larger constituency. Like his predecessor, Nixon would claim intimate knowledge of their character, which he derived from his upbringing in Southern California. They were a fast-growing group—just how fast was often unclear, thanks to a lack of federal data—and they were a major presence in the swing states of the Sunbelt, states whose economic and political power were on the rise. Now, having won the presidency, Richard Nixon was in the position of having to demonstrate accomplishments for a group that Republicans had for eight years, and at little cost to themselves, accused Democrats of neglecting.

Converting the Mexican-American vote did not require an entirely new set of strategies. Mexican-American leaders had long been highly focused on receiving presidential appointments, and the White House expected that they would respond favorably to seeing their people in high government positions. In February 1969, Nixon named Hilary Sandoval Jr., an El Paso businessman and John Tower supporter, to lead the Small Business Administration (SBA). He was the first in a long line of Spanish-speaking Americans to occupy this post, representation on which was to become the Republicans' capitalist analog to liberal Democrats' desire for status within the government's anti-discrimination apparatus.

Later that spring, the White House announced that two Los Angeles attorneys, Martin Castillo and Henry Quevedo, would occupy the top two positions at the Inter-Agency Committee on Mexican American Affairs (ICMAA), which Congress later that year renamed the Cabinet Committee on Opportunities for Spanish-Speaking People.[7] Castillo was a Democrat and Quevedo was the son of MAPA founder and longtime Democratic activist Eduardo Quevedo.[8] In a personal meeting with Nixon a month before the 1968 elections, these men had received "clear commitments" that if elected he would address Mexican Americans' social and economic problems. The two had told the candidate that "the potential for the Republican Party and for the Country is great among the large Mexican-American voter [*sic*] in the years to come." They spoke of the possibility of the GOP "realis[ing] some of this potential with much hard work and some integrity."[9] Overseeing a Cabinet Committee staff that grew to more than thirty, they would have their chance to accomplish both. Their mandate included producing research that would inform policy, recommending the right people for federal jobs, advising congressional committees, and otherwise encouraging federal agencies to direct resources to Spanish-speaking communities.

The White House assigned a pair of higher-level personnel to oversee these minority representatives. Reflecting the administration's aspiration to use Mexican-American outreach as an instrument of disruption, it placed the Spanish-speaking constituency in the portfolio of the bellicose vice president, Spiro Agnew. At the same time, suggesting a softer side and awareness that the Spanish-speaking were still predominantly a Democratic and in many respects liberal constituency, Leonard Garment, Nixon's former law partner in New York and a liberal civil rights advisor to the president, would act as an administration strategist and public contact as well.

In his first months, Nixon added to these appointments a more lasting form of recognition. In April 1969, Secretary of Commerce Maurice Stans announced that the 1970 census would, for the first time, ask Americans nationwide if they were of "Spanish Origin" (see Chapter 4). Martin Castillo recalled that it was "pretty tricky business" to make the change, since the Bureau of the Census was against it and since Mexican Americans had long insisted that they were "Caucasian." But a "lot of White House pressure" had gone into persuading the Bureau, pressure Nixon was willing to apply because, in Castillo's words, the change "was good for everybody."[10] Certainly it was believed to be good for the administration. The new president would be in position to boast that he was the first to officially recognize that Mexican Americans were no longer merely a regional people. The new national data could justify disbursement of additional federal funds to their communities, for which Nixon could claim credit. And the data would clarify these voters' locations and socioeconomic circumstances, enabling Republican campaign strategists to target them more easily during elections.

Affirmation of Mexican Americans' existence was more than a statistical project, however. Those who worked for him recognized that the group's ascent under the Republicans was to be cast as a corrective measure, an end to Democrats' supposed bias in favor of African Americans. In his oft-cited treatise, *The Emerging Republican Majority*, GOP strategist Kevin Phillips observed that "Negro-Democratic mutual identification" was fundamental to the party's 1968 appeal to white voters, and it is no stretch to see in Nixon's early attempts to unmoor the Spanish-speaking constituency from its traditional partisan allegiance an extension of this thinking.[11] As one historian puts it, Nixon "understood that resentment was *the* engine of American politics."[12] And Richard Nixon had surely observed, as in Ronald Reagan's 1966 gubernatorial campaign and in other mid-1960s elections (see Chapter 3), that at least some Mexican Americans were signaling resentment at the nature, and the effectiveness, of black political expression.

Martin Castillo struck a particularly aggressive public posture in service of this agenda. When the black assistant secretary for equal opportunity at the Department of Housing and Urban Development gave the opening remarks at the 1969 convention of the League of United Latin American Citizens in Long Beach, California, "several" of the civil rights group's "most important delegates" boycotted his speech. Castillo sided with the boycotters and criticized the decision to open the conference with an African American and not a Mexican American.[13] He urged the audience to put their ethnic identity ahead of partisan loyalty, claiming that "before this Administration took over, Washington thought in terms of minority or black problems. . . . Now we talk in terms of black and Mexican-American problems."[14]

Inside the beltway, for a president "little interested in the substance of domestic policy beyond its political repercussions," to champion Mexican-American interests was to bludgeon perceived enemies—mostly Jewish and black—in the bureaucracy.[15] The administration's view was that the federal government, especially its civil rights apparatus, was beholden to anti-Nixon forces. It needed to be shaken up. The president had his counselor, John Ehrlichman, investigate the US Commission on Civil Rights (USCCR) for "possible discrimination" against Mexican Americans and Indians. In news that supposedly confirmed Nixon's suspicions, Ehrlichman reported that five Jews and two African Americans comprised the USCCR executive staff. The other populations were "virtually unrepresented," with "budget allocation, outlays and programs reflect[ing] similar imbalance."[16] In another case, the office of the secretary of labor was told that Vice President Spiro Agnew wanted "more visibility" devoted to "the plight of our Spanish-speaking citizens." Agnew, who in one historian's words had been chosen as Nixon's running mate "because the last thing he [Nixon] wanted was peace between the races," had been "disturbed to learn that the Spanish speaking, as the second largest identifiable minority group in this country, has unemployment rates . . . considerably higher than almost every other sector of the country." Given their need, Agnew wanted a Department of Labor weekly publication, "Black News Digest," to devote more attention to "the non-Black minority groups which share similar labor problems." Its title might even be changed to "Minority News Digest."[17]

This racial polarization strategy did not resolve certain dilemmas of partisanship, however. The GOP leader needed to make inroads into an overwhelmingly Democratic electorate, while still rewarding his Mexican-American party loyalists. Southwestern Republican congressmen were furious that Nixon had appointed Castillo, a Democrat, to represent the administration to Mexican Americans, and were outraged by the numerous "unfriendly militant Democrats" serving on the ICMAA staff. Writing for California's Republican delegation and in support of those Mexican-

American Republicans—a group "too loyal to neglect and too important to offend"—Rep. Burt Talcott demanded a White House conference on Mexican Americans—a key campaign promise of Nixon's—run without the ICMAA's involvement, "unless Republicans can have some voice."[18] For more than a year, however, the administration delayed action. In February 1970, a group of impatient San Antonio Republicans then tried to pressure the White House by going to the newspapers. "If we, the registered and working Mexican-Americans toiling the Republican vineyards do not . . . request that he honor his pledge," they argued, "the Democrats will remind him, and the rest of us, around election time." The Texans found it "hard enough to convert garden-variety Mexican-American Democrats to the Republican Party" without having to "use our converting time making excuses for the President not keeping his word." They were happy to hold "a special presidential Southwest Mexican-American Conference" in Texas, if one in Washington could not be arranged.[19]

As the field shifted from the Southwest to Washington, however, partisan divisions became interwoven with ethnic ones. Several southwestern Republicans did not want Puerto Ricans invited to any White House conference. They feared that Puerto Ricans and the liberal northeasterners who tended to represent them would diminish the partisan advantage Republicans stood to gain from hosting a national conference. Responding to their concerns in October 1969, the administration committed that it would exclude Puerto Ricans and Cubans from the White House conference.[20]

However, the administration's efforts to insulate the Mexican-American constituency from political adulteration by the congenitally liberal Puerto Ricans soon ran into problems. When Nixon, reluctant to offend Mexican Americans, signed on to Congress's creation of a Cabinet Committee on Opportunities for Spanish-Speaking People in December 1969, he endorsed a new ethnic reality in which all "Spanish-speaking" people constituted a single constituency. Republicans linked to Puerto Rico or Puerto Rican communities on the mainland were thus emboldened to argue for inclusion alongside Mexican Americans in any presidential outreach activities. An aide to Puerto Rico's resident commissioner in Congress had spent years "wondering why the national Republican Party has not endeavored to tell Puerto Ricans living in the Continental United States why they should 'vote Republican.'" The new Cabinet Committee, he believed, could be the vehicle to incorporate them into the Republican Party en masse. "The Democrats have really done very little for the Puerto Ricans, but they have succeeded in making them believe that it was a lot," wrote the aide. "Lets [*sic*] get our just rewards."[21]

The late 1960s did seem a propitious time for a Republican advance on the Puerto Rican electorate. The island's Democratic Party analog, the Partido Popular Democrático (PPD) of Luis Muñoz Marín, long a factor in the political socialization of the mainland population, was in disarray. In 1968, voters in Puerto Rico had elected as governor the candidate of the Republican-aligned Partido Nuevo Progresista (New Progressive Party), ending the PPD's twenty-eight year reign.[22] The new governor, the industrialist Luis Ferré, applauded Nixon for signing the Cabinet Committee into law, and thus acknowledging "the needs of a silent, loyal, deserving and somewhat neglected minority." Noting that "the concept of the committee has been broadened to include Puerto Ricans" (Ferré counted the island's population among them) and that they were "completely unrepresented at the moment," he asked Nixon to give Puerto Ricans "priority for all vacancies on the staff . . . until their representation is brought to par with that of Mexican-Americans."[23]

While the White House lambasted bureaucratic enemies for having few "Spanish-speaking" employees, other Puerto Ricans joined in criticizing the administration for failing to bring aboard those who could address *their* particular concerns. Ivan González, Special Assistant on Spanish-speaking Affairs to Massachusetts's Republican governor, Francis W. Sargent, had felt "great joy" upon learning that the Congress had expanded the ICMAA to include his people. However, he protested that "there is not even one single Puerto Rican within the agency who could act as a liaison" with the large "Spanish leadership" of the Northeast. Deplorably, he wrote, "although the name has changed, the game is still the same. The only ones receiving any benefit from this agency are still the Mexican-Americans in the Southwest."[24]

Presidential neglect compelled Puerto Rican leaders to form new arguments against national origin as a criterion for administration assistance. The president of the New York-based educational uplift organization ASPIRA, Luis Nuñez, regularly offered moderate views on Puerto Ricans' relationship with the administration.[25] As he told Nixon's civil rights liaison, Leonard Garment, the new Cabinet Committee demonstrated "much

sentiment both in the Congress and in the general public for a united approach" to Mexican-American and Puerto Rican problems. The administration had therefore to choose to satisfy national priorities or parochial
ones. "Any list of arguments" in favor of the pan-Hispanic approach "could
probably be refuted by someone who felt that Mexican-Americans (Chicanos),
have unique problems and for that matter, Puerto Ricans, Cubans, etc.,"
he conceded. But efficient policy and ethnic harmony were more important. Indeed, "the better policy would be one of trying to bring people together into larger grouping," one that recognized them as a "community
representing over 10 million people." For the country's benefit and "for the
future of all these communities," Nuñez appealed to Garment, "it will be
better if the federal government, in all its activities, tried to encourage this
feeling of community." That the numerically smaller Puerto Ricans would
stand to reap greater benefits from being included with Mexican Americans as full members of a national "Spanish-speaking" minority group is
not in itself sufficient reason to doubt Nuñez's sincerity. Nevertheless, the
incentives for reconciling ethnic differences were powerfully conditioned
by the politics of federal assistance.[26]

The problem was that although Congress made Nixon responsible for
managing the distinct "Spanish-speaking" constituencies as one, he and
his staff did not see them as equally valuable. When Leonard Garment cited
the Cabinet Committee's "wider mandate" to justify Puerto Ricans' inclusion in a White House conference, Ehrlichman's assistant gave the White
House's position: "for several reasons, the most important of which is politics I think we should limit to just Mexican-Americans." After all, he reminded Garment, "that's where the votes are."[27]

☆ ☆

As the midterm elections of 1970 approached, the White House's outreach
effort had managed the worst of both worlds: most Mexican Americans
believed that the administration had done nothing for them, while Puerto
Ricans thought that the Mexican Americans had gotten everything. Unwilling to offend southwestern Republicans, but unable to ignore Puerto
Ricans and Cubans due to the Cabinet Committee's mandate, the administration tabled the conference until after the 1970 elections. In place
of substantive negotiation with recognized leaders, the White House intended to convince middle-class members of the nation's Spanish-speaking

communities to view Republican values and appointed officials as means to and manifestations of their own ethnic group's advancement.

One initiative rewarded the Spanish-speaking for embracing entrepreneurship. In August 1970, Vice President Agnew, CCOSS chairman Martin Castillo, SBA director Hilary Sandoval, and Los Angeles businessman Benjamin Fernandez gathered at that city's Century Plaza Hotel. There they unveiled the National Economic Development Agency (NEDA). NEDA was a private nonprofit organization whose aim was to "promote business development among the nation's 10 million Spanish speaking citizens." Fernandez, a Republican fundraiser (and future US presidential candidate), was its first president and chairman of the board. With more than a hint of racial score settling, Agnew praised the new organization as "a clear sign of President Nixon's interest in what we call 'the forgotten minorities.'" It would help ensure that "Americans of Hispanic descent get a fair chance at the starting line" and an opportunity to "share in America's economic miracle." At once an affirmation of the administration's ethnic inclusiveness and America's middle-class promise, the program would "prove that a man born poor, if given a chance, just a little help, can still succeed in the United States." It was definitely "not a handout," Agnew said.[28]

At a time when Puerto Rican and Mexican-American liberals and leftists had difficulty combining their efforts, NEDA's fusion of entrepreneurial ideology and ethnic symbolism, buttressed by federal funds, showed a Republican model for pan-Hispanic cooperation. For its modern mission of "foster[ing] the free enterprise system among Spanish-speaking people," NEDA drew upon icons of the past.[29] Its publications were emblazoned with a sword and morion, the crested helmet commonly associated with the defunct Spanish Empire.[30] Taxpayer dollars provided the material encouragement to bind these communities to one another. An initial grant from the government of more than $600,000 coupled with over a million dollars of further assistance in its first two years allowed the organization to establish offices across the continental United States, as well as in Puerto Rico.[31] NEDA's board reflected the diversity of the nation's Spanish-speaking people. It consisted of "leaders from Mexican American, Puerto Rican and Cuban Communities [sic]," a collaboration Agnew celebrated as historic. Indeed, it was one of the only major organizations of its time to successfully connect these various communities to one another.[32]

NEDA served several purposes. It advanced the ongoing redefinition of the Spanish-speaking American as a national minority, and gave the White House a rebuttal to charges it only was concerned for Mexican Americans. By aiding small businessmen, the administration would also be supporting role models whose moderate values would compete with the militant Chicano and Puerto Rican social movements. Furthermore, NEDA's beneficiaries would be expected to provide campaign contributions, which Ben Fernandez would be in position to process. NEDA thus represented the potential of pan-Hispanic capitalism to link middle-class and establishment values to ethnic empowerment, in turn promoting social stability and Republican politicians along the way.

The project was not without certain biases. During its first two years, NEDA claimed to have helped thousands of clients to receive guarantees of leases or bonding, lines of credit, or minority set-aside contracts. It took credit for facilitating more than $36 million in debt and equity financing for nearly seven hundred proposals in a single ten-month period. National numbers concealed what were becoming familiar distributional inequalities, however. More than one-third of NEDA's financing went to Miami, where Cuban Americans had over the previous decade used the Cuban Refugee Program and other coordinated aid to make rapid progress in the banking and commercial sectors. Of the remainder, three-quarters went to the Southwest. More funding went to Albuquerque and El Paso, for example, than to New York and Chicago, a virtual guarantee that Puerto Ricans would receive only a small benefit from NEDA.[33]

Meanwhile, the Cabinet Committee proposed a respectable version of Hispanicity that seamlessly complemented NEDA's market-centric view of ethnic empowerment. Its 1970 annual report contained images of Mexican agricultural laborers and Puerto Rican slum dwellers, but suggested that the solutions lay not in strikes or other collective action but in education, and in trusting the government to promote small business. Several photos celebrated CCOSS and SBA employees fighting for federal resources on behalf of their constituents. Another, captioned "A Puerto Rican Couple Proudly Display Their Small Cafe Built on Resourcefulness and Enterprise," illustrated what the Spanish-speaking could become with hard work, helpful bureaucrats, and the business savvy of groups like NEDA.[34] Though previous governments had offered mere "token participation," the seventies were

In 1970, the Nixon administration chose Benjamin Fernandez, a California financial consultant and Mexican American, to lead its outreach to the Spanish-speaking business community. Photo by John Rous, courtesy of Associated Press.

poised to be "the dawn of achievement and progress" for Spanish-speaking Americans thanks to the current administration.[35]

The White House's appeal to the Spanish-speaking American as a culturally distinct and dignified guardian of mainstream values was of a piece with its larger attempt to use the "social issue" in the 1970 elections. Richard Scammon and Ben Wattenberg's *The Real Majority* (1970), effectively the administration's handbook for the midterms, argued that the day's politics pivoted on the "social issue." This they defined as a fear of wholesale cultural transformation and an instability in social mores. The vast "real majority" of American voters were the "unyoung, unpoor, and unblack" voters—otherwise attracted to Democrats' economic message, and they would reject the party if they associated it with permissiveness toward crime, pornography, drugs, black militants, protestors, or other menaces of the day.[36]

The Nixon administration's attempt to heighten a group's ethnoracial consciousness—aggressively tried with white voters—by framing its values as diametrically opposed to both black Americans and their liberal patrons was certainly evident in its Spanish-speaking outreach.

Yet while the White House portrayed the "Spanish-speaking Americans" as a single, national group whose common culture aligned with mainstream values, the persistent belief that its policies aided specific national origin or regional populations largely prevented it from establishing a unified "Spanish-speaking" campaign message for the 1970 congressional elections. Republicans were warned to "tailor the use" of materials to the audience in question. The Cuban Refugee Program, for example, was "not particularly appreciated by Mexican-Americans." "Mexican-American advancements," in turn, were "not as enchanting to the Cubans or to Puerto Ricans in the northeastern United States." "In sum," the word went out, "a Spanish speaking opportunity program does not touch every American whose mother tongue was Spanish."[37]

When the voting was done, Democrats retained a ten-vote Senate majority and a seventy-three-vote edge in the House. They scored notable wins in governors' races.[38] In states of consequence for Mexican-American strategy, the outcome had not been good for Republicans. In Texas, Rep. George H. W. Bush lost his US Senate bid to Lloyd Bentsen, a conservative Democrat and John Connally protégé. Joseph Montoya, the Senate's lone Spanish American, defeated a Goldwater conservative in New Mexico to earn another six-year term. Finally, in California, liberal Democrat John Tunney won his race, defeating Republican incumbent George Murphy. In one bright spot, Manuel Luján Jr. of New Mexico, the lone Republican of Spanish heritage then serving in the national legislature, was reelected.[39] Louis Nuñez's report that 64 percent of New York's Puerto Rican voters had helped return Gov. Nelson Rockefeller to Albany for a fourth term would have registered as very little consolation in the Oval Office.[40]

An irritated President Nixon demanded to know why Republicans had not gained greater traction with Mexican Americans, a group he believed was ripe for the political taking. Leonard Garment viewed the outcome as "a really unfortunate story of misfires, inaction and bad luck."[41] But the president's reelection campaign was up next, and it was clear that the administration's Spanish-speaking program would have to undergo a significant transformation. Shortly after the 1970 elections, Hilary Sandoval was forced to resign his position at the SBA.[42] Martin Castillo and Henry Quevedo resigned two weeks later, with Quevedo blaming "old-line bureaucrats" for obstructing their mission in Washington. "They think of civil rights as a black-white issue and just don't know that the nation's second largest minority is also suffering. That's 10 million people," he said.[43] Garment was relieved of his responsibilities for dealing with the Spanish-speaking Americans in February 1971. According to chief of staff H. R. Haldeman, the change was made "because his [Garment's] overriding concern is for Blacks."[44]

Haldeman then designated Robert Finch "the responsibility for the exploitation of our Mexican American accomplishments."[45] Until recently the Secretary of Health, Education, and Welfare (HEW), Finch was a chain-smoker and moderate Republican. A softer touch than the belligerent Agnew, he had served as California's lieutenant governor before joining the administration, and thus was also more familiar with Mexican Americans than Garment. He was a logical choice for his new role.

As Finch took on "Spanish-speaking" outreach, the administration was rolling out a second plan to secure middle-class Mexican Americans' loyalty. In response to their leaders' belief that the number of federal jobs they held reflected an administration's respect for them and indicated their own progress in society, Nixon proposed expanding Mexican-American participation in the civil service. Back in July 1970, Agnew and Martin Castillo had held a White House meeting with eleven federal "Spanish-speaking officials." It was intended to demonstrate Nixon's interest in, as Castillo put it, "parity of attention" for this group in Washington. While assuring reporters that he did not support the use of "quotas," the vice president concluded that it was fair for minority groups to expect federal employment at "a reasonably equivalent ratio to [their percentage of the] population."[46] Given that more than nine million "Spanish-speaking Americans" lived in the United States, there was much work to do. However, the White House delayed announcing any initiative to increase the group's representation until after the midterms, likely out of fear that doing so would alienate the conservative white voters who were its major target in 1970.

Just a few days after the voting, though, the situation was different. With eyes turning toward the president's reelection campaign, the administration introduced its "Sixteen Point Program" to extend affirmative action to this long-neglected minority. Eager to confirm this constituency's best image of itself, and aware of conservatives' disdain for affirmative action, the White House insisted that the plan constituted no "preferential treatment." Rather, it was a "special emphasis program." And it was needed to prevent discriminatory policies like height and weight requirements, or the use of "an 'accent' . . . as a screen-out factor," from denying otherwise "highly qualified" people a chance at "rightful competition."[47] The Sixteen Point Program pledged to boost federal recruitment of Spanish speakers using "selective placement on bilingual basis," and by reaching out to Spanish-speaking veterans who were eligible for "noncompetitive appointments." It called upon agencies to employ Spanish-speaking high school and college teachers in summer jobs. Continuing a demand of the ICMAA, the program called for improving and expanding minority employment statistics to show "special information relating to employment and upward mobility of Spanish surnamed persons in the Federal Government." The plan required agencies to incorporate this minority group in their existing affirmative action (EEO) plans. And it mandated a full-time staffer in the Civil Service Commission to ensure compliance.[48] In December 1970, the administration appointed a New Mexico Republican named Fernando E. C. De Baca to implement the new program.[49]

While the program was superficially pan-Hispanic and national, it advanced a more specific White House mission. Like NEDA, it was a foundation of the administration's Mexican-American patronage network for 1972. Its work began in earnest in early 1971, when the White House's new Special Assistant for Personnel, former HEW undersecretary Fred Malek, established something called the "Spanish-Speaking Ad Hoc Committee." Again, despite its name, it was primarily designed to place Mexican Americans in visible positions in the federal service, where they would "form a nucleus" for the wider recruitment of their people.[50] Malek wanted individuals who were "politically in concert with the Administration and generally sophisticated executives in their own right," people with "the ability to reach into the pertinent states"—Arizona, California, Colorado, New Mexico, and Texas—to recruit others. His staff assembled an initial cadre of fourteen Mexican-American professionals, whom they expected to screen out federal job applicants unfriendly to the administration's goals. All were Republicans under 50 years old. They were doctors, lawyers, and businessmen. They were to act as the administration's conduits to the sensible, winnable, Mexican Americans.[51]

☆ ☆

Even as it developed more sophisticated and superficially pan-Hispanic mechanisms for reaching Mexican Americans, the White House remained vexed by its obligations to the broader "Spanish-speaking" constituency. The Cabinet Committee was supposed to be the principal means by which the executive would manage aid to these populations. But lacking formal authority and informal White House backing, it had like its predecessor been largely ineffective. Unable to convince federal agencies to hire and devote many more resources to Spanish-speaking Americans, it was not much of an asset in the 1970 elections. It lay moribund for months after, evidence of administration neglect that could prove costly in the 1972 elections, should the situation continue unchanged. Democratic congressmen were pressing the White House to appoint a new chairman and to fill staff vacancies.[52] Asian Americans were reportedly demanding a Cabinet committee of their own, which only increased the pressure on Nixon to do something about the CCOSS. Mexican Americans and Puerto Ricans began coordinated lobbying, not necessarily for any specific policy, but rather to convince the White House to revive the Cabinet Committee.[53]

Counselor Robert Finch investigated the administration's options. His deputy, George Grassmuck, observed that "many 'grass roots' individuals" considered the CCOSS "the most important Federal body which exists solely for their benefit." It was "the primary point of contact between the community" and Washington, and a "beacon" for people "otherwise . . . lost in the Federal labrynth" [sic]. It seemed to be "the focal point for the emerging role of the Mexican Americans, Puerto Ricans, Cubans, and Latins" in national affairs. Eliminating it would certainly anger voters.[54]

However, Grassmuck also recognized that "the combination of all government and Administration concern" about Mexican Americans, Puerto Ricans, and Cubans "into one effort" was deeply complicated. "While all are Spanish speaking, and have some religious, and other cultural aspects that are alike, they do not share these in common," he wrote. Rather, to organize these communities together primarily reflected "the Anglo's way of looking at these people from the outside."[55] Cubans felt toward Mexicans and Puerto Ricans a "polite disdain—certainly not a willingness to follow" their leaders in the Cabinet Committee "or in other Spanish speaking matters." This led Grassmuck to conclude that they "probably need to be handled separately" from the others.[56]

On the other hand, many leaders had embraced what he called the "Spanish-speaking concept"—out of a clear-eyed quest for power. They did not always like it, or each other, but they believed it was "a foundation on which they can build." Moreover, since "none of the three communities want[ed] to see either of the other two" in charge of the Cabinet Committee, and since Mexican Americans and Puerto Ricans were sure to "react with a violent negative" if the administration scrapped it, the groups were, to an extent, stuck with each other.[57] Both pragmatic national origin alliance as well as national origin rivalry helped keep the institution alive.

The problem for Republicans was in making the CCOSS both politically useful and at least superficially equitable. Mexican Americans constituted the bulk of its staff, a "constant source of divisiveness," especially embittering to Puerto Ricans.[58] The "factionalism within the brown community" made finding Castillo's replacement more difficult still. The new chairman had to come from "the Mexican-American sector of the Spanish-Speaking population," and was preferably a Republican, although the "right kind of Democrat" was a possibility.[59] Robert Finch even looked into appointing two additional deputy chairmen who could provide ethnic balance. But the Office of Management and Budget shot down that plan, calling it "unwarranted," likely to lead to dysfunction, and contrary to the CCOSS's enacting legislation, which had assumed that the Spanish-speaking were a single minority group.[60]

Though the group's internal divisions were great, White House staff believed that the gulf between the Spanish-speaking and African Americans would be decisive in its cohesion. Twelve Democratic congressmen who had formed a Congressional Black Caucus had held meetings with the president in March 1971, during which they called for changes to foreign and domestic policy.[61] Grassmuck observed that, "Spanish Speaking community spokesmen were watching closely" for the administration's response. It was clear that "they want the same type of opportunities as Negroes, and do not want 'to play second fiddle to any minority.'"[62] Republicans could "champion the Spanish speaking groups," partly because "the Democratic Party appears to be the champion of the Blacks." This perception, he believed, did "not go down well with the Spanish-speaking."[63] Months of

White House planning had led again to making "Negro-Democratic mutual identification" the core of its "Spanish-speaking strategy."

When the administration rolled out its new appeal to Spanish-speaking Americans in the summer of 1971, few of the nuances exhibited in its internal deliberations were present. The Cabinet Committee's 1971 Annual Report described a "disadvantaged minority" numbering perhaps twelve million, "a diverse amalgam of Mexican, Puerto Rican, Cuban and other Spanish derivation." The Cabinet Committee anchored this people's collective history in the Southwest, noting the existence of Spanish settlements before Plymouth Rock, then still the central physical referent in American nationalist mythology. It also made an uncommon assertion—for a government entity, at least—about the group's racial makeup, referring to "the white population of the Southwest" in 1790 as "practically all Spanish." Whereas others had assimilated, the report found that Spanish-speaking Americans "remain the least 'Americanized'" of the country's ethnic groups. The "remarkable phenomenon" of Spanish language maintenance was supposedly "a singularly unique element of their character," and not the consequence of either persistent immigration, or social or racial exclusion. "They simply have not been willing to abandon their cultural and linguistic heritage," these attributes that, as "whites," most clearly distinguished them.[64] After compiling the new census figures that the White House had ordered to be generated along with other federal statistics and data gleaned from "on-site visits by CCOSS personnel," the report illustrated them as a single element in America's ethnic map.

To complement its narrative of the Spanish-speaking constituency, the Nixon administration anointed the group a host of new leaders. Nixon selected forty-two-year-old Henry M. Ramirez to carry his message forth in the role of Cabinet Committee chairman. Ramirez was an active Republican and a conservative Catholic who had grown up in a family of migrant workers. He had taught high school in Nixon's hometown of Whittier until the last months of the Johnson administration, when he accepted a job with the US Commission on Civil Rights' Mexican American Studies Division.[65] He first caught the Nixon White House's attention in a lengthy memo he wrote on federal outreach to Spanish-speaking Americans. Ramirez's perspective dovetailed with Republican hopes, describing this group as "generally characterized by a strong family structure, deep religious ties," and "a rather conservative political outlook." The Nixon administration could do

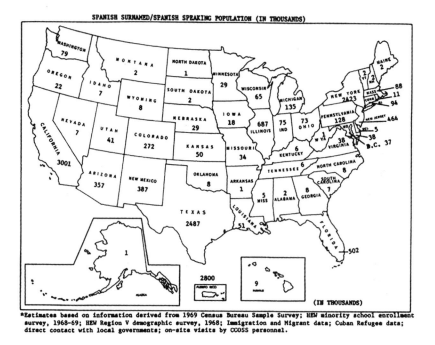

SPANISH SURNAMED/SPANISH SPEAKING POPULATION (IN THOUSANDS)

\*Estimates based on information derived from 1969 Census Bureau Sample Survey; HEW minority school enrollment survey, 1968-69; HEW Region V demographic survey, 1968; Immigration and Migrant data; Cuban Refugee data; direct contact with local governments; on-site visits by CCOSS personnel.

The Cabinet Committee on Opportunities for Spanish-Speaking People furnishes its own portrayal of a national minority. "Annual Report of the Cabinet Committee on Opportunities for Spanish-Speaking People, Fiscal Year 1971," Box 15, Robert H. Finch Files, SMOF, NPM.

much to help these people, he claimed. Steps included distinguishing them in all federal statistics, honoring their church leaders, and supporting farm workers. No doubt angling for the job, he declared that the Cabinet Committee must have "a competent and imaginative chairman" who came from the Mexican-American population.[66] The White House was attracted to Ramirez's moderate views. "He is not a militant, and he is not a soap-box advocate," read one administration vetting report. He was "perhaps . . . an opportunist," but not "just for himself. He is also ambitious for his people," it claimed.[67]

If Ramirez's appointment conveyed the primacy of Mexican-American interests, the White House nonetheless paid respect to the "Spanish-speaking concept." It finally filled the Cabinet Committee's advisory board, which had been mandated by its enacting legislation but never yet established.

Richard Nixon with Henry Ramirez and the Advisory Board to the Cabinet Committee on Opportunities for Spanish-Speaking People, 1971. Courtesy of Nixon Presidential Library and Museum, Yorba Linda, California.

Careful to preserve ethnic balance, the administration selected four Mexican Americans, three Puerto Ricans, and three Cubans. They came from California, New Jersey, Arizona, New Mexico, Florida, Texas, Washington, DC, and Puerto Rico. In a newspaper editorial intended to promote "a climate of unity," one of the Cuban advisors, Manuel Giberga, stressed that the people they represented all shared "a common dominator . . . not only ethnic but also spiritual, cultural and psychological." Their "many hopes and things in common," he argued, "must be coordinated in collective actions." Such coordination in turn needed "to have as starting point the gratitude and loyalty to the United States of America, the country where they have found liberty and opportunity to decorously unfold their lives."[68] Efforts to provide unity through geographical and ethnocultural representation leavened with an immigrant patriotism did not mask that the committee did not reflect the population's electoral preferences. While the Spanish-speaking Americans were overwhelmingly registered Democrats, only one advisory committee member was a Democrat.[69]

The administration's appointed representatives competed with Democratic elected officials in the fluid struggle to define the leadership of Spanish-speaking America. To create a scene comparable to his March summit with the Congressional Black Caucus, Nixon introduced Ramirez and the advisory committee to several members of his Cabinet on August 5, 1971. During the meeting, the president suggested ways for those hand-picked leaders to pursue their claims. The Mexican Americans he had known from his childhood in Whittier had been "family oriented, law abiding people," he said. And "although they did need attention—that wheel was not squeaking much." He urged them to form a lobby so that their people would have better access to federal programs and employment. In the interim, he would do what he could to foster their advancement. "The government has the responsibility," he said. "Private business does not move as fast in developing opportunities." Nixon admonished his Cabinet to "get off their duffs," and to provide assistance to this deserving group, not just to "those who tear up the place and pound fists."[70] The president also spent a few minutes in the Oval Office coaching Ramirez on how to stand up for himself and his goals. The subject was not in the president's talking points, but Nixon ad-libbed a more explicit comparison between blacks and Mexican Americans. "They just raise the devil, and as a result they've got a congressional lobby to send in," but "you fellas, you've just sat too long." "The responsible people," he told Ramirez, "you've got to really get organized, and just raise as much hell as they do." They faced a "language barrier," of course. But "the Mexican American has an enormous advantage over the blacks" because "you do not have the racial" barrier to overcome, said Nixon, in a remark either hopelessly optimistic toward, or willfully ignorant of, the nature of anti-Mexican bigotry in the United States. "You shouldn't be penalized for not being a bunch of bomb throwers. But what will it take?"[71] Ramirez contended it was the progress and inclusion of people like himself. "We have to become an integral part of the fabric of our country and our government. . . . It happens by being in positions of authority . . . to be inside."[72]

For Nixon, making this humble and patriotic son of immigrants into an American minority leader was of a piece with the administration's broader quest to appear the champion of humble and patriotic people of all backgrounds, encapsulated in his invocation of the Silent Majority. Nixon's

Mexican-American appointees were intended to have particular resonance in an era when the United Farmworkers of America presented a potent left-liberal image of the ethnic Mexican laborer. Ramirez was thus exemplar and counterpoint. One of eleven children, forced into migrant labor after an injury to his father, he claimed to have "picked every crop there is to pick in California." The press portrayed him as embodying several seemingly conflicting tendencies. Challenging yet conformist, he was "a Chicano activist with some Establishment views."[73] He had little to say about past injustices, and even less to say about revolution. He told reporters that his people's problem was that it lacked a bourgeoisie: "that's the trouble. . . . The stability of our community, as well as the nation, depends on development of a middle-class."[74] Ramirez's focus on upward mobility in the national context reflected a broader mindset, he said. He was glad to have left California, for doing so afforded him perspective on his people's problems and the capacity to do something about them. Ramirez called for "a brain drain from the barrios into positions of responsibility." Chicanos brought into the system would return to their communities with new ideas and useful experience. "They won't just know about Los Angeles, but also about Texas, Colorado, and New Mexico."[75] By shifting the focus of community empowerment from the local to the regional and national, and connecting with activists and administrators elsewhere, they would have a better chance to make a difference in the barrios.

The administration selected additional envoys to spread the message that Republicans valued hard-working Mexican Americans and the expertise their lives had conferred.[76] A few weeks after resurrecting the CCOSS, the president chose a forty-one-year-old Fresno Republican named Philip V. Sánchez to lead the Office of Economic Opportunity, the agency created to coordinate Lyndon Johnson's War on Poverty. Newspapers latched on to another rags-to-responsibility story. The *Los Angeles Times* related how Sánchez, "whose appearance is distinctly Mexican," had been just "a scrawny 6-year old" when he "joined his Mexican migrant family . . . picking fruit and cotton" during the Depression. Abandoned by his father, he had come a long way.[77] Indeed, the *Washington Post* declared him on the verge of becoming the "highest ranking official of Mexican heritage in the federal government," an assertion bound to irritate Senator Joseph Montoya.[78]

To symbolize the triumphs of minority capitalism under his leadership, President Nixon nominated Romana Bañuelos to be US Treasurer in the fall of 1971. Courtesy of Nixon Presidential Library and Museum, Yorba Linda, California.

The White House's true public relations masterstroke was a Los Angeles entrepreneur named Romana Bañuelos. In September, after what the administration claimed was a twenty-four-hour search, Nixon nominated her to be treasurer of the United States. The feel-good story practically wrote itself. The *Chicago Tribune* described a business genius who without as much as a high school diploma had turned a home-based tortilla venture into a multimillion-dollar Mexican food empire.[79]

Nixon took time on multiple occasions to meditate on the rise of this woman, on her tremendous authenticity, and what it all meant for his own reelection campaign. He was glad she was "born in Mexico, [and] therefore not a Spanish type. She isn't old [unintelligible], like [the actor] Cesar Romero. Not an aristocrat."[80] He returned to the subject with Haldeman, his chief of staff, basking in the glow of her ethnic credibility. "I think the Mexican lady thing was a good one," he said. "She talked with a Mexican accent. She looks like a Mexican." Indeed, Haldeman remarked, "She's got Indian blood in her. She isn't just a high level, you know." "She's not a Spanish Mexican," the president replied, "she's a *Mexican* Mexican." It had been "a hell of an appointment."[81] Like Henry Ramirez, Romana Bañuelos epitomized the kind of Mexican American that White House officials wanted on their side. Haldeman considered her "a good American success story. Built her own little tamale stand up into a growing business." "Damn right," said Nixon. As if Bañuelos's free enterprise credentials were not enough, her sons were Los Angeles county sheriffs. The president and his deputy could almost not believe their good fortune. She scored a political hat trick, appealing to small businesspeople, proud Mexican Americans, and even "law and order" types. "That was the most dramatic example," Haldeman marveled, where "we sort of pushed a button, and said come up with a Mexican woman, and in fact four days later we ended up with a Mexican woman. Who was chairman of the board of a bank, and runs around with scholarship foundations for Mexican kids. She's a hell of a story! And they run all of this in the paper, made it out like—yeah, she's a good Horatio Alger type."[82]

Even better, the political exchange rate for Mexican-American patronage was surely favorable. The two men believed that the appointment would go farther with Mexican Americans than a comparable appointment would have gone with blacks. "I have a feeling that that helps with the Mexicans [voters]. I don't think it helps one damn bit with the Negroes," said Nixon.

"Well, they think it's their divine right," replied Haldeman. "The Mexicans haven't gotten enough of it to be able to think that."[83] Nixon thrilled at his fortune. "If we can't make something out of that, that the Treasurer of the United States is a Mexican. She signs every goddamned bill: Romana Bañuelos."[84] Recognition of a group's political utility hardly made the president's circle into racial liberals, however. When, on another occasion, Nixon mused about the political benefits of seeing, "Romana Bañuelos on every dollar bill," an advisor cracked that, "They'll start calling it the peso."[85]

☆ ☆

By late 1971, the Nixon administration had committed itself to a comprehensive attempt to win over the "Spanish-speaking" minority group. It sought to convince Spanish-speaking Americans that certain aspects of Nixon's approach to governance—an emphasis on personal independence, family, and small business—reflected that their ethnic values were honored and incorporated in government. The new knowledge and institutions created about and for this minority *population* did not necessarily make it an *electorate*, however, let alone mobilize it to vote for a particular party or candidate. A strong emphasis on the symbolism of appointed leadership characterized the Republican appeal. The administration, with its force of upwardly mobile political surrogates, believed it was poised to capture the parts of the "Spanish-speaking vote" it deemed most essential, remaining committed to securing the middle class of Mexican America above all others. Nonetheless, leaders from a variety of Spanish-speaking communities seemed more accepting of the "Spanish-speaking concept" than ever before, provided it was fairly applied. The Nixon team was not the only one trying to convert "Spanish-speaking" identity into political power, however. Liberal Mexican Americans and Puerto Ricans in Congress saw themselves as the rightful leaders of the nation's Spanish-speaking people. They, too, hoped to consolidate the Spanish-speaking vote.

# 6

# Liberal Democrats and the Meanings of "Unidos"

In September 1969, Senator Joseph Montoya was called upon to lead the nation's Spanish-speaking people. Carlos Alvarez, former leader of a Puerto Rican veterans' group, wrote to him of an urgent need for a prominent national figure to convene "a *high level nationwide conference* of Spanish leaders," and to establish "a large master organization or federation of Hispanic Societies." Alvarez envisioned an inclusive federation, one "representative of all, without regard to creeds, color of skin, or political beliefs." It would be rooted in the ethnic bond shared by these "close to fifteen (15) million citizens and residents who live, work and pay taxes in the world's most important nation." While conceding that their "traditions and cultures vary as among the very people of the United States of America because of regions and ancestry," Alvarez avowed that, "to all intent and purposes we are all *one* and the *same*, descendants in the great majority of the mother country Spain."[1]

Montoya's reply to this assertion of ethnic sameness was to affirm his support for "unity among the Spanish-speaking organizations." The senator had worked to that end, he said, by sponsoring legislation to create a Cabinet Committee on Opportunities for Spanish-Speaking People (CCOSS). As envisioned, it would act as "a permanent body to serve all Spanish Americans and represent all organizations of Spanish-speaking people."[2] After Montoya's bill passed, a Carlos Alvarez, probably the letter writer, was to join the new Cabinet Committee as a consultant. Yet he and the organization's congressional liaison (also a Puerto Rican) were fired in the fall of 1971. They were surplus to a White House directive to turn the committee into a full-fledged arm of Nixon's 1972 reelection campaign. Despite Montoya's hope that the CCOSS would foster Hispanic unity, and Alvarez's faith in the fundamental sameness of Spain's descendants in

America, it was revealing of the state of play of Spanish-speaking politics as practiced by the White House that Alvarez's attorney was to accuse the executive branch body of engaging in "a pattern of discrimination and practices that excluded Puerto Ricans."[3]

There was powerful incentive for Democrats to provide an alternative to presidential Spanish-speaking politics. While President Nixon appointed a coterie of upwardly mobile Mexican Americans as official guardians of a racially charged and individualistic Spanish-speaking political identity, Montoya and a small group of congressmen—including, crucially, the first Puerto Rican to represent a mainland district—sought to mobilize a broader Spanish-speaking electorate around a different set of political values. Working with a range of allies, including community organizers, social workers, and civil servants, they attempted to construct a nationwide and ostensibly nonpartisan "Spanish-speaking coalition" in late 1971. There existed a stunningly broad and fervent interest in the power to be gained from national pan-Hispanic organization, as more than a thousand individuals—overwhelmingly Mexican American and Puerto Rican—attended the congressmen's "Unidos" conference in Washington, DC. As participants of diverse geographical, ideological, strategic, partisan, and ethnic orientations met one another, learned from one another, debated one another, and devised means of justly distributing resources and representation among their communities, they brought forth contending visions of "unity." Some envisioned the "coalition" as a means to achieve *shared* policy goals of Mexican Americans and Puerto Ricans. Others saw in it a strategy to advance each group's *specific* causes. For others, though, political unification reflected something more—the crystallization of a community consciousness and sense of peoplehood, validation of the sameness of which Carlos Alvarez had written. The relationship between coalition and community was less a question to be resolved in a weekend and more a central ambiguity that was creatively and productively exploited by planners and participants alike.

The Unidos conference thus constituted a pivotal event in the early "doing" of Latino politics. First, its deliberations proved that a left-liberal Spanish-speaking policy agenda could be derived from a nationwide base of Puerto Ricans and Mexican Americans. Second, against a history of presidential engagement that subordinated the former to the latter (Johnson) or excluded them altogether (Nixon), the Unidos collaboration formalized a new and more egalitarian representational structure for Spanish-speaking politics.

In this vision emerging from the congressmen and the communities, Mexican Americans and Puerto Ricans existed as *equal groups* given discrete and equally powerful geographic spheres of influence, while Cubans received no explicit representational allocation in the coalition. At the same time, the Unidos conference showed its leaders were unable to reckon with the demands of Puerto Rican independence and Chicano third-party advocates within their imagined political community. Leftists' participation in the conference drove the congressmen to withdraw their support for the Spanish-speaking electoral coalition, and as a result the conference's left-liberal template would not be deployed for independent political action.

Nevertheless, having stimulated popular desire for pan-Hispanic electoral mobilization, the impulses and forms of Latino politics on display at the Unidos conference lodged themselves within the comparatively safe confines of the Democratic Party. As the legislators transferred their leadership to a Democratic Party "Latino Caucus," they brought the logic of equal representation for Mexican Americans and Puerto Ricans to the party's Latino structures. Paired with a thoroughly liberal presidential candidacy, Democratic "Latino" politics in 1972 had a central economic component, fusing labor and employment concerns and group identity in powerful ways. Moreover, the Unidos conference's egalitarian representational vision of Latino politics characterized the "Spanish-speaking" wing of the party's 1972 presidential campaign, "Unidos con McGovern/Shriver," completing the integration of this vision of pan-ethnic power sharing within a formally multicultural and economically just Democratic Party.

☆ ☆

By the early 1970s, the politics of Latino pan-ethnicity were being redefined by an ever-shifting set of relationships among Congress, the federal bureaucracy, and the White House. As of the end of 1969, the CCOSS and the "Spanish Origin" statistic had clearly institutionalized a pan-ethnic Latino constituency in the federal bureaucracy. But the Nixon administration's southwestern orientation and aversion—if not hostility—toward Puerto Rican voters, as well as its sense that Cubans belonged in a different political category, ensured that Mexican Americans were to be the face of the "Spanish-speaking" people.

However, a change in Congress raised the possibility of a more representative Spanish-speaking political presence in Washington. In 1970, the former Bronx borough president and the country's leading Puerto Rican politician, Herman Badillo, stood for election in a newly created "Puerto Rican District" in the House of Representatives. The congressional district encompassed zones of Puerto Rican residence in the South Bronx and East Harlem, as well as a white working-class area in the borough of Queens. Its significant pockets of Italian, Greek, black, and Jewish voters, not to mention Irish and German ones, joined to its Puerto Rican core to make it a most polyglot constituency. Showing the persistence of an interracial coalition politics characteristic of the New Deal era, and the strategy of a politician eager to one day hold the mayor's office, Badillo declared his candidacy to address the crises then afflicting the nation's cities: "It is time we challenge those in Washington so fascinated with war strategies, southern strategies and the like and present them with a new, more urgent one: the urban strategy." Badillo took on five opponents in the Democratic primary, a cohort of challengers that included two other Puerto Ricans, two Italians, and one African American. He ended up prevailing by some 556 votes out of roughly 25,000 cast. He counted the support of the labor-backed Liberal Party, as well as two of the top liberal Republicans in the state, Governor Nelson Rockefeller and New York City's mayor, John Lindsay. Running without Republican opposition (and against a relatively unknown Conservative Party challenger) in the general election, he became the first Puerto Rican elected to serve as a voting member in the national legislature.[4]

Sent to Washington in early 1971, he encountered Los Angeles congressman Edward Roybal. The congressmen shared a history and sensibility. Going back to John F. Kennedy in 1960, they had been involved in presidential politics through parallel campaigns to turn out the Democratic vote in Spanish-speaking districts. Both were urban liberals, raised to influence by interracial coalitions forged from a combination of civic nationalism and ethnic pride. Both men spoke perfect English, inflected by regional accents. Yet it was clear that the two men had grander ambitions than their congressional districts could hold. First elected in 1962, Roybal's decade in Congress had seen great changes in his city and district. Although a broad New Deal coalition put him in office, a continued in-migration of Mexican people and the surging activist energies of the Chicano movement increased his incentive to portray himself as a leader of this group, and indeed of all Spanish-speaking Americans. Badillo, in contrast, was biding his time in Congress. He hoped to exchange his rented room in Washington, DC, for Gracie Mansion in Manhattan after the city's next mayoral election, which would come in 1973. Positioning himself as a champion for woebegone urban America, with which the plight of mainland Puerto Ricans was inextricably bound, was a means of maintaining a broad appeal, a continuity with the interracial coalition building that had defined his career. At the same time, demonstrating his ethnic bona fides while avoiding divisive questions about Puerto Rico's political status would allow him to appear authentically connected to his core constituency. A perennial mayoral candidate, national politics was for him a means to a local end.[5]

Eschewing Chicano and Puerto Rican nationalism while maintaining an identification as spokesmen for their respective communities, Roybal and Badillo thus were working on distinct but compatible projects. Brought together in the Congress in 1971, the two politicians from the great coastal metropolises would seek to move beyond the political battles and community boundaries of Mexican Americans in Los Angeles and Puerto Ricans in New York, toward a politics built on shared interest and a new, nationwide "Spanish-speaking" solidarity.

The two legislators viewed the Nixon administration's revitalized Spanish-speaking outreach program with frustration and suspicion. As Henry B. González had predicted, the Cabinet Committee had proven weak and subject to White House manipulation. Many liberals believed that it might prove helpful to their cause under a different president, however, and so Roybal and Badillo tried to use their own ethnic credibility to influence its activities. They wrote to President Nixon in August 1971, expressing relief that a chairman and advisory committee had at last been named. "Clearly," stated the congressmen, such a committee was "essential" for Spanish-speaking Americans to receive a fair share of federal resources and "enjoy full equality with other Americans." Nevertheless, the administration's previous neglect meant that a group numbering sixteen million people—a third more than even the Cabinet Committee had estimated—suffered poorer quality of health, housing, welfare, jobs, education, as well as a lack of "equal justice under the law and basic human dignity." Nixon had met with the Congressional Black Caucus in March. Roybal and Badillo now wanted their own meeting with the president, to discuss making the CCOSS an advocate for all Spanish-speaking people, and not simply for the administration. Nixon had already anointed spokespeople for this group, however. The two elected officials who in effect represented the largest urban concentrations of ethnic Mexicans and Puerto Ricans in the United States waited months for a simple reply to their request for an audience.[6]

Nixon's actions only reinforced the lessons of the last decade, which had made plain that custody of the "Spanish-speaking concept" could not be entrusted to the executive or party officials, who routinely manipulated and demobilized it to suit their narrow needs and interests. Roybal and Badillo thus set out to organize an ostensibly nonpartisan alliance of the sort that Carlos Alvarez had called for two years earlier. In September 1971, they joined Senator Joseph Montoya and Representative Manuel Luján Jr., the New Mexico Republican, to announce that they would be convening a "National Spanish-Speaking Coalition Conference" the following month in the nation's capital. Declaring their conference theme to be "Unidos" (united), they aimed to weld the diverse sectors of Spanish-speaking America into a common force and mount a serious challenge to their collective political, social, and economic exclusion. "Our expectations over the last decade in terms of social justice have not materialized," the leaders announced.[7] "The continuous deterioration of conditions in which the Spanish-speaking live," Badillo told the *New York Times,* "and the apathy shown to their problems by governmental institutions make the calling of this conference imperative."[8]

The politicians wanted to create at least the impression that Spanish-speaking Americans were a national swing vote, a condition made more plausible by the Nixon administration's highly public courtship of Mexican Americans. Joined with Puerto Ricans, they could control one hundred electoral votes and hold the balance of power in presidential elections, agonizingly close in 1960 and 1968. Such a potent ethnic bloc would be in a position, Roybal believed, to obtain the sorts of "concessions and promises from national politicians" that had long eluded them and caused their people to suffer. The congressmen thus generalized the Republican critique of their status with Democrats to the entire political system. "We've been taken for granted by both parties for too long," Roybal fumed. They wanted autonomy and respect. They planned "to set up an organization with political muscle" and to create "a united political front." No longer content merely to turn out the vote for others, they planned to influence matters themselves with a "permanent coalition" organized "in every state," according to Badillo.[9]

Reflecting their own diverse sensibilities and loyalties, the congressmen intended an ascent to leadership of a national ethnic bloc, but were cautious about upending existing relationships in bringing about a more multicultural democracy. Roybal, for instance, claimed that the Unidos conference would be a means by which the elected officials would be recognized as the leaders of a national Spanish-speaking minority. "When we speak in the House," he told assembled reporters of the coalition-building effort, "we no longer will be speaking only for ourselves but for the whole Spanish-speaking community." While one *Los Angeles Times* reporter called the conference an effort to put "brown power" on the map, the ever-cautious Senator Montoya downplayed any racial or radical overtones: "We seek to utilize our location, numbers and access to American political institutions to bring America's attention to the previously ignored plight of our Hispano-American population."[10] And at its outset, Luján, the Republican, registered his concern about the conference's partisan potential, saying he preferred to see it develop "solutions for problems, not political strategy."[11]

The Nixon administration was divided in its response. Having spent months designing a "Spanish-speaking" outreach plan to cultivate Mexican Americans' loyalty, White House aide George Grassmuck argued that "our need is to cut the ground out from under this gathering and this group before these people can seize the initiative for the heavily Democrat Puerto Rican population in the northeast." Grassmuck's boss, Robert Finch, and CCOSS chairman Henry Ramirez recommended meeting with the congressmen before their conference, presumably to blunt their criticism of the administration.[12] White House political guru Charles Colson appears to have been less concerned. One of his subordinates informed him that the conference was an effort by "the Spanish-speaking types in the Congress" to "follow the Black Caucus' lead." Scribbled on the memo was a pungent reply: "The Hell they will! *They'll* never follow the lead of the blacks!"[13] Colson refused to sanction a meeting between the congressmen and the president. Instead, he proposed that Nixon convene the Cabinet Committee and invite the "Spanish surnamed members of Congress" to attend.[14] Other White House aides wanted all congressmen with sizeable Spanish-speaking constituencies included. This meant inviting conservative Republicans Barry

Goldwater and John Tower, as well as James Buckley, the Conservative Party senator from New York and brother of *National Review* editor William F. Buckley. This was plainly not the meeting that the liberal Democrats Roybal and Badillo requested. But by creating the Cabinet Committee, Roybal and his fellow congressmen had given the president the tools to safely ignore them. The onus was on the Democratic legislators to prove that they could be ignored no more.[15]

☆ ☆

The arrival of Friday, October 22, 1971, revealed an extraordinary number and range of individuals committed to exploring or otherwise influencing the process of Spanish-speaking political unification. While officials had originally imagined having "200 leaders" in attendance, the number of people who descended upon the Hospitality House Motor Inn, located in the Washington suburb of Arlington, Virginia, was probably closer to 1,200.[16] They were a geographically diverse assembly. Some made the trip from California, Texas, and New York, of course. But a vocal contingent from Chicago was joined by smaller groups from as far away as Utah and Washington. Some represented white-collar occupations and moderate organizations. University professors and social workers and federal employees came in from around the country. Leaders from the Puerto Rican Forum, the League of United Latin American Citizens (LULAC), and the American G.I. Forum (AGIF), as well as representatives from the Ford Foundation–supported Southwest Council of La Raza and the Midwest Council of La Raza attended. But leftists believed they, too, had a stake in "Spanish-speaking" politics. Chicano student activists and Puerto Rican independence advocates, including the Young Lords, showed up. So did José Angel Gutiérrez, the Mexican American Youth Organization activist and founder of La Raza Unida Party, the budding Chicano political party. He traveled with the radical land grant activist Reies López Tijerina, fresh out of prison and now under the same roof as Nixon's new CCOSS chairman, Henry Ramirez. Some locals simply came on a whim. Working in Washington, DC, as a lobbyist and organizer, Willie Vazquez recalls getting a phone call about the nearby event, hopping in the car and heading over. The scene struck the young Puerto Rican as unprecedented. "Remember," he said, all these Spanish people are in the nation's capital in extraordinarily large numbers. And these are not just your local community organizers. They were doctors and lawyers and professors and those guys that run all those cultural programs. . . . It was an incredible cross section of people. Had I ever seen that before? Hell no! . . . This was national and this was Spanish people and it was just incredible.[17]

José Angel Gutiérrez recalled arriving with Tijerina to a scene of excited turmoil. "It was chaos. The Puerto Ricans were yelling all over the damn place. . . . I walked into a crazy house. Everybody was yelling and screaming and jumping up."[18] The 160-room motel was bursting at the seams. An overwhelmed food service staff closed its kitchen, and the building's ventilation system proved no match for the cigarette smoke that came to enshroud the proceedings.[19]

For the planners, simply to have gotten Mexican-American and Puerto Rican leaders and activists to consider adopting a shared platform was a novel and creative accomplishment. The Johnson and Nixon administrations each mostly paid lip service to collective engagement with the moderates of the two communities, an approach that stemmed at least in part from a reluctance to ask Mexican Americans to share the presidential limelight with the numerically smaller Puerto Ricans. The task had been no easier when grassroots activists of leftist orientations were involved, however. Frank Espada, a Puerto Rican antipoverty activist who helped organize the event for Badillo and who chaired the political strategy panel, recalled that, "prior to that time, these groups were not talking to each other at all." The reason, he said: "nationalism." The New York Puerto Rican activists whom Espada knew were involved in or gravitating toward the island's independence movement, which had a strong socialist orientation. Chicano cultural nationalism, which tended to downplay internal class differences, did not resonate with them. Furthermore, the notion of "La Raza," with its emphasis on the Chicano's indigenous heritage, did not directly speak to many Puerto Ricans' conception of their community as one with a strong African heritage. José Angel Gutiérrez, the Chicano leader, recalls the problem as doubly complicated: "back in the 60s and 70s if you walked into a meeting of Mexicans you could derail the whole damn thing by asking, 'can someone tell me what a Chicano is?'" The issue was "the identity politics" of "who are we? Are we Latino, Hispanic, Chicano, are we Indo-Hispano?" But not only were Chicanos divided. As Gutiérrez saw it Puerto Ricans were "the same way," with a divide among independence activists, statehood supporters, and Commonwealth backers. "You've got to know who you're talking to," he remembers. "Otherwise you're spending another hour debating the merits of each one of those positions." Despite these obstacles, Espada knew a few Chicano leaders and had called to invite them to the conference anyway. "I simply said, 'why not? We have nothing to lose.'" And, as it turned out, "they were hot to trot."[20]

The conference environment and agenda reflected an effort to represent the diverse backgrounds and objectives of liberal Mexican-American and Puerto Rican participants, exposing all involved to a controlled degree of difference while maintaining the search for common ground. The planners had named some of the motel's conference rooms for nineteenth-century Puerto Rican independence heroes, and others to honor legendary explorers of the Southwest.[21] A southwesterner and a New Yorker would give the two keynote speeches. Two chairpersons—one representing Mexican Americans and the other Puerto Ricans, apparently—presided over each session, meetings devoted to topics the planners believed the two constituencies could care about: political strategy, job training, equal opportunity, unions, and education, along with housing and economic development. Neither immigration nor Puerto Rico's political status appear to have been official meeting items (though they would force themselves onto the agenda). If all went according to plan, conference participants would gather on Sunday morning to vote on resolutions that would be the basis of a coalition platform. And that afternoon they would establish an organizational structure and plan a strategy for their coalition. On Monday morning, the congressmen would tell the press of the many gains made over the weekend, and about how 1972 was going to be the year when the Spanish-speaking people became a real player in American politics.[22]

☆ ☆

Opening the conference and laying their claim to leadership, the congressmen set about instilling in their audiences a sense of shared purpose. In his initial remarks, Herman Badillo set out a modest overarching goal: "We are not here to resolve problems but to show that unity is possible . . .

to discuss and discover what unites us rather than what divides us."[23] Roybal was more ambitious, challenging the assembled to show "mutual respect for each other," to look beyond "past disagreements . . . differences in ideology, status or party affiliation," and to "end once and for all" the "envidias [jealousies]" that kept them from uniting. Far too long had they allowed themselves to be "drained politically and culturally," to be "overwhelmed" and left "weak and isolated." They needed more than "symbolic cultural solidarity." They needed political solidarity.[24]

But the cultural and the political were never so far apart. In order to build the *coalition* they wanted to lead, the congressmen and their allies spoke in ways that imagined Mexican Americans and Puerto Ricans on the mainland as already members of the same *community*. This necessitated a selective interpretation of the past and the present to succeed. It also rested upon the unspoken exclusion of Cubans, whose different experiences troubled the narrative of community belonging then under construction.

In the first keynote address, for example, Senator Joseph Montoya articulated his own conception of the conference participants' collective identity, a "peoplehood," the New Mexican said, which consisted of three elements: "Hispanos, Chicanos, and Boricuas." He told their story. "We are here as founders whose forebears settled America before the Pilgrims began their voyages," he opened, with "a better claim to recognition on the basis of prior occupancy" than all but "the Indian." He spoke delicately of conquest. Montoya mentioned the "Mexican War," after which "many of our people have lived as second-class citizens." The senator then referred to 1898, the year since which "others of them [Puerto Ricans] have led lives distinguished solely by economic exploitation and denial of equal opportunity." It seems that for Montoya the link between these complex and divergent histories was not colonialism, however. Such a critique would demand decolonization, expulsion of the *gringo,* and national liberation. Instead, he argued, it was exclusion from American civic institutions that held them together. His was a vision of pan-ethnic community forged in its quest to share equally in the economic benefits and the legal protections of US citizenship.[25]

Envisioning collective organization as the fulfillment of their common American citizenship and their overlapping ethnic histories, Montoya spoke against the potential for radical politics to captivate the group. In his vision, a secular code of upright conduct defined their collectivity. They were marked by their virtue, patience, and essential reasonableness. Other groups had "pounded upon portals of American life with gun butts and clenched fists," but Montoya called upon his people to "show our culture, heritage and maturity by calmly and collectively calling upon the American people for full justice." They had endured unspeakable violence at the hands of police and vigilantes, he acknowledged. Someone in the audience demanded "an eye for an eye," to wild applause. The senator mildly reiterated his call for maturity, moderation, and nonviolence.[26]

That his people's suffering was deplorable Montoya did not deny. He decried police brutality, bigoted judges, unrepresentative draft boards, devious employers, insensitive doctors, and indifferent teachers. He criticized condescension and stereotyping by advertising firms, and excoriated banks for refusing to lend to Spanish-speaking businesspeople. "Yet of all the second class treatment inflicted upon our communities," he claimed, "the worst has come from the national government itself." It was a "true national disgrace" that "we are qualified to die for America and be mentioned in holiday speeches, but not good enough to rise to the top by merit in our own government's civil service." Particularly shameful was the government's antidiscrimination apparatus, whose equal employment opportunity programs, under current leadership, were "usually shells and shams."[27] Against a backdrop of widespread poverty, the farmworker movement, Vietnam protests, deep distrust in the justice system, and dilapidated housing, that Montoya saw the Civil Service Commission as perhaps the greatest offender was revealing. It was an argument for middle-class inclusion as the best means to group progress, a liberal way of supporting the government while appearing to attack it.

It was essential to Montoya's vision that America's mistreatment of the Spanish-speaking people had been ugly, but that this ugliness was exceptional to the national character. Therefore, despite his stated disappointment in American government, he called upon the assembled to "retain faith in this country, its ideas and institutions." Their unification would purify American institutions, push the nation further "away from the old melting pot ideal" and toward an America defined by "diversity and cultural pluralism." "Within the institutional framework of this nation, we must create a new path," he argued. To secure their place in a revived America, the three branches of his imagined Spanish-speaking community—the

Hispano, Chicano, and Boricua—must unite and mobilize. "We shall, in unity, be free! Unidos!" he closed.[28]

Montoya drew respectful applause. One man began to shout "Unidos!" over and over again but failed to rally others. Soon enough, a woman rose to the microphone and denounced the speech as "a lot of empty rhetoric" and the conference as "just an enhancement for your political ambitions." Judging by the crowd's reaction, more than a few agreed. For many, the senator, with his high-pitched voice and clipped diction, seems to have epitomized the establishment politician out of touch with his constituents. Here was the antithesis of the hip and impassioned grassroots activists who reserved their support for more charismatic and forceful critics of the status quo.[29] As José Angel Gutiérrez reflected, the small group of elected officials were trying to build a national network, but without ceding power to the activists. "We were the tree shakers . . . they saw themselves as the apple catchers." They hoped "that we would raise the issues and cause the problems and the demonstrations . . . and they could negotiate for us. Well, that didn't fly."[30]

Someone called for Reies López Tijerina to take the microphone, hailing Montoya's bitter foe as "our leader." The land grant activist came to the stage amid great adulation. "All the time he wants!" screamed a supporter. For Tijerina, it was delicious revenge. "I bet he [Montoya] never imagined that his organizational work at uniting all the different groups at the nation's capital would be so that I would speak to them," he remembered. "Montoya was crushed, and I thought this was but a dream." Despite this triumphant memory, Tijerina's remarks were not a stirring call to the land grant struggle for which he was known, but a subdued protest accusing New Mexico police of drugging and raping his wife while he was imprisoned. The only reason he attended the conference, he said at the time, was to unburden himself of the crime they had committed against his family. No doubt to the officials' chagrin, several newspapers ran this story rather than provide coverage of the policy and strategy debates taking place in the meeting rooms.[31]

While Montoya's argument for a tripartite Hispanic community forged through the collective exercise of American citizenship left many attendees uninspired, the audience had far more praise for the conference's second major speechmaker, Joseph Monserrat. An old ally of Herman Badillo, Monserrat had been born in Bayamón, Puerto Rico. His family migrated to New York, and he grew up in East Harlem during the Great Depression. From 1950 to 1969, he directed the New York office of the Puerto Rican Department of Labor's Migration Division, the principal agency charged with ameliorating Puerto Ricans' conditions on the mainland.[32] And standing before the second day of the Unidos conference he was a revelation. His "Bronx Yiddish accent" conveying his passion, he struck all the right notes in a rollicking, unscripted half-hour sermon on the many cultural affinities of Mexican Americans and Puerto Ricans. Switching suddenly from shout to whisper, building from prose to song, he stirred the crowd.[33]

Monserrat was a unifier. He acknowledged that Mexican Americans and Puerto Ricans might perceive differences in their ranks, but claimed that any "heated discussions" occurred primarily "because we've never sat down this way before and talked in a large group," and because, as a people, "we've got a lot to say." Like Montoya, Monserrat endeavored to articulate a common historical narrative that would harmonize the stories of Puerto Ricans and Mexican Americans in the United States. Primacy of place was essential for Monserrat as well. He portrayed his people as predecessors of Anglo America, calling Ponce De León "the first Puerto Rican migrant." The crowd erupted with cheers and laughter when he explained their shared history of having preceded the Mayflower, "that very overcrowded little ship from whom everyone in America wants to be a descendent of." Had they known it would later be so important, "we would have been there to greet them not only with frijoles, we would have greeted them in Spanish."[34] In contrast to Montoya, proud descendent of Spanish explorers, the New Yorker Monserrat explicitly embraced their people's shared history of migration. Unlike previous immigrants, however, whom he described as having been swallowed up by Americanization, his people would amass the power to defend their language, their culture, and their community. They would break the tradition of a coercive melting pot. They would transform the shame that generations of immigrants had felt at being outsiders, redeeming their sacrifice and the nation at the same time through their pursuit of cultural and political autonomy.[35]

For Monserrat, racial thinking was a resource. Whereas Montoya avoided talk of racial difference, situating his imagined political community within a story of unfolding American citizenship, Monserrat cast his gaze beyond the nation's borders to embrace and redefine their collective racial position.

Mexican Americans and Puerto Ricans were participating in a "worldwide social revolution," he said, in which "the nonwhites of the world are saying we're tired of carrying the white man's burden and we're going to shift some of that burden over onto him." Their unification required rejecting "the whole crazy scheme around skin color" practiced in the United States. In a dramatic moment, he situated Puerto Ricans within the ethnoracially hybrid family central to Chicano peoplehood, and said that this "familia de la raza" was "beginning to unite itself, and united it is." At the same time, Monserrat incorporated ethnic Mexicans into a conception of raceless belonging that had long been a staple of racial discourse in Puerto Rico. "We, who are the integrated people of the country, because we are black and we are white and we're Mexicano and we are Indio" must not accept "the color values" of blacks or whites, he argued. To do so would "divide our own family in half," and lead the family to "begin to use terms we have never permitted ourselves to use." Denying that they had sought to benefit from the establishment or maintenance of America's color line, or that Mexico or Puerto Rico each had its own racial hierarchies, was a powerful act of forgetting. On the other hand, given the tendency of others to build "Spanish-speaking" solidarity out of anti-black sentiment, the argument represented a step toward ethnic inclusiveness and interracial cooperation. The Spanish-speaking people were a multiracial and therefore putatively nonracial family.[36]

In Monserrat's telling, they were a timeless group, extant prior to the American nation. And yet they were a new people poised to shower their gifts of enlightenment and tolerance upon the country, educating and enabling it to meet a new day in world history. What remained was just to recognize the latent truth of their connectedness and to convert their familial/ethnoracial bond into a political one. All they had to do was unite.[37]

To sustained shouts of approval, Monserrat concluded by leading the crowd in a version of "La Cucaracha," its lyrics reconfigured to commemorate the coming together of Chicanos and Boricuas. The crowd began to chant, "Unidos! Unidos! Unidos!" What had changed since Montoya's address? The Saturday planning sessions or the socializing that evening may have convinced the conference's diverse constituents to see each other and their presence there in a more positive light. Monserrat may have been a better speaker. No matter, there was good feeling heading into the conference's last hours.

Sen. Joseph M. Montoya, Rep. Edward Roybal, and Rep. Herman Badillo *(standing)* conferring during the Unidos Conference, October 1971. Courtesy of Universidad de Alcalá, Spain.

☆ ☆

Much was accomplished during the two days. Throughout the weekend, in a largely deliberative and democratic process, participants in the nascent coalition reached consensus on most principles and objectives set before them. The bulk of the panels had evinced "quiet, semi-scholarly discussion of social service issues," rooted in common needs.[38] Their committees presented more than 100 resolutions to the wider assembly, usually broad statements appealing to all, and the overwhelming majority of these were accepted. They called for an end to the Vietnam War. They demanded fair funding in antipoverty programs. They criticized all levels of government for failing to achieve "acceptable patterns of employment" for their people, and to enforce equal opportunity legislation in the private sector.[39] They insisted upon control of the educational process, open admission to universities, and the training of bilingual and bicultural teachers. They called for official recognition "that the language of our people is Spanish" and for HEW Title VII bilingual programs so that their people could "retain

a Spanish language identity."[40] Furthermore, they resolved to create lobbying and political action groups in Washington to spur government responses to these and other needs. In an important demonstration of common
ground on a volatile issue that affected Mexican Americans and Puerto
Ricans differently, they defeated a resolution supporting Roybal's efforts
to place sanctions on employers who hired undocumented workers.[41]

When differences born of national origin rivalry had emerged, democratic processes at times kept them in check, and the session still trained
on removing obstacles to unity. In the Federal Systems workshop, for instance, a vocal Puerto Rican contingent demanded that the conference focus
on correcting the "alleged imbalance in Federal employment and other benefits between Puerto Ricans and Mexican-Americans." The result appears
to have been a resolution in favor of a "fair share formula" so that government jobs and public resources allocated would "reflect the ethnic population
served," and that federal statistics be specific enough to ensure a reasonable
distribution of funds to both Mexican Americans and Puerto Ricans. And
when some Puerto Ricans disrupted the proceedings and demanded "a
separate Cabinet Committee for Puerto Ricans" and for the Senate to refuse to confirm Henry Ramirez, who had fired two Puerto Ricans as one
of his first acts in charge, a large number of Puerto Ricans worked to defeat the resolution, which went down 22–20.[42]

Puerto Rico's political status was a more difficult issue, however, one that
raised a number of logistical, strategic, and philosophical questions for the
nascent coalition. First, a vocal minority of the attendees adamantly rejected Herman Badillo as a leader. Frank Espada recalled the congressman
from the event's beginning being "booed down" by Puerto Rican *indepen-
dentistas* in the crowd, who considered him a "piti-yankee," a sellout to the
imperialists.[43] In addition, Puerto Rican independence activists challenged
Badillo's injunction that coalition meant to "discover what unites us rather
than what divides us," as well as those visions of community that blended
Chicanos and Boricuas into a single story of peoplehood.[44] This was clear
when during an open session, Gilberto Gerena Valentín, an ally early on
in Badillo's career, grabbed the microphone and set down a "militant"
marker. Along with an end to the fighting in Vietnam, for prison reform,
a cessation of police brutality, he called for, crucially, Puerto Rican independence. In his understanding of coalition, unity did not mean surrendering

each group's specific issues. The groups must be "juntos, pero no re-vueltos," he declared, that is "together but not scrambled."[45]

In the political strategy committee session, the meeting's most popular but "least genteel" panel,[46] some activists put forward resolutions asking the United Nations to take up the case of whether Puerto Rico constituted a colony. This raised a fundamental question: was the colonization of *a* Spanish-speaking people a common concern for *all* Spanish-speaking people in the United States? The conference planners took the position that the island's political status was for its residents alone to determine. This was hardly satisfactory for those in attendance who considered themselves Puerto Ricans, despite their residence on the mainland. "So we're second-class Puerto Ricans, and second-class Americans?" one woman asked. Another Puerto Rican argued that the conference was not the place for such a resolution, and urged political action in New York and Chicago instead. But for others, the coalition's stance on Puerto Rico was a defining test of the Spanish-speaking people as a common enterprise. Someone insisted that the audience had an ethnic obligation to align with Puerto Rican independence. "We want you to understand that they are part of the raza, although they are in the Caribbean," he said.[47] In by far the closest vote that the committee took, the resolution went to a recount and was finally defeated by two votes out of more than one hundred cast. Several minutes of applause mixed with uproar followed the vote, further straining the coalition.[48]

The question of whether Puerto Rico's status constituted a "Spanish-speaking" American's issue did not die there, however. By Sunday afternoon, with votes on the final resolutions pending, the departure of many participants for distant destinations altered the conference's political balance. Federal employees in attendance observed that radical voices, especially those of Puerto Ricans from the Northeast who were able to stay longer, came to dominate the proceedings.[49] It was then that the independence issue came before the floor again. Conference chairman Roybal tried to deny the motion for a United Nations inquiry into the island's status, but soon was overruled "by an enormous hand vote." An hour of "very tense debate" ensued, during which one of Roybal's own Los Angeles constituents spoke against him for holding up the motion. Roybal, the man who had dreamt of uniting the Spanish-speaking, was instead "creating a division among us that has not previously existed," said the constituent. Finally put to a vote, the motion passed. "A truly thunderous cheer" erupted. The Puerto Rican national anthem rang out in song.[50]

Gaining in sway as the hours went on, Puerto Ricans crucially shaped the distribution of power within the national Spanish-speaking political organization being formed, though in this case by working to restrict access to the coalition rather than by expanding its menu of issues. While delegates fought over the board's composition, a forceful group refused to admit Cubans at all. One participant recalled that "when the Cubans were mentioned as possible delegates, the Puerto Rican delegates rose up in arms," with the Young Lords and other youth activists threatening "to overcome and crowd out the Conference Chairman's control of the assembly."[51] "We're being racist against our own people," pleaded defenders of Cuban involvement, but they were "shouted down" by those claiming that, "they [the Cubans] don't share our problems."[52] The conference's eventual plan established a fifty-three-member committee with a carefully apportioned membership. Fifteen Chicanos and two Puerto Ricans would be selected from the Southwest, fifteen Puerto Ricans and two Chicanos from the Northeast, and eleven Mexican Americans and Puerto Ricans from the Midwest.[53] The remaining quota would be allocated among "other Latin American citizens."[54] In a tense atmosphere dedicated to unifying the Spanish-speaking peoples of the United States, no places were reserved for Cubans, who remained a Spanish-speaking people apart.

What seems to have been most disquieting to the congressmen who had brought them together, however, was that many who remained until Sunday seemed genuinely poised to reject Democrats and Republicans alike, that is to pursue the political independence that the conference advertised itself to be about. José Angel Gutiérrez's political party, La Raza Unida, had won control of two counties and had begun campaigning statewide in Texas. It was a clear alternative model for independent political action.[55] In the end, however, third-party advocates were forced to accept a compromise resolution promising to "study" the feasibility of such a move.[56] But even this proved too much for the leaders. Badillo and Roybal infuriated the crowd by asserting that they were not bound to endorse any resolution with which they disagreed. Shouts of "vende patria" or "traitor" convinced Roybal to bring the conference to an abrupt adjournment.[57]

From the perspective of the elected officials, the "pioneering coalition" predicted at the opening of the conference was much less than that by its end.[58] The politicians checked out of the hotel within minutes of the adjournment, and canceled their Monday press conference.[59] Newspapers reported that Roybal and Badillo "left the conference discouraged, even angry." Unity was "an idea whose time has not yet come," lamented the latter.[60]

☆ ☆

While engaged in a different project, the congressmen had learned several lessons that would have been familiar to Lyndon Johnson, Richard Nixon, or any national figure trying to harness "Spanish-speaking" politics. Roybal and Badillo had needed a large crowd to show other power brokers that they were to be respected and courted. But big events to bring the populations together required great expenditures of time and effort, and offered highly uncertain gains. As Democrats, they could hardly endorse calls for a third party. Puerto Rican independence was yet another political minefield. The mainstream politicians were also vulnerable to being outshone by more charismatic leaders like Reies Tijerina. They could not have enjoyed being ridiculed as self-interested hacks, and could not count on their supporters to defend them successfully against the radicals. "Unless the moderates stop being afraid of offending somebody," Badillo grumbled, "coalition will have to wait—another generation maybe."[61] Years later, Badillo would still blame "radical groups . . . the ones who shot members of Congress . . . who believed in Puerto Rican independence" for having "made it impossible to settle on realistic goals" during the two-day event.[62]

While attacked from the left, the congressmen did not avoid the scorn of traditionalists either. Congressman Henry B. González—who did not attend the conference—spoke out against its particularism. He said that "we should not pretend that the problems of the Spanish-surnamed are so unique that the program would not benefit all Americans." He expressed his fear that the organizers were isolating their constituents and making it difficult to find ways "to enlist majority support" for their goals.[63] Montoya faced a more complicated political terrain still. Radicals were deriding him as a do-nothing or enemy, yet he would be criticized for allowing them to attend his conference in the first place.[64] A Las Cruces woman called his attempt to be an ethnic leader "belittling." "Yes, you are Spanish-American," she wrote, "but heretofore you have been bigger than Spanish-American, Anglo. . . . You have represented *all* of us and that is why we vote for you." "Do not, I beg of you, at this late date become a Chicano."[65]

The dean of "Spanish-speaking" federal legislators, Montoya was to abjure further involvement in coalition activities, citing "restrictions upon the use of congressional offices and staffs for other than strictly congressional business." He directed activists' inquiries to Paul Sedillo, a leader in the United States Conference of Catholic Bishops and chairman of the Unidos conference's task force.[66]

Sedillo called for an interest-based organizing to avoid the conflicts that beset the October event. The goal was to identify "platforms . . . to support without having to get into any cultural differences between Puerto Ricans, Cubans and Mexican Americans," he said. They would continue to pursue the balance of power in national elections by limiting their leadership to those without party ties. "We have to form a block and not be traditional Democrats or traditional Republicans because they have given us a job every now and then," he said. Instead, he encouraged the coalition to pursue a class-based ethnic strategy. They should address themselves to the poor, for these were "the real experts on housing and unemployment." "Spanish-speaking" power could not be achieved "by continually supporting individuals who are going to address themselves only to the elite."[67]

Although Sedillo planned a follow-up conference in Washington at the end of April 1972 to "implement the policies of the entire Spanish-speaking people of the country," no record of it exists in the major US newspapers. Instead, the Mexican American Political Association, LULAC, and the AGIF held a "National Chicano Political Caucus," ostensibly including Puerto Ricans, in San José, California, during that last week in April. At that event, opponents of these "traditionalist" groups led a walkout in which they endorsed the La Raza Unida Party to organize nationwide. They supported a series of resolutions focusing on "all Chicano organizations working for the liberation of Chicanos." An independent electoral politics rooted in region and national origin, however complicated, continued to proceed more easily than Spanish-speaking politics.[68]

☆ ☆

Despite the politicians' discouragement and turn away from establishing an independent coalition invested in the grassroots—if such was ever a true goal of theirs—the Unidos conference still tapped into a growing interest in pan-Hispanic alliances, and encouraged organizing across the country. A Colombian in New York wrote Montoya of his excitement "that so many Hispanic people of all nationalities" had shown "enthusiasm" for a common goal, and offered to raise funds for the coalition.[69] A LULAC leader from El Paso praised "the principles of the conference, especially in uniting all of our forces . . . to eliminate the thorny problems that have plagued our ethnic group for so long."[70] A councilman from Pueblo, Colorado, reported that the event had "attracted attention from all levels of society in our state and community." He had arranged a tape of Montoya's speech to be played on the radio and was planning to hold a state follow-up conference the next month.[71] Vilma Martínez, who later became general counsel of the Mexican American Legal Defense and Educational Fund, congratulated Roybal "for having conducted the first meeting" of its kind. She argued that "without unity we will undoubtedly remain on the bottom of the totem pole, even if 100% of us were to be educated."[72] The cooperation shown in the conference suggested a business opportunity as well. A New York–based educational publisher found it "beautiful to have the opportunity of meeting our Chicano brothers" and requested a conference mailing list so that she could send catalogs to the bilingual educators in attendance. Puerto Rican teachers from the area had met "to discuss the results and future" of the coalition. They had been angry about "the involvement and disruptions of political groups" at the event, and were concerned that the "continuance of this National organization" might be in jeopardy.[73]

Even those frustrated by the fractiousness they observed in October could argue that moderate voices had to take charge because, for better or worse, the groups were stuck with each other. One Unidos participant had learned "that the Hispano-Chicano elements of the Southwest, Northwest and Mid-West" had better "sharpen up their political acumen" and learn "to compete against the sharper and keener political minds of the Puerto Ricans, Cubans and other Latin Americans, who have been oppressed peoples and have lived in controversy most of their lives." He urged an end to "the easygoing methods and 'hasta mañana' ways of the Hispano-Chicano," and called on them "to study, learn and associate more with other ethnic minority members who compose 'LA RAZA COSMICA, LATINA U BRONCE.'" If the Hispano-Chicano subgroup did not "compete against them to make a better and more unified plan to win the many battles ahead," none would "obtain an equal share of our goals" or receive "our civil and human rights guaranteed under the constitution and Laws of the United States of America."[74]

Others inspired by the Unidos conference viewed "Spanish-speaking" politics not as a productive competition among regions and ethnicities but the transcendence of their differences. This perspective had strong appeal in the Midwest, home to large but not overwhelming populations of Mexican Americans and Puerto Ricans. Indeed, one participant remarked that "the Chicano and Boricua of the Midwest displayed a stronger unity than any other region" at the conference. "The Midwest, without a doubt, will be the laboratory for the 'Unidad' between the Mexican-Americans and the Puerto Ricans," he predicted.[75] Chicago activist Samuel Gonzales similarly argued that "the key to a strong coalition of Latinos across this nation lies in the Midwest, where large communities of Chicanos and Boricuas live and struggle for common concerns." He was impatient, and angry at the congressmen's apparent abdication of leadership. Midwesterners, lacking a "national level" representative of their own, needed the officials' help to continue advancing the coalition project.[76]

Unlike those who viewed national origin as a building block in a panethnic coalition, Gonzales saw it as a transitory phase and called upon all his people to embrace a new primary identity. He argued that "acting alone as Chicanos, Boricuas, etc., we can never make it as a political power," and urged them to *Unite* and *Act* as *One People* and support each other nationwide, as well as on a state and local level." The process was simple: "We strengthen the unity between us, first. Then we rid ourselves of the detrimental practice of separatism thru national identity (like Chicano, Boricua, etc.; which the astute Anglo will try to use to split us), and instead, embrace the universality of La Gente Latina." Regardless of nationality or region, their common connection was their suffering in the United States. In Gonzales's vision, it would propel them forward: "We all feel the painful flames of oppression into which we have all been cast by the Anglo society. But what they (Anglos) do not [know] is that those same flames have welded our people together in an unbreakable bond of unyielding determination to see all our people *free* of social discrimination and all that it entails."[77]

The event also resonated strongly among federal employees, one of its major audiences. After all, these civil servants had much in common heading into the weekend. Regardless of region or nationality, they had the same employer. They operated within roughly the same pay grades, they encountered the same affirmative action programs not designed to include them, and they most often did so in the same city, Washington. As the conference neared, Roybal explicitly linked the cause of Spanish-speaking unity to the fight for the group's incorporation in the civil service. In fact, the day before the conference, Roybal had joined LULAC and the AGIF of California in suing the federal government for discrimination. Only 2.9 percent of federal workers had a Spanish surname, compared to 7 percent of the country's population. It was evidence, they argued, that the Civil Service Commission and a number of federal agencies were violating civil rights law.[78] Roybal angrily accused federal officials of acting "immorally and illegally" maintaining an American "caste system," and rendering "the ideal of equal employment" simply "another American myth."[79]

Employees of the Office of Economic Opportunity (OEO) were particularly disposed to the conference planners' message that unity was the means by which they could at last enjoy the fruits of Americanism. Most were based in the Washington, DC, headquarters, but others came from offices in Denver, Dallas, Chicago, New York, and San Francisco. They were Mexican Americans, Puerto Ricans, and Cuban Americans. With few exceptions, the event gave them tremendous hope. "History was made at this past weekend," wrote one OEO worker. "Never before had 2,000 Spanish-Speaking ethnically diverse individuals of the 'Latino' communities across the nation met to discuss differing problematic issues and at the same time strive for common goals," he enthusiastically reported.[80] Another OEO staffer remarked that, while the conference's resolutions were important, "the simple fact that two thousand people, separated ideologically and ethnically came together for a common goal, which was unity, and attained it, marks that occasion as a success."[81] A field representative based in Minnesota believed he had witnessed "a major turning point" and "one of the most historic moments of the Spanish-speaking community, and our society as a whole." He was thrilled to have been part of a "union" that he felt "was not motivated by dissent, hate or anti-American feeling" but one "full of hope and a desire to make the dream of America a reality to everyone."[82]

Indeed, the weekend was personally transformative and professionally rejuvenating, reminding many why they had gone to work for the government in the first place. One federal worker expressed his great thanks for being allowed to attend, since he had "achieved a better understanding of my fellow 'Latino brothers' of all ethnic groups."[83] Another reflected that "it was indeed a momentous occasion for me to observe and participate in a bipartisan effort to unite" all of the groups. She celebrated "the growth process that is occurring in our people," their ability to "come together to express frustrations, injustices, needs and problems . . . to develop goals, set priorities, establish measurable objectives, evaluative processes . . . united in a common cause which transcends factions, geography, etc." For her, it "was no more and no less than the OEO philosophy as I see it."[84] Considering that this was not necessarily a day off, but a weekend spent in a smoky and hot motel, such words take on added significance.

These government workers were self-aware agents of group uplift, which they hoped to achieve via their people's incorporation in American institutions. They were beginning to organize themselves to promote their interests and gradualist politics. One public employee in Denver had listened to tapes of the conference, and agreed with Senator Montoya that "there has been too much militancy, and organized civil delinquency." (Indeed, most federal workers who mentioned the conference's overt expressions of nationalism did so disapprovingly.) He declared his support for Montoya's "kind of leadership," and said that a similar philosophy had "produced a large Union in 'IMAGE' *Incorporated Mexican American Government Employees.*" IMAGE was then uniting Mexican-American public employees throughout the West. Soon it would expand east and change its name to accommodate the sensibilities of Puerto Ricans and other Spanish-speaking Americans in the federal civil service. In line with the conference's animating spirit, they would argue as one people in the federal battle for affirmative action.[85]

☆ ☆

As the above statements indicate, the failure of Edward Roybal and Herman Badillo to consolidate an independent Spanish-speaking political coalition at the Unidos conference did not mark the end of a left-liberal pan-Hispanic politics. Rather, the coalition logic, policy orientation, and the relationships forged in the Unidos conference would continue to integrate the nation's diverse Latino political communities within the Democratic Party.

An important stimulus to this process of ethnopolitical coalescence was the McGovern–Fraser reforms. Changes to party rules initiated after the

Democrats' catastrophic 1968 convention in Chicago, the reforms aimed to open the doors to people traditional party organizations had long marginalized, if not actively excluded. To these advocates of a "New Politics," the old party machines and structures were undemocratic and unprincipled. They reeked of cronyism and were polluted by bigotries of all types. The path forward, the reformers held, meant incorporating women, the young, and minorities, and giving them greater visibility in party functions. In 1972, the most visible of party functions was the Democratic National Convention. When it came to selecting delegations, the reforms compelled state parties to take "affirmative steps to encourage . . . representation" of these constituencies "in reasonable relationship" to their percentage of the state population.[86] As implemented for the party's 1972 national convention in Miami, proportional representation rules greatly altered the makeup of state delegations. These became far less white, less male, less straight, and, with fewer unionists, a sign of the party's postindustrial future.

The party's self-reconstruction meant that more Spanish-speaking Democrats than ever had a voice in the 1972 convention. California's 1972 delegation was 17 percent Mexican American. The percentage of Puerto Ricans in New York State's delegation had tripled (to six) since the last convention.[87] Texas sent twenty-seven Mexican-American delegates and alternates in 1972.[88] In comparison, the number of Spanish-speaking delegates to the Republican convention was extraordinarily small. The Republican delegations from New York, Texas, and New Mexico each counted a solitary "Spanish-surnamed" member.[89]

The Democratic National Committee channeled its inclusive delegate roster into pan-Hispanic organization. In advance of the convention, a newly created Office of the Spanish Speaking summoned all "delegates of Mexican, Puerto Rican, and other Spanish heritage" to assemble as a single caucus. When the convention opened, reporters observed the Spanish-speaking contingent as a vital element in a new type of convention, one marked by "the emergence of proud and vocal clusters of people bound together less by geographical or even ideological interests than by a sense of common identity and shared grievances." The party had invited the Latino delegates to draft their own "separate, detailed Raza Platform" to submit to candidates. All told, "some 150 [Latino] delegates packed tightly into a small room" of Miami's Deauville Hotel, in order to set a national agenda for their people.[90]

This process of negotiating for influence within the party was inseparable from the ongoing redefinition of the Latino community. The delegates had—as in many past gatherings—begun by disputing the name of
their collective enterprise. Yet they rather quickly moved beyond this question, with growing levels of familiarity among activists and newly formalized mechanisms for their political participation no doubt playing a role.
Even the naming dispute signaled a certain ideological convergence around
a left-liberal identifier. Both of the terms reportedly debated ("Latino" or
"La Raza") attested to their people's Western Hemispheric origins. This
was a far cry from the traditional practice of valuing pure European descent so commonly associated with "Hispano" or "Spanish-American" elites,
and less calculated to appeal to a more conservative ethnic sensibility than
other labels such as "Spanish-speaking."[91] The term "La Raza" further reflected a Chicano racial orientation, in which *mestizaje*, the mixing of indigenous and European blood, played a central role. Neither identity, in
other words, was for the highborn.

Accepting the moniker "Latino" in Miami, the Democratic delegates
nonetheless delimited their constituency further, and in ways that borrowed
from the logic of the Unidos conference. The new "Latino Caucus" delivered its agenda in the name of the "Boricua-Chicano community." This fusion of two labels associated with Puerto Ricans and a younger generation
of Mexican Americans, respectively, implied a fundamental equality of the
two groups. At the same time, like the Unidos conference, it pointedly excluded the Cubans whose influence was becoming unmistakable in the
Miami that lay just outside their hotel windows, but whose typically more
conservative political sensibilities set them at odds with those activists then
defining the Democratic version of *Latinidad*.[92]

The Democratic platform reflected much of these activists' vision and
enfolded the constituency in the national party's support for a blend of cultural difference and social justice. It celebrated the "Spanish-speaking" as
one of "the racial, national, linguistic and religious groups which have contributed so much to the vitality and richness of our national life" and recognized their place within a larger culture that treasured "the magnificence
of the diversity" in the United States.[93]

This was not simply about recognizing ethnic difference in the abstract;
material gains were at stake. The platform reinforced their "right to be different" by promising to identify the Spanish-speaking as a separate group

in government statistics, an as-yet incomplete process but one deemed necessary for the group to be "assured their rights under federal programs." Both by supporting bilingual educational programs and by accommodating Spanish in its daily administration would the government nurture their linguistic difference and promote their economic advancement. The platform also addressed long-festering injustices that spoke to the group's twinned ethnic and working-class ambitions. It backed McGovern supporter Cesar Chavez and his United Farmworkers in "the struggle for unionization by the poorest of the poor in our country—America's migrant farm workers." It even referenced rights to land that were "due American Indians, and Americans of Spanish and Mexican descent," the great hope of Reies López Tijerina and his "Indo-Hispanic" land grant movement.[94]

Cubans were conspicuous for their location. Just as in the Unidos conference, the New Politics Democrats did not treat the most important Cuban issue—relations with the island—as a Spanish-speaking issue but rather within a wider call to remake US foreign policy. In October 1971, George McGovern had called for normalization of relations between the United States and Cuba, and had done so in Miami no less. Massachusetts senator Edward Kennedy, brother of the slain president who had sent Cuban exiles into battle and who had once pledged to return these soldiers' flag to a "free Havana," talked not only of establishing relations but about withdrawing from the US naval base at Guantanamo Bay.[95] Democrats' 1972 platform said that "the time has come to re-examine our relations with Cuba and to seek a way to resolve this cold war confrontation on mutually acceptable terms."[96]

Though the party's platform bore the distinctive imprint of the Mexican-American and Puerto Rican grassroots, the Latino Caucus wanted more. This much was clear a month after the convention, when Edward Roybal and Herman Badillo, having assumed the caucus's leadership, presented Democratic nominee George McGovern with the group's twenty-three demands for meaningful inclusion in the party, the campaign, and what they hoped would be the ensuing Democratic administration. Their first two points emphasized visible group representation, requesting that McGovern appoint "top level Latino campaign staff," and grant their group both a Cabinet post and a Supreme Court nomination. But the document also looked to the Democratic standard-bearer for assistance in drawing average Spanish-speaking people into America's democracy. It called for him to endorse political education and training programs, and to expand voter registration "machinery" to bring more to the polls. It even sought Mc-Govern's aid in the creation of a "Spanish-speaking lobby," which had been another objective of the Unidos conference.[97]

Yet the Latino Caucus devoted more space to ensuring that the candidate understood that labor and employment issues were, in effect, "Latino" issues. Labor-centric ethnic demands proposed to aid blue-collar workers by calling for McGovern to support farmworker unionization and the lettuce boycott, bilingual job training programs, and better access to union membership. For the middle classes, and those on whose behalf these individuals would work as civil servants, the Latino Caucus demanded "parity" for Spanish-speaking Americans in the relatively comfortable offices of the federal bureaucracy. This was an agenda to bring all Latinos into a more central position in national economic life, not simply to confer cultural prominence.[98]

George McGovern's Spanish-language flyers portrayed him as the heir to the legacies of John and Robert Kennedy.[99] Now, he confronted the ultimatum of the political community that the Kennedy brothers had, in concert with Mexican-American and Puerto Rican leaders, helped summon into existence. As that constituency grew in numbers and self-awareness, patronage and policy demands that John F. Kennedy would have laughed at were becoming an accepted feature of the Democratic Party landscape. McGovern responded with a six-page letter assenting to virtually the entire Latino Caucus platform.[100]

Organizing themselves into a single constituency did not erase nationality's significance to Latino Democrats any more than embracing the "Spanish-speaking concept" did for Republicans. But whereas Nixon's men would pay lip service to a singular "Spanish-speaking" constituency, while ignoring if not denigrating Puerto Ricans in their search for Mexican-American votes, the McGovern campaign—adopting the name "Unidos con McGovern/Shriver"—echoed the Unidos conference's structural organization as well. This national campaign recognized a single Latino electoral unit, one composed of ostensibly equal parts. McGovern's advisors deputized Texas native and educator Luis Velazquez as its "National Chicano Coordinator." The campaign's "National Boricua Coordinator" was a US Commission on Civil Rights staff member named Gabriel Guerra Mondragón. And the man overseeing their efforts was the new director of the Democratic National Committee's (DNC) Office of the Spanish Speaking, an Oakland attorney named Richard Beserra.[101]

Establishing a representative structure within the campaign was a pre-lude to defining authentic Latino political representation in other spheres. The DNC's Latino campaign publication, "Mano en Mano" (Hand in Hand), denounced Nixon's attempt to create a cohort of upwardly mobile Spanish-speaking appointees. The administration "paraded out the few La-tinos who were appointed to the fat salary, low-power positions," expecting this to serve as "appeasement" for years of policy neglect.[102] To any Latino Democrats who might be drawn in by this transparent tokenism, Beserra asked them to consider what "political power" really consisted of: "Is it being appointed to a position by someone who can 'unappoint' you as soon as the election is over and you've served his political needs? Or is it being elected to office and having a vote in policy making matters and programs that affect your community?" The point, then illustrated in a large chart with names like Montoya, Roybal, and Badillo, was supposed to be clear: "The Democratic Party *ELECTS* Spanish Speaking Officials."[103]

The superiority of elected leadership in connecting the broader "com-munity" to power was fundamentally connected to the Latino citizen's re-sponsibility to aid those community members in the greatest need. As Democrats imagined it, ethnic solidarity required that voters and the leaders they chose stood with the poor of their own group. The *Wall Street Journal* had asked Henry B. González and Edward Roybal in April 1972 to com-ment on Nixon's Spanish-speaking outreach. The two congressmen instead pointed out Nixon's de facto opposition to the United Farmworkers' organ-izing campaigns. It was rank hypocrisy, they argued, for Nixon to be with "one hand wooing the Mexican-American and Puerto Rican voters, and with the other using every means at its command to smash the only effec-tive hope for the poorest among them." The AFL-CIO agreed, calling Nixon's middle-class program "an attempt to convince Mexican-Americans that an administration which has consistently turned a deaf ear to the problems of the poor really cares about the Chicano."[104] Seeking the Mex-ican American Political Association's endorsement, a McGovern surrogate similarly argued that Republicans "have no understanding of people that are powerless," and that such facts required the political group's support for the Democrat.[105] McGovern's Chicano campaign coordinator, Luis Velazquez, likewise took aim at Romana Bañuelos. The Treasurer of the United States, she was urged by Nixon's campaign team not to mention the word "discrimination," and to stick to handing out signed one-dollar bills to gleeful audiences. "Can autographing dollar bills feed one empty stomach?" Velazquez pleaded in the pages of "Mano en Mano."[106]

McGovern's strategists did not expect a massive turnout of impoverished Latinos, however. Rather, the Democrats' invocation of solidarity with workers and the poor was by September 1972 aimed at much the same voter segment that Nixon would pursue with his middle-class appeal. It was the "older Chicanos and Boricuas who have been involved in past elections," the "more middle class Latinos," the challengers needed to persuade. These voters, they hoped, might still be convinced "to remain in the Democratic camp" and throw their support behind the national ticket.[107] This middle-class strategy, then, relied upon fastening that group to those beneath them in communities like the ones from which they themselves had emerged.

When November arrived, however, not only was McGovern soundly defeated but Nixon gained notably among Mexican Americans, prompting Latino Democrats to assess what a multicultural Democratic Party could do to secure Latino loyalty. Leader of the party's Office of the Spanish-Speaking, Richard Beserra interpreted the results as "telling the Democratic Party to shape up, showing it that we want more than tokenism."[108]

His campaign postmortem coupled skepticism that Latino politics could be directed on a nationwide scale with a firm belief that Latino unity was the overarching objective needed to animate the group's members to achieve political power. Casting doubt upon the concept of a top-down, national Spanish-speaking campaign, Beserra argued for a "national decentralization program." This meant carving out distinct Latino political territories in the East, Midwest, and Southwest, and empowering local communities in those places to define Latino politics. Even as they organized locally, he argued, Democrats could use the dream of Latino solidarity to attract voters who otherwise lacked strong party loyalties. And a renewed effort to "stress unity amongst Spanish Speaking" Americans might bring about his goal of "a highly visible and well-coordinated body of Latinos throughout the United States," one integrated in the party "as a unified body that is politically sophisticated." Thus even while devolving authority to local communities and dividing the Latino electorate into geographically (and thus often ethnically) distinct units, the Democrats would not surrender the animating hope that a united Latino voting bloc was possible. Indeed, it was becoming the glue that bound the constituency as much as any strong sense of community.[109]

☆ ☆

To obtain power and independence in the US political system, Mexican-American and Puerto Rican congressmen had tried to create something new. A liberal "Spanish-speaking coalition" that could advance a democratically derived policy agenda and establish a robust and durable electoral coalition to extract commitments from both major parties was an ambitious objective. The congressmen's project was at its core a community-building endeavor. Like all such efforts, it necessitated a selective interpretation of the past and the present to succeed. It required people to reconsider, transform, or shed deeply held personal beliefs. And given the variety of understandings of unity that participants brought to the discussion, the process would certainly take more than a weekend.

The Unidos conference was a turning point in several respects, however. Not only did most of its output confirm Edward Roybal and Herman Badillo's vision of Latino politics as a coalition bonded by culture and the search for *common* objectives, not a coalition built on reciprocity (e.g., Chicano support for Puerto Rican independence and the latter's support for, as an example, the land grant movement), but it furthered a vision of political *Latinidad* in which Mexican Americans and Puerto Ricans existed as equal *peoples* and members of a national community, or in some cases a family, a relationship forged through the exclusion of Cubans. It also sharpened the sense among mainstream Latino political leaders that "Spanish-speaking" political deliberations could not be so public, lest radical activists challenge the elected officials' agenda and authority.

Though this ostensible movement for Spanish-speaking political independence faltered, many of the personal relationships, policy visions, and power-sharing ideas of the Unidos conference would help transform the Democratic Party in 1972. As the Democratic congressmen advanced the party's multicultural reconfiguration, they still worked to infuse its official diversity with a strongly inclusive economic agenda that resonated with both their urban, New Deal roots, and the ambitions of a growing Latino bureaucratic class. Their attempt to pull the Latino constituency to the left coincided with President Nixon's landslide reelection, in which the administration would fuse ethic and class agendas in a different alignment to secure Republicans' largest-ever percentage of the "Spanish-speaking Vote."

# The "Brown Mafia" and Middle-Class Spanish-Speaking Politics in 1972

Richard Nixon deemed his prejudices thoroughly justified. A trove of lessons accumulated in his youth and over his decades in public life, time spent reading, meeting with dignitaries in foreign lands, they all led him to believe that the globe was divided into several racial civilizations, each at a different stage of development. Now, though, presiding over a country whose history of colonization, enslavement, and immigration had made it a home for myriad representatives of these supposedly unequal civilizations, this worldview posed acute challenges for the man in the White House. In a country formally committed to the idea of equal opportunity for all, what to do about Americans who the president and many others still believed belonged to inferior races?

During the homestretch of the 1972 campaign, Nixon held forth on the matter. His audience, gathered in the Oval Office, was an American Dental Association delegation. "There's always a question these days saying environment is everything," the president told the dentists. "Now we're beginning to find that inheritance makes a great deal of difference." Searching for validation of his hypothesis, Nixon then asked if African Americans made good dentists, and about Howard University's dental program in particular. His guests seemed uncomfortable at the question. Still, they informed the president that Howard, the Washington institution that had been training black professionals for a century, did not in fact turn out many top-flight dentists. A parallel question about Mexicans elicited a similar response. The president felt that Cubans must be different, but let the matter go. In any event, he said, leading a nation that clamored for equality in everything was a real challenge when some groups were just not up to standard. But what was a president to do?

Do you tell the Brown and the Black that he's destined to [fail]? No, you don't tell him that. . . . I have a different theory about this. My view is sort of a combination of genetics and environment. What is the oldest civilization? The oriental? What is the next oldest? Well, it sure ain't the blacks. It's probably the whites, but we aren't very old. Western Europe? We were still eating each other, you know, and they had a great civilization in China and Japan. Then, the blacks. My God, they're very close to the savage business. You see? When we talk about these things . . . if we just give them enough education and the same opportunity, that all of a sudden they are going to be equal? It's not going to happen.

Instead, he declared, "What's going to happen is over a period of time, they may develop the potential but it's going to take, we're not talking in terms of 5 years or 10 years or 25 years. We're talking here in terms of hundreds of years."[1]

However warranted Nixon believed his racial verdicts to be, he recognized the harm in broadcasting them too widely. As he had explained to his domestic policy advisor, Daniel Patrick Moynihan, in the autumn of 1971,

My theory is that the responsibility of a president, in my present position, first is to know these things. . . . But also, my theory is, that I must do everything that I possibly can to deny them. . . . I'm putting it out all over this place that we have got to proceed on the assumption, not that everybody is equal, but that everybody should have an equal opportunity, and that anybody *might* go to the top.

The president believed that every benighted civilization inevitably produced a few talented individuals who could hold their own with anyone regardless of race. The Irishman Edmund Burke and the black football star Gayle Sayers he sometimes cited as examples. Edward Brooke, US senator from Massachusetts and an African American, was for Nixon another such "exception."[2]

The "exceptions" chosen and made by Nixon would loom large in the 1972 campaign to incorporate the "Spanish-speaking vote" in the president's "New Majority." For an administration intent on redefining the Spanish-speaking people as a nationwide middle-class constituency, the White House's Mexican-American appointees, migrant-workers turned professionals among them, were key electorate-makers. They hailed the president's emphasis on individual social mobility, entrepreneurialism, professional networking, and white-collar affirmative action as the solutions for the social inequality of the Spanish-speaking American. Their stories of success and association with the presidency intended to demonstrate that Nixon honored cultural difference as an important dimension of American life, yet still showed that an ethos of competitive individualism remained at the core of the nation's identity. Moreover, and in important contrast with what would follow from the GOP, the administration appeared to back this symbolic inclusion by making the central government the engine of their incorporation. Federal support flowed in the form of jobs to individuals and aid to community organizations and programs that were willing to play ball with the White House. However, while rhetorically invested in a nationwide Spanish-speaking campaign driven by middle-class patronage and racial polarization, the White House cared little for the cause of Latino unity. Its short-term electoral objectives in the Southwest and its disdain for Puerto Rican voters reflected the now-customary presidential impulse to rank and segment Spanish-speaking America. The Republican campaign's enlistment of Cubans in the Watergate conspiracy and the ways in which that drama played out in Miami furthered heightened perceptions of national origin difference within what became in the early 1970s an institutionalized nationwide "Spanish-speaking" electorate.

☆ ☆

The White House's 1972 campaign for the Spanish-speaking vote took shape just a stone's throw from the White House, at 1701 Pennsylvania Avenue NW, in the offices of the Committee to Re-elect the President (CREEP). Under the leadership of Nixon's political counselor, Charles W. Colson, the CREEP grew quickly to nearly two-dozen staff members after being established in the spring of 1971. Consolidating control over the 1972 presidential campaign, the CREEP appropriated functions previously undertaken by the Republican National Committee (RNC). The RNC's programs for Mexican-American and Catholic outreach, for example, were cut drastically, absorbed into and subordinated to the president's reelection effort.[3]

By late 1971, Colson had learned enough to consider the "Spanish-speaking" as one of four "Interest Groups" (along with Labor, "Middle America," and the "Ethnic-Catholic" group) that the White House would make special efforts to target in 1972.[4] This constituency was, in his view, "fertile ground to be plowed hard."[5] A recent campaign poll of Mexican Americans in Orange and Los Angeles Counties hinted at the potential payoff. It showed that even though they trusted Democrats to "keep the country prosperous," a full 75.9 percent—a slightly greater percentage than among nominal whites and 20 percent more than among blacks—self-identified as members of "the silent majority." Their party allegiances were flexible as well. Overwhelmingly Democratic in registration, at least 30 percent indicated that they nevertheless voted for Republicans at least half of the time.[6] Colson called upon Domestic Council director John Ehrlichman to improve the administration's "identification" with these voters. And he wanted Ehrlichman to push "the Spanish-speaking press" and "the Spanish-speaking organizations with whom we have been developing contacts" to do more to help the administration.[7] As Mexican-American and Puerto Rican congressmen were planning the Unidos conference and aiming to prove that their people were a swing vote, the evidence that Colson and the Republicans had thus far assembled pointed in a similar direction.

But if Edward Roybal and Herman Badillo understood the "Spanish-speaking" as a potential liberal and urban bloc vote, Colson's crew imagined other values animating their politics. Imagination mattered greatly, because despite some initial polling, Republicans possessed few hard facts about this tantalizing electorate-in-formation. "We do not even have a very firm idea of their number or location," let alone a solid grasp of the characteristics required for a "firm statistical analysis," reads one campaign memorandum submitted to the president, likely in the fall of 1971. Republicans thus justified an aggressive pursuit of this voter group by a more ethnographic set of observations. One confidential memorandum spoke hopefully of tapping into this up-and-coming electorate's "unifying qualities," particularly the "innately conservative social outlook" that predisposed it to a right-of-center appeal.[8] "All Spanish-speaking Americans share certain characteristics—a strong family structure, deep ties to the Church, a generally hard-line position on the social issue," claimed another GOP analysis from December 1971.[9]

The entire group was further bound together by its shared "isolation" from the US mainstream. Because they had yet to be "dealt in" by government, the fall 1971 memo contended, the group "will take whatever they can get from whomever will give it." Improving upon Nixon's predecessors' record would be "relatively costless." Moreover, because African Americans had—at least by comparison—been brought into the system, a delicious opportunity to split the Democratic coalition presented itself. Republicans, the confidential memo recommended, "should exploit Spanish-speaking hostility to blacks by reminding Spanish groups of the Democrats' commitment to blacks at their expense."[10]

Campaign higher-ups who beheld the incipient Spanish-speaking constituency as a culturally conservative, racially homogeneous (and anti-black), cheap political date, nevertheless knew enough to take stock of its internal differences. Republican analysts made plain by December 1971 their view that "each group must be handled separately with specially-tailored appeals." Cuban Americans, for starters, were "upwardly mobile and avidly anti-Communist," and were the most likely to support Nixon. Though most Cubans were registered Democrats, Nixon had been cultivating a following among them through his longtime, loyal friend, Charles Gregory Rebozo. A Cuban-American real estate figure and Key Biscayne bank president who first met the future president in 1950, "Bebe" Rebozo had helped start a small "Cubans for Nixon" campaign in 1968. It traded on Nixon's staunch anti-Communist credentials; in 1967, its leader, Bay of Pigs veteran and Rebozo ally Edgardo Buttari, had called Nixon "our great hope for liberation and justice." While most Cubans in South Florida had not yet naturalized, yet alone registered, Nixon had made a modestly decent showing in 1968 among those who had sought the ballot. Thus appeared to Republicans "the first indication of the importance of this vote."[11]

President Nixon would direct federal patronage their way, but his greatest appeal to Cubans was in his presumed implacability in the face of Castro's Communism. Nixon had told staff at his first meeting on Latin America to "follow a very tough line on Cuba." He then had almost nothing public to say about Cuba in his first two years as president and made only a couple of mentions of the island in 1972.[12] But with Rebozo serving as an important link between the White House and Miami, and with the president's summer White House established on Key Biscayne, there was a sense of proximity and access that further reassured Miami's Cuban power brokers. Many were comfortable in vouching that even though the president would cross the globe to pursue détente with China and the Russians, he would never soften his stance on Cuba.[13]

In 1972, there were allegedly 80,000 registered Cuban-American voters in Miami's Dade County. The group was a "key swing vote" and essential to taking Florida, if the state's Republican Party chairman was to be believed. They remained mostly registered Democrats (Republicans supposedly lacked even an office in Dade County), but this allegedly owed more to convenience and habit than ideology or strong partisan loyalty. Moreover, their conservatism on foreign policy and law and order favored the GOP candidate. Suggesting their distance from the overall realm of "Spanish-speaking" politics, Miami's Cubans revived the "Cuban American Clubs for Nixon in '72," and were enlisting volunteers and carrying out the business of registration. Nixon analysts believed they needed a boost. Delivering the right amount of federal funds, while somehow circumventing the Democratic officials who ran Miami (possibly through the Cuban Refugee Program), Republicans could sunder the connections between Cuban-American voters and the Democrats. In June 1971, Edgardo Buttari, the former head of the 1968 Cuban Americans for Nixon effort and current Cabinet Committee on Opportunities for Spanish-Speaking People (CCOSS) advisory member, quietly assumed the number two position at the Cuban Refugee Program, a $25,000 a year title that he managed to keep shielded from the press, and even some program employees, for more than a year. According to news reports, he was both a budget aid and an "informal liaison with Cuban groups throughout the United States." Republicans looked to enlist another faction of Cuban supporters, led by another Cabinet Committee advisor, Manuel Giberga. Strategists expected him to use his position to "assure maximum political benefit" from the "federal activity" ongoing in the Miami area. Said to have "invaluable organizational lists and even a list of every Cuban voter in Miami," Giberga was also thought to be capable of "deliver[ing] his weight in money" to the Nixon campaign.[14]

In contrast to the striving and successful Cubans, Puerto Ricans, "the nation's most impoverished minority," were the Republicans' "least attractable" Spanish-speaking population.[15] Yet Nixon strategists did not at first view them as a lost cause. A sector of "upwardly mobile, educated young" Puerto Ricans who had assumed leadership in various public and quasi-public enterprises over the past decade of civil rights and governmental expansion looked promising. And those born on the mainland were, GOP strategists believed, turning against their traditional leaders, whom they regarded as "bought off" by urban machine politicians. As evidence of this trend, the group had in recent elections thrown increasing support to New York Republicans such as Governor Nelson Rockefeller and New York City mayor John V. Lindsay. Lindsay and Rockefeller were outspoken liberals, however, members of the party's "Eastern Establishment" that Nixon so detested. For the president, that Puerto Ricans gave these men their votes was hardly a mark in the group's favor. He communicated his doubts about their "New Majority" bona fides on his advisors' lengthy strategy memorandum. To the recommendation of setting up a Cabinet Committee office in New York City, the country's main Puerto Rican hub, Nixon, who surely understood the intention, replied simply: "why." In the margins just after the memo's section on Puerto Rican support for Rockefeller and Lindsay, he made his preference even clearer: "We shouldn't waste our time."[16]

Mexican Americans were much nearer to the president's heart, and his strategists knew it. Nixon's naming of a cadre of Mexican Americans, Californians all, to high-profile positions in the Spanish-speaking campaign's rollout in August 1971 had confirmed this group's centrality in his thinking. If the Spanish-speaking vote was important, Mexican Americans were a substantially larger segment of the population and "of pivotal importance" in more states than either Cubans or Puerto Ricans. The family orientation, religiosity, and social conservatism found in all "Spanish-speaking" people were "particularly" evident in this group as well. A "fertile target group" of Mexican-American Nixonites could be found among the "local community leaders, professionals and upwardly mobile lower-class Mexican-Americans." Not only did the Nixon campaign judge them to be more influential in their communities than prominent Mexican-American leaders such as Cesar Chavez, José Angel Gutiérrez, Reies Tijerina, or Corky Gonzales, but these local leaders could be, like the Cuban Americans, "influenced by programs, dollars, and jobs." Such inducements the administration could offer in spades. But beyond appealing to the pragmatic orientation of local leaders, the campaign expressed optimism at exploiting the group's "deep religious ties" to the Catholic Church. More than the other main Spanish-speaking constituencies, it seems, the administration could reach Mexican Americans through "active and persistent cultivation of church leaders," especially in the Southwest.[17]

Tensions inherent in making Mexican Americans the primary target of a national "Spanish-speaking" campaign were manifest almost from the get-go, however. First, the aggressive drive to reorganize the Cabinet Committee for electoral duty made it more difficult to balance the claims of Puerto Ricans and Cubans with those of Mexican Americans. Days after being named chairman, Henry Ramirez fired two Puerto Rican staff members. The jilted employees then publicly accused the CCOSS of pervasive discrimination against their people.[18] In response, Senators Jacob Javits of New York and Charles Percy of Illinois, both liberal Republicans, held up Ramirez's confirmation. The administration promised additional Puerto Rican representation in the Cabinet Committee staff, and named Ed Aponte, a New Yorker, as executive director. This failed to squelch the problem, however. In Ramirez's telling, Aponte insisted on controlling the CCOSS east of the Mississippi River, where Puerto Ricans were more likely to live. He also wanted the committee to develop programs for the island's population.[19] Ramirez resisted both demands, and soon announced that Aponte was out as executive director. His choice of Aponte's replacement again angered the senators. A Puerto Rican from California, Reynaldo Maduro was in their view ill-equipped to address the problems of Puerto Ricans from the East.[20] Going forward, the White House had to warn its surrogates that, "the most sensitive area of the entire Spanish-speaking picture is the resentment of Puerto Ricans against Mexican Americans." A briefing memorandum for Puerto Rican areas instructed them "not to mention Henry Ramirez," the Cabinet Committee, "any Mexican American, or any issue seen as wholly Mexican, such as bilingual education."[21]

Believing that national origin rivalries made a White House "Spanish-speaking" conference likely to "end in disorder," Nixon's staff set out to court the various communities in their home regions.[22] Nevertheless, the administration's liaisons stumbled in their unfamiliarity with local ethnic nuances. Ramirez, for instance, failed to take the measure of nationalist sentiment among the Cuban community of Miami. He apparently committed the cardinal sin of telling the exiles to focus on US politics and "to forget about the return to the homeland." According to Miami power broker Edgardo Buttari, "a Democrat properly instructed, would have caused less harm than he [Ramirez] did." Even Ramirez's choice of meeting place had been disastrous. He reportedly convened the gathering at a former "Mexican restaurant that went bankrupt precisely for being Mexican and located in . . . Little Havana." Buttari warned the administration to "avoid any handling" of Cuban affairs by "Mexican functionaries" such as Ramirez, since "the

Cubans feel greatly hurt by the Mexicans for their pro-Castrism [*sic*] and the persecution to which they have subjected the Cubans" since the Cuban Revolution.[23]

Chicago, where Mexican Americans and Puerto Ricans could both be found in sizable numbers, presented different problems. In October 1971, presidential counselor Robert Finch, Henry Ramirez, Office of Economic Opportunity (OEO) director Philip Sánchez, and Department of Health, Education, and Welfare staff traveled to the Windy City, promising to make sure federal jobs and dollars flowed to its Spanish-speaking communities.[24] The delegation was met with no shortage of anger and resentment, however. "Verbal assaults, punctuated at times by cursing and walkouts" characterized their meetings. According to one witness, "both Ramirez and Sánchez got roasted." The two served as "punching bags for" the disgruntled Chicagoans, who bitterly resented that federal jobs and programs for the Spanish-speaking all seemed to go elsewhere, especially to the Southwest. Puerto Ricans had an added grievance against what appeared to be Ramirez's attempt to purge them from the Cabinet Committee.[25]

Yet Finch remained sanguine about converting Spanish-speaking resentment into Republican gains. Those "two miserable damn days with that Cabinet on Spanish-speaking" left him with this impression of the city's Mexican-American and Puerto Rican voters: "I think they're up for grabs." "There are four-hundred thousand of them in Chicago alone," he marveled. Instead of being brought into Cook County politics as their population grew, they had been gerrymandered out of any influence. They were properly angry about it, too. "We've got a little something going there," Finch reported to Nixon. "You can get a big chunk of that vote." "You really think it is [so]?" asked the president. "It's not what we've done," Finch replied. "It's what the others haven't."[26]

Still, the White House's nascent Spanish-speaking program foundered. The president had pinned great hopes on Treasurer Romana Bañuelos, the quintessential American success story whose hard work and determination had allowed her to rise from nothing to a position of economic and community prominence, and now, thanks to Nixon's recognition, national prestige. However, within weeks of her nomination the press identified another ingredient in her ascent: undocumented immigrants. In October 1971, Immigration and Naturalization Service (INS) agents raided her Gardena, California factory, accompanied by a *Los Angeles Times* reporter. A sensational *Times* editorial told of "workers cower[ing] in lavatories and lockers, sprint[ing] across the yard to scale fences, scattering aprons and hats as they ran" from the authorities. All told, thirty-six of the plant's three hundred employees were held on suspected immigration violations. Some were deported that very evening. Suddenly, Bañuelos threatened to become the face of all the unscrupulous employers who exploited unauthorized immigrants at the average American's expense.[27] Indeed, her business practices continued to attract undesirable attention in 1972. An economic strike by Teamsters Local 630 begat a National Labor Relations Board (NLRB) complaint against Bañuelos's firm for bargaining in bad faith. The NLRB eventually found the company guilty of unfair labor practices (though not until after the election), determining that Bañuelos's son had threatened to call the immigration authorities on any undocumented strikers.[28]

These fiascoes only fed the administration's paranoid instincts. When the story of the raid broke, an irate Nixon demanded vengeance upon the *Los Angeles Times*. "I want this whole goddamn bunch gone after," he instructed his chief of staff, H. R. Haldeman. The enraged president called upon his secretary of the treasury, John Connally, to summon an IRS audit of *Times* publisher Otis Chandler's tax returns, and those of the entire Chandler family while they were at it. Of his attorney general, John Mitchell, he ordered that the INS chief responsible for the raids—"a kike by the name of Rosenberg," said the president—be transferred, and that a punitive immigration raid be made on the *Times*, as well as an investigation into whether Chandler's gardener was a "wetback."[29] The situation was undoubtedly more uncomfortable for Nixon since just a day after the INS hit Bañuelos's factory the *Washington Post* reported an untidy bit of presidential gossip. An undocumented immigrant gardener had been discovered working on Nixon's own San Clemente estate the year before.[30]

Greater discipline and coordination were needed. The CREEP set about putting in place a new Spanish-speaking campaign structure, and by March 1972 it had assembled the "White House Spanish Speaking Constituent Group Task Force." It was known to its members by a playful moniker: "The Brown Mafia."[31] Its self-described "Godfather" was the former teacher and current Cabinet Committee chairman, Henry Ramirez. Joining him was Antonio Rodríguez, a young San Antonio businessman and the former CCOSS executive director. A White House press staffer and former *Houston Chronicle* reporter named Carlos Conde took on media relations.

Managing their efforts was a veteran of several Republican congressional campaigns, the Chicago-born political consultant Alex Armendariz. All were Mexican Americans. Linking them to the CREEP was Colson's subordinate, William "Mo" Marumoto, a Japanese American who had himself been raised in a Mexican neighborhood in Santa Ana, California.[32] In Marumoto's estimation, the group (composed of "a southwesterner, a California educator, a journalist, a midwesterner and a non-Hispanic") possessed a sufficiently broad perspective to provide the best possible campaign advice. If the Brown Mafia's four Mexican Americans and one Japanese American constituted "good balance," as Marumoto claimed, it is further evidence that the CREEP's national campaign had a very specific core constituency.[33]

But if the "Spanish-speaking" task force was by all right a Mexican-American task force, it still found the "Spanish-speaking concept" handy. In claiming a place of prestige in the larger campaign, the Brown Mafia's ethnic experts set about defining the vast bloc and then dividing it into usable pieces. Submitted in the spring of 1972, the group's confidential "Plan to Capture the Spanish Speaking Vote" illustrates this analytical strategy. The plan describes this pan-ethnic population in singular terms, as "a community apart." It attributes to this people a singular racial identity and common aspiration for inclusion. The group was "most conscious of the fact that they are treated differently from other white populations," the campaigners argued, but "want[s] very much to belong." And thanks to Nixon's census intervention of 1969, the Brown Mafia drew upon newly available data to nationalize the Spanish-speaking electorate. The plan identified five crucial states (California, Texas, Illinois, New York, and New Jersey) and one less important state (New Mexico) where Spanish-speaking voters could tip 179 electoral votes and thus "easily determine the outcome of the election." Jockeying for prestige within the campaign, the Brown Mafia pointed out that the number of Spanish-speaking Americans eighteen years of age and over—and thus potential 1972 voters—was in most of these states far larger than another swing constituency the administration had its eye on, Americans who had in 1968 cast a presidential vote for Alabama governor George Wallace and his brand of racist, law and order populism. Of course, attainment of majority age did not alone confer the right to vote. But with the campaigners fighting for recognition and resources, this was not the time to point out such facts, even if Spanish-speaking Americans

Table 7.1. Nixon Campaign Poll of Major States in "The Plan to Capture
the Spanish Speaking Vote"

| State | "No. SS 18 and Over" | "Republican or Democrat Plurality" (1968) | "Wallace" (1968) |
|---|---|---|---|
| California | 2,107,895 | 223,346 (R) | 487,270 |
| Texas | 1,081,527 | 38,960 (D) | 584,269 |
| New York | 1,065,831 | 370,538 (D) | 358,860 |
| Florida | 296,632 | 210,010 (R) | 624,207 |
| New Mexico | 254,117 | 39,611 (R) | 25,737 |
| Illinois | 195,196 | 134,960 (R) | 390,958 |
| Arizona | 202,176 | 96,207 (R) | 46,573 |
| Colorado | 182,511 | 74,171 (R) | 60,813 |
| New Jersey | 244,922 | 61,261 (R) | 262,187 |

Source: Confidential Memorandum, "The Plan to Capture the Spanish Speaking
Vote," in Senate Select Committee, *Watergate and Related Activities, Book 19*
(Washington DC: US Government Printing Office, 1974), 8620.

in New Mexico were far more likely to be citizens, and thus possible voters,
than those in California or Florida. For the Brown Mafia, more worth mentioning was the Spanish-speaking campaign's efficiency. Almost 60 percent
of Spanish-speaking voters in those six states lived in forty-four counties,
making them comparatively easy to pursue.[34] Selling themselves and their
electorate, the Brown Mafia argued that Nixon's overall record on behalf
of the wider Spanish-speaking group was so impressive when compared to
that of previous presidents, that their young campaign could overcome
weakness on any given issue.[35] In sum, the Spanish-speaking were numerous, they were located in all the right places, and they were winnable.[36]

The Brown Mafia's portrait of a national electorate devoid of meaningful
phenotypic variation or citizenship distinctions coexisted with an admission that the "community" was "highly segmented." It was a truth that called
for focusing the campaign among the group's most politically profitable segments. For the Mexican Americans of the Brown Mafia, this meant putting Cuban Americans in their place. In their estimation, there were far
fewer "qualified Cuban voters" than Florida Republicans had previously asserted. Notwithstanding the Cubans' high rates of support for Nixon, they
were inessential to carrying even Florida, the only state in which they were

**Table 7.2.** Mexican-American and Puerto Rican Campaign Issues

| Spanish-speaking middle-class issues | Spanish-speaking urban poor issues |
| --- | --- |
| Economic development | Bilingual education |
| Bilingual education | Job training programs |
| Higher education | Unemployment |
| Job improvement programs | Discrimination |
| Senior citizen programs (noninstitutional) | Housing |
| Law and order | Police brutality |

*Source*: Confidential Memorandum, "The Plan to Capture the Spanish Speaking Vote," in Senate Select Committee, *Watergate and Related Activities, Book 19* (Washington DC: US Government Printing Office, 1974), 8622.

of any great consequence.[37] Having downplayed Cubans' potential to influence the election, the Brown Mafia set about explaining what drove the Mexican Americans and Puerto Ricans. It determined that for these groups, "income or class" divisions were more salient than nationality in determining their "main concerns." But again, lacking even "satisfactory polling information," the Brown Mafia was left to "speculate" as to the precise issues of importance (shown in the table above).[38]

Showing a sensitivity to the Spanish-speaking working class, and at least implicitly and at first more optimism about reaching out to Puerto Ricans than Nixon had, the Brown Mafia recommended get-out-the-vote activities for the group's middle-class sector, and for "all segments of the voter group" to be targeted in the wider "media and public relations aspect of the campaign."[39]

The Brown Mafia sought hard polling data to strengthen its powers of interpretation. As the summer of 1972 approached, the group commissioned a "top reputable political survey company" to ask hundreds of Spanish-speaking people in Los Angeles, San Antonio, Chicago, and New York City their views on the president, government, and several policy issues.[40] Almost 85 percent of the interviews were conducted in Spanish, despite census data indicating that a majority of "Spanish Origin" Americans were English dominant. If Spanish language ability was thought to define the Spanish-speaking American, the survey firm considered common nationality of interviewer and interviewee a prerequisite for valid results. Therefore, "Mexican Americans interviewed Mexican Americans and Puerto

Ricans interviewed Puerto Ricans."[41] On the other hand, the polling firm expected that respondents shared common racial orientations. It asked them leading questions about their "neighborhoods," and whether "blacks had been given too much advantage."[42] The results showed very low rates of support for the president, including 75 percent disapproval in New York, 70 percent disapproval in Chicago, and only 29 percent approval in Los Angeles.[43]

It is the Brown Mafia's reading of the data that stands out. What ecumenism existed in the spring of 1972 seems to have evaporated by the time the polling returned. Though Nixon was not much more popular in East Los Angeles than in East Harlem, the verdict on the latter was caustic. "A New York Puerto Rican does not look like a promising constituent for anybody," the analysis began. The New Yorkers provided responses that were often quite similar to those cited as given in the other cities. Yet the Brown Mafia singled them out as a people apathetic toward their lives and their government. The survey allegedly showed that Puerto Ricans were "undermotivated" and "easily self-divided." They did not care about education, desired money and gifts above all other goals, and were sustained in large part by the hope of winning the lottery. Even worse, "since some Puerto Ricans are black—and no one knows how many," Republicans could not employ two favorite polarizers—busing and the "black/brown issue"—with them. Calling a positive campaign in New York "hopeless," the Brown Mafia recommended a concentrated "effort to denigrate the opposition and keep the electorate home, leaving them with no candidate." They argued that "simple slogans" could prevent this "uneducated a political [*sic*] audience, addicted to media" from casting its ballots. Puerto Ricans prioritized ridding their community of narcotics and ending the war in Vietnam. The Brown Mafia proposed hitting Democratic presidential candidate George McGovern's record on drugs. They then offered variations on attacks, such as "McGovern, the rich man's candidate, McGovern, the college kids [*sic*] candidate." The latter two slogans suggested an awareness of New York Puerto Ricans' economic plight, even as the rest of the memo ignored the role of class in painting them as a culturally backward electoral wasteland.[44]

San Antonio, in contrast, was a model of the possible. Nearly one-half of the respondents there approved of Nixon. Just as encouraging, the analysts noted, the city was "surprisingly reflective" of the state's overall politics, conservative and trending Republican. Moreover, a healthy 40 percent of respondents were middle class. Having lamented the administration's inability to play the race card with Puerto Ricans, the Brown Mafia now cheered a similar circumstance with San Antonians. Race, it reported, was not a major issue among this "self-confident" group. In fact, the strategists had been caught off guard to find that the *neighborhood* question was taken literally," with a "surprising" number of respondents wanting the streets to be paved and a decent sewer system installed,[45] not someone to keep African Americans from moving in next door.[46] Even the popularity of La Raza Unida Party (RUP), the electoral standard bearers of Chicano nationalism, recommended additional resources be devoted to the Texas campaign. The RUP's existence illuminated two new electoral segments. First, there were the 62.3 percent of San Antonians who approved of the third party. If encouraged to vote for RUP, they would surely represent a net loss for Democrats. More important, however, were the nearly 20 percent of respondents who disapproved of the party. These conservative Mexican Americans were "a natural Republican target." The Brown Mafia suggested sending John Connally to reach out to them, transferring some of the Kennedy magic to Republicans in the process. "After all," the report concluded, "he was shot too in Dallas."[47]

Influential Republicans appear to have been won over by such analyses. Pressed by a skeptical campaign director, John Mitchell, Nixon's head pollster, Robert Teeter, cited the Brown Mafia's survey results in defending the "high potential" for gains among the "Spanish-American Bloc." Rather than casting doubt on the idea of a national "Spanish-speaking Vote," the diversity of opinion shown in the survey convinced Teeter "that the attitudes of Spanish-Americans toward the president are flexible." That flexibility combined with Nixon's "quite favorable" personality ratings to indicate that "a significant number" of these voters were "well on their way to completing" the "attitude change" required to ultimately switch their votes to the Republican in the White House. The party that had seen "Negro-Democratic mutual identification"[48] as a key to winning over white voters need not fear defections from their own ranks simply because the party was making "positive overtures" to this "minority." Teeter was "confident" that Republicans could enlist the "Spanish-American" group in Nixon's coalition "without alienating others who might otherwise vote for the President."[49]

With a sense that their stock within the party was rising, the Brown Mafia further endeavored to reshape the Spanish-speaking people's image for August's Republican National Convention in Miami. Turning back the clock on the 1960s, they rejected inclusion in the party's "minority plank." To be "lumped into a heterogeneous division called 'minorities'" was unacceptable, Armendariz explained to one of Chuck Colson's assistants. It particularly angered the middle class, whose pride of "culture and origin" led them to associate the concept of "minority" with that of "an inferior sub-class." At its heart, labeling them such raised the "real 'Black/Brown' issue." "The nation's second largest minority," simply put, "often resents the largest."[50]

The Brown Mafia prepared a statement to the platform committee that further repositioned their people within the party's conceptualization of difference. "They believe in God and in the family," read the proposed declaration of group values. "They know religion and family are strong weapons against drugs and crime." They were doggedly independent. "They would rather help themselves than ask for help. They look for work. They do not wait for work to look for them." Unlike those minorities from whom they were disassociating themselves, the Brown Mafia's statement implied, they were a people seeking "no special favors" in pursuit of a "fair share of the greatness of America."[51]

For the Brown Mafia, curating the Spanish-speaking electorate's image was a full-time job. It involved not only praising the group's values to the heavens but also policing any negative conceptions of its place in the nation. In July 1972, chief strategist Alex Armendariz attempted to suppress the publication of census reports that he feared suggested that the group was not making such rapid progress under Nixon. He informed Marumoto that *Our position is that any statistical data which show the Spanish-Speaking community lagging behind other elements of the population will be construed as the fault of the incumbent government* and that their publication "would amount to supplying the Democrats with more campaign material." Considering anything but "straight demographic material potentially damaging to our current objectives," he urged that the census findings be concealed "until after the election."[52]

Denying the unequal existence of Spanish-speaking America went hand in hand with denying its causes. The Brown Mafia instructed surrogates to "refrain" from pointing out "current problems," which were "always blamed on current administrations."[53] Romana Bañuelos in particular was something of a loose cannon. She had to be ordered to "avoid statements deploring 'discrimination.'" According to Armendariz, she was told instead to "shift emphasis" in her remarks to "the concept of 'opportunities'" and to Nixon's "record of achievements for the Spanish-speaking."[54]

As it constructed the Spanish-speaking electorate along Nixon's preferred lines, the Brown Mafia looked for outlets to spread its message. The operatives found an ally and beneficiary in Dr. Daniel T. Valdes. A Denver sociologist who had written his University of Colorado doctoral dissertation on the political behavior and voting patterns of "Americans with Spanish names," Valdes had spent several years in academia before taking an interest in ethnic publishing.[55] In search of financing for his own magazine dreams, he wrote to the Nixon administration, which seemed to have money to burn. The Brown Mafia saw in Valdes's proposed journal, *La Luz* (The Light), an excellent opportunity. It would be the first of its kind, a national "SS magazine" (Spanish-speaking) modeled on the "*Ebony-Life* format." In March 1972, the campaign helped get this promising publication off the ground.[56] With *La Luz* still in need of cash, Nixon operatives connected Valdes to national advertisers known to be friendly to Republicans.[57] The publisher soon agreed to print several positive articles on the administration's Spanish-speaking initiatives, including flattering profiles of its high-ranking appointees.[58] The Brown Mafia then went to work, designing covers and cranking out content for the fledgling magazine, which ran to more than seventy pages an issue.[59] Within a year, *La Luz* claimed a circulation of more than 115,000, and it would publish into the 1980s.[60]

The synergy between *La Luz*'s approach to ethnic marketing and the Nixon administration for capturing an electorate was striking. Valdes aimed the magazine at "the lower middle and middle classes and the emerging upper middle income Hispanos," the same population the administration was targeting. While Nixon considered himself a friend to the "forgotten minorities," the publisher was catering to an "underserved national ethnic group" of "twelve million highly ethnic Americans" hitherto "reading Anglo magazines only" and left "without a national magazine of their own."[61]

The safe version of Hispanic identity on display in *La Luz* was also consistent with the White House's effort to portray Spanish-speaking Americans as an emerging subset of the nation's diverse population, one possessed of mainstream values. Valdes, the publisher, wrote in the magazine of a "new consciousness" developing among the country's Mexican Americans, Cubans, Puerto Ricans, as well as its Central and South Americans. It could be seen in "the positive sense of self-development, self-determination, and self-control" that they were beginning to exert within America's politics, culture, and economy. The magazine elided the difference between national identity and pan-ethnicity to suggest that this "new consciousness" was a lot like "German pride, Irish pride, Italian pride," all of which had "propelled these groups into the full stream of American life." The Nixon administration preferred this kind of approach. Invoking a broad cultural solidarity led to discussions of family, religion, and tradition, where Republicans might compete—instead of nationalism, which raised questions about conquest, racial difference, and separatism.[62]

The magazine cast Hispanic identity both as a fundamental truth and a means of elevating the Spanish-speaking American's importance in the market and polity. For *La Luz*, nationalism was an obstacle to be overcome. Its pages took aim at the "restrictive political perspective" or the "restrictive, regional perspective," which defined the group's members by nationality. These failed to grasp how "the Hispano in America and throughout the world exists simultaneously" on both "political and cultural levels." Instead, it was the "cultural common denominator" that served as "a binding force which transcends all politics or nationalistic feelings." This sentiment had a sort of "mystical quality," known only to its possessors. *La Luz* did not dwell on many particulars, but defined this "Hispanidad—the essence of Hispanic culture" as a collection of "language, religion, values, [and] customs."[63] Despite the significance the publisher ascribed to language, the vast majority of the magazine was in English.

A recurring collection of leadership profiles, "Here Comes La Gente," was conceived to show that "despite the diversity of national, cultural, and racial types among our people, we all fuse into a single 'peoplehood,' an integrated entity, under the umbrella concept of 'La Raza.'" Its subjects varied, and defied easy political classification. The inaugural issue profiled Mexican-American journalist Ruben Salazar, who had been killed by police in 1970 while reporting on Chicano antiwar protests in Los Angeles. It spotlighted Mexican muralist Diego Rivera, Colorado priest Joseph Lara, and Casimiro Barela, an influential Spanish-American politician during Colorado's first decades of statehood. The mini-biographies of Hispanic luminaries, collected in one place, taught a larger lesson to the Americans of Spanish origin: to see themselves as "a microcosm of the vast Hispanic world in all its complexity."[64]

The magazine encouraged readers to see the Nixon administration's advocates for "La Raza" in this tradition. Readers who learned a thing or two about golfer Lee Trevino, or Diego Rivera, or a nineteenth-century statesman, could turn the page and read about Henry Ramirez and his Cabinet Committee on Opportunities for Spanish-Speaking People. Large photos of Nixon and Ramirez appeared alongside quotes conveying the administration's concern for the Spanish-speaking in an inaugural issue profile of the CCOSS. The second issue devoted its cover to Leona Saenz, a regional director in the Department of Labor's Women's Division and one of those many exceptional Spanish-speaking officials whom Nixon claimed credit for raising to prominence in government. Her story showed there was no contradiction between serving the country and being a full member of America's second-largest minority. "In addition to holding down an important job, she is an outstanding mother and wife," reported *La Luz*. In short, she was the perfect example of "our modern U.S. Hispana."[65]

☆　☆

Images were one thing; votes another. Behind the Brown Mafia's promotion of a national Spanish-speaking population (led by Mexican Americans) fully embracing middle-class values were much more targeted attempts to move the political needle. The president's men would convey Nixon's attention, at times generously and at times ruthlessly, and almost always through the medium of taxpayer dollars. The plan was laid out in a March 1972 memorandum entitled "Increasing the Responsiveness of the Executive Branch." In it, White House patronage chief Fred Malek called for executive branch departments to "systematically but discreetly seek out opportunities for improving services to target groups and geographic areas" where the campaign hoped to make inroads. In moments when discretion was deemed unnecessary, Malek would present federal officials with color-coded maps indicating where to direct government money for maximum political return.[66]

The Brown Mafia pursued Malek's vision for "capitalizing on the incumbency." The White House had set aside more than forty million tax dollars for distribution to supporters. To ensure that their share of money went to the right places, the Brown Mafia helped put dozens of allies in regional offices of Cabinet agencies, the federal antipoverty program, and the Small Business Administration.[67] The campaigners instructed them to distribute federal resources and jobs in ways that helped to "fill in any gaps in the President's record." Federal agency heads were, of course, to publicize those efforts widely. Well-placed appointees should provide valuable political intelligence, too. Programs "which serve as havens for opposition political operatives" were, in particular, to be "closely supervised." In a moment of cheek that stood out, even in the 1972 campaign, the Brown Mafia argued that these government units had to "devot[e] all their energies toward solving the problems of the Spanish speaking poor (particularly in September and October)," rather than politicking.[68]

At the same time, the CCOSS became "closely allied with" political strategist Chuck Colson's "shop." The CREEP made no bones about calling upon the CCOSS staff of thirty-five to support the campaign.[69] CREEP deputy director Jeb Magruder prioritized its "full politicization" and deployment of its budget—slated to increase from $800,000 to $1.3 million in July—in service of Nixon's reelection.[70]

The Brown Mafia used the withdrawal of federal dollars to punish perceived opponents as well. Antonio Rodríguez worked on "reidentifying SS [Spanish-speaking] groups who have applied for federal grants . . . who are unfriendly toward the Administration." One such malefactor was Development Associates, a minority-owned firm based in Washington, DC. Armendariz suspected that it had "close ties with the DNC and Cesar Chavez." Marumoto called it "a classic example of a firm, not necessarily on our team, which is making a comfortable living off us." The Brown Mafia recommended terminating the company's contracts. First, however, they invited the firm's president to the White House, in order to ascertain his willingness to donate money and free printing services to the reelection campaign. After he reportedly refused, he received a congratulatory notice. Development Associates had "graduated" from the Small Business Administration's minority contracting program. This "graduation" bestowed upon it the privilege of competing against all other government contractors, and the loss of any grants received once the fiscal year ended.[71]

If the White House expected recipients of federal contracts to be on the "team," Benjamin Fernandez, the California moneyman and National Economic Development Association cofounder, established a means for them to prove it. In March 1972, he launched the "National Hispanic Finance Committee for the Reelection of President Nixon" (NHFC), aiming to raise $1 million for the campaign. Edward Roybal and Herman Badillo had sought to build an ostensibly nonpartisan grassroots electoral coalition. Fernandez, in contrast, envisioned his Republican fundraising network as the foundation of true "Spanish-speaking" power. "Under the umbrella of the Republican Party," he claimed, "we can have a greater voice in the governing of our own." Collaboration in fundraising, he said, was "the basis for a national political coalition of Spanish-speaking minorities."[72]

The NHFC, government agencies, and federal grant recipients soon developed a close relationship. The case of J. A. Reyes, chairman of the Washington, DC, area NHFC, is instructive. His consulting firm qualified for minority contractor status and received hundreds of thousands of dollars in federal grants in 1971. In 1972, however, the firm doubled its haul of federal dollars, including a $200,000 noncompetitive grant from the OEO to evaluate an emergency food and medical services program for migrants. Lower-level OEO staff had rejected the evaluation as unnecessary, since similar studies had been performed recently. However, Peter Mirelez, appointed head of OEO's migrant division in February 1972 in the White House effort to incorporate southwestern community elites, overrode them.[73] The contract was then canceled for substandard work, only for OEO higher-ups to have it reinstated. Administration staffers directed another $200,000 grant, this time from the Office of Minority Business Enterprise (OMBE), to Ultrasystems, Inc., which the CREEP claimed "strongly supports the Administration." Indeed, the vice president of Ultra-Systems, Inc. was Fernando Oaxaca, national treasurer of the National Hispanic Finance Committee to Re-elect the President.[74]

But "capitalizing on the incumbency" meant more than simply rewarding the more conservative segments of Mexican America. The campaign pursued means of influencing the Chicano left as well. The Nixon campaigners sought to aid the La Raza Unida Party in a variety of ways. Early in 1972, Antonio Rodríguez, Alex Armendariz, and William Marumoto all lobbied the administration to grant $75,000 for the political party to hold its convention. The Brown Mafia believed that the party leader, José Angel Gutiérrez, would try to "maintain a balance of power in the two major parties," a strategy that they perceived would be to Nixon's advantage. White House documents state that Gutiérrez had approached them over the summer "for a quiet Republican contribution" to RUP—something Gutiérrez later denied[75]—in exchange for the party's willingness to condemn Democratic presidential nominee George McGovern at its convention.

Cesar Chavez, who had already endorsed McGovern, later had his invitation to speak at the event rescinded. Furthermore, a CREEP memorandum states that "in a meeting off the convention floor" unnamed sources again pledged "to publicly condemn McGovern" in exchange for an $8,000 contribution to the campaign of Ramsey Muñiz, the RUP candidate in the 1972 Texas gubernatorial race. Gutiérrez also killed in committee a "dump Nixon" resolution that had enjoyed wide support. In September, people claiming to be RUP members heckled Ted Kennedy as he stumped for McGovern in Los Angeles, holding signs proclaiming, "What have we gained from the Democrats?" and "Raza sí, Kennedy no." Another placard read, "send the Irish back to Ireland." In October, RUP forced California's Mexican American Political Association (MAPA) convention into a deadlock that prevented the organization Edward Roybal helped found from endorsing a presidential candidate. In the campaign's homestretch, OEO director Phillip Sánchez intervened to ensure that RUP affiliates in Texas would receive funding for health centers they were planning to operate.[76]

In another twist, the Brown Mafia tried to make New Mexico land grant activist Reies López Tijerina into an administration asset. Tijerina's occupations of federal land and shootouts with law enforcement officers had made him at once a Chicano movement hero and a federal prisoner. Out on parole since July 1971, Tijerina met with Henry Ramirez in the chairman's office and discussed his "probation, parole, and the possibility of a full Executive pardon." Tijerina claimed confidence that a strong majority of Spanish-speaking Americans would favor his receiving a pardon from Nixon. Although no deal appears to have been reached, Ramirez informed his superiors of his belief that Tijerina "would work with us in return for due considerations."[77]

The White House looked to co-opt or "neutralize" mainstream activists as well. The goal was not obtaining the endorsement of groups like the Southwest Council of La Raza (SWCLR) but rather "keeping them from supporting the Democrats." In the spring of 1972, the CCOSS hired SWCLR's E. B. Duarte to augment its Public Information Office. And in what was considered "a beginning effort to de-politicize" the group, the Brown Mafia advocated for it to obtain $30,000 from the Department of Labor to hold its national conference, at which administration surrogates would plan to deliver pro-Nixon remarks. The Southwest Council had also submitted a $6 million dollar proposal to the Department of Housing and Urban Development, along with another sizable grant request to the Office of Minority Business Enterprise. The OMBE proposals were well received within the agency, but the administration refused to finalize them before the election, hoping to maintain SWCLR's neutrality.[78]

Though the White House prioritized the conversion of Mexican-American voters, and few outside of their Florida backers imagined the relatively small number of Cuban voters would be an influential factor in 1972, Cubans were noteworthy allies in Nixon's reelection. Campaign contributions poured in from South Florida, as Ben Fernandez's National Hispanic Finance Committee to Re-elect the President furnished Cubans a chance to translate into political influence the economic strength they had amassed as a result of more than a decade of federally underwritten and coordinated aid to their professional and business sectors, including that which they had derived from Fernandez's own National Economic Development Agency. The heavily Cuban Florida chapter of the NHFC was said to have raised $105,000, somewhere approaching a third of the national organization's entire haul.[79] This participation confirmed that a sector of Cuban America was taking important first steps into the world of GOP pan-Hispanic politics.

Cubans played clandestine roles in Nixon's reelection as well. Drawing upon exiles' anti-Communism, and the years of CIA training invested in the community for the original purpose of destabilizing Cuba, the CREEP employed Cubans in an array of efforts to challenge or discredit administration critics. Some were strange but comparatively small public relations events. For example, the campaign enlisted Miamians to launch public demonstrations in support of the administration's war policies. In May 1972, as antiwar activists protested the administration's mining of Vietnamese ports, seven hundred Cubans turned out to endorse the president's hardline approach. A four-hundred-car-long motorcade jammed the streets of Miami, with Cubans honking horns, waving flags, and bearing signs that encouraged Nixon to "use the big stick."[80] In the wake of Nixon's 1972 visits to the People's Republic of China and the Soviet Union—moves expected to stir opposition in Miami—Spanish-speaking campaign manager Alex Armendariz paid a visit. Subsequently, allies in the National Hispanic Finance Committee to Reelect the President "spontaneously" produced an "informal" signature-gathering campaign backing Nixon's diplomacy.[81]

Then there were the Cubans recruited to more aggressive actions against the antiwar movement. The man the CREEP placed in charge of these clandestine missions was E. Howard Hunt. He had been the CIA's point person during the Bay of Pigs invasion, and remained to a section of devoted Cubans the personification of American anti-Communist commitment. Bernard Barker, a Cuban who had served as Hunt's lieutenant at the Bay of Pigs, was to say that Hunt "represents to the Cuban people their liberation."[82] Barker and many other exile counterrevolutionaries had remained on the CIA payroll throughout the decade after the Bay of Pigs, and on the tenth anniversary of the failed overthrow he met once more with his handler, "Eduardo." With Hunt seemingly now working out of the White House, he engaged Barker to raise a team of like-minded Cubans for a "national-security job." A "traitor" was said to be passing sensitive papers to the Russians, and higher powers needed help to stop it. The "traitor" in question was Daniel Ellsberg, an outspoken war critic and the press's source for the Pentagon Papers, the Defense Department's explosive and damning top-secret history of US involvement in Vietnam. Ellsberg saw a psychiatrist, and Barker's team flew to Los Angeles in September 1971, broke into the doctor's office, and attempted to steal medical records in order to smear the patient's reputation.[83] Then, in May 1972, as FBI director J. Edgar Hoover's body lay in state at the Capitol rotunda, the White House learned that an antiwar demonstration was going to take place at the national mall. Ellsberg would be one of those reading off the names of dead soldiers. Soon enough, Cuban operatives under Barker's command were flying first class from Miami to Washington to break up the protest. Barker told his henchmen that the "Hippies, traitors, and Communists" intended to "perpetrate an outrage on Hoover." Identifying Ellsberg, he directed them to attack the "traitor" and run.[84] Instigating a brawl, and decking any "longhaired hippie" in sight, the Cubans did their level best to break up the event.[85]

The Cubans' involvement in the Ellsberg break-in and the Hoover protest beatings was prelude to their stealing documents and bugging the telephones of the Democratic National Committee headquarters located at the Watergate hotel. After a series of misadventures, Barker and two other Cubans (Barker's real estate partner, Eugenio Martinez, and locksmith Virgilio Gonzalez), were among the five men arrested for the break-in on June 17, 1972. Miami was abuzz with theories. Some speculated that the Republicans or the CIA were behind it; others simply believed the Cubans were free-lancing. The *Washington Post* sent reporters to Miami. They relayed that "leaders of militant anti-Castro groups" were busy distancing themselves from the crime. The head of the paramilitary outfit Alpha 66 could not fathom the break-in being managed from on high: "It was so badly done, so amateurish," he remarked, positing that "if it had been ordered by the White House, it would have been done better."[86]

The White House saw in the Cubans' image as fanatical anti-Communists a handy means to distance Nixon from responsibility for the crime. On June 20, 1972, as the administration's cover-up began to take shape, the CREEP's Chuck Colson was explaining to Nixon a plausible picture. It was remarkable, he told the president who needed no such bulletin, just how much Miami's Cubans despised McGovern and feared his possible presidency. They believed that the Democrat would recognize Castro's government and then the exiles would lose political asylum and face eventual repatriation to a Communist Cuba. It was only natural that the Cubans, said Colson, would "resort to something pretty serious." "We are just going to leave this where it is, with the Cubans," replied the president. He counted the Cubans among those who needed to "plead guilty and get this stuff behind them."[87] Later that evening, the president called his chief of staff, H. R. Haldeman, with a feeling that Watergate might not only be "under control" but perhaps even exploitable for gain:

> A lot of people think the break-in was done by anti-Castro Cubans. . . . I'm going to talk to Bebe and have him round up some anti-Castro Cubans. . . . Those people who got caught are going to need money. . . . I'm going to have Bebe start a fund for them in Miami. Call it an anti-Castro Fund, and publicize the hell out of the Cuban angle. That way we kill two birds with one stone. Get money to the boys to help them, and maybe pick up some points against McGovern on the Cuban angle."[88]

Nixon operatives instructed the Cubans to emphasize that their actions in the break-in were the product of their fierce opposition to Castro.[89] And some time before the conspirators' fall 1972 indictment, Manuel Artime, a Bay of Pigs leader and the CIA's one-time exile "golden boy," told his friend Howard Hunt that he was putting together a committee to support the defendants.[90] Payments began to flow. In July, Hunt's wife, Dorothy, distributed tens of thousands of dollars in bail money and "income replacement" funds to the conspirators.[91] She had a code name (Chris), and she made clear that the envelopes of cash were provisional, with guilty pleas expected for payment to continue.[92] On August 1, 1972, Nixon checked on the matter with Haldeman, who reported that "everybody's satisfied. They're all out of jail, and they've all been taken care of." According to Haldeman, there had been "a lot of discreet checking to be sure there's no discontent in the ranks, and there isn't any." "Well, they have taken all the risk and they have to be paid. That's all there is to that," replied the president.[93] That was hardly the end of the matter, however. Payment had to continue to ensure the proper result. It was then that occurred a tragedy tailor-made for conspiracy theorizing. Dorothy Hunt was carrying $10,000 in cash intended for the Miamians when her Chicago-bound United Airlines jet crashed, killing her and forty-four others, in December 1972, a month before their plea would take place.[94] Artime picked up the slack. He received $21,000 in "support" funds from Howard Hunt and other unknown sources, to be distributed to the four Miami defendants during and after their trial.[95]

Meanwhile, the White House comforted itself that the media accepted the Cubans' version of the break-in. The nation watched televised interviews in which the burglars declared that sincere fear of Communist subversion—and they were the experts in its consequences—motivated their actions against McGovern and the Democrats.[96] Thanks in part to the Cubans' cooperation, the president and his allies were able to keep the scandal at bay for the remainder of 1972.

☆ ☆

With the Brown Mafia working behind the scenes and McGovern's foundering campaign unable to convince the media or the American people that Watergate was a White House crime, Nixon took his campaign into the Democratic strongholds that had rebuked him in 1968. In late September, he made a quick visit to the largely impoverished border towns of South Texas. According to reporters, "the streets of Laredo . . . were jammed with a surging, happy crowd,"[97] as "thousands of thousands of smiling brown faces" beheld their president. Before two hours had passed, the presidential entourage's Chinook helicopters were whipping up dust, "descend[ing] in awesome formation" on a high school baseball field a hundred miles away in Rio Grande City. Inside the school's auditorium, the young audience gave the president a rapturous reception. Having learned that there was a piano in the room, Nixon unexpectedly began to play and sing "Happy Birthday" to local congressman Eligio "Kika" de la Garza, a Democrat forty-five years old that day and running unopposed in November.[98] De la Garza deserved it, Nixon said, because he was one of those who had "proved that you can go clear to the top if you have the will." Indeed, to young people raised in one of the nation's poorest areas, Nixon offered a different theory of wealth and national inclusion. In it he rhetorically joined Mexican people with America's "white ethnics."

> We are rich because all the cultures of the world are here. We are proud of those of Mexican background who have added their wonderful warmth and all of their talent and all of their spirit and all of their hard work to make this a great country. We are proud of those of Italian background, of Polish background, Irish, you name it, whatever it is. The important thing is this: I often hear people say, when they are speaking of this person or that person, he is an Italian or he is a German or he is a Mexican. What I say is, he is an American. That's what he is.[99]

Nixon concluded by reminding the kids to work hard, respect their parents, and show love for their country. Through their efforts, they would command the world's respect by proving "that here in this country that any boy or girl, whatever his background, has a chance to go to the top in whatever occupation he chooses."[100]

After extolling the American dream, the president spent a few hours living it up at the Floresville ranch of John Connally, his former treasury secretary and now the chairman of "Democrats for Nixon." "Under a red and gold tent erected on Connally's oak-shaded lawn," the First Family joined "about 200 wealthy guests" for a sumptuous dinner. The Nixons banqueted in good company. Budweiser's August A. Busch Jr. and the actress Eva Gabor were there. So was Mario Procaccino, who as a law-and-order candidate for mayor of New York in 1969 had been a favorite of white ethnics. The guests satisfied their elite sensibilities with "prime ribs in wine sauce" and "pastry stuffed with crab meat." Lest anyone mistake this for a rich man's affair, black-eyed peas offered a taste of the down home.[101]

About twelve miles away on the Floresville courthouse lawn, Democratic vice presidential candidate Sargent Shriver addressed a rally over beans, tamales, and cold beer. Shriver had flown down to contrast McGovern's

Richard Nixon delivers motivational remarks to Mexican-American high school students during the last weeks of the 1972 campaign. Courtesy of Nixon Presidential Library and Museum, Yorba Linda, California.

campaign—for the working man, the poor, and the minorities—with Nixon's for the blue bloods. "Don't let it worry you what the millionaires are doing," over at Connally's, he told the crowd. "All of us are more numerous than the millionaires and we will win if we stick together."[102]

The Nixon campaign, however, rested on an assessment that a significant number of middle-class Mexican Americans did not share the view that ethnic authenticity manifested itself in attention to the poor. They were paying attention to the political system's responsiveness to their class ambitions and interests, their urges for status and recognition, their pride at seeing their own in high places. Armando Mena, who claimed to have been an alternate delegate for Robert Kennedy in 1968, now saw things differently and was working on the Nixon campaign in East Los Angeles. "I'm tired of people like Sargent Shriver . . . coming here and telling us how poor we are," he said in the last days of the campaign. "He and all the others are giving us a psychological whipping. . . . They [the Democrats] had plenty of years in the White House and they didn't show us much." For all the media controversy surrounding her undocumented employees, Romana Bañuelos ranked as one of the most visible members of the administration, an icon of incorporation in the establishment. "The militants kind of do us a favor when they criticize" her, Mena said, "because everybody loves Mrs. Bañuelos."[103]

The administration's Mexican-American appointees scolded Democrats for making working-class-conscious appeals to their coethnics. The self-described "ex-farm worker," Philip Sánchez, admonished the Democrats for their convention's vociferous support of the United Farmworkers' lettuce boycott. "To me," the OEO director told a Los Angeles audience in late September, "it meant that they consider that every Spanish-speaking American, or the majority thereof, are laborers."

> Let me suggest to you, ladies and gentlemen, we are not all farm laborers. We know a lot about the dignity and the sweat of working in the sun and producing food and fiber. But we also can be architects. We can be attorneys. We can be artists. And we can be business people. And we can be even bureaucrats like myself.[104]

They were not "tokens," either, said Sánchez. They were in "positions of influence and control . . . where we deserve to be."[105] In contrast to what his OEO predecessor, Shriver, might say, that any individual could go to the top *was* a sign of group progress. That Mexican-American and Puerto Rican leaders had for so long equated high-level appointments from Democratic administrations with advancement for their people only reinforced the claim.

Even lower-level Nixon campaign workers were now able to take their message directly to the upwardly mobile Mexican Americans. Improved federal data collection demonstrated that there was a growing sector of prosperous individuals in Mexican America, but also that this group was geographically dispersed. A creative response was required. Thus was born the Brown Mafia's "Camiones Por Nixon" program, a flying squadron of five Winnebago motor homes deployed to suburbs and shopping centers, places "where middle class Spanish-speaking persons are known to congregate." These "mobile headquarters" helped Republicans to register their target constituents. If campaign operatives are to be believed, they also "capture[d] the imagination" of GOP chairmen "in several states."[106]

Republicans sensed that White House patronage and a carefully crafted middle-class ethnic appeal, delivered by the administration's exceptional appointees, might deliver powerful results. Two weeks before the election,

Nixon greeted his administration's high-ranking Spanish-speaking Americans in the Cabinet room, grandly and clumsily: "Around this table are the most appointees at this level of, shall we say, Spanish-speaking background, or, that we have ever had in this government." They represented a different kind of minority, he said:

> I think that what really distinguishes the group that all of you come from some of the other minority groups, and particularly the Negro group, which all of us, of course, feel deserves special attention because of the historical background . . . but what distinguishes you, is that you do not face the problem of racism. . . . Our Mexican-Americans, most of them are poor . . . they have lower income than blacks. . . . But, on the other hand, they are proud. They just don't want to sit there on their fannies and take the welfare. They will, like anybody else. But they'd rather not. . . . It's the character. They're proud. They will work. They have the drive. They have the ability to go up.

After praising his audience's character and determination, Nixon confidently reflected on his prospects, not just for victory, but for establishing a new base among the Spanish-speaking people. "We're going to get a bigger percentage of the voters than we've ever gotten before. . . . Whatever the percentage is . . . we believe that this group should be on our side, should be with us, should be part, should act, so we're going to continue to work on it. . . . In the next four years, we want to use you as a beginning." He exhorted them to serve as role models for young children in the barrios and to recruit more doctors and lawyers and other professionals to the civil service. Revealing how much the administration viewed its "Spanish-speaking" outreach as a southwestern project, Nixon described the need to establish further "representation in this government that is worthy of the region you come from." They were like Jackie Robinson breaking baseball's color barrier, he said, making the president by implication a wise Branch Rickey. It was an odd twist considering his invidious black/brown comparisons only moments earlier. Regardless, together they would keep America great. The best and brightest of the group could be a national asset, even if the president of the United States left unsaid his belief that the great majority of them remained decades, if not centuries, behind.[107]

☆ ☆

A few days before voters headed to the polls, the Brown Mafia report ridiculing Puerto Ricans and calling for a negative campaign leaked to the press. Democratic spokesmen immediately denounced it as a "model of bigotry." Luis Velasquez, McGovern's "Chicano coordinator," said that it showed "the low esteem in which Nixon really regards the Latino community."[108] More than anything else, however, it demonstrated that Republican operatives viewed the "Latino community" as a rather differentiated political entity. At least as far as Republicans were concerned, there was no single Latino political "community."

Indeed, campaign postmortems reveal that the Nixon campaign had allocated few resources to winning over Puerto Ricans. Despite providing staff for Mexican-American communities in California and Texas, the CREEP refused to dedicate a comparable campaign worker to Puerto Rican voter turnout. The campaign also declined to run Spanish-language television advertisements in New York, devoting its funds to California instead. New York "Spanish-speaking" outreach was passed off to Governor Rockefeller's organization. It was clear that "personality conflicts" and perceived campaign bias against Puerto Ricans produced much "distrust" and "hostilities" between the Spanish-speaking New York Republicans and the Brown Mafia in Washington.[109]

None of this nuance prevented the "Spanish-speaking" as a whole from receiving credit for helping Nixon to win forty-nine states, however. In the weeks after the election, numerous analyses appeared on the voting behavior of the nation's Mexican Americans, Puerto Ricans, and Cubans. Several heralded the emergence of a Spanish-speaking vote, but did little to clarify the concept. In fact, they reported significantly different outcomes, depending on their chosen unit of analysis. The day after the election, the *Washington Post* reported that "Latin voters, which means Puerto Ricans in New York, Cubans in Florida and Mexican-Americans in Texas and California" gave Nixon 24 percent of their vote, an increase of 7 percent from 1968.[110] A few days later, the paper reported a CBS analysis giving Nixon 31 percent of the nation's "Spanish-speaking vote," and 49 percent of that vote in Texas and Florida. Puerto Ricans, so maligned by the Brown Mafia, still tendered Nixon 24 percent of their votes, according to CBS.[111] Aided by an infusion of Cuban voters, South Florida precincts that had gone two to one for the Democrat Hubert Humphrey in 1968 reversed themselves in 1972, with Nixon carrying them by a two-to-one margin. The *Miami*

*Herald* reported that in Little Havana, the 141st precinct—"probably the most predominantly Cuban precinct" in Dade County—went for Nixon, 426 to 99.[112] The White House remained cautious, predicting that when all was said and done, Nixon's share of the nation's Spanish-speaking vote would probably amount to between 26 and 30 percent.[113]

Privately, however, White House staff felt a special pride at the outcome. The Texas results were especially gratifying. Operatives had been fixated on San Antonio, which they believed had provided the decisive margins for Kennedy in 1960 and Humphrey in 1968. Back in 1960, Nixon picked up 17 percent of the city's Mexican-American vote. In 1968, however, that number was down to 6 percent, only one point better than Barry Goldwater had performed with those same voters in 1964.[114] In 1972, though, the president carried Bexar County by almost 40,000 votes out of roughly 210,000 ballots cast, suggesting a strong showing among Mexican Americans.[115] The CREEP sampled San Antonio Mexican-American voters by class, and concluded that Nixon had won 20 percent of the vote in a low-income precinct, almost half in a middle-income area, and nearly 70 percent of those in an upper-income precinct.[116] The president took majorities in three lower Rio Grande Valley counties as well (Hidalgo, Willacy, Cameron). Nixon's staff took these results as evidence of a larger trend. With

**Table 7.3.** Sampling of Nixon Results in Texas

| County | % Mexican American | % Nixon in 1972 |
| --- | --- | --- |
| Starr | 98 | 42.0 |
| Webb | 86 | 41.9 |
| Hidalgo | 79 | 52.6 |
| Willacy | 77 | 62.0 |
| Cameron | 76 | 59.6 |
| El Paso | 57 | 53.8 |
| Bexar | 45 | 60.5 |
| Nueces | 44 | 54.9 |
| Harris | 11 | 61.7 |

*Source:* Memorandum, Herbert G. Klein for Richard M. Nixon, November 13, 1972, Box 48, Confidential Files, Political Affairs, White House Special Files, White House Central Files, Nixon Presidential Materials Project, College Park, Maryland.

"continued communication and cultivation," the gains made in 1972 "can be translated into broader support for the President and the party," wrote communications director Herbert Klein. "We will follow through."[117]

Ignacio López, a coordinator of Los Angeles' "Hispanos with Nixon," was not sure that the Republicans' gains would be durable. A former anti-poverty worker and a registered Democrat, he felt that a good amount of Nixon's support came as a result of voters' disenchantment with McGovern. After all, he had encountered many voters who "cared very little for either candidate." Nevertheless, many had switched, and "if they [Republicans] want to keep these new friends . . . they'll have to follow up consistently," he said. López planned to remain a registered Democrat for the time being. However, this could change, depending on that follow-up. For him, it was "up to the Republicans now."[118]

☆ ☆

Yet it was unclear if Republicans led by Richard Nixon were willing, or even capable, of continuing the work of bringing the "Spanish-speaking" into the president's New Majority. The federal funds earmarked for convincing grassroots activists and nonprofit organizations of the White House's beneficence were slow in arriving, if they arrived at all. As one Republican analyst put it, there were "a few courtesy meetings . . . and other non-substantive gestures" after the election, but no new programs or improvements to existing ones. Many loyalists felt abused. Nixon's campaign had employed a number of Spanish-speaking Americans as campaign surrogates, showcase examples of their people's progress in government. Having served this purpose, however, many found themselves in professional limbo after the election. Nixon turned the OEO, which had been led by Philip Sánchez, over to a right-wing activist named Howard J. Phillips. His charge was to dismantle the body, spelling trouble for incumbent officeholders within what remained of the federal War on Poverty. Patronage was also limited. The LULAC leader for whom a federal judgeship was dangled as inducement to support the incumbent received instead an offer to sit on a consumer safety commission, a moderate insult he declined.[119]

Congressional inquiries began into Nixon's campaign as well. These attempted to discredit the administration's 1972 appeals as hollow, improper, or unlawful. In 1973, the House of Representatives held hearings into the administration's politicization of the supposedly neutral advocacy body, the Cabinet Committee on Opportunities for Spanish-Speaking People.[120]

Watergate was bigger, of course. Documents subpoenaed from the CREEP exposed the strong-arm tactics of the administration's Spanish-speaking campaign. The administration's "Responsiveness Program," its misuse of public funds earmarked to aid the minority poor, and its patronage system conducted in the name of affirmative action, made the Spanish-speaking constituency look like just another transactional interest group, belying the image of proud and independent people that its leaders cultivated. Senator Joseph Montoya inveighed against Nixon's "blatant attempt to buy the Spanish-speaking voters." It was an "incredible insult," he said, this "concerted effort to try to convince them that there was money in the trough if they just lined up." Montoya, whose New Mexico had its own rich tradition of patronage politics, insisted that "the Spanish-speaking people" were "not that kind of voter."[121]

Vote-buying accusations were mundane when compared to what the Senate inquiry revealed about the Nixon campaign's workings in Miami's Cuban community, however. Throughout the criminal investigation of the break-in, the Watergate burglars maintained that they were acting to protect the United States from Communism, and that no one had bought their silence. And in January 1973, Cubans Bernard Barker, Eugenio Martinez, and Virgilio Gonzalez joined another Miamian with an anti-Castro and CIA resume, Frank Sturgis, in pleading guilty in DC court to burglary, eavesdropping, and conspiracy charges. They were "provisionally" given maximum prison sentences of forty years (E. Howard Hunt got thirty-five).[122] The true sentence, however, would depend on the extent of the burglars' cooperation with the wider investigations into campaign wrongdoing. In the coming months, as various witnesses came forward, the Cubans' involvement in staged prowar rallies, the spying on and physical abuse of dissenters, and the bizarre and sensational links between the Bay of Pigs and a supposed "third-rate burglary attempt" were to become front-page news.

While Nixon's defenders came from all walks of life, Watergate had a particular influence on many Cubans in the United States for whom the patriotic cause of Cuban freedom, and loyalty to—in many cases exculpation of—Nixon came to be twinned concepts. Indeed, the Senate hearings, watched at least in part by an overwhelming majority of Americans, provided another stage on which the drama of Cuban patriotism and betrayal, so central to Cuban exile self-understanding since the Bay of Pigs, could be enacted. Testifying before the Senate committee in late May 1973, Bernard Barker situated the break-in within the long history of his involvement on behalf of Cuban freedom. As he understood it, this was no dirty trick, but rather "a matter of national security," one being orchestrated "above FBI and CIA" levels. Barker's justification proceeded from his community and his experience: "The fact that the Castro Government was aiding the Democratic party had been rumored and had been spoken of freely in Miami from different organizations of personalities that I had confidence in."[123] He claimed that E. Howard Hunt, trusted ally in his life's cause of Cuban liberation, needed his team's help to obtain proof of that involvement. Of course he was willing to break the law. In his mind he was, as he had long been, working in the service of the United States, a man simply "there to

Four accused Watergate burglars and their lawyer *(middle)* outside of district court in Washington, DC. During their trials and the contemporaneous Watergate hearings, the four Cuban-American defendants insisted their work was intended to expose traitors in government and to substantiate rumored financial links between Democratic officials and Cuban communists. *Left to right:* Virgilio Gonzalez, Frank Sturgis, attorney Henry Rothblatt, Bernard Barker, and Eugenio Martinez. Photo by © Wally McNamee/CORBIS/Corbis via Getty Images.

follow orders, not to think." On the verge of being overcome with feeling, he told the senators of his great pride in working with his fellow conspirators: "We'll have to live with the term 'burglar.' But we resent, very emotionally, the words that we were 'hired.' There was no need to buy our silence. We were not for sale. . . . We're just plain people who very truthfully believed that Cuba has a right to live."[124]

While the Senate gallery chuckled at Barker, the braiding of Cuban freedom and defense of Nixon was common coin in Miami. A woman watching the Watergate hearings outside of a television store in Little Havana stood dumbfounded by what she was witnessing: "It is a new world," she said. "I don't understand how they can do this to this great President and to these patriots."[125] Cuban exile press commentators, too, vigorously defended the president. Some outlets argued that it was an unthinkable action for the legislature to judge the president, despite the Constitution's clear provision for just that. Others made the case that American democracy differed so much from Soviet Communism and that Nixon's critics were "useful idiots, or worse, traitors who play the communists' game." And still another tack was the apologist defense that the misdeeds of Watergate were just a part of politics, that anyone, or everyone, could be doing it.[126]

With White House encouragement, Cuban leaders had been busy playing these chords, turning the burglars' cause into one that affirmed the Cuban community's sense of solidarity and oneness, all the while minimizing the significance of their transgression. In April 1973, just a month before Barker was to testify before the Senate, a fourteen-member "Committee of Help" started up "The Miami Watergate Defendants' Relief Fund." The committee included Bay of Pigs invasion heroes, a Catholic priest, and an attorney, among others. Reinaldo Vergara, a committee leader and engraver by trade, made clear the group's business was not to render judgment but to defend Cuban freedom. "We are not concerned if they are guilty or not," said Vergara. "They are decent people. Whatever they did, if they did anything, was to help the country in the fight against Communism. We are a group of Cubans helping other Cubans." Appearing on conservative commentator William F. Buckley's television program (alongside E. Howard Hunt), a committee member praised the defendants. They were "heroes who believed they were fighting communism." They deserved "a medal instead of throwing them in jail."[127]

While the fundraising group's leader, Vergara, said the effort had "nothing to do with any political thing,"[128] the public activities of the relief committee wove together defense of the Cuban conspirators not only with the cause of Cuban freedom but also the defense of Richard Nixon. In January 1974, Rev. Ramón O'Farrill delivered an invocation at a two-hundred-guest defendants' fundraising dinner that clearly tied Miami and Washington: "May God bless President Nixon so he can endure the attacks upon him so the nation may survive." Vergara, too, cast the break-in as a virtual duty of *Cubanidad:*

> There were not any more Cubans involved in the Watergate because no one else was asked. . . . Because we know if any Cuban had been told that there were Castroite documents in an office in Washington, there would have been not just four Cubans in the Watergate, there would have been thousands of Cubans in the Watergate.[129]

If any Cuban would have willingly committed the same crime, how seriously could they judge Nixon?

Dogged reporting and investigative work led to mounting pressure on Nixon to release the recordings of his conversations about Watergate and made plain how enmeshed the White House had been in supporting that image. While the "Watergate Defendants' Relief Fund" registered as a charity in February 1973, the investigation indicated that members of this committee, including the prominent exile leader Manuel Artime, had in the summer of 1972 formed an earlier "committee" in support of the burglars as they awaited trial in DC court. It also became public knowledge that thousands of dollars had been mailed to Artime by people connected to the campaign and that he had distributed it to the defendants and their families.[130]

And the story went to the top. After the Supreme Court forced the administration to turn over Nixon's secret White House recordings in July 1974, the tapes revealed the president's awareness that hush money was being funneled through a "Cuban committee" and his preference for using it as "cover."[131] "Is the Cuban committee an obstruction of justice if they want to help?" asked the president in March 1973. The man with whom Nixon was speaking that day, White House counsel John Dean, had heard in passing that a committee had been formed to ensure cooperation from the defendants. Only much later did he learn that it was the president himself who had first proposed such a committee just a few days after the June 1972 arrests.[132]

The Cuban protagonists in the burglary maintained their story of loyalty and patriotism to the administration's end. The month before Nixon's resignation, Bernard Barker, who along with Eugenio Martinez claimed to owe $60,000 in legal fees and who faced up to ten years in prison for executing the Ellsberg break-in that Nixon ordered, denied any knowledge of White House involvement. He maintained "the highest respect" for the American president.[133] When Nixon finally did resign, in August 1974, Barker praised him for acting "like a man," claiming that "everyone in the country respects him for" resigning, an action taken for "the welfare of the nation." Nevertheless, Barker worried, now, that the cause of toppling Castro had been set "several years back," so confident was he that "in his second term, with no re-election to worry about" Nixon "would have aided us to liberate Cuba."[134] Writing later that fall, Eugenio Martinez further blended the Cuban cause and Watergate. The latter was "a repetition of the Bay of Pigs," a "fiasco for the United States and a tragedy for the Cubans," the outcome being that "everyone landed in the hands of Castro—like a present." The rumors that helped inspire Martinez's most fateful mission for the US government, that the Cuban leader was financing George McGovern's campaign against Nixon, were "nothing new" to the Cubans in Miami at the time, or even two years later. "We believe that today," he wrote.[135]

☆ ☆

Thus did the 1972 presidential campaign at once institutionalize and suggest the fragility of a "Spanish-speaking" politics, while simultaneously tarring it with scandal. With vast resources at its disposal, and little guilt about deploying them for the president's benefit, the Nixon campaign could target the Mexican-American middle class with recognition and rewards. If their coethnics followed, so much the better. McGovern's weakness as a candidate makes it difficult to assess the extent to which the administration's campaign was capable of fundamentally reorienting the outlook of this vast and differentiated group of voters. Moreover, it was clear by election time that Nixon's team did not view all Spanish-speaking Americans as equally worthy. As the administration's cynical politics became more fully understood through the Watergate investigation and other congressional inquiries, and as it seemed to fail in extending its inclusiveness beyond the campaign, Hispanic Republicans and their elite allies would have to devise their own Hispanic strategy. They would do so in dialogue with a Cuban-American constituency still deeply nationalistic but now increasingly invested in US domestic politics. All the same, the notion of the Spanish-speaking voter as possessing the "balance of power" would persist far beyond 1972. Both parties had become obligated to appeal to these many populations as a single bloc, however complicated that task might be.

# 8

# The "Impossible Dream" of the Hispanic Republican Movement

Summoned to testify before the Senate committee investigating the Watergate affair in late 1973, Benjamin Fernandez was at once reflective, proud, and defiant about his role in the 1972 campaign. "To work the Spanish-speaking people into a cohesive unit," said the California businessman, Republican activist, and Nixon fundraiser, was "the toughest thing I have ever done in my life." He explained: "We have a tradition of not working together. Indeed, among ourselves we joke that the Mexican-American does not talk to the Puerto Rican, the Puerto Rican does not talk to the Cubano, the Cubano talks to no one." But as he happily observed, Republicans were writing a new history. The Nixon administration's aid program for Spanish-speaking entrepreneurs, the National Economic Development Agency (NEDA), had proved that these groups "could indeed work together on a unified basis." And by this discovery Fernandez had been transformed. "My future was determined," he declared. The fundraiser's life would henceforth be "devote[d] . . . to working with the Spanish-speaking people."[1] The practical, class-based alliance of NEDA was only a first step, however. Fernandez wished to lead a much broader transformation of both the Republican Party and the mindset of its newest constituency. As he would vow two years later as leader of a new Republican National Hispanic Assembly, "the unification of the Spanish-speaking people from coast-to-coast" was "the impossible dream" he aimed to achieve.[2]

In the wake of Nixon's 1972 landslide and the Watergate scandal, Benjamin Fernandez vied with Democrats and with other Republicans to politicize the middle class and upwardly mobile members of an increasingly heterogeneous nationwide "Spanish-speaking" constituency. He and likeminded Hispanic Republicans were armed with a faith that Hispanic unity, individual economic advancement through "free enterprise," and their party could be mutually reinforcing. The most influential of these party activists were, like Fernandez, Mexican Americans from the Southwest. But in 1974 they joined hands with Cubans—by this time increasingly committed to domestic political participation—and Puerto Ricans to establish the party's official Hispanic auxiliary, the Republican National Hispanic Assembly (RNHA). Though strong in the Southwest, the RNHA was intent on expanding beyond the territory the Nixon administration considered the incubator of Hispanic Republicanism. While Republican activists nationalized their efforts, they did so in an unequal dialogue with a new president, Gerald Ford, whose patronage was vital to their project. Yet pressure from a "New Right" and Ronald Reagan's insurgency began to change the internal calculus of Republican Hispanic politics. Coupled with the growth of undocumented immigration, conservative pressure created a welter of new challenges for both Ford and the RNHA. Reagan's attack on détente magnetized Cubans to him and away from Ford, while border questions emboldened hardliners within Ford's administration to take stances that jeopardized the administration's and the RNHA's effort to continue Nixon's outreach to the moderate Mexican-American middle class, the core element of GOP "Spanish-speaking" strategy. Woven together, the internationalization of GOP Hispanic politics and pressure from the Right greatly complicated the party's Hispanic unification project and foreshadowed a coming challenge to moderate Mexican-American influence in Republican Hispanic affairs.

☆ ☆

The 1972 elections returned a verdict that Spanish-speaking Republicans would proudly cite for years to come. Richard Nixon achieved his forty-nine-state victory thanks to many groups, of course, but media reports immediately claimed that perhaps a third of Spanish-speaking voters—traditionally strong Democrats—had cast a ballot for the incumbent. Benjamin Fernandez's fundraising campaign, the National Hispanic Finance Committee, raised more than $300,000, well short of its $1 million target, but still certainly no pittance.[3] The White House and Nixon's Spanish-speaking supporters, the bulk of whom were Mexican Americans, reveled in the outcome.

But as we have seen, the coming months would be far from simple for the leaders of Hispanic Republicanism. Though Richard Nixon had brought them into the system, their patron was in retreat from his commitments to them. And as the investigation into Watergate and its related crimes did increasing damage to his presidency, not to mention cast some of their own campaigning in a less than flattering light, many might have wondered how to respond.

Yet as was the case for the Cuban burglars and their defenders, the leaders of Hispanic Republicanism resolutely defended the president's actions (and theirs on his behalf) as fully justified and in the interests of their people. His Senate inquisitors painted Benjamin Fernandez, emblem of minority business success and Nixon's top Hispanic fundraiser, as a shady influence peddler, a conduit between favor seekers and crooked administration operatives who only provided state services in exchange for campaign contributions.[4] All he had done, he testified in November 1973, was sacrifice his time and put his business career on hold to bring his people into the nation's mainstream and democratic life. Through his efforts, "hundreds of thousands of Spanish-speaking voters became viable participants in our two-party system of Government." In fact, being grilled by the Senate committee only inspired him to more ethnic activism. "I am more convinced than ever," he said, "that I must continue to work with the Spanish-speaking people, that this must be a lifetime commitment on my part."[5]

Thanks to George H. W. Bush, he would have his chance. Following Nixon's reelection, the president had tapped Bush, then his ambassador to the United Nations, to serve as chair of the Republican National Committee (RNC). Bush had his hands full defending the scandal-plagued president from charges of official misconduct. Still, the Texan considered it essential to build upon the gains Nixon had made with the Spanish-speaking constituency. As the president had shown, the executive's short-term needs and biases regularly divided the Latino electorate against itself. The Republican Party, with different needs, required alternatives to a Hispanic outreach program driven by presidential prerogatives.

Seeking to attract a national pan-ethnic constituency, not simply to the top of the ticket but to Republicanism as a whole, Bush's RNC formed a "Spanish Speaking Advisory Committee" in April 1973. Its preliminary set of "recommendations," published in English and Spanish, articulated a fuller spectrum of "Spanish-speaking" policy positions than the Nixon White House had ever identified. For example, while Nixon's 1972 Spanish-speaking campaign avoided foreign policy themes in its pursuit of Mexican-American votes, the new committee took these matters on. Reflecting the growing importance of Cuban Americans within the party, and likely also their fears that détente-minded Secretary of State Henry Kissinger would pursue a new direction toward the island, the new committee called for the White House to "consult closely with leaders of the Cuban-American community in formulating any new policy . . . toward the Cuban-Castro regime." As Cubans anchored Republican Spanish-speaking politics to a conservative foreign policy agenda, the need to maintain Mexican Americans' sympathetic ear on border questions restrained the shift right. The committee expressed the need for a humane response to what was becoming recognized as a significant increase in the country's undocumented population. Describing them as "aliens who have lived and have paid taxes in America for many years, but whose entry was never recorded," the GOP cautiously moved that the Congress investigate the possibility of the undocumented "becom[ing] legal residents without fear of reprisal for their previous illegal status." Bush himself claimed that such a move "would have great impact on bettering the living standards of Spanish Speaking families."[6]

The following year, Republicans set themselves to formalize the Hispanic presence within the GOP. Activists and elected officials met on April 8, 1974, in Washington, DC, to found an official party auxiliary, which they named the Republican National Hispanic Assembly. Benjamin Fernandez was chosen the assembly's first chairman. His stated goal was to "organize the Hispano people into a dynamic, viable political force." His two touchstone requirements: "Unity and Organization."[7]

Fernandez was studied in class-specific understandings of these concepts. Like his earlier ventures in small business development and campaign fundraising, the RNHA attracted those who married a pan-Hispanic outlook with a passion for business. RNHA founding members included the former Peruvian diplomat Pedro de Mesones, by 1974 a Washington, DC–based political consultant. A man who reportedly judged that "Latins do not make the most" of their chances in the United States, Mesones's idea of group uplift was to hold welfare recipients' payments in escrow while the poor were taught the virtues and habits of "free enterprise." The merit of providing "loans, not a handout" spoke for itself.[8] Then there was the chairman of the RNHA's Florida chapter, José Manolo Casanova. A stockbroker and bank president, Casanova was the son of a Cuban senator whose family's sugar plantation was so vast as to accommodate one hundred miles of railroad track. He was also a prodigious fundraiser in Florida's National Hispanic Finance Committee to Re-Elect the President. A protégé of the president's friend and advisor Charles "Bebe" Rebozo, and heavily involved in Cuban-American political affairs, he nonetheless disclaimed the title of "politician." "I consider myself a businessman, basically," he said.[9] This combination of detachment and involvement was likely shared by the all-male RNHA executive committee, made up of businessmen, medical doctors, and other prosperous figures from Los Angeles, Dallas, New York, Miami, Chicago, and other nodes of Hispanic America.[10]

The prominence of Cuban Americans in the orbit of Hispanic Republicanism after 1972 deserves further explanation. Prior to 1972, Cuban leaders had, by and large, set themselves apart from the currents of Spanish-speaking politics. Their exile mentality set their focus on effecting their return to Cuba above all else. Moreover, the predominance of businessmen and professionals in their midst and, for some, their skin color, made them reluctant to identify with a political program that was largely advanced by Mexican Americans and Puerto Ricans, mainly domestic in nature, and principally justified by claims to be a permanent and disadvantaged "minority." Rather than lobby in conjunction with the other groups, then, they related to the federal government primarily through the Cuban Refugee Program.[11] Their main interface with the Republican Party, too, had been its anti-Communist auxiliary, the Republican National Heritage Groups Council. By 1972, however, Cubans had begun participating in the National Hispanic Finance Committee to Re-Elect the President, and serving as advisors to the Cabinet Committee on Opportunities for Spanish-Speaking People. These gingerly steps into pan-Hispanic politics were part of a broader shift in Cuban America. In August 1971, Castro had begun the process of extinguishing the program of "freedom flights," under which almost 300,000 Cuban refugees had been admitted to the United States since 1965,[12] and the hopes for an imminent return seemed sufficiently remote that many Cubans began to participate in mainstream US electoral politics at once to improve their situations in the United States and effect change in Cuba. The number of Cubans who planned to remain in the United States grew quickly between 1973 and 1976, and a surge of naturalizations accompanied this sentiment. Whereas only 25 percent of Dade County's eligible Cubans had become citizens as of 1970, that number was 55 percent a decade later. In fact, Cubans constituted a disproportionate 12 percent of the nation's new Americans in the decade. Breakthroughs in local representation came as early as 1973, when two Cuban Democrats (Bay of Pigs veterans, naturally) won election to Miami's City Commission and school board. That same year, Dade County's commissioners passed an ordinance declaring the jurisdiction officially bilingual and bicultural. Dade would promote the Spanish language in its official workings and Spanish-speakers in public employment, moves justified by the taxpayer claims and the record of increasing civic engagement on the part of the county's Cubans and other Latinos.[13] Though many Cubans aspired to return to their homeland, never again would they return to being considered purely an externally oriented constituency.

Given their increasing integration in domestic politics, Ben Fernandez recognized the need to bring Cuban Americans more fully into the pan-Hispanic consensus. And so this Mexican American advocated for Cuban interests, complaining to New Mexico congressman Manuel Luján in September 1974 of the perpetual "lack of representation of one of the major Hispanic Groups, the Cuban-Americans" in White House functions. He protested their absence from high federal offices. The RNHA's success, he argued, depended on "all the groups that comprise our Hispanic brotherhood" achieving "proper participation and representation in the Federal government." Resolving the matter was, he said, "a very important factor in unity."[14] Invoking Hispanic solidarity in support of Cuban-American aspirations also had the unmistakable advantage of making the RNHA into a gatekeeper of Cuban Americans' ascent in the federal leadership structure.

☆ ☆

Fernandez's effort to channel Cuban-American political energies into a Hispanic unification project centered on patronage politics and a business orientation was but one force vying to influence the GOP's direction, however. As the RNHA organized to make the Republican Party multi-cultural, a loose network of right-wing groups and forces was on the ground, raising money, supporting candidates, drafting policy papers, and generally beating the drum against any compromise with liberalism. Collectively known as the "New Right," this movement was committed to advancing conservatism in foreign and domestic affairs. Strong in the South and West, it combined a revulsion at détente with antitax, antigovernment populism, strident defense of traditional gender roles and morality, unyielding hostility to abortion, and a commitment to restore what its backers felt was the central place of (Christian) religion in the public square. The decades-long assault on liberalism in which many of them participated had only enjoyed momentary victories, such as when conservatives propelled Arizona senator Barry Goldwater to the Republican presidential nomination in 1964. Richard Nixon's championing of "law and order," his strategic obstruction of civil rights enforcement, and his outreach to blue-collar Catholic voters had appealed to them, and had certainly helped remake the prospects for the Republican Party in both the South and in northern cities. But while conservatives defended Nixon in Watergate, this was not out of love for the man or his policies. After all, the latter included such heresies as endorsing an Occupational Safety and Health Administration, controlling wages and prices, not to mention proposing a welfare "reform" that, had it been enacted, would—just in its very first year—have enlarged the federal commitment to welfare by some thirteen million persons and four billion dollars. Moreover, New Right activists found Nixon's entreaties to Communist nations craven and detestable, for in their view no accommodation could be made to the Red menace. As the Nixon administration collapsed, New Right activists redoubled their efforts to seize the initiative, either by starting a third party or by capturing the GOP.[15]

In a Republican Party facing significant organized pressures from the right, the RNHA had to harmonize its conception of the Hispanic-American collectivity with that increasing conservatism. When roughly 250 RNHA members convened in Washington, DC, in July 1974 to plan for that year's midterm elections, New Mexico congressman Manuel Luján explained to reporters that the gathering was a natural fit: the GOP and the Spanish-speaking American were "both conservatives." The two, he claimed, "respect traditional institutions, especially the family, and reject the moral permissiveness espoused by so many present-day Democrats."[16] Luján explained that organizing as a bloc to defend "Hispanic" social conservatism still meshed neatly with the party's ideology of personal advancement. The group's coordinated electoral participation, said Luján, was "vital for us Hispanos, if we are to receive greater consideration as individuals."[17] Hispanic politics was indeed a group politics; but it was also a conservative politics.

While espousing a Hispanic social conservatism, RNHA activists did not fall in lockstep with the New Right's clamor for color-blindness in public life. New York's RNHA chairman, Michael Carbajal Jr., saw no reason for Hispanic Republicans to downplay their ethnic difference in search of party recognition. Instead, he called for full inclusion based upon their unique characteristics and heritage.

> I hear some people say, "Why do you need a separate organization? Why not operate within the existing structure?" . . . The answer is simple. Hispanics have different temperaments and customs. They are proud people and they do not go where they are not wanted. It is not enough to open party doors to them, they must be invited in and they must feel they belong. The only way this came about is through the Republican Hispanic Assembly.

By sponsoring the RNHA, the party had "transformed an ideal [unity] into a reality." But far from promoting separatism, this Hispanic unity would be channeled so that "we can all," he said, "get into the political mainstream of our great country."[18] Their ethnic assembly was an essential tool in achieving status within the party—and by extension the nation.

The Republican Party's opening to them was a means to acquaint group members with one another and to project visions of ethnic politics forged in local contexts onto the national level. Ben Fernandez described that same 1974 RNHA convocation as a watershed moment for Hispanic unification, "the first time, Mexican-Americans, Puerto Ricans, Cuban-Americans and other citizens of Latin heritage came together under a common Republican umbrella . . . for the attainment of Republican principles and the election of GOP candidates." Over two and a half days filled with seminars and cocktail hours, shared meals and bull sessions, RNHA activists representing the country's various Latino communities received an education in the art of political organizing. The RNHA designed sessions to integrate members into the party's "Grassroots '74" election effort and fundraising programs. It devoted time for them to share their previous campaign experiences with one another. The event would conclude with an hour on the finer points of actually "winning elections."[19] Seeking to maintain the momentum, Fernandez argued that victories in the midterms and "the development of Hispano political power through unity among the Spanish-speaking" would go hand in hand.[20]

Even absent the political headwinds of Watergate, to leave a "Hispanic" imprint on the 1974 midterms required a certain amount of imagination. After all, the geographical limitations of congressional races did not tend to invoke the alliance of distinct Hispanic communities in the same way that a presidential campaign did. When aggregated, however, varied candidacies from across the country could furnish an image of Hispanic unity. Profiled in "El Republicano," the RNHA's newsletter, is a pan-Hispanic array of aspiring congressional Republicans. There was the city councilman and pharmaceutical firm sales manager, running in Southern California on a record of "promoting workable social programs . . . while consistently holding the line against increased taxes." In Brooklyn, New York, there was the insurance business owner, the holder of an MBA. He was discussed in the same space as the affirmative action officer employed at the defense contractor Rockwell, who was seeking a seat representing Los Angeles. In Miami, there was the Cuban-American insurance agent and former Green Beret running against the seventy-four-year-old Claude Pepper, and calling the onetime New Deal Democrat "Mr. Inflation."[21] Victories by these men, RNHA members and leaders hoped, would give them clout within the party and allow the GOP to compete symbolically with the Democrats—most notably Edward Roybal and Herman Badillo—who dominated the discourse on the Spanish-speaking American in the House of Representatives.

Although all of the RNHA's celebrated candidates went down in defeat in a brutal election cycle for Republicans, Fernandez and others continued to build the organization in 1975. They established its constitution and bylaws, elected officers, and integrated several women into its leadership ranks.[22] They expanded the organization's geographic reach as well. By September 1975, Fernandez could praise his onetime NEDA colleague, "a former dishwasher and now a successful businessman" named Monte Montez, for running a five-state RNHA conference out of his Kansas home. In Florida, the growth of the RNHA showed that "on a national basis, the Cubans make up with enthusiasm and enterprise what they lack in numbers." Calling to "respect them for their suffering and for their swift embracing of the free enterprise system of our country," Fernandez predicted that the Florida group "will be a front runner in the drive for national leadership." And not to play favorites, he could report with pride that the assembly's first local chapter had been founded in New York and that it was "on the threshold of leading the Hispanic Republican movement in our country."[23]

☆ ☆

While the RNHA forces attempted to forge an influential place for themselves within a multicultural post-Watergate GOP, they did so in dependent dialogue with a new president and party leader, Gerald R. Ford. The Ford administration's outreach reflected an attempt to preserve continuity with the organized factions of Hispanic Republicans brought into the party by Richard Nixon and RNC chairman George Bush, but also how mounting pressure from conservatives, including the New Right's darling, former California governor Ronald Reagan, was altering the internal chemistry of Hispanic Republicanism in ways that made its traditional ambitions of incorporating the constituency more complicated.

When Ford became president in August 1974, the White House's own channels to the wider Spanish-speaking constituency were in flux. Congress had envisioned the Cabinet Committee on Opportunities for Spanish-Speaking People serving as a pan-ethnic lobby within the executive branch, but its political manipulation, laid bare during Watergate and other congressional hearings, fatally damaged its support among legislators. Despite lobbying by Latino organizations and individuals, the committee was set to die out once its five-year authorization concluded at the end of 1974.

Facing pressure to demonstrate that Spanish-speaking Americans remained an administration priority, in the summer of 1974, the capsizing Nixon White House designated a special assistant to the president whose portfolio would be "Hispanic Affairs." The administration's choice was Fernando E. C. de Baca, a thirty-six-year-old New Mexico native and self-described "fourth generation Republican."[24] He had been the first director of the Sixteen Point Program, the Nixon administration's affirmative action program for Spanish-speaking civil servants.[25] Nixon's resignation in August 1974 meant that Gerald Ford occupied the White House when De Baca assumed his role. His task, however, remained the same: bolster the president's standing among Spanish-speaking Americans by embodying "Hispanic" aspirations and progress in the White House. Underscoring the symbolism, his appointment was made official on September 16, 1974, Mexican Independence Day, which in turn coincided with National Hispanic Heritage Week celebrations.

Though he hailed from Albuquerque, New Mexico, De Baca presented himself as more than a southwestern figure. He claimed membership in a variety of Hispanic groups, including the League of United Latin American Citizens (LULAC), the American G.I. Forum, the Puerto Rican Forum, and the public employee organization IMAGE. He also pointed to his association with the American Legion and Veterans of Foreign Wars (he was a Vietnam veteran). His biographical sketch portrayed a man straddling communities in search of racial and cultural authenticity. He was directly descended, on his father's side, from "the Spanish explorer Nunez [sic] Cabeza de Vaca who landed at Tampa Bay, Florida, in 1527." And thanks to his Mexican immigrant mother (described in his bio as "a Mestizo"), De Baca was also "of Mexican and Indian descent."[26]

De Baca's experiences in New Mexico and in Washington taught him what countless politicians have known, that public sector employment was a crucial means of winning constituent support, in this case incorporating middle-class Spanish-speaking Americans in the Republican Party. He built ties to IMAGE, the government worker organization. He included its leaders in a meeting with the new president in October 1974, along with the traditional civil rights organizations LULAC and the American G.I. Forum. Following up, De Baca explained that the president had "instructed me to work closely with you" and policymakers, to address ways of bringing more Spanish-speaking people into government employment. In turn, IMAGE drafted memoranda for De Baca to have distributed to heads of federal departments to accelerate the implementation of affirmative action for their people. Lending the prestige of the presidency to the budding group, De Baca spoke at IMAGE's events, and cultivated its leaders' support with laudatory personal messages, autographed photos of Ford, and preferential access for White House tours. He also raised IMAGE's profile within the administration, calling it "one of the largest, most responsible and effective Spanish Speaking organizations in the country." He urged White House schedulers to put its annual convention on Ford's calendar. No sitting president had ever addressed such an event for a national Hispanic civil rights organization, and IMAGE was a plausible choice for this symbolic breakthrough.[27]

Using public employment to incorporate an ethnic group in one's coalition was an old political strategy, of course. Yet De Baca and the Ford administration were discovering an arena of pan-Hispanic politics far more nuanced than that which had existed when Lyndon B. Johnson appointed Vicente Ximenes to lead an Inter-Agency Committee on Mexican American Affairs in 1967, or even when Richard Nixon named Henry Ramirez chairman of the Cabinet Committee on Opportunities for Spanish-Speaking People in 1971. De Baca's office, which consisted of himself and a secretary, claimed to be keeping tabs on more than five hundred organizations.[28] His position's "increased visibility" and status encouraged these groups, as well as legislators, their constituents, and a host of federal agencies, to inundate him with requests for information or advocacy.[29] The Cabinet Committee had operated with a staff of more than thirty. But De Baca alone was the primary federal contact for the vast and diverse constituency. It was overwhelming. As he wrote to White House counselor Anne Armstrong, "I am asked to be everybody's Congressman, Senator, and Cabinet Committee and advisor all rolled into one. . . . I hate to see the day when some major issue arises for which I will not be able with my very small staff to reply, much less provide any kind of useful responses."[30]

Any plan "to address the multi-faceted 'Hispanic issue' with integrity," judged De Baca, required a significant increase in resources.[31]

☆ ☆

A surge in unauthorized migration from Mexico added greatly to the Ford administration's challenges in balancing its Hispanic appeal—traditionally centered on Mexican Americans—with its primary need to defend itself from the conservative insurgency. In the mid-1960s, liberal congresses had ended the US–Mexico agricultural guest worker Bracero Program. They had also imposed new ceilings on legal migration from the Western Hemisphere. With Mexican labor demanded, but with fewer legal means for workers to migrate, many chose to cross the border without legal permission. They gained greater incentive to leave their homes after 1973, when Mexico's leadership began to withdraw its economic support for rural communities and instead embraced an export economy and an industrial complex growing up around the country's border with the United States. Along with a contemporary population explosion in Mexico, the restructuring attendant to this new era of economic integration led vast numbers of these migrants to enter the United States in search of stability.[32]

The national media played an important role in generating public anxiety over their presence. In the pages of *U.S. News and World Report,* for example, one read of "great waves of Latin-American immigrants" who "appear well along the way to accomplishing what their Spanish ancestors couldn't: the 'conquest' of North America." "Already the nation's second-largest minority, America's Spanish-speaking population—estimated at 12 million or more—is increasing by more than a half million a year." It reported "estimates . . . that about 1.2 million Spanish-speaking 'wetbacks' illegally entered" the country in 1973, from Mexico alone.[33]

Hard-liners in Ford's government fueled a wider sense of panic. The commissioner of the Immigration and Naturalization Service (INS), General Leonard F. Chapman, was particularly outspoken. In 1974, the former Marine Corps commandant told the national press that the problem of the undocumented was "very serious and getting worse," and that in a matter of years the country could have "15 or more million" illegal aliens. Some, he said, came "surreptitiously at night," whereas others entered "through organized smuggling rings," thus abetting crime. He further intimated that the group was responsible for straining America's resources, from gasoline to potable water, raising the "fundamental question" of how to regulate the size of the American population so as to preserve Americans' way of life. The country had to "[turn] off the magnet," said Chapman. By penalizing employers who hired the aliens, Americans could stop "the flood that's coming in every day."[34]

In 1975, Chapman conducted a speaking tour and media blitz to amplify public concern over the "silent invasion" he claimed was occurring.[35] Migrants were "milking the U.S. taxpayer of $13 billion annually," stealing jobs away from their rightful occupants, consuming costly government services, and evading taxes, said the INS commissioner. His emphasis on the pernicious fiscal consequences of undocumented immigration were no doubt calculated for maximum impact at a time of rising joblessness, tax-payer revolts, and government debt crises.[36]

Other high administration officials were busy securing Ford's right flank. Just days before the 1974 mid-term elections, Attorney General William Saxbe declared illegal migration a "severe national crisis" and called for a sweeping change in immigration enforcement. The nation's top law enforcement officer declared the firing of "1 million persons now holding jobs" without authorization—a group understood to be over-whelmingly Mexican in origin—and "stem[ming] the flow of illegal im-migrants" to be his top two priorities.[37] Embarked upon his own speaking tour, he told South Texas audiences that the undocumented "mock our system of legal immigration," taking jobs, using social services, and draining funds from the American economy through their remittances to Mexico. He intimated that they were also quite possibly "a substantial factor in our growing crime rates." Millions of additional dollars in the INS budget and thousands more border patrol agents would be needed to deport the one million current jobholders, "and then find those who have burrowed more deeply into our society," reported the attorney general.[38]

The challenges of the Mexico–US border were fast becoming a "His-panic" issue. The major Mexican-American civil rights organizations, LULAC and the American G.I. Forum, had jointly proclaimed them-selves in support of undocumented aliens' human rights.[39] Church leaders in the Northeast were warning De Baca that abuses stemming from the crackdown had gone national, with "even Puerto Ricans" being "asked to produce citizenship papers."[40]

Though De Baca had risen to some prominence in a state where "Spanish Americans" had historically distanced themselves from Mexican immigrants, and though his surname came from a Spanish explorer, his credibility as a national "Hispanic" leader was at stake. He worked to co-ordinate a response with advocacy organizations. As he wrote to the Forum of National Hispanic Organizations, a coalition formed in 1974 and encompassing dozens of groups, "We need to seriously sit down and begin to more precisely articulate for the benefit of the Executive Branch and for the Congress of the United States concise position statements" on a variety of "important issues." The first matter he cited was "the illegal alien question."[41]

De Baca conducted his own public relations campaign, attempting to improve the White House's reputation with Hispanic Americans while countering the harshest rhetoric of his administration colleagues. He presented undocumented immigration as a great national challenge, one that demanded a thoughtful response. He called for actions "to discourage the tremendous wave of people who illegally stream across our borders daily" but also tried to convince skeptical Americans that "thousands of illegal aliens" were taxpayers as well. Moreover, he argued that "it would be impossible to apprehend the millions of undocumented persons in the U.S. without turning the U.S. into a police state," and thus it was "imperative to regularize the status of such persons so that they will not be exploited and they can better integrate themselves into society as a whole." He reminded the country that, "Americans have confronted problems of staggering dimensions before and have overcome them." What was necessary, "above all else," was to "look at the human needs of the problem."[42]

Conservative opponents responded to De Baca's invocation of a humane nationalism with scorn. His call to legalize undocumented aliens on US soil outraged one El Paso man, who saw in it an example of "permissiveness" and a "reward" for the "deluge of Mexican aliens that is storming our boundaries." Highlighting the extent to which immigration was rendering all Hispanic Americans—even the descendants of Spanish explorers—as one group in the public imagination, the writer characterized De Baca's position as a function of his desire to "take care of his own nationality."[43] INS commissioner Chapman was incensed as well. He complained to Ford's head aide for interest groups, Theodore Marrs, about De Baca's remarks in favor of citizenship for the undocumented. De Baca's comments "debunking statements made by other administration officials" about the number of jobs that could be opened "by acting against illegal aliens" were dangerous, argued the commissioner. De Baca's words "only tend[ed] to stir emotions," wrote Chapman, and appeared "at odds with efforts to find viable solutions" to "the illegal alien problem." The former Marine commandant suggested a sit-down meeting with the special assistant for Hispanic affairs, closing his letter formidably: "I'm available."[44]

☆ ☆

If the White House's embodiment of Hispanic Republicanism, De Baca, acted as a counterweight to conservative opinion on immigration, he positively inflamed it on another international subject: Cuba. In this case, conservative opinion and Cuban-American opinion were for the most part indistinguishable. As Ben Fernandez was learning in painful measure, what most strongly distinguished Cubans from the Mexican Americans and Puerto Ricans who had long focused pan-Hispanic politics on jobs, grants, elite access, and other forms of recognition was the extent to which foreign policy questions dominated their political outlook.

De Baca attempted to exclude their most urgent concerns from the established framework of "Hispanic" politics. As he saw it, the Office of Hispanic Affairs was first and foremost "a vehicle for enhancing the nation's domestic interest and affairs, specifically addressing questions of policy as these pertain to Hispanic Americans' development within the United States." In contrast, the Cubans who contacted his office "have been primarily concerned with matters pertaining to foreign relations with Cuba." Rather than burden "Hispanic Affairs" with the seemingly extraneous details of Cubans' foreign policy agenda, he sought "a proper and ongoing relationship . . . to be established with the State Department, in order that these interests are properly channeled."[45]

But the State Department was itself transforming De Baca's task in managing Hispanic Affairs. As Ford ascended to the White House, Cuba's international isolation was waning, and Secretary of State Henry Kissinger urged in August 1974 for the United States to "loosen up" with respect to the island, lest the Americans find themselves unable to influence events there. In early 1975, Kissinger made public statements that appeared to endorse détente with Cuba, saying that "We see no virtue in perpetual antagonism between the United States and Cuba."[46]

Echoing the Kissinger position later that year, De Baca attempted to use his national prominence as a Hispanic leader to diminish the extent to which a hard line on Cuba constituted the essence of even Cuban-American politics. Having toured the country and taken the measure of the group's attitudes toward their homeland, he concluded publicly in late summer of 1975 that while "the Cuban leaders have made it clear they are adamantly opposed to normal relations with Cuba" the "rank-and-file Cuban families . . . don't necessarily agree." Noting Ford's "certain empathy" for the exiles, he also explained that the president "recognizes reality and understands the need to get along with all our neighbors." As he called for "the Spanish-speaking community" he represented to "take a good look at the Cuba issue in terms of what's in our best interest and the best interest of the hemisphere," he observed that it was certainly "inconsistent . . . to have detente with the Soviet Union and to treat Cuba differently."[47] The *Spanish-speaking* position was to be open to a relationship that *Cuban* Republicans would never entertain.

A swift backlash ensued. The front page of the *Miami Herald* carried the news under the headline "Exiles Reconciled to Cuba Ties?"[48] The implied answer was decidedly in the negative. The National Association of Cuban Lawyers dashed off a telegram to the president, in which it called De Baca's remarks "wrong" and a "disservice" to Ford's "political image."[49] A Republican state committeeman from Dade County, Mike Thompson, read the comments and immediately "arranged for a random telephone survey of approximately two hundred Miami-area Cubans," asking their views on normalization and renewed trading ties between the nations. The results were damning. "While Mr. DeBaca carries the title of 'Hispanic-affairs adviser,' it is obvious that his knowledge of the Cuban-American community is either nonexistent or, worse, deviously misconstrued. In either case," wrote Thompson, "he is unworthy of his position." The sentiment from Miami was clear: "Mr. DeBaca is wrong on Cuba . . . and Cuban-Americans. Dr. [Henry] Kissinger [Ford's secretary of state] is wrong on just about everything else. Your nation and your Party pray that you will recognize your advisers for what they are."[50]

The consequences of such moments revealed a changing calculus within GOP Hispanic circles. The Republican Party under Nixon and Ford had consistently promoted Mexican Americans such as De Baca and showed little concern about the consequences for Puerto Ricans, whom they envisioned as unalterably liberal and thus unlikely Republicans. Ford's White House could not afford to look like it was subordinating Cuban Americans, however. In November 1975, Ronald Reagan announced he was challenging Ford for the Republican Party's nomination the following year, and the insurgent's Cold War bellicosity would be the heart of his appeal to the increasingly influential Cuban-American constituency. According to one administration strategist, instead of drawing Florida's Cuban Americans into a Hispanic consensus in support of détente, De Baca "did irreparable damage" to Ford's standing with the group. Reflecting upon the upcoming primary challenge in Florida, he judged that

Cubans were "strongly pro-Reagan, and . . . not likely to be wooed back easily."[51] In December 1975, the Republican National Hispanic Assembly pressed Ford in the White House for "a firm statement that will end speculation on coexistence with the Cuban Communist government within the foreseeable future."[52] Ford found himself offering Cuban-American Republicans in particular his reassurances "categorically and emphatically" that "the United States will have nothing to do with Castro's Cuba—period."[53]

Although Florida's RNHA pledged its support to Ford in the primary season,[54] less than ten days before the Florida primary, De Baca announced that he would be stepping down from his position as the Ford administration's conduit to Hispanic America.[55] There were costs to rewarding Cuban exceptionalism. While it may have placated some Cubans, the departure of the White House special assistant for Hispanic affairs—to work for the Democratic governor of New Mexico, no less—hardly solved the problem. According to one administration official, De Baca's exit led to "an outburst of expressed malcontent" from Cubans (and Puerto Ricans) who demanded "a representative from their areas rather than having the Mexicans dominate American/Hispanic matters."[56] Theodore Marrs advised the president of the need to find a replacement quickly, thereby "preventing traumatic competitive reactions amongst the various Hispanic segments."[57] Ford was "being hurt" by the vacancy, wrote Marrs again in May 1976, and needed someone "to pick up the astonishing number of loose ends" on Hispanic affairs before too long.[58] "A person with knowledge as to the routes in the maze would be most helpful," he argued.[59]

Indeed, a replacement might have kept the president from the embarrassment he suffered on the campaign trail in Texas in early April. Some of Ford's advisors believed that Mexican Americans held certain sympathies for Latin America that might cause them to reject Reagan, who was then battering the president for renegotiating terms of US control over the Panama Canal. San Antonio seemed a good place to test their theory, yet the message was lost almost immediately. Presented a tamale during a visit to the Alamo, the eager Ford showed his unfamiliarity with the food. Photographers captured his first bite—the inedible corn husk wrapper and all—a statement of cultural ignorance prime for national news consumption.[60]

President Gerald R. Ford attempts to consume an unshucked tamale on the campaign trail in San Antonio, April 1976. Ford's gaffe exposed his unfamiliarity with Texas culture and created a sensation for local and national media. Photo courtesy of Associated Press.

☆ ☆

All the while, the RNHA maintained hope that the 1976 presidential election would build upon the triumphs of 1972 and confirm their people as a meaningful piece of the party's future. They counted on the prestige and authority of the presidency to grow their organization and facilitate their rise in the ranks of Republican power brokers. With Reagan challenging Ford from the right, an organized ethnic constituency might even be the difference maker. Thus Fernandez and the RNHA offered the incumbent public support, if not an endorsement, in his battle for renomination and reelection. When the RNHA secured an audience with Ford in December 1975, shortly after Reagan's announcement, Fernandez called it "monumental" and "a historic meeting." According to Fernandez, "never in the history of the Republican [Party] has the President of the United States met with a permanent Republican organization consisting of a cross-section of Americans of Hispanic origin." Fernandez was careful to praise the man whose help he needed, telling the party's Hispanic activists that Ford was "a good man; a sincere man; one who is trying to be a good President."[61]

The main commodity the Hispanic Republican movement sought from Ford was federal jobs. As "the largest employer in the land," a bastion of nondiscrimination "long before the private sector," and the means by which Spanish-speaking Americans received "services and programs" from Washington, Ford's bureaucracy was, the RNHA of California reported, an entity "of great importance to the Spanish-speaking people."[62] The national RNHA called upon the president to reinvigorate the federal Spanish-speaking affirmative action program begun under Nixon.[63] High positions were more important still. Ben Fernandez warned Republican heavies that "presidential appointments" had fallen to a "deplorable" level since the heights of the Nixon reelection campaign. He stressed that these appointments—"accomplishments which can be quantified"—were in fact "the swiftest way to earn credibility with the people."[64]

While referring to the president's credibility, Fernandez undoubtedly had his own in mind as well. He defended Ford's hiring record in public, even as he pressured the administration to place his allies in visible jobs in federal agencies, and on boards and commissions.[65]

The RNHA's orchestration of Hispanic unity via presidential patronage appears to have exacerbated the intense factionalism then animating the Cuban exile community, divisions that took on additional layers as exile Republicans sorted themselves into Ford and Reagan blocs. The Cuban Refugee Program (CRP) had a $90-million annual budget, and thus great material as well as symbolic influence among the exiles. No Cuban had ever held the reins in the CRP's fifteen-year history. In August 1975, though, President Ford named a Cuban American connected to the RNHA, Ricardo Nuñez, to manage the program.[66] An anti-RNHA faction of Cuban Americans revolted. Lillian Giberga, widow of prominent Nixon fundraiser Manolo Giberga, blamed Ben Fernandez's out-of-touch Washington-based "Mexican clique" for helping to elevate Nuñez.[67] In March 1976, after Reagan took over 70 percent of the Cuban vote in Florida's Republican primary, Giberga was quick to cite the outcome as proof that Ford had backed the wrong faction. The "devastating political results" of the primary constituted a "repudiation" of his support for the RNHA affiliates, she wrote the president.[68]

To Giberga, even though Reagan did not carry Florida, his success in Miami was a clear sign that pan-Hispanic politics was a failure. Although she had been "consistently spurned" in previous attempts to counsel the White House on Cuban strategy, she reiterated that "the Cubans are *unlike any other ethnic group* and *unlike other Spanish-speaking ethnics with whom they are consistently and wrongly grouped*, and, therefore, should be dealt with in a completely different manner. Their distinct individualities make this new voter *unique in character*". She reminded the president that continuing to misunderstand this reality threatened the loss of 100,000 Cuban electors, "the swing vote in Florida."[69]

Fernandez and the RNHA hoped that Ford would resist any such retreat from pan-Hispanic politics. Indeed, the president's patronage and the celebration thereof informed the construction of GOP Hispanic politics as the primary season neared completion. As was becoming the custom with an election approaching, Ford did appoint Spanish-speaking Americans to a handful of prominent federal posts (including, of course, the Cuban Refugee Program). The RNHA, in turn, arranged for these men of status to serve as honored guests at its first annual banquet and fundraiser in July 1976, just weeks before the hotly contested Republican National Convention. By attending the event, President Ford and his vice president, the former New York governor Nelson Rockefeller, validated the organization's significance to the party and the nation. Blessing the RNHA's self-image as a true nationwide constituency, the president declared that the GOP he led would be "a channel for a new era of Hispanic involvement, from California and the Southwest, from Florida, from New York, from Arizona, and from all over this great land."[70]

Fernandez and the RNHA took their message to the Republican National Convention in Kansas City the following month. In his speech before the convention, the first such oration in party history, Fernandez performed the ritual construction of "Hispanic culture" in tune with ascendant party personalities and values. The "American of Hispanic origin," he said, was "conservative in fiscal matters, conditioned from childhood to live within his means," was "wary of the power of the 'federales'" and those "monstrous government agencies which would infringe on his individual rights." Fernandez linked "individual personal integrity"—supposedly Ford's hallmark and clear counterpoint to his predecessor—to the Hispanic American's simple request for participation in the system. By adopting the "recommended Hispanic plank," declaring the party against Castro, and recognizing the RNHA as an "official auxiliary," the convention could build upon the Republican gains of 1972 and deliver a victory in November, he promised. Reflecting both the RNHA's professional and class-conscious orientation and perhaps a sense that many in the audience were suspicious of any formalized (particularly nonwhite) ethnic politics, Fernandez vowed that the assembly's integration in the campaign would "be with dignity, with integrity, and with honor."[71]

Not all were convinced, even among Hispanic Republicans. A group of Cuban-American delegates for Reagan opposed the RNHA's bid to become a recognized party auxiliary, offering a blend of color-blind politics and Cuban exceptionalism as counterpoint to Fernandez's claims. The RNHA argued that a separate organization facilitated Hispanic Americans' entry into the core of American life. Miami's Alberto Cardenas, however, emphasized the need to build coalitions with other Republicans; his colleague, Carlos Salman, called the practice of establishing a Hispanic auxiliary akin to being put "in a closet . . . not part of the mainstream." The men pointed to their equal but integrated participation in Dade County's "Reagan-For-President" committee—and to Reagan's success in South Florida—as evidence that for Hispanic Americans there was a model far more effective than forming "minority splinter groups."[72] For Hispanic Americans to prosper in the GOP, the Miami Cubans judged, they needed to arrest their urge to formalize the party's multiculturalism.

It was hardly the case that Cubans did not have specific convention goals derived from their own experience, however. Cardenas and other Miami supporters of Reagan were drawn first and foremost to the challenger's foreign policy views. They had planned for months to use their presence at the convention to "alert our fellow delegates about pending dangers of worldwide Communist usurpation as seen through the eyes of those of us who have experienced this horror first hand." Having called for the party to take "a strong anti-Communist stand in international affairs," their presence contributed to the party's uncompromising Cuba plank. They also saw their chosen candidate use his delegate strength to force adoption of the "Morality in Foreign Policy" plank that censured the Ford administration's pursuit of détente.[73] The Cuban delegates' denunciations of the RNHA's "splinter[ing]" of Republicanism were thus probably less a criticism of ethnically inspired politics but rather of the RNHA's particular leadership and its basic alignment with the more moderate candidate in the race.

☆ ☆

After Ford fought off Ronald Reagan's convention challenge and secured renomination, the RNHA sought to assume a central role in the general election. Ben Fernandez submitted the outlines of "a legitimate, bona fide Hispanic campaign" he intended to run in coordination with the President Ford Committee (PFC), Ford's 1976 campaign organization, as well as with various Republican state party chairmen. His "bare bones budget" outlined the party's first truly egalitarian Hispanic campaign, devoting equal funding to California, Texas, New York, New Jersey, Florida, and Illinois.[74]

To presidential advisors, however, it was not at all clear that Fernandez's initiative would aid Ford's reelection. The Republicans' foremost expert on such matters, Alex Armendariz, expressed his skepticism. The man who ran Nixon's 1972 Spanish-speaking campaign warned the Ford administration that although that effort had relied upon "a centralized and standardized organization," Latino communities had not then—just four years earlier—possessed "the degree of sophistication and diversity that exists today." For this election, it was clear that "unrelated groups in each target area know their communities better than anyone in Washington." In echoes both of what Democrats proposed following McGovern's loss and what Reagan's Cuban delegates were arguing, Armendariz called for a strategy that empowered this "local leadership" to create its own campaign events, but "force[d]" it to "work closely with the local and state GOP structure, rather than acting independently as an appendage of the party." He recommended a "very low-profile effort" and, almost certainly with Fernandez in mind, warned the administration to "avoid creating supermen—focus on local Republicans rather than on Washington-based personalities."[75] Decentralization of Hispanic outreach was the recommendation.

Ford campaign advisors debated whether Hispanic political unity was even worth fostering. Taking into account the president's position within his party and the types of policies and patronage he could deliver, one campaign strategist doubted it. Because Puerto Ricans were, the strategist wrote, "urbanely [*sic*] concentrated and overwhelmingly Democrats," Ford did not have "much more to offer them." This analysis was consistent with Nixon's view of Puerto Ricans' place in Hispanic politics. However, a fundamental change was the analyst's suggestion to shift priority away from Mexican Americans as the main recipients of "Spanish-speaking" patronage. "Mexican Americans (Chicanos) are well represented in government posts; more than they deserve, considering their help to us. I would side with the Cuban element—most Republican—and their legitimate wish to be *more* considered within our councils," wrote the operative. And no doubt stung by Ford's poor showing in Dade County during the Florida primary, he recommended more active cultivation of those Cuban Americans unaffiliated with the RNHA.[76]

This did not mean that Mexican Americans had no role to play in Republican victory, however. As the analyst explained to his superiors,

> *let's not forget* that Mexican Americans in California & Texas are different from one another (*and* jealous) and can be played off. But better still they can be played off *against the negroes* to break the monolithic low class mass that goes Democrat [*sic*]. We should do all in our power to encourage this division—splitting the opposition—by doing what we can ON A LOCAL BASIS, however, to show the Chicanos we'll do more for them and not prefer the negroes (as the Democrats do). The terrain is ripe for this since the Chicanos are acquiring greater cognizance of their strength and heritage and the fact they figure last on the "minority" totem pole.[77]

Precisely when to accentuate Hispanic America's internal differentiation, and when to use race to bring parts of that national community together, was a decision for higher Republican powers.

The President Ford Committee chose to side with the decentralists, prohibiting the RNHA from running its own Hispanic general election campaign against the Democrat, former Georgia governor Jimmy Carter. Adding to the insult, the Ford campaign actively shunned the auxiliary and its expertise in key states. An infuriated Ben Fernandez wrote that the Ford campaign's tight rein on Hispanic voter outreach had "emasculated the Hispanic effort begun by our people as early as 1974." He predicted doom for Ford in Texas and Florida, and an unnecessarily narrow margin of victory in California. Although an important segment of the group had once been practically "in the palm of our hands," Fernandez was declaring that "the President has lost the Spanish Speaking vote." Seven weeks remained until the election.[78]

☆ ☆

Whether Ben Fernandez was correct at the time, he did predict the outcome. The scope of Ford's losses among Hispanic Americans was already becoming apparent as the 1976 results were still being finalized, with reporters describing "enormous margins among both blacks and Latin-Americans" going to Jimmy Carter.[79] One more thorough analysis gave Carter about 81 percent of Latino ballots, including "crucial vote margins" in Texas and New York, both "pivotal electoral states."[80] For the first time in eight years, Hispanic Republicans would be cut off from the White House patronage and access they required to fortify and grow their movement.

As the next two chapters show, Latino Democrats were hard at work at a mutually reinforcing project of legislatively institutionalizing their constituency and organizing its Democratic elected officials in a coherent national body. And soon enough the onus for recognizing and nurturing the Hispanic constituency, or as the case may have had it, containing and managing it, would again fall upon a president of their party.

# 9

# Securing Representation
# in a Multicultural Democracy

If the 1972 election appeared to mark the full institutionalization of the "Spanish-speaking vote" in both parties, the years that followed witnessed immediate contests over its character and relationship to those parties. While Watergate encouraged the conservative ascendancy that in turn shaped the self-image and internal workings of Hispanic Republicanism, George McGovern's landslide loss to Nixon intensified the contest over the future of the Democratic Party in ways that also bore directly on Latino participation. Having failed to stop McGovern's nomination, a core of Democratic regulars had imagined that "a big enough . . . loss" in 1972 would allow them to retake the Democratic National Committee (DNC) from the candidate's "New Politics" allies, and to regain control over presidential candidate selection and the party's ideological orientation. While many in this "conservative counterinsurgency" focused on reviving the party's hawkish Cold War internationalism, another key objective was to undo the McGovern-Fraser reforms. Taking effect after 1968, these party rules guaranteed participation of women, young people, and minorities in important party structures, and expanded rank-and-file participation in electing party leaders. For many in the anti–New Politics faction, "the crazies" and an "activist elite" had taken over, alienating the white working class and marginalizing organized labor, leading the party to ruin.[1]

The Latino Caucus saw it differently. It joined in the struggle to block any effort to "turn back the clock," as one black DNC member had put it, on the party's transformation.[2] The party's candidate had suffered an extraordinary defeat, but the Latino Caucus had no intention of abandoning its collective numbers. Speaking for a community he said was fifteen million strong, Herman Badillo called upon new DNC chairman Robert S. Strauss, a Texan backed by the anti-McGovern forces, to "renew" the party's "commitment to Puerto Ricans, Mexican-Americans, Cubans, Dominicans, and other Spanish-speaking peoples and take affirmative action to insure that it represents the best interests of our community." The party's Office of Spanish Speaking Affairs and the Latino Caucus itself needed unequivocal backing from the top. And any effort to revise the composition of party structures must have at its heart "proportional representation" of their people. Having garnered McGovern's campaign pledges that Latinos would be fully included in Democratic affairs, the Latino Caucus now "urge[d] that these positions remain the fundamental commitment of the Democratic Party to the Latino community."[3] If those promises were not kept, given all that Republicans had been doing to convert Spanish-speaking voters, the party would likely fall further behind in the race for national power.

When the Nixon presidency collapsed amid Watergate and a wave of Democratic "Watergate Babies" swept into Congress in 1974, it furnished a potential reprieve for the Democratic elites whom Herman Badillo had petitioned. The Latino constituency, having given an unprecedented percentage of its ballots to a Republican in 1972, might not have needed placating after all. Yet the 1974 congressional victories, which strengthened the party's northern and liberal wing, also bolstered the chances of a breakthrough in the Latino political project.

As the Watergate scandal toppled a president who divided and disorganized the Spanish-speaking vote for his own benefit, Latino congressmen pressed ahead to transform the United States into a truly multicultural democracy, with a unified and recognized "Latino" people as a central element. Their work proceeded on a number of mutually reinforcing fronts, though each possessed its own conception of democratic participation. In the middle years of the 1970s, Edward Roybal and Herman Badillo advanced a series of legislative reforms that extended the safeguards of representation they had won in the Democratic Party to the nation's electoral system and the federal statistical bureaucracy. Facing opposition to recognizing Latinos as a permanent national minority—some of that opposition emerging from within their own party—they employed their coalition-building traditions in an alliance with black elected officials and civil rights organizations. Together they extended the reach of American democracy, broadening the Voting Rights Act to protect "language minorities" as well as African Americans. To enforce new voting rights protections required new forms of state knowledge. Thus did voting protection abet the contemporary project of securing statistical recognition of the national "Spanish Origin" population, something only provisionally achieved in the 1970 census. Adopting an expansive vision of democratic participation, one that more fully recognized the large numbers of noncitizens in their imagined political community, Latino elected officials and a cadre of Washington-based lobbyists argued that consistent national enumeration of their people and their collective socioeconomic condition was essential to the workings of American democracy. Finally, to bring these and other advances back to bear on the Democratic Party itself, to strengthen its commitment to a multicultural future, Roybal and Badillo also constructed a new national network of the party's Latino elected officials. At once broadly democratic and wary of certain forms of grassroots mobilization, the intertwining of legal, bureaucratic, and organizational recognition of a national minority— whether called Latino or Hispanic—helped consolidate the transformation in the political landscape and national self-image temporarily illuminated by the bipartisan emergence of the Spanish-speaking vote in the 1972 election.

☆ ☆

Although they had emerged from the 1972 campaign season widely regarded as a national minority electoral constituency, Latinos collectively lacked the ballot protections that African Americans had won during the 1960s. The Voting Rights Act of 1965 had outlawed literacy tests and poll taxes, and introduced federal oversight of elections, steps that cumulatively broke the back of the decades-long organized disfranchisement of black voters. But the act focused on the Deep South. And while it also barred New York officials from applying that state's literacy test to most Puerto Ricans, its deliberate exclusion of Texas (as well as the Southwest) meant it did little to alleviate voting barriers that many Mexican-American communities faced. These electorates remained vulnerable to gerrymandering or at-large election schemes, as well as to economic and physical threats. The county that provided Spanish-language voting materials, too, was exceedingly rare before 1975. Together, these facts ensured that Latinos, Mexican Americans especially, would remain politically underrepresented. National voting rights legislation did not, by and large, apply to them.

The Voting Rights Act would come up for renewal in 1975. But many congressmen and President Gerald Ford's attorney general at first supported simply extending the law for five years, keeping its focus on seven states in the Deep South.[4] However, Hispanic Americans were in a stronger position than ever to make a claim on its protections. They had become a sought-after constituency of both parties. They had also developed greater coordination among themselves and with the wider community of civil rights organizations. The American G.I. Forum, the League of United Latin American Citizens (LULAC), IMAGE, and "all the major national Spanish-speaking organizations" had recently formed a Washington, DC–based lobbying organization, the National Congress of Hispanic American Citizens, which claimed to speak for three million members in ninety-five organizations.[5] It, in turn, had affiliated with the Leadership Conference on Civil Rights, a coalition of major civil rights groups, including the NAACP and the Urban League. In addition, the Ford Foundation–sponsored Southwest Council of La Raza, an umbrella organization of Mexican-American groups, had in late 1972 renamed itself the National Council of La Raza and begun the process of relocating its headquarters to Washington, DC, where it could be closer to the decision makers and allies most vital to its future.[6]

Latino elected officials had reason to believe that African American legislators might join with them to expand the Voting Rights Act. Roybal and Badillo could take solace in knowing that the seventeen members of the Congressional Black Caucus pledged to support "extend[ing] the act's coverage to Spanish speaking and other minorities who face severe problems of disenfranchisement."[7] They would find a strong partner in Houston congresswoman Barbara Jordan. In the long line of liberals who labored to fuse Texas's Mexican Americans and blacks into a progressive powerhouse, she introduced voting rights legislation in February 1975 that made English-only elections in Latino areas a trigger for federal supervision.[8] Addressing congressional colleagues, Jordan vouchsafed that the two groups experienced "the same, or similar experiences" of disfranchisement.[9]

Seeking changes in national election law to bring about representation comparable to that which they had secured within the Democratic Party, Roybal and Badillo introduced their own legislation on February 20, 1975. Beyond extending the Voting Rights Act for a decade, the bill, H.R. 3501, expanded the Act's coverage. It required the Bureau of the Census to identify political jurisdictions in which people of "Spanish origin" comprised at least 5 percent of the voting-age citizenry, had voter turnout lower than the national averages in 1964 or 1968, and that also conducted elections only in the English language. By subjecting these jurisdictions to federal oversight, and in particular the requirement that electoral changes be submitted to the Department of Justice for "pre-clearance," Roybal believed that the bill would finally reform electoral practices in Texas, Arizona, and California, practices that had for so long muzzled Mexican Americans' political voices.[10]

The justification for expanding federal voting protections to all the nation's "Spanish origin" people revealed a progressive intertwining of Mexican Americans' and Puerto Ricans' local political and legal histories. When Vilma Martínez of the Mexican American Legal Defense and Educational Fund (MALDEF) testified before Congress, she did so on behalf of six million "United States citizens of Mexican ancestry." The group she called "the second largest minority in America" was simultaneously "65 percent" of the nation's "Spanish-surnamed community."[11] Moreover, central to MALDEF's arguments in support of the expansion was Section 4(e) of the 1965 voting law. As discussed in Chapter 3, liberal senators from New York had included this "American Flag" provision on the premise that because US policy fostered Spanish as Puerto Rico's language of instruction, Puerto Ricans who had completed the sixth grade ought not be subject to their state's English literacy test. In the early 1970s, Puerto Rican activists mobilized along with advocates from the Puerto Rican Legal Defense and Education Fund to file various class-action lawsuits on behalf of plaintiffs in Chicago, New York, New Jersey, and Philadelphia. In these cases, federal courts had affirmed the need for bilingual election materials in order for Puerto Rican plaintiffs to truly exercise the franchise under Section 4(e). Reflecting the significance of these Puerto Rican legal challenges, in its brief to the Justice Department, MALDEF cited three such decisions: *Arroyo v. Tucker* (1974), *Torres v. Sachs* (1974), and *Puerto Rican Organization for Political Action v. Kusper* (1972). The Puerto Rican cases, MALDEF's brief states, showed "that where *Spanish-speaking Americans* reside, the conducting of an election only in the English language is a 'device' which abridges or denies the right to vote of such citizens."[12]

Federal officials, too, endorsed the transferability of Puerto Rican precedents to all "Spanish-speaking" voters. Analyzing the bills pending before Congress, the US Commission on Civil Rights (USCCR) held "other language minority persons" to be "similarly situated to the Puerto Rican plaintiffs in *Torres v. Sachs*," and thus concluded that "a similar case can be constructed so that English language elections are definable under Section 4(c) as 'tests or devices.'"[13] The Commission's 1975 report, *The Voting Rights Act: Ten Years After*, was even clearer. The report cited the *Torres* ruling that "It is simply fundamental that voting instructions and ballots, in addition to any other material which forms part of the official communication to registered voters prior to an election, must be in Spanish as well as English, if the vote of Spanish-speaking citizens is not to be seriously impaired."[14] The Department of Justice weighed in on April 8. Erasing any of its previous skepticism, it declared that "Based on case law, our investigation of discrimination of various types against persons of Spanish origin, and the evidence submitted to the Subcommittee, there seems little doubt that such persons suffer from extensive barriers to the exercise of their franchise."[15] When it came to justifying extension of the Voting Rights Act, Puerto Rican cases unlocked doors for all persons of "Spanish origin."

While knitting Latino legal communities together around common experiences judged analogous to those of African Americans, the Voting Rights Act extension served as the backdrop for a debate over the Latino's place in the American ethnoracial order. Roybal and Badillo's bill was grounded in the Fifteenth Amendment's prohibitions on racial restriction of the franchise. But sensing an "apparent confusion over whether Mexican Americans and Puerto Ricans fall within the term 'race or color,'" the legislators chose to justify the bill based upon the Fourteenth Amendment's equal protection clause as well.[16] Mexican Americans stood to benefit most from expansion, but their lack of racial fixity provoked the greatest amount of concern. Testifying on behalf of the Leadership Conference on Civil Rights in March 1975, attorney Joseph Rauh worried that the Fifteenth Amendment might not easily apply to "the Mexican Americans in the Southwest." Rauh was a pillar of postwar US liberalism, a champion of labor, and a supporter of expanding the bill. But he worried because Mexican Americans themselves appeared of many opinions "as to whether that group is covered by 'race or color.'" He had "asked that question repeatedly and . . . gotten different answers."[17] The matter was no easier for Puerto Ricans. When asked directly if he believed Puerto Ricans "constitute[d] a race," a Puerto Rican Legal Defense and Education Fund attorney said the matter was "very personal," but that "probably [they did] not."[18] From his seat on the Judiciary Committee's Subcommittee on Civil and Constitutional Rights, Herman Badillo pointed out that Puerto Rican leaders sought unity of their people first and foremost, and could gain nothing in trying to "say which Puerto Ricans are white, which are black, or which are mixed."[19] He warned of an impending legal challenge in which

> you will get some Puerto Rican on the witness stand and they will be asked what race they are, and if the wrong fellow says that he is white, then the court might rule that there is no way of determining what race a Puerto Rican is any more than there is any way of determining what race a New Yorker is or a Washingtonian is,

thereby costing the group its legal protection.[20]

Federal officials attempted to adjudicate "Spanish origin" peoples' place in the American ethnoracial order. The United States Commission on Civil Rights backed a racial understanding of Latino identity. Referencing dictionaries and court decisions, its staff explained that

> Population groups distinguished by, and discriminated against on the basis of, their language, their common cultural heritage, and their physical characteristics meet the anthropological / sociological definition of race. In using such racial characteristics to identify a class for 14th amendment purposes, the courts have gone far in supporting the definition of such groups as "races" for purposes of 15th amendment protection. Based on such reasoning, Spanish origin minority groups should be defined as a race for purposes of protection under the Voting Rights Act.[21]

The Department of Justice, too, counseled legislators that even if their racial "status" was "less clear" than, for instance, that of Native Americans, it was nonetheless "fully consistent with the spirit of the [Voting Rights] Act as amended to treat Mexican Americans and Puerto Ricans as racial groups."[22]

African American organizations feared it was not so clear. Secure in a Voting Rights Act grounded in the Fifteenth Amendment, they dreaded that opponents would exploit the reworked legislation to eliminate existing protections for black voters. According to NAACP Washington Bureau director Clarence Mitchell, southern opponents were seeking any means "to open the door for real damage" to the bill's main areas of coverage. Six years of Republican control of the White House also meant that any new wave of legal challenges to voting rights would come before an increasingly conservative judiciary. Mitchell warned that states would be emboldened to "believe they could now get out from under the act with respect to blacks." Won only through the sacrifice of countless lost lives and battered bodies, the Act had also engendered a certain proprietary feeling in black America. Some African Americans, he claimed, would perceive any attempt to change "so sacred" a law as an act of "sabotage."[23]

It was not that black organizations did not want Spanish-speaking Americans included, their representatives said. Urban League executive director Vernon Jordan testified that

> After centuries of exclusion and oppression, black Americans can ill afford not to support such an expansion to provide equal protection to a people who, like ourselves, know full well the demeaning, frustrating and immoral acts which have been perpetrated upon minorities in this country when we have tried to exercise our right to register and to vote. We can ill afford to forget from whence we came. We can ill afford to turn our backs on a people seeking that freedom which we have long sought—freedom to participate in the American way of life.[24]

But they wanted to see it done by including the Spanish-speaking under a separate title of the legislation. That way, reasoned the NAACP's Mitchell, they would minimize risk that the new parts of the law might be found unconstitutional, thus jeopardizing the whole of the law. The goal was to "get others on board," but without "sink[ing] the ship."[25]

Roybal and Badillo took these concerns to heart, and cosponsored a new bill with Barbara Jordan. Their H.R. 6219 extended the act for seven years, and separately expanded protection of the law to a new class of "language minorities." These were defined in broad pan-ethnic terms, as "persons who are American Indian, Asian American, Alaskan Natives or of Spanish heritage." H.R. 6219 was reported out in May 1975, and in June passed with an impressive House margin of 341 to 70. An amended version passed the Senate in late July, 77 to 12, and after resolution of differences the legislation was signed by President Ford on August 6, 1975.[26] Ford's assistant for Hispanic affairs, Fernando De Baca, called it "a historic document which signals a major breakthrough for the nation's 10 million Spanish-speaking Americans."[27]

He was not overstating the case. By the end of the month, the Department of Justice was informing 464 counties across twenty-seven states that they would be required to print bilingual election materials. Forty counties in California faced a new federal mandate. Furthermore, the entire state of Texas was now required to submit any changes to its election law to federal courts or the attorney general for "pre-clearance."[28]

☆ ☆

As momentous as the Voting Rights Act's extension would be, potential voting power could not be the sole basis for this "language minority's" claims on society. The large number of Latinos who were immigrants meant that many in the group also lacked US citizenship, and thus the ability to cast a ballot. In the matters of legislative apportionment and the distribution of federal funds, however, Latinos could register their presence, and do so irrespective of their citizenship. As we have seen, many individuals and organizations recognized that obtaining an accurate picture of their numbers and circumstances was essential to improving the Latino condition. Ricardo Zazueta, the director of a LULAC and American G.I. Forum joint job-training program, expressed this view when testifying before Congress in 1974. "There is no doubt," he said then, "that in statistics, as in our children, lies our future."[29]

The 1970 decennial census encouraged this sentiment. When the Bureau of the Census released preliminary findings of its 1970 count, organs such as *U.S. News and World Report* told of a nation undergoing rapid change. The "bigger than expected" population shifts caused by the exodus of rural America to the cities and suburbs, and the great movement of Americans to the South and West, portended a "significant transfer of power" to the growing areas.[30] According to the *Los Angeles Times*, California's "Latin American heritage" population had doubled since 1960, and was now more than twice as large as the state's black population.[31] Across the country, while few would have been surprised to learn that 811,843 of New York State's 872,471 Puerto Ricans lived in New York City, the new "Spanish Origin" identifier also revealed some altogether new populations. In New York City alone, it highlighted the existence of almost 400,000 persons who might have been Dominican, Cuban, Spanish, or of some other "Hispanic extraction," as the *New York Times* put it.[32]

For Mexican Americans, whose greatest concentrations lay in the growing Sunbelt, the results were potentially positive news. With a "good" count of their people, they stood to gain in legislative reapportionment, federal aid dollars, and, less directly, political influence. For those in the struggling cities of the Rust Belt, where most Puerto Ricans lived, the stakes were probably higher. Population decline, if overestimated, would deal further damage to communities suffering amid the multifaceted urban crisis. Getting every person counted mattered greatly.

With so much on the line, Latino activists and urban politicians' stance toward the census findings was one of extreme skepticism. In New York State, community leaders could not fathom that the national measurement of first- and second-generation Puerto Ricans in the 1970 census— 1,379,043—was smaller than the 1,454,000 Puerto Ricans who had been identified by the 1969 Current Population Survey (CPS).[33] And in California, even before preliminary state totals were released, federal lawsuits were already seeking to enjoin the Bureau from publishing its 1970 Spanish Heritage statistics. The plaintiffs argued that the Bureau's use of a mail-out/mail-back system of enumeration, and discrimination against their group in census employment, had led the census to miss more than five million of their people.[34]

The conflict over national statistics begat further organization. In California, representatives of the American G.I. Forum, LULAC, IMAGE, and MALDEF joined together, forming the "Mexican-American Population Commission of California." They accused the Bureau of "abdicat[ing] its responsibility" to hold a fair count in 1970, and placed themselves in the "quasi-governmental role" of overseeing its findings. Compiling data from census surveys, the California Department of Education, and the US Department of Labor, they generated their own set of facts with which to dispute the 1970 count. In June 1973, they announced that 3.75 million "Spanish-surnamed" people lived in the state, almost twice as many as the two million "persons of Spanish Origin" announced by the 1970 census.[35]

New techniques of counting the population, designed in part to placate such critics, made the Bureau of the Census even more vulnerable to their charges. In 1973, census officials had reassigned all children under fourteen years of age to the Spanish Origin category if their mothers belonged to it, regardless of what the "head of household" had listed.[36] The change produced roughly 300,000 additional Spanish Origin children, and instantly boosted the larger group's population by about 3 percent.[37] The Bureau's March 1973 CPS was another flashpoint. It showed about 1.5 million more Spanish Origin people—a 17 percent increase—than had been counted in the decennial census taken in April 1970. The Bureau claimed that some of the growth came from its use of new identifiers, and that two-thirds was likely due to a combination of immigration and an increase in births over deaths. The Mexican-American Population Commission argued, however, that the new numbers were the Bureau's admission of "past mistakes." The change "vindicated" their earlier criticism. It was proof that a bureaucracy without their involvement, a "totally academic approach," would fail to incorporate their people, whose "different lifestyles and outlooks" demanded "new mechanisms to accurately count population."[38] Newspapers followed this line and mistakenly called the 1973 CPS a "recount" that had "discovered" the population gain, or suggested that it was a revision of the 1970 census, rather than a new survey conducted at an entirely different point in time.[39]

The campaign to discredit traditional practices of counting Latinos gained allies among federal civil rights advocates. Louis Nuñez was one. A Puerto Rican who was named deputy staff director of the USCCR during Nixon's reelection campaign, he proposed in 1973 that the USCCR investigate a potentially massive undercount of Spanish Origin people in the 1970 census. The inquiry produced *Counting the Forgotten: The 1970 Census Count of Persons of Spanish Speaking Background in the United States.* A 112-page indictment of Census Bureau ineptitude and insensitivity, the report transformed what statisticians saw as a technical problem into a civil rights question, and a manifesto for institutionalizing Hispanic identity in government.[40] *Counting the Forgotten* found "strong evidence" that the country's "Spanish-speaking background population was substantially undercounted" in 1970, and "probably . . . by appreciably more than" the 7.7 percent that the Bureau acknowledged having undercounted the nation's blacks.[41] While national origin ruled in electoral circles, the report made language the core characteristic of "the nation's second largest minority population." It criticized the Bureau for not mailing out Spanish-language questionnaires, for failing to provide sufficient Spanish instructions, and for not hiring enough bilingual enumerators. Furthermore, the Bureau had been "insensitive" to use a "variety of indices" to measure the group. The report called upon it henceforth to employ "a uniform measure" to identify this population, and to furnish it "the same consideration given to nonminorities in the Bureau's methodology and data collection techniques." Indicating the mutually reinforcing nature of the institutionalization of pan-ethnicity within the bureaucracy, one of the important pieces of evidence cited was a Cabinet Committee on Opportunities for Spanish-Speaking People report estimating that twelve million people of "Spanish-speaking background" resided in the United States in 1971.[42]

The search for "a uniform measure" was crucial. It led the government's civil rights advocates to seek out the federal government's Office of Management and Budget (OMB). Its Statistical Policy Division (SPD) served as the "central coordinating agency" for federal data.[43] A 1971 OMB report noted that the "proliferation of statistical collection activities" in dozens of federal agencies had led to "wide disparities" in data quality, among other "operational inefficiencies."[44] One agency might report as many as fifteen ethnoracial categories while another reported only one ("minority"). Most agencies used "various categories for persons of Spanish heritage."[45] The SPD expected to provide "leadership" in these matters, and standardization would be the answer.[46]

Faced with the "problem" that one SPD statistician called "identifying Spanishness," standardization had specific implications. As Mexican-American activists had found when attempting to form their own coalitions in the early 1960s, and as they later discovered when interacting with Puerto Ricans and Cubans, the first problem was picking a term that would include them all. Different federal agencies used different terms to measure this population, and their techniques for reporting also varied. Some government departments obtained data by visual observation. Others used self-identification. This difference complicated the range of identifiers available—could one visually observe a "Spanish-speaking" American?—and raised other questions. Like the legislators, statistical managers noted that the population itself did not always agree about the race to which it belonged. Some group members desired to identify themselves racially as "white," while others preferred "brown" or "Indian," and still others chose "black."[47]

The solution to these dilemmas was to be selectively superficial. The government needed to create, in historian David Hollinger's words, a sort of "race equivalent."[48] According to the OMB, its new category "should yield consistent results" whether using self-identification or visual observation, "and be sufficiently general to encompass all minority groups." Terms had to be "those that an observer can readily apply, e.g., a general category of persons of Spanish origin, versus a particular national origin such as Cuban." Besides diminishing the importance of national origin, reliance on a visual cue to "Spanishness" was also broadly consistent with the OMB's objective of "identify[ing] the individual as a member of the group even though he may no longer be conscious of his origin or even if he may be actively trying to avoid identification with the racial or ethnic group." These quasi-racial requirements led OMB to reject existing identifiers such as "Spanish surnamed," or the increasingly popular "Spanish-speaking." Such characteristics did not define the population that managers were most concerned about measuring, those whose physical appearance marked them for different treatment in society.[49]

OMB officials acknowledged the pressure coming from a great many "minority interest groups," and that they expected "the 'women' groups" to soon demand "additional sexual data." "Despite prior, intensive efforts," however, SPD staff admitted lacking a "cohesive, well-thought-out policy in these areas." As of 1973, they had no real idea of the quantity of racial and ethnic data the government gathered, the cost of its collection and storage, the percentage that ever got evaluated, and what, if any of it, was useful. The OMB was adrift, but it could not remain so for long. As one internal analysis concluded, "continuing external pressures, political sensitivities and potential programmatic benefits all seem to demand that OMB provides some guidance and soon—or at least determine internally where we stand."[50]

While statisticians debated, Latino legislators did their best to ensure that federal statistics reflected their people's place in the nation. It was not just the census that was suspect, after all. The absence of a single standard for federal data denied their importance in other ways. For example, the unemployment rate was catalogued every month for blacks and whites, but not for their group. Since the fall of 1971, Roybal and Badillo had been introducing resolutions to compel the Bureau of the Census and the Bureau of Labor Statistics to take regular stock of their group's position in American life. Badillo wanted to know "exactly where we stand," so that America's second largest minority could receive the "full and fair share" of federal resources that its collective numbers deserved.[51] In 1973, Roybal cited the "racial, social, economic, and political discrimination" his people suffered, and argued that they could not "lift themselves out" of their despair because the lack of "regular, nationwide evaluation" prevented policymakers from making an accurate assessment of their "urgent and special needs."[52]

Latino groups lobbied to convince Congress that consistent national enumeration of their socioeconomic condition was essential to the workings of American democracy. In hearings on the subject in 1974, Alex Zermeno of the National Council of La Raza (NCLR) testified that proper data would promote impartial administration. Without good statistics, minorities were at the mercy of any administration bent on "politicizing the government services" that were its obligation to provide. By shedding light on Nixon's Spanish-speaking strategy, the Watergate investigation showed what it was like when groups "couldn't make [their] case on facts, on statistics" and thus were "forced to play the patronage game." It was time to end the government's "statistical atrocities" and fulfill the public's "right to quality information."[53]

Essential to achieving efficiency and realizing this "right," according to advocates, was the creation of an official category that would place all Spanish-speaking people under a single banner. The NCLR argued that a "common identifier" would "reduce confusion" and "provide for increased accuracy." The US Commission on Civil Rights too deemed it "very important" for census and OMB officials to jointly establish "a standard Spanish origin category." Roybal called for the OMB to take the lead in establishing a consistent identifier, with "Spanish origin or descent" or "Spanish-speaking background" as possible options.[54]

A mandate that collectively distinguished these populations from the mainstream did not sit well with some House members, however. Congressmen such as Texas Democrat Richard White portrayed themselves as allies of the cause, but skeptics of the method. For White, assimilation was desirable, the byproduct of improved material condition. He thus wondered if the group's economic advancement would render a national Spanish-speaking statistic obsolete. Years before, he recalled, civil rights groups had sought to eliminate "Mexican" as a designation on birth certificates. The moniker was thought prejudicial, an impediment to individual and group inclusion. Would not reviving such a practice make it difficult for this group to assimilate, a problem since, White said, "we're all Americans."[55]

If White feared sowing division among Americans, other congressmen believed that a standard national statistic might not divide them enough. William Lehman, a freshman Democrat from South Florida, objected to including his constituents and their "success-oriented Cuban culture" in the same category as another "minority." He cautioned against any effort to view "all Spanish surnames as a monolithic thing," claiming that there existed "more difference between the Cubans and the Mexicans or the Puerto Ricans and the Cubans than there is between the Anglos and the Cubans, or the blacks and the Mexicans, and so forth." Cubans' rapid structural assimilation—their "mobility of class," Lehman called it—raised doubts about considering the country's Spanish-speaking populations "as a kind of a block group." As far as he was concerned, it was an open question if government could even produce a statistic of "any value to help us solve our problem."[56]

Aided by a new Washington-based lobbying apparatus, Roybal continued to press his case. In January 1975, he introduced H.J. Res. 92, which requested that the OMB "develop a Government-wide program for the collection of data with respect to Americans of Spanish origin or descent."[57] Advocacy groups lined up behind the effort, displaying the type of organizational unity that they wished to see reflected in the statistics. The National Congress of Hispanic American Citizens weighed in for a single, "Spanish Origin or descent" category, one that would also allow people to indicate their national origin.[58] An even more vocal supporter of a national and pan-Hispanic approach to data collection was the NCLR. Its report on *The Hispanic American: A National Planning Policy Issue for the 1980 Census,* condemned policymakers for their faulty "regional conceptualization" of what the NCLR now called the "Hispanic issue." Legislators and bureaucrats had divided New York, South Florida, and the Southwest "into Puerto Rican, Cuban and Mexican American spheres of influence," asserted the report. Federal statistics, however, showed that more than a million Cubans, Puerto Ricans, and Mexicans lived beyond "the regions with which they are 'ethnically' identified." These facts necessitated a new way of thinking about the country that was devoid of "regional ethnocentricity." According to NCLR, a uniform countrywide statistic would recognize and publicize the fact that "the Hispanic American issue is a national question."[59]

After four years, it appeared that the Congress agreed. On October 29, 1975, the Roybal resolution passed the House, and the Senate ordered it out of committee by a voice vote. It was the only law to mandate data collection for a specific ethnoracial group. It required the use of more Spanish-language questionnaires and bilingual enumerators during censuses. It demanded monthly instead of quarterly unemployment statistics for this group. The goal was "a reliable and comprehensive socioeconomic profile," one "on par with that available for the general population of the United States."[60] On May 21, 1976, the resolution passed the Senate, and on June 7, the House concurred. President Ford signed it in the Rose Garden little more than a week later, with Roybal and Badillo looking on.[61]

Together, the Roybal resolution and Congress's extension of the Voting Rights Act had a cascading effect. They provided legislative endorsement of this minority group's emergence as both a national electoral constituency and a statistical entity. These in turn bolstered other efforts to standardize the "Hispanic" American's bureaucratic identity. In response to congressional pressure, the OMB "instructed" the Equal Employment Opportunity Commission (EEOC) and the Department of Health, Education, and Welfare's Office of Civil Rights (OCR) to adopt "a single set of racial and ethnic categories" for educational reporting, beginning in the fall of 1975.[62] After ten months of work, the Federal Interagency Committee on Education (FICE), of which the EEOC and OCR were a part, accepted "Hispanic" as one of five racial/ethnic classifications.[63] The category was defined as "a person of Mexican, Puerto Rican, Cuban, central or South American, or other Spanish culture or origin, regardless of race." The FICE also permitted asking if a person belonged to one of four races, followed by the question, "is your ethnic heritage Hispanic?"[64] The federal government continued to refine its approach, and in late 1976 the OMB and the US Government Accountability Office released a draft of new racial and ethnic categories that included a "Hispanic" option.[65] On May 12, 1977, Jimmy Carter's OMB director, Bert Lance, approved the categories as part of something called "Statistical Directive 15." Effective immediately for new and revised federal surveys, the regulation demanded that all federal statistics be brought into conformance by January 1, 1980. Statistical Directive 15 received very little attention at first. Statisticians appreciated its importance, however. In an article explaining the changes, a lead OMB statistician wrote that the revision created, "for the first time, standard categories and definitions for use at the Federal level in reporting on racial and ethnic groups."[66] Backed by the authority of the federal government, it would play a central role in organizing the benefits and burdens of Americans' ethnic identities, and in constructing the national image, for decades.

☆ ☆

Fresh from amalgamating the Latino constituency in the realms of voting rights and national statistics, Roybal and Badillo again trained their quest for Latino unity on the Democratic Party. In November 1975, they and a handful of prominent Latino Democrats invited a group of 175 individuals to Washington, DC, where they aimed to lay the foundation for what Badillo called a "historic new Latin organization," one that would enable the exercise of "Latin Power." In what the *New York Times* described as "a ringing speech" to the assembled representatives, Arizona governor Raúl Castro—a self-proclaimed "establishment" figure narrowly elected in the Democratic wave of 1974—declared at once their shared origin and the imperative of unity. "Somos del mismo barro—we are of the same clay," he told them. "We have no other way but to unite and demand our rights."[67]

Setting the ground rules for unity, however, was a political act in and of itself, one that reflected a narrowed realm of participants. Their failure to control the grassroots activists at the Unidos conference still fresh in memory, the planners limited the event to Latino officials at the local, state, and federal levels. After all, reasoned Badillo, these individuals had been "chosen to represent the very diverse communities they serve" and thus could "best articulate their constituents' needs, and mobilize the kind of action" that would produce positive legislation and electoral results. Such a view was in keeping with Roybal's contention that his people had moved beyond "the confrontation politics of the '60s" and had embraced "active participation in the system." Distancing Latino politics from "confrontation" helped justify the event's clearly partisan nature. While the 1971 Unidos conference's ostensible objective was to forge a nonpartisan "Spanish-speaking coalition," the 1975 event took place under the auspices of the Democratic National Committee and its Latino Caucus.[68]

An organization of Democratic elected officials could realize geographic diversity, but the qualification of office-holding made gender inclusivity as well as ideological and strategic variety more difficult to achieve. Badillo spoke excitedly of creating a "vehicle for political discussion between Hispanics of the Southwest, Florida, Puerto Rico, and the Midwest and the

Northeast." And conceiving of unity in terms of representation afforded to the group's "various geographic segments," organizers established a steering committee with members from eleven states and the Commonwealth of Puerto Rico. Having divvied up turf, the group failed in its attempts to ensure female representation from each state. In a sign of just how few women had been invited to join in the official Latino political project, certain state rosters contained the words "woman delegate to be determined." Similarly, the emphasis on elected officialdom would produce a group more cautious in its tactics. When Badillo remarked about this "harmonious, constructive, and exciting" gathering of leaders, he could not help but note the changes that had taken place since the Unidos conference. The responsible elected officials assembled had come to terms with the need for unity, he said, and agreed that the most useful "exercise [of] 'Latin Power'" would come "through the electoral process." Their people were "definitely on the move."[69]

In January 1976, its leaders christened their new assembly the National Association of Latino Democratic Officials. Edward Roybal served as its first chairman. Raúl Castro was vice chairman, and Herman Badillo was secretary-treasurer. Brimming with ambition after the recent extension of the Voting Rights Act, the new group voiced its goal of adding one million Hispanic voters to the rolls, and to use their coalition's power to exercise a meaningful voice in their party in time for the 1976 elections.[70]

☆ ☆

While Democrats' recriminations over the debacle of the 1972 campaign often centered around how much to empower the party's "minority" constituencies, the Nixon administration's collapse and the Democratic triumphs of 1974 facilitated a rapid and enduring consolidation of Hispanic or Latino pan-ethnicity in American elections and official statistical practices, a change in national status that was in turn reflected in the workings of the Democratic Party. Employing multifarious conceptions of democratic participation and representation, Latino elected officials along with allies in African America and in a burgeoning world of Washington-based Hispanic lobbyists remade the United States ever more into a multicultural democracy. Just four years after devastating defeat to Richard Nixon in 1972, the Democratic practitioners of Latino politics could be justifiably confident that their people were more central than ever to the nation's political future.

# 10

# Latino Liberalism in an Era of Limits

Latino Democrats entered the nation's bicentennial year full of expectation. As part of the ongoing revolution in minority rights, their elected officials had won them new federal ballot protections that seemed certain to increase their share of the nation's vote total. Their legislators and lobbying groups had institutionalized their place in the bureaucracy as well, prevailing upon government skeptics to count them as a permanent minority in national statistics. Clearly distinguished from white and black America, their people's unique needs would become more apparent, their claims more easily justified. Scores of Latino elected officials now belonged to a new national organization, Edward Roybal's National Association of Latino Democratic Officials (NALADO), and their numbers could only grow. And in another sign of greater prominence in Democratic Party affairs, theirs was the only protected party constituency (these included women, blacks, and youth) to head to the 1976 Democratic National Convention with a larger number of delegates than it had brought in 1972. The party's "Latino Caucus" excitedly predicted that with the support of elected officials, the party, and its presidential nominee, "this 1976 Democratic and Bicentennial Year should be the breakthrough for Latinos in the electoral process."[1]

Yet even as their growing numbers and organizational sophistication seemed to betoken a necessary and almost automatic increase in power, Latino Democrats found no easy breakthrough forthcoming. In this moment, the power of the Democratic leader to act both as a focal point for, and brake on, the Latino political enterprise remained strong. Georgia Democrat Jimmy Carter validated this electoral constituency's distinctiveness as a candidate but, seeking to present himself as a new type of Democrat unbeholden to the party's "special interests," offered it the cold comfort of color-blindness upon his ascension to the Oval Office. The generation of Hispanic activists and elected officials led by Edward Roybal and Herman Badillo perceived in Carter a manifold threat to their community's place within the nation. First, he was unwedded to his party's New Deal commitment to a broad federal role in bringing about economic justice. Second, Carter's selective color-blindness closed doors they had pried open by securing party and legislative recognition as a permanent minority—the positive use of their quasi-racialization—even as his immigration policies promised to racialize them negatively through hostile state action. Defending their vision of an economically egalitarian and multicultural party, Latino Democrats fused economic claims with deep roots in the New Deal Era to assertions of cultural and familial autonomy then becoming central to 1970s politics. And they complemented this blending of material and cultural considerations with a full-on embrace of their physical distinction from white society.

Their creative synthesis forced the Carter White House to abandon its pretensions to color-blind liberalism and to enlist its allies in establishing new Hispanic institutions and political appeals that incorporated the objectives of both cultural and economic security, but that also acted to defend Jimmy Carter's record. As new leaders emerged to redefine the terms of power sharing among "Hispanic American Democrats," their ascent demonstrated the enduring acceptance of the "Spanish-speaking concept," but also how its malleability would feature in the party's future. Not only could Latino political identity be made to promote a traditionally liberal agenda, it could be used to insulate a Democratic administration from liberal criticism.

☆ ☆

Testifying before the Democratic Platform Committee in May 1976, Edward Roybal challenged his party's self-image and its relationship to his rising constituency. As he had argued in securing voting rights and statistical recognition for Latinos, he claimed that it was unacceptable to regard the group as anything other than a deeply rooted and permanent feature in American life. Accordingly, Democrats needed to develop policies with their specific needs in mind. Simply waiting for them to succeed within the existing arrangement, the party's "comfortable reliance on the dogma that time equals progress," was an old trope for European immigrants, and unacceptable when it came to Latinos.[2]

Roybal yet again sought to educate Democrats in the commonality of the Latino struggle, defining the group anew in the nation's bicentennial year. In Roybal's telling, language was one feature that defined their difference. NALADO denounced a public school system willing to "'de-educate' our Latino children instead of nurturing their ability and pride" in speaking Spanish. The "Latino" perspective on the administration of justice was also unique. Roybal connected the suffering of Puerto Ricans in the prisons and jails in New York State to the police killing of journalist Ruben Salazar in East Los Angeles. He further tied these tragedies to "the memories of Border Patrol 'raids' on our communities," and "urban 'sweeps' by Immigration officials," and linked these to the Texas Rangers' ruthless enforcement of white supremacy in South Texas. "The symbols and memories of this victimization are to be found everywhere where Latinos have resided," he informed his fellow Democrats.[3]

As Roybal and NALADO rejected the imposition of borders within and among their communities, his remarks reflected how even a mainstream formulation of Latino political identity had grown more international in character over the 1970s. Showing this broadened perspective, Roybal claimed that "what we advocate for the Latino community in this country can be applied equally to the developing countries of Latin America." It was time, he argued, to resolve the "clear contradiction, which is growing more conspicuous every year, between the espousal of American democratic principles and our government's failure to oppose the denial of human rights in the hemisphere and even in our own country."[4]

While conservatives were then busily employing family values to roll back government programs,[5] Roybal's conceptualization of the "Latino community" and family operated to decidedly different ends. Far from purely "cultural" and certainly not conservative, it was inseparable from his call for a reinvigorated Democratic commitment to a broad program of liberal economic reform. He spoke of the "certain core values which the Latino community holds deeply," first of which was "a strong and vibrant FAMILY structure."[6] He argued that "economic security is the social cement which holds the family together." Full employment, domestic economic development banks, and affirmative action too were essential to supporting the Latino family, as was good housing and "full comprehensive national health insurance." It was "unemployment, underemployment, and job discrimination," and not the state, that were "inherently anti-family," Roybal declared.[7]

Roybal beheld a party whose willingness to pursue economic justice was wavering during the difficult economic times of the 1970s, and asked for "direct commitments" to support this agenda, steeped in fundamentally interlocking ideas of economic and cultural security. He was "firmly convinced that the Latino community" would "respond" favorably.[8]

The man who would become the Democratic presidential nominee and party leader, who would ultimately "commit"—or not—to an economically just and multicultural party, was Jimmy Carter. The former governor of Georgia, Carter was rural in origin, evangelical in faith, restrained in his liberalism, and deeply southern. Though these attributes did not automatically align him with the core constituencies of Latino Democrats, Carter's civil rights record suggested some appeal. After his 1970 gubernatorial election, Carter had gained notoriety for speaking out against racial discrimination, and he actively incorporated African Americans in state government. He became symbolic leader of a wave of "New South" officials, moderate Democrats capable of forging biracial coalitions and turning back the Southern Strategy.[9] Yet while representing civil rights progress for his state and region—his gubernatorial predecessor, Lester Maddox, had become famous earlier for chasing black patrons away from his segregated restaurant with an ax handle—Carter was cut from a different cloth than the leading Latino liberals. A leader of the Democratic opposition to the liberal George McGovern's 1972 nomination, he was uneasy around labor, and a fiscal conservative who instinctively distrusted the massive programs of the Great Society. An advocate of "good government," Carter was also known to denounce "selfish special interests" for warping federal priorities. In his run for president, his advisors lamented a "balkanization of politics that has made it hard to muster a majority for important causes" and counseled Carter to "speak clearly for the common good."[10] In the party's presidential primaries, Carter situated himself between the party's liberal and conservative presidential aspirants, hardly a bigot but eager to present himself as a new type of Democrat, one not beholden to the party's traditional organized constituencies.[11] And running against a general election opponent, Gerald Ford, who was by party and pardon associated with the disgraced Richard Nixon, Carter further played up his independence. His campaign persona was of the honest and pious man, an outsider or "anti-politician" who could through his expertise bring about a more moral, efficient, and responsive federal government.[12]

It was in dialogue with Carter's vision of liberalism, which accepted a certain amount of civil rights progress but also sought to move the party beyond the programs and expectations of the New Deal and Great Society, that Democratic Latino politics was again constructed. When the party's Latino Caucus was reunited before the Democratic National Convention that nominated Carter in New York City in the summer of 1976, it elaborated an expansive interpretation of its constituency's common will. Distilling its vision in a "National Issues Working Paper," it accommodated both a traditional liberal economic sensibility and a new cultural liberalism. For the former, the statement endorsed a full employment program with government as "employer of last resort." And in the direction of the latter, it called bilingual and bicultural education fundamental for "maintaining the strong family and cultural ties so essential to all Latinos." Even more, broadening the party's conception of leadership, caucus members committed themselves to equal representation for women within the group. Their declaration of principles sought for the "double burden of discrimination borne by Latinas" to "be addressed from within the Latino community itself as well as by the national community."[13]

As the Democratic Party's ongoing redefinition stretched Latino liberalism to encompass a fuller range of domestic issues and constituencies, the foreign policy ambitions of presumptive nominee Carter favored its internationalizing as well. Carter had inherited McGovern's brand of internationalism, which rejected "Cold War obsessions" and saw US diplomatic aims advanced by prioritizing human rights and economic development, rather than by propping up morally reprehensible (but pro-US) regimes.[14] In this vein, Carter delegates and other members of the Latino Caucus displayed their new consciousness of the role they could play as guardians of American morality, and as agents of peace and friendship in the hemisphere. They spoke out in the name of human rights in Latin America and denounced injustices committed in the name of winning the Cold War, such as the "extreme American interference in the internal politics of Chile and other nations in this hemisphere."[15]

As Republicans had found, foreign policy's increasing prominence in US Latino politics also obliged the Latino Caucus to delineate a stance on

Cuba-US relations. Liberal Mexican Americans and Puerto Ricans had long been the party's central Latino constituencies, and Roybal and Badillo, the party's most influential Latino leaders, favored normalization of relations with the island. However, Cuban Americans were by 1976 a growing factor, one whose views complicated the caucus's left-liberal homogeneity on diplomatic affairs. In caucus deliberations, a Cuban member rejected proposals for normalization with Castro. He urged the body to take a position instead on behalf of prisoners of the Cuban regime, as well as press freedoms in Latin America. Jaime Benítez, Puerto Rico's resident commissioner in the US Congress, seemed to favor this approach, remarking upon the need to "demonstrate solidarity between all the rest of us and the Cubans residing in this country." In the end, however, the Latino Caucus endorsed the liberal position of normalization, provided the Cuban government "refrain[ed] from interference in the internal affairs of other nations"—Cuba was then petitioning the United Nations on behalf of Puerto Rican independence, and aiding armed revolutions in sub-Saharan Africa—and that it release its political prisoners.[16] This position was strongly similar to that which the party ultimately adopted in its platform.[17]

Although the nation's immigration laws affected each of its national origin groups in different ways, the Latino Caucus displayed a significant degree of unity in deliberations over undocumented immigrants. The decade's poor economic climate—its low economic growth and high inflation—and high levels of undocumented immigration had led to increased pressure on policymakers to take action. With Gerald Ford's attorney general, William Saxbe, and with the INS commissioner, Leonard F. Chapman, deportation was a popular measure. The caucus resisted. It resolved in favor of "a General Amnesty for any undocumented person who is present in the United States on or before July 4, 1976," and for an immediate cessation to deportations of the undocumented. But the Latino Caucus also rejected Democratic legislation that purported to solve the problem. Under pressure from organized labor, liberals in Congress had for several years been debating bills that would penalize employers who knowingly hired the undocumented, in theory freeing up jobs for citizens and legal residents. The Latino Caucus resolved that the best known of these, belonging to New Jersey Democrat Peter Rodino, would "have the effect of discriminating against all brown people in the United States." As Rodino was a rumored running mate for the party's choice for president, Carter, the caucus

Presumptive Democratic presidential nominee Jimmy Carter taking notes alongside Rep. Herman Badillo during a 1976 Democratic National Convention meeting of the party's Latino Caucus. Photo courtesy of Bettmann Archive/Getty Images.

determined that his "infamous" legislative proposal disqualified him from a place on the ticket.[18]

Even as the racialized policing of immigration status was pushing Latino Democrats to imagine a racial sameness and shared destiny, the Latino Caucus worked through a set of structures that acknowledged its members' heterogeneity. It contained a distinct "Chicano Caucus" and comparable bodies for Puerto Ricans and Cubans. Puerto Ricans further divided themselves, with one camp addressing "urban Puerto Rican problems" and another, led by New York's Badillo, representing the "views of Puerto Ricans from the Island." In a sign that despite their agreement, distinct subgroup agendas still existed, Mexican Americans and Puerto Ricans planned to deliver separate position papers from their respective groups during the caucus's penultimate day audience with Jimmy Carter.[19]

Internal heterogeneity could divide the group while simultaneously co-inciding with a fear that other minorities were privileged in the campaign. According to news reports, as Carter attempted to deliver remarks to the Latino Caucus, Mexican Americans seized the floor and produced "a list of Chicano issues which they feel have been overshadowed by the dominance of Puerto Ricans" within the wider caucus. Carter was forced to take his seat. David Almada, the Chicano Caucus spokesperson, demanded that Chicanos be named to high positions in the campaign, that Carter support a "general amnesty for Mexican farmworkers" lacking in documents, and that, if elected, he name Chicano presidential advisors, Cabinet secretaries, and Supreme Court justices. Carter's reputation for racial moderation put him ahead of most southern governors, but this had not satisfied the Chicano Caucus. "'Minority doesn't mean just black,'" Almada told the candidate, "to a roar of cheers and applause."[20] The point was apt. The party platform addressed Puerto Rico, but made no explicit mention of a domestic Latino (or Hispanic or Spanish-speaking or Chicano) constituency, opting to consolidate ethnoracial difference under broader headings, such as "women and minorities" or "minority and language-minority citizens."[21]

☆ ☆

While Carter wished to transcend the Democrats' image as a congeries of "special interests," his campaign still mobilized voters in more specific ways. Turning to the general election and away from the more critical of the party's Latino activists, Carter advisors invited a select group of Latino Democrats to form a "small" and "manageable" committee that would "include the Spanish-speaking people" in the campaign. This committee, the National Hispanic Advisory Board, would be composed of party activists and elected officials from the traditional power centers of Latino America in the Southwest and New York, and now Florida as well. The advisory board's official campaign status provided it, in theory, a means to build the Latino electorate. Inclusion meant a chance to use the candidate's celebrity and resources as a lever with state and local parties. It would have also held out the promise of the status of association with power and the expected furtherance of its members' own careers.[22]

In the dance of validation between the candidate and his supporters, a white man from Georgia whose family had set foot in North America in the 1630s became the vessel of Latino political unity.[23] From the Carter campaign's perspective, the advisory board would be "reflect[ing] the entire spectrum of Latin American Nationalities, political ideologies and geographic distribution." Such a broad membership would "in itself constitute a symbol of the unified Latino support in behalf of the candidate." Supposedly despite "the peculiar needs of our various Hispanic groups" the body was also itself "integrated by" its shared commitment to the Georgian. The National Hispanic Advisory Board, in turn, saw itself as the true "leadership" of Hispanic America and the embodiment of *Latinidad* through its association with Carter. In late September, the board explained that "Mexican-Americans, Puerto Ricans, Cubans—all different Hispanics—are working together" on Carter's behalf "because he is the only one to recognize the leadership of the Latinos in this country." An advisory board member further claimed that, "though there may be regional differences among the groups, there was a common cause among the differences—they all [support] JC." "We declare *being one*," resolved the committee, "in our determination to elect Jimmy Carter as Chief Executive of the United States."[24] A shared political ambition reflected the overcoming of differences and the construction of ethnic harmony.

To be sure, the members of the advisory board were at least as dependent upon the national campaign for inculcating a feeling of Latino solidarity as the campaign was upon them to deliver it in tangible vote form. For some, new ethnic orientations were indeed emerging through the mechanism of the national campaign. National Hispanic Advisory Board member Alicia Chacón remembered that heading into the 1976 campaign, "All of us . . . had been philosophically Chicanos . . . we weren't Latinos, we weren't Hispanics. We were Chicanos." Traveling the country to vouch for Carter, however, alongside Puerto Ricans and Cubans, offered insight into a Latino political world beyond the familiar. Chacón recalled the experience as "the first time that I got to know more Latinos, you know—*de otras razas. Yo siempre andaba nomas con Chicanos* (and of other races. I was always with the Chicanos.). But I got to know, a lot of the Puerto Rican leadership, the Cuban leadership and . . . kind of appreciated where they were coming from."[25]

Though Carter's Georgia-bred campaign leadership was educated in politics far from the core Latino communities, the challenges of a collective Latino mobilization were far from unknown. In August 1976, advisory board cochair Maurice Ferré confided to Democratic vice presidential nominee Walter Mondale that the "apathy, division and jealousy, traditional in us of the Spanish culture," had produced "splintering effects" for the party's Latinos. Their attempts to forge "unity," he informed the Minnesotan, "officially and unofficially, have in the past met with disaster, tragedy, [and] comedy." Only recently had they achieved some "modest success."[26] Herman Gallegos, one of the founders of the Southwest Council of La Raza and a Carter campaign worker, too explained in a "Hispanic strategy memorandum" that "although Hispanics constitute a significant percent of the vote *potential* they have been incapable or unwilling to employ their vote with the same degree of effectiveness as other groups." The situation needed to be "drastically changed and quickly so," with Gallegos urging the Carter campaign to "inspire the Latino/Chicano to raise that percentage."[27]

Then in his early forties, Maurice Ferré had an elite perspective on pan-Hispanic politics, one that was born of experiences vastly different from those of his older, more traditionally liberal fellow elected officials, Roybal and Badillo. Ferré's family had roots in Cuba, but he had been born in Puerto Rico and educated in the United States. His uncle, Luis Ferré, was an industrialist and the Commonwealth of Puerto Rico's third governor, serving from 1969 to 1973 as the standard bearer of the Republican-aligned New Progressive Party. Maurice Ferré shared in the bounty of his family's international real estate and cement businesses, reportedly valued in 1975 at upwards of $100 million.[28] With ample resources upon which to draw, he served in Florida state and Miami city government before being elected mayor of Miami in 1973. His exposure to the city's increasingly prominent Cuban population convinced him that there was a "bilingual revolution and rebirth of ethnic pride" not only in Miami but "sweeping through the entire 13 million strong Latin population of the continental United States."[29] In 1975, a few months before Latino Democratic elected officials were to form NALADO, the ambitious Ferré proposed to lead his own "American Coalition for Hispanic Action." Ferré claimed that "political pressure and militancy" were in order. He intended his group to foster a "common identity and diminish divisions that have for decades hampered our advancement." Suggesting the extent to which Ferré's constituency was a different one—a more affluent one—from that of either Herman Badillo or Edward Roybal, he announced his initiative at a Cuban American Chamber of Commerce meeting in Chicago.[30]

From a wealthy family, coming of age amid the postwar boom, and representing a Sunbelt city, Ferré interpreted the Latino electorate in ways congenial to a Carter campaign eager to form a new type of Democratic Party. His formulation of the class and culture mix that defined Latinos partook far less of the focus on economic marginalization that underpinned the McGovern campaign's appeal to Latinos. Essential was his interpretation of the "social and economic distinctions in all Latino communities," which he dubbed "even more clear-cut than with the Blacks." For Ferré, there existed the "Americans of Latino origin," the type of people "who have made the grade into the system (professionals, semi-professionals, skilled, semi-skilled, etc.)." And there existed "the Latino who is disenfranchised and alienated." Though Carter's "normal constituency" would include the latter as well as other poor people, Ferré argued that the campaign should focus on the former, "appeal[ing] to the emotional need of those that feel *a part of the system but discriminated*, rather than . . . the angry non-voters." Though accepting the larger Latino population's tendency to be affected by "emotional issues," appeals to the "more sophisticated Latino electorate" had to channel that emotionality "through subjects such as bilingual education, job opportunities, upward mobility, reduced discrimination, etc." Ferré labeled these types of concerns—not, for example, school prayer, abortion, or gay rights—as Latino "social issues."[31]

While dividing the electorate along class lines, Ferré's analysis revealed a renewed interest in defining the Latino political constituency along religious and familial axes. Although pundits often spoke of Carter as having a "Catholic problem" (though this was almost always a reference to his difficulty among white, blue-collar voters in the Northeast and Midwest), Ferré considered the candidate's Baptist faith an asset in wooing Latinos, the majority of whom were Catholic. In Ferré's view, Carter's fundamentalism had "a definite appeal to Latins who are from large families and mostly either Catholic or Fundamentalist in their religion." He recommended, further, to "strongly stress" Carter's "large and unified family, which has Latino appeal."[32] Candidate Carter did take time to identify his values with those he claimed inhered among Latinos, praising "the strong and tight family unit that is maintained among the families who come from Spanish-speaking countries" and suggesting that the country's poor (marked by "loosely knit family structures") could learn a thing or two from these people.[33]

Although such advice adapted earlier depictions of the religious and family oriented "Spanish-speaking" American electorate to a born-again Democratic nominee, new levels of engagement with Latino religiosity as such did characterize the Carter campaign. In addition to creating a separate "Hispanic Desk" within its "Minority Affairs" division, the campaign employed Herman Gallegos in its "Urban Ethnic Affairs" unit. Headed up by a Trinitarian nun named Sister Victoria Mongiardo, it aimed to solidify white ethnic support for Carter in the major industrial states of the Northeast and Midwest, where the Southern Baptist candidate's "Catholic Problem" was likely to be most injurious.[34] But the desk also recognized the need to be "concentrating in several states with a high percentage of Catholic Hispanic residents," a list that included Texas, Florida, and, of lesser priority, Colorado, Arizona, and New Mexico.[35] It repeatedly urged campaign higher-ups to recognize that, "in terms of the Catholic Vote, the Hispanics comprise 25% of the Catholic population."[36] Franklin Delano López, a Puerto Rican and Carter's Hispanic Field Coordinator in the Northeast and Midwest, also warned the campaign that it was "conservative Catholics" who comprised "the vast majority of" the nation's "Spanish Speaking population." But suggesting the extent to which the campaign had not developed a language to talk to Hispanics *as Catholics*, López's optimistic solution was for the campaign to "drop" any discussion of abortion in favor of "bread and butter issues" such as jobs and education.[37]

With little more than a month remaining before the 1976 election, the Carter campaign considered the states of Florida, Texas, New York, New Jersey, California, and possibly Illinois its best opportunities to summon a decisive Hispanic vote. It devoted particular energy and resources to expanding the electorate in Texas, efforts that combined with the Voting Rights Act's new application to the state to produce record Mexican-American registration. Florida was another priority, and registrations in Dade County were "the most successful of the program," according to one Carter operative.[38] When it came to getting out the vote elsewhere, however, the campaign devoted relatively few resources. "National Hispanic Field Coordinator" Franklin Delano López complained that he had "practically had no budget" to work with in the Northeast and Midwest. State parties offered him little aid either. Ohio Democrats ponied up $250 for the entire Latino statewide effort, according to López.[39]

Despite such paltry assistance, López was to claim that "the hispanic [*sic*] vote was a decisive factor" in Carter's victory.[40] Indeed, a detailed analysis of the results gave the Democrat about 81 percent of the group's votes. While Carter failed to win a southwestern state besides Texas, Mexican-American support in that state, which had also saved John F. Kennedy's 1960 campaign, proved again decisive. It seemed that Puerto Rican voters were essential to Carter's taking New York as well. Moreover, the winner's plurality among Latinos in Ohio, a state he carried by only about 11,100 votes and whose Electoral College value surpassed that of Nevada, Utah, Colorado, Arizona, and New Mexico combined, was an estimated (and implicitly decisive) 18,000.[41]

☆ ☆

The 1976 elections restored a Democrat to the White House after eight years and left the party in command of huge congressional majorities. For observers of the country's racial politics, Carter's recapture of the South for Democrats was highly notable, for it seemed to arrest the region's Republicanization, which had been accelerated by the backlash to civil rights. The *New York Times* editorialized that "If President-elect Carter can turn his personal triumph in the South into a viable biracial coalition, the Republican Southern strategy will be wrecked for a long time to come."[42]

For Latino Democrats, however, the dawn of a Democratic presidency was a moment to ensure that their party and the American government were not simply biracial but truly multicultural. Carter had promised a government "as good as its people," but his Latino supporters believed that their people's inclusion in that government was a key determinant of its goodness. And success in their own undertaking, as always, was measured in jobs. Acting upon the transition team's request, the National Hispanic Advisory Board put forward those individuals it deemed best qualified to serve in the administration. It got little in the way of response.[43] Democratic lawmakers, including Edward Roybal, submitted some six hundred names; none received a significant job offer during the transition.[44] Civil society groups bristled at this cold shoulder. ASPIRA and the Puerto Rican Legal Defense and Education Fund wrote of being "much disturbed that no Puerto Ricans or other Hispanics" had received "even nominal consideration" for Cabinet or other senior positions.[45] Mexican-American labor activists in San Antonio expressed their "deep disappointment" in Carter for snubbing their people, "despite the fact that Texas saved your election and Mexican Americans were the deciding factor."[46] Texas activist and National Hispanic Advisory Board member Alicia Chacón recalled how the scores of resumes Latinos sent to Washington sat filed away, unorganized and unread. "The campaign had been easy because they were courting us, but then after the election was won . . . all the phone numbers were disconnected," she remembered. Carter's Latino supporters had been made to feel "like clowns."[47] It sounded like 1960 all over again.

Observing the extent of Carter's neglect, Democratic elected officials founded yet another pan-Hispanic organization in the hopes of holding the new president to account. In December 1976, Edward Roybal, Herman Badillo, Henry B. González, Kika de la Garza, and Puerto Rico's resident commissioner, Baltasar Corrada del Río, formed the Congressional Hispanic Caucus.[48] At its inception, the caucus called for "strengthening the Federal commitment to Hispanic citizens."[49] Though their community was "at the bottom of the ladder," the federal commitment started at the top. Badillo observed that while Carter had been "talking about women and blacks" a great deal, he had "omitted Hispanics."[50] As spring of 1977 came and the new administration had still not given them anything to take back to their constituents, Roybal denounced the White House's "complete lack of sensitivity to the problems of the Spanish-speaking and Latinos."[51]

Protests also bubbled up from white-collar workers who saw Carter's slights first hand. A generation of activist-minded Latino civil servants had ensconced itself in the federal bureaucracy and planned to send the White House an unambiguous declaration of their own presence in the capital, and in the nation. Gilbert Chávez, the president of the public employee organization IMAGE, informed Carter that Hispanic federal workers were "very concerned" about his poor record of including their people in federal decisionmaking positions. He warned that there was a "nationwide effort now underway to assemble Hispanics Americans [sic]" to register their displeasure in the capital come April.[52]

In the spring of 1977, organizing themselves as "Concerned Hispanic Citizens of the United States," IMAGE joined with the National Council of La Raza (NCLR) to plan a "Marcha de Reconocimiento" or "March of Recognition." Federal workers implored their colleagues to join the protest, urging them to make a powerful statement "to our president, Jimmy Carter, who received 82% of our votes."[53] Linking the ongoing fight for public jobs, the development of a Hispanic constituency, and the advent of new governmental initiatives, they demanded "a comprehensive national policy for this country's second largest minority group."[54]

Thousands reportedly gathered on the National Mall for the April 1977 event. They carried the flags of the United States and of many nations, striding past the White House en route to the Lincoln Memorial. There they attended a mass and heard local and national Latino leaders exhort the new Democratic administration to bring their community truly into the national fold by allowing its members a place in their government. Drawing comparisons to another transcendent moment that occurred on the same spot, *La Luz,* the Hispanic magazine started with aid from Nixon's Brown Mafia, called their protest the "Hispanic March on Washington," an historic moment in Latino unity and assertiveness.[55]

Carter had enlisted Latinos in a multicultural campaign, but offered the constituency a color-blind façade with respect to governance. Indeed, Carter went to lengths to ignore its particular claims once in office. The new president resisted designating a "Latino" or "Hispanic" point person in the executive branch, even though every president since Lyndon Johnson had done so. Carter did name Los Angeles attorney Joseph Aragon as one of sixteen "top presidential advisers" and gave him an office in prime White House real estate. And Aragon had come to the White House from the Democrats' Office of Spanish Speaking Affairs. But he strenuously denied that he was the "White House Chicano." Rather, he presented himself as a living example of Carter's view that "the age of tokenism" and "the ghettoizing of the White House" were in the past. His portfolio, he said, included an array of important (i.e., nonethnic) issues. Aragon further claimed to resent when Hispanic organizations brought their concerns to him "because I have a Spanish surname and they assume I'm the guy who's supposed to handle it." For Aragon, it was as if Latinos had been "almost brainwashed" into believing "that we are a minority, that we will always be one and that we should act like one."[56] More than a year into his term, the president demurred when asked if he might appoint an assistant whose portfolio would be "Latino concerns." He replied that "to segment" his staff by special constituencies, be they "old people or farmers or labor or business or women or blacks or Spanish-speaking people" was "contrary to what I want."[57] Here was the man whose technocratic vision and managerial expertise supposedly made him a new type of Democrat.

Carter's liberalism was selectively color-blind, however. The president developed a strong record of appointing African Americans to his Cabinet and to the federal bench. His Equal Employment Opportunity Commission also vigorously pursued racial discrimination cases, further testifying to his priorities.[58] The appearance that Carter had room for only one "minority" in his governing coalition was intensely irritating to Edward Roybal, for Carter's narrow biracialism undermined years of his work building a multicultural party. After more than a year observing Carter in office, Roybal found it necessary to meet with the president to protest "the fact that Hispanics in this country are not being properly recognized as an ethnic minority with distinct characteristics." He had spent years fighting to make the powerful recognize that "Spanish-speaking Americans" were distinct from both black and white America, and not merely "the latest of immigrant groups." It was galling to once again have to make the case. That it was to his own party leader made it all the worse. Only a few weeks after reiterating this fundamental problem of recognition to Carter, the president's secretary of housing and urban development, Patricia Roberts Harris, gave a long interview (with Roybal's hometown *Los Angeles Times*, no less) in which she argued that Hispanics' social problems stemmed primarily from linguistic difficulties. These, she claimed, would likely be overcome within twenty years. An African American, Harris also downplayed racism's impact on Latinos, pointing out that they were "classified as white in a society that values whiteness and devalues blackness." Roybal found this inexcusable. A high administration official's view that Hispanics were, as he put it, "at a temporary stage of assimilation or acculturation into American life" was deeply offensive. It was more evidence of a "lack of understanding . . . that 'minority problems' encompass more than the Black population," he wrote, and yet another example of the White House's "insensitivity to this nation's second largest minority." It was "clear and convincing proof," Roybal told the president, that Hispanic voices were needed at the highest levels of the executive branch.[59]

One critical exception to Carter's initially color-blind stance toward Latinos lay in the area of immigration. The president's choice for Commissioner of the Immigration and Naturalization Service (INS), Leonel Castillo, was a clear concession to a belief in aligning government administrator with affected constituency. A Mexican American appointed in March 1977 at thirty-eight years of age, he replaced Leonard F. Chapman, the former

President Jimmy Carter meets with the Congressional Hispanic Caucus, 1978. Carter's immigration proposals and initially colorblind posture toward the Latino constituency caused great resentment among Caucus leaders. *Left to right:* Rep. Robert García (D-NY), Rep. Edward Roybal (D-CA), Carter, Rep. Eligio "Kika" de la Garza (D-TX), (probably) Baltasar Corrada del Río (NPP-PR), and (probably) Carter aide Tim Kraft. Courtesy of the Jimmy Carter Library/National Archives and Records Administration.

Marine Corps commandant whose hard-line direction of the INS had deeply strained what was already a difficult relationship with Mexican Americans (see Chapter 8).[60] Unlike Chapman, Castillo supported a vast program of legalization for the undocumented.[61] And his appointment convinced Herman Badillo to bestow the seal of Hispanic approval. The INS commissionership was "the one job that we [the Congressional Hispanic Caucus] specifically targeted as one that must be filled by a Hispanic," affirmed the congressman. Castillo's "Hispanic background," Badillo claimed, would endow him with "the necessary sensitivity and awareness needed to deal with the increasingly critical problems surrounding illegal immigration." His nomination, said Badillo at the time, represented nothing less than "a major breakthrough in relations between the new administration and the Hispanic community."[62] The Congressional Hispanic Caucus's emphasis on securing the INS appointment suggested the extent to which immigration—and specifically the matter of undocumented border crossing—had become inextricably linked with the Latino image in American politics.

☆ ☆

Immigration would put the Carter administration's attempt to neutralize Latino identity to the test. During the 1976 campaign, there appeared to have been an understanding in favor of muting the issue, which had the potential to divide the party's labor and Latino constituencies. Edward Roybal made only oblique reference to immigration in his testimony before the Democratic Platform Committee, for example. And while the Latino Caucus condemned Peter Rodino and his legislation at the convention, the group omitted immigration from its final "National Issues Working Paper." The Democratic platform, too, fell conspicuously silent on what to do about the millions of undocumented newcomers. All it offered was a vague pledge to "support a provision in the immigration laws to facilitate the acquisition of citizenship by Resident Aliens."[63] It was notable that in September of the 1976 campaign, with Carter in California, his advisors urged him "*not mention or comment on the Rodino bill unless pressed.*"[64] And as of mid-October, Carter's Hispanic campaign manager, Rick Hernandez, would note that they had still not "made any definitive statements" concerning the "border problems" in the Southwest.[65]

Immigration was not simply an ethnic issue. It was fundamentally related to questions of economic management that exposed the inconsistency of Carter's vision and political strategy. The nation's ongoing post-1973 economic turmoil, in which low growth and high inflation—together "stagflation"—was the context in which the administration addressed what was becoming the central "Hispanic" issue of the day. In the spring of 1977, as the White House took up the topic in earnest, the unemployment rate was over 7 percent, having risen slightly in Carter's first full month.[66] Liberals demanded stimulus to bring jobs to the masses, labor law reform that would challenge deunionization, and an urban policy that would heal the nation's Rust Belt after years of deindustrialization and white flight to the suburbs. Candidate Carter had endorsed government's responsibility to bring about full employment.[67] Yet President Carter showed little taste in fighting for union goals, urban aid, or a broad and costly package of economic security reforms, including liberals' cherished goal of national health insurance. He prioritized fiscal conservatism and the fight against inflation instead. However, Carter had shown himself eager to recover the trust of American—here mostly white—workers. And for several years, commentators and officials had been beating the drum against a job-stealing "invasion" of the nation's borders, advocating harsher penalties and increased deportations. The White House could not delay action on immigration for long.

Immigration was proving a baffler, though. Early in Carter's term, top domestic advisor Stuart Eizenstat expressed frustration at his inability to find a workable policy. "No issue that I have encountered since January 20 seems so to defy resolution," declared Eizenstat.[68] As congressional leaders, civil rights organizations, organized labor, and countless average people living in fear of deportation awaited Carter's direction, staff members hastened to preserve presidential command of the issue. It was essential to prevent "the proliferation of state-mini-Rodino bills."[69] In late March, a Carter administration "task force" circulated drafts of a proposed immigration policy. The first element listed in the plan was to penalize employers who hired undocumented workers. This was followed by an amnesty provision, then a new and more secure Social Security card, and "increased enforcement." Ideas about "Economic Development for sending countries" were then included among the latter provisions. Though the plan appeared comprehensive, it was clear to domestic policy staff member Annie Gutiérrez that it had not been sufficiently vetted. As she reported to Eizenstat, the administration's review of its options failed to

> point out any of the negative aspects of the proposed policy. There has been no examination of the fiscal impact, no discussion with experts as to the feasibility, cost, or timing problems of the proposed Social Security card. . . . Unless definite steps are taken to neutralize the bad publicity, and positive steps taken to talk about "UNDOCUMENTED," not "illegal" aliens, families, contributing (as they do) to taxes and social security, the President would suffer much political grief.[70]

Patience was not in the offing, however. Within two days of Gutiérrez's warning, below headlines blaring "Alien Crackdown" and "TOUGH POLICY PROMISED," the *San Antonio Light* reported that the administration was "ready to move on the alien problem." The paper quoted Secretary of Labor Ray Marshall expressing sympathy for the undocumented, but readying the public for a new Social Security card intended to render them unemployable. "If American Express and Bank Americard can make a card to give you money in an airport, I bet we can make one just as fool-proof," said the secretary.[71]

☆ ☆

As the administration sought to separate the illegal from the legal, the Congressional Hispanic Caucus sought their coalescence. The precise objective was to make what most considered a "Mexican" problem into one that all "Hispanics" should take a common interest in resolving. The Puerto Rican Herman Badillo had been taking this approach for several years. In 1974, he had warned his colleagues that "illegal alien" had, dangerously, "become a code word for Spanish-speaking." He spoke of immigration "dragnets" ensnaring those of "Latin background," not just in the southwestern borderlands but also in the Northeast. And he explained how aggressive apprehension campaigns rippled outward, so that "all too often Puerto Ricans, Mexican Americans, Cubans, and other Spanish-speaking citizens are needlessly embarrassed, inconvenienced, and intimidated" in their daily lives.[72] As details of the administration's plans emerged throughout the spring of 1977, Badillo implored his colleagues to show greater generosity. Identifying himself "as a member of the Spanish-speaking community," he called for a "Bicentennial Amnesty" for all those undocumented aliens who had been present in the United States on July 4, 1976. No longer, he protested, should those lacking papers be made into "scapegoats for our country's economic ills."[73]

Debating immigration with an administration that often disputed Latinos' ethnoracial permanence, Latino leaders explored new ways of representing their collective community that reasserted that permanence by acknowledging that a certain physical type was emblematic of the group (even if it was not all-controlling). In the past, Roybal and Badillo tended to avoid basing political claims on their constituents' physical appearance. In lieu of a "racial" conception of the Hispanic American, they preferred culture and sometimes language—hence the term Spanish-speaking—to define these peoples in the quest to be recognized as a distinct public policy constituency. This made a certain amount of sense, as no singular Hispanic phenotype existed. Plans to penalize employers who hired undocumented workers presented a new reality, though. Badillo took aim at the racial nature of these penalties, explaining to Secretary of Labor Marshall in April 1977 that

> there are well over 1,000,000 Hispanics living in New York who are American citizens by birth—emigrants from Puerto Rico—to say nothing of the thousands of naturalized citizens from Caribbean and Latin American countries. Many of them are poor, and hold un-skilled or low-skill jobs. It is they who will suffer when they are no longer hired because they have accents or look Hispanic, and employers do not want to take the chance of hiring an illegal alien.[74]

And in a letter to President Carter, he and Roybal reiterated their contention that "many employers will be likely to request identification only from individuals who are assumed to be 'foreign' because of their language, appearance or manner."[75]

The notion that sanctioning employers guaranteed civil rights violations had significant support in civil society. The bishops of the United States Catholic Conference were on record as predicting that employer sanctions would "create a civil rights problem of horrendous magnitude" and "assuredly . . . lead to discrimination against any person belonging to a minority group whose legal status might be called into question."[76] The Spanish Information Network, a Spanish-language cable television network that went nationwide in the 1970s, had also denounced the Rodino bill "on the basis that it 'discriminates against Mexican Americans, Puerto Ricans and all citizens of Spanish heritage." A force in creating a positive image of the nationwide Hispanic consumer, it blamed the INS for "mak[ing] 'illegal alien' synonymous in the public mind with 'criminals,' 'dope smugglers,' 'Communists' and 'job stealers'"—a false "image" that was "overtly anti-Hispanic."[77]

All this was known in October 1977, when the White House released an immigration proposal that included employer sanctions. In response, lawyers representing the National Council of La Raza and other advocacy groups asserted that the plan will have a discriminatory effect upon the Latino Community with little regard for their status as United States citizens or permanent residents. . . . Employers are unlikely to ask a person with Aryan looks for proof of the right to work. But when employers see a Brown face or hear a Spanish accent, the request for documents will be predictably swift. In effect, Hispanics will have to carry their documents with them, thus creating a de facto national identification system for them and them alone.[78]

The NCLR joined with the American G.I. Forum, LULAC, MALDEF, IMAGE, and other civil rights organizations (though not ASPIRA or the Puerto Rican Forum) in a "Hispanic Ad Hoc Coalition on Immigration." Sanctions, the coalition argued, "will unavoidably cause increased employment discrimination against brown-skinned, or non-English-accented persons."[79]

A lobbying posture that diminished the importance of language and a dignified culture as the defining traits of group membership illustrated important changes underway in Hispanic politics. The civil rights groups' suggestion that the Hispanic was "brown" no doubt reflected the preponderance of Mexican Americans in the coalition, and the extent to which Chicano activism and ideology had influenced their willingness to espouse a nonwhite racial identity. On one hand, this characterization of Hispanic racial identity submerged life's reality, particularly for those of a distinctly Afro-Latino background. Yet it also largely put to bed the image of the pure-blooded Spanish American as the iconic "Hispano," and with it at least some of the claims to "whiteness" that at times and in places attached themselves to a "Hispanic" identity in the United States. Moreover, while Puerto Rican civil rights groups appear to have been aloof from these early efforts, their most important elected official was not. A man whose birth had conferred him citizenship and whose olive complexion had led him at least once to be mistaken for an Italian, Herman Badillo's advocacy posed a compassionate and solidaristic rejoinder to the racist and jingoistic fearmongering of a Hispanic invasion.[80] These were important steps for those who recognized "Hispanics" as a group national in dimension, American in character, yet unlikely to be assimilated into "white" America.

If the acceptance of physical difference was integral to the "Hispanic" stance on immigration policy, so too were economics. And in this, the leaders' critique once again reflected the growing internationalism of Latino politics. Herman Badillo argued that any sound policy to address the undocumented "must include diplomatic initiatives and foreign policy planning that will help alleviate the problem at its sources," most importantly Mexico.[81] On an issue most relevant to Mexicans, Puerto Rico was particularly instructive. Citing the consequences of the island's Operation Bootstrap as evidence that US-sponsored capital-intensive growth would simply promote more migration, Badillo and Roybal called upon Carter to foster policies "which will promote human development and the expansion of labor-intensive jobs in Latin America." In search of "a humane immigration and international development policy in the Western Hemisphere," Badillo and Roybal called for a "long-term economic commitment to Latin America," not a mass crackdown on the undocumented.[82] Again, ethnic advocacy had a clear material dimension.

Advocates looked beyond the borders in other respects. The discourse of human rights, which Carter had embraced as a presidential candidate, was a crucial asset. MALDEF invoked the president's reputation as a "staunch advocate of human rights" to argue against his policy's emphasis on enforcement as the solution to "the undocumented alien 'problem.'"[83] In a resolution presented to IMAGE's executive board, its founder, Ed Valenzuela, addressed "the plight of millions of Hispanics who have migrated to the United States." He spoke for those "Americans of Hispanic heritage who feel that we can no longer allow the continuing neglect of this group which has been treated as inferior and in some cases, suffered sub-human treatment." It was clear that "at a time when this nation is advocating the human rights of people of all nations of the world, we must focus in on a critical problem in our own backyard."[84]

Such pan-Latino political collaboration increased the risk for officials who might have supported immigration legislation such as Carter's. In order to forestall additional disputes among their labor and minority constituents, congressional Democrats and the White House put off the reckoning. Toward the end of 1978 they created a Select Commission on Immigration and Refugee Policy (SCIRP), and charged it with issuing policy recommendations in late 1980.[85] Although the SCIRP allowed the White House to avoid continued conflict over legislation, enforcement of existing laws remained a thorn in Carter's relations with Latino activists and elected officials throughout his term.

☆ ☆

It was not long before Latino legislators had lost all patience with the Democratic White House. After a year of Carter, Henry B. González complained that he had been "treated like 'crap' by the President, his administration, and staff."[86] Congressional Hispanic Caucus chairman Edward Roybal publicly branded the Democratic administration "passive and insensitive to our needs." Signaling a posture of greater independence, he dropped the "Democratic" affiliation from his lobbying organization, NALADO. The renamed National Association of Latino Elected and Appointed Officials (NALEO) was, he said, "the last vehicle that we can use to tell the Carter Administration that we are not happy with their performance."[87] In the summer of 1979, NALEO announced plans for its own nationwide nonpartisan Latino voter registration drive. It would be independent of the Democratic National Committee's own effort, which was expected to bolster Carter's reelection hopes.[88]

Roybal and the Latino leadership's discontent stemmed from particular feelings of neglect, but also from sources similar to those fueling a wider liberal rebellion against Carter. Such tensions came to the fore at the party's mid-term conference in Memphis in December 1978. Liberals were up in arms, assailing Carter's domestic austerity program as a betrayal of their party's creed. They were irate that the White House had reduced the Humphrey–Hawkins Full Employment Act, their comprehensive attempt to put Americans back to work and hold their minority and labor constituencies together, to a bland nothingness.[89] Massachusetts senator Edward M. Kennedy brought delegates to their feet with calls for national health insurance and the protection of social programs then under threat from Carter's plans to increase defense spending.[90] Kennedy was edging closer to openly challenging the president for the party's nomination in 1980. By the summer of 1979, Carter's overall approval rating was at 29 percent. Nixon's had been higher during Watergate. Kennedy was far more popular with Democrats than was Carter. A youthful social liberal from California, Governor Jerry Brown, also prepared his campaign to unseat the unpopular president.[91]

Jimmy Carter could no longer afford to alienate Latinos. Presidential assistant Tim Kraft, soon to be named manager of Carter's reelection campaign, made clear the group's centrality to the incumbent's prospects in the summer of 1979: "Suffice it to say that in the three states where their number exceeds 1.5 million (Texas, California, New York), we need them badly."[92] If the administration intended to win those states, it had so far failed to placate Latino power brokers, for whom representation through patronage had historically mattered as much if not more than policy. Kraft lamented that only 3 out of 355 White House staff positions belonged to this key constituency.[93] Worse still, the Latino presence in other parts of the executive branch was shrinking, exactly the wrong direction for it to be heading before an election. The most prominent member to depart was Leonel Castillo, the INS chief. Expected to be sensitive to Latino concerns yet pressured to take a hard line in defense of administration policy, it was a thankless job for anyone, but especially so for a Mexican American. According to Kraft, Latino leaders were in no rush to "put another Chicano through what Castillo has suffered over the last two and one half years."[94]

To thwart the liberal insurgency, the "ghettoizing of the White House" that Carter supposedly disdained would become his policy.[95] In August 1979, the White House reversed itself and created an Office of Hispanic Affairs. It would be headed by a special assistant for Hispanic affairs, who would in turn join a previously named special assistant for black affairs, another representing women, and, after January 1980, a special assistant for white ethnics. Empowered to make policy recommendations, the office had a political purpose that was quite obvious. Carter even candidly admitted to a Congressional Hispanic Caucus gathering in September 1979 that the advisor would be furnishing "advice on many things, one of which is how to get votes."[96]

The White House asked that advice of Esteban E. Torres. Born in the copper-mining community of Miami, Arizona, in 1930, he was an ideal choice for an administration criticized for ignoring Hispanics' plight *and* for abandoning the Democratic commitment to economic justice. Torres's father was a Mexican immigrant, union activist, and Depression-era *repatriado*. His family survived the decade thanks to the New Deal's Works Progress Administration. Growing up in Los Angeles, Esteban Torres took work on a Chrysler assembly line and became active in the United Auto Workers. His quick ascent in the union's ranks landed him a position in its international affairs desk in Washington, DC. He learned about Latin

America and the capital culture, but returned to California in the late 1960s to lead the East Los Angeles Community Union (TELACU), a labor-backed community development corporation. After 1976, he again left, this time for a diplomatic post, his reward for backing Carter for president. In short, Torres was a fixture in a pivotal Mexican-American community, credible in labor circles, and practiced in the ways of Washington. And if previous administrations are any guide, White House staff would have considered his mestizo features to be legitimating assets. Finally, for maximum public relations impact, his tenure officially began during Hispanic Heritage Week in 1979.[97]

As the latest presidential appointee in such a position, Torres became enmeshed in the familiar but still delicate work of both representing the diverse Hispanic populations in the White House and representing the White House to them. He assembled a staff that reflected at least some of the core constituencies of Hispanic America, blending a handful of Californians, including future Secretary of Labor Hilda Solis (then just an intern), with two island-born Puerto Ricans who possessed connections in New York and Chicago, respectively.[98] Torres then positioned the office as the fulcrum of a new "Hispanic" assertiveness. Thanks to it, he announced, "Hispanics will no longer have to go hat in hand to ask to be heard. We will demand it." Even as he proclaimed the dawn of a "challenge era for Hispanics," however, Torres defended Carter's record, claiming that his boss had "done more for Hispanics than any other president in history and plans to do more."[99]

Latino elected officials and organizations truly expected more. Wiser about the workings of executive branch power as they had become, the idea of a special assistant to the president for Hispanic affairs no longer impressed them. They wanted their people in policymaking roles. They were lobbying for Cabinet posts, the number two or three slot at the justice department, and the ambassadorship to Mexico.[100]

Carter did not lack for opportunities to name the nation's first Latino Cabinet member. But though he considered Herman Badillo and Miami mayor Maurice Ferré to lead the Department of Housing and Urban Development, he awarded the job to a fellow southerner, former New Orleans mayor Moon Landrieu. The newly created Department of Education offered another opening. Yet in October, the president nominated a San Francisco federal appeals court judge, Shirley Hufstedler, instead. A victory for women's groups nevertheless angered Latinos. In passing over a Hispanic, charged Roybal, White House decision makers once again revealed themselves to be "political amateurs." "I can't see how 189 electoral votes can just be set aside," he complained. MALDEF's president called it just another example of the administration's "failure to treat us as anything other than peons."[101]

☆ ☆

While the White House embraced the symbolism of multicultural governance, a contest for the loyalty of Latino party activists was brewing. Every presidential election since 1960 had stimulated Democrats to pursue some form of Latino unification, but the expected intraparty contest of 1980 accelerated the process. As well as previewing the Kennedy insurgency, the party's 1978 midterm conference witnessed the founding of a group called Hispanic American Democrats (HAD).[102] Roughly two hundred Memphis delegates established the new party organization, pledging to "unify the diverse interests of all Hispanics—*Chicanos, Cubans, Puerto Ricans, and others*—into one strong voice."[103] Like Ted Kennedy, HAD appeared to stake out a position to Carter's left. Its leaders declared their intention to hold the president accountable to his commitments to the poor, to full employment, and to the creation of a national health insurance system. What was more, HAD vowed to work with African Americans to achieve those goals.[104]

It was unclear just how much HAD would hold Carter's feet to the fire, however. One news report credited Rick Hernandez, a Carter aide and soon-to-be deputy campaign chairman, with having "launched" the group.[105] HAD's top leadership, too, was drawn from party "establishment" figures who held strong incentives to support Carter. HAD chairman David Lizárraga came from the same organization, TELACU, as Esteban Torres, Carter's Hispanic Affairs assistant. And TELACU had grown ever more powerful thanks to Carter administration grants.[106] Despite its vow to avoid "presidential politics" until Democrats chose a nominee, HAD's request to "oversee" the party's Hispanic outreach also implied coordination with the Carter White House.[107] In at least one case HAD provided the White House with membership lists upon request, presumably facilitating Carter's aides' access to this organized constituency.[108]

There were other linkages. Polly Baca Barragán, a Colorado state senator, occupied posts in HAD and as a regional coordinator of Carter's reelection campaign. Joining her was the Cuban-American chairman of Florida's Democratic Party, Alfredo Durán. Under his leadership, Florida Democrats took steps favorable to Carter, bumping up their primary's date to provide the incumbent, who expected to do well there, some good early publicity in the campaign against Kennedy and Brown.[109]

Moreover, as HAD took shape over the course of 1979, it was clear that it would be composed with calculation. Indeed, Hispanic American Democrats altered the terms of Latino political representation within left and liberal circles. The 1971 Spanish-speaking coalition had treated Mexican Americans and Puerto Ricans as equal groups, and divided membership accordingly. The party's previous embodiment of Hispanic political unity, its Latino Caucus, had supported distinct and theoretically equal Chicano and Puerto Rican caucuses, as well as a Cuban caucus gaining in importance. In contrast, the thirty-five-member steering committee formed in Memphis structured HAD according to population: 60 percent Mexican American, 23 percent Puerto Rican, 12 percent Cuban, and 5 percent "Other."[110] Procedures for establishing HAD state delegations further shifted the balance of power within these national origin categories. Each "state" (Puerto Rico counted) received a delegate "for every 5% of Hispanic population residing in each Congressional District," based upon the findings of the 1970 census. This recipe gave California, home of chairman David Lizárraga, 132 of HAD's 557 delegates. And it allotted Puerto Rico a 120-delegate trove. This last fact meant that HAD allocated the overwhelming majority of the "Puerto Rican" quota not to the highly liberal New York community, which would vote in the presidential election, but to the island, where the president's supporters were reported to have been "firmly in control" of Democrats' "delegate-selection machinery."[111] HAD regulated access to influence in other ways. Although Democratic voters elected Edward Roybal and those officeholders he had organized into NALEO, elected officials would not automatically have a vote in HAD without first becoming elected delegates of that organization.[112]

Summoning their members to Denver for a national convention in December 1979, Hispanic American Democrats interpreted the quest for unity as a novel undertaking. They chose a conference theme, "IT'S ABOUT

TIME," that reflected a belief that unity was long overdue. HAD's script-writers could at times profess their ambition as wholly new, claiming that the convention would be creating the "first nationwide Hispanic Demo-cratic organization."[113] Similarly, Lizárraga referred to the conference as "the first time that Hispanic political leaders from throughout the country have come together for the benefit of Cubans, Puerto Ricans, Mexican Americans, and all Hispanics alike."[114] Such characterizations neglected the myriad assemblies of Latino Democrats and Republicans alike since at least the 1971 Unidos conference.

To cast the HAD moment as unprecedented implicitly blamed estab-lished leaders for the group's previous inability to coalesce and achieve its manifest potential. According to the conference program, in prior years the nation's Hispanics grew in numbers while remaining "an essentially leader-less giant moving in many different directions."

> No national organization had emerged to serve as a forum for Hispanic interests—as had the NAACP for blacks—and no national leader has stepped forward to speak for the urban Hispanic—as Cesar Chavez had so skillfully done for the agrarian Hispanic. In short, in 1976, the His-panic movement was on a road to nowhere.[115]

The HAD leadership's narrative of the "leaderless giant" thus disparaged the many efforts of Roybal and Badillo. Indeed, as one political writer put it, "the young Turks" within HAD believed Roybal's Congressional His-panic Caucus "moves too slowly and represents the past." The mention of Cesar Chavez points to a similar effort to marginalize. The month before the Denver convention, the labor leader had announced his opposition to Carter's renomination. HAD's characterization, while appearing to honor him, consigned the unionist to the realm of the "agrarian" rather than the "urban Hispanic" that the new organization claimed to represent.[116]

At the convention itself, HAD members offered their own candid di-agnoses of their longstanding inability to unite. Some pointed to class dif-ferences, particularly the perceived affluence of Cuban Americans. Others noted a past fixation on separate concerns, in the words of one delegate that "the burning issue to Chicanos has been undocumented workers, while the issue for Cubans has been political prisoners, and for Puerto Ricans, state-hood." Perceived territorial boundaries reinforced such senses of difference. David Lizárraga cited a customary belief that "New York belongs to the

Puerto Ricans, Florida belongs to the Cubans, the Southwest belongs to the Chicanos."[117]

HAD spokesmen were unanimously confident that they could render these differences obsolete by structuring Hispanic politics as a politics of common ground. Lizárraga dismissed the history of "turf problems." All the national origin groups now realized, he submitted, that "the power we have is so limited, we can't afford to divide it." Esteban Torres stated that to recognize Latinos' particularities without letting these "impede" the group's "economic and political goals" was an "evolutionary process," but it was a process nonetheless underway. Robert García, the man who replaced Herman Badillo in Congress when the latter rejoined New York City government in 1977, described how past efforts had always begun by focusing on areas of disagreement. In contrast, HAD's approach was premised on "starting with things we can agree on." As a result, he said, "we're finding out we really do have a lot in common."[118]

As in years past, this was largely true from a policy perspective. Denver delegates adopted resolutions on more than three-dozen subjects "most crucial and critical to Hispanics" in the coming decade, a set of stances that they intended to present in condensed form for inclusion in the party's 1980 platform. The product of their deliberations, HAD's "1980 Hispanic National Platform," said little about the defining issues for many Puerto Ricans and Cuban Americans, for instance avoiding mention of Puerto Rico's status or Cuba's leadership. Devoting themselves to areas of agreement meant instead a collective endorsement of "vigorous enforcement" of civil and voting rights laws, affirmative action, full employment, bilingual education for language maintenance, as well as an end to police brutality against Hispanics.[119]

As evidence that a Hispanic consensus on immigration transcended the party's Latino elected officials, HAD too rendered sympathy with the undocumented population a quintessentially "Hispanic" stance. Noting that "Hispanic immigrants have been unjustifiably scapegoated and blamed for the ills of society," the platform defended this "severely exploited" class of laborers. It rejected warrantless immigration raids and denounced "the inappropriate" use of local police as enforcers of the nation's immigration laws. HAD went on record demanding "blanket or unconditional amnesty" and protection of Hispanic families from the ravages of deportation. And it contested any attempt to deny a public education to the children of those without papers. Pairing immigration and "human rights," it remonstrated against the ways that "citizens and non-citizens alike" suffered "unconstitutional scrutiny" of their place in the country. And at a time when conservatives worked to deny state services to undocumented people, it made scarce distinction between the benefits an undocumented Hispanic and a US citizen Hispanic could justly access.[120]

Where HAD broke new ground was in its social liberalism. Seemingly for the first time in a national Latino forum, activists made sexual orientation a "Hispanic" issue. In its call for civil and human rights, HAD advocated on behalf of "Hispanics in the gay community who suffer discrimination two-fold due to their mode of lifestyle." The platform decried their victimization at the hands of police, as well as the ways that discrimination hindered their ability to immigrate. In what truly stands out in the history of pan-Hispanic politics, HAD "pledge[d] an end to all social, economic, psychological, and legal oppression of the Hispanic Gay Community."[121]

In establishing a vision for the coming decade, the "1980 Hispanic National Platform" was the most detailed compendium of "Hispanic" political positions on record. Given how many previous unity efforts had failed, it was indeed an impressive accomplishment, one that reflected organizational development, new levels of socialization within the Democratic Party, and growing individual political acumen. It went some way toward, as Florida party chairman Alfredo Durán put it, "caus[ing] Hispanic issues to become Democratic issues."[122]

While Durán maintained that HAD's efforts would result in "the Hispanic voter . . . be[ing] wooed more ardently by both political parties," the establishment of a national organization and platform should not be mistaken for Latino political independence.[123] Hispanic American Democrats, as its name implied, abandoned virtually any pretense of pursuing the "balance of power" strategy. Ignoring the more than a third of Latino voters who had cast a ballot for Nixon, HAD chairman David Lizárraga portrayed the group's position this way: "We've always given our votes to the Democratic Party. Now we have to make that party responsive to us."[124] Moreover, the platform HAD defined as the true product of a national community's deliberation—in which the "Hispanic" position was socially liberal and pro-immigration—found fewer takers across the aisle, where the Hispanic agenda was cast as socially conservative and anticommunist. Indeed, it was becoming anathema to an ever-larger share of the Republican Party that would nominate the conservative Ronald Reagan for president in 1980.

Constructing a collective agenda was not the same as creating Hispanic political unity either. In the matter of Democrats' contested presidential nomination, HAD members disagreed strongly. An informal newspaper poll showed Carter enjoying the support of nearly 40 percent of HAD delegates in Denver, with Kennedy counting roughly 24 percent, and Jerry Brown mustering 6 percent. Almost a third of HAD delegates proclaimed themselves uncommitted. Brown and Kennedy backers wanted the group to pledge to make an endorsement, which could become an official "Hispanic" repudiation of Carter. But pro-Carter forces wanted HAD to adopt a no-endorsement policy, expecting that neutrality would favor the incumbent. The assembly listened as representatives of the three candidates sought their support. Ultimately, a compromise permitted HAD to endorse, but did not require it to do so.[125]

As the Democratic candidates bruised each other over the ensuing months, they drew the leaders of Hispanic America into opposing camps. By April 1980, HAD leaders including David Lizárraga, Polly Baca Barragán, Alfredo Durán, and Robert García would form the overwhelming majority of Carter's National Hispanic Campaign Committee.[126] Kennedy, unable to corral HAD's endorsement, attempted to recreate the Mexican-American–Puerto Rican liberal coalition that had propelled his brother John to the White House two decades before, and that supported his brother Robert in 1968. Herman Badillo and Fernando Chavez, the son of the farmworker leader, launched the latest "Viva Kennedy" movement in February 1980.[127]

Kennedy spoke for those left behind. The senator toured the South Bronx, a bombed-out symbol of the nation's urban crisis. As a freezing March rain poured down on that benighted district, Herman Badillo stood beside Kennedy as the candidate blistered the White House for its broken promises to revive urban America. A New York victory reinvigorated the challenger's flagging campaign. Jerry Brown's exit from the race then opened the door for the United Farmworkers of America to endorse Kennedy in April. The union helped push Kennedy to victory in Arizona the following week. Just a few weeks after that win, Cesar Chavez barnstormed the barrios of Texas with the Democratic insurgent. Though the president trounced the challenger in the Lone Star state's May primary, early polling indicated that

Carter's worst showing came among Mexican Americans. Carter continued to amass a delegate lead throughout the spring, but UFW support again helped Kennedy to a surprise victory in California, prolonging his challenge. Even after Carter had effectively sewed up the nomination, Kennedy's strength among Latinos, as well as Jews, blacks, and Catholics, constituted a key barrier to any chance of Carter's consolidating enough Democratic support to win reelection.[128]

The rift that ran all the way to the August 1980 party convention was amply represented among the nation's second largest minority. Carter and Kennedy each maintained a "Hispanic Caucus" at the convention. Kennedy forces were hoping to convince Carter's delegates to switch their votes to the senator. As they battled to change convention rules to make that easier, Kennedy pleaded with the Hispanic American Democrats to support his call for "una 'convencion abierta'"—an open convention—and for delegates to "vote their consciences," rather than according to the will of primary voters. Yet as "shouts of '¡Viva!' mingled with polite applause and a few boos," it became clear that Kennedy would not sway the majority of the Democrats' Hispanic vote. In the end, Hispanic American Democrats abstained from endorsing a candidate and took no position on Kennedy's attempt to release the delegates of their obligations. "The fact is that unity is the No. 1 concern in our community and not who will be the candidate," said HAD chairman and Carter delegate David Lizárraga.[129]

☆ ☆

In Jimmy Carter, Latino Democrats encountered a familiarity, a president who honored the cause of Latino unity in service of his election, but who appeared mostly uncommitted to recognizing their ethnoracial permanency, and centrality to a multicultural Democratic Party, at least until reelection time. Yet and still, the dependent dialogue between party activists and candidate further transformed the content of Latino politics. During a decade in which global forces came to play an increasingly decisive role in shaping the US economic and political landscapes, candidate Carter's emphasis on human rights as a central foreign policy tenet reinternationalized Democratic Latino politics by encouraging activists to coalesce around their vision of a just US presence in the hemisphere. Moreover, his administration's neglect served to advance the institutionalization of Latino politics. Confronting the president's superficial color-blind liberalism, elected officials organized new institutions to represent "Hispanic" interests and developed new ways of linking ethnic concerns and liberal economic demands. As the decade's economic uncertainty thrust new international issues—none more important than immigration—to the fore, it required Latino Democrats to articulate collective "Hispanic" or "Latino" stances with respect both to their president and the Republican Party. These creative intraparty challenges forced the Carter White House to abandon its pretensions to color-blind liberalism, and to enlist its allies in establishing new Hispanic institutions and political appeals that reflected concern for both cultural and economic security.

The widespread practice of pan-Hispanic politics had unintended consequences as well. The Hispanic American Democrats' response to the Kennedy insurgency showed that the Hispanic impulse was now popular enough, as well as malleable enough, to be used by individuals and to ends that its original practitioners opposed. A new generation of Hispanic leaders, who surrounded Democrats' economic message with a Latino social liberalism, was preparing to supplant the generation of leaders forged in the long era of the New Deal. By the end of the decade, then, the pan-Hispanic impulse and its institutions straddled the line between insurgent force and establishment appendage, true testament to the institutionalization of the "Hispanic Vote" in the party. Meanwhile, similar processes of leadership succession were underway in the GOP, as the founders of Hispanic Republicanism fought to retain their foothold in a party moving fast to the right.

# 11

# The "New Hispanic Conservatives"

For the Hispanic Republican movement, the weeks following Gerald Ford's loss to Jimmy Carter had been times of reflection. Benjamin Fernandez and the Republican National Hispanic Assembly (RNHA) had pleaded for permission to campaign as a nationwide bloc in support of Ford's reelection, seeing in such a mobilization evidence of their full acceptance as equal members of the party. But they had been denied. And now, for the first time in eight years, they could not count on a Republican White House to deliver the patronage and other forms of recognition essential to nurturing their organization. In a somber note he penned to the outgoing administration, Fernandez promised that, despite his disappointment, he fully intended to continue "working very hard to develop a two-party system among Hispanos."[1] Yet, as conservatives began to exercise ever more power within the party, it was far from certain that there would be tolerance of, let alone support for, the RNHA's brand of middle-class multicultural Republicanism going forward.

As Latino liberals of various stripes and factions were competing for space in a Democratic Party disoriented by the structural and ideological challenges of the 1970s, Ben Fernandez's movement collided with the GOP's conservative takeover spearheaded by Ronald Reagan. Fearful for his faction's status, Fernandez attempted to prove his relevance to Republican elites by launching a pathbreaking run to the presidency in 1980. The Hispanic conservatism he elaborated was eclectic. It celebrated government aid as a means to individual upward mobility, rejected a color-blind public sphere in favor of ethnically inclusive institutions, blended these with an orthodox conservative's critique of taxes and regulation, and wedded all to a hard-line foreign policy agenda. Hispanic conversion would not come from one candidacy, however. Fernandez's limited success with Republican voters and Ronald Reagan's capture of the party and presidency augured a new direction in GOP "Hispanic strategy." While adopting the moniker of "the New Hispanic Conservatives," the RNHA and its Mexican-American leadership continued to advocate *marketing* the party to Hispanics—primarily Mexican Americans—by the traditional means of ethnically inclusive government. However, an administration espousing antigovernment positions was set on *transforming* the constituency, by advancing new issues and elevating new leaders. With administration support, Reaganite Cubans fused their own self-assertion and emergence from beneath the shadow of Mexican-American leadership to achieve supremacy in GOP Hispanic affairs. Their articulation of Hispanic Republicanism was steeped in antigovernment and social conservatism, and hawkish foreign policy views toward the hemisphere. In placing ideological purity and party loyalty—Cuban Republicans' calling cards—over conversion of moderate Mexican Americans, their ascent helped end the first period of Hispanic politics in the Republican Party.

☆ ☆

Even more than their Democratic counterparts, Hispanic Republicans found the late 1970s a time of uncertainty concerning their place within their party. Having been sidelined during the election of 1976, the Republican National Hispanic Assembly could not reasonably be blamed for Gerald Ford's poor showing with Hispanic Americans. At the same time, the nearly 15 percent drop in Hispanic support for the Republican ticket since 1972 did not strengthen the group's hand in the party. In the aftermath of an election that seemed to some to have dealt a heavy blow to the Southern Strategy, some of the party's leaders publicly acknowledged that the GOP needed to improve its standing among women, minorities, and Catholics.[2] Yet whether the party, out of the White House and badly outnumbered in Congress, would put resources into converting a fast-growing but historically Democratic constituency was another matter.

In the months after the 1976 election, Ben Fernandez grew increasingly weary of what he called the "patronizing" attitude of Bill Brock, the conservative Tennessean who chaired the Republican National Committee (RNC). Seeking to prove their worth, Fernandez and the RNHA set their sights on the 1980 presidential election. By the summer of 1978, the RNHA discussed recruiting a talented Hispanic Republican to run for president, someone who could act as a focal point for their quest to unify Hispanic America in the name of Republicanism. To little surprise, Fernandez emerged as the front-runner. The businessman pledged that his forthcoming candidacy would "help legitimize" his people's place in the Republican Party. He vowed to "bring in Hispanics to the party in our way, with our own methods."[3] Whether this was a serious long-shot campaign, a Fernandez vanity project, a simple party-building maneuver, or a combination of the three was unclear.

Fernandez's confidence, however, was unmistakable. Addressing a crowd of potential voters in November 1978, he predicted his run would inaugurate an "absolute, total revolution in American politics." It was through him, he remarked, that "the Hispanic-American vote of the United States" would break from what he alleged was a self-inflicted apathy (and Democratic loyalty) and transform the country.[4] Fernandez's official campaign announcement took place at the National Press Club in Washington a few weeks later. It too showed the brashness that would define his run. Fernandez declared then with no hesitation: "I fully expect to be the next president of the United States."[5]

Not all Republicans were as enthusiastic, and Fernandez's presidential campaign precipitated a conflict over the RNHA's place in the party. Republicans accustomed to having the group in its "auxiliary" role viewed its act of independence with consternation. For some party elites, Fernandez's crusade was a distraction. They wanted the RNHA to focus on the 1978 congressional races instead. Fernandez's rivals accused him of squandering precious dollars and political capital. The leader of the RNHA in California went a step further and denounced Fernandez's ambition as an instance of ethnic betrayal. "He's acting like an individual, like a gringo," said the Cuban exile George Adams. Fernandez, though, responded that his determination was but the height of ethnic authenticity. "I guess it's just the individualism of the Hispanic coming out in me," he retorted.[6]

And individualism did rule his run. Fernandez's campaign was premised on an incredible story of upward mobility—he called it his "Horatio Alger" tale.[7] As he explained to reporters and audiences, he had been born in a converted Kansas City railroad boxcar in 1925, the son of Mexican immigrants from Michoacán. He joined his migrant family picking sugar beets in the Midwestern fields at the tender age of five. When his father at last found better work in a steel mill, the family settled in East Chicago,

Indiana.[8] Fernandez graduated from high school and entered military service at the tail end of World War II. College followed at the University of Redlands, across the country in sunny Southern California. One of five ethnic Mexicans enrolled there in 1949, Fernandez later proudly recalled "break[ing] every academic record on that campus" and graduating in two years at the top of his class. General Electric took notice of his accomplishments and provided him elite training in finance and management in New York. Earning a New York University MBA in the process, he was on the fast track to success in one of America's premier corporations during the 1950s.[9]

His individual rise continued in a decade of group consciousness. In 1960, the year that Mexican Americans and Puerto Ricans launched the Viva Kennedy drive, Fernandez founded his own management consultancy.[10] And in 1965, while the forerunners of the United Farmworkers of America marched in the epic Delano grape strike, Fernandez was helping to form a Mexican-American Chamber of Commerce in the San Fernando Valley, just north of the Hollywood Hills.[11]

When California's own Richard Nixon assumed the presidency in 1969, vowing to support minority capitalism, Fernandez was invited to a White House dinner. The businessman's thank you note, by way of a letter to the editor of the *Los Angeles Times*, showed how this self-described "son of an illiterate immigrant from Mexico" interpreted his invitation to the table of power. It was proof, he opined, of "the fantastic opportunities open to any American who has the ambition and desire to succeed." His gratitude was to the nation for making such possible. He further "pray[ed] that our minority groups, in their rush for fair play, do not lose sight of the principles of the free enterprise system, a system which I fully understand and love."[12] Such attitudes led him to become, in 1970, the face of "Brown capitalism" in the Nixon administration. As chairman of the National Economic Development Agency, then the National Hispanic Finance Committee to Re-Elect the President, and later of the Republican National Hispanic Assembly, he was a walking example that business success, ethnic pride, and patriotism went hand in hand in the Republican Party.

At the time of his campaign, the very remote possibility of "a Fernández for president" inspired a budding national Hispanic media to reflect on the status of their emerging pan-ethnic group. A magazine called *Nuestro*, which was geared toward middle-class and English-dominant Latinos, praised this "intensely serious . . . man of poise and assurance who has already achieved a great deal both in business and in politics." Though it gave him "a candle's chance in a snowstorm" of taking the presidency, the magazine told its upwardly mobile audience that a strong showing for Fernandez would no doubt make it easier for the next Latino who would seek the highest office. Meanwhile, his candidacy would demonstrate, to "Anglos and Latinos" alike, "the growing power of our people."[13]

Mainstream media outlets viewed Fernandez through a different lens. National reporters poked fun at his self-assurance. "He is convinced he is a phenomenon," read a fairly typical profile. "He moves and speaks as though some omniscient force had assured him that Abraham Lincoln's log cabin, the symbol of humble origins and great deeds for the last 100 years, is about to be replaced by a boxcar," it continued.[14] Another writer called him a man of "little fame but a great deal of self-confidence."[15] Political scribes appear to have found Fernandez's braggadocio more risible because of his physical appearance. They often mentioned his slightness of stature—he stood about five feet, six inches tall. One *Chicago Tribune* writer even bluntly identified him as a "stocky, dark-haired candidate."[16]

Undeterred by such criticisms, Fernandez sought to redefine the location of Hispanic leadership and success for a conservative era. In his vision, ethnic victories would manifest themselves in the marketplace. On the stump, he could and did switch into Spanish when it served his purposes. But the majority of his remarks he delivered in the relentlessly optimistic tones of the corporate motivational seminar. Fernandez was unabashed in describing his business success. Speaking of his years as a consultant, he informed one audience, "[I] made a whole bunch of money and I loved it."[17] Indeed, that he was supposedly a millionaire was central to his appeal. His own story gained a broader meaning through his quest for office, though. "It will prove to the whole world that the system works," said the candidate. "It will be an inspiration to every poor kid in the country."[18]

Bearing a winner's disposition, he proclaimed the economic doldrums of the late 1970s to be self-inflicted. High unemployment and inflation could, in his view, be overcome with attitude adjustments. He called for Americans, and Hispanic Americans especially, to embrace "four fundamental values," which he identified as "the work ethic, freedom of choice, opportunity and free enterprise."[19] Considering the first of these, he argued that the road to economic recovery was built by those "working 60–70 hours a week . . . starting their own business," and "risking everything." Proposals for shorter workweeks, which might reduce unemployment by spreading work around, were evidence to him that America was "getting too soft." The country's people, Fernandez opined, did not need "more time to go fishing."[20] "Freedom of choice" meant an individual's willful *decision* to escape barrio poverty. The son of an illiterate who even in dark financial times resisted welfare payments, who recalled a youth surrounded by classmates destined for prison, he himself had made an active choice "not to be poor." Others were free to make that same choice.[21]

Fernandez's third fundamental value, "opportunity," was a concept in transition. When he announced his candidacy, an early version of his statement had "equal" preceding it. It was telling, then, that in his campaign kickoff and in subsequent addresses to the American people, Fernandez made a point of severing that liberal watchword from the concept of "opportunity."[22] This principle dovetailed with the fourth: "free enterprise." Fernandez's business experience taught him that life was about competition, the healthy process of sizing up a market and finding a way to profit. "Apply the principles of business to what you're doing," he counseled a group of Texas college students he hoped to enlist in his campaign.[23]

With "stagflation" whipsawing liberal economic policy options, Fernandez's principles mapped neatly onto the ascendant conservative economic thinking that stressed "liberating" the market from government intervention. He advocated deregulation of industry.[24] He vowed to "give it ["big business"] a big hug," advising voters that, "when I'm President, you better buy some stock."[25] He adopted a number of other conservative economic stances, placing blame for inflation on the government, pledging a balanced budget,[26] and calling himself, "unshakably opposed to socialized medicine."[27] He combined endorsement of unionization in principle with support for "right-to-work" laws designed to weaken unions.[28]

But for a candidate who envisioned "Americans of Hispanic origin" as his donor and electoral base, not all could be about getting government out of the way.[29] For example, to some audiences he spoke of his role in founding the Nixon's administration's National Economic Development Agency. He talked of expanding its government-assisted small business model to the Anglo and the factory worker, to "middle America," as he put it, so that they too could jolt the US economy back to life and fulfill their own personal dreams. In addition, before his campaign officially began, college students heard him vow to direct the Department of Justice to investigate the high number of deaths of Texas Mexicans in police custody, which he called a "mass violation of civil rights."[30]

Fernandez also rejected the notion of a color-blind public sphere in favor of ethnically inclusive institutions. Latino professionals reading *Nuestro* magazine learned his view that if placed in public sector personnel or procurement offices, people like them could "change things overnight" for their coethnics. With particular respect to justice, having a person "who interprets the law in favor of the *hispano* immediately affects 16 million of our lives."[31] Challenged on whether his personal success was broadly replicable, or rather an exceptional story that proved the need for liberal government to champion the needs of the poor and minorities, Fernandez criticized his party for "not [being] representative of the people of the United States." It was "a dying party" as a result. He denounced the attitudes of the party's "far right wing" and pledged "to go around" conservative Republicans who stood in the way of his people's advancement.[32] In part to separate himself from such reactionary Republicans, Fernandez called himself a "people's conservative."[33]

While Fernandez carved out a place just to the left of most conservative Republicans on domestic matters, he proposed a hard-line foreign policy. He denounced the Panama Canal treaty and the SALT II arms-reduction initiatives. On another occasion he promised, "If I saw Nicaragua going communist, I'd send in the Marines," remarks that Ronald Reagan's campaign researchers dutifully recorded. The candidate's strident anti-Communism led *Washington Post* columnist George Will to offer that Fernandez "may be the fiercest conservative in the crowd, any crowd."[34]

Portraying himself as an expert on Latin America, Fernandez had distinct ideas for Mexico. By virtue of his Mexican parentage, Fernandez envisioned himself as the central protagonist in building a new alliance with that nation, a "special relationship," he said, "similar to what we have to Israel."[35] Two great questions of a globalizing age converged in that country, he said: undocumented immigration and the energy crisis. On the first, Fernandez vowed to enact policies that showed "compassion and toughness." Undocumented aliens would be allowed to register with immigration authorizes and reside in the United States, "under the protection of the US Constitution." They would be permitted to apply for citizenship if they wished. Fernandez spoke against fencing the US-Mexico border, citing the lack of interest in a comparable fortification of the frontier with Canada. He suggested that legal limits of Mexican immigration would possibly have to be increased. He covered his right flank, however. After an initial legalization of the undocumented, he promised to "slam the door shut." He pledged to "enforce the law of the land," denouncing the "anarchism" of a nation that did not apply its rules. Such was a place of "no civilization whatsoever." Fortunately, for the candidate and the country, Fernandez's solution to the immigration dilemma lay in Mexico's vast energy supplies. He envisioned a program by which the poorer country's laborers could work in the United States in exchange for Americans receiving preferential access to Mexican crude. He asked voters to consider the question: "Who better in the White House to deal with Mexico on oil than a Fernandez?"[36]

While the issues of the day drew him to Central America and Mexico, Fernandez's electoral strategy depended on the Caribbean. Specifically, it all rested on him foregoing the Iowa caucuses and coming out on top of Puerto Rico's winner-take-all primary. Riding that momentum to a decent showing in New Hampshire, he would gain a national profile, he hoped. Then he would find it easy to achieve the threshold of support necessary to access the federal matching funds his campaign required to enter the full slate of GOP primaries.[37]

As he toured key states in the summer and fall of 1979, Fernandez's story and stances gained notoriety. After a hit speech before the National Federation of Republican Women, the *Chicago Tribune* political editor called him "the surprise of various GOP presidential forums."[38] George Will penned his column delighting in Fernandez and "the jaunty chauvinism of . . . the fastest growing ingredient in the tangy American broth." He called Fernandez a "natural Republican."[39] Even the resident soothsayer at the *Washington Post* saw his promise. Having consulted Fernandez's charts, astrologer Svetlana Godillo found him both "idealistic and pragmatic" with "judgment . . . balanced and tempered," a man capable of great leadership. "His chart indicates that he is one dark horse who may pay off," gushed the fortuneteller, who nonetheless suggested that the Cabinet was Fernandez's most likely landing spot.[40]

In late 1979, Fernandez projected a soaring confidence. He claimed that three of "the so-called front-runners" for the Republican nomination had already offered him the vice presidency, a position for which he avowed no desire.[41] "I can hardly wait to tangle with Reagan in California," he boasted.[42] Reagan campaign researchers were not so sure Fernandez hadn't lost it. They reported that the insurgent had "gone beyond the impossible dream to the obsessive illusion."[43]

The Reagan team's assessment was indeed the more accurate. Despite his enthusiasm and fund-raising experience, Fernandez found it difficult to finance his campaign. A candidate was required to raise $5,000 in twenty states in order to qualify for federal matching funds. But as the pivotal Puerto Rico primary neared, Fernandez was still far short of his objective.[44] Equally distressing was his inability to generate enthusiasm from Hispanic Americans. During his brief ascent in the fall of 1979, he had waxed that party loyalty mattered little, "porque lo que vota es la sangre"; that is, because it is the blood that votes.[45] But whether it was because comparatively few Hispanic Americans were registered Republicans or whether his message did not appeal to them, ethnic loyalty was clearly an insufficient resource to power his campaign. As this became clear, Fernandez blamed Hispanic Americans. They had, he complained, some kind of "mental block" that prevented them from supporting one of their own when he had a genuine chance. They viewed his ambition as presumption, seeing only a man who did not "know his place."[46]

Although Hispanic Americans were not flocking to Fernandez's campaign, he still predicted his heritage would help him take Puerto Rico's primary "by a landslide."[47] Instead, he finished a very distant fourth. According to one tally, he had managed only 1,912 votes. In comparison, the winner, George H. W. Bush, took 123,217.[48] In previous weeks, Bush's bilingual son, Jeb, had worked diligently to cultivate the island's nearly 1700 party precinct leaders. In "flowing Spanish," the younger Bush had backed up his father's pledges to support statehood for Puerto Rico.[49] And while Fernandez, a Mexican American, had hoped to lead the march of Hispanics into the GOP, it was the Anglo, Jeb Bush, who played the part of pan-Hispanic political mobilizer, predicting that his father's win would "be transferable to the Cuban community in Miami and the Puerto Rican community in New York."[50]

Fernandez was deeply embittered. He charged that fraud and intimidation were behind his disappointing results. He vowed to file electoral complaints and even criminal complaints against Republican officials on the island.[51] Demonstrating a lack of self-awareness, the man called to account before the Senate Select Committee investigating Nixon even referred to the situation as a "Puerto Rican Watergate."[52]

Defeat in Puerto Rico betokened a string of poor showings in the Northeast, leaving Fernandez to ponder what had gone wrong with his strategy. "Frankly, I thought the Hispanic community would be getting really excited right about now, but they haven't," he candidly told one reporter. His inability "to fire up the Latino community" was, he admitted, "a crushing experience for the campaign."[53] With little money coming in, and an inability or unwillingness to tap his own bank account, Fernandez had to limit the number of primaries he entered. He ultimately qualified in fifteen states, and Puerto Rico. But he failed to win a single delegate and never topped 1 percent in any primary. His campaign ended nearly $150,000 in debt. Embarrassingly, he even struggled to get on the ballot in his home state of California, whose primary was to be held in early June 1980. In the end, Fernandez was able to vote for himself, and then to concede.[54]

☆ ☆

Fernandez's poor campaign showing and the ongoing advance of conservatives within the party left his faction of Hispanic Republicans scrambling to maintain influence. The task fell primarily to the new leader of the RNHA, Fernando Oaxaca. Born to Mexican immigrant parents in 1927, Oaxaca was raised a bookish child in a bilingual El Paso household. His upbringing was sufficiently more secure than many of his Mexican-American peers, and public college and military service routed him upward in postwar America. Engineering training led him out of West Texas and toward Los Angeles, where a successful career in the defense industry awaited. His politics were essentially moderate. He had once been affiliated with the liberal faction in California's Democratic Party, had supported John F. Kennedy in 1960, and had believed in 1964 that Barry Goldwater "was an absolute nut." His own growing prosperity and disillusionment with the Vietnam War, however, drew him to the Republican Party in the late 1960s. He was very much one of those white-collar Mexican Americans that the Nixon administration had made special efforts to court. Indeed, he had served as an informal aide to Martin Castillo, a fellow southern Californian and Nixon's first chairman of the Cabinet Committee on Opportunities for Spanish-Speaking People. The knowledge of government that Oaxaca acquired through that association, along with patronage in the form of Nixon administration contracts, supported Ultrasystems, Inc., his fledgling consultancy. He in turn served as treasurer of Ben Fernandez's National Hispanic Finance Committee to Reelect the President. Oaxaca's fund-raising and party activism coupled with his managerial acumen led Gerald Ford to appoint him to the Office of Management and Budget. There, he oversaw the Statistical Policy Division as it developed the "Hispanic" category. Conscious that this diverse group's parts need to "coalesce our interests," he was devoted to using mainstream politics as the means to Hispanic unity and power. As he said in the nation's bicentennial year, "I am absolutely and totally convinced that the only way the Hispanic community will ever really progress is to be in office" and "to become honest-to-God players in . . . making . . . financial contributions to parties to push candidates, to behave like the majority of society behaves."[55]

Having gained little from Fernandez's presidential run, Oaxaca and the RNHA attempted to exert influence on the remaining GOP presidential contenders, a group that included George H. W. Bush, the former RNC chairman under whose leadership the RNHA was founded, as well as former California governor Ronald Reagan. While convention delegates remained up for grabs in the summer of 1980, the RNHA outlined an agenda it wished to see the candidates adopt. Similar to Latino Democrats, the RNHA sought high appointments, including the pledge of a Cabinet post and for the future president's first Supreme Court nomination to go to an Hispanic American. Upward mobility and economic security measures provided the policy backbone, though. The RNHA proposed that candidates rally behind a class-based home ownership aid program, "catastrophic illness" insurance for those earning less than 50,000 per annum, as well as "low interest loans for the *families* of college age youth to facilitate attendance" at colleges and universities.[56]

The RNHA staked out an especially unorthodox position on immigration. It called for the abolition of the Immigration and Naturalization Service, and the placing of its border patrol duties under the auspices of the United States Coast Guard. The latter body had "a much better image and past policies of 'helping' people." Lest party elites doubt the feasibility of these plans, Oaxaca argued that "*No Congressman will vote against a pro-Hispanic initiative.*"[57]

After Reagan wrapped up the nomination (and chose Bush as his running mate), much of this moderate agenda was off the table. Benjamin

Fernandez's remarks to the Republican National Convention that July in Detroit showed him in retreat from the unabashedly ethnic yet conservative figure he cut during the campaign. Aside from a few words in Spanish, the assembly chairman's speech was mostly absent any cultural content. It did not explain the alleged compatibility of Hispanic peoplehood and Republicanism, as Fernandez had in 1976. For 1980, his people were distinguished less by any particular ethnoracial or cultural markers and more by their demographic potential. They were "ethnics," albeit "the fastest growing ethnics." He made almost no request of the platform at all. The closest to what might be considered a statement of ethnic politics was his denunciation of a burgeoning "communist movement in the Western Hemisphere," seen in an onrush of "Marxist Communist governments" in the Caribbean basin. Whereas his confident address in 1976 had sought the convention's action to "confirm" that the GOP was "the party [of] the Spanish-speaking people," what remained for 1980 was excoriation of Jimmy Carter and twinned reverence for Reagan and "the free enterprise system." The speech could have been given by most any Republican in 1980.[58]

If Ben Fernandez had to mute his *Hispanidad* for Reagan's convention, Cubans found that their Republicanism and their *Cubanidad* accentuated one another. Right from the convention's kickoff, Florida's two Cuban delegates (and seven alternates) made their presence felt by staking out the doorways of the Joe Louis Arena and distributing literature opposing the despised Castro regime. Florida delegates delivered a thousand information packets to the convention floor, urging the party's leaders to commit to deepening Cuba's economic isolation and permitting "freedom-loving Cuban fighters to eradicate the Communist regime." They kept rapt attention as the platform was delivered and "studied with approval its hard-line foreign policy." Its only shortcoming with respect to Cuba was its omission of a pledge of noninterference with Cuban-American paramilitary operations against Castro. As they would choose the leader of Cuba, by violence if necessary, so did they imagine they might choose the US president, by democratic means. "The Cuban vote could give Reagan Dade, and Dade County could give Reagan Florida. And Florida, as you know, is a swing state," opined Carlos Salman, a forty-seven-year-old real estate figure and leader in Reagan's Cuban effort.[59]

☆ ☆

With the Mexican-American leaders of the RNHA fighting a rear-guard effort to conserve their clout in the party and Cuban Americans brimming with confidence in their exceptional compatibility with Reagan, the former intensified their efforts to convince the party's right wing that conservatism and their "Hispanic" agenda were compatible. Oaxaca advised party leaders that "hundreds of thousands of key Hispanic votes beyond the normally expected 20% can swing to the Republican side in 1980." With the GOP lacking any "scientifically polled data," Oaxaca filled in the gaps, providing an education intended to appeal to the party's hardliners. He described an ideal Republican voter group, "individualistic," "honest, hard working, entrepreneurial in spirit . . . self-sufficient," and more. Despite their cultural and linguistic differences, as well as their pride in their national origins, they were "deeply patriotic" believers "in the 'American Dream.'" Republicans risked peril by regarding them as "some 'foreign' entity" and not "as full and equal partners in the building of America." Of Hispanics, said Oaxaca, *"They are Americans first."* And no doubt with Reagan's conservative advisors in mind, he mentioned how Hispanics had grown concerned about "the growing burden . . . particularly on the little businessman, of needless government regulation, paperwork and general interference in the marketplace." It was these beliefs, Oaxaca argued, that were "impressive confirmation that Hispanics think much like 'mainstream' Americans."[60]

If in Oaxaca's telling Hispanics were not unlike the white, suburban voter, Republicans had still to reckon with the group's internal "strains of opinion." For Oaxaca, these mapped onto national origin. He portrayed Puerto Ricans and Cubans as largely focused on their island homelands. Mexican Americans, in contrast, were far more interested in domestic policy. Health care, voting rights, education, and affirmative action mattered to them. They also cared about protection from violent crime, drugs, juvenile delinquency, "terrorists," and, "conversely, police 'brutality.'" The RNHA leader showed caution in addressing issues that were clear-cut to conservatives but very complicated for Mexican Americans. He referred obliquely to "all the questions around the complex subject of undocumented workers." He vaguely mentioned "the questions about bilingual/bicultural programs and their true effectiveness" and "the question of neighborhood schools and [the] alternative of busing."[61]

As the general election began, the RNHA struggled once again to occupy a central place in the campaign's Hispanic outreach. Learning that Reagan's advisors were considering separate appeals to each main Latino constituency, the RNHA strongly resisted. Oaxaca repeatedly informed the officials that

> a separate campaign for Mexican-Americans, for Puerto Ricans, for Cuban-Americans, etc. does not make managerial or cultural sense. It is divisive and flies in the face of what the RNC has worked on for years in supporting *one* Hispanic Auxiliary within it. What binds the Hispanics in this country together is our language, our common heritage in Spain, tempered and modified by colonial effects and, more importantly, common characteristics of pride, love of family, church and work, and a deep and abiding patriotism.

There was, he said, only one "Hispanic Political 'Market.'"[62]

Inseparable from the RNHA's single Hispanic campaign concept was that conversion of Mexican Americans—and by extension Mexican-American leaders such as himself—would receive top billing. Oaxaca claimed that courting Puerto Ricans would yield a relatively tiny "payoff" and that Cuban voters ought to be already "in the bag." Three-quarters of Hispanic America was the "Mexican / 'Other'" population, however. They would be a great prize to convert to the GOP. As the businessman Oaxaca told Reagan's campaign manager, William Casey, "There is a big payoff here . . . good R.O.I.!" (return on investment). Impatient for Reagan's commitment to utilizing his people's expertise in the campaign, Oaxaca let his exasperation slip: "The RNHA and I and, I am sure, hundreds of leaders around the U.S. have troops, wagons, horses and we're all just waiting for a goddam general!"[63]

☆ ☆

A general was on his way. By early August 1980, campaign manager Casey had grown reportedly "quite upset" at the state of Reagan–Bush Hispanic outreach.[64] Shortly thereafter, the campaign turned not to the RNHA but to Alex Armendariz. The veteran political operative had been rewarded for managing Nixon's 1972 Spanish-speaking campaign by being named director of the Office of Minority Business Enterprise, where he served two

Republican administrations advancing the causes of black and brown capitalism, and particularly in deepening Republican linkages with the Hispanic business community. After Ford's departure from office, Armendariz founded a communications firm that linked big corporations to the budding "Hispanic market." The skillsets of ethnic advertising and political campaigning overlapped considerably, and Armendariz soon returned to active political work on Texas senator John Tower's successful 1978 reelection bid. The foremost expert in GOP Hispanic campaigns, he was thus an architect of the "Hispanic Vote" itself. Now he would apply his expertise for Reagan.[65]

Because trustworthy polling was initially unavailable, Armendariz's judgments about the Hispanic constituency served in its stead. In his vision, this remained an electorate defined by attributes many Republicans valorized, a people "very patriotic and pro-American" and "strongly family-oriented."[66] The politics of minority envy that Republicans had encouraged for years remained in play in 1980 as well. Armendariz rated President Carter's third-greatest vulnerability (after inflation and unemployment) as Hispanics' "growing resentment" at the "surge in Black programs and participation in all facets of government" under the president. The contrast between Carter's "preferential treatment for Blacks"[67] and Reagan's courtship of an up-and-coming Latino constituency was favorable for the Republican, the consultant believed.[68]

The electorate was changing, though, growing more nuanced. In 1972, Armendariz identified the Latino voter bloc as composed of "three distinct classes": a "middle class," the "urban poor," and the "migrant worker."[69] For 1980, he included a fourth influential Hispanic constituency: the "Undocumented Aliens." Though not voters themselves, these "undocumented persons" engendered "a decided sympathy" from other Hispanics, especially Mexican Americans. He warned that there was little hoping a "national get-tough policy toward immigrants"—without whose labor so many businesses cease to function—would resonate with Hispanic voters. Although Mexican Americans were the most affected, Armendariz stated that, "a wide-ranging resolution of this matter" was "a key issue with Hispanics." It was more important than ever to understand the electorate, because Hispanic political influence now extended well beyond its customary spheres and could very well decide states like Michigan, Ohio, and Pennsylvania, Armendariz commented.[70]

The return of preliminary polling suggested Reagan's challenges. First of all, and contrary to many Republicans' hopes, the campaign would learn that the group did "not see themselves as conservative as they are sometimes described." Rather, half were "somewhat" or even "very" liberal. Polls showed that Mexican Americans "place[d] more stress on the importance of religion in the home than other Hispanic cohorts," seemingly favorable news. But these findings had to be reckoned against results that called them the Latinos least likely to exhibit "distrust of government programs and their helpfulness." Moreover, while "strong majorities" of Latinos perceived efficacy in voting, the feeling—"interestingly," Republican analysts observed—was "strongest among the urban poor." These were precisely the voters the GOP operatives wanted to stay home, because they were "heavily Democratic-oriented" and "not likely Reagan prospects."[71]

In search of a sweet spot for Latino Reaganism, the campaign located it where, as historian Robert O. Self has observed, so many of the era's political contests had coalesced: "the family."[72] It was, Armendariz contended, the "traditional family values" such as "hard work, self-reliance, and education" that presented Republicans with a great opportunity to cash in with Hispanic voters, no matter their region or national origin. This was consistent with polls indicating that the group's "value structures" led its members to interpret issues such as "better education, health, and living conditions as important things to happen to the family." The decade's economic turbulence, and inflation especially, had precipitated a family crisis. It was "the first time," according to Armendariz, that "many Hispanic mothers are being forced to enter the labor market" simply "to meet the essential family needs." This was "contrary to traditional Hispanic values," and especially disruptive because it was happening "often without the husband's approval."[73]

As it had for Edward Roybal and many Latino liberals, Armendariz's understanding of the Hispanic family blurred simple distinctions between "economic" and "social" issues. But whereas liberals had advocated expansive federal economic policies to strengthen the Latino family, Armendariz viewed making the Hispanic family a Republican commodity by, as Ben Fernandez's candidacy had suggested, making success in the free market appear consistent with ethnic family values. In one instance, as candidate Reagan prepared for a September campaign address to Mexican-American businessmen in San Antonio, Armendariz insisted to the candidate's speechwriters that the gospel of economic freedom was not enough. Reagan had to acknowledge that "Mexican Americans are family people first, and businessmen second," and that "the traditional Hispanic values of family, hard work and strong neighborhood" were precisely "the qualities which encourage entrepreneurship."[74] Rendered in the language of the family, the Republican ticket's antigovernment economic message—to which a stagflation-weary Hispanic electorate already was susceptible—had the potential to go far.

Such instructions were essential to humanizing Reagan for the Hispanic constituency. Republican polls reported that half of Latinos viewed the candidate as "cold" or "very cold."[75] Campaign materials hoped to counter this perception, portraying Reagan instead as "warm and sympathetic to the problems of a bilingual minority."[76] One Hispanics for Reagan–Bush pamphlet cast Reagan as "a man who knows us," and a believer in "all of the values important to the integrity of Hispanic culture in America." It warned that the treasures of "family," "neighborhood," "work," "peace," and "freedom" were under assault from "the crushing burden of double-digit inflation." The antidote for Hispanics was to join in the struggle to "halt the growth of runaway government."[77]

Reagan's conservative Hispanic appeal nonetheless highlighted the public sector as a means of social and economic inclusion. Advertisements announced that California government under Reagan was a haven of "opportunity" for Hispanics, an implicit criticism of Carter's patronage record, imbalanced in favor of African Americans. The dawning of a new era for the nation and a people was complete in a spot declaring that, "In this decade, only one man can give hope to the Hispanic community." "Reagan," it said: "He recognizes our time has come."[78]

There would be ample resources to spread such messages. The cash-flush Reagan organization embraced Armendariz's assessment that Reagan–Bush was poised to make "unprecedented inroads" in this traditionally Democratic constituency.[79] With less than two months remaining until the election, Reagan–Bush allocated a staggering $125 million to the Hispanic "voter group" and placed at Armendariz's disposal $25 million in "program" funds.[80]

☆ ☆

As the Reagan–Bush campaign appealed to national "Hispanic" values and interests, it simultaneously fostered an opportunity for Cuban Americans with ties to Reagan to renegotiate their position with respect to the Hispanic political project. In the weeks following the party's convention, Miami attorney Alberto Cardenas laid out for Reagan his argument for a new national political role for Cuban Miami. Cochairman of Reagan's Dade County campaign in 1976, a 1978 GOP congressional candidate, and an RNHA vice chairman, he broke with a tendency within his community and willingly accepted that his people, the Cubans, were a "minority." He claimed they were "the perfect example to all minorities," in fact, for having "retain[ed] their unique culture, language and ethnic identity while at the same time joining the main stream" of American life. He also allowed that his people belonged with other "Hispanics," as his participation in the RNHA suggested. All the same, Republicans could not pretend that Cubans did not have "issues and positions of priority . . . which differ greatly from the priorities or philosophy of the rest of our hispanic [sic] friends throughout the United States," particularly with respect to foreign policy. Getting to his point, Cardenas argued that the party could no longer allow "the voice of Hispanics" to be "carried by the representatives of the numerically largest group within the Hispanic communities," Mexican Americans. Given the proper backing, he contended, a strong Miami-based Cuban-American effort for Reagan could mobilize tens of thousands of Cuban voters, not only in Florida, but also in Illinois, New Jersey, and New York. In terms of "political philosophy," he professed, the Cubans of the Empire State were as distinct from Puerto Ricans "as Governor Reagan's philosophy is different from Ted Kennedy's." He implored Reagan to authorize a distinct "Cuban-American" campaign.[81]

Not waiting for official approval, Cuban Americans laid the groundwork for mobilizing their own, nationally and locally. By early September, they had established a "National Cuban American Council" for Reagan, a leadership structure weighted toward Florida, but with state chairmen from such far-flung states as Louisiana, Colorado, and California.[82] In Dade County, their "Comite Reagan–Bush" planned a direct mail operation to inform forty thousand households that Jimmy Carter was Fidel Castro's preferred choice for president. Twenty-thousand Spanish-language brochures—adapted to include Reagan's "thoughts on Castro and Central America"—were set to go out to area malls, coffee shops, and residences. And Cuban-American professionals—"Dentists, Doctors and Accountants"—planned to mail signed three-by-five index cards to their client lists on behalf of the GOP ticket.[83] All this was already set in place when, on September 30, 1980, the Reagan campaign informed Cuban-American leaders that it had given approval to a "National Cuban Advisory Committee," with Cardenas serving as its chairman.[84]

Cubans' mobilization began to alter the procedures of GOP Hispanic politics. Although Alex Armendariz remained nominally superior—any "planned activity" or publicity from the Cuban committee was supposed to require his written approval—the campaign manager would have recognized their growing influence.[85] Managing Nixon's reelection just eight years prior, he had argued that the Hispanic electorate cared very little about foreign affairs, describing Cubans as "exceptions to this rule."[86] In 1980, campaign polling revealed that attracting Latino support necessitated avoiding "hawkish positions on VietNam, China, etc."[87] Yet sure enough, Armendariz began to oversee campaign advertisements for Cuban areas that endorsed their exceptionalism and contradicted the latter claim. Channeling the *Star Wars* blockbuster film, these ads told Cubans that Reagan was "our only hope" against "the insidious spread of Castro-style Communism" in the hemisphere.[88] The campaign manager, too, had little recourse when Cuban Advisory Committee leaders reportedly spoke on behalf of the larger group that "Hispanics believe a stronger stance is needed against Fidel Castro's Communist expansionism in the Carribean [*sic*] and Central America."[89]

While Cuban Americans further injected hard-line foreign policy stances into the wider GOP Hispanic appeal, they were not the only Hispanic Republicans to enter into a dialogue with Reaganism. Tejanos contributed their own "raza" conservatism, this of a social nature. The state chairman of the Mexican American Republicans of Texas (MART), L. G. "Brownie" Trevino, wrote to Ronald Reagan in late August 1980, explaining that "Mexican Americans have been mistakenly stereotyped as liberals but nothing can be further from the truth—we are pro work ethic, pro family, pro prayer in the schools and pro right to life."[90] The MART issued a "Raza Declaration" for the 1980 campaign. The manifesto spun Mexican-American pride into a religious and masculine call to dump liberalism. Conservative bêtes noires in academia, social work, and the public school system came in for criticism. The declaration expressed a deep anxiety about

what the government is doing in our schools "ya no le dan lugar a Dios," [they give no place to God anymore] they put our kids on buses and ship them all over town to be counted as whites, away from the barrio. And now they may even have maricones [derogatory for homosexuals] for teachers. They teach our girls how easy it is to avoid getting pregnant and have abortions. Our fathers' teachings "Los hombres no lloran," [men don't cry] . . . are being pushed aside against our wishes and being replaced with liberal "throw-away" gringo values that destroy la familia.[91]

For all its traditionalism, the code-switching in the Raza Declaration indicated that this was hardly a statement of 100 percent Americanism. Even while espousing conservative positions, the declaration explicitly embraced a "minority" identity, taking pride in the group's "double heritage" and condemning those who did not as "elitists." It also validated the group's connection to the undocumented immigrants, those "Raza" "who don't have their papers fixed."[92]

The Reagan campaign reflected this eclectic conservatism back to the constituency in the field. When Hispanic Heritage week came around, Reagan took to South Texas. Visiting the Rio Grande Valley city of Harlingen, the candidate and his wife, Nancy, arrived in a downtown plaza "on a horse-drawn carriage, decorated with colorful paper flowers." They were joined by an elite cadre of Texans, including the state's Republican governor Bill Clements, former Democratic governor John Connally, US senator John Tower, and Dallas Cowboys quarterback Roger Staubach. The thousands in attendance on that Mexican Independence Day saw Reagan dressed in a white guayabera for maximum climatic and cultural sensitivity. They heard him laud their heritage as "a vital force in American life today." "You have preserved the fundamental values of the Hispanic community—not merely the immediate family, but the extended family linking the generations," he told them. He offered his take on the notion of human rights, praising their "firm attachment to the great human right of property ownership," as well as their efforts in "labor[ing] long and hard to own your homes, your farms, your business enterprises, your own piece of America."[93]

An early version of Reagan's Harlingen speech appears to the contemporary reader deeply humane on the question of the undocumented migrant:

We cannot erect a Berlin Wall along our southern border. We cannot rely on traps and dogs and other brutal and inhuman techniques to hunt down fellow human beings whose only crime is the desire to work and to provide for their families. . . . These are people, poor people, people with hungry families and undernourished children. We must never lose sight of this fact.[94]

The text officially released to reporters contained a more modest plea to regard immigration as "a matter that demands the utmost sensitivity and spirit of cooperation on both sides." The candidate was to say that, "we are talking here not just about statistics, but human beings, families, the hopes and dreams for a better life."[95] Newspapers reported that Reagan's audience applauded the candidate's stated desire to "document the undocumented workers and make them legal coming into our country with a visa."[96] Reagan also went on record in Harlingen that "You don't build a nine-foot fence along the border between two friendly nations."[97]

This was not the last effort to present a softer side of conservatism to Mexican Americans. A couple of weeks later, Reagan returned to East Los Angeles, whose Mexican Americans he had wooed during his 1966 run for governor of California. There, in 1980, he claimed to support bilingual education. He said that it was "necessary in those communities where Spanish is the native tongue" and that he "would oppose any legislative attempts to eliminate it."[98]

While Reagan reassured average Hispanic voters that he was sensitive to their unique circumstances and culture, his campaign had a clear class constituency. In advisor Elizabeth Dole's view, "business people" were its "number one priority among Hispanics." In previous years and in part through the impetus of minority business programs begun under Nixon, businessmen had built a nationwide "Hispanic Chamber of Commerce," yet another one of the decade's new pan-Hispanic institutions. As of fall 1980, the Chamber claimed twenty-five thousand members in eighteen states.[99] Though once enthusiastic supporters of Carter, the Chamber's leadership had soured on the incumbent. Directed by Kansas City businessman Hector Barreto, the group gathered in Miami for the "First Hemispheric Congress of Latin Chambers of Commerce and Industry," where as many as two thousand "Cubans, Puerto Ricans, Central and South Americans and Mexican Americans" united to criticize Carter's poor approach to Hispanic businesses. The Chamber excoriated the Small Business Administration, particularly its Minority Business Development Agency (MBDA).

Under the incumbent, it had become "an 'Ebony-Black' elite that disen-franchises minorities, especially Hispanics," and known for "practic[ing] an elitist racism of the highest form." Its actions had "downgraded the minority status of Hispanics in the United States."[100]

Class similarity and the sense of common victimization by seemingly privileged blacks in the minority business bureaucracy were a powerful stimulus to unity and political action. The business leaders viewed the MBDA in a manner akin to how Spanish-speaking Democrats regarded the Equal Employment Opportunity Commission in the 1960s. Its functioning was both essential to group improvement and a fundamental test of a government's inclusiveness. Carter's MBDA was failing that test. Elizabeth Dole, whose husband Robert was US senator from Barreto's state of Kansas, secured the Chamber's endorsement of Reagan, which his campaign announced just before the election.[101] In its quest for a "fair share," the Chamber called "it imperative that all Hispanics see the light" and vote for Reagan.[102]

☆ ☆

And yet the vast majority did not. More than two million Latinos voted in November 1980, an all-time high. An in-depth analysis conducted by the Southwest Voter Registration Education Project indicated that only a quarter of Latinos voted for Reagan. Roughly 70 percent still voted for Jimmy Carter (down from 81 percent in 1976), with the remaining 5 percent supporting other candidates, most notably Illinois congressman and independent candidate John Anderson. Unsurprisingly, Reagan fared considerably worse in New York State, where Puerto Ricans predominated, pulling only 13 percent of Latino votes to Carter's 85 percent. The Republican's showing was even worse in Illinois. Still, Reagan outperformed his national numbers with Michigan's Latinos, and in New Jersey, where a large Cuban population was no doubt influential. Predictably, Reagan's strongest showing among Latinos came in Florida, where almost 60 percent of Latino voters preferred him to Carter. Stronger still in South Florida, the challenger received 84.3 percent of the vote in one heavily Latino precinct in Miami, according to the report. Meanwhile, Carter's high (89 percent among the group in Illinois) and low (37 percent in Florida) state totals further illustrated just how differentiated the "Latino vote" had become.[103]

Republicans, however, believed that Reagan's victory had been more sweeping. A *New York Times*/CBS News exit poll had put Reagan's

Hispanic tally at roughly 36 percent, and it was this number that GOP insiders repeatedly cited in their assessments of whether to continue to reach out to the constituency.[104]

The task was thus to safeguard and potentially expand upon these imagined gains. In the new administration, Elizabeth Dole became director of the Office of Public Liaison, the White House entity charged with interest group outreach. For Dole and others invested in party "Hispanic strategy," the fundamental question going forward was twofold: given that Reagan's governing approach would be deeply conservative (if not as conservative as many on the right hoped), what means would be available to maintain and even build upon these levels of minority support, and which individuals and Hispanic constituencies could serve as the focal point and image makers of a Reaganized Hispanic Republicanism?

It was clear from the start that the Reagan Revolution's attempt to roll back the limited welfare state laid down in the New Deal and the multicultural democracy born during the civil rights era constituted a challenge to the philosophies and functioning of the core national Hispanic organizations. Reagan's first budget slashed some $47 billion from Carter's last one, with the pain inflicted primarily on the most vulnerable members of society. Not only to be felt at the individual level in Latino America, the cuts also figured to hit existing Latino organizations very hard, for they relied upon such federal dollars to provide a range of community health, educational, and vocational services.[105]

In February 1981, the White House also revoked federal education rules, initiated in the waning months of the Carter administration, that would have greatly expanded the number of students who received bilingual instruction.[106] Reagan's new education secretary, T. H. Bell, characterized the requirements, which many in the Latino political establishment considered essential to their people's achievement of equality, as "harsh, inflexible, burdensome, unworkable and incredibly costly," and "symbolic of the many ills that have plagued the Federal Government."[107]

The Voting Rights Act was set to expire the next year, as well. The White House was committed to weakening it by requiring individuals to provide proof of discriminatory "intent" and not merely discriminatory "effect." Given the longstanding use of seemingly neutral maneuvers such as gerrymandering and at-large elections to prevent meaningful Latino electoral mobilizations, and how recently Latinos had won protections as a "language minority," policies that would make it more difficult to prove discrimination constituted a clear threat to the group's tenuous place in American democracy.[108]

As the administration established its conservative program, it was simultaneously evaluating which sectors of the nation's Hispanic leadership to empower. One debate was whether to reach out to the liberal representatives of what was still a mostly Democratic constituency or continue to punish them. In February 1981, the new administration invited the leaders of several mainstream Latino organizations to the White House, hoping to "alleviate their current concerns."[109] However, what some deemed necessary "coalition-building" clearly angered many Latino Republicans. Tirso del Junco, the conservative Cuban exile and Reagan ally who served as California's Republican Party chairman, attended the meeting but questioned the wisdom of "lend[ing] credibility, or provid[ing] a platform for," people or groups critical of the president.[110] The sting was far worse for the moderate Mexican Americans in charge of the Republican National Hispanic Assembly. Excluded from the meeting, RNHA chairman Fernando Oaxaca called himself "shocked and almost amazed by the insensitivity or naivete" of Dole's attempt to court these "alleged Hispanic leaders." "The Assembly and yours truly," he wrote, "loyal to the core and, figuratively, still perspiring a bit from the campaign," had been shut out of all recognition. They deserved to be the ones, Oaxaca believed, with a chance to shape Reagan's program "to deal with and market to Hispanics."[111]

For traditional party insiders such as Oaxaca, the new administration's antistatist conservatism undermined the means by which they had attracted their people to the party for more than a decade. For example, the Small Business Administration was slated for a significant budget reduction, leaving Ben Fernandez and others to wonder if their businesspeople would be left behind in the contest for valuable minority contracts.[112] Neither could Hispanic Republicans count on using federal employment for partisan recruitment. Ominous rumors circulated that the White House planned to eliminate the federal workforce's Latino affirmative action program, which dated back more than a decade to the first Nixon administration. Fearing the rumors founded, Elizabeth Dole had to inform the Director of the Office of Management and Budget (OMB), David Stockman, that the program's future was "a very important issue to our Hispanic Constituency."[113] And even though often identified as a Democratic concern, moderate

Republicans feared heavy fallout from Reagan's proposed cuts to bilingual education programs. For Fernando Oaxaca, Stockman's OMB had showed neither "sensitivity to the needs of people" nor an awareness of the political consequences of such an action.[114]

But the White House's actions suggest that it interpreted the candidate's 1980 Hispanic results as evidence that it could begin to reconstruct the Hispanic electorate in Reagan's image, rather than cater to the image and policy expectations advocated by its traditional leaders, whether Democratic or Republican. That is, rather than seeking to "market to Hispanics," as Fernando Oaxaca imagined, the administration was testing to see if it could bend Hispanics into marketing Reagan.

It soon became clear that whatever White House recognition Reagan's Hispanic supporters received, they would have to earn by demonstrating loyalty to Reaganomics. In March, the White House began "an all-out public relations offensive, both on television and Capitol Hill," to pressure legislators to support its economic program, which gave tax cuts for the wealthy and axed aid for the poor, hungry, unemployed, and disabled. Later that month, nearly three-dozen Hispanic Republicans met with Reagan and found that with that access came the request to "help sell the President's economic package" back home. They could anticipate "tough questions" in their communities. People there were worried about cuts to bilingual education and job training programs.[115]

Still, many enlisted in the cause. They established a "Hispanic Coalition for Economic Recovery." Ostensibly a "nonpartisan" group (though working with Dole's office and led by prominent Hispanic Republicans such as Fernando De Baca and congressman Manuel Luján), the coalition aimed to mobilize Hispanic businesspeople, civic groups, and organizations to support Reagan's budget and small business agenda. It planned to raise money for a direct mail campaign, newspaper and magazine ad buys, and to fund a speakers' bureau to defend the administration's proposals before a variety of Latino audiences across the nation.[116]

And sell the administration's program it did. Blaming government for "spending beyond its means" and criticizing "skyrocketing Federal entitlements," the Hispanic Coalition for Economic Recovery touted the benefits of lower taxes for overall economic health.[117] Though not long on how "bringing inflation under control . . . strengthening our national defense and . . . holding the line on excessive Federal entitlement funding" reflected ethnic priorities, the Hispanic Coalition's newspaper advertisements declared their loyalty: "We Support You, Mr. President."[118]

The White House also enlisted the Hispanic Chamber of Commerce to drape Reagan's economic program in an ethnic mantle. Under Hector Barreto's leadership, the Chamber had been the solitary national Hispanic organization of any consequence to endorse Reagan–Bush in 1980, and Barreto personally enrolled in the Hispanic Coalition for Economic Recovery. In April 1981, he brought more than one hundred local presidents of Hispanic chambers of commerce to the White House. There, the group praised Reagan's budget cuts, new business tax incentives, and other reductions in individual tax rates, as well as anticipated "relief from costly and unnecessary regulations."[119]

The Chamber embraced its economic mission in a particularly ethnic fashion. In what amounts to the organized Hispanic business community's position paper on Reaganomics, it deployed the long-used language of Hispanic patriotism to the novel end of dismantling the social safety net:

> We members of the Hispanic community have been rather late in developing an effective voice in American government. We love this country. We have fought and died for its ideals. Hence we respond positively to an appeal to sacrifice for the economic good of our country. We respond even more positively when we are assured that we are not asked to sacrifice to any greater extent than other Americans.[120]

The Chamber took comfort in Reagan's placing of two Latinos in the top posts in the Small Business Administration and the Minority Business Development Agency.[121] After the unfair treatment they endured during the Carter years, they were willing to accept as progress the president's restoration of a seat at the table and his vow to make black and Hispanic businessmen partake equally in a shrinking pie.

In Reagan's first year, the most optimistic Republicans could see important gains being made in what Elizabeth Dole called their "effort to build a lasting coalition among middle-class Hispanics."[122] A June 1981 poll, conducted in the wake of a survived assassination attempt that bolstered Reagan's popularity across the board, indicated that Hispanics gave Reagan 63 percent approval ratings. Dole swooned at the "remarkable 38 percent" of self-identified Republicans in this same group, supposedly "up from a base of less than 10 percent."[123] This 28 percent jump was all the more impressive considering the general population's identification with Republicanism had risen only 3 percent since Reagan took over, according to party sources.[124] Cuban Americans were reporting especially phenomenal success in extending Republicanism in South Florida. Registration drives yielded what the Office of Public Liaison believed was "an unprecedented occurrence": registered Hispanic Republicans now outnumbered registered Hispanic Democrats in pivotal Dade County.[125] The White House had named a growing number of appointees of Hispanic origin, to whom they could point as evidence of Reagan's inclusiveness. The upper echelons of the administration seemed to think "that 'all is well'" among Hispanics.[126]

The joy was not to last. Dole would report in May 1982 that Reagan's "initial upsurge [among Hispanics] has since reversed itself and is now declining at an alarming rate."[127] Over the previous fall and winter, Reagan's Hispanic disapproval ratings rose 15 percent, and his approval numbers dropped 9 percent.[128] General economic factors certainly played a role, as the administration's budget plans and drive to squelch inflation produced a painful recession and an unemployment rate near 10 percent throughout 1982.[129]

More specific factors were jeopardizing the administration's Hispanic appeal, however. As Dole explained to Chief of Staff James A. Baker III in March 1982, "Hispanics are beginning to view the Administration as racist and as one with little concern for the poor." The administration had put forward "unqualified or controversial" individuals for important civil rights jobs. Moreover, its stance on the Voting Rights Act's renewal—Reagan opposed provisions that would have made it easier to prove violations of the law—appeared "unacceptable" to Latino groups. And at a time of great economic distress, cutting funds from "programs for the needy," which were considered both "very successful and cost effective," was not going over well with Hispanics.[130] Hostility to affirmative action was yet another Reagan liability. Dole warned Reagan's "troika"—Baker, White House Counselor Edwin Meese III, and Deputy Chief of Staff Michael Deaver—that the Justice Department's "statements equating quotas with goals and timetables have antagonized" potential supporters who sought jobs and contracts from Washington.[131] And minority enterprise programs, "once a major attraction for Hispanics, are now considered in a shambles by them." The White House's budget cuts, especially to bilingual education, struck at the "Hispanic upward mobility" that was foundational to expanding Reagan's support among the Latino middle classes. On top of it all, the White House had done a poor job of that time-honored political cure-all: rewarding Hispanic loyalists with meaningful positions in government.[132]

It was not only the Hispanic middle class who felt threatened under the new administration. In late April, Reagan's Immigration and Naturalization Service initiated a week-long campaign of immigration sweeps. Publicized in advance as a means of returning "desirable"[133] work to the unemployed American, the program, "Operation Jobs," included hundreds of workplace raids and, ultimately, the rounding up of thousands of undocumented workers.[134] Dole informed the troika that this action, along with the administration's decision to revoke temporary residency permission to tens of thousands of Mexican nationals, a status they had held since 1977,[135] exposed the White House to "extensive political damage." For the administration's Hispanic outreach, it was, she said, a "crisis of major proportions."[136]

The situation was so dire that White House staff proposed a "Hispanic Crisis Intervention." One option the Office of Public Liaison entertained was a hard turn right, particularly in the realm of social questions. According to Dole's assistant, Henry Zuniga, this would mean devising a new "comprehensive Hispanic Strategy" that would build upon the supposedly "natural" affinity "between Hispanics and conservative issues." These included "anti communist [sic] actions in foreign affairs, tuition tax credit, and anti-abortion issues; anti-gun control issues and school prayer."[137]

But the task of uniting Hispanics with the broader conservative movement's agenda was easier said than done. Dole's office soon learned as much from a sizable survey of Mexican-American adults in San Antonio and East Los Angeles. More than 80 percent in each city (90 percent in Los Angeles) endorsed the Voting Rights Act and bilingual education. They supported the Equal Rights Amendment. And pluralities believed the Reagan administration's funding of "welfare," the "environment," and even "blacks" to be insufficient. In cities that both parties had long considered bellwethers of Hispanic political opinion, Reagan had disapproval rates above 60 percent, far worse than his 35 percent disapproval rating among the general population. The surprise takeaway for Dole's staff: "the Mexican-American is more progressive than expected."[138]

☆ ☆

Still with the primary aim of converting Hispanic Americans into Reagan constituents, Dole urged the troika in May 1982 to endorse a "Hispanic strategy" targeted, as the longstanding RNHA tradition had it, at the upwardly mobile Mexican American. Indeed, despite the evidence of Mexican Americans' stubborn resistance to conservatism, the Office of Public Liaison still argued that they above all Hispanic groups continued to deserve "primary strategic emphasis." After all, they continued to hold the greatest numbers of all the major Hispanic populations, and to evince a "high potential" for conversion. Puerto Ricans both differed "ideologically" from Reagan and would require "slightly more effort" to reach, all with no certain rewards. They would be second in line. Cubans, judged already prosperous, were already likely to support Reagan. Little attention needed to be directed their way. Overall, the White House needed a concerted effort to reach the types of Hispanics "moving up the economic ladder and who have a stake in their communities and the economy in general." Businessmen and professionals were the "target Reagan Hispanic supporters."[139]

Yet the recommendation that Republicans direct themselves to converting the upwardly mobile Mexican American clashed with the party's treatment of its very own upwardly mobile Mexican-American supporters. In January 1982, RNHA chairman Fernando Oaxaca anxiously wrote to Reagan that party leaders were engaged in "a conscious, or worse, inadvertent effort to destroy or emasculate" his organization. In the roughly fifteen months since the election, Oaxaca reported that the RNC had "cast the RNHA out into the street, literally and truly, by cutting its funding and support to zero." The group had even been banished from the Republican Party's Washington headquarters. While using the RNHA's membership lists for fundraising purposes, the RNC nonetheless handed control of its newsletter to a "Southern Anglo." The RNHA soon disappeared from its own publication's pages.[140]

The party leadership's cold treatment of the RNHA was not accidental. It appeared to be a systematic campaign by conservatives to reorient the Assembly away from its fairly moderate Mexican-American leadership, and toward a Cuban-American faction with strong ties to Reagan and the conservative movement. At the head of the rival faction was Dr. Tirso del Junco. His conservative credentials had been long established since his founding of the "very right-wing" American Committee to Free Cuba, and his active backing of Barry Goldwater's 1964 presidential campaign.[141] His political acumen and friendship with Reagan had helped him ascend to the chairmanship of California's Republican Party. In the winter of 1981–1982, he helped found the California Republican Hispanic Council as an alternative to the RNHA in the state.[142] Claiming two thousand members, the Council was organized into geographical units in order, del Junco said, "to bring them inside the party and to be part of the whole structure and not just to be . . . separate Spanish groups."[143] His attempt to subordinate what Ben Fernandez had called the "Hispanic Republican Movement" to Republican Party organization and discipline soon moved beyond the state. With the support of the RNC leadership, del Junco took command of an "Advisory Committee" that began to replicate the RNHA's national functions. Fernando Oaxaca reported that the doctor had "made numerous trips to Texas, Florida and, perhaps other states, to 'organize' Hispanic Republicans."[144]

For Oaxaca, the Cubans were both culturally and philosophically out of step with the Hispanic electorate that Republicans needed to convert. Their growing influence on the party's Hispanic thinking threatened the GOP's chance at expanding their Hispanic base. "We don't need advice for Mexican-American candidates put out by Cuban-American 'experts,'" he argued to the president, likely with del Junco in mind. Whether the RNC leadership and its new "Hispanic experts like it or not," Oaxaca explained, the Hispanic voter was "mostly Democrat, biased against and suspicious of our Party." Republicans could not "reel in this big fish," without employing "competent and non-doctrinaire Hispanic Republicans" to defend its policies. None of this changed what had drawn the constituency to Reagan in the first place, which Oaxaca called "*the fundamental conservative nature of the Hispanic community, particularly vis-a-vis foreign policy and its revulsion for government dependency.*" But what was needed was for "the dollar-laden" Republican Party to "get off their insensitivity and blind idealogy [*sic*] kicks and get some common sense people out there to explain what in the hell is going on!" Time was wasting, the embattled RNHA chairman contended. "*We have lost the 1982 Hispanic vote and the 1984 vote is going fast* unless we *do* something."[145]

As his frustration mounted, Oaxaca took the fateful step of criticizing the administration in public. Published in the March 1982 issue of *Caminos,* his essay entitled "The New Hispanic Conservatives" lambasted "the amazingly insensitive approach to governing of a few misguided Reagan faithful." What they failed to understand was that this "new cultural blend of Americans" did "NOT FIT NEATLY INTO THE FOSSILIZED PARTY IDEALOGY [*SIC*] AND DOGMA OF EITHER MAJOR NATIONAL PARTY." The group was both conservative *and* liberal, claimed Oaxaca.

> So a warning to President Ronald Reagan and company; the Hispanics who voted for you and Mr. Bush in 1980 expected change but not as much change. They still feel they have problems that they know only Washington can work on. And they voted for a tougher foreign policy but they won't buy armed intervention in Latin America. They voted for a new look at the undocumented worker issue but not renewed and insensitive "sweeps" in Latino neighborhoods . . . and they sure didn't expect an apparent erosion of concern about civil rights enforcement—regardless of paperwork reduction or "regulatory reform" goals or dogma.

In the eyes of this national spokesperson for Hispanic America, it was clear that out of the experiences of the past decade and now with a President Reagan, "A NEW HISPANIC POLITICAL IDENTITY IS EMERGING AND CRYSTALLIZING."[146]

This challenge to Reaganism would not be tolerated. Oaxaca intended to bring party activists together during Hispanic Heritage Week of 1982, "to plan intelligently and with foresight, the rebuilding of" the RNHA, and "to define the issues of importance to our community."[147] But his intentions to reforge "a true Hispanic partnership with the Republican Party"[148] under Mexican-American leadership were dashed after the 1982 elections. On January 8, 1983, in Dallas, a well-organized group of Cuban Americans led by Tirso del Junco seized the reins of the RNHA, sweeping nearly every important organizational post. Cubans managed even to take over auxiliary offices in Texas and the Northeast, by tradition reserved to Mexican Americans and Puerto Ricans, respectively.[149] The majority of Mexican Americans and a number of Puerto Ricans walked out upon seeing how badly they had been beaten.[150] Oaxaca described the rout as the result of "a stunning series of maneuvers, some illegal, and according to many, some fraudelent [*sic*]." The extent of party elites' involvement is not clear, though Oaxaca believed that the RNC likely played a role.[151] The RNHA's new leaders did claim to have delighted in Reagan's "words of encouragement and support" in the wake of the coup.[152] The president had supposedly called Tirso del Junco "immediately" to offer congratulations when the Cubans' victory had been assured.[153]

It was difficult not to view the power grab in ethnic terms. For Oaxaca, it had been perpetrated by "forces insensitive to the need for involvement of Mexican-American Republicans in Party affairs."[154] For another analyst, the clash was between "the friends of the President, and the followers of Vice President George Bush, this latter group led by the Mexican Fernando Oaxaca." The takeover was especially important to the Cubans, for it put an end to "ten years of the National Hispanic Assembly being dominated by those of Mexican descent." Home was never far from Cubans' involvement in Hispanic politics, however. It was considered "very beneficial for the cause of the liberation of Cuba" to have a Cuban directing Republican Hispanic activities, wrote the observer.[155]

Considering the takeover from the White House, Elizabeth Dole remarked that it was "regrettable, but frightfully obvious, that our Republican Hispanic leaders are likely to be spending more time fighting one another than working to advance the party in the Hispanic community." For Dole, this "sub-group animosity" was nothing new. But testifying to the full institutionalization of a "Hispanic" politics, nor was it reason to cast doubt upon viewing Hispanic America as a single "community."[156]

☆ ☆

Indeed, the Cuban Americans who seized the RNHA still paid homage to the notion of a Hispanic collectivity. In preparing a Hispanic strategy for party leaders, new chairman Tirso del Junco laid out his vision of the constituency in more than thirty pages. In it, he argued that this group, "so diverse . . . so 'different' . . . so little understood," did in fact "share one thing above all in common: *a sense of Hispanic identity*." And he implored his fellow Republicans to "give clear evidence of our respect for Hispanics' self-identity, for their culture, and for their traditions."[157]

Such pronouncements had become required of any national "Hispanic" leader. But they were not enough for a conservative age. As a newly empowered group mythmaker, del Junco sought to recast his people's political identity as a sort of blank slate. Drawing on demographic data made

President Ronald Reagan at a 1981 White House meeting of Hispanic supporters, his close friend and California Republican state chairman Dr. Tirso del Junco at his side.
Photo by Ron Edmonds, courtesy of Associated Press.

possible by new census procedures, he observed that 60 percent of Hispanic adults had, like himself, been "born outside the U.S." Because so many had yet to naturalize and others were so young, he stressed that, "*Most Hispanics do not—and cannot—vote.*" As a result, he contended, "there are more first-time voters among Hispanics than among any other group. And most of them inherit neither loyalty to the Democratic Party nor commitment to its candidates." They were, at their core, an "un-socialized electorate."[158]

Imagining the Hispanic vote as unmoored from its history was the first step. But what was more important was finding a strategy to supplement the support of GOP Hispanic die-hards with what del Junco argued were the roughly 15–20 percent of Hispanics who could support the party under the right circumstances. These "additional votes" were only meaningful, of course, if Republicans secured them "without losing the votes we presently win from other elements of the Republican Party's support." Given the GOP's rightward turn, this meant abandoning whole sectors of Hispanic America.

> Let's face it! Republicans can not win—and should not try to win—votes from low-status Hispanics who are economically dependent on the full package of economic protection programs authored by the Democrats. Nor should we seek votes from Hispanics who are ideologically committed to expanding federal spending on such programs.[159]

It was not enough for del Junco to disclaim Republicans' historical participation in constructing the limited American welfare state. Del Junco then proceeded to absolve the GOP of its tentative Nixon–Ford era endorsements of affirmative action for Latinos. The Hispanics that Republicans could hope to recruit to a conservative party viewed it, in the main, as "a program that 'helps blacks.'" Rather than supporting affirmative action's effective extension to Hispanics, though, del Junco recommended the party train its fire "on the unfairness of" such "'preferential treatment' and quotas.'" He lumped affirmative action together with "bussing and other primarily black-oriented programs."[160]

An alternative set of Hispanic issues would bring home the "additional" Hispanic votes that del Junco sought. Foremost among these, according to the Cuban, was "a more vigorous national defense" and "more assertive foreign policies." Meting out discipline for America's enemies abroad joined with protecting families at home through tax credits for parochial schools and tough policies on crime. This was a "Hispanic" agenda for the 1980s.[161]

While the RNHA leader proposed a Hispanic political identity harmonized with Reaganism, little stopped the contests for power ongoing *within* the broader framework of GOP Hispanic politics. These put the notion of a commonly held "sense of Hispanic identity," as del Junco called it, to the test.

In the summer of 1983, the Cuban Americans active in the 1980 campaign met with Alex Armendariz to assert their distinct place in the Hispanic political landscape heading into Reagan's reelection run. Previous Republican administrations had increased funding to existing Hispanic civic and educational organizations in advance of their reelection campaigns, hoping to improve their own levels of Hispanic support. But, argued the Cubans, these Latino groups were "primarily liberal and anti-Republican."

Federal dollars thus went to activities such as voter registration, which meant that Republican administrations ended up fostering the growth of "liberal political machines." Having determined that "such liberal Democrat politicization" of federal funding mechanisms was "not only wrong, but illegal," the Cuban Americans called for Reagan to direct those funds instead to Cuban Americans, who "already ha[d] in place an array of social, civic and educational organizations that would be able to utilize federal program monies in ways most advantageous to the Administration." The Cubans argued that there was simply no time to find effective organizational conduits to conservatives in Mexican America, whose leaders they labeled as "highly political" and "anti-Reagan." It was better for the White House to treat Mexican Americans, they concluded, "in a manner similar to the way it reacts to the union vote," that is "bypassing" leadership "and appealing directly to the rank and file."[162]

Such judgments suggested the continued salience of national origins when compared to pan-ethnic categories such as "Hispanic" or "Latino." But as if they were not sufficient, each mention of the word "Hispanic" in the meeting summary was placed in quotes, as if to mock the very concept of a national community, political or otherwise.[163]

☆ ☆

Despite these subsurface rivalries, the public image of a conservative Hispanic collective was resolute, and moving in lockstep with Reagan. Twenty years after partaking of electoral catastrophe in "Latin Americans for Goldwater–Miller," Tirso del Junco stepped to the podium to endorse Reagan's renomination at the 1984 Republican National Convention, now as chairman of the Republican National Hispanic Assembly. As leader of a national pan-ethnic constituency, speaking in the name of "Hispanic Americans," he denounced liberal economic and social policy as pure transactional politics. His people were not "another special interest sold to the highest bidder." He asserted ethnic pride in principle. His were not "a people who would trade equality of opportunity for the empty promises of affirmative action" or one "who will confuse educational excellence with racial quotas." He praised Reagan's economy and his inclusion of Hispanics in government. And he credited the president with precipitating "a rebirth of traditional religious family values," citing Reagan's support for school prayer, tax credits for religious education, and limits on abortion.[164]

As del Junco picked up and rewove various threads animating Latino politics over the past decades and added new issues, he returned to one of its earliest notions. This was that the US Hispanic population had a unique perspective on freedom in the hemisphere and a central role to play in safeguarding it. His people knew well "the shattered illusions" of revolution in Cuba and elsewhere, he said. They stood with the American president and with "our brothers and sisters in Central America" then resisting "the threat imposed upon free people" by leftist forces.[165]

A quarter of a century before, it was this same "struggle for freedom" that had animated some to join in the nascent alliance of "Viva Kennedy" campaigners. Then, the members of this inchoate constituency had little national presence, few notions of even what to call themselves, but a basic commitment to civil rights and liberal economic reform. In 1984, however, del Junco could express this Cold War ethnic patriotism on behalf of the most conservative president of his lifetime, fuse it to an anti-civil rights and antigovernment economic agenda, and do so in the name of "a people." In del Junco's telling, his people's support for Reagan came naturally. They gave it, he said, "as Hispanics."[166]

# Epilogue

During the 1960s and 1970s, a broad range of Americans—activists, politicians, artists, educators, and more—advanced a vision of national identity in which the country's ethnic and racial diversity constituted its very essence. The recognition of the Hispanic or Latino American as a core element of the nation's mosaic was pivotal to this reconstruction of Americanism. The people now known as the country's "largest minority" had emerged as a political community, shattering any chance of an American politics defined solely in black and white terms—or in which US leaders could expect Latinos' ethnoracial distinctions to lose their salience over time. A multicultural democracy was established.

Yet the "united political front" of Hispanics, as Edward Roybal had described his cherished goal in 1980, remained elusive. "One of the things we find is that Hispanics many times divide among themselves instead of coordinating activities," lamented Roybal, the foremost architect of national Latino politics. It was an explanation that suggested that petty or foolish rivalries, or at best a lack of political sophistication, prevented an otherwise natural cohesion from occurring.[1] The search to find an explanation for Latinos' comparative political weakness only grew as the population, now fully recognized in national statistics, exhibited substantial demographic growth.

Observers took to calling Latinos the "sleeping giant." It was a term Roybal had used in the late 1950s in reference to California's Mexican-American population. It was a particularly optimistic appellation then, reflecting the Los Angeles city councilman's hopes that new organization had led his people to the brink of bringing real "strength" to bear on California politics.[2] By the 1980s, the "sleeping giant" had in many cases become synonymous with the national Latino vote, which Roybal, by then two decades a congressman, had worked to bring into existence.

A malleable metaphor, the "sleeping giant" found purchase at all levels of US politics. In the early 1980s, some applied the term to the millions of Latino resident aliens eligible to naturalize. It was they who could almost immediately alter the balance of power in big and important states during presidential elections.[3] Others cast it as that "mythical monster," the national "Latino vote." After twelve years of Republican control of the White House, an analyst in the early 1990s bemoaned his people's "ambivalence and disunity," and posited that "the fabled Sleeping Giant" appeared to have "lapsed into a coma, from which he may never awaken."[4] Yet the giant came to represent state electorates as well, with new opportunities arising for it to demonstrate its verve. Speaking of California Latinos who turned out in droves for Democrats in 1996, in part as a response to the anti-immigrant Proposition 187 passed in their state two years prior, the executive director of the National Association of Latino Elected and Appointed Officials (NALEO) declared that, "The giant is awake and boy is he angry!"[5] It was not only state electorates, though. From Los Angeles to New York City, local Latino communities, according to commentators, were capable of becoming giants in various stages of awakening.[6]

Dissenters found it difficult to get a word in edgewise. A Houston political scientist attempted to explain that his area's Latino electorate was neither dormant nor gigantic, but rather "a normal-sized political animal." He was contradicted by the political operative who insisted that, "The giant is waking up, and he is making a pot of coffee."[7] Even those who mocked the term found it difficult to avoid. As Richard Nixon's "Brown Mafia" media operative Carlos Conde facetiously remarked after Antonio Villaraigosa's election as mayor of Los Angeles in 2005, "It's beginning to sound a bit tedious but the 'sleeping giant' has awakened. Again and again and again!"[8] Reinforced by its application at the local level, the metaphor maintained its utility for describing national races. Said labor leader Eliseo Medina as Latino voters were being credited for Barack Obama's 2012 reelection: "The sleeping Latino giant is wide awake, cranky, and it's taking names."[9]

The expectation of Hispanic power waiting to be realized once Latinos "awoke," put aside their rivalries and apathy, and acted as one, has persistently obscured a complicated set of intragroup relationships, as this book shows. Indeed, the image of ethnic sameness embodied by the "sleeping giant" was, at best, an imperfect reflection of Latino America's true self-perceptions. One major survey conducted in 2002, for example, suggested that Hispanic solidarity was at most a secondary proposition. Indeed, although 81 percent of respondents said they had used pan-ethnic terms such as "Hispanic" or "Latino" to describe themselves, national origin designations remained far more popular as the first or only way that Latinos described themselves. Only 14 percent believed that they shared "one Hispanic/Latino culture." And nearly half believed that "Hispanics from different countries" were "not working together politically."[10] More recent studies tend to echo these findings, indicating that "Hispanic" identity may be gaining in popularity, but that it remains mostly an "undefined form of secondary collective identification."[11]

Meanwhile, the Latino political project faces other pressing challenges. Immigrants have accounted for much of the group's recent population increase. Assuming the new arrivals can obtain citizenship—no sure thing, even in time, given their varying legal statuses—converting their presence into votes (or awaiting their children's majority) will still take time. Though many advocates have fought to make immigration the defining issue of Latino politics, border crossing, documented or not, further diversifies the Latino constituency. What was once mostly a conversation among Mexican Americans, Puerto Ricans, and occasionally Cubans must now incorporate Dominicans, Salvadorans, Bolivians, and Colombians, to name just a few. It must take place in ever more dialects, accommodate a greater array of historical self-understandings, national symbols, and racial schema. It must continue to negotiate the divide between old-comer and newcomer embedded in all stories of migration. And it must do so in a political climate in which powerful voices are rejecting cultural pluralism, dismantling voting rights protections for minorities, and taking aim at the foundations of citizenship for a host of Americans born into immigrant families.

The accumulated challenges of Latino politics have reinforced Latino leaders' tendency to base their appeals on their group's aggregate numbers and economic contributions. In 2003, the Bureau of the Census reported that Hispanics had become the country's largest minority, with upward of thirty-seven million members. Hector Flores, the president of the League of United Latin American Citizens (LULAC), declared then that the census had only stated the obvious. Latinos were "working everywhere, paying taxes, trying to reach the American dream." Their numbers, upright conduct, and commitment to the country justified the devotion of more resources to their communities. Since their group comprised such a large share (then almost 13 percent) of the American people, advocates said that officials would be foolish to neglect them. To one representative of the National Council of La Raza, this young group included the country's "future taxpayers and voters." They were therefore worthy of public investment. Similarly, for the executive director of NALEO, "because such a large section of the country is Latino" it was "in America's self interest" to ensure their success.[12]

Of course, it had never been sufficient for Latino leaders to argue that numbers alone entitled their people to benefits and power. They still labored to fashion the country's largest minority into a cohesive unit capable of deciding elections and winning policy victories. Said one LULAC official in 2003, "I'm not sure how long it is going to take us," adding that, "we Latino leaders are very much aware that we've got to find the keys to unlock our passion as an interest group."[13]

The notion of a Latino community whose collective "passion" waits to be "unlocked" is a powerful testament to the multifaceted struggle undertaken by activists and elected officials during the 1960s and 1970s. So, too, are the numbers and, in the case of certain individuals, the visibility of the current generation of Latino officeholders. In 1960, there were two "Spanish American" congressmen with voting privileges. As of this writing, some three dozen members of the House of Representatives are Latino, the overwhelming majority of them Democrats. Four US senators are Latinos. Two of them, Cuban Republicans Ted Cruz and Marco Rubio, were serious presidential candidates in 2016. It is reasonable to expect each presidential election going forward to feature credible Latino candidacies in one or both parties. In that event, we can expect copious analysis about whether these aspirants can count on the Latino vote to deliver them victory. Yet the variations in ideology, political styles, and national origin reflected in the current crop of Latino officeholders show the continued differentiation of Latino politics, one that will complicate any single candidate's ability to marshal that pan-ethnic allegiance in decisive fashion.

In the end, the image of a nationwide Latino political community that these candidacies will again invoke—a people on the cusp of making a definitive statement of national influence—not only reflects that community.

It helps constitute it, in politics and beyond. Every two to four years, the story draws the diverse Latino populations into contact with one another. It offers an alternative to the demands of national origin identity as well as other more local solidarities, and to the rivalries born of these. Political identity, for a time at least, defines the group. A people still on the margins of American society, primed to make its collective voice heard, yet frustrated time and again by insensitive parties or internal disunity. If only we join forces, the leaders and activists say, this could be the year, our year. It is a narrative of community, albeit a highly imperfect one.

Yet as this book has shown, the extent to which the entire system of American democracy creates a genuine space for a Hispanic, Latino, or Latinx politics—by whatever designated name—matters, too. All political movements are susceptible to co-optation and manipulation by elites, but the Latino unity project has been especially so, given its reliance upon those elites to facilitate the networking of an extraordinary range of geographically, ideologically, and ethnoracially diverse political communities. And as before, the currents of the wider contest for power with which Latino politics is dialogically constructed will determine much about its future character and direction. The specific attraction of Latinos to liberalism, for example, will probably have as much to say about contemporary liberalism as it does about Latinos.

It is certain that a vast array of individuals and organizations, grassroots activists, advocacy lobbies, and public relations firms will be constantly reexamining *Latinidad,* molding it, pushing at its edges, infusing it with perspectives and aligning it with policies—left, right, or center—that they believe will make this pan-ethnic sentiment operative for some faction in the political system. New generations of activists and elected officials will give voice to these conceptions of a community nationwide or, in some cases, extending beyond the country's borders. They will, again, seek alliances and recognition from the most powerful people in the land. For all the questions it raises, the notion of the "Latino vote" is here to stay.

It has been more than 150 years since Whitman's prophecy to the citizens of Santa Fe. Then, with a nation gashed and bloody from the Civil War, the great poet spoke of a people who could redeem the nation by the "nature of their being." He wrote that they would, "like a giant stream that for generations and years and centuries flows underground unseen by human eye . . . suddenly arise to the full surface, in full flood and majestic grandeur."[14] Those who expect the country's Latinos to experience a sudden and nationally restorative political awakening will most likely be disappointed. But beneath the image of a "sleeping giant," there will continue the hard work of forging many versions of—and uses for—"Latino" or "Hispanic" politics. Some of these political projects will demand safety and dignity for individuals and communities suffering terrible injustices, whether in this country, in Latin America, or at the border where the two meet. Others will convince a reluctant alderman to fix a pothole. Whatever its ends, may the work of Latino politics continue without the burden of redeeming a nation for which all Americans are responsible.

# Notes

## Abbreviations

| | |
|---|---|
| AAP | Albert A. Peña, Jr. Papers, MS 37, University of Texas at San Antonio Libraries Special Collections |
| APP | The American Presidency Project |
| DLK | Files of David L. Kaplan, Coordinator of the 1970 Decennial Census, RG 29, Records of the Bureau of the Census, National Archives, Washington, DC |
| EDF | Elizabeth Dole Files, Ronald Reagan Presidential Library and Museum, Simi Valley, California |
| FAHA | Fernando Edward C. De Baca and Christine Gauvreau, The Ford Administration and Hispanic America: The Office Files of Fernando E. C. De Baca (Woodbridge, CT: Primary Source Media, 2009) |
| GISP | George I. Sánchez Papers, Benson Latin American Collection, General Libraries, University of Texas at Austin |
| GRFL | Gerald R. Ford Presidential Library and Museum, Ann Arbor, Michigan |
| GSMP | George S. McGovern Papers, 1939–1984 (mostly 1968–1979), Public Policy Papers, Department of Rare Books and Special Collections, Princeton University Library |
| HBGP | Henry B. González Papers, 1946–1998, the Dolph Briscoe Center for American History, University of Texas at Austin |
| HPG | Dr. Hector P. García Papers, Special Collections and Archives, Bell Library, Texas A&M University–Corpus Christi |
| JAGP | José Angel Gutiérrez Papers, Benson Latin American Collection, University of Texas Libraries, University of Texas at Austin |
| JCL | Jimmy Carter Presidential Library and Museum, Atlanta, Georgia |
| JFKL | John F. Kennedy Presidential Library and Museum, Boston, MA |
| JJB | Joe J. Bernal Papers, Benson Latin American Collection, University of Texas Libraries, University of Texas at Austin |
| JMMP | Joseph M. Montoya Papers, University of New Mexico Center for Southwest Research |

JSP         Julian Samora Papers, Benson Latin American Collection, Univer-
            sity Libraries, University of Texas at Austin
JVLP        John Vliet Lindsay Papers (MS 592), Manuscripts and Archives,
            Yale University Library
LBJL        Lyndon Baines Johnson Presidential Library and Museum, Austin,
            Texas
MADT        Mexican American Democrats of Texas Records, 1962–1987,
            University of Texas at San Antonio Libraries Special Collections
NPL         Richard Nixon Presidential Library and Museum, Yorba Linda,
            California
NPM         Nixon Presidential Materials Project, College Park, Maryland
OMB         RG 51, Records of the Office of Management and Budget, National
            Archives, College Park, Maryland
PFC         President Ford Committee Records, 1975–1976
RAC         Rockefeller Archive Center, Sleepy Hollow, New York
RRL         Ronald Reagan Presidential Library and Museum, Simi Valley,
            California
SMOF        Staff Member and Office Files
WHCF        White House Central Files
WHSF        White House Special Files

## Introduction

*Epigraph:* Quoted in Henry B. González, "It's Our Choice to Make,"
*entrelíneas,* n.d., Box 327, Henry B. González Papers, the Dolph Briscoe
Center for American History, University of Texas at Austin.

1. "It's Your Turn in the Sun," *Time,* October 16, 1978.
2. Michael Scherer, "Yo Decido: Why Latinos Will Pick the Next President,"
   *Time,* March 5, 2012; See, for example, Cindy Y. Rodriguez, "Latino Vote
   Key to Obama's Re-Election," CNN, November 9, 2012, http://www.cnn
   .com/2012/11/09/politics/latino-vote-key-election/; Donna St. George and
   Brady Dennis, "Growing Share of Hispanic Voters Helped Push Obama to
   Victory," *Washington Post,* November 7, 2012, https://www.washingtonpost
   .com/politics/decision2012/growing-share-of-hispanic-voters-helped-push
   -obama-to-victory/2012/11/07/b4087d0a-28ff-11e2-b4e0-346287b7e56c
   _story.html?utm_term=.4edcf3bcb309; or Nate Cohn, "This Time, There
   Really Is a Hispanic Voter Surge," The Upshot, *New York Times,* November 7, 2016, https://www.nytimes.com/2016/11/08/upshot/this-time
   -there-really-is-a-hispanic-voter-surge.html?_r=0; Andrew O'Reilly, "The
   Year of the Latinos: Hispanic Voting Surge Shaking Up Presidential
   Election," Fox News, November 7, 2016, http://www.foxnews.com/politics
   /2016/11/07/year-latinos-hispanic-voting-surge-shaking-up-presidential
   -election.html; and Patricia Mazzei and Nicholas Nehamas, "Florida's
   Hispanic Voter Surge Wasn't Enough for Clinton," *Miami Herald,* November 9, 2016, http://www.miamiherald.com/news/politics-government
   /election/article113778053.html.

3. Cristina Beltrán, *The Trouble with Unity: Latino Politics and the Creation of Identity* (New York: Oxford University Press, 2010), 5.

4. See, for example, Gary Gerstle, *American Crucible: Race and Nation in the Twentieth Century* (Princeton, NJ: Princeton University Press, 2001).

5. Beltrán, *The Trouble with Unity*, 19.

6. Political theorist Beltrán's excellent work *The Trouble with Unity* adopts this general chronology, while G. Cristina Mora's valuable study *Making Hispanics* looks mostly to post-1968 events in its effort to explain Hispanic pan-ethnicity's institutionalization. Beltrán, *The Trouble with Unity*, 7, and chaps. 1, 4; Mora, *Making Hispanics: How Activists, Bureaucrats, and Media Constructed a New American* (Chicago: University of Chicago Press, 2014).

7. Neil Foley, "Becoming Hispanic: Mexican Americans and the Faustian Pact with Whiteness," in *Reflexiones: New Directions in Mexican American Studies*, ed. Neil Foley (Austin: University of Texas Press, 1998), esp. 55–56; Sonia Song-Ha Lee, *Building a Latino Civil Rights Movement: Puerto Ricans, African Americans, and the Pursuit of Racial Justice in New York City* (Chapel Hill: University of North Carolina Press, 2014), 214 and chap. 6.

8. See Suzanne Oboler, *Ethnic Labels, Latino Lives: Identity and the Politics of (Re)Presentation in the United States* (Minneapolis: University of Minnesota Press, 1995), xv, xvi, xvii, 15; Juan Gómez-Quiñones, *Chicano Politics: Reality and Promise, 1940–1990* (Albuquerque: University of New Mexico Press, 1990), 184–185.

9. Beltrán, *The Trouble with Unity*, 7, 14, chap. 3; Mora, *Making Hispanics*, 6; Oboler, *Ethnic Labels, Latino Lives*, xviii.

## 1. The Many Political Communities of Latino America

1. George I. Sánchez to Kyle Haselden, May 22, 1963, Box 42, Julian Samora Papers, Benson Latin American Collection, University Libraries, University of Texas at Austin (hereafter JSP).

2. "Book Review," George I. Sánchez to Julian Samora, February 20, 1952, Box 42, JSP.

3. George I. Sánchez, *Forgotten People: A Study of New Mexicans* (Albuquerque: University of New Mexico Press, 1940).

4. Helen Rowan, "A Minority Nobody Knows," *Atlantic Monthly*, June 1967, 47–52.

5. See Mary Dudziak, *Cold War Civil Rights: Race and the Image of American Democracy* (Princeton, NJ: Princeton University Press, 2002); and Thomas Borstelmann, *The Cold War and the Color Line: American Race Relations in the Global Arena* (Cambridge, MA: Harvard University Press, 2001).

6. George J. Sánchez, *Becoming Mexican American: Ethnicity, Culture and Identity in Chicano Los Angeles, 1900–1945* (New York: Oxford University Press, 1993), 231; On the "American Standard of Living" in Arizona's copper mines, see Katherine Benton Cohen, *Borderline Americans: Racial Division and Labor War in the Arizona Borderlands* (Cambridge, MA: Harvard University Press, 2009), esp. 89–90.

7. Leo Grebler, Joan W. Moore, and Ralph C. Guzman, *The Mexican-American People: The Nation's Second Largest Minority* (New York: Free Press, 1970), 235, 181; see also William S. Clayson, *Freedom Is Not Enough: The War on Poverty and the Civil Rights Movement in Texas* (Austin: University of Texas Press, 2010), 15.

8. Julie L. Pycior, *LBJ & Mexican Americans: The Paradox of Power* (Austin: University of Texas Press, 1997), 15–19; Grebler, Moore, and Guzman, *The Mexican-American People*, 252, 144; Armando Navarro, *Mexicano Political Experience in Occupied Aztlán: Struggles and Change* (Walnut Creek, CA: AltaMira Press, 2005), 254; Brian D. Behnken, "The Movement in the Mirror: Civil Rights and the Causes of Black-Brown Disunity in Texas," in *The Struggle in Black and Brown: African American and Mexican American Relations during the Civil Rights Era*, ed. Brian D. Behnken (Lincoln: University of Nebraska Press, 2012), 51.

9. Rodolfo Rosales, *The Illusion of Inclusion: The Untold Political Story of San Antonio* (Austin: University of Texas Press, 2000), 28; Juan Gómez-Quiñones, *Chicano Politics: Reality and Promise, 1940–1990* (Albuquerque: University of New Mexico Press, 1990), 83–84.

10. See Ramón A. Gutiérrez, "Unraveling America's Hispanic Past: Internal Stratification and Class Boundaries," *Aztlán* 17, no. 1 (Spring 1987): 79–80; and Charles Montgomery, "Becoming 'Spanish-American': Race and Rhetoric in New Mexico Politics, 1880–1928," *Journal of American Ethnic History,* 20 no. 4 (Summer 2001): 59–84. David Montejano suggests that, prior to the Chicano Movement, "a unity of class or even of ethnicity could not be assumed," even within largely Mexican-American neighborhoods in San Antonio. These, he finds, were "a complex aggregation of . . . local worlds" in which, at least for the young, "kinship and intimate peer relationships" were more relevant than national identity. See David Montejano, *Quixote's Soldiers: A Local History of the Chicano Movement* (Austin: University of Texas Press, 2010), 54.

11. On Texas voting restriction, see David G. Gutiérrez, *Walls and Mirrors: Mexican Americans, Mexican Immigrants, and the Politics of Ethnicity* (Berkeley: University of California Press, 1995), 27–28.

12. Gutiérrez, *Walls and Mirrors,* 27–28; Pycior, *LBJ & Mexican Americans,* 23–24, 65, 48, 43, 47; Juan Gómez-Quiñones, *Roots of Chicano Politics, 1600–1940* (Albuquerque: University of New Mexico Press, 1994), 333–338; David Montejano, *Anglos and Mexicans in the Making of Texas, 1836–1986* (1987; repr., Austin: University of Texas Press, 1999), parts 2 and 3.

13. John R. Chávez, *The Lost Land: the Chicano Image of the Southwest* (Albuquerque: University of New Mexico Press, 1984), 54; Daniel Valdes y Tapia, *Hispanos and American Politics* (New York: Arno Press, 1976), 57; Jack E. Holmes, *Politics in New Mexico* (Albuquerque: University of New Mexico Press, 1967), 49–50. Gómez-Quiñones, *Roots of Chicano Politics,* 327; F. Chris García, Paul L. Hain, Gilbert K. St. Clair, and Kim Seckler, *Gov-*

*erning New Mexico* (Albuquerque: University of New Mexico Press, 2006), 226; Gómez-Quiñones, *Roots of Chicano Politics*, 331.

14. Ernest B. Fincher, *Spanish-Americans as a Political Factor in New Mexico, 1912–1950* (New York: Arno Press, 1974), 132–135, 103–105; Valdes, *Hispanos and American Politics*, 80.

15. Maurilio E. Vigil, *Los Patrones: Profiles of Hispanic Political Leaders in New Mexico History* (Washington, DC: University Press of America, 1980), 149–151; Chavez was actually the second Hispano elected to the US Senate. Octaviano Larrazolo, a Republican, had been elected in 1928 but served only six months due to illness. "LARRAZOLO, Octaviano Ambrosio (1859–1930)," in *Biographical Dictionary of the United States Congress*, http://bioguide .congress.gov/scripts/biodisplay.pl?index=l000101 (accessed March 16, 2014).

16. Hispanos were already junior partners in state politics. Despite turning out in great numbers, and occasionally electing candidates such as Chavez, they held only a minority of Democratic and Republican Party leadership positions between the World Wars. Rarely were they elected governor. Almost totally excluded from judicial positions, they also had to scratch and claw to obtain state appointed offices. Gómez-Quiñones, *Roots of Chicano Politics*, 332; During the period from 1916–1948, they held only a minority of Democratic and Republican Party central committee positions, and usually less than a third of those in the reigning Democratic Party. Fincher, *Spanish-Americans as a Political Factor*, 125; a 1949 state antidiscrimination bill required all Spanish-American legislators to vote in favor for a mere one vote margin of victory. Gómez-Quiñones, *Chicano Politics*, 47–50.

17. Chavez fought to preserve Roosevelt's Fair Employment Practices Commission—which prohibited discrimination in war industry—against evisceration by southern senators after World War II, and sponsored a legislative ban on employment discrimination as a whole. Kevin Allen Leonard, "Dennis Chavez: The Last of the Patrones," in *The Human Tradition in America between the Wars, 1920–1945*, ed. Donald W. Whisenhunt (Wilmington, DE: Scholarly Resources, 2002), 117.

18. See Montejano, *Anglos and Mexicans*, part 3, esp. 228–244.

19. Quoted in Montejano, *Anglos and Mexicans*, 232.

20. Quoted in Mario T. García, *Mexican Americans: Leadership, Ideology, and Identity, 1930–1960* (New Haven, CT: Yale University Press, 1989), 31.

21. On Mexicans and whiteness, see Neil Foley, "Becoming Hispanic: Mexican Americans and the Faustian Pact with Whiteness," in *Reflexiones: New Directions in Mexican American Studies*, ed. Neil Foley (Austin: University of Texas Press: 1998), 53–70; and Neil Foley, *Quest For Equality: The Failed Promise of Black-Brown Solidarity* (Cambridge, MA: Harvard University Press, 2010).

22. Quoted in Gutiérrez, *Walls and Mirrors*, 77.

23. Gutiérrez, *Walls and Mirrors*, 77–78.

24. Benjamin H. Johnson, "The Cosmic Race in Texas: Racial Fusion, White Supremacy, and Civil Rights Politics," *Journal of American History* 98, no. 2 (September 2011): 408.

25. On "Acquiescent" and "Transformational" incorporation, see Gary Gerstle, "Historical and Contemporary Perspectives on Immigrant Political Incorporation: The American Experience," *International Labor and Working-Class History* 78 (Fall 2010): 110–117.

26. Minorities were a rarity in the state capital of Sacramento as well, with only one black and one Jew serving in the state legislature in 1939. Kenneth C. Burt, *The Search for a Civic Voice: California Latino Politics* (Claremont, CA: Regina Books, 2007), 16, 20.

27. García, *Mexican Americans*, 158.

28. Burt, *The Search for a Civic Voice*, 14.

29. Quoted in Gutiérrez, *Walls and Mirrors*, 112.

30. Virginia E. Sánchez Korrol, *From Colonia to Community: The History of Puerto Ricans in New York City* (Berkeley: University of California Press, 1983, repr. 1994), 143; Lorrin Thomas, *Puerto Rican Citizen: History and Political Identity in Twentieth-Century New York City* (Chicago: University of Chicago Press, 2010), 51–53; see also 161–162, 211.

31. Liberal members, including the group's first president, Eduardo Quevedo, were appalled when, after the Soviet Union signed a nonaggression pact with Nazi Germany in late 1939, El Congreso quickly dropped its vocal antifascism and began calling for nonintervention in the European war. García, *Mexican Americans*, 158, 165, 171–173; Sánchez, *Becoming Mexican American*, 245–246.

32. See Vicki L. Ruiz, *Cannery Workers, Cannery Lives: Mexican Women, Unionization, and the California Food Processing Industry, 1930–1950* (Albuquerque: University of New Mexico Press, 1987): chap. 6; and Zaragosa Vargas, *Labor Rights Are Civil Rights: Mexican American Workers in Twentieth-Century America* (Princeton, NJ: Princeton University Press, 2005): chaps. 3 and 4; Gutiérrez, *Walls and Mirrors*, 173.

33. The labor-centric Mexican-American movement was revived for a few years by the Asociación Nacional México-Americana (ANMA), which maintained the connections between Mexican people and the US left, most notably the Independent Progressive Party of Henry Wallace. But ANMA suffered a similar fate as El Congreso. Its unapologetic challenges to Mexican people's economic and cultural exclusion, as well as to US Cold War foreign policy, caught the US attorney general's eye, and by 1954 ANMA was tarred as a Communist "front" organization. The stakes of participation considerably raised, another vigorous attempt to bring unity to the Southwest was thwarted. Gómez-Quiñones, *Chicano Politics*, 51.

34. US Department of Labor, Bureau of Labor Statistics, "Employment Status of the Civilian Noninstitutional Population, 1942 to Date," http://www.bls.gov /cps/cpsaat01.htm (accessed February 4, 2014); Gutiérrez, *Walls and Mirrors*,

141; Navarro, *Mexicano Political Experience,* 231, 251; Gary Gerstle, *American Crucible: Race and Nation in the Twentieth Century* (Princeton: Princeton University Press, 2001), 199; Montejano, *Anglos and Mexicans,* 280.

35. See Vernon Carl Allsup, *The American G.I. Forum: Origins and Evolution* (Austin: University of Texas Press, 1982): 40, and chap. 3; and Patrick J. Carroll, *Felix Longoria's Wake: Bereavement, Racism, and the Rise of Mexican American Activism* (Austin: University of Texas Press, 2003).

36. Pycior, *LBJ & Mexican Americans,* 58–60.

37. Rosales, *Illusion of Inclusion,* 46.

38. It was not until the 1970s that most middle-class neighborhoods and schools opened up to Mexican Americans, Rosales, *Illusion of Inclusion,* 5, 9–10; During the war years, Mexican people died of tuberculosis at three times the rate Anglos did; their infant mortality rates were double and triple those of Anglos; and Mexican-American women died giving birth at an even more alarming rate. Edwin Larry Dickens, "The Political Role of Mexican-Americans in San Antonio, Texas" (PhD diss., Texas Tech University, 1969), 63–65, 67.

39. Rosales, *Illusion of Inclusion,* 31, 35, 49.

40. George Green, *The Establishment in Texas Politics: The Primitive Years, 1938–1957* (Westport: CT: Greenwood Press, 1979), 17.

41. Leonides González also managed a silver mine in Durango. Eugene Rodriguez Jr., *Henry B. González: A Political Profile* (New York: Arno Press, 1976), 31; Brenda Haugen, *Henry B. González: Congressman of the People* (Minneapolis: Compass Point Books, 2006), 21, 27.

42. Rodriguez, *Henry B. González,* 42.

43. Rodriguez, *Henry B. González,* 47–48; Dickens, "The Political Role of Mexican-Americans in San Antonio, Texas," 104–106.

44. Rodriguez's translation of "nuestra raza" was "our race." Quoted in Rodriguez, *Henry B. González,* 53, 56, 54.

45. Rodriguez, *Henry B. González,* 53, 56–58; Dickens, "The Political Role of Mexican-Americans in San Antonio, Texas," 108–109.

46. Rodriguez, *Henry B. González,* 71.

47. The margin was less than 300 votes. Rosales, *Illusion of Inclusion,* 57–58, and Rodriguez, *Henry B. González,* 75.

48. While the liberal coalition had expanded the electorate, with less than 30,000 of the 140,000 eligible voters in the 1956 elections Mexican Americans (and 10,500 African American), González could not have won with a singular message of Mexican, or even "minority" empowerment. Turnout jumped 13 percent from 1948, pushing the total to 68.7 percent. Rodolfo F. Acuña, *Occupied America: A History of Chicanos,* 5th ed. (New York: Pearson / Longman, 2004), 280; Rodriguez, *Henry B. González,* 74; Peña won a seat on the Bexar county commission as well. Dickens, "The Political Role of Mexican-Americans in San Antonio, Texas," 112.

49. Governor Price Daniel suggested that at least one of the bills would not be used against Mexican Americans, but there was ample reason for them to be suspicious. The state's education officials had a long history of segregating Mexican-American children, often citing language deficiencies to consign them to inferior schools. Mexican-American civil rights groups had spent years litigating for their children to go to school with Anglo children. See Guadalupe San Miguel Jr., *"Let All of Them Take Heed": Mexican Americans and the Campaign for Educational Equality in Texas, 1910–1981* (Austin: University of Texas Press, 1987), esp. part II.

50. Quoted in Brian Behnken, *Fighting Their Own Battles: Mexican Americans, African Americans, and the Struggle for Civil Rights in Texas* (Chapel Hill: University of North Carolina Press, 2003), 59.

51. Rodriguez, *Henry B. González*, 81.

52. Also, see "Texas Curbs Near for Integration," *New York Times*, November 24, 1957. See Behnken, *Fighting Their Own Battles*, 58.

53. Thomas O'Neill, "Politics and People," *Baltimore Sun*, June 4, 1958; "Texas Race Poses Integration Test," *New York Times*, May 11, 1958.

54. "The González Candidacy," *Texas Observer*, May 16, 1958, Henry B. González Papers, 1946–1998, The Dolph Briscoe Center for American History, University of Texas at Austin (hereafter HBGP), Box 50.

55. Gail Beagle, "Henry B. González, Candidate for Governor, Says He Doesn't Believe in Waving False Flags," *Port Neches Chronicle*, July 1958, HBGP, Box 50.

56. Rodriguez, *Henry B. González*, 87.

57. Friends of González, "Go with González for Governor!," HBGP, Box 50.

58. For a friend's critical appraisal of this practice, see George I. Sánchez to Henry B. González, May 9, 1958, Correspondence and Subject Files, 1931–1972, Box 17, GISP.

59. Liborio Rodríguez Zapata, "Nuestro Homenaje a Henry B. González," HBGP, Box 50.

60. "Conservatives Gain Control of Party in Texas," *Los Angeles Times*, July 28, 1958.

61. "González, Henry Barbosa," http://www.tshaonline.org/handbook/online/articles/fgo76 (accessed October 1, 2011).

62. Shana Bernstein, "Interracial Activism in the Los Angeles Community Service Organization: Linking the World War II and Civil Rights Eras," *Pacific Historical Review* 80, no. 2 (May 2011): 231, 238–239.

63. Katherine Underwood, "Pioneering Minority Representation: Edward Roybal and the Los Angeles City Council, 1949–1962," *Pacific Historical Review* 66, no. 3 (August 1997): 401.

64. The last Mexican American to serve on the council before Edward Roybal departed in 1881; When the future president of El Congreso, Eduardo Quevedo, ran in 1938, he is said to have been "the first Mexican American candidate in the twentieth century to aspire actively to local office." Sánchez, *Becoming Mexican American*, 250.

65. Burt, *Search for a Civic Voice*, 54; George J. Sánchez, "Edward R. Roybal and the Politics of Multiracialism," *Southern California Quarterly* 92, no. 1 (Spring 2010): 57; Underwood, "Pioneering Minority Representation," 404–405.

66. Before the war Boyle Heights' Jewish population was more than double the Mexican population, a key factor in its reputation for left-wing politics. George J. Sánchez, "'What's Good for Boyle Heights Is Good for the Jews': Creating Multiracialism on the Eastside during the 1950s," *American Quarterly* 56, no. 3 (September 2004): 635; Underwood, "Pioneering Minority Representation," 402.

67. Burt, *Search for a Civic Voice*, 57–58.

68. On the birth of the CSO, see Burt, *Search for a Civic Voice*, chap. 3; and Bernstein, "Interracial Activism in the Los Angeles Community Service Organization."

69. Soon it claimed 800 members, split between men and women, three quarters of whom had US citizenship. Underwood, "Pioneering Minority Representation," 406; Bernstein, "Interracial Activism in the Los Angeles Community Service Organization," 245–248.

70. Underwood, "Pioneering Minority Representation," 408, 409.

71. Bernstein, "Interracial Activism in the Los Angeles Community Service Organization," 244; Underwood, "Pioneering Minority Representation," 409.

72. Burt, *Search for a Civic Voice*, 65; Underwood, "Pioneering Minority Representation," 409.

73. Gutiérrez, *Walls and Mirrors*, 169.

74. Quoted in Underwood, "Pioneering Minority Representation," 411.

75. Gutiérrez, *Walls and Mirrors*, 169.

76. Quoted in Burt, *Search for a Civic Voice*, 96.

77. Quoted in Sánchez, "Edward R. Roybal and the Politics of Multiracialism," 63.

78. Burt, *Search for a Civic Voice*, 124, 133.

79. Quoted in Burt, *Search for a Civic Voice*, 99.

80. Sánchez, "Edward R. Roybal and the Politics of Multiracialism," 52.

81. Quoted in Burt, *Search for a Civic Voice*, 96, 94.

82. Burt, *Search for a Civic Voice*, 146; Navarro, *Mexicano Political Experience*, 272–273.

83. Quoted in Burt, *Search for a Civic Voice*, 161.

84. Burt, *Search for a Civic Voice*, 176–180.

85. Mario T. García, *Memories of Chicano History: The Life and Narrative of Bert Corona* (Berkeley: University of California Press, 1994), 197.

86. On the composition of the Fresno convention, see García, *Memories of Chicano History*, 198; Quoted in Ernesto Chávez, *"¡Mi Raza Primero!" (My People First!): Nationalism, Identity, and Insurgency in the Chicano Movement in Los Angeles, 1966–1978* (Berkeley: University of California Press, 2002), 34.

87. Burt, *Search for a Civic Voice,* 180–183.

88. Burt, *Search for a Civic Voice,* 149; García, *Memories of Chicano History,* 197.

89. Corona, who was from California, claimed that the use of the term "Latin American" was "an attempt to obscure our true identity as *Mexicans*" and a surrender to past discrimination and political subordination. García, *Memories of Chicano History,* 197–199.

90. Oscar Handlin, *The Newcomers: Negroes and Puerto Ricans in a Changing Metropolis* (Garden City, NY: Anchor Books, 1962), 51, 95; César J. Ayala and Rafael Bernabe, *Puerto Rico in the American Century: A History since 1898* (Chapel Hill: University of North Carolina Press, 2007), 64–68.

91. Sánchez Korrol, *From Colonia to Community,* 173–175.

92. Quoted in Sánchez Korrol, *From Colonia to Community,* 186.

93. Alexander Keyssar, *The Right to Vote: The Contested History of Democracy in the United States* (New York: Basic Books, 2000), 145–146.

94. Dan Wakefield, "Politics and the Puerto Ricans: Getting Out the Vote in Spanish Harlem" *Commentary,* March 1, 1958.

95. José Cruz, "The Political Incorporation of (In)Migrants in the United States: The Case of Puerto Ricans," August 22, 2011, https://ssrn.com/abstract =1914477 or http://dx.doi.org/10.2139/ssrn.1914477, 12.

96. Thomas, *Puerto Rican Citizen,* 94.

97. Quoted in Thomas, *Puerto Rican Citizen,* 104.

98. Quoted in Thomas, *Puerto Rican Citizen,* 102, 125–126.

99. Marcantonio often ran on the line of the American Labor Party, a social democratic party that was active in New York at the time, but he became so popular in his district that he sometimes swept the Democratic and Republican primaries.

100. See Gerald Meyer, *Vito Marcantonio: Radical Politician, 1902–1954* (Albany: State University of New York Press, 1989), chap. 7; and Sánchez Korrol, *From Colonia to Community,* 188–190.

101. Ayala and Bernabe, *Puerto Rico in the American Century,* 136–137.

102. And although wages improved over the decade, the lure of better opportunities on the mainland, where the minimum wage would rise to $1 an hour in 1956, was strong (in Puerto Rico in 1953, wages for male manufacturing workers averaged $18 a week, while women earned about $12). Ayala and Bernabe, *Puerto Rico in the American Century,* 180–194.

103. Michael Lapp, "Managing Migration: The Migration Division of Puerto Rico and Puerto Ricans in New York City, 1948–1968," (PhD diss., Johns Hopkins University, 1991), 46–47. Gilberto Gerena Valentín, *Gilberto Gerena Valentín: My Life as a Community Activist, Labor Organizer, and Progressive Politician in New York City* (New York: Center for Puerto Rican Studies, 2013), 114.

104. José E. Cruz, "Puerto Rican Politics in New York City during the 1960s: Structural Ideation, Contingency, and Power," in David F. Erickson, ed., *The Politics of Inclusion and Exclusion: Identity Politics in Twenty-First Century*

*America* (New York: Routledge, 2011), 67; Sánchez Korrol, *From Colonia to Community*, 213; and US Bureau of the Census, "Table 17. Population of the 100 Largest Urban Places: 1940," http://www.census.gov/population/www /documentation/twps0027/tab17.txt; "Table 18. Population of the 100 Largest Urban Places: 1950," http://www.census.gov/population/www /documentation/twps0027/tab18.txt; "Table 19. Population of the 100 Largest Urban Places: 1960," http://www.census.gov/population/www /documentation/twps0027/tab19.txt (all accessed May 28, 2012).

105. In 1960, Puerto Rican men with labor market experience in New York had median annual earnings of $5,430, as compared to $8,140 for whites and $6,241 for blacks. Experienced female workers from Puerto Rico earned far less than men, but fared better than Puerto Rican men relative to blacks and whites, with median earnings of $3,861, whereas white women earned $5,131 and black women $4,572. Clara E. Rodríguez, "Economic Factors Affecting Puerto Ricans in New York," in Centro de Estudios Puertor-riqueños, *Labor Migration under Capitalism: The Puerto Rican Experience* (New York: Monthly Review Press, 1979), 205.

106. Thomas, *Puerto Rican Citizen*, 134–135.

107. Lapp, "Managing Migration," 50 and 51n85.

108. José Ramón Sánchez, *Boricua Power: A Political History of Puerto Ricans in the United States* (New York: New York University Press, 2007), 110; Quoted in Sonia Song-Ha Lee, *Building a Latino Civil Rights Movement: Puerto Ricans, African Americans, and the Pursuit of Racial Justice in New York City* (Chapel Hill: University of North Carolina Press, 2014), 50–51.

109. Quoted in Lapp, "Managing Migration," 56.

110. Thomas, *Puerto Rican Citizen*, 135.

111. Meyer, *Vito Marcantonio*, 173.

112. Thomas, *Puerto Rican Citizen*, 97.

113. Quoted in Lapp, "Managing Migration," 111, 112–113.

114. Sánchez, *Boricua Power*, 107–108.

115. The number of Puerto Rican staff grew from 20 to 250 in just two years. Thomas, *Puerto Rican Citizen*, 153–154.

116. Lapp, "Managing Migration," 115.

117. Lapp, "Managing Migration," 105, 119; Ayala and Bernabe, *Puerto Rico in the American Century*, 195–196.

118. Lapp, "Managing Migration," 268–269.

119. Lapp, "Managing Migration," 265, 221–222, 256, 237.

120. Quoted in Lapp, "Managing Migration," 223.

121. The Migration Division routinely publicized among the migrants the progress being made in development back home, the new housing being built, the coming of American stores, and the anniversary of the Common-wealth. Lapp, "Managing Migration," 269; Ayala and Bernabe, *Puerto Rico in the American Century*, 208–210.

122. Lapp, "Managing Migration," 302.

123. Gerena Valentín, *Gilberto Gerena Valentín*, 111.
124. "Hispanic Parade Livens up Fifth Ave," *New York Times*, May 4, 1959; Thomas, *Puerto Rican Citizen*, 161–162.
125. Gerena Valentín, *Gilberto Gerena Valentín*, 126–130; Alexander Feinberg, "Fifth Ave. Echoes to Puerto Ricans," *New York Times*, April 14, 1958; In early May, a "Spanish-American parade" was also held, though Puerto Ricans made up most of its ranks as well. "Rain Raises Pace of Latin Parade," *New York Times*, May 5, 1958.
126. Thomas, *Puerto Rican Citizen*, 211.
127. Ayala and Bernabe, *Puerto Rico in the American Century*, 238.
128. In 1950, the sociologist C. Wright Mills observed Puerto Ricans' embrace of "Latino," and contended that it was a strategic move to align with "some larger and more favored minority." Quoted in Lee, *Building a Latino Civil Rights Movement*, 91; Harvard historian Oscar Handlin, in a 1959 book, noted Puerto Ricans' "incentive to pass," and their sometimes tendency to self-identify as "Latinos or Hispanos." Handlin, *The Newcomers*, 112–114.
129. Thomas, *Puerto Rican Citizen*, 186–187.
130. See Lee, *Building a Latino Civil Rights Movement*, chap. 3.
131. Jonathan C. Brown, *Cuba's Revolutionary World* (Cambridge: Harvard University Press, 2017), 13–14; Louis A. Pérez Jr., *Cuba and the United States: Ties of Singular Intimacy*, 2nd ed. (Athens: University of Georgia Press, 1997), 238–239.
132. María de los Angeles Torres, *In the Land of Mirrors: Cuban Exile Politics in the United States* (Ann Arbor: University of Michigan Press, 2001), 42; María Cristina García, *Havana USA: Cuban Exiles and Cuban Americans in South Florida, 1959–1994* (Berkeley: University of California Press, 1996), 16, 13.
133. Brown, *Cuba's Revolutionary World*, 1; Miguel A. De La Torre, *La Lucha for Cuba: Religion and Politics on the Streets of Miami* (Berkeley: University of California Press, 2003), 33.
134. De La Torre, *La Lucha for Cuba*, 33; García, *Havana USA*, 13.
135. Michael J. McNally, *Catholicism in South Florida, 1868–1968* (Gainesville, FL: University of Florida Press, 1982), 137.
136. García, *Havana USA*, 85, 84.
137. Mauricio Fernando Castro, "Casablanca of the Caribbean: Cuban Refugees, Local Power, and Cold War Policy in Miami, 1959–1995" (PhD diss., Purdue University, 2015), 16–17.
138. García, *Havana USA*, 15.
139. Chanelle N. Rose, *The Struggle for Black Freedom in Miami: Civil Rights and America's Tourist Paradise, 1896–1968* (Baton Rouge: Louisiana State University Press, 2015), 170–172.
140. Rose, *The Struggle for Black Freedom in Miami*, 3.
141. Chanelle N. Rose, "Beyond 1959: Cuban Exiles, Race, and Miami's Black Freedom Struggle," in *Civil Rights and Beyond: African American and*

*Latino/a Activism in the Twentieth-Century United States,* ed. Brian D. Behnken (Athens: University of Georgia Press, 2016), 64–65.

142. McNally, *Catholicism in South Florida,* 142.

143. McNally, *Catholicism in South Florida,* 143.

144. George Southworth, "State Must Regulate Migrant Employment," *Miami Herald,* August 8, 1958.

145. García, *Havana USA,* 44.

146. Rose, *The Struggle for Black Freedom in Miami,* 175, 183–185, 187.

147. See the variety of brief articles on June 17, 1954, including "These Recommendations May Help on Puerto Rican Woes," *Miami Herald.*

148. George Southworth, "Dade Group Considering Puerto Ricans' Problems," *Miami Herald,* August 8, 1958.

149. Transcript, "Crisis, Amigo," in Senate Committee on the Judiciary, *Cuban Refugee Problems: Hearings before the Subcommittee to Investigate Problems Connected with Refugees and Escapees,* 87th Cong., 1961, 138, 182.

150. "They're OK," *Newsweek,* December 4, 1961, 59.

151. Indeed, in 1963, the *Baltimore Afro-American* headlines blared "AFRO FINDS 20,000 DARK CUBAN EXILES." James Williams, *Afro-American,* January 19, 1963.

152. Carl J. Bon Tempo, *Americans at the Gate: The United States and Refugees during the Cold War* (Princeton, NJ: Princeton University Press, 2008), 114.

153. De los Angeles Torres, *In the Land of Mirrors,* 51.

154. Quoted in de los Angeles Torres, *In the Land of Mirrors,* 68.

155. Castro, "Casablanca of the Caribbean," 28–29; García, *Havana USA,* 16.

156. Quoted in Castro, "Casablanca of the Caribbean," 34.

157. García, *Havana USA,* 84.

158. De La Torre, *La Lucha for Cuba,* 58.

159. García, *Havana USA,* 123.

160. García, *Havana USA,* 122–123; Brown, *Cuba's Revolutionary World,* 120; Lars Schoultz, *That Infernal Little Republic: The United States and the Cuban Revolution* (Chapel Hill: University of North Carolina Press, 2009), 110–112.

161. Brown, *Cuba's Revolutionary World,* 113; García, *Havana USA,* 123–124.

162. Castro, "Casablanca of the Caribbean," 31–32.

163. García, *Havana USA,* 17–18.

164. Castro, "Casablanca of the Caribbean," 35, 56.

165. García, *Havana USA,* 22.

166. García, *Havana USA,* 29.

167. Castro, "Casablanca of the Caribbean," 36.

168. Castro, "Casablanca of the Caribbean," 36–37, 31; McNally, *Catholicism in South Florida,* 146.

169. Quoted in Rose, *The Struggle for Black Freedom in Miami,* 214; Castro, "Casablanca of the Caribbean," 42–43.

170. Castro, "Casablanca of the Caribbean," 44–45.

171. Quoted in Castro, "Casablanca of the Caribbean," 51.

172. Tracy S. Voorhees, "Report to the President of the United States on the Cuban Refugee Problem" (Washington, DC: US Government Printing Office, 1961), 1.

## 2. Viva Kennedy and the Nationalization of "Latin American" Politics

1. Edward T. Folliard, "1960 'Battleground,'" *Washington Post,* June 18, 1960.

2. Ignacio García claims that only the "possibilities" of appointments were explored. According to Max Krochmal, however, Albert Peña received explicit assurances that "some top level appointments" would go to Mexican Americans. Ignacio M. García, *Viva Kennedy: Mexican Americans in Search of Camelot* (College Station: Texas A&M University Press, 2000), 44, 55, 48; Max Krochmal, *Blue Texas: The Making of a Multiracial Democratic Coalition in the Civil Rights Era* (Chapel Hill: University of North Carolina Press, 2016), 224–225.

3. McCormick married into the family of Ralph Estrada, head of the Arizona-based fraternal society Alianza Hispano-Americana. Kenneth C. Burt, *The Search for a Civic Voice: California Latino Politics* (Claremont, CA: Regina Books, 2007), 185–187.

4. Letter, Hector García to Viva Kennedy Clubs, November 3, 1960, University of North Texas Libraries, The Portal to Texas History, texashistory.unt.edu; crediting Houston Metropolitan Research Center at Houston Public Library, texashistory.unt.edu/ark:/67531/metapth249116/.

5. García, *Viva Kennedy,* 55.

6. García, *Viva Kennedy,* 95–96.

7. Burt, *The Search for a Civic Voice,* 188–191.

8. Burt, *The Search for a Civic Voice,* 188–191; García, *Viva Kennedy,* 94–95, 102.

9. Quoted in Mario T. García and Sal Castro, *Blowout! Sal Castro & the Chicano Struggle for Educational Justice* (Chapel Hill: University of North Carolina Press, 2011), 78, 80.

10. Quoted in Krochmal, *Blue Texas,* 224–225.

11. Letter, Hector García to Viva Kennedy Clubs, November 3, 1960.

12. Born in 1930, his mother was a professor and writer, while his father was a composer who founded Havana's Philharmonic orchestra. His father-in-law was Edwin McCammon Martin, a State Department official and later ambassador to Argentina. Adam Bernstein, "Pedro A. Sanjuan, U.S. Official Who Fought Discrimination, Dies at 82," *Washington Post,* October 2, 2012.

13. Pedro A. Sanjuan, interview by Dennis O'Brien, Washington, DC, August 6, 1969, transcript, John F. Kennedy Presidential Library and Museum, Boston, MA (hereafter JFKL), https://www.jfklibrary.org/Asset-Viewer/Archives/JFKOH-PAS-01.aspx, 13.

14. Fears that this battle might jeopardize the campaign's ability to mobilize Puerto Rican voters and thus carry New York state had indeed driven the party to hire Sanjuan in the first place. Sanjuan, interview by O'Brien, 3.

15. Christopher Bell, *East Harlem Remembered: Oral Histories of Community and Diversity* (Jefferson, NC: McFarland and Company, 2013), 147.

16. Public Broadcasting System, "Latino Americans," http://www.pbs.org/latino -americans/en/watch-videos/#2365053287 (accessed November 11, 2016); Gerena Valentín, *Gilberto Gerena Valentín*, 102; Robert D. McFadden, "Herman Badillo, Congressman and Fixture of New York Politics, Dies at 85," *New York Times*, December 3, 2014.

17. Sanjuan, interview by O'Brien, 9.

18. Herman Badillo, telephone interview by the author, March 3, 2011.

19. Peter Kihiss, "Democrat Tours Harlem," *New York Times*, August 24, 1960.

20. "Kennedy's Day," *New York Times*, October 12, 1960.

21. Sanjuan, interview by O'Brien, 19.

22. "Remarks of Senator John F. Kennedy, 116th Street Rally, New York, New York," October 12, 1960, Papers of John F. Kennedy, Pre-Presidential Papers, Senate Files, Speeches and the Press, Speech Files, 1953–1960, JFKSEN-0913-008, JFKL.

23. Herman Badillo, *One Nation, One Standard: An Ex-Liberal on How Hispanics Can Succeed Just Like Other Immigrant Groups* (New York: Sentinel, 2006), 146–147.

24. Milton Bracker, "Rockefeller a Hit in Spanish Speech: Puerto Rican Crowd Enjoys Even a Mistake at Talk in East 108th Street," *New York Times*, October 25, 1958.

25. Jack Murphy, "Rockefeller's Son Opens Drive to Woo Harlem to the G.O.P.," *New York Times*, August 27, 1960.

26. Edward C. Burks, "Negro in Cabinet Pledged by Lodge," *New York Times*, October 13, 1960; Pedro Sanjuan recalled that the audience was "terrible to Lodge. They threw things at him, and they booed him." Sanjuan, interview by O'Brien, 20.

27. Sanjuan, interview by O'Brien, 5.

28. Peter Kihiss, "City Spanish Vote at a Record High," *New York Times*, November 2, 1960.

29. Sanjuan, interview by O'Brien, 16.

30. Douglas Dales, "City Registration Sets a New Mark with Final Spurt," *New York Times*, October 16, 1960.

31. José Ramón Sánchez, *Boricua Power: A Political History of Puerto Ricans in the United States* (New York: New York University Press, 2007), 120.

32. "1960 Presidential Election Results," JFKL, https://www.jfklibrary.org /learn/about-jfk/life-of-john-f-kennedy/fast-facts-john-f-kennedy/1960 -presidential-election-results.

33. Burt, *The Search for a Civic Voice*, 193–194.

34. García, *Viva Kennedy*, 105.

35. Homer Bigart, "Democrats Criticize Foe's Campaign," *New York Times*, November 13, 1960.

36. Layhmond Robinson, "Voting Gain Made by Puerto Ricans," *New York Times*, November 23, 1963.

37. Quoted in Julie L. Pycior, *LBJ & Mexican Americans: The Paradox of Power* (Austin: University of Texas Press, 1997), 120–121.

38. Sanjuan, interview by O'Brien, 13.

39. John F. Kennedy, "Speech of Senator John F. Kennedy, Cincinnati, Ohio, Democratic Dinner," October 6, 1960, APP, https://www.presidency.ucsb.edu/documents/speech-senator-john-f-kennedy-cincinnati-ohio-democratic-dinner.

40. John F. Kennedy: "Excerpts of Remarks by Senator John F. Kennedy, Johnstown, PA," October 15, 1960, APP, https://www.presidency.ucsb.edu/documents/excerpts-remarks-senator-john-f-kennedy-johnstown-pa.

41. Jonathan C. Brown, *Cuba's Revolutionary World* (Cambridge, MA: Harvard University Press, 2017), 115.

42. William M. Leogrande and Peter Kornbluh, *Back Channel to Cuba: The Hidden History of Negotiations between Washington and Havana* (Chapel Hill: University of North Carolina Press, 2015), 42.

43. Quoted in Lars Schoultz, *That Infernal Little Cuban Republic: The United States and the Cuban Revolution* (Chapel Hill: University of North Carolina Press, 2009), 152.

44. Schoultz, *That Infernal Little Cuban Republic*, 139.

45. Brown, *Cuba's Revolutionary World*, 120.

46. Silvia Pedraza, *Political Disaffection in Cuba's Revolution and Exodus* (New York: Cambridge University Press, 2007), 95.

47. Brown, *Cuba's Revolutionary World*, 118–119.

48. See, among others, Schoultz, *That Infernal Little Cuban Republic*, 146–148; Haynes Johnson et al., *The Bay of Pigs: The Leaders' Story of Brigade 2506* (New York: W. W. Norton, 1964); Peter Wyden, *The Bay of Pigs: The Untold Story* (New York: Simon and Schuster, 1980); Howard Jones, *The Bay of Pigs* (New York: Oxford University Press, 2008).

49. Brown, *Cuba's Revolutionary World*, 116–117.

50. Richard Reeves, *President Kennedy: Profile of Power* (Norwalk, CT: Easton Press, 2000), 91.

51. Jones, *The Bay of Pigs*, 121–122.

52. Julian Zelizer, *Arsenal of Democracy: The Politics of National Security from World War II to the War on Terrorism* (New York: Basic Books, 2010), 150.

53. Reeves, *President Kennedy*, 169.

54. Quoted in Reeves, *President Kennedy*, 103.

55. Quoted in Leogrande and Kornbluh, *Back Channel to Cuba*, 47.

56. Quoted in Reeves, *President Kennedy*, 106; Schoultz, *That Infernal Little Cuban Republic*, 173.

57. Senator Thurston Morton quoted in Zelizer, *Arsenal of Democracy*, 150.

58. Quoted in Schoultz, *That Infernal Little Cuban Republic*, 162.

59. "I don't want the U.S. to get involved in this," said Kennedy to his Navy chief of staff. Reeves, *President Kennedy*, 93.

60. Quoted in Jones, *The Bay of Pigs*, 123.

61. Quoted in Brown, *Cuba's Revolutionary World*, 128.

62. Schoultz, *That Infernal Little Cuban Republic*, 169.

63. Reeves, *President Kennedy*, 94.

64. Quoted in Reeves, *President Kennedy*, 96–99.

65. John F. Kennedy: "Address before the American Society of Newspaper Editors," April 20, 1961, APP, https://www.presidency.ucsb.edu/documents /address-before-the-american-society-newspaper-editors.

66. "Resignation Letter of José Miró Cardona to the Revolutionary Council of Cuba," April 9, 1963, History and Public Policy Program Digital Archive, Archivo Histórico Diplomático Genaro Estrada, Secretaría de Relaciones Exteriores, Mexico City, obtained by Jorge Mendoza Castro, translated by Anita Harmer and Tanya Harmer, http://digitalarchive.wilsoncenter.org /document/115208.

67. Mauricio Fernando Castro, "Casablanca of the Caribbean: Cuban Refugees, Local Power, and Cold War Policy in Miami, 1959–1995" (PhD diss., Purdue University, 2015), 117.

68. Foreword, "Counter Revolutionary Handbook," October 10, 1962, Papers of Robert F. Kennedy, Attorney General Papers, Attorney General's Confidential File, 6-6: Cuba: Counter Revolutionary Handbook, JFKL.

69. Quoted in Castro, "Casablanca of the Caribbean," 117.

70. Leogrande and Kornbluh, *Back Channel to Cuba*, 43.

71. Don Bohning, *The Castro Obsession* (Washington, DC: Potomac Books, 2005), 129; Castro, "Casablanca of the Caribbean," 94; Schoultz, *That Infernal Little Cuban Republic*, 186.

72. Quoted in Piero Gleijeses, *Conflicting Missions: Havana, Washington, and Africa, 1959–1976* (Chapel Hill: University of North Carolina Press, 2002), 19.

73. Memorandum, Richard Helms for Robert F. Kennedy, n.d. (filed January 21, 1963), Papers of Robert F. Kennedy, Attorney General Papers, Attorney General's Confidential File, 6-6: Cuba: Counter Revolutionary Handbook, JFKL.

74. Central Intelligence Agency, "Major Cuban Exile Organizations," attached to John McCone to Maxwell D. Taylor, May 3, 1962, Papers of Robert F. Kennedy, Attorney General Papers, Attorney General's Classified File, 71-4-16-32: Cuban Government in Exile, February 25, 1961–May 3, 1962, JFKL.

75. Foreword, "Counter-Revolutionary Handbook," Papers of Robert F. Kennedy, Attorney General Papers, Attorney General's Confidential File, 6-6: Cuba: Counter Revolutionary Handbook, JFKL.

76. Quoted in Castro, "Casablanca of the Caribbean," 116.

77. *Foreign Relations of the United States, 1961–1963,* vol. 10, *Cuba,* January 1961–September 1962 (Washington, DC: U.S. Government Printing Office, 1997), Document 399.

78. Quoted in Castro, "Casablanca of the Caribbean," 116.

79. María Cristina García, *Havana USA: Cuban Exiles and Cuban Americans in South Florida, 1959–1994* (Berkeley: University of California Press, 1996), 33.

80. Johnson, *The Bay of Pigs,* 343.

81. Juanita Greene, "A Wave of Hope Sweeps Exiles in Orange Bowl," *Miami Herald,* December 30, 1962; Joy Reese Shaw, "First Lady Spoke as a Mother," *Miami Herald,* December 30, 1962; Johnson, *The Bay of Pigs,* 343–344; Wyden, *The Bay of Pigs,* 303.

82. Press Release, "Remarks of the President and Mrs. John F. Kennedy at Presentation of the Flag of the 2506th Cuban Invasion Brigade," December 29, 1962, Papers of John F. Kennedy, Presidential Papers, President's Office Files, Speech Files, Remarks on presenting Cuban Invasion Brigade flag, Orange Bowl, Miami, Florida, December 29, 1962, JFKL.

83. Press Release, "Remarks of the President and Mrs. John F. Kennedy at Presentation of the Flag of the 2506th Cuban Invasion Brigade."

84. Greene, "A Wave of Hope Sweeps Exiles in Orange Bowl," *Miami Herald,* December 30, 1962.

85. "An Editorial—Turning of the Corner," *Miami Herald,* December 30, 1962.

86. "Resignation Letter of José Miró Cardona to the Revolutionary Council of Cuba."

87. Quoted in Schoultz, *That Infernal Little Cuban Republic,* 189–191, 210.

88. Tracy S. Voorhees, *Report to the President of the United States on the Cuban Refugee Problem* (Washington, DC: US Government Printing Office, 1961), 1.

89. John F. Kennedy, "Letter to Secretary Ribicoff Requesting Him to Undertake Direction of Cuban Refugee Activities," January 27, 1961, APP, https://www.presidency.ucsb.edu/documents/letter-secretary-ribicoff -requesting-him-undertake-direction-cuban-refugee-activities.

90. "Statement by the President Following a Conference with Secretary Ribicoff on Cuban Refugee Problems," February 3, 1961, APP, https://www .presidency.ucsb.edu/documents/statement-the-president-following -conference-with-secretary-ribicoff-cuban-refugee.

91. Castro, "Casablanca of the Caribbean," 78.

92. Castro, "Casablanca of the Caribbean," 93.

93. García, *Havana USA,* 23.

94. Silvia Pedraza-Bailey, *Political and Economic Migrants in America* (Austin, University of Texas Press, 1985), 43.

95. Castro, "Casablanca of the Caribbean," 78.

96. See, for instance, "Statement by the President Following a Conference with Secretary Ribicoff on Cuban Refugee Problems" February 3, 1961.

97. García, *Havana USA,* 30.

98. Brown, *Cuba's Revolutionary World,* 126; Senate Committee on the Judiciary, *Cuban Refugee Problems: Hearings before the Subcommittee to Investigate Problems Connected with Refugees and Escapees,* 87th Cong., 1961, 73, 132.

99. Carl J. Bon Tempo, *Americans at the Gates: The United States and Refugees during the Cold War* (Princeton, NJ: Princeton University Press, 2008), 122.

100. García, *Havana USA,* 37.

101. Democratic Party Platforms: "1964 Democratic Party Platform," August 24, 1964, APP, https://www.presidency.ucsb.edu/documents/1964-democratic -party-platform.

102. "Resignation Letter of José Miró Cardona to the Revolutionary Council of Cuba."

103. Quoted in Castro, "Casablanca of the Caribbean," 119.

104. "Latin Criticizes State Department," n.d., Box 152, Dr. Hector P. García Papers, Special Collections and Archives, Bell Library, Texas A&M University–Corpus Christi (hereafter HPG).

105. Kaplowitz, *LULAC,* 74.

106. Quoted in Michelle Hall Kells, *Héctor P. García: Everyday Rhetoric and Mexican American Civil Rights* (Carbondale: Southern Illinois University Press, 2006), 67.

107. Quoted in Kaplowitz, *LULAC,* 72–73.

108. Russell Baker, "Kennedy Agrees on Puerto Rico as a 'Workshop' in Latin Policy," *New York Times,* January 19, 1961.

109. "Puerto Rico's Uplifter: José Teodoro Moscoso Mora Rodríguez," *New York Times,* March 30, 1961.

110. Quoted in Kells, *Héctor P. García,* 67.

111. Quoted in García, *Viva Kennedy,* 111.

112. Telles was named ambassador to Costa Rica. Kaplowitz, *LULAC,* 72.

113. "Spanish-American Leaders Assail Administration Patronage Policy," *Colorado Federation of Latin Groups* 10, no. 1 (February 1962), Box 233, HPG.

114. Pycior, *LBJ & Mexican Americans,* 122.

115. Mario T. García, *Memories of Chicano History: The Life and Narrative of Bert Corona* (Berkeley: University of California Press, 1994), 209.

116. Nicholas Lemann, "The Unfinished War," *The Atlantic,* December, 1988, http://www.theatlantic.com/past/politics/poverty/lemunf1.htm.

117. García, *Viva Kennedy,* 126–128.

118. Quoted and translated in Kells, *Héctor P. García,* 190.

119. García, *Viva Kennedy,* 127. "Political Association of Spanish Speaking Organizations (PASO) Board Meeting Held April 28th and 29th, 1961," Box 152, HPG.

120. It endorsed Henry B. González in the Democratic primary to fill Lyndon Johnson's seat in the Senate, and supported a Viva Kennedy campaigner for

the federal bench in South Texas. García, *Viva Kennedy*, 123–129; "Political Association of Spanish Speaking Organizations (PASO) Board Meeting Held April 28th and 29th, 1961," Box 152, HPG.

121. "World Eyes Texas Vote, Johnson Says," *Washington Post*, November 4, 1961.

122. Pycior, *LBJ & Mexican Americans*, 126.

123. Quoted in Rodolfo Rosales, *The Illusion of Inclusion: The Untold Political Story of San Antonio* (Austin: University of Texas Press, 2000), 72.

124. "Democrat Wins Texas House Seat," *Los Angeles Times*, November 5, 1961; Juan Gómez-Quiñones, *Chicano Politics: Reality and Promise, 1940–1990* (Albuquerque: University of New Mexico Press, 1990), 58.

125. For his part, the loser suggested economics played a larger role, that "in a low-income metropolitan area, you just can't beat Santa Claus." Robert D. Novak, "Sound GOP Defeat in Texas Raises Doubts of Party Strategy for '62 House Election," *Wall Street Journal*, November 6, 1961.

126. "Roybal to Seek Thirtieth District Congress Seat," *Los Angeles Times*, January 23, 1962.

127. Gómez-Quiñones, *Chicano Politics*, 73.

128. Katherine Underwood, "Process and Politics: Multiracial Electoral and Representation in Los Angeles' Ninth District, 1949–1962 (PhD diss., University of California, San Diego, 1992), 258.

129. Burt, *Search for a Civic Voice*, 204–206.

130. "Roybal to Seek Thirtieth District Congress Seat," *Los Angeles Times*, January 23, 1962. "Recapitulation of Congress and Governorship Races, with Vote Percentages," *New York Times*, November 11, 1962.

131. One of the first announcements he made after being sworn in was to announce his opposition to extending the Bracero program. "Bracero Plan to be Opposed by Rep. Roybal," *Los Angeles Times*, January 10, 1963; Two years later, Eligio "Kika" de la Garza, a Johnson loyalist, was elected to represent Texas's 15th Congressional District, drawn from a strip of agricultural counties in the Rio Grande Valley. He took nearly 70 percent of the vote. That same year, Joseph Montoya, New Mexico's at-large representative in the House, reclaimed the US Senate seat long occupied by that chamber's lone Spanish American, the late Dennis Chavez. With his victory, Montoya not only preserved Hispano representation in the Senate but became, to many, the highest-ranking ethnic Mexican in government. Texas Legislative Council, "Texas Congressional Districts, 1958–1964 Elections," http://www .tlc.state.tx.us/redist/pdf/congress_historical/c_1958_1964.pdf; "Votes for Contests for House of Representatives Are Listed," *New York Times*, November 8, 1964.

132. Island voters ostensibly had recourse to a nonvoting Resident Commissioner in the House of Representatives.

133. Layhmond Robinson, "New Harlem Club Opposing De Sapio," *New York Times*, December 11, 1960.

134. John Sibley, "Court Voids Vote for Santangelo," *New York Times,* January 11, 1962.

135. Paul Crowell, "Mayor Gives Jobs to 7 Who Helped to Elect Him," *New York Times,* January 1, 1962; Charles G. Bennett, "New City Agency Planned to Spur Relocation Task," *New York Times,* July 8, 1962.

136. US Bureau of the Census, "No. HS-7. Population of the Largest 75 Cities: 1900–2000," www.census.gov/statab/hist/HS-07.pdf.

137. José Cruz, "The Political Incorporation of (In)Migrants in the United States: The Case of Puerto Ricans," August 22, 2011, https://ssrn.com/abstract =1914477 or http://dx.doi.org/10.2139/ssrn.1914477, 30–31; US Bureau of the Census, "No. HS-7. Population of the Largest 75 Cities: 1900–2000," www.census.gov/statab/hist/HS-07.pdf.

## 3. Civil Rights and the Recognition of a "National Minority"

1. "Text of Speech by Albert Peña, Jr. . . . . Paso State Convention," June 8, 1963, Box 233, Dr. Hector P. García Papers, Special Collections and Archives, Bell Library, Texas A&M University–Corpus Christi.

2. "Text of Speech by Albert Peña, Jr."

3. "The Mexican American: A New Focus on Opportunity" (Washington, DC: Inter-Agency Committee on Mexican American Affairs, 1968).

4. Cuban exiles' combination of advantaged racial position, presumed temporariness, and federal assistance secured through the Cuban Refugee Program, ensured that they remained far removed from these conversations.

5. Democratic Party Platforms, "Democratic Party Platform of 1960," July 11, 1960, The American Presidency Project (hereafter APP), http://www.presidency.ucsb.edu/ws/index.php?pid=29602#ixzz1SBm Qy9o3.

6. John F. Kennedy, "Statement by the President upon Signing Order Establishing the President's Committee on Equal Employment Opportunity," March 7, 1961, APP, http://www.presidency.ucsb.edu/ws/index.php?pid =8520&st=10925&st1=#ixzz1LQ5tz4Tv.

7. Hugh Davis Graham, *The Civil Rights Era: Origins and Development of National Policy, 1960–1972* (New York: Oxford University Press, 1990), 13–31.

8. John Skrentny, *The Minority Rights Revolution* (Cambridge, MA: Harvard University Press, 2002), 101–102.

9. Hugh Davis Graham, *Collision Course: The Strange Convergence of Affirmative Action and Immigration Policy in America* (New York: Oxford University Press, 2002), 137.

10. Skrentny, *The Minority Rights Revolution,* 109.

11. Graham, *The Civil Rights Era,* 45–46.

12. Graham, *The Civil Rights Era,* 54, 59–60.

13. "Information for Workshop Chairmen," Box 20, Office Files of George Reedy, Lyndon Baines Johnson Presidential Library and Museum, Austin, Texas (hereafter LBJL).

14. Quoted in Julie L. Pycior, *LBJ & Mexican Americans: The Paradox of Power* (Austin: University of Texas Press, 1997), 128.

15. Quoted in Nancy MacLean, *Freedom Is Not Enough: The Opening of the American Workplace* (New York: Russell Sage Foundation, 2006), 168.

16. Brian Behnken, *Fighting Their Own Battles: Mexican Americans, African Americans, and the Struggle for Civil Rights in Texas* (Chapel Hill: University of North Carolina Press, 2003), 72–73.

17. Paul Weeks, "Great Negro Tide Surges into Melting Pot of West," *Los Angeles Times,* September 17, 1962.

18. Ruben Salazar, "Negro Drive Worries Mexican-Americans," *Los Angeles Times,* July 14, 1963.

19. Ruben Salazar, "Johnson to Hear Plaint of Minority," *Los Angeles Times,* July 29, 1963.

20. Gladwin Hill, "Coast Minority Found Suffering," *New York Times,* August 9, 1963.

21. Memorandum, George Reedy to Lyndon Baines Johnson, n.d., Box 20, Office Files of George Reedy, LBJL.

22. Making no allowances for the status of those appointments, the pamphlet indicated that Kennedy had named fourteen "Spanish-speaking Americans" from New Mexico, eight from Texas, seven from California, five from Puerto Rico, four from Arizona and Colorado, and three from New York. See George Reedy to Lyndon Baines Johnson, n.d., Box 21, Office Files of George Reedy, LBJL; and "Spanish-speaking Americans: A People Progressing," Box 20, Office Files of George Reedy, LBJL.

23. George Reedy to Lyndon Baines Johnson, n.d., Box 20, Office Files of George Reedy, LBJL.

24. Ruben Salazar, "Latins Here to Protest Bracero Law," *Los Angeles Times,* August 5, 1963.

25. George Reedy to Lyndon Baines Johnson, n.d., Box 21, Office Files of George Reedy, LBJL.

26. Frank X. Paz, "Federal Civilian Employment"; Martin Ortiz, "Mexican Americans in the Los Angeles Region"; Anthony P. Rios, "Statement Presented to the Honorable Lyndon Johnson"; and "Recommendations Presented to Vice President Lyndon B. Johnson," all in Box 20, Office Files of George Reedy, LBJL.

27. Graham, *The Civil Rights Era,* 106–110.

28. "Remarks by Vice President Lyndon B. Johnson," August 9, 1963; "Johnson Offers Equal Opportunities," *La Opinión,* August 10, 1963, *trans.* Elizabeth Hanunian, Box 21, Office Files of George Reedy, LBJL.

29. Ruben Salazar, "Johnson Speaks Here for Fair Employment," *Los Angeles Times,* November 15, 1963; Bill Becker, "Minority in West Seeks Job Gains," *New York Times,* November 15, 1963.

30. Memorandum, George Reedy to Lyndon B. Johnson, August 20, 1963, Box 21, Office Files of George Reedy, LBJL.

31. Ruben Salazar, "Johnson Speaks Here for Fair Employment," *Los Angeles Times,* November 15, 1963; Bill Becker, "Minority in West Seeks Job Gains," *New York Times,* November 15, 1963.

32. J. B. Clinton, "Notes on California Conference, 11/14–11/15/63," Box 890, Office Files of John Macy, LBJL.

33. *Los Angeles Times,* November 15, 1963.

34. Philip Potter, "Goldwater's 'Aim' Ignored," *Baltimore Sun,* September 18, 1963.

35. "Goldwater Rally Will Be 'Fiesta,'" *Los Angeles Times,* August 20, 1963.

36. *Baltimore Sun,* September 18, 1963.

37. "Text of a speech by Senator Barry Goldwater before a Young Republican Rally, Dodger Stadium," September 16, 1963, Series II, Box 134, The Personal and Political Papers of Senator Barry M. Goldwater, Arizona Historical Foundation.

38. Kenneth Burt, "Latinos con Eisenhower: 'Me Gusta Ike' or 'Yo Quiero Ike'," February 6, 2010, http://kennethburt.com/blog/?p=436; "Spanish Drive Backs Johnson," *The Odessa American,* July 10, 1960; *Baltimore Sun,* September 18, 1963; Ruben Salazar, "Viva Kennedy Leader Switches to Goldwater," *Los Angeles Times,* September 19, 1963.

39. See Lisa McGirr, *Suburban Warriors: The Origins of the New American Right* (Princeton, NJ: Princeton University Press, 2001).

40. "Cuban Exile Will Speak to Clubs," *Los Angeles Times,* November 5, 1961; Dan Thrapp, "Cuban Says U.S. Apathy Can Bring Communism," *Los Angeles Times,* October 30, 1961; Louis Fleming, "Probe into 'Muzzling' of Military Asked: 15,700 at Anti-Red School Rally," *Los Angeles Times,* August 31, 1961; "Latin American GOP Group Seeks Members," *Los Angeles Times,* January 12, 1964.

41. "Latin Goldwater Unit Will Tell Progress," *Los Angeles Times,* October 8, 1964; Richard A. Santillán and Frederico A. Subervi-Vélez," Latino Participation in Republican Party Politics in California," in *Racial and Ethnic Politics in California,* eds. Bryan O. Jackson and Michael B. Preston (Berkeley: IGS Press, 1994), 292.

42. "Background," n.d. but likely from 1962, Box 16, Series 33, Speeches, Nelson A. Rockefeller gubernatorial records, Rockefeller Archive Center, Sleepy Hollow, New York (hereafter RAC).

43. "Governor Nelson A. Rockefeller Informal Meeting with Leaders of Puerto Rican Community," June 22, 1961, Box 51, Series 34, Diane Van Wie, Nelson A. Rockefeller gubernatorial records, RAC.

44. Santillán and Subervi-Vélez, "Latino Participation in Republican Party Politics in California," 291.

45. The administration's race policies posed dilemmas for his relationship with Governor Connally, a Johnson protégé aligned with conservatives, while his disputes over patronage and policy matters alienated important liberals such

as US senator Ralph Yarborough. Robert Dallek, *Flawed Giant: Lyndon Johnson and His Times, 1961–1973* (New York: Oxford University Press, 1998), 44–45.

46. Robert Dallek, *An Unfinished Life: John F. Kennedy 1917–1963* (Boston: Little, Brown and Company, 2003), 691–692.

47. John F. Kennedy, "Remarks in Houston to the League of United Latin American Citizens," November 21, 1963, APP, https://www.presidency.ucsb.edu/documents/remarks-houston-the-league-united-latin-american-citizens.

48. Dan William Dickey, *The Kennedy Corridos: A Study of the Ballads of a Mexican American Hero* (Austin: University of Texas Center for Mexican American Studies, 1978), 64–65. A portion of this is also cited in Pycior, *LBJ and Mexican Americans*, 138–139.

49. "Ray Botello Film," http://www.jfk.org/index.cfm?objectid=39F28DEE-1D09-33F3-C8C7AD185317303C (accessed April 4, 2012).

50. Dickey, *The Kennedy Corridos*, 3, 76.

51. Quoted in Randall B. Woods, *Prisoners of Hope: Lyndon B. Johnson, the Great Society, and the Limits of Liberalism* (New York: Basic Books, 2016), 224; "Californian Will Be Named Assistant Army Secretary," *New York Times*, February 25, 1964, 18.

52. Pycior, *LBJ and Mexican Americans*, 146.

53. Pycior, *LBJ and Mexican Americans*, 149; "Letter template from John J. Herrera," May 21, 1964, University of North Texas Libraries, The Portal to Texas History, texashistory.unt.edu/ark:/67531/metapth249233/.

54. The "typical" campaign weekend hit all the stops, including "Polish and German sausage barbeques, Mexicano matanzas, a Negroes [*sic*] beef barbeque, and a Baptist Church Americano picnic." "The Association of President Lyndon Johnson and EEOC Commissioner and Cabinet Committee Chairman Vicente Ximenes," Box 3, Papers of Vicente T. Ximenes, LBJL.

55. The campaign did have a foothold in Florida. Pycior, *LBJ and Mexican Americans*, 149.

56. Pamphlet, Democratic National Committee, "Continuemos Adelante Viva Johnson y Humphrey," n.d., University of North Texas Libraries, The Portal to Texas History, texashistory.unt.edu/ark:/67531/metapth249040/m1/3/?q=%22Viva%20Johnson%22 (accessed July 14, 2016).

57. Letter, Viva Johnson Club, "Invitation to join the Viva Johnson Club," n.d., (http://texashistory.unt.edu/ark:/67531/metapth249033/ (accessed May 20, 2016), University of North Texas Libraries, The Portal to Texas History, http://texashistory.unt.edu; crediting Houston Metropolitan Research Center at Houston Public Library, Houston, Texas.

58. Levy and Kramer, *The Ethnic Factor: How America's Minorities Decide Elections* (New York: Simon and Schuster, 1972), 78–79.

59. Pycior, *LBJ and Mexican Americans,* 151.
60. Quoted in Michelle Hall Kells, *Vicente Ximenes, LBJ's Great Society, and Mexican American Civil Rights Rhetoric* (Carbondale: Southern Illinois University Press, 2018), 175.
61. Pycior, *LBJ and Mexican Americans,* 154, 155, 163.
62. Lyndon B. Johnson, "Radio and Television Remarks upon Signing the Civil Rights Bill," July 2, 1964, APP, https://www.presidency.ucsb.edu/documents /radio-and-television-remarks-upon-signing-the-civil-rights-bill.
63. "The Equal Employment Opportunity Commission during the Administration of President Lyndon B. Johnson, November 1963–January 1969," 27, Box 1, "Volume I Administrative History [1 of 2]," Administrative History, Equal Employment Opportunity Commission, Volume I, Volume II, Part I, LBJL; Graham, *The Civil Rights Era,* 178; "Monthly Personnel Record," Box 1, "Volume I Administrative History [2 of 2]," Administrative History, Equal Employment Opportunity Commission, Volume I, Volume II, Part I, LBJL; whether the "national origin" complaint was the aggrieved party's preference or that of the EEOC staff, very few Mexican Americans or other "Latins" were designated as having made a complaint on "race discrimination." See "Complaint Statistics: July 2, 1965–June 30, 1966," Box 1, "Volume I Administrative History [1 of 2]," Administrative History, Equal Employment Opportunity Commission, Volume I, Volume II, Part I, LBJL; Equal Employment Opportunity Commission, "Shaping Employment Discrimination Law," http://www.eeoc.gov/eeoc/history/35th/1965-71 /shaping.html.
64. "Description of Events Preceding the EEOC Meeting at the University of New Mexico, Albuquerque, New Mexico, March 27–28, 1966," Box 2, Albert A. Peña, Jr. Papers, MS 37, University of Texas at San Antonio Libraries Special Collections (hereafter AAP).
65. Skrentny, *The Minority Rights Revolution,* 121; Paul Beck, "Mexican American Walkout Mars U.S. Job Conference," *Los Angeles Times,* March 29, 1966; Its executive board, the "Joint National Committee," consisted of the heads of the major Mexican-American organizations: Corona (MAPA), Flores (AGIF), Hernández (LULAC), and Albert Peña (PASO). Most were Democrats, and California and Texas were the states best represented on the committee. A California educator, Armando Rodríguez, was chairman of the larger coalition, which included Henry B. González's brother, Dr. Joaquin González; also included were Ralph Guzman, a California political science professor, and a young antipoverty worker from Denver named Rudolph Gonzales. Pycior, *LBJ & Mexican Americans,* 165–167; "Minutes of Delegates Assembled at University of New Mexico Albuquerque, New Mexico Monday, March 27, 1966," Box 2, AAP.
66. The labor and political activist Bert Corona considered the confrontation a turning point for his more conservative colleagues. It was the first time these "professional people and educators" had "displayed their anger and disgust

with the government," he remembered. Mario T. García, *Memories of Chicano History: The Life and Narrative of Bert Corona* (Berkeley: University of California Press, 1994), 224.

67. "Banquet Memo," Box 2, AAP.

68. Jack Jones, "Mexican-Americans Vow New Area Unity," *Los Angeles Times,* April 29, 1966.

69. "Banquet Memo," Box 2, AAP.

70. Robert A. Reveles to Lyndon B. Johnson, March 31, 1966, Box 2, AAP.

71. "Banquet Memo," Box 2, AAP.

72. Jack Jones, "Social Ferment Stirs Mexican-Americans," *Los Angeles Times,* May 8, 1966.

73. Rudy L. Ramos to John Macy Jr. April 22, 1966, Box 2, AAP; "EEOC Named in Complaint by Latin Unit," *Los Angeles Times,* April 30, 1966; While no part of government disappointed them more than the EEOC, their view on representation extended to other agencies. With only one Mexican American at the DC headquarters (and none in its migrant branch), the Office of Economic Opportunity could never achieve victory in the War on Poverty, they argued. Similarly, petroleum companies leasing federal lands hired few if any Mexican Americans because there were none on the Secretary of the Interior's staff. The offices charged with monitoring employment within the agencies had to "hire a proportionate number of Mexican-Americans" and empower them to redress the inequities in staffing. If the Civil Service Commission (in charge of equal employment policy for the federal government) could not secure representation for Mexican Americans in the federal workforce, they wanted a new agency created. "Federal Departments' 'In-Shop' Equal Employment Opportunity Program," Box 2, AAP.

74. George I. Sánchez to Franklin Roosevelt Jr., April 5, 1966, Box 2, AAP; for a sampling of Sánchez's views on the heterogeneity of Mexican America in the early 1950s, see George I. Sánchez to Julian Samora, undated, Box 42, Julian Samora Papers, Benson Latin American Collection, University Libraries, the University of Texas at Austin; and George I. Sánchez to Julian Samora, February 20, 1952, Box 42, Julian Samora Papers, Benson Latin American Collection, University Libraries, the University of Texas at Austin.

75. Rowland Evans and Robert Novak, "Inside Report . . . The Mexican Revolt," *Washington Post,* March 31, 1966.

76. Leo Grebler, "Neglect by the Federal Government of Mexican-Americans Deplored," *Los Angeles Times,* April 5, 1966.

77. "Transcript of President's Conference on Domestic and World Affairs," *New York Times,* May 22, 1966.

78. Rudy Ramos to Augustine Flores, n.d.; "Washington, D.C. Report 'Information for Progress'"; and "Washington, D.C. Report, May 17, 1966," all in Box 2, APP.

79. In fact, the chairman of the group's "National Committee for Militant Action," LULAC president Alfred Hernández, called off the protest. Maclovio Barraza to Rudy L. Ramos, May 13, 1966, Box 2, APP.

80. García, *Memories of Chicano History*, 218; Craig A. Kaplowitz, *LULAC, Mexican Americans, and National Policy* (College Station: Texas A & M Press, 2005), 104–105.

81. García, *Memories of Chicano History*, 219.

82. Memorandum, David S. North to Joseph A. Califano, October 21, 1966, Box 6, Office Files of Joseph A. Califano, LBJL.

83. "We are thru' with all Whit House [*sic*]—call them conf. on Mex Am Problems," he scrawled on a September memorandum to Califano. Memorandum, Joseph A. Califano to Lyndon Baines Johnson, September 24, 1966, Box 6, Office Files of Joseph A. Califano, LBJL.

84. Transcript of phone call to Joseph A. Califano, December 31, 1966, EX HU 2 MC, Box 23, White House Central Files (hereafter WHCF), LBJL.

85. Harvey Bernstein, "Federal Rights Panel for Latins Expected Soon," *Los Angeles Times*, September 27, 1966.

86. Jack Jones, "How About That White House Conference? Latins Wonder," *Los Angeles Times*, January 25, 1967.

87. The number was 68.6 percent in 1960. Carmen Teresa Whalen and Víctor Vázquez-Hernández, *The Puerto Rican Diaspora: Historical Perspectives* (Philadelphia: Temple University Press, 2008), 3, table 1-2.

88. Sonia S. Lee, "I Was the One Percenter: Manny Diaz and the Beginnings of a Black-Puerto Rican Coalition," *Journal of American Ethnic History* 26 (March 2007): 56–57.

89. Xavier F. Totti, "Marching with Martin Luther King," http://centropr .hunter.cuny.edu/centrovoices/chronicles/marching-martin-luther-king (accessed August 7, 2016).

90. Gilberto Gerena Valentín, *Gilberto Gerena Valentín: My Life as a Community Activist, Labor Organizer, and Progressive Politician in New York City* (New York: Center for Puerto Rican Studies, 2013), 134–135.

91. Sonia Song-Ha Lee, *Building a Latino Civil Rights Movement: Puerto Ricans, African Americans, and the Pursuit of Racial Justice in New York City* (Chapel Hill: University of North Carolina Press, 2014), 117–118.

92. Lee, *Building a Latino Civil Rights Movement*, 119–121.

93. Gerena Valentín, *Gilberto Gerena Valentín*, 136–138.

94. Lee, *Building a Latino Civil Rights Movement*, 133, 144–145.

95. "President Lyndon B. Johnson's Special Message to the Congress: The American Promise," March 15, 1965, http://www.lbjlib.utexas.edu/johnson /archives.hom/speeches.hom/650315.asp.

96. House Committee on the Judiciary, *Hearings on H.R. 6400 and Other Proposals to Enforce the 15th Amendment to the Constitution of the United States*, 89th Cong., 1st sess., 1965, 508–513.

97. Phone conversation, Lyndon B. Johnson and Nicholas de.B. Katzenbach, April 2, 1965, Citation 7312, WH6504.01, accessed at millercenter.org.

98. Phone conversation, Lyndon B. Johnson and Nicholas de.B. Katzenbach, April 7, 1965, Citation 7323, WH6504.02, accessed at millercenter.org.

99. Martin Shefter, *Political Crisis / Fiscal Crisis: The Collapse and Revival of New York City* (New York: Basic Books, 1985), 77.

100. Quoted in James Thomas Tucker, *The Battle over Bilingual Ballots: Language Minorities and Political Access under the Voting Rights Act* (New York: Routledge, 2016), 33.

101. Warren Weaver, "Plan to Widen Puerto Rican Vote Is Added to Rights Bill by Senate," *New York Times,* May 21, 1965.

102. Peter B. Edelman Oral History Interview—RFK #5, January 3, 1970, http://www.jfklibrary.org/Asset-Viewer/Archives/RFKOH-PBE-05.aspx.

103. Weaver, "Plan to Widen Puerto Rican Vote," *New York Times,* May 21, 1965.

104. One source indicates the number as close to 5,000, while the Migration Division of the Office of Puerto Rico held that the number was 8,107. Charles G. Bennett, "Lindsay Presses Fight to Protect Voter Rights," *New York Times,* April 12, 1966; José E. Cruz, "Puerto Rican Politics in New York City during the 1960s: Structural Ideation, Contingency, and Power," in David F. Erickson, ed., *The Politics of Inclusion and Exclusion: Identity Politics in Twenty-first Century America* (New York: Routledge, 2011), 73.

105. Peter Kihss, "Badillo Holding 141-Vote Lead," *New York Times,* September 16, 1965, 1.

106. Quoted in José E. Cruz, "The Political Incorporation of (In)Migrants in the United States: The Case of Puerto Ricans" (August 22, 2011). Available at SSRN: http://ssrn.com/abstract=1914477 or http://dx.doi.org/10.2139/ssrn .1914477., 32.

107. *El Diario-La Prensa,* November 4, 1965.

108. José Cruz, "The Political Incorporation of (In)Migrants in the United States: The Case of Puerto Ricans," August 22, 2011, https://ssrn.com/abstract =1914477 or http://dx.doi.org/10.2139/ssrn.1914477, 30–31.

109. Vincent J. Cannato, *The Ungovernable City: John Lindsay and His Struggle to Save New York* (New York: Basic Books, 2001), 70.

110. Stanley Ross, "Democratas Hispanos Para Rockefeller," n.d., Box 27, Series 5, Campaigns, Nelson A. Rockefeller gubernatorial records, RAC.

111. Memorandum, John Flores to John Lindsay, February 21, 1966, Series XV, Box 388, John Vliet Lindsay Papers (MS 592), Manuscripts and Archives, Yale University Library (hereafter JVLP).

112. John Lindsay, "Representation-Puerto Rican," Series VI, Box 98, JVLP; "John Lindsay on the Puerto Rican Community," Series VI, Box 98, JVLP.

113. Flyer, "John Lindsay Para Alcalde," Series VI, Box 98, JVLP; trans. by author.

114. "John Lindsay on the Puerto Rican Community," Series VI, Box 98, JVLP.

115. Press Release, John V. Lindsay for Mayor, "Text of Remarks by Congressman John V. Lindsay . . . ," July 8, 1965, Series VI, Box 103, JVLP.

116. Press Release, John V. Lindsay for Mayor, "Text of Remarks by Congressman John V. Lindsay . . . ," July 8, 1965, Series VI, Box 103, JVLP; "Mayor Lindsay Will Name 152 Spanish Speaking Employees," January 11, 1966, Series XV, Box 388, JVLP.

117. Charles G. Bennett, "Lindsay Rejects Ethnic Job Rule," *New York Times,* February 3, 1966.

118. Paul Hofmann, "Mayor Criticized by Puerto Ricans," *New York Times,* February 5, 1966.

119. Paul Hofmann, "Puerto Rico Head Will Aid Lindsay," *New York Times,* March 22, 1966; A. W. Maldonado, "The 'New Badillo' Speaks Out," *San Juan Star,* April 19, 1960, in series XV, Box 388, JVLP.

120. A. W. Maldonado, "Lindsay Aide Hits Badillo's Criticism," *San Juan Star,* April 13, 1966; Memorandum, John Flores to John Lindsay, February 18, 1966, both in Series XV, Box 388, JVLP; Paul Hofmann, "Hispanic Leaders Form New Group," *New York Times,* March 14, 1966.

121. Michael Lapp, "Managing Migration: The Migration Division of Puerto Rico and Puerto Ricans in New York City, 1948–1968," (PhD diss., Johns Hopkins University, 1991), 322; Bernard Weinraub, "New Police Board Has Two Negroes and Puerto Rican," *New York Times,* July 12, 1966; "Puerto Rican Leader Named to City Rights Post," *New York Times,* May 2, 1966.

122. Henry Raymont, "Mayor Will Seek More Advice Here on Puerto Ricans," *New York Times,* January 23, 1967.

123. Quoted in Joseph H. Boyd Jr. and Charles R. Holcomb, *Oreos and Dubonnet: Remembering Governor Nelson A. Rockefeller* (Albany: State University of New York Press, 2012), 64–65.

124. Pamphlet, Comité Accion Hispano Americano, "Rocky Se Preocupa Por Usted," Box 67, Series 5, Campaigns, Nelson A. Rockefeller gubernatorial records, RAC (trans. by author); Democratos Hispanos Para Rockefeller, "Political Committee Statement," Box 35, Series 5, Campaigns, Nelson A. Rockefeller gubernatorial records, RAC; Press Release, Salvatore R. Almeida, "Democrats Have Always Taken Puerto Ricans for Granted," Box 32, Series 5, Campaigns, Nelson A. Rockefeller gubernatorial records, RAC; "Harlem Democrats for Rockefeller," Box 67, Series 5, Campaigns, Nelson A. Rockefeller gubernatorial records, RAC; See also Eric Pace, "2 Lawyers Being Considered by Lindsay for Review Board," *New York Times,* June 1, 1966.

125. Stanley Ross to Eugene Rossides, November 14, 1966, Box 27, Series 5, Campaigns, Nelson A. Rockefeller gubernatorial records, RAC.

126. Richard Bergholz, "Reagan Matches Forces with Brown on East L.A. Tour," *Los Angeles Times,* October 2, 1966.

127. See Mark Brilliant, *The Color of America Has Changed: How Racial Diversity Shaped Civil Rights Reform in California, 1941–1978* (New York: Oxford University Press, 2010), chap. 7.

128. Jules Tygiel, *Ronald Reagan and the Triumph of American Conservatism,* 2nd ed. (New York: Pearson/Longman, 2006), 115.

129. Kenneth C. Burt, *The Search for a Civic Voice: California Latino Politics* (Claremont, CA: Regina Books, 2007), 232; Brilliant, *The Color of America Has Changed*, 219–220.
130. *Los Angeles Times*, October 2, 1966.
131. William Roberts, quoted in Brilliant, *The Color of America Has Changed*, 219.
132. See Ronald Reagan, Campaign Speech 200, "Mexican-American Democrats for Reagan Headquarters East L.A.," October 1, 1966; and Campaign Speech 218, "East Los Angeles J.C. Mexican-American Speech," October 14, 1966 in Ronald Reagan Gubernatorial Audiotape Collection, Ronald Reagan Presidential Library and Museum, Simi Valley, California (hereafter RRL).
133. *Cong. Rec.*, 89th Cong., 2nd sess., 1966, 112: 13157.
134. *Cong. Rec.*, 89th Cong., 2nd sess., 1966, 112: 9534.
135. Pycior, *LBJ & Mexican Americans*, 177.
136. Ben Goodwin, "Latin Demos Considering Support of Sen. Tower," *Corpus Christi Times*, August 3, 1966, EX PL ST 43, Box 70, WHCF, LBJL.
137. Kaplowitz, *LULAC*, 110.
138. *LULAC Extra*, October, 1966, Box 889, Office Files of John Macy, LBJL.
139. Kaplowitz, *LULAC*, 110; The estimate was "between thirty and thirty-five percent." John R. Knaggs, *Two-Party Texas: The John Tower Era, 1961–1984* (Austin, TX: Eakin Press, 1986), 104.
140. Kaplowitz, *LULAC*, 110; Lou Cannon, *Governor Reagan: His Rise to Power* (New York: Public Affairs, 2003), 160.
141. Quoted in Pycior, *LBJ and Mexican Americans*, 196.
142. Memorandum, Hubert Horatio Humphrey to Lyndon Baines Johnson, March 1, 1967, EX HU 2 ST 5, Box 25, WHCF, LBJL.
143. Attachment to Memorandum, Hubert Horatio Humphrey to Lyndon Baines Johnson, March 1, 1967.
144. Quoted in Hugh Davis Graham, *The Civil Rights Era*, 226–227.
145. Quoted in Kaplowitz, *LULAC*, 108.
146. Memorandum, John Macy to Lyndon Baines Johnson, March 10, 1967, Box 889, Office Files of John Macy, LBJL; Memorandum, John Macy to Lyndon Baines Johnson, January 30, 1967, Box 889, Office Files of John Macy, LBJL; Quoted in Pycior, *LBJ and Mexican Americans*, 197.
147. Memorandum for the President (unsent), December 13, 1966, Box 774, Office Files of John Macy, LBJL.
148. Seth Kantor, "President Johnson to Give Oath to Ximenes on Friday," *Albuquerque Tribune*, June 7, 1967, Box 2, Papers of Vicente T. Ximenes, LBJL.
149. Memorandum, Lyndon B. Johnson to W. Willard Wirtz . . . Vicente T. Ximenes, June 9, 1967, Senate Subcommittee on Executive Reorganization, *Establish an Interagency Committee on Mexican-American Affairs: Hearings on S. 740*, 91st Congress, June 11–12, 1969, 175.
150. Lyndon Johnson Phone Conversation with Clinton Anderson, March 24, 1967, Conversation No. 11652, WH6703.04, http://millercenter.org/scripps /archive/presidentialrecordings/johnson/1967/03_1967.

151. Report to the President by Certain Members of the Cabinet, "The Mexican American: A New Focus on Opportunity," *Weekly Compilation of Presidential Documents*, vol. 3, 842–846.

152. Lyndon B. Johnson, "Memorandum Establishing the Inter-Agency Committee on Mexican American Affairs," June 9, 1967, APP, https://www .presidency.ucsb.edu/documents/memorandum-establishing-the-inter-agency -committee-mexican-american-affairs.

153. See Report to the President by Certain Members of the Cabinet, "The Mexican American," 3:846; and Lyndon B. Johnson "Remarks at City Hall, Cumberland, Maryland," May 7, 1964, APP, http://www.presidency.ucsb .edu/ws/?pid=26223.

154. "Keynote Speech by Vicente T. Ximenes . . . before the 20th Annual Convention of the American G.I. Forum of the U.S.," August 8, 1968, Box 2, Papers of Vicente T. Ximenes, LBJL.

155. Vicente Ximenes, "Address to the G.I. Forum National Convention, Denver, CO, August 2–August 6, 1967," Box 58, Henry B. González Papers, 1946–1998, The Dolph Briscoe Center for American History, University of Texas at Austin.

156. Nicolas Avila, "Panorama Angelinos," *La Opinión*, June 11, 1967, Box 2, Papers of Vicente T. Ximenes, LBJL.

157. Senate Committee on Labor and Public Welfare, *Nominations: Vicente T. Ximenes, New Mexico, to be a Member of the Equal Employment Opportunity Commission*, 90th Cong., 1st sess., 1967, 1.

158. García, *Memories of Chicano History*, 199, 217–218. The MAPA alliance with Puerto Ricans was in addition to new MAPA chapters promised for Chicago and other industrial towns along Lake Michigan, which had been announced in May 1967. See Carl Greenberg, "MAPA Plans for National Voting Bloc in '68 Told," *Los Angeles Times*, May 15, 1967; Carl Greenburg, "Latin Groups in State, N.Y. Forge Voting Link," *Los Angeles Times*, July 16, 1967.

159. ICMAA Press Release, "Mexican American Affairs Agency Chairman Deplores Ethnic Slurs in Advertisement," September 16, 1968, Box 8, Papers of Vicente T. Ximenes, LBJL.

160. José A. Chacon, "A Report: Accomplishments of the Inter-Agency Committee on Mexican American Affairs, June 9, 1967 to June 1, 1969," in Senate Subcommittee, *Establish an Interagency Committee*, 100, 95.

161. Senate Subcommittee, *Establish an Interagency Committee*, 96–98; "Address by Vicente T. Ximenes . . . before the Interagency Advisory Group of the Civil Service Commission," February 14, 1968, Box 2, Papers of Vicente T. Ximenes, LBJL.

162. Memorandum, Vicente Ximenes to Lyndon Baines Johnson, September 7, 1967, Box 7, Papers of Vicente T. Ximenes, LBJL.

163. "Statement by Vicente T. Ximenes," and "Speeches Given by Vicente Ximenes, 1969–1971," Box 3, Papers of Vicente T. Ximenes, LBJL.

164. "New York Speech, January 11, 1968," Box 2, Papers of Vicente T. Ximenes, LBJL.

165. Vicente T. Ximenes, "Before HEW Employees," February 8, 1968, Box 2, Papers of Vicente T. Ximenes, LBJL.

166. "Draft Memorandum for the President," n.d., Box 6, Office Files of Joseph A. Califano, LBJL.

167. "Draft Memorandum for the President," n.d., Box 6, Office Files of Joseph A. Califano, LBJL.

168. Memorandum, David S. North to Joseph A. Califano, December 2, 1966, Box 6, Office Files of Joseph A. Califano, LBJL.

169. Memorandum, David S. North to Joseph A. Califano, November 9, 1966, Box 6, Office Files of Joseph A. Califano, LBJL.

170. Jack Jones, "How About That White House Conference? Latins Wonder," *Los Angeles Times,* January 25, 1967.

171. Memorandum, Joe Califano to the President, February 13, 1967, quoted in Lorena Oropeza, *¡Raza Sí! ¡Guerra No! Chicano Protest and Patriotism during the Viet Nam War Era* (Berkeley: University of California Press, 2005), 56.

172. "Hearing Set on Problems of U.S. Latins," *Los Angeles Times,* September 13, 1967.

173. Chacon, "Accomplishments," 93.

174. Senate Subcommittee, *Establish an Interagency Committee,* 170.

175. Senate Subcommittee, *Establish an Interagency Committee,* 204.

176. Oropeza, *¡Raza Sí! ¡Guerra No!,* 55; "Mexican-American Unit to Boycott Conference," *Los Angeles Times,* October 17, 1967; García, *Memories of Chicano* History, 237–238.

177. Ruben Salazar, "Humphrey Asks Action by Mexican-Americans," *Los Angeles Times,* October 28, 1967.

178. Quoted in *Cong. Rec.,* 90th Cong., 1st sess., 1967, 113: 33024–33025.

179. Salazar, "Humphrey Asks Action by Mexican-Americans," *Los Angeles Times,* October 28, 1967; Oropeza, *¡Raza Sí! ¡Guerra No!,* 57.

180. "Hearings End with Disunity," *Baltimore Sun,* October 29, 1967.

181. García, *Memories of Chicano History,* 227.

182. Quoted in Gómez-Quiñones, *Chicano Politics,* 110.

183. Quoted in Pycior, *LBJ and Mexican Americans,* 212.

## 4. Becoming Spanish-Speaking, Becoming Spanish Origin

1. *Cong. Rec.,* 90th Cong., 2nd sess., 1968, 114: 27512.

2. Public Law 90-498, http://www.loc.gov/law/help/commemorative -observations/pdf/Pub.%20L.%2090-498.pdf (accessed April 29, 2012).

3. *Cong. Rec.,* 90th Cong., 2nd sess., 1968, 114: 27512–27513.

4. *Cong. Rec.,* 90th Cong., 2nd sess., 1968, 114: 27513.

5. *Cong. Rec.,* 90th Cong., 2nd sess., 1968, 114: 22800.

6. Ramón A. Gutiérrez, "Unraveling America's Hispanic Past: Internal Stratification and Class Boundaries," *Aztlán* 17, no. 1 (Spring 1987): 96.

7. Neil Foley, *Mexicans in the Making of America* (Cambridge, MA: Harvard University Press, 2014), 167.

8. Juan Gómez-Quiñones, *Chicano Politics: Reality and Promise, 1940–1990* (Albuquerque: University of New Mexico Press, 1990), 115–116.

9. Quoted in Gordon Mantler, *Power to the Poor: Black-Brown Coalition and the Fight for Economic Justice, 1960–1974* (Chapel Hill: University of North Carolina Press, 2013), 72–73.

10. Ignacio M. García, *Chicanismo: The Militant Forging of an Ethos* (Tucson: University of Arizona Press, 1997), 33.

11. Frankie McCarty, "Tijerina Denounces Sen. Joseph Montoya," *Albuquerque Journal*, December 24, 1967, Box 47, Reies Tijerina Papers, University of New Mexico, Center for Southwest Research.

12. Howard Bryan, "Sen. Montoya Is Target of Pickets," *Albuquerque Tribune*, April 5, 1968.

13. Mantler, *Power to the Poor*, 190–191.

14. Carlos Muñoz Jr., *Youth, Identity, Power: The Chicano Movement* (New York: Verso, 2000), 57.

15. Quoted in García, *Chicanismo*, 34.

16. Rodolfo Gonzales, "I am Joaquin," http://www.latinamericanstudies.org /latinos/joaquin.htm (accessed September 8, 2011).

17. Quoted in David Montejano, *Quixote's Soldiers: A Local History of the Chicano Movement* (Austin: University of Texas Press, 2010), 59–60, 88.

18. Montejano, *Quixote's Soldiers*, 81, 86, 92–94.

19. Lorrin Thomas, *Puerto Rican Citizen: History and Political Identity in Twentieth Century New York City* (Chicago: University of Chicago Press, 2010), 229, 215, 216, 218, 223, 225, 230–231; Johanna Fernández, "The Young Lords and the Social and Structural Roots of Late Sixties Urban Radicalism," in *Civil Rights in New York City: From World War II to the Giuliani Era*, ed. Clarence Taylor (New York: Fordham University Press, 2011), 143–145.

20. Fernández, "The Young Lords," 142–143. Thomas, *Puerto Rican Citizen*, 232; Lilia Fernández, *Brown in the Windy City: Mexicans and Puerto Ricans in Postwar Chicago* (Chicago: University of Chicago Press, 2012), 175–176, 180–183.

21. Quoted in Fernández, *Brown in the Windy City*, 199–200.

22. Fernández, *Brown in the Windy City*, 176, 199–200.

23. José Angel Gutiérrez, telephone interview by the author, February 6, 2015.

24. Although the conference was interracial, its most powerful group was clearly African Americans, who successfully required the 80 percent of delegates who were not black to grant them 50 percent of the conference's votes, and to adopt more than a dozen "black power principles" without any changes. Mantler, *Power to the Poor*, 66; Ernesto B. Vigil, *The Crusade for Justice: Chicano Militancy and the Government's War on Dissent* (Madison: University of Wisconsin Press, 1999), 39.

25. Mantler, *Power to the Poor*, 72.

26. Mantler, *Power to the Poor*, 72–73.

27. Warren Weaver Jr., "Parley on New Politics Yields to Militant Negroes' Demands," *New York Times*, September 3, 1967. Quoted in Patricia Bell Blawis, *Tijerina and the Land Grants: Mexican Americans in Struggle for Their Heritage* (New York: International Publishers, 1971), 99.

28. Quoted in Mantler, *Power to the Poor*, 97; Gilberto Gerena Valentín, *Gilberto Gerena Valentín: My Life as a Community Activist, Labor Organizer, and Progressive Politician in New York City* (New York: Center for Puerto Rican Studies, 2013), 199–200; Mantler, *Power to the Poor*, 110.

29. Gutiérrez recalled that "one of the first demands we made with King" was to say "wait a minute you're not going to really do this thing as white poor, black poor and leave us out again are you?" Gutiérrez, interview by the author; Gerena Valentín, *Gilberto Gerena Valentín*, 199–200.

30. William N. Curry, "Poor March Aided by Puerto Ricans," *Washington Post*, June 16, 1968.

31. Mantler, *Power to the Poor*, 142, 147–148, 152, 156.

32. Mantler, *Power to the Poor*, 198, 201.

33. Lorena Oropeza, *¡Raza Sí! ¡Guerra No!: Chicano Protest and Patriotism during the Viet Nam War Era* (Berkeley: University of California Press, 2005), 85.

34. A cooperative economics for "the liberation of La Raza" called all classes to action, the workers "who plant the seeds, water the fields, and gather the crops" as well as "the middle class, the professional." "El Plan Espirtual de Aztlán," http://www.sscnet.ucla.edu/00W/chicano101-1/aztlan.htm (accessed September 29, 2011).

35. Quoted in Fernández, *Brown in the Windy City*, 199.

36. Quoted in Mantler, *Power to the Poor*, 202.

37. Thomas, *Puerto Rican Citizen*, 228–231.

38. Quoted in Thomas, *Puerto Rican Citizen*, 231.

39. The document was strongly influenced by the Black Panther Party's "Ten-Point Program."

40. "13 Point Program and Platform of the Young Lords Organization (October 1969)," in *The Young Lords: A Reader*, ed. Darrel Enck-Wanzer (New York: New York University Press, 2010), 9–11.

41. "13 Point Program and Platform of the Young Lords Organization (October 1969)."

42. "13 Point Program and Platform of the Young Lords Organization (October 1969)."

43. Cristina Beltrán, *The Trouble with Unity: Latino Politics and the Creation of Identity* (New York: Oxford University Press, 2010), 40.

44. Hundreds of thousands of Cuban exiles, it scarcely needs mentioning, had a particular place in mind when they thought of home.

45. See Montejano, *Quixote's Soldiers*, 92, 96, 106, 108.

46. A reference to the Mississippi senator and notorious white supremacist Theodore G. Bilbo, who had died in 1947.

47. *Cong. Rec.*, 91st Cong., 1st sess., 1969, 115: 9058, 10526, 9059, 9952–9953, 8590.

48. *Cong. Rec.,* 91st Cong., 1st sess., 1969, 115: 10523, 9953, 8591, 9953, 10522–10524, 10527.
49. Paul R. Wieck, "Sen. Montoya Calls Tijerina an 'Enemy,'" *Albuquerque Journal,* December 16, 1967; Vina Windes and John Crenshaw, "Reies Lacks Big Backing—Montoya," *The New Mexican,* December 29, 1967, Box 47, Reies Tijerina Papers, University of New Mexico, Center for Southwest Research.
50. Letter, Joseph M. Montoya to Alfred B. Martinez, January 8, 1969, Box 47, Reies Tijerina Papers, University of New Mexico, Center for Southwest Research.
51. *Cong. Rec.,* 91st Cong., 1st sess., 1969, 115: 1958–1959.
52. *Cong. Rec.,* 91st Cong., 1st sess., 1969, 115: 27119–27120.
53. Telegram, Louis P. Tellez to Senator Joseph Montoya, n.d., in Senate Committee on Government Operations, *Establish an Interagency Committee on Mexican-American Affairs,* 91st Cong., 1st sess., 1969, 228.
54. Telegram, José P. Lopez to Senator Abraham Ribicoff, June 11, 1969 in Senate Committee, *Establish an Interagency Committee,* 233.
55. Telegram, Aldo Bairo to Abraham Ribicoff, June 11, 1969, in Senate Committee, *Establish an Interagency Committee,* 233.
56. Francisco Bravo, M.D. to Joseph Montoya, June 10, 1969, in Senate Committee, *Establish an Interagency Committee,* 227.
57. Senate Committee, *Establish an Interagency Committee,* 204.
58. Letter, José Antonio Vasquez to Abraham Ribicoff, June 10, 1969, in Senate Committee, *Establish an Interagency Committee,* 229.
59. Letter, Armando Rodriguez to Abraham Ribicoff, June 10, 1969, in Senate Committee, *Establish an Interagency Committee,* 228–229.
60. Letter, Jesus Rodriguez to Abraham Ribicoff, June 10, 1969, in Senate Committee, *Establish an Interagency Committee,* 231.
61. *Cong. Rec.,* 91st Cong., 1st sess., 1969, 115: 1958–1959.
62. Senate Committee, *Establish an Interagency Committee,* 19.
63. *Cong. Rec.,* 91st Cong., 1st sess., 1969, 115: 1958–1959.
64. Senate Committee, *Establish an Interagency Committee,* 4.
65. Senate Committee, *Establish an Interagency Committee,* 3–4, 72.
66. Senate Committee, *Establish an Interagency Committee,* 14, 209, 213.
67. Senate Committee, *Establish an Interagency Committee,* 14–15, 220, 196, 194, 218–220.
68. Senate Committee, *Establish an Interagency Committee,* 219.
69. Senate Committee, *Establish an Interagency Committee,* 158.
70. Senate Committee, *Establish an Interagency Committee,* 158.
71. Senate Committee, *Establish an Interagency Committee,* 17–18.
72. *Cong. Rec.,* 91st Cong., 1st sess., 1969, 115: 1958–1959.
73. *Cong. Rec.,* 91st Cong., 1st sess., 1969, 115: 39393, 39395.
74. *Cong. Rec.,* 91st Cong., 1st sess., 1969, 115: 39393.
75. *Cong. Rec.,* 91st Cong., 1st sess., 1969, 115: 39396.

76. *Cong. Rec.,* 91st Cong., 1st sess., 1969, 115: 39398, 39400.

77. *Cong. Rec.,* 91st Cong., 1st sess., 1969, 115: 39395.

78. *Cong. Rec.,* 91st Cong., 1st sess., 1969, 115: 39398, 39400, 39395, 39399.

79. Thomas, *Puerto Rican Citizen,* 219.

80. Ernesto Chávez, *¡Mi Raza Primero! (My People First!): Nationalism, Identity, and Insurgency in the Chicano Movement in Los Angeles, 1966–1978,* (Berkeley: University of California Press, 2002), 47–51.

81. *Cong. Rec.,* 91st. Cong., 1st sess., 1969, 115: 39393–39401.

82. *Cong. Rec.,* 91st Cong., 1st sess., 1969, 115: 39394.

83. *Cong. Rec.,* 91st Cong., 1st sess., 1969, 115: 27118–27121.

84. *Cong. Rec.,* 91st Cong., 1st sess., 1969, 115: 39401.

85. Richard Nixon, "Statement on Signing the Bill Establishing the Cabinet Committee on Opportunities for Spanish-Speaking People," December 31, 1969, The American Presidency Project, https://www.presidency.ucsb.edu /documents/statement-signing-the-bill-establishing-the-cabinet-committee -opportunities-for-spanish.

86. Staff Report, "The Census—What's Wrong with It, What Can Be Done," *Trans-Action* 5 (May 1968): 50, 53.

87. Jacob S. Siegel and Jeffrey Passel, "Coverage of the Hispanic Population of the United States in the 1970 Census: A Methodological Analysis," *Current Population Reports,* special studies, P-23, no. 82 (Washington, DC: U.S. Government Printing Office, 1979), 6; Ariela J. Gross, "Texas Mexicans and the Politics of Whiteness," *Law and History Review* 21, no. 1 (Spring 2003): 198; on immigration, see Victoria Hattam, *In the Shadow of Race: Jews, Latinos and Immigrant Politics in the 20th Century* (Chicago: University of Chicago Press, 2007).

88. Peter Buechley, "A Reproducible Method of Counting Persons of Spanish Surname," *Journal of the American Statistical Association* 56, no. 293 (March 1961): 88–97, cited in Griselda Cristina Mora, "De Muchos, Uno: The Institutionalization of Latino Panethnicity, 1960–1990" (PhD diss., Princeton University, 2009), 151.

89. U.S. Bureau of the Census, *We, the Mexican Americans/Nosotros, Los México Americanos* (Washington, DC: Government Printing Office, 1970), 4.

90. U.S. Department of Commerce, "Form P-103, Abridged Instructions to Enumerators, Population," http://www.census.gov/history/pdf/1940abridged .pdf (accessed April 15, 2012), 7.

91. Siegel and Passel, "Coverage of the Hispanic Population of the United States in the 1970 Census," 6–7.

92. Philip Hauser to George I. Sánchez, December 6, 1949, Box 36, George I. Sánchez Papers, Benson Latin American Collection, General Libraries, University of Texas at Austin (hereafter GISP).

93. Ian F. Haney López, "Race, Ethnicity, Erasure: The Salience of Race to LatCrit Theory," *California Law Review* 85 (1997): 1148n20, 1170–1171, and 1179n115, cited in Steven H. Wilson, "Brown over 'Other White': Mexican

Americans' Legal Arguments and Litigation Strategy in School Desegregation Lawsuits," *Law and History Review* 21, no. 1 (Spring 2003): 154.

94. George I. Sánchez to Philip Hauser, December 10, 1949, Box 36, GISP.

95. George I. Sánchez, "The U.S. Census—1950," Box 36, GISP.

96. George I. Sánchez to Howard G. Brunsman, July 15, 1953, Box 36, GISP.

97. U.S. Bureau of the Census, *U.S. Census of Population: 1950,* vol. 4, *Special
Reports,* part 3, chap. D, "Puerto Ricans in Continental United States"
(Washington, DC: Government Printing Office, 1953), 4; for 1960, see *U.S.
Census of Population: 1960,* vol. 2, *Subject Reports, Report No. 1D, Puerto Ricans
in the United States* (Washington, DC: Government Printing Office, 1963).

98. David E. Hayes-Bautista and Jorge Chapa, "Latino Terminology: Concep-
tual Bases for Standardized Terminology," *American Journal of Public Health*
77, no. 1 (January 1987): 64.

99. Since more than 90 percent of second-generation Puerto Ricans on the
mainland were under thirty years old, Bureau statisticians later concluded
that the "Puerto Rican Birth or Parentage" question covered "practically all
of the population of Puerto Rican origin" residing on the mainland in 1970.
Siegel and Passel, "Coverage of the Hispanic Population," 6.

100. Census Advisory Committee on Population Statistics, "Summary of Eighth
Meeting—September 29, 1967," Box 3, Census Advisory Committee on
Population Statistics, 1948–1980, RG 29, Records of the Bureau of the
Census, National Archives, Washington, DC.

101. Ruben Salazar, "U.S. Mexicans Seek Separate Census Listing," *Philadelphia
Inquirer,* May 16, 1969, in Box 17, Files of David L. Kaplan, Coordinator of
the 1970 Decennial Census, RG 29, Records of the Bureau of the Census,
National Archives, Washington, DC (hereafter DLK).

102. Salazar, "U.S. Mexicans Seek Separate Census Listing."

103. Sam Kinch Jr. "Census Omissions Bother Yarborough," *Dallas Morning
News,* April 4, 1969, in Box 17, DLK.

104. Memorandum, Herman Gallegos, May 13, 1969, Box 162, Joseph M.
Montoya Papers, University of New Mexico Center for Southwest Research
(hereafter JMMP).

105. The Mexican American Study Project was a Ford Foundation-financed
initiative begun in 1964 to fill in many of the gaps left by the census. The
project would culminate in the 1970 release of *The Mexican-American People:
The Nation's Second Largest Minority,* a more than six-hundred-page tome on
the experience of urban Mexican Americans; House Committee on Post
Office and Civil Service, *1970 Census and Legislation Related Thereto,*
91st Congress, 1st sess., 1969, 520, 481, 482.

106. House Committee, *1970 Census,* 484, 520, 481.

107. House Committee, *1970 Census,* 484–486.

108. House Committee, *1970 Census,* 484, 466, 563, 561.

109. Staff Report, "The Census—What's Wrong with It, What Can Be Done,"
*Trans-Action* 5 (May 1968): 54.

110. However, they reintroduced the "Spanish Mother Tongue" identifier, along with their other ostensibly objective measures, for 1970. Harvey Choldin, "Statistics and Politics: The 'Hispanic Issue' in the 1980 Census," *Demography* 23, no. 3 (August 1986): 407.
111. Census Advisory Committee on Population Statistics, "Summary of Thirteenth Meeting—March 21, 1969," Box 3, Census Advisory Committee on Population Statistics, 1948–1980, RG 29, Records of the Bureau of the Census, National Archives, Washington, DC.
112. The term employed at the time was "Spanish Origin."
113. Conrad Taeuber, interview by Robert Voight, April 12, 1989, www.census .gov/prod/2003pubs/oh-Taeuber.pdf.
114. "Latin Americans Will Be Counted," *Corpus Christi Times,* May 28, 1969, in Box 17, DLK.
115. Ruben Salazar, "Census Unit Plans Nationwide Count of All Spanish-Speaking," *Los Angeles Times,* May 28, 1969.
116. "Census Checks Latins in U.S.," *Federal Times,* June 25, 1969, in Box 17, DLK.
117. "Latin Data Needed," *Dallas Morning News,* June 19, 1969, in Box 17, DLK.
118. "A Spanish-American Suit to Stop the U.S. Census," *San Francisco Chronicle,* February 27, 1970; "'Racial' Suit Hits Census," *San Francisco Examiner,* February 27, 1970, both in Box 17, DLK.
119. "Census Race Question Hit," *Houston Post,* April 17, 1970, in Box 17, DLK.
120. The senators also criticized the Bureau for not hiring sufficient numbers of bilingual enumerators, and for not printing sufficient quantity of bilingual questionnaires. *Cong. Rec.,* 91st Cong., 2nd sess., 1970, 116: 6710–6711.
121. U.S. Bureau of the Census, *Persons of Spanish Origin in the United States: November 1969* (Washington, DC: U.S. Government Printing Office, 1971), 1–2.
122. US Bureau of the Census, *Persons of Spanish Origin in the United States,* 7.
123. US Bureau of the Census, *Persons of Spanish Origin in the United States,* 9, 14, 2.
124. US Bureau of the Census, *Persons of Spanish Origin in the United States,* 2.
125. Steven V. Roberts, "5% in U.S. Cite Spanish Origins," *New York Times,* April 18, 1971.

## 5. Mastering the "Spanish-Speaking Concept"

1. Barry Goldwater to Bryce Harlow, January 6, 1969, EX HU 2, Box 1, White House Central Files (hereafter WHCF), Nixon Presidential Materials Project, College Park, Maryland (hereafter NPM).
2. Mark R. Levy and Michael S. Kramer, *The Ethnic Factor: How America's Minorities Decide Elections* (New York: Simon and Schuster, 1972), 79.
3. While he benefited from appearing on the ticket with David F. Cargo, a popular Republican governor whose wife (the former Ida Jo Anaya) helped

him among the state's Hispanos, the results suggested, at the very least, that these voters were not congenitally anti-Nixon. Levy and Kramer, *The Ethnic Factor,* 79.

4. Richard Nixon, "Address Accepting the Presidential Nomination at the Republican National Convention in Miami Beach, Florida," August 8, 1968, The American Presidency Project, https://www.presidency.ucsb.edu /documents/address-accepting-the-presidential-nomination-the-republican -national-convention-miami.

5. Rick Perlstein, *Nixonland: The Rise of a President and the Fracturing of America* (New York: Scribner, 2008), 252; Stephen E. Ambrose, *Nixon: The Education of a Politician, 1913–1962* (New York: Simon and Schuster, 1987), 302.

6. Influential Republicans of the day did not consider even these staunchly anti-Communist communities certain to be swayed by too hard right an appeal. In his 1969 manifesto *The Emerging Republican Majority,* GOP strategist Kevin Phillips locates them in a liberal "Latin Crescent" that ran from El Paso to Miami. The "Latin refugees and fortune-hunters of southern Florida" may have in time become outspoken in support of Ronald Reagan. But the bulk of the Cubans, Phillips claimed in 1969, were not "right-wing conservatives." Kevin Phillips, *The Emerging Republican Majority* (New Rochelle, NY: Arlington House, September 1970), 282–284.

7. Since the position offered no salary, Castillo would also be appointed as deputy staff director of the US Commission on Civil Rights.

8. Dan Oberdorfer, "Mexican-American Seen Slated to be Head of SBA," *Washington Post,* February 20, 1969; Ruben Salazar, "Nixon to Name L.A. Attorney Head of U.S. Latin Agency," *Los Angeles Times,* April 17, 1969; "Nixon Swears in L.A. Attorney to U.S. Post," *Los Angeles Times,* May 29, 1969.

9. Memorandum, Martin Castillo and Hank Quevedo to Robert H. Finch, "Paper in re: the Mexican-American and the New Administration," November 26, 1968, Box 63, Daniel Patrick Moynihan, Staff Member and Office Files (hereafter SMOF), NPM.

10. Richard Nixon Foundation, "Creating Opportunities for Latino Americans," Nixon Foundation Website, Video File, 1:06, http://blog.nixonfoundation .org/2010/10/white-house-and-campaign-officials-discuss-rns-latino -initiatives/ (accessed November 8, 2011).

11. Kevin Phillips, *The Emerging Republican Majority,* updated ed. (Princeton, NJ: Princeton University Press, 2015), 547.

12. Kenneth O'Reilly, *Nixon's Piano: Presidents and Racial Politics from Washington to Clinton* (New York: Free Press, 1995), 279.

13. Ruben Salazar, "Talk by Negro Opens Latin League Meeting," *Los Angeles Times,* June 28, 1969.

14. Ruben Salazar, "Nixon Aide Pledges More Help in Solving Problems of Latins," *Los Angeles Times,* June 29, 1969.

15. Quoted in O'Reilly, *Nixon's Piano,* 318.

16. Memorandum, Ehrlichman to Nixon, September 29, 1969, Box 16, Robert H. Finch Files (hereafter Finch Files), SMOF, NPM.

17. Memorandum, C. D. Ward to Secretary of Labor, November 5, 1970, Box 17, Finch Files, SMOF, NPM. On Agnew and his racial qualifications for selection to the Nixon ticket, see O'Reilly, *Nixon's Piano,* 286–290.

18. Burt Talcott to Harry S. Dent, July 1, 1969, HU 2, Box 6, WHCF, NPM.

19. "Republican Group Petitions Nixon for Mexican-American Conference," *San Antonio Express/News,* February 22, 1970, Box 16, Finch Files, SMOF, NPM.

20. Gordon Brownell, Bill Casselman, Steve Hess to John Ehrlichman, October 1, 1969, Box 21, Finch Files, SMOF, NPM.

21. Orville Watkins to Bryce Harlow, January 22, 1970, Box 15, Finch Files, SMOF, NPM.

22. César J. Ayala and Rafael Bernabe, *Puerto Rico in the American Century: A History since 1898* (Chapel Hill: University of North Carolina Press, 2007), 224–226.

23. Luis A. Ferré to Richard Nixon, January 29, 1970, Box 18, Finch Files, SMOF, NPM.

24. Ivan González to Richard Nixon, March 25, 1970, HU 2, Box 6, WHCF, NPM.

25. Memorandum, Leonard Garment to Kenneth R. Cole Jr., September 14, 1970, Box 16, Finch Files, SMOF, NPM.

26. Luis Nuñez to Bradley H. Patterson Jr., September 8, 1970, Box 16, Finch Files, SMOF, NPM.

27. Ken Cole's response is handwritten on Memorandum, Leonard Garment to Kenneth R. Cole Jr., September 8, 1970, Box 16, Finch Files, SMOF, NPM.

28. Office of the Vice President, "News Release," August 21, 1970, Box 18, Finch Files, SMOF, NPM; For those curious why Agnew was so concerned with minority business, the vice president reminded the audience that his father was Greek, and therefore "a member of a minority." Richard West, "Agnew Announces Economic Aid Plan for Latins in U.S." *Los Angeles Times,* August 22, 1970.

29. National Economic Development Agency, "NEDA Performance Record, April 1972," Box 18, Finch Files, SMOF, NPM.

30. National Economic Development Agency, "NEDA Performance Record, April 1972.

31. *Cong. Rec.,* 92nd Congress, 2nd. sess., 1972, 118: 15815–15817; National Economic Development Agency, "NEDA Performance Record, March 1972," Box 18, Finch Files, SMOF, NPM.

32. Office of the Vice President, "News Release," August 21, 1970, Box 18, Finch Files, SMOF, NPM.

33. "NEDA Performance Record, March 1972," Box 18, Finch Files, SMOF, NPM.

34. Carlos Conde, ed., *The Spanish Speaking People of the United States: A New Era* (Washington, DC: Cabinet Committee on Opportunities for Spanish Speaking People, 1970), 1–16.

35. Conde, *The Spanish Speaking People of the United States*, 9, v.

36. Quoted in Jefferson Cowie, *Stayin' Alive: The 1970s and the Last Days of the Working Class* (New York: New Press, 2010), 92.

37. Memorandum Robert Finch to John R. Brown III, October 17, 1970, Box 21, Finch Files, SMOF, NPM.

38. Richard Reeves, *President Nixon: Alone in the White House* (New York: Simon and Schuster, 2001), 272.

39. He had joined the House in 1968, when the end of the state's at-large congressional voting meant the creation of a new district for the heavily Hispanic northern part of the state. He was a moderate, a former insurance salesman, and the son of the mayor of Santa Fe. Martin Tolchin, "Manuel Lujan Jr.: Secretary of the Interior," *New York Times*, December 23, 1988.

40. "Boricuas Ayudaron con un 64% al Triunfo de Nelson Rockefeller," *El Diario/La Prensa*, November 30, 1970; Luis Nuñez to Garment, December 9, 1970, Box 16, Finch Files, SMOF, NPM.

41. Leonard Garment to Richard M. Nixon, February 5, 1971, Box 65, Bradley H. Patterson Jr. Files, SMOF, NPM.

42. "SBA Head Quits, Cites Poor Health," *Chicago Tribune*, November 20, 1970.

43. James M. Naughton, "James Farmer to Resign as a Nixon Welfare Aide," *New York Times*, December 5, 1970.

44. H. R. Haldeman to Robert H. Finch, February 2, 1971, Box 65, Bradley H. Patterson Jr. Files, SMOF, NPM.

45. H. R. Haldeman to Robert H. Finch, February 2, 1971.

46. James M. Naughton, "Agnew Sees Need to Aid a Minority," *New York Times*, July 8, 1970.

47. "Sixteen Questions on the Sixteen-Point Program," Box 4, Central File, Records of the Cabinet Committee on Opportunities for Spanish-Speaking People, RG 220.15.6, National Archives, College Park, MD.

48. "President Nixon's Sixteen Point Program," Box 4, Central File, Records of the Cabinet Committee on Opportunities for Spanish-Speaking People, RG 220.15.6, National Archives, College Park, MD.

49. "New Chicano Adviser," *Los Angeles Times*, December 10, 1970.

50. Memorandum, Malek to Haldeman, "Mexican-American Recruiting Status Report," January 25, 1971, Box 16, Finch Files, SMOF, NPM.

51. The administration created a similar committee for blacks, and one for "ethnics," the latter chaired by the RNC's Laszlow Pastor. Memorandum, Fred Malek to H. R. Haldeman, January 6, 1971, Box 16, Finch Files, SMOF, NPM.

52. Chet Holifield and Frank Horton to Richard M. Nixon, June 21, 1971; Alan Cranston to Richard M. Nixon, March 1, 1971; and Henry M. Jackson to Richard M. Nixon, July 23, 1971. All in EX FG 145, Box 7, WHCF, NPM.

53. Memorandum, Antonia Pantoja to Robert Finch, May 21, 1971, Box 15, Finch Files, SMOF, NPM.

54. George Grassmuck to Neal Ball, August 4, 1971, Box 16, Finch Files, SMOF, NPM.

55. George Grassmuck, "On the Spanish Speakers: Caveats and Concerns," June 15, 1971, Box 16, Finch Files, SMOF, NPM.

56. George Grassmuck, "On the Spanish Speakers: Caveats and Concerns," June 15, 1971, Box 16, Finch Files, SMOF, NPM.

57. George Grassmuck, "On the Spanish Speakers: Caveats and Concerns," June 15, 1971, Box 16, Finch Files, SMOF, NPM.

58. "An Overview of Spanish Speaking Affairs for White House Perspective, May, 1971," Box 21, Finch Files, SMOF, NPM.

59. Memorandum, Russ Deane to Clark MacGregor, June 16, 1971, EX HU 2, Box 4, WHSF, WHCF, NPM; Frank P. Rocco to Fred Malek, March 19, 1971, Box 18, Finch Files, SMOF, NPM.

60. Dwight A. Ink to George Grassmuck, July 14, 1971, Box 16, Finch Files, SMOF, NPM.

61. Paul Delaney, "Blacks in House Get Nixon Pledge," *New York Times*, March 26, 1971.

62. Edward Roybal and newly elected Representative Herman Badillo would not officially form the Congressional Hispanic Caucus for another five years, but they were beginning to collaborate on issues of shared concern, pressing the administration to do more for their communities. George Grassmuck to Clark MacGregor, May 10, 1971, Box 15, Finch Files, SMOF, NPM.

63. George Grassmuck, "On the Spanish Speakers: Caveats and Concerns," June 15, 1971, Box 16, Finch Files, SMOF, NPM.

64. "Annual Report of the Cabinet Committee on Opportunities for Spanish Speaking People, Fiscal Year 1971," Box 15, Finch Files, SMOF, NPM.

65. "Nixon Appoints Former Whittier Teacher to Post," *Los Angeles Times*, August 5, 1971; Dan Oberdorfer, "Nixon, Buckley Meet to Soothe Conservatives," *Washington Post*, August 6, 1971.

66. "An overview of Spanish speaking affairs for White House perspective May, 1971," Box 21, Finch Files, SMOF, NPM.

67. George Grassmuck to Robert Finch, May 18, 1971, Box 18, Finch Files, SMOF, NPM.

68. "Schedule Proposal," July 28, 1971, EX FG, Box 7, WHCF, NPM; Manuel R. Giberga to Henry M. Ramirez, n.d.; and Manuel Giberga, "Importance of the Unity of the Latins in the United States," *Diario Las Americas*, August 10, 1971, Box 15, Finch Files, SMOF, NPM.

69. "Schedule Proposal," July 28, 1971, EX FG, Box 7.

70. "Draft Minutes of Cabinet Committee Meeting on Spanish Speaking," August 5, 1971, Box 16, Finch Files, SMOF, NPM; and CAB 67-13, August 5, 1971, White House Tapes, NPM.

71. OVAL 555-3, August 5, 1971, White House Tapes, NPM.

72. OVAL 555-3; August 5, 1971, White House Tapes, NPM.

73. Frank Del Olmo, "Nixon Appointee Wants Mexicans to Get Involved," *Los Angeles Times*, September 13, 1971.

74. Seth Kantor, "New Cabinet Panel Head Will Boost Chances for his People," *Fort Worth Press*, August 12, 1971, Box 15, Finch Files, SMOF, NPM.

75. Frank Del Olmo, "Nixon Appointee Wants Mexicans to Get Involved," *Los Angeles Times*, September 13, 1971.

76. Shortly after Ramirez's public debut, Nixon nominated El Paso's former mayor and Kennedy's Ambassador to Costa Rica, the Democrat Raymond Telles, for a five-year term as Vicente Ximenes's replacement on the EEOC. "SEC Staff Aide Named Commissioner," *Washington Post*, August 8, 1971.

77. Nick Thimmesch, "New OEO Chief Brings Poor Background to Poverty Agency," *Los Angeles Times*, February 17, 1972.

78. Don Oberdorfer, "Noted Negro, Mexican-American May Get Top Administration Jobs," *Washington Post*, August 27, 1971.

79. Louise Hutchinson, "Recruiting Big Job for Nixon Aides," *Chicago Tribune*, September 26, 1971.

80. EOB 279-14, September 22, 1971, White House Tapes, NPM, transcript posted at www.gwu.edu/~nsarchiv/NSAEBB/NSAEBB95/mex14.pdf.

81. OVAL 577-17, September 20, 1971, White House Tapes, NPM.

82. EOB 279-14, September 22, 1971, White House Tapes, NPM.

83. EOB 279-14, September 22, 1971, White House Tapes, NPM.

84. OVAL 577-17, September 20, 1971, White House Tapes, NPM.

85. OVAL 576-6, September 18, 1971, White House Tapes, NPM.

## 6. Liberal Democrats and the Meanings of "Unidos"

1. Who better to bring them together than the eminently respectable senator from New Mexico, whom Alvarez flattered as "a man totally divested of personal ambitions or self-aggrandizement," and as a "solid, living example of self-made (Hombre) who through courage and dedication has raised an exemplary family." Carlos Alvarez to Joseph Montoya, September 25, 1969, Box 162, Joseph M. Montoya Papers, University of New Mexico Center for Southwest Research (hereafter JMMP).

2. Joseph Montoya to Carlos Alvarez, October 3, 1969, Box 162, JMMP.

3. Associated Press, "Puerto Ricans Charge Bias in Nixon Unit," *Washington Post*, September 5, 1971.

4. Clayton Knowles, "Creation of a New 'Puerto Rican' District Stirs Controversy," *New York Times*, January 22, 1970; Alfonso A. Narvaez, "Badillo Expected to be in Close House Race," *New York Times*, June 20, 1970; Richard Phalon, "Governor Is Said to Back Badillo," *New York Times*, April 24, 1970; "Badillo Endorsed by Lindsay in Race for Seat in Congress," *New York Times*, May 1, 1970; Richard L. Madden, "Badillo Wins House Race," *New York Times*, June 24, 1970; "Rerun in the 21st," *New York Times*, September 24, 1970; Will Lissner, "Appellate Division Upholds Badillo's Nomination in 21st District," *New York Times*, October 1, 1970.

5. Stephen Isaacs, "Rep. Herman Badillo and His Strange Bedfellows: The Most Ardent Striver in New York Politics," *Washington Post*, November 14, 1971; Richard L. Madden, "8 New House Members Split Evenly in Outlook," *New York Times*, November 5, 1970.

6. Edward Roybal and Herman Badillo to Richard Nixon, August 9, 1971, Box 16, Robert H. Finch Files, Staff Member and Office Files (hereafter SMOF), Nixon Presidential Materials Project, College Park, Maryland (hereafter NPM).

7. AP, "Latin Parley is Called by Four from Congress," *New York Times*, September 26, 1971.

8. Will Lissner, "Coalition Sought by Puerto Ricans," *New York Times*, September 30, 1971.

9. Memorandum, Joe Alarid to Bob McNeill, September 30, 1971, Box 158, JMMP; Thomas J. Foley, "'Brown Power' Parley Opens This Weekend," *Los Angeles Times*, October 22, 1971.

10. Foley, "'Brown Power' Parley Opens This Weekend."

11. *Los Angeles Times*, October 22, 1971.

12. George Grassmuck to Dave Parker, October 5, 1971, Box 16, Robert H. Finch Files, SMOF, NPM.

13. Doug Hallett to Charles W. Colson, October 8, 1971, Box 4, EX HU 2, White House Central Files (hereafter WHCF), NPM.

14. W. Richard Howard to Dave Parker, October 8, 1971, Box 4, EX HU 2, WHCF, NPM.

15. Bud McFarlane to William E. Timmons, October 12, 1971, Box 4, EX HU 2, WHCF, NPM.

16. Press reports conflict as to the number, and some boasted of 2,000 participants. Quoted in Jack Agüeros, "It Was 'Herman's Show' Till Curtain Time," *Village Voice*, November 11, 1971.

17. Willie Vazquez, telephone interview by the author, March 16, 2015.

18. José Angel Gutiérrez, telephone interview by the author, February 6, 2015.

19. Donald Maldonado, Untitled Report, October 1971, Box 158, JMMP.

20. Gutiérrez, telephone interview by the author; Frank Espada, telephone interview by the author, February 23, 2011.

21. See room chart in Box 21, Robert H. Finch Files, SMOF, NPM.

22. National Spanish Speaking Coalition, "Agenda, National Spanish Speaking Coalition Conference, October 23–24, 1971," Box 158, JMMP.

23. *Village Voice*, November 11, 1971.

24. Edward Roybal, "Guest Editorial," *Las Nuevas*, vol. 1, ed. 7, November, 1971, Series III, Box 85, Edward R. Roybal Papers, California State University, Los Angeles.

25. Joseph Montoya, "Unidos," Box 76, JMMP; Tape #10 "D.C.," Box 108, José Angel Gutiérrez Papers, Benson Latin American Collection, University of Texas Libraries, University of Texas at Austin (hereafter JAGP).

26. Tape #10 "D.C.," Box 108, JAGP.

27. Tape #10 "D.C.," Box 108, JAGP.

28. Tape #10 "D.C.," Box 108, JAGP.
29. Tape #10 "D.C.," Box 108, JAGP.
30. Gutiérrez, telephone interview by the author.
31. Gutiérrez, telephone interview by the author; Reies López Tijerina, *They Called Me "King Tiger": My Struggle for the Land and Our Rights,* trans. José Angel Gutiérrez (Houston: Arte Público Press, 2000), 169.
32. Monserrat later became the head of the New York City Board of Education. Wolfgang Saxon, "Joseph Monserrat, 84, Leader in Efforts to Unify Latinos," *New York Times,* November 19, 2005.
33. Joseph Wershba, "Daily Closeup, Joseph Monserrat, Director, P R Migration," *New York Post,* January 29, 1959, in Series III, Box 7, Joseph Monserrat Papers, Archives of the Puerto Rican Diaspora, Centro de Estudios Puertorriqueños, Hunter College, City University of New York.
34. Tape #11, Side A, Box 108, JAGP.
35. Tape #11, Side A, Box 108, JAGP.
36. Tape #11, Side A, Box 108, JAGP..
37. Tape #11, Side A, Box 108, JAGP.
38. *Village Voice,* November 11, 1971.
39. Tape #11, Side A, Box 108, JAGP.
40. Tape #11, Side A, Box 108, JAGP..
41. Thomas J. Foley, "Latin Conference Votes to Set up Political Power Base in Capital," *Los Angeles Times,* October 25, 1971.
42. José Toro to Phillip Sanchez, October 27, 1971, Box 158, JMMP; Tape #11, Side B, Box 108, JAGP.
43. Espada, telephone interview by the author.
44. *Village Voice,* November 11, 1971.
45. *Village Voice,* November 11, 1971.
46. *Village Voice,* November 11, 1971.
47. Tape #12, Box 108, JAGP.
48. Tape #12, Box 108, JAGP.
49. Aurora Arredondo to Phillip Sanchez, October 27, 1971, and Leonor Muñoz, "Memorandum for the Director," both in Box 158, JMMP.
50. *Village Voice,* November 11, 1971.
51. Thomas H. Martinez to Joseph Montoya, November 5, 1971, Box 158, JMMP.
52. Foley, "Latin Conference Votes to Set up Political Power Base in Capital."
53. *Los Angeles Times,* October 25, 1971.
54. Thomas H. Martinez to Joseph Montoya, November 5, 1971, Box 158, JMMP.
55. Montejano, *Quixote's Soldiers,* 192.
56. Nick Kotz, "U.S. Latin Coalition Plans Convention," *Washington Post,* October 26, 1971.
57. *Village Voice,* November 11, 1971.
58. Jack Rosenthal, "Unity Urged for All of Spanish Origin," *New York Times,* October 24, 1971.

59. *Village Voice,* November 11, 1971.

60. Jack Rosenthal, "The Goal among the Spanish-Speaking: 'Unidos,'" *New York Times,* October 31, 1971.

61. *New York Times,* October 31, 1971.

62. Herman Badillo, telephone interview by the author, March 3, 2011.

63. *Los Angeles Times,* October 22, 1971.

64. Joseph J. Quintana Jr. to Joseph Montoya, October 25, 1971, Box 158, JMMP.

65. Such correspondence appears more frequently in Montoya's records as he became more outspoken against discrimination, especially in the many federal workplaces that drove New Mexico's economy. Doris M. Mawson to Joseph Montoya, October 29, 1971, Box 158, JMMP.

66. Joseph Montoya to Samuel Gonzales, November 30, 1971, Box 158, JMMP.

67. Jim Maldonado, "Chicano Movement: Political Aims," *Santa Fe New Mexican,* February 15, 1972, Box 163, JMMP.

68. Maldonado, "Chicano Movement." The *Baltimore Sun, Chicago Tribune, Los Angeles Times, New York Times, Wall Street Journal,* and *Washington Post* were those the author consulted. On the San José convention, see Armando Navarro, *La Raza Unida Party: A Challenge to the U.S. Two-Party Dictatorship* (Philadelphia: Temple University Press, 2000), 147–149.

69. Luis Vargas to Joseph Montoya, October 27, 1971, Box 158, JMMP; trans. by author.

70. E. J. Moreno to Joseph Montoya, October 26, 1971, Box 158, JMMP.

71. Henry G. Reyes to Montoya, October 28, 1971, Box 158, JMMP.

72. Vilma Martínez to Edward E. Roybal, January 13, 1972, Box 163, JMMP.

73. Dolores Armada to Joseph Montoya, October 27, 1971, Box 158, JMMP; Armada to Montoya, November 9, 1971, Box 158, JMMP.

74. Memorandum, Thomas H. Martinez to Joseph Montoya, November 5, 1971, Box 158, JMMP.

75. Donald Maldonado, Untitled Report, October, 1971, Box 158, JMMP.

76. "We find it alarming to read your letter which sounds like a speech to an interested, but uncommitted audience. We are past that here. We do not have to be sold on the concepts. We accept them and the challenge of organizing. We are now throwing the ball back to you for the leadership and push that this Coalition must have," he wrote. Samuel Gonzales to Joseph Montoya, November 17, 1971, Box 158, JMMP.

77. Samuel Gonzales, "Only Through *Unity* Will We Get *Equality* and *Justice,*" Box 163, JMMP.

78. *League of United Latin American Citizens, et al. v. Robert E. Hampton, et al.,* 501 F.2d 843 D.C. Cir. 1974).

79. Jack Rosenthal, "Latin-Americans Sue U.S. on Rights," *New York Times,* October 23, 1971; The lawsuit would be dismissed by the old United States District Court for the District of Columbia, and three years later by the United States Court of Appeals for the DC circuit. Both courts found that the plaintiffs lacked standing in the case for not identifying a specific

instance in which they or their members had been discriminated against. The appeals court also held that the plaintiffs had failed to exhaust their administrative remedies, in the appeals to the Civil Service Commission itself. See *League of United Latin American Citizens, et al. v. Robert E. Hampton, et al.*

80. Carlos A, Guffain, "Memorandum for the Director," October 26, 1971, Box 158, JMMP.
81. Frank Fuentes Jr., "Memorandum for the Director," October 27, 1971, Box 158, JMMP.
82. Donald Maldonado, Untitled Report, October, 1971, Box 158, JMMP.
83. Carlos A, Guffain, "Memorandum for the Director," October 26, 1971, Box 158, JMMP.
84. Vilma Gorena-Guinn to Phillip Sanchez, October 27, 1971, Box 158, JMMP.
85. Leo A. Espinosa, to Joseph Montoya, November 6, 1971, Box 158, JMMP.
86. Theodore H. White, *The Making of the President, 1972* (New York: Atheneum, 1973), 31–32.
87. White, *The Making of the President, 1972*, 177–178, 132.
88. Benjamin Márquez, *Democratizing Texas Politics: Race, Identity, and Mexican American Empowerment* (Austin: University of Texas Press, 2014), 96.
89. Memorandum, Alex Armendariz to Bob Marik, "Campaign Report," November 14, 1972, in Senate Select Committee on Presidential Campaign Activities, *Presidential Campaign Activities of 1972: Executive Session Hearings on Watergate and Related Activities, Book 19*, 8760.
90. Memorandum, Polly Baca Barragán, "National Convention Activities and Events," June 20, 1972, Box 15, Joe J. Bernal Papers, Benson Latin American Collection, University of Texas Libraries, University of Texas at Austin (hereafter JJB); Robert B. Semple Jr., "Caucuses Are Bound by Common Identity," *New York Times*, July 11, 1972, 19.
91. *New York Times*, July 11, 1972.
92. "Presented to Senator George McGovern, by the National Latino Caucus, August 9, 1972," Box 15, JJB.
93. Democratic Party, "1972 Democratic Party Platform," July 10, 1972, The American Presidency Project, https://www.presidency.ucsb.edu/documents/1972-democratic-party-platform (accessed November 24, 2016).
94. Democratic Party, "1972 Democratic Party Platform," July 10, 1972.
95. Don Bohning, "Exiles Adjusting to U.S.-Cuba Ties?," *Miami Herald*, October 21, 1971.
96. Democratic Party, "1972 Democratic Party Platform," July 10, 1972.
97. "Presented to Senator George McGovern, by the National Latino Caucus, August 9, 1972," Box 15, JJB.
98. "Presented to Senator George McGovern, by the National Latino Caucus, August 9, 1972," Box 15, JJB.
99. "George McGovern para Presidente," Box 97, George S. McGovern Papers, 1939–1984 (mostly 1968–1979), Public Policy Papers, Department of Rare Books and Special Collections, Princeton University Library (hereafter GSMP).

100. Christopher Lydon, "McGovern Assures Party Bloc Leaders," *New York Times* August 10, 1972. The nominee committed to their people a Cabinet post or federal judgeship (though not one on the Supreme Court). He promised to recognize them with a distinct category on national censuses (still only occasionally done), one that would distinguish among national origin subgroups. He also vowed to bolster support for bilingual education. He committed himself to equality within the Spanish-speaking population, and a strengthened Cabinet committee "serving *all* Latinos." George McGovern to Joe Bernal, September 28, 1972, Box 15, JJB.

101. He oversaw a staff of twelve volunteers, who worked on voter registration and analysis, translation, fundraising, scheduling of speakers, and providing of relevant educational and publicity materials to local groups. "Unidos con McGovern," in Democratic National Committee Office of the Spanish Speaking, *Mano en Mano* Vol. 1, Issue 3, October 1972, Box 97, GSMP.

102. "¡Basta Ya!," in Democratic National Committee Office of the Spanish Speaking, *Mano en Mano* Vol. 1, Issue 4, November 1972, Box 156, GSMP.

103. Democratic National Committee Office of the Spanish Speaking, *Mano en Mano* Vol. 1, Issue 2, June 1972, Box 51, JJB.

104. They specifically cited Nixon's desire to limit the union's ability to use the boycott to bring intransigent employers to the negotiating table. Tony Castro, "Republican 'Chicano Strategy' Eyes Mexican-American Vote," *Washington Post*, January 24, 1972; John Pierson, "Senor Nixon Makes a Pitch for the Votes of Mexican-Americans," *Wall Street Journal*, April 11, 1972.

105. Frank del Olmo, "Chicanos Hear Pleas from Major Parties," *Los Angeles Times*, October 15, 1972.

106. Years of neglect had justified any "anger and grievance against our party," but comparing McGovern and the Democrats to Nixon was, argued Velazquez, like "the difference between meat and bones." Luis Velazquez, "Is Anybody Looking?," in Democratic National Committee Office of the Spanish Speaking, *Mano en Mano* Vol. 1, Issue 3, October 1972, Box 97, GSMP.

107. Memorandum, Richard Beserra to Spanish-Speaking Delegates, September 15, 1972, Box 15, JJB.

108. Frank del Olmo, "Election Reflects Growing Political Power for Latins," *Los Angeles Times*, November 14, 1972.

109. Memorandum, Richard Beserra to Latino Steering Committee, November 21, 1972, Box 15, JJB.

## 7. The "Brown Mafia" and Middle-Class Spanish-Speaking Politics in 1972

1. OVAL 801-19, October 17, 1972, White House Tapes, Nixon Presidential Materials Project, College Park, Maryland (hereafter NPM).

2. WH 10-116, October 7, 1971, White House Tapes, NPM.

3. See Richard Reeves, *President Nixon: Alone in the White House* (New York: Simon and Schuster, 2001), 297; and Robert Mason, *Richard Nixon and the Quest for a New Majority* (Chapel Hill: University of North Carolina Press, 2004), 131–132.

4. Committee for the Re-Election of the President, "Memorandum for the Attorney General," December 16, 1971, in Senate Select Committee on Presidential Campaign Activities, *Presidential Campaign Activities of 1972: Hearings on Watergate and Related Activities, Phase III: Campaign Financing, Book 13,* 93rd Cong., 1st sess., 5533.

5. Memorandum, Charles W. Colson to John Ehrlichman, December 20, 1971, Box 4, EX HU 2, White House Central Files (hereafter WHCF), NPM.

6. "Mexican American Analysis of Survey Taken in Orange and Los Angeles Counties—October 1971," in Senate Select Committee on Presidential Campaign Activities, *Presidential Campaign Activities of 1972: Executive Session Hearings on Watergate and Related Activities, Book 19,* 8678–8679.

7. Memorandum, Charles W. Colson to John Ehrlichman, December 20, 1971, Box 4, EX HU 2, WHCF, NPM.

8. "Confidential," n.d., in Hugh Davis Graham, *Civil Rights during the Nixon Administration, 1969–1974* (Bethesda, MD: University Publications of America, 1989), Part I, Reel 3, Frames 901–952.

9. Nixon could produce "some movement" in their voting patterns if he convinced them that he "has recognized their social and economic problems." "Memorandum for the Attorney General," December 16, 1971, in Senate Select Committee, *Presidential Campaign Activities of 1972, Book 13,* 5533.

10. "Confidential," n.d., in Graham, *Civil Rights during the Nixon Administration, 1969–1974,* Part I, Reel 3, Frames 901–952.

11. "Memorandum for the Attorney General," December 16, 1971, in Senate Select Committee, *Presidential Campaign Activities of 1972, Book 13,* 5533; Roberto Fabricio, "Cubans Left without Homeland or Hero," *Miami Herald,* August 9, 1974; "Confidential," n.d., in Graham, *Civil Rights during the Nixon Administration, 1969–1974,* Part I, Reel 3, Frames 901–952.

12. Lars Schoultz, *That Infernal Little Republic: The United States and the Cuban Revolution* (Chapel Hill: University of North Carolina Press, 2009), 245.

13. *Miami Herald,* August 9, 1974.

14. Roberto Fabricio, "Nixon Backer Gets $25,000 as Cuban Aide," *Miami Herald,* July 1, 1972; "Confidential," n.d., in Graham, *Civil Rights during the Nixon Administration, 1969–1974,* Part I, Reel 3, Frames 901–952.

15. "Memorandum for the Attorney General," December 16, 1971, Senate Select Committee, *Presidential Campaign Activities of 1972, Book 13,* 5533.

16. "Confidential," n.d., in Graham, *Civil Rights during the Nixon Administration, 1969–1974,* Part I, Reel 3, Frames 901–952.

17. "Confidential," n.d., in Graham, *Civil Rights during the Nixon Administration, 1969–1974,* Part I, Reel 3, Frames 901–952.

18. "Latin Panel Biased, Puerto Ricans Assert," *Los Angeles Times,* September 4, 1971.

19. Henry M. Ramirez, interview by the author, Bethesda, MD, February 7, 2011.

20. In New York's Spanish-language press, Javits stated his displeasure. He claimed that Maduro, who had been living in Mexico for the previous decade, "does not know the Puerto Rican communities in the United States very well, especially those living in New York City; he could not represent them since he does not know its necessities; how to meet their objectives, and how to help them obtain the recognition that they are entitled to." Luisa Quintero, "In Spite of Ramirez, Edward Aponte is still on the Job," *El Diario/La Prensa,* December 30, 1971, Box 21, Robert H. Finch Files (hereafter Finch Files), Staff Member and Office Files (hereafter SMOF), NPM.

21. "Briefing for Puerto Rican Areas," Box 17, Finch Files, SMOF, NPM.

22. Russell Dean to Clark MacGregor, June 16, 1971, quoted in Hugh Davis Graham, *The Civil Rights Era: Origins and Development of National Policy: 1960–1972* (New York: Oxford University Press, 1990), 318.

23. Edgardo Buttari to Charles G. Rebozo, n.d., Box 21, Finch Files, SMOF, NPM.

24. Their stated aim was "to upgrade the Spanish Speaking people's position in the federal government by assuring that they have access to positions of power" and to ensure that "programs, grants, and dollar expenditures, reach Hispanic communities in numbers proportionate to their population." Press Release, "Statement by Acting Chairman Henry M. Ramirez before a group of Spanish speaking community leaders on the eve of the Regional Council meeting in Chicago, Illinois," October 14, 1971, Box 19, Finch Files, SMOF, NPM.

25. Jerome Watson, "Stormy Sessions of US Officials with Latins Here Told," *Chicago Sun-Times,* October 21, 1971.

26. OVAL 594-5, October 18, 1971, White House Tapes, NPM.

27. "Justice in the Immigration Problem," *Los Angeles Times,* October 8, 1971; "Treasurer's Firm Raided for Aliens," *Chicago Tribune,* October 6, 1971; "The Illegal Alien: Growing Threat to U.S. Workers," read one 1972 *Los Angeles Times* headline by Harry Bernstein, the reporter who had accompanied INS agents on their raid of Bañuelos's factory. *Los Angeles Times,* October 22, 1972; the publicity ultimately led to passage of a California state law, signed by Governor Ronald Reagan, making it a crime to knowingly employ an undocumented worker. Reagan pronounced the bill fully compatible with a recent change to state law that made undocumented aliens ineligible to receive welfare payments. Using language that would be familiar decades later, Reagan justified state enforcement of immigration law by criticizing "the federal government's failure to meet its own obligations in this regard," and because it had "become increasingly clear that we can no longer wait for

Congress to enact legislation to effectively cope with the problem." Richard West, "Reagan Signs State Ban on Hiring Illegal Aliens," *Los Angeles Times,* November 9, 1971.

28. Harry Bernstein, "Bañuelos Firm Found Guilty in Labor Case," *Los Angeles Times,* November 22, 1972. Ramona's Mexican Foods was raided for the seventh time, just after the elections. See Harry Bernstein, "53 Illegal Aliens Seized in Plant Run by Son of U.S. Treasurer," *Los Angeles Times,* December 9, 1972; Harry Bernstein, "Bañuelos Food Firm Struck by Teamsters," *Los Angeles Times,* March 9, 1972.

29. Jack Nelson, "Nixon Targeted the Times, Tapes Show," *Los Angeles Times,* March 22, 1997. http://articles.latimes.com/1997-03-22/news/mn-40969_1 _otis-chandler.

30. Ken W. Clawson, "Illegal Alien Worked Briefly at San Clemente," *Washington Post,* October 7, 1971.

31. According to Brown Mafia member William Marumoto, this was supposedly in reference to JFK's "Irish Mafia." Senate Select Committee, *Presidential Campaign Activities of 1972, Book 13,* 5278.

32. John R. Knaggs, *Two-Party Texas: The John Tower Era, 1961–1984* (Austin, TX: Eakin Press, 1986), 138; Memorandum, Fred Malek to Bob Haldeman, "Mexican American Visibility," August 11, 1972, Box 37, Committee for the Re-Election of the President (CRP): Frederic Malek Papers, Series III, Richard Nixon Presidential Library and Museum, Yorba Linda, California (hereafter NPL).

33. Memorandum, Bill Marumoto to Chuck Colson and Fred Malek, "Priorities in the Spanish Speaking Area," July 14, 1972, Box 36, Committee for the Re-Election of the President (CRP): Frederic Malek Papers, Series III, NPL.

34. Likewise, the Brown Mafia made little attempt to distinguish Mexican-American and Puerto Rican populations, even though the former often included high numbers of immigrants while in the latter most were US citizens from birth. According to CREEP documents, Nixon would take Florida, Colorado, and Arizona "without heavy reliance on the Spanish speaking." Confidential Memorandum, "The Plan to Capture the Spanish Speaking Vote," in Senate Select Committee, *Presidential Campaign Activities of 1972, Book 19,* 8620–8625.

35. Confidential Memorandum, "The Plan to Capture the Spanish Speaking Vote."

36. Confidential Memorandum, "The Plan to Capture the Spanish Speaking Vote"; The Brown Mafia's analysis complemented administration research which in April 1972 showed that Nixon had ninety electoral votes safely secured. Although the White House was confident of winning New Mexico and Colorado, it still appeared that the "large key swing states," including California, Illinois, and Texas, would demand "all-out effort." In addition, Pennsylvania, Michigan, New York, and Connecticut, at least two of which

were likely to have substantial numbers of Puerto Rican voters, constituted "major opportunity states," those Nixon had lost in 1968 but that looked promising for 1972. Memorandum, Cliff Miller to John N. Mitchell, April 25, 1972, Box 46, CF PL, White House Special Files (hereafter WHSF), WHCF, NPM.

37. Confidential Memorandum, "The Plan to Capture the Spanish Speaking Vote," 8624–8625.

38. Confidential Memorandum, "The Plan to Capture the Spanish Speaking Vote," 8617–8640, 8622.

39. Confidential Memorandum, "The Plan to Capture the Spanish Speaking Vote," 8626.

40. Memorandum, Alex Armendariz for Fred Malek, "Spanish-speaking study," in House Committee on Government Operations, *Activities of the Cabinet Committee on Opportunities for Spanish-Speaking People*, 93rd Cong., 1st sess., 1973, 28.

41. Memorandum, Alex Armendariz for Fred Malek, "Spanish-speaking study," 28.

42. Memorandum, Alex Armendariz for Fred Malek, "Spanish-speaking study," 30.

43. Memorandum, Alex Armendariz for Fred Malek, "Spanish-speaking study," 28–33.

44. Memorandum, Alex Armendariz for Fred Malek, "Spanish-speaking study," 28–29.

45. Annual flooding of the city's largely Mexican-American West Side persisted into the decade. See David Montejano, *Quixote's Soldiers: A Local History of the Chicano Movement* (Austin: University of Texas Press, 2010), 25.

46. Memorandum, Alex Armendariz for Fred Malek, "Spanish-speaking study," 31–32.

47. Memorandum, Alex Armendariz for Fred Malek, "Spanish-speaking study," 32–33.

48. Kenneth O'Reilly, *Nixon's Piano: Presidents and Racial Politics from Washington to Clinton* (New York: Free Press, 1995), 313.

49. Memorandum, Robert M. Teeter to John N. Mitchell, "Spanish-American Bloc," June 12, 1972, Box 36, Committee for the Re-Election of the President (CRP): Frederic Malek Papers, Series III, NPL.

50. Memorandum, Alex Armendariz to Bill Rhatican, "Platform Plank for Spanish-Speaking," July 24, 1972, Box 37, Committee for the Re-Election of the President (CRP): Frederic Malek Papers, Series III, NPL.

51. "Proposed Statement by Dr. Henry Ramirez to the Platform in Miami," Box 37, Committee for the Re-Election of the President (CRP): Frederic Malek Papers, Series III, NPL. The GOP platform did not go this far. But it did contain a Spanish-speaking section that praised "the significant contributions to our country by our proud and independent Spanish-speaking citizens," their incorporation in the administration, and the ways the government was

promoting bilingualism, near but not of the part addressing "Ending Discrimination." Republican Party Platforms, "Republican Party Platform of 1972," August 21, 1972, The American Presidency Project, https://www .presidency.ucsb.edu/documents/republican-party-platform-1972.

52. Memorandum, Alex Armendariz to William Marumoto, "Selected Characteristics of Persons and Families of Mexican, Puerto Rican, and Other Spanish Origin: March 1972," July 12, 1972, Box 37, Committee for the Re-Election of the President (CRP): Frederic Malek Papers, Series III, NPL.

53. Memorandum, Alex Armendariz to Spanish-speaking Surrogates, July 24, 1972, Box 37, Committee for the Re-Election of the President (CRP): Frederic Malek Papers, Series III, NPL.

54. Memorandum, Alex Armendariz to Frederic Malek, "Romana Banuelos," August 31, 1972, Box 36, Committee for the Re-Election of the President (CRP): Frederic Malek Papers, Series III, NPL.

55. The title of the 1964 dissertation was "A Sociological Analysis and Description of the Political Role, Status, and Voting Behavior of Americans with Spanish Names." See "Studies in Race and Culture, 1964," *Phylon* 26, no. 4 (4th Qtr. 1965): 403.

56. Memorandum, Bill Marumoto to Chuck Colson, "Weekly Report for Brown Mafia," March 17, 1972, in Senate Select Committee, *Presidential Campaign Activities of 1972, Book 13,* 5546.

57. Memorandum, Bill Marumoto to Chuck Colson, "Weekly Report for Spanish Spea [*sic*]," April 28, 1972, in Senate Select Committee, *Presidential Campaign Activities of 1972, Book 13,* 5566.

58. Memorandum, Bill Marumoto to Chuck Colson, "Weekly Report for Brown Mafia," March 17, 1972, 5546.

59. Memorandum, Bill Marumoto to Chuck Colson, "Weekly Report of the Spanish Speaking," July 28, 1972; and Memorandum, Bill Marumoto to Chuck Colson, "Weekly Report of the Spanish Speaking," September 1, 1972 in Senate Select Committee, *Presidential Campaign Activities of 1972, Book 13,* 5647, 5671.

60. Memorandum, Marcella to Joseph Montoya, January 11, 1973, Box 163, Joseph M. Montoya Papers, University of New Mexico Center for Southwest Research.

61. "La Luz Proposal" and "Publisher's Statement," *La Luz,* April 1972, 7, both in Box 16, Finch Files, SMOF, NPM.

62. Daniel T. Valdes, "Personal Letter" and "Publisher's Statement," in *La Luz,* April 1972, 6, 7; both in Box 16, Finch Files, SMOF, NPM.

63. "Here Comes La Gente," *La Luz,* April 1972, 56–57, Box 16, Finch Files, SMOF, NPM.

64. "Here Comes La Gente."

65. "This Month's Cover," *La Luz,* May 1972, 1. Box 16, Finch Files, SMOF, NPM.

66. Senate Select Committee on Presidential Campaign Activities, *The Final Report of the Select Committee Presidential Campaign Activities* (Washington, DC: Government Printing Office, 1974), 367–368, 379.

67. On the $40 million in grants, see Memorandum, Bill Marumoto to Chuck Colson, "Weekly Report for Spanish Spea [*sic*]," April 28, 1972; and Memorandum, Bill Marumoto to Chuck Colson, "Weekly Report for Spanish Speaking," June 2, 1972, both in Senate Select Committee, *Presidential Campaign Activities of 1972, Book 13*, 5569, 5588.

68. "Capitalizing on the Incumbency," n.d., in Senate Select Committee, *Presidential Campaign Activities of 1972, Book 19*, 8652.

69. Confidential Memorandum for the Attorney General, "Interest Group Reports," December 16, 1971, in Senate Select Committee, *Presidential Campaign Activities of 1972, Book 13*, 5534.

70. Senate Select Committee, *The Final Report of the Select Committee*, 395.

71. Senate Select Committee, *The Final Report of the Select Committee*, 386–389.

72. Frank del Olmo, "L.A. Latins Help Form Nixon Funding Group," *Los Angeles Times*, March 16, 1972. Some reports called it the "National Hispanic Finance Committee to Reelect the President."

73. Mirelez was once a member of the Mexican-American ad hoc committee that had protested the EEOC's indifference to Mexican Americans in 1966.

74. Senate Select Committee, *The Final Report of the Select Committee*, 385–386.

75. Gutiérrez, conversation with author, October 5, 2013.

76. For Kennedy and MAPA, see Carl Greenberg, "La Raza Unida Members Heckle Kennedy at Rally for McGovern," *Los Angeles Times*, September 11, 1972 and Frank Del Olmo, "Latin Group Won't Take Position in Race for President," *Los Angeles Times*, October 16, 1972, respectively; for others, see Memorandum, William Marumoto to Chuck Colson, June 2, 1972; Memorandum, Alex Armendariz to Frederic Malek, September 8, 1972; Memorandum, Alex Armendariz to Chuck Colson, September 14, 1972; Memorandum, Alex Armendariz to William Marumoto, September October 30, 1972, all in Senate Select Committee, *Watergate and Related Activities, Book 13*, 5589, 5677, 5679, 5678.

77. Henry Ramirez to Alex Armendaris, August 29, 1972, quoted in Senate Select Committee, *Watergate and Related Activities, Book 13*, 5316.

78. Memorandum, Bill Marumoto to Chuck Colson, "Weekly Activity Report for the Spanish Speaking," June 9, 1972 in Senate Select Committee, *Watergate and Related Activities, Book 13*, 5601; "Obtaining Support of Independent Spanish Speaking Political Organizations," in Senate Select Committee, *Watergate and Related Activities, Book 19*, 8657; Memorandum, Bill Marumoto to Chuck Colson, "Weekly Activity Report for the Spanish Speaking," June 23, 1972, and Memorandum, Bill Marumoto to Chuck Colson, "Weekly Activity Report of the Spanish Speaking," July 28, 1972, both in Senate Select Committee, *Watergate and Related Activities, Book 13*, 5614, 5644; and Memorandum, David J. Wimer to Richard Wise, June 29,

1972, in Senate Select Committee, *The Final Report of the Select Committee*, 392–393.

79. Roberto Fabricio, "Political Intrigue Had Latin Connection," *Miami Herald*, June 30, 1974.

80. Bea L. Hines and Arnold Markowitz, "Cubans Support Nixon's War Stand as Dissenters Pop Balloons into Bay," *Miami Herald*, May 14, 1972.

81. Roberto Fabricio, "Criticism 'Hushed' on Nixon's Trips," *Miami Herald*, May 19, 1973.

82. Walter Rugaber, "Barker Asserts He Sought Proof of Cuba Aid to Party," *New York Times*, May 25, 1973.

83. Eugenio Martinez, "Mission Impossible: The Watergate Bunglers," *Harper's*, October 1, 1974.

84. Quoted in Rick Perlstein, *Nixonland: The Rise of a President and the Fracturing of America* (New York: Scribner, 2008), 654–655; Anthony Summers, *The Arrogance of Power: The Secret World of Richard Nixon* (New York: Viking, 2000), 404.

85. William Montalbano and Roberto Fabricio, "'Watergate Team Formed for Hoover Rites,'" *Miami Herald*, April 22, 1973.

86. Peter Jay and Kirk Scharfenberg, "Exiles' View of 'Bugging,'" *Washington Post*, June 23, 1972.

87. Quoted in John W. Dean, *The Nixon Defense: What He Knew and When He Knew It* (New York: Viking, 2014), 7, 24, 28.

88. Quoted in Summers, *The Arrogance of Power*, 431.

89. Perlstein, *Nixonland*, 679.

90. John M. Crewdson, "Nixon in Apparent Conflict on Hush Fund: 4 Miamians Identified," *New York Times*, June 9, 1974.

91. Memorandum, Dorothy Hunt to William O. Bittman, October 2, 1972, in House Statement of Information, *Hearings before the Committee on the Judiciary, House of Representatives, Ninety-Third Congress, second session, pursuant to H. Res. 803, a resolution authorizing and directing the Committee on the Judiciary to investigate whether sufficient grounds exist for the House of Representatives to exercise its constitutional power to impeach Richard M. Nixon, President of the United States of America, May–June 1974* (Washington, DC: Government Printing Office, 1974), 233.

92. Jack Anderson, "Hush Money Pay to Hunt Detailed," *Washington Post*, May 9, 1974.

93. Quoted in Dean, *The Nixon Defense*, 123.

94. Enstad, Robert, "Watergate Tape Links Hunt's Wife to Payoff," *Chicago Tribune*, May 2, 1974.

95. Rob Elder, "Miamian Says He Got Coverup Funds," *Miami Herald*, July 10, 1973; Cuban Reportedly Links Convicts' Funds to Hunt," *New York Times*, July 9, 1973.

96. Stanley I. Kutler, *Abuse of Power: The New Nixon Tapes* (New York: Free Press, 1997), 66, 144–145.

97. Robert C. Toth, "Nixon Invades Texas Democratic Stronghold," *Los Angeles Times,* September 23, 1972.

98. Richard Reeves, "How Nixon Outwits the Press," *New York Magazine,* October 9, 1972, 49.

99. Richard Nixon, "Remarks to the Student Body of Rio Grande High School, Rio Grande City, Texas," September 22, 1972, APP, https://www.presidency.ucsb.edu/documents/remarks-the-student-body-rio-grande-high-school-rio-grande-city-texas.

100. Richard Nixon, "Remarks to the Student Body of Rio Grande High School, Rio Grande City, Texas."

101. Ken Ringle, "President Takes Campaign to Texas," *Washington Post,* September 23, 1972.

102. "Shriver Joins in Texas 'Tamalada,'" *Los Angeles Times,* September 23, 1972.

103. Bruce Winters, "Republicans Try to Make Chicanos 2-Party Voters," *Baltimore Sun,* October 28, 1972.

104. "Remarks Prepared for Delivery by Phillip V. Sanchez," September 26, 1972, Box 36, Committee for the Re-Election of the President (CRP): Frederic Malek Papers, Series III, NPL.

105. "Remarks Prepared for Delivery by Phillip V. Sanchez."

106. Memorandum, Alex Armendariz to Frederic Malek, "Spanish-Speaking Mobile Campaign Headquarters," September 20, 1972, Box 36, Committee for the Re-Election of the President (CRP): Frederic Malek Papers, Series III, NPL.

107. CAB 109-1, October 27, 1972, White House Tapes, NPM.

108. Frank del Olmo, "Democrats Say Memo Is 'Model of Bigotry,'" *Los Angeles Times,* November 3, 1972.

109. Memorandum, Alex Armendariz to Bob Marik, November 14, 1972, in Senate Select Committee, *Presidential Campaign Activities of 1972, Book 19,* 8777, 8763, 8791.

110. Stephen Isaacs, "Nixon Gains Over '68 in All Segments," *Washington Post,* November 8, 1972.

111. Tony Castro, "Texas Chicanos Voted GOP; New La Raza Unida Got 6%," *Washington Post,* November 13, 1972.

112. Leo Adde, "Voters Shop Selectively, but Spend $553 Million," *Miami Herald,* November 8, 1972.

113. Frank del Olmo, "Election Reflects Growing Political Power for Latins," *Los Angeles Times,* November 14, 1972.

114. Tony Castro, *Chicano Power: The Emergence of Mexican America* (New York: Saturday Review Press, 1974), 198.

115. Memorandum, Herbert G. Klein for Richard M. Nixon, November 13, 1972, Box 48, CF PL, WHSF, WHCF, NPM.

116. Castro, *Chicano Power,* 212.

117. Memorandum, Herbert G. Klein for Richard M. Nixon, November 13, 1972, Box 48, CF PL, WHSF, WHCF, NPM.

118. Frank del Olmo, "Election Reflects Growing Political Power for Latins," *Los Angeles Times,* November 14, 1972.

119. Frank del Olmo, "Discontent Seen among Nixon Latin Appointees: Loss of Positions, Failure to Deliver on Promises," *Los Angeles Times,* February 26, 1973; "Background," in Fernando Edward C. De Baca and Christine Gauvreau, *The Ford Administration and Hispanic America: The Office Files of Fernando E. C. De Baca* (Woodbridge, CT: Primary Source Media, 2009), Reel 7, Frame 890; Senate Select Committee, *The Final Report of the Select Committee,* 402.

120. See House Committee on Government Operations, *Activities of the Cabinet Committee on Opportunities for Spanish-Speaking People,* 93rd Cong., 1st sess., 1973.

121. Senate Select Committee, *Presidential Campaign Activities of 1972, Book 13,* 5308.

122. Walter Rugaber, "McCord Expected by His Lawyer to Tell Judge Sirica . . . ," *New York Times,* March 25, 1973; David Hosansky, ed., *Eyewitness to Watergate: A Documentary History for Students* (Washington, DC: CQ Press, 2007), 10.

123. Walter Rugaber, "Barker Asserts He Sought Proof of Cuba Aid to Party," *New York Times,* May 25, 1973.

124. Quoted in Rick Perlstein, *The Invisible Bridge: The Fall of Nixon and the Rise of Reagan* (New York: Simon and Schuster, 2014), 101–102.

125. Roberto Fabricio, "Implicated Cubans are Heroes to Miami's Exile Community," *Miami Herald,* May 25, 1973.

126. Frank Calzon, "El Exilio Cubano y la Crisis Norteamericana: La Mentalidad Watergate y la Liberación de Cuba," *¡Cuba Va!* 1 (Autumn 1974): 5.

127. Gene Miller, "Miami Cubans Assist Watergate Defendants," *Miami Herald,* April 20, 1973, 21-A; Fabricio, "Implicated Cubans Are Heroes to Miami's Exile Community."

128. Gene Miller, "Miami Cubans Assist Watergate Defendants."

129. Roberto Fabricio, "3 Now Face Ellsberg Charges," *Miami Herald,* January 27, 1974.

130. Elder, "Miamian Says He Got Coverup Funds"; "Cuban Reportedly Links Convicts' Funds to Hunt."

131. John M. Crewdson, "Nixon in Apparent Conflict on Hush Fund: 4 Miamians Identified," *New York Times,* June 9, 1974.

132. Dean, *The Nixon Defense,* 322, 317.

133. Dan Neuharth, "Two 'Plumbers' Seek Defense Money," *Miami Herald,* July 16, 1974.

134. Roberto Fabricio, "Barker: I Tried to Stop Burglary," *Miami Herald,* August 9, 1974.

135. Eugenio Martinez, "Mission Impossible: The Watergate Bunglers," *Harper's,* October 1, 1974.

## 8. The "Impossible Dream" of the Hispanic Republican Movement

1. Senate Select Committee on Presidential Campaign Activities, *Presidential Campaign Activities of 1972: Hearings on Watergate and Related Activities, Phase III: Campaign Financing, Book 13*, 93rd Cong., 1st sess., 5398–5399, 5362.

2. Benjamin Fernandez to Alma Green, September 15, 1975, in Fernando Edward C. De Baca and Christine Gauvreau, *The Ford Administration and Hispanic America: The Office Files of Fernando E. C. De Baca* (Woodbridge, CT: Primary Source Media, 2009) (hereafter FAHA), Reel 2, Frame 288.

3. Tony Castro, "Texas Chicanos Voted GOP; New La Raza Unida Got 6%," *Washington Post*, November 13, 1972; Senate Select Committee, *Presidential Campaign Activities of 1972, Book 13*, 5277.

4. See Senate Select Committee, *Presidential Campaign Activities of 1972, Book 13*, 5327–5402.

5. Senate Select Committee, *Presidential Campaign Activities of 1972, Book 13*, 5360, 5362.

6. Press release, Republican National Committee, "The Republican Party Recommends Solutions to Important Issues in the Spanish Speaking Community," n.d., Gwen A. Anderson Files: 1974 (hereafter Anderson Files), Box 118, Gerald R. Ford Presidential Library and Museum, Ann Arbor, Michigan (hereafter GRFL).

7. Benjamin Fernandez to Pedro (probably de Mesones), n.d., President Ford Committee Records, 1975–1976 (hereafter PFC), Chairman's Office: DeBolt Subject File (hereafter "DeBolt Subject File"), Box A13, GRFL. New Mexico congressman Manuel Luján, chairman of its advisory committee, declared that the new RNHA would be a vehicle for "Spanish-speaking Republicans at the state and local level to actively participate in all GOP activities and thus gain political power." Press release, Republican National Committee, "RNC's Spanish Speaking Advisory Committee Auxiliary Unit Formed," n.d., Anderson Files, Box 117, GRFL.

8. Benjamin Fernandez to Pedro (probably de Mesones), n.d., PFC; Peggy Ann Bliss, "'Marshall Plan' for Needy Urged," *San Juan Star*, October 21, 1972, PFC, DeBolt Subject File, Box A13, GRFL.

9. Rob Elder, "Ford Victory Would Seal Cuban Banker's Clout," *Miami Herald*, February 22, 1976, PFC, DeBolt Subject File, Box A13, GRFL.

10. Press release, Republican National Committee, "RNC's Spanish Speaking Advisory Committee Auxiliary Unit Formed."

11. See María Cristina García, *Havana USA: Cuban Exiles and Cuban Americans in South Florida, 1959–1994* (Berkeley: University of California Press, 1996).

12. García, *Havana USA*, 43.

13. Alejandro Portes and Rafael Mozo, "The Political Adaptation Process of Cubans and Other Ethnic Minorities in the United States: A Preliminary Analysis," *International Migration Review* 19, no. 1 (Spring 1985): 60; María Cristina García, "Exiles, Immigrants, and Transnationals: The Cuban

Communities of the United States," in *The Columbia History of Latinos in the United States since 1960*, ed. David G. Gutiérrez (New York: Columbia University Press, 2004), 174; García, *Havana USA*, 114.

14. Benjamin Fernandez to Manuel Luján Jr., September 20, 1974, J. Stanley Pottinger Files, Box 140, GRFL.

15. Sean Wilentz, *The Age of Reagan: A History, 1974–2008* (New York: Harper-Collins, 2008), 85; Laura Kalman, *Right Star Rising: A New Politics, 1974–1980* (New York: W. W. Norton, 2010), 27–28; Marissa Chappell, *The War on Welfare: Family, Poverty, and Politics in Modern America* (Philadelphia: University of Pennsylvania Press, 2010), 69.

16. "A Republican Future for the Spanish Speaking," *El Republicano* 1, no. 1 (October 1974), PFC, DeBolt Subject File, Box A13, GRFL.

17. "A Republican Future for the Spanish Speaking."

18. Michael Carbajal Jr. "A New Beginning," FAHA, Reel 2, Frames 292–293.

19. "Chairman's Message," *El Republicano* 1, no. 1 (October 1974), PFC, DeBolt Subject File, Box A13, GRFL; "Republican National Hispanic Assembly Organizational Conference," Anderson Files, Box 117, GRFL.

20. "Chairman's Message."

21. "Hispano Republicans Run For Congress," *El Republicano* 1, no. 1 (October 1974), PFC, DeBolt Subject File, Box A13, GRFL.

22. See "Businesswoman Heads California RNHA," *El Republicano* 1, no. 1 (October 1974), PFC, DeBolt Subject File, Box A13, GRFL, and untitled list of RNHA leaders, n.d., Robert T. Hartmann Files, Box 28, GRFL.

23. Ben Fernandez to Members et al., September 30, 1975, FAHA, Reel 2, Frames 283–285.

24. Fernando E. C. De Baca to Mike Thompson, October 24, 1975, FAHA, Reel 10, Frame 474.

25. De Baca's credentials in public service also included a number of state-level positions in New Mexico and a stint running the Department of Health, Education, and Welfare's west coast region. White House Press Release, July 19, 1974, Anderson Files, Box 117, GRFL.

26. "Biographical Sketch of the Honorable Fernando E. C. De Baca, Special Assistant to the President," FAHA, Reel 6, Frame 328.

27. Edward Valenzuela, "The Spanish Speaking and Government Employment" (PhD diss., Union Graduate School—West, 1977), 123; Fernando E. C. De Baca to Edward Valenzuela, November 18, 1974, FAHA, Reel 9, Frame 29. See Edward Valenzuela to Fernando E. C. De Baca, November 25, 1974, and "Memorandum for Heads of Departments and Agencies," November 25, 1974, both in HU 2, White House Central Files, Box 2, GRFL; Fernando E. C. De Baca to Edward Valenzuela, May 1, 1975, FAHA, Reel 1, Frame 385; Fernando E. C. De Baca to Edward Valenzuela, September 4, 1975, FAHA, Reel 10, Frame 211; Memorandum, Fernando E. C. De Baca to Anne Kamstra, September 4, 1975, FAHA, Reel 6, Frame 194; Memorandum, Margaret Dress to Michael J. Farrell, November 20, 1975, FAHA,

Reel 6, Frame 154; Memorandum, Fernando E. C. De Baca to Warren Rustand, March 25, 1975, FAHA, Reel 9, Frame 598.

28. Forum of National Hispanic Organizations, "Record of Proceedings," May 23, 1975, Box 8, Thomas Aranda Files, GRFL.

29. Memorandum, Fernando De Baca to Ann Armstrong, n.d., FAHA, Reel 5, Frame 517.

30. Memorandum, Fernando De Baca to Ann Armstrong.

31. "Recommended Staffing Structure and Rationale," n.d., FAHA, Reel 5, Frame 516.

32. Aristide Zolberg, *A Nation by Design: Immigration Policy in the Fashioning of America* (New York: Russell Sage Foundation / Harvard University Press, 2006), 340–341.

33. "The Newest Americans: A Second 'Spanish Invasion,'" *U.S. News & World Report,* July 8, 1974, Box 26, Theodore C. Marrs Files, GRFL.

34. Chapman acknowledged that most were "not criminals" but rather "good people who are in an impoverished condition and are trying to find work . . . so they can support their families." Nonetheless, he blamed public assistance programs ("our welfare system") in part for allowing low-level jobs in the United States to go unfilled by natives. "How Millions of Illegal Aliens Sneak into U.S.," *U.S. News & World Report,* July 22, 1974, Box 26, Theodore C. Marrs Files, GRFL.

35. James Strong, "Stop 'Silent Invasion' of Aliens: U.S. Aide," *Chicago Tribune,* March 27, 1975.

36. Quoted in David G. Gutiérrez, *Walls and Mirrors: Mexican Americans, Mexican Immigrants, and the Politics of Ethnicity* (Berkeley: University of California Press, 1995), 188.

37. Bob Kuttner, "Saxbe Urges New Plan on Illegal Aliens," *Washington Post,* October 31, 1974; Ronald J. Ostrow, "Saxbe Calls Illegal Aliens a U.S. Crisis: Cites Job, Crime, Welfare," *Los Angeles Times,* October 31, 1974.

38. "Saxbe Calls Illegal Aliens a U.S. Crisis: Cites Job, Crime, Welfare," *Los Angeles Times,* October 31, 1974.

39. "Alien's Rights Are Said Violated," *San Antonio Express,* September 5, 1975, Box 4, Fernando E. C. De Baca Files; GRFL.

40. "*Immigration* (Illegal Alien Question)," February 12, 1975, Box 4, Fernando E. C. De Baca Files, GRFL.

41. Fernando E. C. De Baca to Daniel Archuleta, May 8, 1975, FAHA, Reel 4, Frame 112; David Vidal, "Hispanics Allege U.S. Insensitivity," *New York Times,* December 14, 1975.

42. "New Policies on Aliens Urged," *Independent* (Long Beach, CA), December 11, 1975; "Aliens Rob Economy," *Clovis News-Journal,* December 18, 1975. See also Fernando E. C. De Baca to Joseph E. Stanton, December 18, 1975, Box 4, Fernando E. C. De Baca Files, GRFL.

43. Chris P. Fox to Gerald Ford, January 14, 1975, Box 4, Fernando E. C. De Baca Files, GRFL.

44. L. F. Chapman Jr. to Theodore C. Marrs, February 18, 1975, Box 4, Thomas Aranda Files, GRFL.

45. Draft Memorandum, Fernando E. C. De Baca to Donald Rumsfeld, n.d., FAHA, Reel 5, Frame 513.

46. Lars Schoultz, *That Infernal Little Republic: The United States and the Cuban Revolution* (Chapel Hill: University of North Carolina Press, 2009), 262–263.

47. Phil Gailey, "Exiles Reconciled to Cuba Ties?," *Miami Herald,* September 3, 1975, FAHA, Reel 7, Frame 640.

48. Gailey, "Exiles Reconciled to Cuba Ties?"

49. Telegram, Humberto Quiñones to Gerald Ford, September 4, 1975, FAHA, Reel 10, Frame 538.

50. Mike Thompson to Gerald R. Ford, September 5, 1975, FAHA, Reel 10, Frames 558–559.

51. Alex Armendariz, "Hispanic Strategy Considerations," n.d., PFC, DeBolt Subject File, Box A13, GRFL.

52. "Ford: Cuba Intervention Delays Ties," *Miami Herald,* December 12, 1975.

53. Gerald R. Ford, "Remarks at a President Ford Committee Reception in Miami," February 14, 1976, The American Presidency Project (hereafter APP), https://www.presidency.ucsb.edu/documents/remarks-president-ford-committee-reception-miami.

54. José Manolo Casanova et al. to Gerald R. Ford, December 30, 1975, FAHA, Reel 10, Frames 1125–1126.

55. Fernando E. C. De Baca to Gerald Ford, March 1, 1976, FAHA, Reel 10, Frame 1224–1225.

56. "Draft" (dated "April 1976?"), Box 26, Theodore C. Marrs Files, GRFL.

57. Memorandum, Ted Marrs to Bill Baroody, April 7, 1976, PFC, Political Office: Norman Watts Subject File, Box C24, GRFL.

58. Memorandum, Ted Marrs to Doug Bennett, May 13, 1976, Box 1, Foster Chanock Files, GRFL.

59. Memorandum, Ted Marrs to Bill Baroody, April 7, 1976.

60. Samuel L. Popkin, *The Reasoning Voter: Communication and Persuasion in Presidential Campaigns,* 2nd ed. (Chicago: University of Chicago Press, 1994), 1; James M. Naughton, "Ford, in Texas, Requests Stronger Drug Penalties," *New York Times,* April 10, 1976.

61. Benjamin Fernandez to RNHA Executive Committee, January 27, 1976.

62. Albert C. Zapanta to Judy Harbaugh, August 27, 1975, PFC, Chairman's Office: Calloway Subject File, Box A4, GRFL.

63. Fernandez and the RNHA did also urge Ford to adopt a position of "no détente with Cuba." Benjamin Fernandez to RNHA Executive Committee, January 27, 1976.

64. Benjamin Fernandez to Robert Hartmann et al., October 6, 1975, Robert T. Hartmann Files, Box 28, GRFL.

65. Benjamin Fernandez to Orlando Hoed, May 21, 1976, PFC, DeBolt Subject File, Box A13, GRFL; as a sample, see Benjamin Fernandez to Gerald R.

Ford, May 5, 1976, Anderson Files, Box 21, GRFL; and Benjamin Fernandez to Douglas P. Bennett, March 25, 1976 and May 7, 1976, both in J. Stanley Pottinger Files, Box 140, GRFL.

66. George Volsky, "Inquiry Is Reopened on Cuban Nominee." *New York Times,* August 15, 1975, 36.

67. Lillian Giberga to Gerald R. Ford, August 18, 1975, Thomas Aranda Files, Box 3, GRFL. The widow of a major Cuban fundraiser, she eschewed the pan-Hispanic network of the RNHA for her late husband's seat on the party's anti-Communist National Republican Heritage Groups (Nationalities) Council, where Greeks, Poles, and Hungarians (rather than Mexicans) would be her political peers. National Republican Heritage Groups (Nationalities) Council, "Officers," FAHA, Reel 2, Frame 254–255.

68. Memorandum, Lillian M. Giberga to the President, April 6, 1976, PFC, DeBolt Subject File, Box A13, GRFL.

69. Memorandum, Lillian M. Giberga to the President, April 6, 1976.

70. Gerald R. Ford, "Remarks at the First Annual Banquet of the Republican National Hispanic Assembly," July 29, 1976, APP, http://www.presidency.ucsb.edu/ws/?pid=6247.

71. Benjamin Fernandez, "Remarks," in *Official Report of the Proceedings of the Thirty-First Republican National Convention* (n.p.: Republican National Committee, 1976), 33–34.

72. John McDermott, "Minorities Should Get into the Mainstream of GOP Action, 2 Miami Latin Leaders Say," *Miami Herald,* August 21, 1976.

73. Republican Party Platforms: "Republican Party Platform of 1976," August 18, 1976, APP, https://www.presidency.ucsb.edu/documents/republican-party-platform-1976; John McDermott, "Castro as Issue Urged by Reagan Supporters," *Miami Herald,* May 19, 1976; Kalman, *Right Star Rising,* 169–170.

74. Benjamin Fernandez to Stuart Spencer, August 25, 1976, Thomas Aranda Files, Box 5, GRFL.

75. Alex Armendariz, "Hispanic Strategy Considerations," n.d., PFC, DeBolt Subject File, Box A13, GRFL.

76. Memorandum, Charles Katsainos to Mrs. Peterson, n.d., PFC, Box F24, People for Ford Office: Ethnic Desk Files, GRFL. Special thanks to J. P. Schmidt at the Ford library for his graphological intervention in service of this footnote's accuracy.

77. Memorandum, Charles Katsainos to Mrs. Peterson, n.d.

78. Fernandez claimed not to have sent this letter. Benjamin Fernandez to Robert T. Hartmann, September 13, 1976, Robert T. Hartmann Files, Box 45, GRFL.

79. RW Apple Jr. "Georgian Wins South," *New York Times,* November 3, 1976.

80. Andrew Hernandez, *The Latino Vote in the 1976 Presidential Election: A Political Research Report,* 3rd ed. (San Antonio: Southwest Voter Registration Education Project, July 1980).

## 9. Securing Representation in a Multicultural Democracy

1. Jeffrey Bloodworth, *Losing the Center: The Decline of American Liberalism* (Lexington: University of Kentucky Press, 2013), 143; Bruce Miroff, *The Liberals' Moment: The McGovern Insurgency and the Identity Crisis of the Democratic Party* (Lawrence: University of Kansas Press, 2007), 262, 264.

2. Bill Robertson, "Leon Ralph Approves Robert Strauss as Party Head," *Los Angeles Sentinel,* December 21, 1972.

3. Herman Badillo to Robert Strauss, December 14, 1972; Memorandum, Richard Beserra to Latino Steering Committee, November 21, 1972, Box 15, Joe J. Bernal Papers, Benson Latin American Collection, University of Texas Libraries, University of Texas at Austin.

4. Memorandum, "Voting Rights Act Extension," Presidential Handwriting File, Box 24, Gerald R. Ford Presidential Library and Museum, Ann Arbor, Michigan.

5. The previous year, this organization was known as Raza Association of Spanish Surnamed Americans (RASSA). El Congreso, as the renamed group was known, was headed by Manuel D. Fierro. Its name paid homage to El Congreso del Pueblo de Habla Española (the National Congress of the Spanish-speaking People), the popular front–era organization headed by Fierro's mother, the labor and civil rights organizer Josefina Fierro de Bright. House Committee on Post Office and Civil Service, *Economic and Social Statistics for Spanish-Speaking Americans,* 94th Cong., 1st sess., 1975, 36.

6. G. Cristina Mora, *Making Hispanics: How Activists, Bureaucrats, and Media Constructed a New American* (Chicago: University of Chicago Press, 2014), 57.

7. Bill Boyarsky, "Latins in Fight over Renewal of Rights Act," *Los Angeles Times,* April 7, 1975.

8. Memorandum, U.S. Commission on Civil Rights, "Analysis of H.R. 3247 . . . ," in House Committee on the Judiciary, *Extension of the Voting Rights Act: Hearings on H.R. 939, H.R. 2148, H.R. 3247, and H.R. 3501,* Part II, 94th Cong., 1st sess., 1975, 938.

9. Senate Committee on the Judiciary, *Extension of the Voting Rights Act of 1965: Hearings on S. 407, S. 903, S. 1297, S. 1409, and S. 1443,* 94th Cong., 1st sess., 1975, 234.

10. House Committee, *Extension of the Voting Rights Act,* Part II, 942–943.

11. "Testimony of Vilma S. Martinez," in House Committee on the Judiciary, *Extension of the Voting Rights Act: Hearings on H.R. 939, H.R. 2148, H.R. 3247, and H.R. 3501,* Part I, 94th Cong., 1st sess., 1975, 853.

12. Emphasis added. On the Puerto Rican cases, see Lorrin Thomas and Aldo A. Lauria Santiago, *Rethinking the Struggle for Puerto Rican Rights* (New York: Routledge, 2019), 152; and Ariel Arnau, "Suing for Spanish: Puerto Ricans, Bilingual Voting, and Legal Activism in the 1970s" (PhD diss., CUNY, 2018); on MALDEF, see House Committee, *Extension of the Voting Rights Act,* Part I, 864.

13. House Committee, *Extension of the Voting Rights Act,* Part II, 948.
14. Report reproduced in House Committee, *Extension of the Voting Rights Act,* Part II, 1006.
15. Senate Committee, *Extension of the Voting Rights Act,* 709–710.
16. Senate Committee, *Extension of the Voting Rights Act,* 267.
17. House Committee, *Extension of the Voting Rights Act,* Part I, 906.
18. House Committee, *Extension of the Voting Rights Act,* Part I, 603.
19. According to one US Census report he cited, 93 percent of mainland Puerto Ricans studied identified themselves as "white," even though Puerto Rico's government refused to collect racial data on the island. House Committee, *Extension of the Voting Rights Act,* Part I, 770.
20. House Committee, *Extension of the Voting Rights Act,* Part I, 787.
21. House Committee, *Extension of the Voting Rights Act,* Part II, 965–967.
22. House Committee, *Extension of the Voting Rights Act,* Part I, 89, 92.
23. House Committee, *Extension of the Voting Rights Act,* Part I, 908–910.
24. Senate Committee, *Extension of the Voting Rights Act,* 846.
25. House Committee, *Extension of the Voting Rights Act,* Part I, 920.
26. Public Law 94-73—Aug. 6, 1975, http://www.gpo.gov/fdsys/pkg /STATUTE-89/pdf/STATUTE-89-Pg400.pdf; "Major Actions: H.R. 6219—94th Congress (1975–1976) https://www.congress.gov/bill/94th -congress/house-bill/6219/actions.
27. Cynthia Gorney, "Ford Hails Gain in Voting Rights," *Washington Post,* August 7, 1975.
28. Ronald J. Ostrow, "Bilingual-Voting Areas Identified," *Los Angeles Times,* August 28, 1975; John M. Goshko, "U.S. Orders Bilingual Voting Rules," *Washington Post,* August 28, 1975.
29. House Committee on Post Office and Civil Service, *Economic and Social Statistics for Spanish-Speaking Americans,* 93rd Cong., 2nd sess., 1974, 94.
30. "Furor over the '70 Census," *U.S. News & World Report,* July 27, 1970, in Box 3, Subject File of Director Manuel D. Plotkin, 1966–1979, RG 29, Records of the Bureau of the Census, National Archives, Washington, DC.
31. Vincent J. Burke, "1 of 6 Californians of Latin Heritage," *Los Angeles Times,* March 8, 1972.
32. Peter Kihss, "Those of Spanish Origin in City Are Put at 15% by 1970 Census," *New York Times,* July 9, 1972.
33. Kihss, "Those of Spanish Origin in City Are Put at 15% by 1970 Census."
34. "Census Bureau Sued; Chicano Groups Say Count Was Inaccurate," *Wall Street Journal,* April 30, 1971. In *Confederacion de la Raza Unida v. Brown,* the injunction was denied. U.S. Commission on Civil Rights, *Counting the Forgotten: The 1970 Census Count of Persons of Spanish Speaking Background in the United States* (Washington, DC: Government Printing Office, 1974), 17n52.
35. Frank Del Olmo, "City, County to be One-Fourth Latin by 1980, Study Predicts," *Los Angeles Times,* June 22, 1973.

36. Previously, a child under fourteen was assigned to the Spanish Origin category if the "head of household" identified himself as "Spanish Origin."

37. Jacob S. Siegel and Jeffrey Passel, "Coverage of the Hispanic Population of the United States in the 1970 Census: A Methodological Analysis," in *Current Population Reports,* special studies, P-23, no. 82 (Washington, DC: US Government Printing Office, 1979), 8.

38. Frank Del Olmo, "Spanish-Origin Census Figure Revised by U.S.," *Los Angeles Times,* January 15, 1974.

39. "New Count Finds More U.S. Spanish," *Washington Post,* January 16, 1974.

40. U.S. Commission on Civil Rights, *Counting the Forgotten,* vii.

41. U.S. Commission on Civil Rights, *Counting the Forgotten,* vi.

42. U.S. Commission on Civil Rights, *Counting the Forgotten,* iii, iv, 48, 11, 100.

43. Julius Shiskin and Marie D. Wann, "The Federal Statistical System of the United States," *Särtryck ur Statistisk tidskrift* (1972): 4, 271, in Box 4, Office of Information and Regulatory Affairs, RG 51, Records of the Office of Management and Budget, National Archives, College Park, Maryland (hereafter OMB).

44. "Reorganization of Federal Statistical Activities," July 19, 1971, Box 1, American Statistical Association Advisory Committee on Statistical Policy, Statistical Policy Division, 1963–1977, OMB.

45. Milo B. Sunderhauf to Margaret E. Martin et al., August 13, 1971, Box 23, Office of Statistical Policy Division Program Records, 1974–1980, OMB.

46. Milo B. Sunderhauf, "Draft," June 22, 1971, Box 23, Office of Statistical Policy Division Program Records, 1974–1980, OMB.

47. Milo B. Sunderhauf to Margaret E. Martin et al., August 13, 1971, Box 23, Office of Statistical Policy Division Program Records, 1974–1980, OMB.

48. David A. Hollinger, *Postethnic America: Beyond Multiculturalism* (New York: Basic Books, 1995), 29.

49. Citing the Bureau's success with "Spanish Origin," statistical manager Milo B. Sunderhauf recommended that a metric for observer identification and national identifiers (Mexican American, Chicano, Puerto Rican, Cuban) be included for self-identification. Sunderhauf to Martin et al., August 13, 1971, Box 23, Office of Statistical Policy Division Program Records, 1974–1980, OMB.

50. "Draft," May 18, 1973, Box 23, Office of Statistical Policy Division Program Records, 1974–1980, OMB.

51. For Badillo's remarks, see *Cong. Rec.,* 92nd Cong., 1st sess., 117: 41901; For Hubert Humphrey's remarks on this matter, see *Cong. Rec.,* 92nd Cong., 1st sess., 117: 41669–41670.

52. House Committee, *Economic and Social Statistics for Spanish-Speaking Americans,* 1974, iii–iv.

53. House Committee, *Economic and Social Statistics for Spanish-Speaking Americans,* 1974, 121–122, 131.

54. House Committee, *Economic and Social Statistics for Spanish-Speaking Americans,* 1974, 123, 174, 90, 81.

55. House Committee, *Economic and Social Statistics for Spanish-Speaking Americans*, 1974, 116, 118, 124, 113.

56. House Committee, *Economic and Social Statistics for Spanish-Speaking Americans*, 1974, 23.

57. House Committee, *Economic and Social Statistics for Spanish-Speaking Americans*, 1975, iv–vi.

58. House Committee, *Economic and Social Statistics for Spanish-Speaking Americans*, 1975, 36.

59. House Committee, *Economic and Social Statistics for Spanish-Speaking Americans*, 1975, 48–52.

60. Senate Committee on Post Office and Civil Service, *Improvement of Economic and Social Statistics Relating to Americans of Spanish Origin or Descent*, 94th Cong., 2nd sess., 1976, S. Rep. 94-896, 2–3.

61. Gerald R. Ford, "Statement on Signing Legislation Relating to the Publication of Spanish-American Economic and Social Statistics," June 16, 1976, The American Presidency Project, https://www.presidency.ucsb.edu /documents/statement-signing-legislation-relating-the-publication-spanish -american-economic-and.

62. Milo B. Sunderhauf to Joseph W. Duncan, July 25, 1974, Box 23, Office of Statistical Policy Division Program Records, 1974–1980, OMB.

63. American Indian or Alaskan native, Asian or Pacific Islander, black / Negro, not of Hispanic origin; Caucasian / white, not of Hispanic origin, and Hispanic were the choices.

64. "FICE Report . . . ," vol. 2, no. 1, May 1975, Box 23, Office of Statistical Policy Division Program Records, 1974–1980, OMB.

65. Like the FICE report, these draft regulations allowed two routes to acceptable data. The first was a two-part question in which respondents indicated their membership in one of four racial categories (American Indian or Alaskan native, Asian or Pacific Islander, black, and white), and then answered an "ethnicity" question, the possibilities being of "Hispanic origin" or "Not of Hispanic origin." The second route was simply to ensure all data could fit within "minimum acceptable catego-ries." These were American Indian or Alaskan native, Asian or Pacific Islander, black, not of Hispanic origin; white, not of Hispanic origin, and Hispanic. Exhibit F, Circular A-46 Revised, and Katherine K. Wallman and John Hodgdon, "Race and Ethnic Standards for Federal Statistics and Administrative Reporting," *Statistical Reporter*, July 1977, 450–454, in Box 23, Office of Statistical Policy Division Program Records, 1974–1980, OMB.

66. Wallman and Hodgdon, "Race and Ethnic Standards for Federal Statistics and Administrative Reporting," 450–454.

67. *Cong. Rec.*, 94th Cong., 1st sess., 1975, 34998; "Latins Announce Creation of National Hispanic Caucus Affiliated with Democratic Party," *New York Times*, November 3, 1975; Daryl Lembke, "Ethnic

Barriers Fall in Southwest Elections," *Los Angeles Times,* November 17, 1974.

68. *Cong. Rec.,* 94th Cong., 1st sess., 1975, 34998; "Latins Announce Creation of National Hispanic Caucus Affiliated with Democratic Party," *New York Times,* November 3, 1975; Emma E. Pullen, "Democrats Urged to Make Use of Latins," *Los Angeles Times,* November 1, 1975.

69. *Cong. Rec.,* 94th Cong., 1st sess., 1975, 34998; "Latins Announce Creation of National Hispanic Caucus Affiliated with Democratic Party"; "Democrats Urged to Make Use of Latins."

70. "Latins Announce Creation of National Hispanic Caucus Affiliated with Democratic Party"; National Association of Latino Democratic Officials (NALADO), "Testimony before the Democratic Platform Committee," May 18, 1976, Box 248, Jimmy Carter Papers–Pre-Presidential, 1976 Presidential Campaign, Ethnic-Urban Affairs—Vickie Mongiardo, Subject File, Jimmy Carter Presidential Library and Museum, Atlanta, Georgia.

## 10. Latino Liberalism in an Era of Limits

1. "National Issues Working Paper of the Latino Caucus," n.d., Box 19, Jimmy Carter Papers—Pre-Presidential, 1976 Presidential Campaign, Issues Office-Stuart Eizenstat, Jimmy Carter Presidential Library and Museum, Atlanta, Georgia (hereafter JCL)

2. NALADO, "Testimony before the Democratic Platform Committee," May 18, 1976, Box 248, Jimmy Carter Papers—Pre-Presidential, 1976 Presidential Campaign, Ethnic-Urban Affairs—Vickie Mongiardo, Subject File, JCL.

3. NALADO, "Testimony before the Democratic Platform Committee."

4. NALADO, "Testimony before the Democratic Platform Committee."

5. See Robert O. Self, *All in the Family: The Realignment of American Democracy since the 1960s* (New York: Hill and Wang, 2012), especially part IV.

6. Others included "A deep and abiding commitment to the DIGNITY OF THE INDIVIDUAL," "A strong SENSE OF COMMUNITY," and "A BILINGUAL-BICULTURAL worldview." NALADO, "Testimony before the Democratic Platform Committee."

7. NALADO, "Testimony before the Democratic Platform Committee."

8. NALADO, "Testimony before the Democratic Platform Committee."

9. Matthew Lassiter, *The Silent Majority: Suburban Politics in the Sunbelt South* (Princeton, NJ: Princeton University Press, 2006), 270–271.

10. Thomas Sugrue, "Carter's Urban Policy Crisis," in *The Carter Presidency: Policy Choices in the Post–New Deal Era,* ed. Gary M. Fink and Hugh Davis Graham (Lawrence: University of Kansas Press, 1998), 139–140.

11. William E. Leuchtenberg, "Jimmy Carter and the Post–New Deal Presidency," in Fink and Graham, *The Carter Presidency,* 7.

12. Laura Kalman, *Right Star Rising: A New Politics, 1974–1980* (New York: W. W. Norton, 2010), 148–151.

13. "National Issues Working Paper of the Latino Caucus," n.d., Box 19, Jimmy Carter Papers-Pre-Presidential, 1976 Presidential Campaign, Issues Office-Stuart Eizenstat, JCL.

14. Bruce Miroff, *The Liberals' Moment: The McGovern Insurgency and the Identity Crisis of the Democratic Party* (Lawrence: University of Kansas Press, 2007), 132–133.

15. "National Issues Working Paper of the Latino Caucus."

16. Minutes, Latino Caucus, July 14, 15, 1976, Box 19, Jimmy Carter Papers-Pre-Presidential, 1976 Presidential Campaign, Issues Office-Stuart Eizenstat, JCL; "National Issues Working Paper of the Latino Caucus." On Cuba, see Lars Schoultz, *That Infernal Little Cuban Republic: The United States and the Cuban Revolution* (Chapel Hill: University of North Carolina Press, 2009), chap. 9.

17. "1976 Democratic Party Platform," July 12, 1976, The American Presidency Project, https://www.presidency.ucsb.edu/documents/1976-democratic-party -platform.

18. Minutes, Latino Caucus, July 12, 1976, Box 19, Jimmy Carter Papers-Pre-Presidential, 1976 Presidential Campaign, Issues Office-Stuart Eizenstat, JCL; Aristide R. Zolberg, *A Nation by Design: Immigration Policy in the Fashioning of America* (Cambridge, MA: Harvard University Press, 2008), 342.

19. Minutes, Latino Caucus, July 14, 1976, Box 19, Jimmy Carter Papers-Pre-Presidential, 1976 Presidential Campaign, Issues Office-Stuart Eizenstat, JCL.

20. Charles Osolin, "Carter: Latins Have a Friend," *Miami News,* July 14, 1976; Sharon Watkins, "Carter Gives Pledge to Latino Caucus," Box 235, Jimmy Carter Papers-Pre-Presidential, 1976 Presidential Campaign, Hispanic Affairs-Rick Hernandez, Subject Files, JCL.

21. "1976 Democratic Party Platform," July 12, 1976.

22. "Jimmy Carter Speech," n.d., Box 313, Jimmy Carter Papers-Pre-Presidential, 1976 Presidential Campaign, Campaign Directors, Minority Affairs Coordinator—Raymone Bain, JCL.

23. "Jimmy Carter: Life before the Presidency," http://millercenter.org/president /biography/carter-life-before-the-presidency (accessed May 13, 2016).

24. H. Alexander Aguiar, "Para America—Por Que No Lo Mejor," Box 19, Jimmy Carter Papers-Pre-Presidential, 1976 Presidential Campaign, Issues Office-Stuart Eizenstat, JCL; Press Release, "Nixon/Ford Administration Neglect and Firm Hispanic Pro-Carter Alliance Established by Committee," September 30, 1976, Box 313, Jimmy Carter Papers-Pre-Presidential, 1976 Presidential Campaign, Campaign Directors, Minority Affairs Coordinator—Raymone Bain, JCL; Draft Minutes, Meeting of the Hispanic Advisory Board, September 29, 1976, Box 235, Jimmy Carter Papers-Pre-Presidential, 1976 Presidential Campaign, Hispanic Affairs-Rick Hernandez, Subject Files, JCL.

25. Alicia Chacón, interview by José Angel Gutiérrez, June 22, 1996, CMAS 2, Special Collections, University of Texas Libraries, http://library.uta.edu /tejanovoices/xml/CMAS_002.xml.
26. Memorandum, Maurice A. Ferré to Walter Mondale, August 13, 1976, Box 315, Jimmy Carter Papers-Pre-Presidential, 1976 Presidential Campaign, Campaign Directors, Minority Affairs Coordinator—Raymone Bain, JCL.
27. Herman Gallegos, "Hispanic Strategy Memorandum," n.d., Box 307, Jimmy Carter Papers-Pre-Presidential, 1976 Presidential Campaign, Director's Office—Urban Ethnic Affairs, Catholic Hispanics Coord.—Herman Gallegos, Subject File, JCL.
28. "Hispanics Create Action Coalition," *New York Times,* June 30, 1975.
29. "Cubans in Miami Stress Heritage," *New York Times,* June 15, 1975, in Box 235, Jimmy Carter Papers-Pre-Presidential, 1976 Presidential Campaign, Hispanic Affairs-Rick Hernandez, Subject Files, JCL.
30. *New York Times,* June 30, 1975.
31. Memorandum, Maurice A. Ferré to Hank Lacayo, September 29, 1976, Box 315, Jimmy Carter Papers-Pre-Presidential, 1976 Presidential Campaign, Campaign Directors, Minority Affairs Coordinator—Raymone Bain, JCL.
32. Memorandum, Maurice A. Ferré to Walter Mondale, August 13, 1976.
33. "Jimmy Carter Speech," n.d.
34. Nick Thimmesch, "Jimmy Carter's Flying Nun" (publication unidentified), September 2, 1976, Box 202, Jimmy Carter Papers-Pre-Presidential, 1976 Presidential Campaign, Political Director—Landon Butler, Subject File, JCL; Andrew Greeley, "Column for University Press Syndicate, for Release the Week of October 4," Box 202, Jimmy Carter Papers-Pre-Presidential, 1976 Presidential Campaign, Political Director—Landon Butler, Subject File, JCL.
35. "Strategy Memo to Landon Butler from Urban Affairs Desk," October 1, 1976; Memorandum, Terry Sundy and Vicki Mongiardo to State Coordinators and Regional Desks, September 20, 1976; both in Box 307, Jimmy Carter Papers-Pre-Presidential, 1976 Presidential Campaign, Director's Office— Urban Ethnic Affairs, Catholic Hispanics Coord.—Herman Gallegos, Subject File, JCL.
36. Handwriting on Letter, Mario J. Paredes to James Carter, September 3, 1976, Box 248, Jimmy Carter Papers-Pre-Presidential, 1976 Presidential Campaign, Ethnic-Urban Affairs—Vickie Mongiardo, Subject File, JCL; Memorandum, Urban Ethnic Desk to Jack Watson, October 28, 1976, Box 307, Jimmy Carter Papers-Pre-Presidential, 1976 Presidential Campaign, Director's Office—Urban Ethnic Affairs, Catholic Hispanics Coord.— Herman Gallegos, Subject File, JCL.
37. Memorandum, Franklin Delano López to Hamilton Jordan et al., September 17, 1976, Box 307, Jimmy Carter Papers-Pre-Presidential, 1976 Presidential Campaign, Director's Office—Urban Ethnic Affairs, Catholic Hispanics Coord.—Herman Gallegos, Subject File, JCL.

38. This is an earlier draft than the one of the same name cited above. "Draft Meeting of the Hispanic Advisory Board," September 29, 1976, Box 235, Jimmy Carter Papers-Pre-Presidential, 1976 Presidential Campaign, Hispanic Affairs—Rick Hernandez, Subject Files, JCL; James P. Sterba, "Growing Mexican-American Vote in Texas Seen as a Major Factor if Ford-Carter Race Is Close," *New York Times,* October 25, 1976.

39. Memorandum, Franklin D. López to Hamilton Jordan et al., November 5, 1976, Box 4, Hamilton Jordan Files, JCL.

40. Memorandum, Franklin D. López to Hamilton Jordan et al.

41. Andrew Hernandez, *The Latino Vote in the 1976 Presidential Election: A Political Research Report,* 3rd ed. (San Antonio: Southwest Voter Registration Education Project, July 1980); "1976 Presidential Election," http://www .270towin.com/1976_Election/ (accessed November 28, 2016).

42. Quoted in Julian Zelizer, *Arsenal of Democracy: The Politics of National Security from World War II to the War on Terrorism* (New York: Basic Books, 2010), 273.

43. David Vidal, "Puerto Rican Aide Sees Statehood Hurt by Ford," *New York Times,* January 5, 1977.

44. Ellen Hume, "Carter Agrees to Put Latins in More Top Posts," *Los Angeles Times,* March 2, 1977.

45. Vidal, "Puerto Rican Aide Sees Statehood Hurt by Ford."

46. Mailgram, Arnold Flores to Jimmy Carter, December 21, 1976, Box 4, Hamilton Jordan Files, JCL.

47. Alicia Chacón, interview by José Angel Gutiérrez, June 22, 1996, CMAS 2, Special Collections, University of Texas Libraries, http://library.uta.edu /tejanovoices/xml/CMAS_002.xml.

48. New Mexico senator Joseph Montoya had been defeated in his 1976 race against the former astronaut Harrison Schmitt. His loss brought an end to four decades of Hispano representation in the national legislature's upper chamber.

49. Though not great in number, they claimed to represent the focal "concentrations of Latino citizens" of the United States, including, of course, those who resided in Puerto Rico. David Vidal, "Congressional Caucus Is Formed to Speak for Hispanic Population," *New York Times,* December 9, 1976.

50. Vidal, "Puerto Rican Aide Sees Statehood Hurt by Ford."

51. Hume, "Carter Agrees to Put Latins in More Top Posts."

52. Mailgram, Gilbert Chávez to Jimmy Carter, March 17, 1977, Box 2, Joseph Aragon Files, JCL.

53. Flyer, "Hispanic-American 'Stand Up,'" n.d., Box 10, Joseph Aragon Files, JCL.

54. Letter, Concerned Hispanic Citizens of the United States to Tim Kraft, n.d. (stamped April 12, 1977), Box 6, Joseph Aragon Files, JCL.

55. "Washington Scene: The Hispanic March on Washington," *La Luz,* July 1977, 69.

56. Frank del Olmo, "Aragon—He's No in-House Chicano," *Los Angeles Times,* May 2, 1977; Paul R. Wieck, "Joe Aragon is Given Job of Checking CSA," probably *Albuquerque Journal,* n.d., Box 9, Joseph Aragon Files, JCL.

57. Transcript, "Interview with the President for Representatives of the Hispanic Media," May 12, 1978, Box 6, Joseph Aragon Files, JCL.

58. James T. Patterson, *Restless Giant: The United States from Watergate to Bush v. Gore* (New York: Oxford University Press, 2005), 113.

59. Edward Roybal to Patricia Roberts Harris, June 30, 1978, and Edward Roybal to Jimmy Carter, June 9, 1978, both in Box 6, Joseph Aragon Files, JCL; For the Harris interview, see Robert Scheer, "Blacks and Poverty: Roots Run Deep," *Los Angeles Times,* May 24, 1978.

60. Passing over the other top choice, who had the backing of Rep. Peter Rodino, whose immigration legislation was anathema to the Hispanic leadership, was lagniappe. Frank del Olmo, "Latin Will Be Named Immigration Director," *Los Angeles Times,* March 8, 1977.

61. Zolberg, *A Nation by Design,* 344.

62. Press Release, "Badillo Hails Appointment of Hispanic to Head Immigration Service," March 9, 1977, Box 9, Joseph Aragon Files, JCL.

63. "1976 Democratic Party Platform," July 12, 1976.

64. "Suggested Responses for Chicano Meeting," September 25, 1976, Box 307, Jimmy Carter Papers-Pre-Presidential, 1976 Presidential Campaign, Director's Office—Urban Ethnic Affairs, Catholic Hispanics Coord.— Herman Gallegos, Subject File, JCL.

65. Memorandum, Rick Hernandez to Governor Carter/Stu Eizenstat, October 17, 1976, Box 235, Jimmy Carter Papers-Pre-Presidential, 1976 Presidential Campaign, Hispanic Affairs-Rick Hernandez, Subject Files, JCL.

66. Press Release, US Department of Labor, "The Employment Situation: March 1977," April 1, 1977, https://fraser.stlouisfed.org/scribd/?toc_id =495873&filepath=/docs/releases/bls/bls_employnews_197703.pdf&start _page=10#scribd-open.

67. Kalman, *Right Star Rising,* 220.

68. Memorandum, Stu Eizenstat for Jimmy Carter, May 23, 1977, Box 12, Joseph Aragon Files, JCL.

69. White House staff believed that Carter informed his Cabinet in early March 1977 that he wanted an administration proposal by April 1. Memorandum, "Timing of Undocumented Worker Proposal," March 8, 1977, Box 12, Joseph Aragon Files, JCL.

70. Memorandum, Annie E. Gutiérrez to Stu Eizenstat, March 25, 1977, Box 12, Joseph Aragon Files, JCL.

71. John Hall and Marianne Means, "Alien Crackdown: Tough Policy Promised," *San Antonio Light,* March 27, 1977, Box 12, Joseph Aragon Files, JCL.

72. *Cong. Rec.,* 93rd Cong., 2nd sess., 1974, 120: 1525–1527; *Cong. Rec.,* 93rd Cong., 2nd sess., 1974, 120: 24814.

73. *Cong. Rec.,* 95th Cong., 1st sess., 1977, 123: H1643–1644, in Box 12, Joseph Aragon Files, JCL.

74. Herman Badillo to Ray Marshall, April 15, 1977, Box 12, Joseph Aragon Files, JCL.

75. Herman Badillo and Edward Roybal to Jimmy Carter, May 12, 1977, Box 12, Joseph Aragon Files, JCL.

76. United States Catholic Conference, "Statement on 'Illegal Alien' Legislation," Thomas Aranda Files, Box 3, Gerald R. Ford Presidential Library and Museum, Ann Arbor, Michigan (hereafter GRFL).

77. Editorial, "Let's Call a Truce in War on Aliens," *San Antonio Light,* November 16, 1975, Thomas Aranda Files, Box 4, GRFL.

78. Final Draft, "Position Paper on President Carter's Immigration Proposal," January 31, 1978, Box 6, Joseph Aragon Files, JCL.

79. Hispanic Ad Hoc Coalition on Immigration, "Response by Hispanics to Changes in Immigration Law Proposed by President Jimmy Carter," January 10, 1978, Box 6, Joseph Aragon Files, JCL.

80. Christopher Bell, *East Harlem Remembered: Oral Histories of Community and Diversity* (Jefferson, NC: McFarland & Company, 2013), 147.

81. Herman Badillo to Ray Marshall, April 15, 1977, Box 12, Joseph Aragon Files, JCL.

82. Herman Badillo and Edward Roybal to Jimmy Carter, May 12, 1977, Box 12, Joseph Aragon Files, JCL.

83. Mexican American Legal Defense and Educational Fund, "Statement of Position Regarding the Administration's Undocumented Alien Legislative Proposal," September 26, 1977, Box 12, Joseph Aragon Files, JCL.

84. Edward Valenzuela, "Hispanic Immigrants," May 18, 1978, Box 6, Joseph Aragon Files, JCL.

85. Zolberg, *A Nation by Design,* 344.

86. Memorandum, Henry B. González, May 24, 1978, Box 6, Joseph Aragon Files, JCL.

87. Edward Roybal, "Speech Given at Chicano Solidarity Conference," March 11, 1978, Box 6, Joseph Aragon Files, JCL.

88. Kenneth Reich, "Hispanics Plan Voter Registration Drive," *Los Angeles Times,* August 5, 1979.

89. Patterson, *Restless Giant,* 112–114.

90. Adam Clymer, "Kennedy Assails Carter on Budget at Midterm Meeting of Democrats," *New York Times,* December 10, 1978; Warren Weaver Jr., "Kennedy Presses for Health Plan," *New York Times,* December 10, 1978.

91. Andrew E. Busch, *Reagan's Victory: The Presidential Election of 1980 and the Rise of the Right* (Lawrence: University of Kansas Press, 2005), 35, 41; George Gallup reported in early August 1979 that Democrats preferred the Massachusetts senator to Carter by a two-to-one margin. George Gallup, "Sen. Kennedy Leads Carter by 2–1 Ratio," *Washington Post,* August 3, 1979;

Memorandum, Tim Kraft and Arnie Miller to Hamilton Jordan, July 20, 1979, Box 47, Hamilton Jordan Files, JCL.

92. Memorandum, Tim Kraft to Hamilton Jordan, July 30, 1979, Box 47, Hamilton Jordan Files, JCL.

93. Memorandum, Tim Kraft to Hamilton Jordan.

94. In addition, Kraft reported, "five of our best Hispanic appointments have left, or are soon leaving government service," but that "no Hispanics have been selected to replace them." Memorandum, Tim Kraft and Arnie Miller to Hamilton Jordan, July 20, 1979, Box 47, Hamilton Jordan Files, JCL; Associated Press, "INS Head Considers Resigning," *Washington Post,* July 13, 1979; Bill Peterson and Christopher Dickey, "Immigration Chief Submits Resignation," *Washington Post,* August 11, 1979; Memorandum, Tim Kraft to Hamilton Jordan.

95. Joseph W. Aragon, interview by David Alsobrook, January 19, 1979, http://www.jimmycarterlibrary.gov/library/exitInt/Aragon.pdf.

96. Jimmy Carter, "Congressional Hispanic Caucus Remarks at the Annual Dinner," September 13, 1979, The American Presidency Project, https://www.presidency.ucsb.edu/documents/congressional-hispanic-caucus-re marks-the-annual-dinner-0.

97. Biographical sketch, "Ambassador Esteban Edward Torres," in *Latino Civil Rights during the Carter Administration, Part I, Records of the White House Office of Hispanic Affairs, 1979–1981, Series A: Esteban Torres Files,* Reel 17, ed. Christian James and Daniel Lewis (Bethesda, MD: LexisNexis, 2007); John R. Chávez, *Eastside Landmark: A History of the East Los Angeles Community Union, 1968–1993* (Stanford, CA: Stanford University Press, 1998), 37–38.

98. Finding Aid, "Records of the Office of Hispanic Affairs: A Guide to Its Records at the JCL," http://www.jimmycarterlibrary.gov/library/find ingaids/Office_of_Hispanic_Affairs.pdf (accessed September 7, 2015); and "Scope and Content Note" in Mark A. Zimmerman, "Latino Civil Rights during the Carter Administration, Part I: Records of the White House Office of Hispanic Affairs, 1979–1981," Series B, https://media2 .proquest.com/documents/102861.pdf.

99. Ralph Winningham, "New Carter Aide Predicts Hispanics' Era of Challenge," n.d., in James and Lewis, *Latino Civil Rights during the Carter Administration, Part I, Series A,* Reel 17.

100. Memorandum, Tim Kraft to Hamilton Jordan.

101. Bill Stall, "Hufstedler Selection Wins Praise; Hispanics Angered," *Los Angeles Times,* October 31, 1979.

102. David S. Broder and Bill Peterson, "Kennedy Warns of a Party Split by Arms Outlays," *Washington Post,* December 10, 1978.

103. *Hispanic American Democrats* 1, no. 1 (May 1979), Box 8, Mexican American Democrats of Texas Records, 1962–1987, University of Texas at San Antonio Libraries Special Collections (hereafter MADT).

104. "Black, Hispanic Dems Unite to 'Eye' Carter," *Afro-American*, December 23, 1978.

105. Neal R. Peirce and Jerry Hagstrom, "The Hispanic Community—A Growing Force to be Reckoned With," *National Journal*, April 7, 1979, 550.

106. Lizárraga had also been named to Carter's National Commission on Neighborhoods. Moreover, as historian John Chávez notes, "increased contacts in Washington and nationwide during the Carter administration made TE-LACU . . . easily the major" Mexican-American community development corporation in the country. As the election grew closer, grants from the Economic Development Administration further allowed Lizárraga to expand his organizational endeavors. Federal aid allowed him to extend his political influence, and by the time HAD was just a few months old, Lizárraga had gained leadership of southern California's Democratic Party organization. Chávez, *Eastside Landmark*, 139–143, 184, 186.

107. Hispanic American Democrats, "Proposal to the Democratic National Committee," April 1979, Box 8, MADT.

108. Hector C. Carreño to Raul Tapia, October 16, 1979, in James and Lewis, *Latino Civil Rights during the Carter Administration, Part I, Series A*, Reel 17.

109. Busch, *Reagan's Victory*, 57.

110. "Bylaws," *Hispanic American Democrats* 1, no. 1 (May 1979), Box 8, MADT.

111. "HAD National Founding Convention," *Hispanic American Democrats* 1, no. 2 (September 1979), Box 8, MADT; Joanne Omang, "Carter May Rue Release of Puerto Rican Nationalists," *Washington Post*, September 17, 1979.

112. "HAD National Founding Convention."

113. "HAD National Founding Convention."

114. David Lizárraga to Jimmy Carter, October 1, 1979, in James and Lewis, *Latino Civil Rights during the Carter Administration, Part I, Series A*, Reel 15; see frames 525–628.

115. Quoted in Kenneth T. Walsh, "Hispanic Dem Goal: Speak as One Voice," *Denver Post*, n.d., Box 78, Hamilton Jordan Files, JCL.

116. Roger Langley, "Hispanics Seek Solid Voter Clout," *The News World*, April 3, 1979, Box 8, MADT; Vernon Jarrett, "Carter Wins One and Loses One," *Chicago Tribune*, November 7, 1979; Walsh, "Hispanic Dem Goal."

117. Joe Seldner, "Hispanic Activists Map Strategy for Political Alliance," *Washington Post*, December 10, 1979.

118. Seldner, "Hispanic Activists Map Strategy for Political Alliance"; Walsh, "Hispanic Dem Goal"; Langley, "Hispanics Seek Solid Voter Clout."

119. Hispanic American Democrats, "1980 Hispanic National Platform," Box 8, MADT.

120. Hispanic American Democrats, "1980 Hispanic National Platform."

121. Hispanic American Democrats, "1980 Hispanic National Platform."

122. The platform was some two-dozen printed pages. In comparison, the 1971 Unidos conference passed a set of resolutions that could be printed on a single page. Hispanic American Democrats, "1980 Hispanic National Platform"; Langley, "Hispanics Seek Solid Voter Clout."

123. Langley, "Hispanics Seek Solid Voter Clout."

124. Walsh, "Hispanic Dem Goal"; Seldner, "Hispanic Activists Map Strategy for Political Alliance."

125. Esteban Torres also claimed a speaking slot in his capacity as head of the Office of Hispanic Affairs, in effect giving Carter supporters two chances to make the administration case. Kenneth T. Walsh and Joseph Seldner, "Carter Holding Edge over Kennedy," *Denver Post*, n.d., Box 78, Hamilton Jordan Files, JCL; Frank del Olmo, "Latino Democrats Attempt to Unite," *Los Angeles Times*, December 9, 1979; Frank del Olmo, "Covina Man to Head Hispanic Political Unit," *Los Angeles Times*, December 10, 1979.

126. Carter/Mondale Presidential Committee, Inc., "Members of the National Hispanic Campaign Committee for Carter-Mondale," Box 4, MADT.

127. Ari L. Goldman, "Cuomo Files Signatures for Carter," *New York Times*, February 7, 1980.

128. Frank Lynn, "Kennedy, in South Bronx, Says Carter Broke Aid Vow," *New York Times*, March 23, 1980; Harry Bernstein, "Chavez Shifts Union's Support from Gov. Brown to Kennedy," *Los Angeles Times*, April 7, 1980; "Surprise Kennedy Win in Arizona Gives Psychological Lift," *Washington Post*, April 14, 1980; Adam Clymer, "Reagan and Carter Win Texas Vote, but Display Weaknesses," *New York Times*, May 5, 1980; Bill Stall, "Kennedy Continues Drive for Minority Group Support," *Los Angeles Times*, May 25, 1980; Robert Shogan, "Carter Goes over the Top but Kennedy Will Press On," *Los Angeles Times*, June 4, 1980; Robert Shogan, "The First Hurdle—Kennedy," *Los Angeles Times*, June 5, 1980.

129. Elaine Kamarck, "A History of 'Super-Delegates' in the Democratic Party," Harvard Kennedy School, Belfer Center for Science and International Affairs, February 14, 2008, https://www.belfercenter.org/publication/history-super-delegates-democratic-party; Laurie Johnson, "Other Conventions Press Their Causes," *New York Times*, August 11, 1980; Ronald Smothers, "Minority Delegates Debate the Use of Their Newly Increased Influence," *New York Times*, August 12, 1980.

## 11. The "New Hispanic Conservatives"

1. Benjamin Fernandez to Robert T. Hartmann, November 16, 1976, Robert T. Hartmann Files, Box 45, Gerald R. Ford Presidential Library and Museum, Ann Arbor, Michigan.

2. Ford's vice presidential running mate, Kansas senator Robert Dole, told Republican governors that his party "need[ed] a Republican version of affirmative action at the grass-roots political level. We need the women, the young, the Hispanics, the ethnics, the Indians," among others. Lou Cannon, "Republican Governors, Optimistic, Are Urged to Woo Minority Votes," *Washington Post*, December 1, 1976.

3. Joel Kotkin, "Ambitions of Hispanic Aide Irk Some in GOP," *Washington Post*, July 12, 1978.

4. "Interview no. 358," Institute of Oral History, University of Texas at El Paso.

5. T. R. Reid, "Hispanic Consultant Seeks Nomination for President in GOP," *Washington Post,* November 30, 1978.

6. Kotkin, "Ambitions of Hispanic Aide Irk Some in GOP."

7. Vivien Hao, "L.A. Hispanic Businessman in Presidential Race," *Los Angeles Times,* November 30, 1978.

8. Warren Weaver Jr., "Mexican Immigrants' Son Enters G.O.P. 1980 Race," *New York Times,* November 30, 1978.

9. "Interview no. 358."

10. Hao, "L.A. Hispanic Businessman in Presidential Race."

11. "Mexican-American Area C of C Forming," *Los Angeles Times,* December 9, 1965.

12. Ben Fernandez, "'I Dined with the President,'" *Los Angeles Times,* May 17, 1969.

13. "¿Qué Pasa?," *Nuestro,* June 1978.

14. Bob Baker, "He Has a Dream—to Be First Latin U.S. President," *Los Angeles Times,* April 23, 1979.

15. Jon Margolis, "Nation: Mexican-American to Seek Presidency," *Chicago Tribune,* November 30, 1978.

16. F. Richard Ciccone, "GOP Upstart Aiming for American Dream," *Chicago Tribune,* October 3, 1979.

17. "Interview no. 358."

18. Baker, "He Has a Dream."

19. "Mexican Immigrants' Son Enters G.O.P. 1980 Race," *New York Times,* November 30, 1978.

20. Baker, "He Has a Dream."

21. "Interview no. 358."

22. Weaver, "Mexican Immigrants' Son Enters G.O.P. 1980 Race."

23. "Interview no. 358."

24. "Benjamin Fernandez," October 3, 1979, Series XXII, Box 886, Ronald Reagan 1980 Campaign Papers, Ronald Reagan Presidential Library and Museum, Simi Valley, California (hereafter RRL).

25. Baker, "He Has a Dream."

26. "Interview no. 358."

27. Ciccone, "GOP Upstart Aiming for American Dream."

28. "Interview no. 358."

29. Hao, "L.A. Hispanic Businessman in Presidential Race."

30. "Interview no. 358."

31. "I Am Presidential Timber," *Nuestro,* March, 1980, 36–38.

32. "Interview no. 358."

33. Margolis, "Nation."

34. George F. Will, "Benjamin Fernandez: A Natural Republican," *Washington Post,* August 23, 1979; "Benjamin Fernandez."

35. "Interview no. 358."

36. *Nuestro,* March 1980, 38; "Interview no. 358"; Ciccone, "GOP Upstart Aiming for American Dream."

37. Weaver, "Mexican Immigrants' Son Enters G.O.P. 1980 Race"; Ciccone, "GOP Upstart Aiming for American Dream."

38. Ciccone, "GOP Upstart Aiming for American Dream."

39. "Benjamin Fernandez," October 3, 1979, Series XXII, Box 886, Ronald Reagan 1980 Campaign Papers, RRL.

40. Svetlana, "Svetlana on Benjamin Fernandez, the Dark Horse," *Washington Post,* August 19, 1979.

41. *Nuestro,* March 1980, 38.

42. Ciccone, "GOP Upstart Aiming for American Dream."

43. "Benjamin Fernandez," October 3, 1979, Series XXII, Box 886, Ronald Reagan 1980 Campaign Papers, RRL.

44. Mark Stein, "Fernandez Refuses to Drop Quest for the Presidency," *Los Angeles Times,* March 6, 1980.

45. "Hispano, republicano, y católico: Benjamin Fernandez: 'Yo Sere Presidente de los Estados Unidos,'" *ABC* (Spain), October 5, 1979.

46. *Nuestro,* March 1980, 36.

47. Stein, "Fernandez Refuses to Drop Quest for the Presidency."

48. "Bush Beats Baker 3–2 in Puerto Rican Primary," *Chicago Tribune,* February 18, 1980.

49. William J. Eaton, "Baker, Bush Have Edge in 1st Primary," *Los Angeles Times,* February 13, 1980; Ward Sinclair, "Bush and Baker Vie for Quick 14 Votes in the P.R. Primary," *Washington Post,* February 17, 1980.

50. *Chicago Tribune,* February 18, 1980.

51. A *Los Angeles Times* reporter cheekily suggested the irony of Fernandez's denunciations with the following passage: "Fernandez, who was principal fund-raiser for Richard Nixon in 1972, called the Puerto Rican primary, which was held without the privacy of voting booths, 'the dirtiest, slimmest, worst campaign I've ever seen.'" Stein, "Fernandez Refuses to Drop Quest for the Presidency."

52. "Fernandez Seeks Recount," *Washington Post,* February 19, 1980.

53. He did say that about 75 percent of fund-raising had come from Hispanics. *Los Angeles Times,* March 6, 1980.

54. Frank del Olmo, "Fernandez' Last Quixotic Gesture," *Los Angeles Times,* June 3, 1980; Stein, "Fernandez Refuses to Drop Quest for the Presidency."

55. Interview with Fernando Oaxaca by Oscar J. Martinez, 1975, "Interview no. 196," Institute of Oral History, University of Texas at El Paso; Interview with Fernando Oaxaca by Oscar J. Martinez, 1976, "Interview no. 416," Institute of Oral History, University of Texas at El Paso.

56. Fernando Oaxaca, "The Elements of Strategy . . . Attracting the Hispanic Vote—1980," May 1980, Series X Box 302, Ronald Reagan 1980 Campaign Papers, RRL.

57. Oaxaca, "The Elements of Strategy."

58. Benjamin Fernandez, "Remarks," in *Official Report of the Proceedings of the Thirty-First Republican National Convention* (n.p.: Republican National Committee, 1976), 34; Benjamin Fernandez, "The Hispanic Community," in *Official Report of the Proceedings of the Thirty-Second Republican National Convention,*" (n.p.: Republican National Committee, 1980), 74–76.

59. Barry Bearak, "Silly and Serious: Florida Delegates Soak up the Glory," *Miami Herald,* July 15, 1980; Barry Bearak, "Cubans Like Reagan's Anti-Castro Stand," *Miami Herald,* July 17, 1980.

60. Fernando Oaxaca, "The Republican Campaign—1980: Hispanics Can Make a Difference!!!!," July 1980, Series V, Box 222, Ronald Reagan 1980 Campaign Papers, RRL.

61. Oaxaca, "The Republican Campaign—1980."

62. Fernando Oaxaca to Max Hugel, July 22, 1980, Series X, Box 310, Ronald Reagan 1980 Campaign Papers, RRL; Memorandum, Fernando Oaxaca to William Casey, July 27, 1980, Series V, Box 222, Ronald Reagan 1980 Campaign Papers, RRL.

63. Memorandum, Fernando Oaxaca to William Casey.

64. Memorandum, Max Hugel to Bill Timmons, "Hispanics," August 1, 1980, Series X, Box 310, Ronald Reagan 1980 Campaign Papers, RRL.

65. Letter, Donald E. Lukens to Stan Anderson, July 23, 1980; and "Alex Armendariz—Political Experience," both in Series VIII, Box 256, Ronald Reagan 1980 Campaign Papers, RRL.

66. Alex Armendariz, "Hispanic Strategy for Reagan," August 6, 1980, Series X, Box 302, Ronald Reagan 1980 Campaign Papers, RRL.

67. Armendariz, "Hispanic Strategy for Reagan."

68. On at least one occasion, he forwarded his supervisors a *Newsweek* article and instructed them to "notice the side-by-side paragraphs describing Carter's attention to Blacks and Reagan's thrust to win over Hispanics." Memorandum, Alex Armendariz to Max Hugel, September 3, 1980, Series X, Box 310, Ronald Reagan 1980 Campaign Papers, RRL.

69. Senate Select Committee on Presidential Campaign Activities, *Presidential Campaign Activities of 1972: Executive Session Hearings on Watergate and Related Activities, Book 19,* 8622.

70. Armendariz, "Hispanic Strategy for Reagan."

71. Puerto Ricans, the quintessentially urban poor Latinos of the Northeast, were said to "differ from other Hispanics in placing greater reliance on good luck, the help of God, and the government to bring about change in their family situations." Implicitly, then, Puerto Rican religiosity was not to be taken as a sign of potential conservatism but rather another manifestation of a lack of "reliance upon the self" that Mexican Americans and Cubans supposedly exhibited with regularity. Memorandum, Vince Breglio to Richard Wirthlin, et al., August 28, 1980, Series X, Box 310, Ronald Reagan 1980 Campaign Papers, RRL; Memorandum, Alex Armendariz to Andy Carter, n.d., Box 310, Ronald Reagan 1980 Campaign Papers, RRL.

72. See again Robert O. Self, *All in the Family: The Realignment of American Democracy since the 1960s* (New York: Hill and Wang, 2012), especially part IV.

73. Memorandum, Alex Armendariz to Martin Anderson, September 15, 1980, Series X, Box 310, Ronald Reagan 1980 Campaign Papers, RRL; Memorandum, Vince Breglio to Richard Wirthlin, et al.

74. Memorandum, Alex Armendariz to Bob Garrick, September 16, 1980, Series X, Box 310, Ronald Reagan 1980 Campaign Papers, RRL.

75. Memorandum, Vince Breglio to Richard Wirthlin, et al.

76. Memorandum, Vince Breglio to Richard Wirthlin, et al.

77. Pamphlet, "The time is now," n.d., Series X, Box 305, Ronald Reagan 1980 Campaign Papers, RRL.

78. Yardang Consultant Services, "Opportunity," n.d., "Inflation," n.d., and "Solutions," n.d., in Series X, Box 305, Ronald Reagan 1980 Campaign Papers, RRL.

79. Alex Armendariz, "Hispanic Strategy for Reagan," August 6, 1980, Series X, Box 302, Ronald Reagan 1980 Campaign Papers, RRL.

80. Memorandum, Eleanor Callahan to V. Orr, et al., September 16, 1980, Series X, Box 310, Ronald Reagan 1980 Campaign Papers, RRL.

81. Alberto R. Cardenas and Carlos Salman to Max Hugel, August 11, 1980, Series X, Box 332, Ronald Reagan 1980 Campaign Papers, RRL.

82. Al Cardenas to Max Hugel, September 9, 1980, Series X, Box 310, Ronald Reagan 1980 Campaign Papers, RRL.

83. Memorandum, Mario J. Elgarresta to Alex Armendariz, September 29, 1980, Series X, Box 332, Ronald Reagan 1980 Campaign Papers, RRL.

84. Memorandum, Juan Woodrofe to Al Cardenas, et al., September 30, 1980, Series X, Box 310, Ronald Reagan 1980 Campaign Papers, RRL.

85. Memorandum, Juan Woodrofe to Al Cardenas, et al.

86. Memorandum, Alex Armendariz to Fred Malek, October 3, 1972, Box 36, Committee for the Re-Election of the President (CRP): Frederic Malek Papers, Series III, Richard Nixon Presidential Library and Museum, Yorba Linda, California.

87. Memorandum, Vince Breglio to Richard Wirthlin, et al.

88. Comite Reagan Bush, "Economy," ca. October 2, 1980; and "Cuba," n.d., both in Series X, Box 332, Ronald Reagan 1980 Campaign Papers, RRL.

89. "GOP Leader Predicts Victory by Hispanics," *Winter Haven News Chief,* December 26, 1980, Series X, Box 332, Ronald Reagan 1980 Campaign Papers, RRL.

90. L. G. "Brownie" Trevino to Ronald Reagan, August 25, 1980, Series X, Box 332, Ronald Reagan 1980 Campaign Papers, RRL.

91. "Raza Declaration," Series X, Box 332, Ronald Reagan 1980 Campaign Papers, RRL.

92. "Raza Declaration," Series X, Box 332.

93. Olivia Carmichael Solis, "Reagan Touts Alien Plan in Stop," *Valley Morning Star,* September 17, 1980, Series X, Box 335, Ronald Reagan 1980 Cam-

paign Papers, RRL; News Release, Reagan Bush Committee, "Address by the Honorable Ronald Reagan . . . ," September 16, 1980, Series X, Box 336, Ronald Reagan 1980 Campaign Papers, RRL.

94. Bob Garrick, "RR Address, Harlingen, TX 9/16/80 Draft 1," Series X, Box 310, Ronald Reagan 1980 Campaign Papers, RRL.

95. News Release, Reagan Bush Committee, "Address by the Honorable Ronald Reagan . . . ," September 16, 1980, Series X, Box 336, Ronald Reagan 1980 Campaign Papers, RRL.

96. Solis, "Reagan Touts Alien Plan in Stop."

97. Jon Margolis, "Reagan Breaks GOP Tradition, Woos Chicanos," *Chicago Tribune,* September 17, 1980.

98. Mike Qualls, "Reagan: Yes on Bilingual Education," *Los Angeles Herald Examiner,* September 27, 1980, Series X, Box 332, Ronald Reagan 1980 Campaign Papers, RRL.

99. Memorandum, Elizabeth Dole to Bill Timmons, October 20, 1980, Series X, Box 332, Ronald Reagan 1980 Campaign Papers, RRL.

100. Telegram, Nelson Malave to Jimmy Carter, September 15, 1980, Series X, Box 333, Ronald Reagan 1980 Campaign Papers, RRL.

101. Memorandum, Elizabeth Dole to Bill Timmons. .

102. Press Release, "U.S. Chamber of Commerce Endorses Reagan–Bush Ticket," October 29, 1980, Series X, Box 332, Ronald Reagan 1980 Campaign Papers, RRL.

103. Choco González Meza and Pamela Eoff, eds., *The Latino Vote in the 1980 Presidential Election* (San Antonio: Southwest Voter Registration Education Project, 1981), 12, 29–33, 39, 35.

104. Adam Clymer, "Displeasure with Carter Turned Many to Reagan," *New York Times,* November 9, 1980; Elizabeth Dole, "Meeting with: Hispanic Community," February 12, 1981; and Fernando Oaxaca to James Baker, February 20, 1981 (original is misdated as 1980), both in Series XII, Box 116, Elizabeth Dole Files, Ronald Reagan Presidential Library (hereafter EDF), RRL.

105. Sean Wilentz, *The Age of Reagan: A History, 1974–2008* (New York: Harper-Collins, 2008), 141; Henry A. J. Ramos, *American GI Forum: In Pursuit of the Dream, 1948–1983* (Houston: Arte Público Press, 1998), 24.

106. See Hugh Davis Graham, "Civil Rights Policy in the Carter Presidency," in *The Carter Presidency: Policy Choices in the Post-New Deal Era,* ed. Gary M. Fink and Hugh Davis Graham (Lawrence: University Press of Kansas, 1998), 213–216.

107. Marjorie Hunter, "U.S. Education Chief Bars Bilingual Plan for Public Schools," *New York Times,* February 3, 1981.

108. John Patrick Diggins, *Ronald Reagan: Fate, Freedom, and the Making of History* (New York: W. W. Norton and Company, 2007), 313; Robert Pear, "Reagan Backs Voting Rights Act but Wants to Ease Requirements," *New York Times,* November 7, 1981; Don Shannon, "Reagan Administration a

Threat to Hispanic Civil Rights, Executive of Ethnic Defense Fund Says," *Los Angeles Times,* February 12, 1981.

109. Dole, "Meeting with: Hispanic Community."

110. Memorandum, Diana Lozano to Elizabeth Dole and Red Cavaney, March 31, 1981, Series I, Box 28, EDF, RRL.

111. Fernando Oaxaca to James Baker.

112. Memorandum, Diana Lozano to Elizabeth Dole and Red Cavaney, March 31, 1981, Series I, Box 28, EDF, RRL.

113. Memorandum, Elizabeth Dole to David Stockman, December 29, 1981, Series I, Box 28, EDF, RRL.

114. Memorandum, Diana Lozano to Elizabeth H. Dole, March 27, 1981, Series I, Box 28, EDF, RRL.

115. Memorandum, Diana Lozano to Elizabeth H. Dole and Red Cavaney; Wilentz, *The Age of Reagan,* 141, 144.

116. It even sought to espouse a "Hispanic" position on the administration's clean air policy. Fernando E. C. De Baca to Elizabeth Dole, November 5, 1981; and Fernando E. C. De Baca to Fellow Concerned Citizen, n.d., both in Series I, Box 28, EDF, RRL.

117. Fernando E. C. De Baca to Fellow Concerned Citizen.

118. Fernando E. C. De Baca, "An Open Letter to President Reagan," n.d., Series I, Box 29, EDF, RRL.

119. Memorandum, Red Cavaney to James A. Baker III, April 15, 1981; and United States Hispanic Chamber of Commerce, "Statement of Endorsement," April 16, 1981, both in Series XII, Box 118, EDF, RRL.

120. United States Hispanic Chamber of Commerce, "Position Paper on President Reagan's Economic Recovery Plan," n.d., Series XII, Box 118, EDF, RRL.

121. United States Hispanic Chamber of Commerce, "Statement of Endorsement," April 16, 1981, both in Series XII, Box 118, EDF, RRL.

122. Memorandum, Elizabeth Dole to Edwin Meese III, July 29, 1981, Series I, Box 28, EDF, RRL.

123. Wilentz, *The Age of Reagan,* 142. While Dole's memorandum dates the poll as June 1980, its references to Hispanic perceptions of Reagan's job performance strongly suggest the poll came from June 1981. Memorandum, Elizabeth Dole to Edwin Meese III, James A. Baker III, and Michael Deaver, May 17, 1982, Series I, Box 28, EDF, RRL.

124. "Edwin Meese Speech Themes before the U.S. Hispanic Chamber of Commerce," Series I, Box 28, EDF, RRL.

125. *"We Finally Made It and It Is Only the Beginning,"* read the local Republican Party's flyer touting this turning point in the political history of Miami's "Hispanic" population. Memorandum, Diana Lozano to Elizabeth Dole, October 2, 1981; and Flyer, Roberto A. Godoy, "Total Registered Voters . . . as of 9-19-81," Series I, Box 28, EDF, RRL.

126. Memorandum, Elizabeth Dole to James A. Baker III, April 6, 1982, Series I, Box 28, EDF, RRL.

127. Memorandum, Elizabeth Dole to Edwin Meese III, James A. Baker III, and Michael Deaver.

128. Memorandum, Elizabeth Dole to James A. Baker III, April 6, 1982.

129. James T. Patterson, *Restless Giant: The United States from Watergate to Bush v. Gore* (New York: Oxford University Press, 2005), 162.

130. Pear, "Reagan Backs Voting Rights Act but Wants to Ease Requirements"; and Memorandum, Elizabeth Dole to James A. Baker III, March 1, 1982, Series VII, Box 91, EDF, RRL.

131. Memorandum, Elizabeth Dole to Edwin Meese III, James A. Baker III, and Michael Deaver.

132. Memorandum, Elizabeth Dole to James A. Baker III, April 6, 1982.

133. Evan Maxwell, "Raids to Hit Aliens Holding Desirable Jobs," *Los Angeles Times,* April 23, 1982.

134. Larry Stammer, "INS Ends Raids on Illegal Aliens," *Los Angeles Times,* May 1, 1982.

135. Evan Maxwell and Leslie Berkman, "Many Mexicans Are Told Their Legal Status in U.S. Has Ended," *Los Angeles Times,* December 24, 1981.

136. Memorandum, Elizabeth Dole to Edwin Meese III, James A. Baker III, and Michael Deaver.

137. Memorandum, Henry Zuniga to Elizabeth Dole, March 31, 1982, Series I, Box 29, EDF, RRL.

138. "Elizabeth H. Dole Meeting with Henry Zuniga," April 1, 1982, Series I, Box 29, EDF, RRL.

139. In the OPL's view, the millions of Hispanics from Central and South America, and even those from Spain, often recent immigrants and noncitizens, would not see any "specific outreach activities" from the White House. Neither would the Hispanic unemployed, the working poor, those with ties to organized labor, or "activist organizations" seeking "increased Federal spending for social welfare programs." Memorandum, Elizabeth Dole to Edwin Meese III, James A. Baker III, and Michael Deaver.

140. Fernando Oaxaca to Ronald Reagan et al., January 25, 1982, Series I, Box 28, EDF, RRL.

141. David E. Kaiser, *The Road to Dallas: The Assassination of John F. Kennedy* (Cambridge, MA: Harvard University Press, 2009), 250.

142. "The State," *Los Angeles Times,* January 11, 1982.

143. Gabrielle Morris, interview with Tirso del Junco, 1982, "California Republican Party Leadership and Success, 1966–1982," Government History Documentation Project, Ronald Reagan Gubernatorial Era, Regional Oral History Office, Bancroft Library, University of California, Berkeley (University of California, 1984), 7–8.

144. Fernando Oaxaca to Ronald Reagan et al.

145. Fernando Oaxaca to Ronald Reagan et al.

146. Fernando Oaxaca, "The New Hispanic Conservatives," *Caminos,* March 1982, Series I, Box 29, EDF, RRL.

147. Memorandum, Fernando Oaxaca to RNHA Executive Committee, August 4, 1982, Series I, Box 29, EDF, RRL.
148. Memorandum, Fernando Oaxaca to RNHA Executive Committee.
149. Memorandum, Elizabeth Dole to Edwin Meese III, January 18, 1983, Series I, Box 29, EDF, RRL.
150. Memorandum, Henry Zuniga to Red Cavaney, January 18, 1983, Series I, Box 29, EDF, RRL.
151. Memorandum, Fernando Oaxaca to Members of the Republican National Committee, January 20, 1983, Series I, Box 29, EDF, RRL.
152. George J. Adams to Ronald Reagan, January 13, 1983, Series I, Box 29, EDF, RRL.
153. Alfredo Izaguirre Horta, "ACUARELA por Colorín," *Noticias del Mundo,* January 14, 1983, Series I, Box 29, EDF, RRL; trans. by author.
154. Memorandum, Fernando Oaxaca to Members of the Republican National Committee.
155. "ACUARELA por Colorín," *Noticias del Mundo,* January 14, 1983, Series I, Box 29, EDF, RRL; trans. by author.
156. Memorandum, Elizabeth Dole to Edwin Meese III, January 18, 1983.
157. Tirso del Junco, "Hispanic Demographics," n.d. Series I, Box 3, Michael McManus Files, RRL.
158. del Junco, "Hispanic Demographics."
159. del Junco, "Hispanic Demographics."
160. del Junco, "Hispanic Demographics."
161. del Junco, "Hispanic Demographics."
162. Memorandum, Manuel Iglesias to Morton Blackwell, n.d., Series I, Box 10, Morton Blackwell Files, RRL; trans. by author.
163. Memorandum, Manuel Iglesias to Morton Blackwell.
164. Address by Tirso del Junco, Chairman, Republican National Hispanic Assembly, in *Official Report of the Proceedings of the Thirty-Third Republican National Convention* (Washington, DC: Republican National Committee, 1984), 46–47.
165. Address by Tirso del Junco, Chairman, Republican National Hispanic Assembly.
166. Address by Tirso del Junco, Chairman, Republican National Hispanic Assembly.

## Epilogue

1. "'United Political Front' Urged: Latino Politicians Look to Miami Cubans," *Los Angeles Times,* July 21, 1980.
2. Quoted in Kenneth C. Burt, *The Search for a Civic Voice: California Latino Politics* (Claremont, CA: Regina Books, 2007), 161.
3. Robert Gnaizda and Mario Obledo, "Latino Vote: The 'Sleeping Giant' Stirs," *Los Angeles Times,* November 13, 1983.
4. Ruben Navarette Jr., "Latinos: The Forgotten Democratic Constituency," *Los Angeles Times,* November 1, 1992.

5. Phil Garcia, "California's 'Giant' Is Awake and Angry," *El Editor* (Lubbock, TX), November 21, 1996.

6. See, for instance, Rueben Martinez, "Will Latino Voter Hear Wake-Up Call," *Los Angeles Times*, September 22, 1992; Juan González, "A Giant Awakes and Votes," *New York Daily News*, November 5, 1998; Albor Ruiz, "A Sleeping Giant May Soon Be Waking Up," *New York Daily News*, July 24, 2000.

7. Alan Bernstein, "Hispanics on Harris County Voter Rolls Triple in a Generation," *Houston Chronicle*, April 28, 2008.

8. Carlos D. Conde, "A New Awakening: Again and Again!," *The Hispanic Outlook in Higher Education*, August 1, 2005.

9. Quoted in Gabriel Arana, "The Mythical Monolith," *The American Prospect*, February 9, 2014, http://prospect.org/article/myth-of-the-sleeping-latino -giant.

10. Whether respondents believed they should be working together is another matter, one that does not appear in the report's summary of findings. Pew Hispanic Center and Henry J. Kaiser Family Foundation, "2002 National Survey of Latinos: Summary of Findings," http://www.pewhispanic.org/files /reports/15.pdf (accessed May 23, 2012).

11. G. Cristina Mora, *Making Hispanics: How Activists, Bureaucrats, and Media Constructed a New American* (Chicago: University of Chicago Press, 2014), 8.

12. Darryl Fears and D'Vera Cohn, "Hispanic Population Booming in U.S.," *Washington Post*, January 22, 2003; Gail Russell Chaddock, "For Hispanics, Cultural Heft and New Tensions," *Christian Science Monitor*, January 23, 2003.

13. D'Vera Cohn, "Hispanics Declared Largest Minority; Blacks Overtaken in Census Update," *Washington Post*, June 19, 2003.

14. Quoted in Henry B. González, "It's Our Choice to Make," Box 327, Henry B. González Papers, 1946–1998, the Dolph Briscoe Center for American History, University of Texas at Austin.

I am also thankful to the North Carolina Association of Historians. Portions of chapter 10 were first published as "'Minority Doesn't Mean Just Black': The 'Hispanic Vote' and the Economics of Identity in the Carter Years," *Journal of the North Carolina Association of Historians* 26 (September 2018): 1–10 and are reprinted here with permission.

There are young minds and spirits to whom I am indebted as well. The bright, inquisitive, and hopeful students I have taught over the years at Canarsie High School, Cornell University, Georgetown, and Western have inspired this project more than they can ever know. I'm grateful that the late Dr. Joel Shapiro gave me my first chance to experience the joys and struggles of being a teacher.

Many other wonderful individuals must also be mentioned by name. Some have volunteered or been coerced into reading all or part of this manuscript. Some are gracious and supportive colleagues and mentors. A few have worked as research assistants or have shared ideas from their own scholarship. Others have given most of their friendship and hospitality. A mighty handful overlap categories. They know who they are. My great thanks goes to Zachary Adams, Saheed Aderinto, Neel Baumgardner, Zach Bernstein, Matt Bowman, Kate Bronfenbrenner, Geraldo Cadava, Mauricio Castro, John Chávez, Robert Clines, Chris Cooper, Jefferson Cowie, José Cruz, Andrew Denson, Darren Dochuk, David Dorondo, Ruth Ann Elmore, Mary Ella Engel, Rodolfo Fernández, Rob Ferguson, Milton and Maria Flores, Neil Foley, Kathy Gallagher, Gary Gerstle, Frederick Gooding Jr., Gael Graham, Andrew Graybill, David Gutiérrez, José Angel Gutiérrez, Andrew Hazelton, Eric Hershberg, Toshi Higuchi, Debbie Jaramillo, Jill Kelly, Justyn Kissam, Alan Kraut, Max Krochmal, Marc Landry, Aldo Lauria Santiago, Alex Macaulay, Joe McCartin, Jamaal McDell, Elizabeth McRae, Carla Mendiola, Brandon Miller, Kathy Orr, Scott Philyaw, Kevin Powers, Julie Reed, Cristina Salinas, Nick Salvatore, Carole Sargent, Pat Scallen, Rebecca Scheidt, Gary Shapiro, Josh Shiffrin, Richard Starnes, Jessie Swigger, Vicki Szabo, Lorrin Thomas, Adam Trien, John Tutino, and Kaitlin Welch. A special thanks is due to Michael Kazin. A humane mentor who encouraged me to transcend my limitations (and in the finest prose I could summon), I treasure his wisdom, friendship, and season tickets.

Two editors at Harvard University Press have made this a much better book. Brian Distelberg's advice on my early chapters helped lay a founda-

# Acknowledgments

This book could not have happened without the aid of many friendly, hard working, and generous people. Among them are the archivists whose va expertise guided my research from the beginning. The staff of six presidenti libraries and their colleagues at the National Archives (I and II) led me to th deliberations, confusions, and manipulations of countless federal official Many thanks, too, to the dedicated archival staffs at Boricua College; Ca State Los Angeles University Library; the UCLA Chicano Studies Researc Center; Princeton University Library; the Dolph Briscoe Center for Amer ican History and the Benson Latin American Collection, both at the Univer sity of Texas at Austin; the Bell Library at Texas A&M–Corpus Christi; th University of Texas at San Antonio Special Collections; the University of New Mexico's Center for Southwest Research; the Center for Puerto Rica Studies at Hunter College (CUNY); the Rockefeller Archive Center; and Yale University Library.

A handful of institutions provided essential money and time. The Department of History at Georgetown University supplied travel funds and a nonservice fellowship that enabled my research to flourish, possibly beyond wise boundaries. Grants from the Lyndon Baines Johnson Foundation and the Gerald R. Ford Presidential Foundation abetted the project's expansionist tendencies. A research fellowship at American University's Center for Latin American and Latino Studies enabled me to clarify its ambitions. The William P. Clements Center for Southwest Studies at Southern Methodist University then extended a fellowship that—in addition to permitting yet more research—supported a manuscript workshop whose participants' thoughtful critiques pivotally shaped the book that was to come. Finally, Western Carolina University furnished financial support and course reductions that allowed me to bring this project to completion.

tion for revision. Andrew Kinney then patiently and perceptively guided the manuscript's expansion and refinement, and engaged reviewers whose insightful critiques have joined with his to greatly strengthen the manuscript. Editorial assistant Olivia Woods was a warm and efficient organizer of the process. Jen Burton navigated a sea of acronyms and other bureaucratic details to produce a fine index. Production editor John Donohue of Westchester Publishing Services was also a genuine pleasure to work with.

The greatest debts are familial. As history teachers themselves, my parents introduced me to the excitement and urgency of learning about the past. My father, Charles Fallon, also instilled in me persistence, no small asset in a job like this. My late mother, Barbara Francis, taught me to be funny, and to be a teacher. My brother Abraham has encouraged, inspired, and laughed with me since forever. Martha and Vincent Chimienti embraced me with the dedication, traditions, and love of their family.

And then there's Liz. She never stopped listening and guiding as I formulated this book's questions and pursued the answers. She read and reread the manuscript, fortifying it at every stage with questions and insights of her own. She never doubted that what I was doing was important. She never even complained that I was spending so much time thinking about Richard Nixon. She has loved and sustained me through everything. Together with Isaac and Julian, our two beautiful boys, we go forward.

# Index